What They Said
in 1971

What They Said In 1971

The Yearbook of Spoken Opinion

•

Compiled and Edited by

ALAN F. PATER

and

JASON R. PATER

MONITOR BOOK COMPANY, INC.

To

The Newsmakers of the World . . .

May they never be at a loss for words

Preface to the First Edition (1969)

WORDS can be powerful or subtle, humorous or maddening. They can be vigorous or feeble, lucid or obscure, inspiring or despairing, wise or foolish, hopeful or pessimistic ... they can be fearful or confident, timid or articulate, persuasive or perverse, honest or deceitful. As tools at a speaker's command, words can be used to reason, argue, discuss, cajole, plead, debate, declaim, threaten, infuriate, or appease; they can harangue, flourish, recite, preach, discourse, stab to the quick, or gently sermonize.

When casually spoken by a stage or film star, words can go beyond the press-agentry and make-up facade and reveal the inner man or woman. When purposefully uttered in the considered phrasing of a head of state, words can determine the destiny of millions of people, resolve peace or war, or chart the course of a nation on whose direction the fate of the entire world may depend.

Until now, the *copia verborum* of well-known and renowned public figures—the doctors and diplomats, the governors and generals, the potentates and presidents, the entertainers and educators, the bishops and baseball players, the jurists and journalists, the authors and attorneys, the congressmen and chairmen-of-the-board—whether enunciated in speeches, lectures, interviews, radio and television addresses, news conferences, forums, symposiums, town meetings, committee hearings, random remarks to the press, or delivered on the floors of the United States Senate and House of Representatives or in the parliaments and palaces of the world—have been dutifully reported in the media, then filed away and, for the most part, forgotten.

The editors of *WHAT THEY SAID* believe that consigning such a wealth of thoughts, ideas, doctrines, opinions and philosophies to interment in the morgues and archives of the Fourth Estate is lamentable and unnecessary. Yet the media, in all their forms, are constantly engulfing us in a profusion of endless and increasingly voluminous news reports. One is easily disposed to disregard or forget the stimulating discussion of critical issues embodied in so many of the utterances of those who make the news and, in their respective fields, shape the events throughout the world. The conclusion is therefore a natural and compelling one: the educator, the public official, the business executive, the statesman, the philosopher—everyone who has a stake in the complex, often confusing trends of our times—should have material of this kind readily available.

These, then, are the circumstances under which *WHAT THEY SAID* was conceived. It is the culmination of a year of listening to the people in the public eye; a year of scrutinizing, monitoring, reviewing, judging, deciding—a year during which the editors resurrected from almost certain oblivion those quintessential elements of the year's *spoken* opinion which, in their judgment, demanded preservation in book form.

WHAT THEY SAID is a pioneer in its field. Its *raison d'etre* is the firm conviction that presenting, each year, the highlights of vital and interesting views from the lips of prominent people on virtually every aspect of contemporary civilization fulfills the need to give the *spoken* word the permanence and lasting value of the *written* word. For, if it is true that a picture is worth 10,000 words, it is equally true that a verbal conclusion, an apt quote or a candid comment by a person of fame or influence can have more significance and can provide more understanding than an entire page of summary in a standard work of reference.

The editors of *WHAT THEY SAID* did not, however, design their book for researchers and scholars alone. One of the failings of the conventional reference work is that it is blandly written and referred to primarily for facts and figures, lacking inherent "interest value." *WHAT THEY SAID*, on the other hand, was planned for sheer enjoyment and pleasure, for searching glimpses into the lives and thoughts of the world's celebrities, as well as for serious study, intellectual reflection and the philosophical contemplation of our multifaceted life and mores. Furthermore, those pressed for time, yet anxious to know what the newsmakers have been saying, will welcome the short excerpts which will make for quick, intermittent reading—and rereading. And, of course, the topical classifications, the speakers' index, the subject index, the place and date information—documented and authenticated and easily located—will supply a rich fund of hitherto not readily obtainable reference and statistical material.

Finally, the reader will find that the editors have eschewed trite comments and cliches, tedious and boring. The selected quotations, each standing on its own, are pertinent, significant, stimulating—above all, relevant to today's world, expressed in the speakers' own words. And they will, the editors feel, be even more relevant tomorrow. They will be re-examined and reflected upon in the future by men and women eager to learn from the past. The prophecies, the promises, the "golden dreams," the boastings and rantings, the bluster, the bravado, the pleadings and representations of those whose voices echo in these pages (and in those to come) should provide a rare and unique history lesson. The positions held by these luminaries, in their respective callings, are such that what they say today may profoundly affect the future as well as the present, and so will be of lasting importance and meaning.

Beverly Hills, California

ALAN F. PATER
JASON R. PATER

Table of Contents

About the 1971 Edition . . .

EACH annual edition of *WHAT THEY SAID* is the culmination of a year's reading, selection, re-reading, editing and verifying what the newsmakers in all walks of life have been saying. The quotes, statements, ideas and opinions expressed in the 1971 issue reinforce the editors' belief—as the two editions before this have—that the thoughts of today's leaders and prominent personalities deserve—indeed, demand—preservation; for today's current events are tomorrow's history, and today's expressed thoughts are tomorrow's echoed wisdom.

The editors wish to thank those educators, librarians and others who have given encouragement and offered suggestions on improving this series. All comments are welcomed, and any ideas deemed practical will be considered for inclusion in future volumes of *WHAT THEY SAID*.

Readers who have used previous editions of *WHAT THEY SAID* will note a few changes in the 1971 volume. These reflect the changing times and the diminishing or increasing importance of certain subjects from year to year. The "Law and Order" section has been combined with "Crime" to form a comprehensive new category: "Crime/Law Enforcement." The "Student Dissent" subsection has been eliminated and combined with "Education." "The United Nations" and "War and Peace" categories are now found in the *International* department. Other features remain unchanged.

Since *WHAT THEY SAID* is a reflection of the constantly-changing world scene, the issues and voices raised from year to year are bound to vary in importance. By comparing each year's edition with those before it, the reader will find some topics receiving either more or less attention, according to their relevance in a given year, and some individuals, more than others, speaking out on the issues. With no intention of being a news summary of 1971, following are some of the happenings reflected in many of this year's quotations . . .

Civil Rights

The most controversial issue in this area was that of court-ordered busing of school children to schools out of their neighborhoods in order to achieve racial balance. The year also recorded the death of Whitney M. Young, Jr., executive director of the National Urban League.

Commerce/Industry/Finance

President Nixon's announcement of a 10% surcharge on virtually all imported products was a controversial issue at home and abroad. Near the end of the year, there was a major revaluation of world currencies in relation to the dollar. The most debated issue was that of a Federally-guaranteed loan to the Lockheed Aircraft Corporation after that firm announced serious financial difficulties.

ABOUT THE 1971 EDITION . . .

Crime/Law Enforcement

Prison riots at San Quentin, Calif., and Attica, N.Y., made prison reform a major subject of discussion and dissension. Police corruption, especially in New York City, garnered much news coverage. Criticism of FBI Director J. Edgar Hoover grew and complaints against FBI surveillance of citizens was a much-debated topic.

Education:

Violent dissent and activism virtually vanished from college campuses in 1971. There was much verbal dissent, however, over courses, curricula and general educational methods, with many expressions of opinion on the future of education in America.

The Environment:

Pollution, conservation and other ecological matters continued to be widely-discussed subjects in 1971.

Foreign Affairs:

The major happening in foreign affairs this year was the Senate's vote against foreign aid, at least in the form aid has been dispensed in the past. President Nixon continued his re-evaluation of America's role in world affairs and, at least verbally, continued the Nixon Doctrine of aid instead of intervention.

Government:

Revenue-sharing and the 18-year-old vote were two major topics of discussion in the realm of government in 1971. Government surveillance of citizens was also a subject of wrangling and dispute that lead to much heated controversy. In the President's State of the Union address, he outlined a major governmental reformation plan that provided for restructuring various parts of governmental machinery. At the end of the year, however, little of this plan had been realized.

Labor and the Economy:

Without doubt, the most talked-about single subject in 1971 was the President's new economic program, announced August 15, which included a 90-day wage-price freeze and a 10% surcharge on imported goods. In November, Phase 2 of the program had been promulgated, with the freeze modified and guidelines taking effect.

Law and the Judiciary:

President Nixon appointed Attorney Edward F. Powell and Assistant Attorney-General William H. Rehnquist as Supreme Court Justices; both won approval of the Senate despite much heated criticism of Rehnquist as being racist.

National Defense:

Most prominent in the area of defense was the reported buildup of Soviet military strength vis-a-vis the American military position. Also much-discussed was the draft, with a volunteer armed force a subject of continued controversy and its ultimate adoption uncertain.

Transportation:

The defeat in Congress of the SST, after much contentious debate and testimony, was the major *cause-celebre* in this field. AMTRAK, the national railroad service, was launched; and mass transit continued to spark interest and opinions.

Politics:

Aside from the usual political verbiage, the coming 1972 Presidential election provided a platform for protracted campaigning and politicking. This year also saw New York Republican Mayor John Lindsay turn Democrat and later announce his candidacy for President.

Urban Affairs:

The financial plight of the cities continued, with government revenue-sharing a possible hope for many Mayors.

Africa:

Attempted coups in Morocco and Sudan both failed in 1971, and ties between Britain and Rhodesia were tentatively re-established.

The Americas:

Attention continued to be focused on Salvador Allende's Marxist government in Chile. The effects of the U.S. imposition of a 10% surcharge on foreign imports touched off criticism in Canada. Attacks on American vessels in international waters, and their capture by several South American nations, continued to be a problem of concern in the hemisphere.

Asia

The No. 1 story in Asia in 1971 was U.S. President Nixon's attempts at thawing relations with Communist China, eluminating in his announcement of a 1972 visit to Peking for discussions with Chinese leaders. India and Pakistan went to war over East Pakistan, and this conflict resulted in Pakistan's losing that area and the establishment of a new nation, Bangla Desh, where East Pakistan used to be. The war in Vietnam seemed to be settling down, while the fighting in Cambodia and Laos continued. On other fronts of the Indochina war, the trial of Lt. William Cally for the My Lai massacre was concluded with his conviction, the U.S. government intervened in Laos, the

ABOUT THE 1971 EDITION . . .

so-called Pentagon Papers case made headlines and South Vietnam conducted a Presidential election with President Thieu running unopposed after his opponents withdrew from the race.

Europe:

The two major stories in Europe in 1971 both involved Britain. The unremitting strife continued in Northern Ireland between those loyal to Britain and those wanting reunification with the Republic of Ireland to the South—between Protestant and Catholic. Britain's entry into the European Common Market climaxed many years of pro and con debate. West German Chancellor Willy Brandt won the Nobel Peace Prize for his efforts toward improved relations with Eastern Europe, and with East Germany in particular. And an agreement on Berlin was finally reached by the East and the West.

The Mideast:

Although war did not break out between Israel and the Arab world this year, as was feared, the rhetoric of war was strong. Face-to-face talks between the opposing sides still were not held.

Journalism:

The publishing by some newspapers of the so-called Pentagon Papers on U.S. involvement in Vietnam stirred pro and con arguments on the legal and ethical implications of printing secret government documents in the public press. CBS-TV's *The Selling of the Pentagon* documentary drew both blasts and praise and resulted in government investigations of fairness in its production. Debate still raged on alleged government repression of the news media.

The United Nations:

The No. 1 event in The United Nations was the admission of Communist China to the world organization and the expulsion of Nationalist China at the same time. U Thant stepped down as Secretary General and was replaced by Austria's Kurt Waldheim.

Editorial Treatment

ORGANIZATION OF MATERIAL

(A) The categories are arranged alphabetically within each of three major sections—

> Part I: "National Affairs"
> Part II: "International Affairs"
> Part III: "General"

In this manner, the reader can quickly locate quotations pertaining to particular fields of interest. It should be noted that some quotations contain a number of thoughts or ideas—sometimes on different subjects—while some are vague as to exact subject matter and thus do not fit clearly into a specific topic classification. In such cases, the judgment of the editors has determined the most appropriate category.

(B) Within each category, the speakers' names are in alphabetical order.

(C) Where there are two or more entries by one speaker within the same category, they appear chronologically by date spoken or date of source.

SPEAKER IDENTIFICATION

The rank, position, occupation, profession or title of the speaker is given as it was *at the time the statement was made*. Thus, due to possible changes in status during the year, a speaker may be shown with different identifications in various portions of the book, or even within the same category. In the case of speakers who hold more than one position or occupation simultaneously, the judgment of the editors has determined the most appropriate identification to use with a specific quotation.

THE QUOTATIONS

All quotations are printed verbatim, as they were originally spoken and reported by the media, except in those cases where the editors of *WHAT THEY SAID* have eliminated extraneous or overly long portions. In such cases, *ellipses* are always inserted—and in no case has the meaning or intention of any quotation been altered. (Material enclosed in parentheses are by the editors and are used to explain or clarify). Special care has been exercised to make certain that each quotation stands on its own merits and is not taken "out of context." *WHAT THEY SAID*, however, cannot be responsible for mistakes made by the original newspaper, periodical or other source, i.e., incorrect reporting, mis-quotations or errors in individual interpretation.

EDITORIAL TREATMENT

DOCUMENTATION AND SOURCES

Documentation (circumstance, place, date) of each quotation is provided as fully as could be obtained, and the sources are furnished with all quotations. In some instances, no documentation details were available, and in these cases only the sources are given. Following are the sequence and style for this information—

> Circumstance of quotation, place, date/Name of source, date: section number (if applicable), page number.
>
> Example: *Before the Senate, Washington, Dec. 4/The New York Times, 12-6:(4)13.*

The above example indicates that the quotation was delivered before the Senate in Washington on December 4. It was taken from *The New York Times,* issue of December 6, section 4, page 13. (In cases where a newspaper publishes more than one edition on the same date, it should be noted that page numbers may vary from edition to edition.)

THE INDEXES

(A) Arranged alphabetically in the *Speakers' Index,* with their respective page numbers, are the names of all speakers whose quotations appear in this volume. This index will be of use to readers wishing to locate all quotations of a particular speaker, regardless of topic.

(B) The reader will find that the basic categorization format of the book itself serves as a useful subject index inasmuch as related quotations are grouped together by their respective categories. However, there is, in addition, a detailed *Subject Index* which provides an in-depth listing of subjects, places, institutions, individuals, etc., mentioned or discussed in the quotations throughout the book, whether directly or indirectly.

ABOUT FAIRNESS

The editors of *WHAT THEY SAID* realize that much of the value of a book of this kind rests in its objectivity. As a result, there has been no conscious editorial bias or influence in the selection of the quotations, the choice of speakers or the manner of editing. Relevance of the statements and the status of the speakers remain the exclusive criteria for inclusion, without any regard whatsoever to the personal beliefs and views of the editors.

Furthermore, every effort has been made to include a multiplicity of opinions and ideas from a wide cross-section of speakers on each topic. Nevertheless, should there appear to be, on some controversial subjects, a preponderance of material favoring one point of view over another, it is simply the result of there having been a preponderance of those views expressed during the year. Also, since persons in politics and government account for a large percentage of the speakers in *WHAT THEY SAID*, there may exist a heavier weight of opinion favoring the political philosophy of those in office at the time, whether in the United States Congress, the Administration, or foreign capitals. This is natural and to be expected and should not be construed as a reflection of agreement or disagreement with that philosophy on the part of the editors of *WHAT THEY SAID*.

Abbreviations

Following are the abbreviations commonly used by the speakers in this book. Rather than spelling them out in full each time they appear in the quotations, this list will facilitate reading and avoid unnecessary repetition.

ABA:	American Basketball Association
ABC:	American Broadcasting Company
AFL-CIO:	American Federation of Labor-Congress of Industrial Organizations
AMA:	American Medical Association
AMTRAK:	United States government subsidized railroad system
ARVN:	Army of the Republic of (South) Vietnam
BIA:	Bureau of Indian Affairs (United States)
CBS:	Columbia Broadcasting System (United States)
CIA:	Central Intelligence Agency (United States)
EEC:	European Economic Community (Common Market)
EFTA:	European Free Trade Association
FBI:	Federal Bureau of Investigation
FCC:	Federal Communications Commission (United States)
GATT:	General Agreement on Tariffs and Trade
HEW:	Department of Health, Education and Welfare (United States)
ICBM:	Intercontinental Ballistics Missile
IMF:	International Monetary Fund
IRA:	Irish Republican Army
MOMA:	Museum of Modern Art (New York)
MPAA:	Motion Picture Association of America
NASA:	National Aeronautics and Space Administration (United States)
NATO:	North Atlantic Treaty Organization
NBA:	National Basketball Association (United States)
NBC:	National Broadcasting Company (United States)
NFL:	National Football League (United States)
NLF:	National Liberation Front-Viet Cong (South Vietnam)
NORAD:	North American Air Defense
OAS:	Organization of American States
POW:	Prisoner of War
SALT:	Strategic Arms Limitation Talks
SEC:	Securities and Exchange Commission (United States)
SST:	Supersonic Transport
TV:	Television
UN:	United Nations
U.S.:	United States
USIA:	United States Information Agency

ABBREVIATIONS

U.S.S.R.:   Union of Soviet Socialist Republics
WASP: White Anglo-Saxon Protestant

Party affiliation of United States Senators and Congressmen—

    C: Conservative-Republican
    D: Democrat
    R: Republican

The Quote of the Year

"It is perfectly clear that people, given no alternative, will choose tyranny over anarchy, because anarchy is the worst tyranny of all."

—ERIC SEVAREID

News commentator, Columbia Broadcasting System; at Stanford University commencement, June 13.

PART ONE

National Affairs

The State of the Union Address

Delivered by Richard M. Nixon, President of the United States, in the House of Representatives, Washington, January 22, 1971.

Mr. Speaker, Mr. President, my colleagues in the Congress, our distinguished guests and my fellow Americans:

This 92nd Congress has a chance to be recorded as the greatest Congress in America's history.

In these troubled years just past, America has been going through a long nightmare of war and division, of crime and inflation. Even more deeply, we have gone through a long, dark night of the American spirit. But now that night is ending. Now we must let our spirits soar again. Now we are ready for the lift of a driving dream.

The people of this nation are eager to get on with the quest for new greatness. They see challenges, and they are prepared to meet those challenges. It is for us here to open the doors that will set free again the real greatness of this nation—the genius of the American people.

How shall we meet this challenge? How can we truly open the doors, and set free the full genius of our people?

The way in which the 92nd Congress answers these questions will determine its place in history. More importantly, it can determine this nation's place in history as we enter the third century of our independence.

'Six Great Goals'

Tonight, I shall present to the Congress six great goals. I shall ask not simply for more new programs in the old framework, but to change the framework itself—to reform the entire structure of American government so we can make it again fully responsive to the needs and the wishes of the American people.

If we act boldly—if we seize this moment and achieve these goals—we can close the gap between promise and performance in American government, and bring together the resources of the nation and the spirit of the people.

In discussing these great goals, I am dealing tonight only with matters on the domestic side of the nation's agenda. I shall make a separate report to the Congress and the nation next month on developments in our foreign policy.

The first of these six great goals is already before the Congress.

I urge that the unfinished business of the 91st Congress be made the first priority of the 92nd.

Over the next two weeks, I will call upon Congress to take action on more than 35 pieces of proposed legislation on which action was not completed last year.

Welfare is No. 1

The most important is welfare reform.

The present welfare system has become a monstrous, consuming outrage—an outrage against the community, against the taxpayer, and particularly against the children it is supposed to help.

We may honestly disagree on what to do about it. But we can all agree that we must meet the challenge not by pouring more money into the old system, but by abolishing it and adopting a new one.

Let us place a floor under the income of every family with children in America—and without those demeaning soul-stifling affronts to human dignity that so blight the lives of welfare children today. But let us also establish an effective work incentive and an effective work requirement.

Let us provide the means by which more can help themselves. Let us generously help those who are not able to help themselves. But let us stop helping those who are able to help themselves but refuse to do so.

The second great goal is to achieve what Americans have not enjoyed since 1957—full prosperity in peace time.

Inflation Turned

The tide of inflation has turned. The rise in the cost of living, which had been gathering dangerous momentum in the late 1960s, was reduced last year. Inflation will be further reduced this year.

But as we have moved from runaway inflation toward reasonable price stability, and at the same time have been moving from a wartime economy to a peace-time economy, we have paid a price in increased unemployment.

We should take no comfort from the fact that the level of unemployment in this transition from a war-time to a peace-time economy is lower than in any peacetime year of the 1960s.

This is not good enough for the man who is unemployed in the 1970s. We must do better for workers in peacetime and we will do better.

To achieve this, I will submit an expansionary budget this year—one that will help stimulate the economy and thereby open up new job opportunities for millions of Americans.

It will be a full employment budget, a budget designed to be in balance if the economy were operating at its peak potential. By spending as if we were at full employment, we will help to bring about full employment.

I ask the Congress to accept these expansionary policies—to accept the concept of the full employment budget.

At the same time, I ask the Congress to cooperate in resisting expenditures that go beyond the limits of the full employment budget. For as we wage a campaign to bring about a widely shared prosperity, we must not re-ignite the fires of inflation and so undermine that prosperity.

With the stimulus and the discipline of a full employment budget; with the commitment of the independent Federal Reserve System to provide fully for the monetary needs of a growing economy; and with a much greater effort by labor and management to make their wage and price decisions in the light of the national interest and their own long-run best interests—then for the worker, the farmer, the consumer, and for Americans everywhere we shall gain the goal of a new prosperity: more jobs, more income and more profits, without inflation and without war.

This is a great goal, and one that we can achieve together.

The third great goal is to continue the effort so dramatically begun this past year; to restore and enhance our natural environment.

Building on the foundation laid in the 37-point program I submitted to Congress last year, I will propose a strong new set of initiatives to clean up our air and water, to combat noise, and to preserve and restore our surroundings.

I will propose programs to make better use of our land, and to encourage a balanced national growth—growth that will revitalize our rural heartland and enhance the quality of life throughout America.

And not only to meet today's needs but to anticipate those of tomorrow, I will put forward the most extensive program ever proposed by a President to expand the nation's parks, recreation areas and open spaces in a way that truly brings parks to the people. For only if we leave a legacy of parks will the next generation have parks to enjoy.

As a fourth great goal, I will offer a far-reaching set of proposals for improving America's health care and making it available more fairly to more people.

Health Care

I will propose:
• A program to insure that no American

family will be prevented from obtaining basic medical care by inability to pay.

● A major increase in and redirection of aid to medical schools, to greatly increase the number of doctors and other health personnel.

● Incentives to improve the delivery of health services, to get more medical care resources into those areas that have not been adequately served, to make greater use of medical assistants and to slow the alarming rise in the costs of medical care.

● New programs to encourage better preventive medicine, by attacking the cause of disease and injury, and by providing incentives to doctors to keep people well rather than just to treat them when they are sick.

I will also ask appropriation of an extra $100 million to launch an intensive campaign to find a cure for cancer, and I will ask later for whatever additional funds can effectively be used. The time has come when the same kind of concentrated effort that split the atom and took man to the moon should be turned toward conquering this dread disease. Let us make a total national commitment to achieve this goal.

America has long been the wealthiest nation in the world. Now it is time we became the healthiest nation in the world.

The fifth great goal is to strengthen and renew our State and local governments.

As we approach our 200th anniversary in 1976, we remember that this nation launched itself as a loose confederation of separate States, without a workable central government.

At that time, the mark of its leaders' vision was that they quickly saw the need to balance the separate powers of the states with a government of central powers.

And so they gave us a Constitution of balanced powers, of unity with diversity—and so clear was their vision that it survives as the oldest written Constitution still in force in the world today.

For almost two centuries since—and dramatically in the 1930s—at those great turning points when the question has been between the states and the federal government, it has been resolved in favor of a stronger central government.

During this time the nation grew and prospered. But one thing history tells us is that no great movement goes in the same direction forever. Nations change, they adapt, or they slowly die.

Time to Reverse

The time has come to reverse the flow of power and resources from the states and communities to Washington, and start power and resources flowing back from Washington to the states and communities and more important, to the people, all across America.

The time has come for a new partnership between the federal government and the states and localities—a partnership in which we entrust the states and localities with a larger share of the nation's responsibilities, and in which we share our revenues with them so they can meet those responsibilities.

To achieve this goal, I propose to the Congress tonight that we enact a plan of revenue sharing historic in scope and bold in concept.

All across America today, states and cities are confronted with a financial crisis. Some already have been cutting back on essential services—for example, just recently San Diego and Cleveland cut back on trash collections. Most are caught between the prospects of bankruptcy on the one hand and adding to an already crushing tax burden on the other.

As one indication of the rising costs of local government, I discovered the other day that my home town of Whittier, Calif.—with a population of only 67,000—has a budget for 1971 bigger than the entire federal budget in 1791.

New Direction

Now the time has come to take a new direction, and once again to introduce a new and more creative balance in our approach to government.

So let us put the money where the needs are. And let us put the power to spend it where the people are.

I propose that the Congress make a $16 billion investment in renewing state and local government—with $5 billion of this in new and unrestricted funds, to be used as the states and localities see fit, and with the other $11 billion provided by allocating $1 billion of new funds and converting one-third of the money going to the present narrow-purpose aid programs into federal revenue sharing funds for six broad purposes—urban development, rural development, education, transportation, job training and law enforcement—but with the states and localities making their own local decisions on how it should be spent.

For the next fiscal year, this would increase total federal aid to the states and localities by more than 25 per cent over the present level.

The revenue sharing proposals I send to the Congress will include the safe-guards against discrimination that accompany all other federal funds allocated to the states. Neither the President nor the Congress nor the conscience of the nation can permit money which comes from all the people to be used in a way which discriminates against some of the people.

The federal government will still have a large and vital role to play in achieving our national purposes. Established functions that are clearly and essentially federal in nature will still be performed by the federal government. New functions that need to be sponsored or performed by the federal government—such as those I have urged tonight in welfare and health—will be added to the federal agenda. Whenever it makes the best sense for us to act as a whole nation, the federal government will lead the way. But where state or local governments can better do what needs to be done, let us see that they have the resources to do it.

Under this plan, the federal government will provide the states and localities with more money and less interference—and by cutting down the interference the same amount of money will go a lot further.

Let us share our resources:

• To rescue the states and localities from the brink of financial crisis.

• And to give homeowners and wage earners a chance to escape from ever-higher property taxes and sales taxes.

Two Other Reasons

Let us share our resources for two other reasons as well.

The first of these reasons has to do with government itself, and the second with the individual.

Let's face it. Most Americans today are simply fed up with government at all levels. They will not—and should not—continue to tolerate the gap between promise and performance.

The fact is that we have made the federal government so strong it grows muscle-bound and the states and localities so weak they approach impotence.

If we put more power in more places, we can make government more creative in more places. For that way we multiply the number of people with the ability to make things happen—and we can open the way to a new burst of creative energy throughout America.

The final reason I urge this historic shift is much more personal, for each and every one of us.

As everything seems to have grown bigger, and more complex; as the forces that shape our lives seem to have grown more distant and more impersonal a great feeling of frustration has crept across the land.

Whether it is the working man who feels neglected, the black man who feels oppressed or the mother concerned about her children, there has been a growing feeling that "things are in the saddle, and ride mankind."

Millions of frustrated young Americans today are crying out—asking not what will government do for me, but what can I do, how can I contribute, how can I matter?

An Answer

Let us answer them. To them and to all Americans, let us say: "We hear you and we will give you a chance. We are going to give you a new chance to have more to say about the decisions that affect your future—to participate in government—because we are going to provide more centers of power where what you do can make a difference that you can see and feel in your own life and the life of your whole community.

The further away government is from the people, the stronger government becomes and the weaker people become. And a nation with a strong government and a weak people is an empty shell.

I reject the patronizing idea that government in Washington is inevitably more wise, more honest and more efficient than government at the local or state level. The honesty and efficiency of government depends on people. Government at all levels has good people and bad people. And the way to get more good people into government is to give them more opportunity to do good things.

The idea that a bureaucratic elite in Washington knows best what is best for people everywhere and that you cannot trust local government is really a contention that you cannot trust people to govern themselves. This notion is completely foreign to the American experience. Local government is the government closest to the people and most responsive to the individual person; it is people's government in a far more intimate way than the government in Washington can ever be.

People came to America because they wanted to determine their own future rather than to live in a country where others determined their future for them.

What this change means is that once again we are placing our trust in people.

I have faith in people. I trust the judgment of people. Let us give the people a chance, a bigger voice in deciding for themselves those questions that so greatly affect their lives.

The sixth great goal is a complete reform of the federal government itself.

Based on a long and intensive study with the aid of the best advice obtainable, I have concluded that a sweeping reorganization of the Executive Branch is needed if the government is to keep up with the times and with the needs of the people.

I propose that we reduce the present 12 Cabinet Departments to eight.

I propose that the Departments of State, Treasury, Defense and Justice remain, but that all the other departments be consolidated into four: Human Resources, Community Development, Natural Resources, and Economic Development.

Let us look at what these would be.

• First, a department dealing with the concerns of people—as individuals, as members of family—a department focused on human needs.

• Second, a department concerned with the community—rural communities and urban—and with all that it takes to make a community function as a community.

• Third, a department concerned with our physical environment, and with the preservation and balanced use of those great natural resources on which our nation depends.

• And fourth, a department concerned with our prosperity—with our jobs, our businesses, and those many activities that keep our economy running smoothly and well.

Under this plan, rather than dividing up our departments by narrow subjects, we would organize them around the great purposes of government. Rather than scattering responsibility by adding new levels of bureaucracy, we would focus and concentrate the responsibility for getting problems solved.

With these four departments, when we have a problem we will know where to go—and the department will have the authority and the resources to do something about it.

Over the years we have added departments and created agencies, each to serve a new constituency or to handle a particular task—and these have grown and multiplied in what has become a hopeless confusion of form and function.

A New Era

The time has come to match our structure to our purposes—to look with a fresh eye, and to organize the government by conscious, comprehensive design to meet the new needs of a new era.

One hundred years ago, Abraham Lincoln stood on a battlefield and spoke of a government of the people, by the people and for the people. Too often since then, we have become a nation of the government, by the government, and for the government.

By enacting these reforms, we can renew that principle that Lincoln stated so simply and so well.

By giving everyone's voice a chance to be heard, we will have government that truly is of the people.

By creating more centers of meaningful power, more places where decisions that really count can be made, by giving more people a chance to do something, we can have government that truly is by the people.

And by setting up a completely modern, functional system of government at the national level, we in Washington will at last be able to provide government that truly is for the people.

I realize that what I am asking is that not only the Executive Branch in Washington but even this Congress will have to change by giving up some of its power.

'Change is Hard'

Change is hard. But without change there can be no progress. And for each of us the question must be not "Will change bring me inconvenience?" but "Will change bring the country progress?"

Giving up power is hard. But 1 would urge all of you, as leaders of this country, to remember that the truly revered leaders in world history are those who give power to people, not those who took it away.

As we consider these reforms we will be acting, not for the next two years or the next 10 years, but for the next 100 years.

So let us approach these six great goals with a sense, not only of this moment in history, but also of history itself.

Let us act with the willingness to work together and the vision and the boldness and the courage of those great Americans who met in Philadelphia almost 190 years ago to create a Constitution.

Let us leave a heritage as they did—not just for our children but for millions yet unborn—of a nation where every American will have a chance not only to live in peace and to enjoy prosperity and opportunity, but to participate in a system of government where he knows not only his votes but his ideas count—a system of government which will provide the means for America to reach heights of achievement undreamed of before.

Those men who met in Philadelphia left a great heritage because they had a vision—not only of what the nation was, but of what it could become.

As I think of that vision, I recall that America was founded as the land of the open door—as a haven for the oppressed, a land of opportunity, a place of refuge and of hope.

'Door of Welcome'

When the first settlers opened the door of America three and a half centuries ago, they came to escape persecution and to find opportunity—and they left wide the door of welcome for others to follow.

When the 13 colonies declared their independence almost two centuries ago, they opened the door to a new vision of liberty and of human fulfillment—not just for an elite, but for all.

To the generations that followed, America's was the open door that beckoned millions from the old world to the new in search of a better life, a freer life, a fuller life, in which by their own decisions they could shape their own destinies.

For the black American, the Indian, the Mexican-American, and for those others in our land who have not had an equal chance, the nation at last has begun to confront the need to press open the door of full and equal opportunity, and of human dignity.

For all Americans, with these changes I have proposed tonight we can open the door to a new era of opportunity. We can open the door to full and effective participation in the decisions that affect their lives. We can open the door to a new partnership among governments at all levels, and between those governments and the people themselves. And by so doing, we can open wide the doors of human fulfillment for millions of people here in America.

In the next few weeks I will spell out in greater detail the way I propose that we achieve these six great goals. I ask this Congress to be responsive. If it is, then the 92d Congress, at the end of its term, will be able to look back on a record more splendid than any in our history.

This can be the Congress that helped us end the longest war in the nation's history, and end it in a way that will give us at last a genuine chance for a full generation of peace.

This can be the Congress that helped achieve an expanding economy, with full employment and without inflation—and without the deadly stimulus of war.

This can be the Congress that reformed a welfare system that has robbed recipients of their dignity while it robbed States and cities of their resources.

This can be the Congress that pressed forward the rescue of our environment, and established for the next generation an enduring legacy of parks for the people.

This can be the Congress that launched a new era in American medicine, in which the quality of medical care was enhanced while the costs were made less burdensome.

But above all, what this Congress can be remembered for is opening the way to a New American Revolution—a peaceful revolution in which power was turned back to the people—in which government at all levels was refreshed and renewed, and made truly responsive. This can be a revolution as profound, as far-reaching, as exciting, as that first revolution almost 200 years ago—and it can mean that just five years from now America will enter its third century as a young nation new in spirit, with all the vigor and freshness with which it began its first century.

My colleagues in the Congress—these are great goals, and they can make the sessions of this Congress a great moment for America. So let us pledge together to go forward together—by achieving these goals to give America the foundation today for a new greatness tomorrow and in all the years to come—and in so doing to make this the greatest Congress in the history of this great and good nation.

The American Scene

Spiro T. Agnew
Vice President of the United States

Young Americans too often are represented as crying out as a class for recognition and as asking for special attentions. In response, many members of the older generation—my generation—have come to regard this cry as a class action and have chosen to shower "youth" generally the special attention that they thought youth wanted. This has been, in my opinion, the wrong response. Our response to your appeal and the appeal of those a bit older than you should not be special attentions. That is not, to me, what young people really want. Rather, they want to be released from the bondage of youth, to be taken seriously as citizens, to compete as full members of the community. And I think they should . . . Our reply should be to accept young men and women—especially those 18 and over—as full members of the community; inexperienced members, perhaps, but still ready to take on a great deal more in the way of responsibilities and burdens than they generally have been given today.

At Hearst Senate (high school) Youth Conference, Washington, Feb. 3/ The Washington Post, 2-4: (C) 2.

(A philosophy of) "let's tell the world how rotten we are and thus expiate our sins" (is being) drummed into our consciousness to such an extent that it is becoming part of our national psyche. If we don't recognize this dangerous attitude for what it is, and overcome it, it will destroy us as a nation. Who are the most rabid critics (of the nation)? We have met the enemy, and they are us.

Before Los Angeles Area Chamber of Commerce, April 7/Los Angeles Times, 4-8: (1)3.

(The American people) don't mind the hard road if they understand the reason for it. And conversely, they don't accept the soft road if that amounts to a total abandonment of the purposes that made this country what it is.

San Francisco Examiner & Chronicle (This World), 4-18:2.

Most of us understand the course our country has embarked on over the years, and approve of it. We may find fault with some specificities of certain actions, but certainly each of us is a patriot in his own way, and we try to serve our country within our understanding of what should be done.

Celebrating American Independence Day, in flight between Seoul and Singapore, July 4/The New York Times, 7-5:3.

The strength of the American system and the reason it is united and free today lies in its ability to restrict its freedom when it absolutely has to, and then to make certain those needed temporary restrictions do not become a habit.

Before Society of Association Executives, Miami Beach, Aug. 25/The Washington Post, 8-26:(A)4.

Respect for our laws and institutions, pride in our jobs, a willingness to work hard, to compete, a desire to achieve and excel—all are under attack today as never before, principally from the liberal and radical left. Our traditional concept of success makes the ultra-liberal nose twitch with distaste, as though it sensed a vaguely unpleasant odor. Gone is the remembrance of the sweet smell of success.

Before Society of Special Former Agents of the FBI, Atlanta, Georgia, Sept. 30/ Los Angeles Times, 10-1:(1)17.

We hear much today about what is called a "crisis of confidence" in America, a spirit of despair, a feeling of hopelessness about the future. If such a mood exists—and I think it is grossly exaggerated—it stems directly from the rhetoric of the utopian leftists who despair at how far we fall short of the ideal instead of how close we have come to achieving it.

Before Association of Life Insurance Counsels, New York, Dec. 15/The Dallas Times Herald, 12-15(A)4.

Harry Ashmore
Executive vice president, Center for the Study of Democratic Institutions; Former editor, "Arkansas Gazette," Little Rock

We have reached a point where anyone who bears any resemblance, in style or outlook, to Thomas Jefferson, Abraham Lincoln, Woodrow Wilson or Franklin Roosevelt is regarded as hopelessly "straight" by the intellectual style-setters, and as a natural enemy by the radical activists. The Puritan Ethic is deemed to be the source of all our ills; patriotism is treated as a loathsome disease; and faith is reserved for a formless utopia to be ushered in by the superior moral consciousness of our children.

At Beverly Hills (Calif.) Man of the Year dinner/The Hollywood Reporter, 2-12:26.

Carl E. Bagge
President, National Coal Association

Somehow, there is abroad in the land a savage, punitive spirit which says that if any institution has flaws, don't improve it—destroy it, and never mind the consequences. If these critics were in a lifeboat with a slight leak, they would not bail out the water; they would chop holes in the bottom to drain it.

U.S. News & World Report, 4-26:53.

Helen Delich Bentley
Chairman, Federal Maritime Commission

Because too many people feel that a living is owed to them and that they need not be productive, an unhealthy malaise is overtaking our nation. Somehow we must reinstill that pride of productivity into the average

American, or we can't help but decay.

Before Propeller Club, San Francisco, March 25/San Francisco Examiner, 3-26:2.

Alan Bible
United States Senator, D–Nev.

America is a nation of mechanization and motorization. Just about everything we do nowadays we do with a motor or an engine, even to cleaning our teeth or brushing our clothes.

Quote, 6-13:554.

Joseph H. Blatchford
Director of the Peace Corps

We Americans are so self-centered. We think people everywhere worry about everything America does.

San Francisco Examiner & Chronicle (This World), 5-9:2.

Warren E. Burger
Chief Justice of the United States

Those who are impatient for change should see that no nation in all history has given more power to the people (than the United States).

Quote, 7-25:73.

Robert C. Byrd
United States Senator, D–W. Va.

In America, any individual of any color can go as high as he wants to go if he just has the drive and a normal amount of common sense.

The New York Times Magazine, 2-28:50.

Jimmy Carter
Governor of Georgia

I . . . think the South has been fairly unyielding in what I would call "enlightened conservatism." We believe very strongly in the autonomy of the individual person, in self-reliance; and we're oriented toward an agrarian philosophy which emphasizes the individual person. I think we share the beliefs of the average American now. There isn't any distinguishable difference between political

(JIMMY CARTER)

philosophy or place in the political spectrum between the average Southerner and the average American voter.

The National Observer, 4-5:5.

Fidel Castro (Ruz)
Premier of Cuba

The United States is a consumer society in decadence. A nation that uses a billion tons of gasoline, which destroys all its natural reserves and has to sack the rest of the world for gasoline to keep 100 to 200 million automobiles moving, which has set up a world police force and on top of that has enormous wastage, cannot maintain itself.

Antofagasta, Chile, Nov. 12/San Francisco Examiner & Chronicle, 11-14:(A)3.

Paddy Chayefsky
Playwright

No matter what our mistakes, with all our faults and stumblings, the United States is still the greatest country in the world. I can't live anywhere else. I get homesick. I've been to Israel three times, and I'll be spending more time there. I'm going to make a movie there this summer, so I'll be away two, three months. I know I won't be able to wait to come home.

Interview, New York/San Francisco Examiner & Chronicle (Datebook), 5-30:14.

Bob Dole
United States Senator, R–Kan.

We are a country where street politics is the order of the day in 1971, just as it was the order of the day in 1931 in pre-Nazi Germany. And the marchers and the vandals and the innocent and the guilty alike are egged on by the clenched-fist salute and the hysterical words of the power-seekers today as they were then. And all this in the name of instant peace.

At Republican fund-raising dinner, Burlingame, Calif., June 12/San Francisco Examiner & Chronicle, 6-13:(A)6.

Helen Gahagan Douglas
Former United States Representative, D–Calif.

We in this country are still free; and those who do not recognize this simply don't know totalitarianism.

Interview, San Francisco/San Francisco Examiner, 4-23:19.

Janet Flanner
Writer

This is a period of demoralization, of anarchy practiced by young people who have so successfully fought off an education that they couldn't spell the word, let alone define it. I find them very depressing. This is a sad period for my country. Much of education and of our structural morality have been destroyed by violence, by a dissipation like the melting of glaciers or rocks turning to lava, and by sheer inertia—which is the extraordinary force of indifference and non-love. There's no sense in talking about learning morality at your mother's knee in America. Mother's knee is very visible because of the miniskirts, but the children are not clustering around it picking up morality.

Interview, New York/The New York Times, 1-30:29.

Joe B. Frantz
Director, Oral History Project, University of Texas at Austin

Life (in the United States) is good today because of the great opening of knowledge, the excitement of being in the middle of the real period of transition. Things are happening. If you have zest for the combat arena, you can't help but enjoy it. I like the mobility we have today—that is, not just physical mobility, but the fact that we can move in any direction. One thing missing is a sense of certainty. But that has its advantages in that there's nothing dull about life today. If all you want is serenity, why then you've picked the wrong time to be born.

Interview/U.S. News & World Report, 1-11:26.

Gilbert Gude
United States Representative, R—Md.

With the bicentennial of our nation just a few years away, Americans should take a fresh look at the older parts of their cities and towns. We should ask ourselves, "What are the features of my town that have character and charm and historic meaning? Is there an old home whose gardens were once the pride of the town? Is there a worthwhile structure connected with a legend or an incident in history? Is there an old building that could be an attractive restaurant or inn?" In preserving and protecting these features, we can show our young people their roots in American traditions. Our older people will also profit, knowing that not everything that is old and comfortable is due to be demolished, to be torn down because it is unappreciated.

Before the House, Washington, March 17/
The Washington Post, 3-28:(B)6.

Paul Harvey
News commentator, American Broadcasting Company

The trouble with parents today is that they are so preoccupied with making money—seeking to spare their children from the deprivation they knew during the Depression—that they're out working when they should be closening family ties. More than *pampering* their offspring, they have *neglected* them. I've been on college campuses constantly. I know there are always professional troublemakers around the fringes who are just there to fan the flames. But the big cross-section of young people are fine. And I think those who survive this era—if they don't rot their guts with alcohol or soften their brains with syphilis or get hooked on some drug they can't shake—having tasted its bitter fruits, are likely to be the strictest generation of parents since Queen Victoria.

Interview, Chicago/TV Guide, 2-20:22.

Theodore M. Hesburgh
President, University of Notre Dame

For the student born in 1950, 21 years old today, one can say that more has hap-pened in his lifetime, more change of every kind more rapidly accomplished during these 21 years, than in the total millennia-long history of mankind before 1950.

Before National Catholic Educational
Association, Minneapolis, April 12/
Los Angeles Herald-Examiner, 4-13:(A)7.

Stephen Hess
Chairman, White House Conference on Youth

As a society, if we fail to employ the idealism and energy of our young people, we do so at great risk. Moreover, if the last year-and-a-half has taught me nothing else, it has certainly taught me to both like and respect this youth generation. I, for one, have absolutely no fear for the future of this country. It will be in capable hands. In the meantime, however, I prescribe a dash of patience and a generous nip of goodwill.

The New York Times, 6-12:29.

Henry M. Jackson
United States Senator, D—Wash.

He (the late Senator Joseph McCarthy) moved in a way in which people literally were denied the Bill of Rights. We had people in this country who didn't dare speak out because of fear. This is a devastating technique, because, of all the forms of tyranny over the mind of man, fear is the worst. Thank God America rose up in its righteous wrath—liberals, conservatives, middle-of-the-roaders, all of us had our tummy full of that. But what we now see (with the current extremism of the left) is another denial, an interference, an attempt to intimidate people in public life who have a responsibility for making decisions, decisions which should be the will of the majority. People have a right to march, a right to protest. But they should understand that when they come out in large crowds they run the risk of that crowd being incited by extremists. What is an extremist? An extremist, whether that person is of the right or the left, is a person who would take the law into his own hands. And there is no place in America for an extremist of any kind . . .

Dallas, May/The Washington Post
(Potomac), 7-25:14.

Barnaby C. Keeney
Chairman, National Endowment for the Humanities

I'm . . . concerned about the humanities, because that's what's lacking in our society: the disinclination to ask why, or to ask to where are we going. That's where we've always had trouble. We've always had a lack of understanding of the past.

Interview, Washington/The Washington Post, 1-14:(G)1.

Walter Lippmann
Former political columnist

I've never known a time when people had so little confidence in the future. They're afraid; they're not sure they're equal to it; and there is a great deal of diffidence about the future . . . But I don't think that that is irremediable. I think even with all our size and complications and so on, if there comes a group of leaders—and there may well—and they can strike the right note, the country will respond.

Interview, Seal Harbor, Me./The Washington Post, 10-17:(C)1.

Marvin Mandel
Governor of Maryland

By any measure of the immediate past, we truly are a troubled nation—sick in spirit, aimless and adrift, overwhelmed by bigness, tortured by a feeling of helplessness, tormented by our own impatience with things as they are.

Inauguration address, Annapolis, Jan. 20/ The Washington Post, 1-21:(B)1.

Marya Mannes
Author, Journalist

To me it is a kind of total fragmentation that is going on in this country. It is a fragmentation as a result of throwing out the past—those who throw out the past entirely, which are the young, and those who refuse to let loose the roots of the past. And there are the countless fakers who want to be "with it," who deliberately abandon standards to be "with it." This goes for the arts

as well as the society . . . I hope profoundly we get someone in the next election who can convey in his philosophy of government and of life a body of living standards, borrowed partly from the past and added to by the young. Then I think we might get on the track again. If this doesn't happen, if we don't get proper leadership, I know I sound like a Cassandra, there will be some kind of catastrophe—it might be some kind of natural catastrophe—to pull us together. We're the only country that has not had one—not been invaded, not been bombed, has not been torn. It's a terrible thing to say, because I don't want to go down in it, but in a sense, adversity—which we haven't had since the Depression—might be very, very healthy for us.

Interview, New York/The Washington Post, 6-3:(B)3.

Charles McC. Mathias, Jr.
United States Senator, R—Md.

The beauty of America, I feel, is that we are not all alike.

Quote, 4-11:337.

Eugene J. McCarthy
Former United States Senator, D—Minn.

People are seeking participation. They feel irrelevant and insignificant. They feel that what they think doesn't matter in deciding how corporations are run, what TV programs are shown, the quality of products they buy. If politics belonged to them, if the government responded, they'd feel a lot better.

Interview, Washington, March 30/ The New York Times, 4-1:41.

George S. McGovern
United States Senator, D—S.D.

In this decade, when we are about to observe the 200th anniversary of our country, we have a new opportunity to square the nation's practices with its founding ideals. As we enter this period, we must undertake a re-examination of our ideas, institutions and the actual conditions of our life which is as fundamental as the discussions of the founding fathers two centuries ago. A public figure today can perform no greater service than to lay bare the proven malfunctions of our society, try honestly to confront our problems in all their complexity and stimulate the search for solutions.

Announcing his candidacy for 1972 Presidential election, Jan. 18/ The New York Times, 1-19:18.

Thoughtful Americans understand that the highest patriotism is not a blind acceptance of official policy, but a love of one's country deep enough to call her to a higher standard.

Announcing his candidacy for 1972 Presidential election, Jan. 18/ The New York Times, 1-19:18.

Golda Meir
Prime Minister of Israel

I owed America much. I arrived a frightened little girl. When I left, aged 23, I was a self-confident young woman. I was not fleeing from oppression and insecurity: I was leaving of my own accord, a good, generous people. I was born under tyranny, but brought up in democracy. It was a country which had fought for independence and had written its own constitution. It was a pioneer's country. It had a dream: the American dream. It still believes in tomorrow.

Interview/Los Angeles Times, 1-24:(F)2.

James Michener
Author

Because I'm much impressed that all great societies have gone down in the course of history, I feel it inescapable that it'll happen here also. However, I'm optimistic that we're good for another 200 to 300 years; because I think we're capable of delaying it, or smoothing it out. I'm sure we don't have to parallel Greece, Persia or Rome, which went from apogee to nadir.

New York/The Christian Science Monitor, 3-4:13.

Arthur R. Miller
Professor of Law, University of Michigan

Consider the implications of these three propositions: First, Americans are scrutinized, measured, watched, counted and interrogated by more government agencies, law enforcement officials, social scientists and poll takers than at any time in our history. Second, probably in no nation on earth is as much individualized information collected, recorded and disseminated as in the United States. Third, the information-gathering and surveillance activities of the Federal government have expanded to such an extent that they are becoming a threat to several basic rights of every American—privacy, speech, assembly, association and petition of government.

Before Senate Subcommittee on Constitutional Rights, Washington, Feb. 25/The New York Times, 2-28:(4)4.

Thomas H. Moorer
Admiral, United States Navy; Chairman, Joint Chiefs of Staff

. . . the most important ingredient in the security of this country is the will of the American people. They must want security, they must want to compete, they must want to be Number 1, if we are going to continue to contribute to the well-being of our fellowman as we have in the past—and at the same time discharge the responsibilities we have as a great and democratic nation. It disturbs me to see people shy away from this because it is a tendency that is developing and it is contrary to the principles on which we've built this country. I worry about this with respect to the young people. In many cases, their tendency is to avoid competition. I think that is bad in any field. I'm not just talking about in the military. We must maintain a burning desire to excel.

Interview, Washington/The Christian Science Monitor, 9-9:9.

Bill D. Moyers
Former Press Secretary to the President of the United States

The myth of American omnipotence, which I cut my teeth on, has faded, and we seem to be taking on a dour outlook about the entire future. The country seems to be

(BILL D. MOYERS)

passing a great kidney stone which will leave us completely changed.

*Before American Library Association, Dallas/
The New York Times, 6-25:40.*

Like members of a religious cult waiting for the sudden reappearance of the Messiah, Americans seem to want a political savior, someone to whom we can transfer our hope for a better day and on whose shoulders we can place the responsibility for achieving it. But it's apparent now that the direction America goes will be decided not by some miracle-working, super-human personality, but by each of us. A nation can be no more truthful than each of us, no more honest than each of us, no more generous, no more worthy than each of us. America is really the whole of its parts.

*At Hofstra University commencement/
The Wall Street Journal, 7-8:10.*

Daniel P. Moynihan
Former Counsellor to the President of the United States

I think it's a moment to be exceedingly impressed by the capacity of democracy to take the people through awful tribulations and terrible strains. You could not conceive a temptation to be stupid or ugly or short-sighted to which the American public has not been exposed in the last decade. To be paranoid, ungenerous, bigoted, frightened. And yet, that is not what it is. It is generous, it is calm, thoughtful, perceptive. If you want to know how strong a democracy it is, I should think this is not the time to read the speeches of our leaders but to read the election returns. Think of what other societies have succumbed to, given comparable strains, comparable tensions and temptations. We have a pretty good country.

*Interview/The New York Times Magazine,
6-27:58.*

Edmund S. Muskie
United States Senator, D—Maine

Almost a century-and-a-half ago . . . a distinguished French observer, Alexis de Toequeville, visited these shores. He was to write that, "America is a land of wonders . . . no natural boundary seems to be set to the efforts of man; and in his eyes, what is not yet done is only what he has not yet attempted to do." That description, I believe, captures the underlying spirit of this nation . . . It is a spirit of hope, of potential, of new directions. It is a spirit which is still valid. It is a spirit we cannot afford to lose. That spirit has beckoned to men and women from the Seventeenth Century to the Twentieth—men and women of different cultures, of different languages, of different beliefs. They came not as oppressors, but as people oppressed. They came not to practice violence, but to live in peace. They came not to destroy a country, but to build—first a home, then a community and finally a nation. In a period of history such as this, in a time of ferment such as this, in a world of change such as this, we need to be reminded of our origins as a nation; of the distance we have traveled; of the progress we have achieved. We are by no means perfect. But we can still take pride in the problems we have solved, in the barriers we have overcome and in the hardships we have weathered . . . Of course, that spirit has not always been tranquil . . . There have been disputes—many of them bitter—over territorial boundaries, over foreign allegiances, over fundamental human rights. But they have never destroyed the promise of America. What is that promise? It is the promise of a free society governed by the rule of law. It is the promise of the right to vote and the right to be secure from extreme conduct. It is the promise of progress through peaceful political means.

*Before New England Historical Society/
The National Observer, 2-8:16.*

Ralph Nader
Lawyer; Consumer rights advocate

Our flag is a beautiful patriotic symbol; and I don't want it associated with military power and jet planes. It should be associated with domestic justice and peace and compassion between one's fellow men.

Los Angeles/
The Hollywood Reporter, 5-5:3.

Richard M. Nixon
President of the United States

. . . if we can get this country thinking not of how to fight a war, but how to win a peace; if we can get this country thinking of clean air, clean water, open spaces, of a welfare reform program that will provide a floor under the income of every family with children in America; a new form, a new approach to government; reform of education, reform of health—if those things begin to happen, if people can think of these positive things, then we'll have the lift of a driving dream. But it takes some time to get rid of the nightmares. You can't be having a driving dream when you're in the midst of a nightmare.

Television interview, Washington, Jan. 4/
The New York Times, 1-5:21.

There can be no generation gap in America. The destiny of this nation is not divided into "yours" and "ours"—it is one destiny. We share it together, we are responsible for it together and, in the way we respond, history will judge us together. There's been too much emphasis on the differences between the generations in America . . . My generation has invested all that it has—not only its love but its hope and its faith—in yours. I believe you will redeem that faith and justify that hope. I believe that, as our generations work together, as we strive together, as we aspire together, we can achieve together, achieve great things for America and the world.

At University of Nebraska, Jan. 14/
The New York Times, 1-15:12.

You know, you can walk around carrying a sign . . . But what does that prove? What does it prove to shout a slogan? What does it prove when you shout just the same thing over and over again? What does it prove unless you do something about it—unless you do something in terms of working with the system to change it?

Television interview/"Today" show,
National Broadcasting Company,
Washington, 3-15.

. . . this is a good time to be alive and not a bad time to be alive. And if you had to choose a place to live, this is the best country in the world in which to live.

Television interview, Washington/"Today"
show, National Broadcasting Company, 3-15.

Night after night on your television, and day after day in your newspapers, you see and you read and you hear those things so often that are wrong about America. We should hear about those things. But we should recognize that the greatness of this country is that we have a system which allows us to correct what is wrong. And I would also remind us all that, as we hear and as we read of what is wrong about America, let's not overlook—as a matter of fact, let's put more emphasis on—what is right about America.

At 80th Continental Congress of the Daughters
of the American Revolution/The Washington
Post, 4-24:(A)18.

Faith in the American future has never been misplaced. It is not misplaced today. In dealing with the future of this country, if you want to be a realist, you have to be an optimist. Two centuries of struggle have earned us a right that is not in our Constitution, but a right that permeates our national life—the right to be confident in our own ability to shape the future.

Before Chamber of Commerce of the United
States, April 26/The Washington Post,
4-27:(A)6.

Sometimes when I see those pillars (on government buildings in Washington), I think of seeing them on the Acropolis in Greece; I think of seeing them also in the Forum in Rome—great stark pillars; and I have walked in both at night. I think of what happened to Greece and Rome, and you see what is

39

(RICHARD M. NIXON)

left—only the pillars. What has happened, of course, is that great civilizations of the past, as they have become wealthy, as they have lost their will to live, to improve, then they have become subject to the decadence that eventually destroys the civilization. The United States is now reaching that period. I am convinced, however, that we have the vitality, I believe we have the courage. I believe we have the strength out through this heartland and across this nation that will see to it that America not only is rich and strong, but that it is healthy in terms of moral and spiritual strength. I am convinced it is there.

Before newspaper, TV and radio executives, Kansas City/Time, 7-19:8;The National Observer, 7-12:2.

The turmoil and uncertainty of the years just past have severely strained America's spirit, and led many to question the nation's purposes, its destiny, even its goodness. We hear the "system" that has produced our abundance and protected our freedom denounced as oppressive and materialist. We hear our defense establishment, which has saved other nations as well as our own from tyranny and conquest, denounced as "militarist" and evil. The right to criticize makes us strong and free. But when so many voices are running down America, the time has come to speak up for America. It's easy to sit back and criticize; it's hard to make the sacrifices, do the work, make the extra effort that makes the difference between a nation on the way down and a nation on the way up. Let no one expect to make his fortune—or his reputation—by selling America short. I see a new confidence in this land, a new birth of faith in ourselves. I see a willingness to face reality, a revival of moral courage, a fresh determination to succeed.

Before Knights of Columbus, New York, Aug. 17/The New York Times, 8-18:23.

There is an insidious line of propaganda that runs through some public commentaries today, and that line is it doesn't matter whether America is Number 1. It matters very much for America to continue to be the leader of the world. There is no other nation in the world that has the strength and potential to defend freedom around the world, to negotiate for peace. So the United States must maintain that strength if we want to have peace. And we shall.

At Veterans of Foreign Wars convention, Dallas, Aug. 19/The Dallas Times Herald, 8-20:(A)1.

Hard work is what made America great. There could be no more dangerous delusion than the notion that we can maintain the standard of living that our own people sometimes complain about, but the rest of the world envies, without continuing to work hard. The "good life" is not the lazy life, or the empty life, or the life that consumes without producing. The good life is the active, productive, working life—the life that gives as well as gets.

Before Congress, Washington, Sept. 9/ The Washington Post, 9-10:(A)12.

The young in America are no longer going to be treated as a mass or a bloc in this country —neither as a generation apart nor as a generation idolized. You deserve better than that. And you will have better. For America is rapidly moving to take you, the young, into full partnership as individuals in our society. Your country knows how much it needs you; and we are proving that, not just with talk but with action. We need your voice first in the political process, as soon as you are prepared for that trust. We need your ideas; we need them in the national debate on issues, goals and directions . . . Certainly, the time when the young are to be seen and not heard is gone in America—and gone for good.

Before National 4–H Congress, Chicago/ The National Observer, 12-11:10.

John J. Riccardo
President, Chrysler Corporation

Two major factors have been suggested as the basic strengths of this country, and I am very much inclined to accept the theory. First is the political stability of the United States. We can and do effect complete changes in state and national administrations without critical disruption of the system. This happens despite the campaign rhetoric by those who are "in" claiming that the whole system will collapse if they don't stay in, and the same claims by the "outs" if they don't get in. The fact is that once the people have decided on change, the change is quiet, orderly and stable. The second major strength of our country operates within the framework of this political stability, and it is an economic system which offers tremendous opportunities for self-improvement, the hope of personal gain and rewards for those who have the motivation, the ability and the willingness to work. It holds the promise of reward for creativity, for personal sacrifice and for dedicated effort. These are just the practical, material answers to the critics and the challengers. We can stand on that record alone. What other economic system can match it? Where in history has there been its equal? . . . The history of this country makes it clear that those two basic strengths—political stability and the best economic system in the world—have combined to make possible more freedom, more choice, more leisure and more opportunity for development of self and soul than anywhere else in the world.

Before Adcraft Club, Detroit, March 12/
Vital Speeches, 5-1:434.

Elliot L. Richardson
Secretary of Health, Education and Welfare of the United States

These are, in Dickens' words, the best of times and the worst of times. Amid unparalleled material prosperity, the nation roils under a bitter and relentless attack on one institution after another. The edge of our personal relations is grim and harsh; and too many of us are retreating into private caves of alienation.

Before National Press Club, Washington/
Los Angeles Times, 5-16:(C)8.

James M. Roche
Chairman, General Motors Corporation

The current disparagement of America holds many ironies. One is that the country is criticized for the relatively narrow area of shortcoming without credit for the broad range of achievement. For example, the nation is credited less with a superior system of public higher education than it is criticized for not making it freely available to all, even the unqualified. The nation is credited less with an incomparable transportation system than it is faulted for its traffic jams. The nation is credited less for having two-thirds of its families own their own homes than it is condemned for its slums.

Before Economic Club of Chicago, March 25/
The New York Times, 3-26:53.

Nelson A. Rockefeller
Governor of New York

When we as a people were conquering an untamed continent, surviving a deep and bitter depression, fighting wars whose aims were understood, we had a strong sense of national purpose, a strong sense of common destiny. We knew where we were going then. Today, we seem, momentarily, to have lost our way. We have undreamed-of material gains. And we have learned that material possessions are not enough; for a man is essentially a spiritual being. I believe there is a new adventure for America—a brave new challenge that can unite us again in common purpose. It is a quest for a new spirituality in our lives. For there is nothing wrong with America that courage, commitment and love cannot conquer. There is nothing wrong with America that we don't have the human and natural resources to overcome. There is truly nothing America can't achieve—if we will only believe in ourselves again.

Inaugural address, Albany, Jan. 1/
The New York Times, 1-2:14.

William J. Ronan
Chairman, New York State Metropolitan Transportation Authority

Today, the problems of urban society must be reckoned with against a backdrop of a rapidly-shifting, surrealistic urban cape. We are

41

(WILLIAM J. RONAN)

forced to decide and to act in a bizarre arena—a kind of theatre of the unreal. We see serious issues treated as fads. Peace, ecology, power, pollution, transportation, civil rights—all dominate the scene like emergency flares, and then fade as the press, television and the public tire of them. In some peculiar form of regression, we seem content to seek expiation—not by ridding ourselves of problems, but by indulging them ritually and transferring the whole mess to communally agreed-upon villains. It's a new form of urban witchcraft.

Before Association of the Bar of the City of New York/The New York Times, 3-24:39.

William L. Safire
Special Assistant to the President of the United States

Despite all the mutterings about the forces of reaction, despite the genuine problems of bureaucratic inertia, the acceleration of improvement is the central fact about American life today; and it is not leaving us in any slack-jawed state of future shock. Bruce Barton used to say, "When you're through changing, you're through." As the prospects for 1972 indicate, this nation is not through changing. On the contrary, our ability to absorb change, to stimulate change, is the reason why the American Revolution, after two centuries, is more vital and exciting than ever.

At "New York Law Journal" Forum/ The New York Times, 12-23:25.

Thomas R. Shepard, Jr.
Publisher, "Look" magazine

If so many people are against free enterprise, is it worth saving? I think it is. With all its faults, it is by far the best system yet devised for the production, distribution and widespread enjoyment of goods and services. It is more than coincidence that virtually all of mankind's scientific progress came in the two centuries when free enterprise was operating in the Western world, and that most of that progress was achieved in the nation regarded as the leading exponent of free enterprise: the United States of America. For in the past 200

years—an eyeblink in history—an America geared to private industry has conquered communicable diseases, abolished starvation, brought literacy to the masses, transported men to another planet and expanded the horizons of its citizens to an almost incredible degree by giving them wheels and wings and electronic extensions of their eyes, their ears, their hands, even their brains.

Los Angeles Times, 8-22:(G)2.

Preston Smith
Governor of Texas

The thing most wrong with America is the attitude of some that it cannot be made better.

Inauguration address, Austin, Jan. 19/ The Dallas Times Herald, 1-20:(AA)1.

Barbara Tuchman
Author, Historian

Our main priority should be the quality of American life, rather than the containment of Communism. We must strengthen our own society. Communism is like a disease; it attacks a rotten body.

Interview, San Francisco/San Francisco Examiner, 3-17:27.

Jack Vaughn
President, National Urban Coalition

There is a terrifying impatience among Americans—instant coffee, instant oatmeal and instant revolution. Everything is always urgency and crisis. Then next year, we will spend months feeling guilty because the projects we hurried into this year didn't really meet the basic issues.

Before New England District, American College Public Relations Association, Hartford, Conn./The Wall Street Journal, 5-19:14.

Lewis W. Walt
General (Ret.) and former Assistant Commandant, United States Marine Corps

America's greatest danger lies in our own country . . . Freedom must be defended 24 hours a day. We can't have peace without spirit and unity, nor liberty without sacrifice . . . Apathy is a national cancer.

At International Orphans, Inc. dinner, Los Angeles/Los Angeles Herald-Examiner 2-11:(B) 7.

Ralph D. Abernathy
President,
Southern Christian Leadership Conference

Some people remember George Washington as the father of our country. But I remember him as a slaveholder. I remember him as a whoremonger. And if he was father of our country, then this country is a prostitute.

On 42nd anniversary of the birth of Dr. Martin Luther King, Jr., New York, Jan. 15/The New York Times, 1-16:35.

(Vice President) Agnew says that black people should take constructive action. I believe the most constructive action black people can take is to help remove from public office irresponsibile, bigoted and irrational politicians such as Spiro T. Agnew.

July 20/The Dallas Times Herald, 7-21:(A)7.

(Regarding violence in relation to civil rights): Violence is not the way. But I understand those who want to burn it down, who want to leave the country or go to Africa. I'm not going anywhere. I didn't ask to come here and I ain't leaving.

Quote, 8-15:146.

Spiro T. Agnew
Vice President of the United States

We in this Administration believe in giving you (American Indians) control over what you have. The reservations are your lands. The lives you lead on them are your lives. The Federal government has (the) obligation to provide financial support. But *you* should establish the priorities; *you* should allocate the funds; *you* should guide the projects.

Before National Conference of American Indians, Kansas City, March 8/ The New York Times, 3-10:17.

(The African leaders of Ethiopia, Kenya and the Congo) have impressed me with their understanding of their internal problems, their moderateness and their recognition of the difficulties (between their countries and the rest of the world). This is in distinct contrast—the quality of this leadership—to many of those in the United States who have arrogated unto themselves the position of black leaders, those who spend their times in querulous complaint and constant recriminations against the rest of society. If you read your newspapers over the past year and see how many of these leaders have been complaining and carping, you'll find out that they comprise a very substantial cross-section of what describes itself as black leadership . . . I happen to believe that there are many, many black people in the United States who are tired of this constant complaining, and who would like to see some constructive action from these people.

News conference en route between Kinshasa and Madrid, July 17/The New York Times, 7-18:1: The Washington Post, 7-18:(A)14.

. . . to be completely candid, one has only to look in the news reports every day to see that some of the more militant black leadership in America are using too much of the tactics of accusation and recrimination about what's not being accomplished. I don't see many cases where black leadership in America has said that "the black medium income has made tremendous strides in the past 10 years and we're encouraged by that and we want to commend people of both races for the work they did to make this happen." Instead, it's never enough and never fast enough. And whatever progress is made is described too often as tokenism. Again, I don't want to lump all of the black leadership into this attitude. There are very fine groups of leaders who don't subscribe to this.

Interview, Washington/The Christian Science Monitor, 8-10:19.

Saul D. Alinsky
Sociologist

When the (Black) Panthers began, I found myself quite sympathetic. But what's wrong or right about them is academic now. The moment Huey Newton glorified the shooting at (the) Marin County (Calif.) Courthouse, they blew it. I think the Panthers are asking for it. They've never been as strong as the press has indicated, and there's a suicidal obsession now. A guy has to be a political idiot to say all power comes out of the barrel of a gun, when the other side has all the guns. A lot of their rhetoric has become a bore. You start saying "whitefascist-racistpig" and people turn off. Here's Newton saying he can't get justice in an American court, and all the time he's saying that he's out on reversal by a superior court. The Panthers will still get a bubble of publicity, but their days are numbered.

Interview/The New York Times, 1-6:33.

James B. Allen
United States Senator, D—Ala.

In Southern states, these (Federal school-integration) agencies literally stomp public schools out of existence, close them down and scatter children and the teachers of these schools all over the countryside. This is the bulldozer approach to compulsory integration of schools used in the South. These agencies see no evil, hear no evil and speak no evil when it comes to racial discrimination in public schools in regions outside the South.

Before the Senate, Washington, April 19/
The New York Times, 4-20:16.

Reubin Askew
Governor of Florida

(Regarding school busing for racial balance): . . . busing, certainly, is an artificial and inadequate instrument of change. Nobody really wants it—not you, not me, not the people, not the school boards—not even the courts. Yet the law demands, and rightly so, that we put an end to segregation in our society. We must demonstrate good faith in doing just that. We must demonstrate a greater willingness to initiate meaningful steps in this area. We must stop *inviting*, by our own intransigence, devices which are repugnant to us. In this way, and in this way only, will we stop massive busing once and for all. Only in this way will we put the divisive and self-defeating issue of race behind us once and for all. And only in this way can we redirect our energies to our real quest—that of providing an equal opportunity for quality education to all our children. If there is another answer, I have yet to hear it.

At University of Florida commencement,
Aug. 28/The New York Times, 9-2:33.

Birch Bayh
United States Senator, D—Ind.

Not since the War Between the States has the subject of race so seriously threatened the fabric of our society. It transcends any other facing us, far beyond the pulse rate of our gross national productivity, beyond even the horror of Vietnam. Richard Nixon has not provided the leadership necessary for a nation to discover the amoral fact that racism is a national hobby we can no longer afford; that racism kills white, black and brown alike, physically and spiritually . . . that racism will survive, individually and institutionally, as long as we refuse to make an individual as well as an institutional commitment to its eradication.

Washington, May 27/Daily World, 6-1:7.

Julian Bond
Georgia State Legislator

(Regarding Alabama Governor George C. Wallace): He's a dangerous man because he is an intelligent man. Now there are many other Southern racists who don't have his mind. I think he's a master politician, and for that reason a dangerous, dangerous man. (It is) dangerous to make him a figure of fun, because he potentially can do so much harm. I mean, the old saying he had in '68 about "if you lie down in front of my car, that's the last car you'll lie down in front of." I think he means that.

Interview/"David Frost Show,"
Westinghouse Broadcasting Company, 8-10.

Edward W. Brooke
United States Senator, R–Mass.

Think what the response could be if, today, millions of white Americans said to those who are black, yellow, red and poor, "We are wrong. We are sorry for years of prejudice, misunderstanding, hatred and discrimination. We accept you as our brothers. We will work with you to achieve what this country ought to be."

At University of Massachusetts at Amherst commencement/The New York Times, 6-14:44.

Robert S. Browne
Professor of Economics, Fairleigh Dickinson University

The black community has erred for too long on the side of subordinating its own best interest to those which were identified as "the national interest." Now that we are reaching our political maturity, we are beginning to discern that there is no such thing as "the national interest." There are merely a number of competing, conflicting, special interests—each greedily seeking to gain control over the largest possible share of the nation's wealth, income and political apparatus. The task which lies before us, as black people, is to devise effective strategies through which we might insure that our lagging, beloved black community at long last obtains an equitable portion of these American prizes.

At luncheon sponsored by Chicago Economic Development Corp., June 4/ The New York Times, 6-7:24.

James L. Buckley
United States Senator-elect, C–N.Y.

It is now clearly against the law—it is not constitutional—to discriminate against anyone on the basis of color. I believe those laws have got to be assiduously enforced. But I don't believe it therefore follows that we should have forced *integration*. We just cannot have forced *segregation*. I am against busing as a means of social engineering.

Interview/The Washington Post, 1-10:(B)2.

Robert C. Byrd
United States Senator, D–W.Va.

(Criticizing court-ordered school busing for racial balance): What kind of national madness has obsessed us? Would the people of this country tolerate this nonsense if it were . . . perpetrated on them by legislative bodies? The answer has to be no, because the people then would have the recourse of the ballot in purging from public office those who would visit upon them and their children such a monstrous and costly madness.

At Young Americans for Freedom convention, Houston, Sept. 3/The Washington Post, 9-4:(A)2.

At some future date—hopefully not too far away—children, both black and white, will no longer be treated as guinea pigs in a social experiment (school busing for racial balance) that amounts to pure folly; and that the needless hauling of them, like cattle, for countless miles and at a wasteful price, will cease to be an obsessional fetish.

Quote, 11-28:507.

Jimmy Carter
Governor of Georgia

We have been afflicted, both personally and in the national press, with, I think, unfair criticism because of the racial problems in the South. Our people have struggled with this problem in a personal way for generations. We have now made—certainly reluctantly in many instances—a major decision to abide by the law. But this hasn't ended the problem, because we're still faced with the daily necessity of assimilating changed social habits. It's still a major problem; but, in effect, our people have decided to face it fairly and on our own initiative now. Politically, I think it would be a serious mistake for a candidate to try to revive racism as a major issue. That's because most of our people, even the arch-segregationists who are in positions of any type of leadership, simply do not want to have to face this traumatic decision all over again.

The National Observer, 4-5:5.

Ramsey Clark
Former Attorney General of the United States

If we had 68 blacks in Congress, we'd solve most of the problems that plague the blacks overnight.
At Southern Methodist University, April 22/
The Dallas Times Herald, 4-23:(B)1.

William Clay
United States Representative, D—Mo.

At one point, the politics of blacks was based on the theory of appeasement to the white majority. Today, that old politics of accomodation has been replaced by the new politics of confrontation. And those providing the leadership for this new politics possess a deep sense of personal commitment to the concept of justice and equality at any cost. Our new politics demands a re-evaluation of the old concept that what's good for the nation is good for minorities. Those who now embrace the new black politics must couch their thinking in the fundamental concept that what's good for minorities is also good for this nation. This position out of necessity requires the development of a new political philosophy. And that philosophy must be practical, sometimes selfish.
Daily World. 6-26:6.

(Regarding Vice President Agnew's recent criticism of black leaders in the U.S.): In my opinion . . . our Vice President is seriously ill. He has all the symptoms of an intellectual misfit. His recent tirade against black leadership is just part of a game played by him called "mental masturbation." Apparently, Mr. Agnew is an intellectual sadist who experiences intellectual orgasms by attacking, humiliating and kicking the oppressed. Mr. Agnew's attack on black leaders . . . assures him of retaining his championship as "buffoon of the year."
Before the House, Washington, July 21/
Los Angeles Times, 7-23:(1)10.

The mass demonstrations, boycotts and marches of the past were appeals to conscience. They are totally ineffective in the nation now. It doesn't have a conscience. If blacks are to get any justice, it will be through political power.
Interview/U.S. News & World Report, 8-23:28.

William M. Colmer
United States Representative, D—Miss.

I think some of the so-called civil rights bills were too hastily enacted. And they went too far under the guise of trying to help some of our colored brethren—I suppose "black" is the word, but my Negro friends wouldn't want to be called "black". . . . It wasn't the Civil Rights Act or the Voting Rights Act that increased the number of Negroes participating in elections in the South. It was the organized effort of the various black organizations and the so-called liberal organizations.
Interview, Washington/
Los Angeles Times, 2-28:(F)2.

Ronald V. Dellums
United States Representative, D—Calif.

You don't have to be black to be a nigger. Anyone who gets kicked, exploited and harmed by this society is a nigger; and they will demand better once thay realize that.
The National Observer, 2-1:2.

Bob Dole
United States Senator, R—Kan.

I've never been able to figure out why people could stand and applause, tears in their eyes, when a black just scored the winning basket—and then have chills go down their spine if they sat next to him at dinner.
Washington/San Francisco Examiner, 1-7:2.

Charles Evers
Mayo Fayette, Miss.; Candidate for Governor of Mississippi

We (black people) got to keep pushing. We got to knock down the racial barriers one by one. People say, "Why do you want to be Governor?" I want to be Governor for the same reason I want to sit in the front of that bus or sleep in a decent hotel; because I have the right.
Interview, Fayette/
The Washington Post, 8-22:(A)2.

James Farmer
Former Assistant Secretary for Administration, Department of Health, Education and Welfare of the United States

The President (Nixon) must address himself to the issues facing black people and make better use of the black talent he has. The black community has grown accustomed to have the President of the United States articulate some of their dreams. We haven't had that the past two years . . . I think words are terribly important. Words help provide direction. The President has said nothing to black people; he has been quiet. If there are no promises, no hope and nothing to look forward to, then frustration builds up. There is hoplessness, and violence is the result.

Philadelphia, Jan. 12/
The Washington Post, 1-14:(A)29.

Walter E. Fauntroy
Delegate to United States House of Representatives, D–D.C.

We (Negroes) have got to stop shucking and jiving and rapping and talking, and start organizing. If we will believe and if we will confront racism and poverty and deal with it as it is, we shall overcome . . . They said to me (during his campaign): "Don't come out here in the ghetto talking about black and white together." They told me, "Revolution is almost here, and we've got to do it ourselves." But I told them now is not the time to go murder-mouthing white people or putting down Negroes who wear shirts and ties. I told them, "You don't take on the Army, Navy, Marines and Air Force —backed up by the metropolitan police—with a .22 pistol." And so I went ahead; and the thing most rewarding was that the majority, given the chance to express themselves quietly, said, "We are tired of polarization."

At Martin Luther King memorial service,
Waldorf, Md., April 18/
The Washington Post, 4-19:(C)1.

Arthur A. Fletcher
Assistant Secretary of Labor of the United States

The preachers and teachers who brought us

(black people) this far played a role in their day. The real leaders of the future are going to be blacks in political office. Blacks recognize that government regulates your life, regulates your business, and is the great dispenser of money.

U.S. News & World Report, 9-20:57.

Joe Frazier
Heavyweight Boxing Champion of the World

We must save our people; and when I say our people, I mean white and black. We need to quit thinking who's living next door, who's driving a big car, who's my little daughter going to play with, who is she going to sit next to in school. We don't have time for that.

Before South Carolina Legislature,
Columbia, April 7/The New York Times,
4-11:(4)7.

Howard A. Glickstein
Staff Director, United States Commission on Civil Rights

. . . I see the increasing racial polarization of our urban areas emerging as the major civil-rights issue of the '70's. As we all know, our cities are becoming increasingly black and poor and our suburbs white and affluent. Jobs and the amenities of city living are moving outward, while blacks are being compressed into the central city, with its aging housing and eroding tax base. We scarcely can hope for better community relations in America so long as this polarization is allowed to continue . . .

Before House Subcommittee, Washington,
Aug. 4/U.S. News & World Report,
8-23:25.

Henry B. Gonzalez
United States Representative, D–Tex.

(Objecting to a "brown caucus" in Congress): We should not pretend that the problems of Mexican-Americans are so unique that programs should not affect all Americans . . . If we cry in an empty room, then we may only hear our own echoes.

The Dallas Times Herald, 10-24:(A)32.

47

Robert P. Griffin
United States Senator, R—Mich.

I am deeply concerned that forced (school) busing solely for the purpose of achieving racial balance is counter-productive. Instead of helping in the effort to promote better race relations, it is resulting in more bitterness and more polarization.

The New York Times, 10-3:(1)67.

Richard G. Hatcher
Mayor of Gary, Ind.

The fact is that, as cities become increasingly black, they are being placed on back burners, and state goals become more popular. The thinking is that anything black is useless.

Airlie, Va., Feb. 22/
The New York Times, 2-23:41.

Theodore M. Hesburgh
Chairman, United States Commission on Civil Rights

One can argue about the costs of equality in America today. But God knows we have known the costs of inequality—wasted talents, frustration, poverty piled on poverty, generation after generation. Laws have been grudgingly passed and more grudgingly obeyed, with every possible legal evasion tested.

San Francisco Examiner & Chronicle
(This World), 9-26:2.

Paul G. Hoffman
Administrator, United Nations Development Program

I have believed for a great many years that the thing America has to realize is the seriousness of a simple little phrase: "regardless of race, creed or color." Until we recognize that as the essential of a first-class country, we are not going to make the progress we should make.

Interview, New York/
The New York Times, 4-25:(1)5.

Roy Innis
National director, Congress of Racial Equality

I had hopes that the change from a Democratic to a Republican Administration would bring a change in styles of dealing with the problems affecting black people; but I haven't seen that change. I've seen only an attempt to try to do some of the same old things in a slightly different way. Neither Administration has really dealt with the fundamental issues affecting the black community: the institutions, the need for a basic restructuring of organizations and the transfer of management and control from people outside the black communities to the people inside those communities. That is not a radical doctrine at all. This is a basic American approach to solving problems through a truly local governmental unit.

Interview/U.S. News & World Report,
1-11:29.

The civil-rights movement is dead—or dying. At least in its old form. I think of movements as happening simultaneously in dynamic relationships. We have two curves, one going up while the other is declining. The civil-rights movement is on the declining curve, while another movement—with different goals and broader strategy—is on the upswing. That is the black nationalist movement . . . the civil-rights movement failed miserably in its other goal—to integrate America. Integration is something quite different from desegregation. What has caused the frustration we see among blacks today is this failure in striving for integration. This is a false goal. Let me make clear: Those blacks who do want to melt in the American melting pot should have that right. All I'm saying is that those who do not want that, but want to aggregate their social, political and economic resources as a group—a separatist group—should also have that right. And I think the majority of blacks will choose that path.

Interview/U.S. News & World Report,
8-23:27.

Daniel K. Inouye
United States Senator, D—Hawaii

We in Hawaii felt we were ready for statehood for 50 years . . . they used every conceivable reason (to deny statehood). But in back of all of this was the unmentionable argument. You would hear, "How would you like to have a Senator named Yakamoto?" In the case of the District of Columbia, at cocktail parties people say, "Oh, yes, we believe in the political philosophy of home rule or whatever; but, Senator, you've got too many Negroes there."

Interview/"Newswatch," WMAL-TV,
Washington, 3-21.

H. J. Jackson
President, National Baptist Convention

Since 1954, there have sprung up in America groups of American leaders and American citizens who have apparently lost sight of the highest goals of civil-rights—that is, the complete achievement of first-class citizenship which carries with it first-class responsibilities. There are among us today Negro leaders who are preaching the gospel of separatism and are advocating a new practice of discrimination and segregation. On this level of life, high goals are never attained, and we can never inherit our promised land.

Before National Baptist Convention,
Cleveland/The National Observer,
10-30:9.

Henry M. Jackson
United States Senator, D—Wash.

There's no reason why a child in one town should have a better education than a child in an adjoining town who is discriminated against just because of where he lives. The problem today is not in the white schools to which black children are bussed. The facts are that those black children get a better education in the schools where pupils are predominately white. The problem is in the black schools to which white children are bussed. Chances for an education are still not equal there.

Los Angeles Herald-Examiner, 11-7:(A)15.

Jesse L. Jackson
Director, Operation Breadbasket, Southern Christian Leadership Conference

The black liberation movement is moving into its final phase, and that's economic. We won the first civil rights battle in the mid-nine-

teen-fifties, and the second one in 1965, with equal voting rights. Now the number one question is black economic power . . . and our solution for liberation is economic. Blacks are just as eager as whites to get their people off the welfare rolls, and the only way that can be done is for the government and business to direct some of their energies to promoting black economic independence.

Interview, Chicago, Oct. 8/
The New York Times, 10-10:(1)56.

Samuel C. Jackson
General Assistant Secretary of Housing and Urban Development of the United States

The fact is that the percentage of high-income blacks living in the suburbs is substantially lower than low-income whites. The fact is that if a black man wants to buy a house in the ghetto, he is courted by both black and white real estate agents. But if he wants to live outside the ghetto, few will service his needs.

Before National Association of Real Estate Brokers, Washington/The Washington Post,
2-27:(D)13.

LeRoi Jones
Playwright, Poet

. . . if someone sees the American Jewish Congress, they don't feel threatened by it. It is an institution for Jews created by Jews. When we speak of black institutions for black people, it becomes some kind of weird concept.

News Conference, Newark, N.J./
Los Angeles Times, 4-1:(1-A)7.

Vernon E. Jordan, Jr.
Executive director-designate, National Urban League

Black people today, for all their righteous anger and forceful dissent, still believe in the American dream. We believe because this is our land, too. Yes, this land is our land; and America will work for black people, too, or it will not work for anyone!

At National Urban League annual conference,
Detroit, July 28/The New York Times,
7-29:16.

(VERNON E. JORDAN, JR.)

In the '60s, we were really talking—at least in the South—about where black people could sit on the bus. Now we talk not about where they sit, because that's settled. Instead, we ask: Can a black man drive the bus? Can he be a supervisor at the bus company? Can a black man sit on the policy-making board of that company? Can he decide the routes of the bus, and to what extent they will facilitate the transportation of black people? What is the relationship of that transportation to accessible job opportunities? And will that transportation company be an equal-opportunity employer? In short, the basic issue has become the implementation of the rights that blacks won in the 1960s.

Interview/U.S. News & World Report,
8-23:28.

Gerald Kennedy
Bishop, Los Angeles area,
United Methodist Church

Some people have criticized the church and the ministry for being too active in this (civil rights) field; but I am very pleased whenever I see the church active in racial affairs and fighting for racial equality. The church in the past has all too often preferred a congregation to be "just our kind of folks." We have been very slow in realizing that the task of the church is not to provide little clubs for like-minded people; but actually to bring to bear upon all of its members the responsibility for racial integration. I do not share the feeling that we're going to make it better if the church stays out of these things. I think the church has been too late and has exercised too little influence in the days past.

Interview/U.S. News & World Report,
1-11:31.

Walter Lippmann
Former political columnist

I thought integration should begin at the top of the age scale, not at the bottom. I wanted to integrate higher education and then move down

from there, and not begin with children who have been bussed around. In other words, you educate and integrate the leaders of the next generation first and they would help integrate the high school people and so on.

Interview, Seal Harbor, Maine/
The Washington Post, 10-17:(C)1.

Peter MacDonald
Chairman, Navajo (Indian) Tribal Council

What is rightfully ours, we must protect. What is rightfully due us, we must claim.

Inaugural address/
The New York Times, 1-10:(4)10.

The Indian today suffers three kinds of depredation: The first is a depredation of the physical needs, which creates hunger, lack of clothing and housing; the second is a depredation of his economy, which keeps him from a good life; and the third is a depredation of his soul, which results in alcoholism, suicide and hopelessness.

The National Observer, 5-3:6.

Do we need to be told more explicitly who the enemy is? It is the Department of the Interior. We (Indians) can never survive as long as we remain the captive of a hostile Department. Right now we are prisoners of war, and the Department of the Interior is holding us, Commissioner (Louis) Bruce and his entire BIA as hostages until we turn over all our remaining land and resources.

Window Rock, Ariz./
The Christian Science Monitor, 9-14:7.

Lester G. Maddox
Lieutenant Governor, and former Governor, of Georgia.

Frankly, I don't believe the American people are so biased and prejudiced that they couldn't look beyond the color of a man's skin to elect a Vice President . . . Find a black conservative candidate for the national ticket—one who is honest and has proved to be a champion of constitutional government, law and order, freedom of choice, private enterprise and private property rights, and a man who will put

America first—and I'll vote for him ten times quicker than I would for a white, sold-out, socialistic liberal.

Anderson, S.C./
Los Angeles Times, 10-28:(1)7.

Robert C. Mardian
Assistant Attorney General, Internal Security Division, Department of Justice of the United States

When the Republicans took office in January, 1969, barely 5 per cent of Southern black children were in unified schools. Today, that figure is 95 per cent. This is probably the untold story of the (Nixon) Administration.

San Francisco Examiner, 1-21:30.

Sam Massell
Mayor of Atlanta

In my civil rights activities over the last 10 years, I had occasion many times to tell white audiences they needed to "think black" . . . I told whites they had to be considerate of the needs and the fears of the blacks. Well, we have reached the point in our history where it is time black audiences, that for their own good, they must be able to "think white." Blacks must learn the needs and fears of the whites if we are to mutually benefit from co-existence.

Before Hungry Club, Atlanta/
The Washington Post, 10-10:(F)1.

James Michener
Author

(In Hawaii) prejudice is a private matter, one which residents realize cannot be legislated for or against. Courts and legislatures in Hawaii do, however, concern themselves with *discrimination* based on prejudice. This, they know, is of public concern and cannot be tolerated. People of the same background tend to dine together, to socialize together. But they'd better not run their banks or their wholesale stores that way. Prejudice based on race, religion and background will probably continue for the rest of the century; and I don't object to this. You can't legislate love. But you can't restrict a person from earning a living. That restricts a nation's advancement. It is what must be handled in the U.S. right now. When it is, I feel we'll be in a position to release a lot of energy for other purposes.

New York/The Christian Science Monitor,
3-4:13.

John N. Mitchell
Attorney General of the United States

We have filed more lawsuits to desegregate schools and to open jobs and housing for the minority community in this country than have ever been filed before. The desegregation of Southern school districts is complete, with the exception of a few areas where strict compliance with court orders may not have been accomplished, but even that is proceeding at an excellent rate . . . The issue is not whether we are satisfied with school desegregation, but whether we are meeting our obligation to enforce the law. We believe we are meeting that obligation in full measure.

Interview, Washington/
U.S. News & World Report, 3-22:42.

Martha Mitchell
Wife of the Attorney General of the United States

People who preach liberalization are the ones who are the least liberal. They are supposed to be against the rich, but they make laws (such as school busing for racial balance) that legislate against the poor instead of the rich. The rich are not hurting—only the backbone of America. The liberals are tearing the backbone of America apart. What they are doing is the opposite of Constitutionality. Freedom of choice is what all my mail says—even from the black community. This thing works in reverse. What they are doing is the opposite of what they are supposed to be doing. When you get far to the left, you begin to move toward totalitarianism.

San Francisco Examiner & Chronicle
(Sunday Women), 5-2:2.

Walter F. Mondale
United States Senator, D–Minn.

The sickening truth is that this country is rapidly coming to resemble South Africa. Native reserves and Bantustans are the inner city; and our apartheid is all the more disgusted for being insidious and unproclaimed.

San Francisco Examiner & Chronicle,
(This World), 5-16:2.

Joseph M. Montoya
United States Senator, D–N.M.

Since the Mexican War, many of our (Spanish-American) people have lived as second-class citizens in a nation whose watchword is liberty. Since the Spanish-American War, others of them have led lives distinguished solely by economic exploitation and denial of equal opportunity. Even now, most are still relegated by today's society to dusty fields, overcrowded barrios and crammed tenements; where children die young and lives are stunted by an unheeding society dangling a golden dream before their eyes. In cities, they occupy areas long since abandoned by earlier groups of immigrants. Used and abused by a system seeking to exploit labor and votes, they are enticed here, squeezed of the juices of life and cast aside . . . We must register protests with utmost vigor in the courts through the legal process. We must let the entire nation know in this manner that the days are finally over when one of us could be killed with impunity or deprived of his rights. We shall *live* in court if necessary to prove our point. Pitiless exposure without letup, relentless publicity and constant legal action, is our unified theme.

Before Coalition Conference of
Spanish-Speaking Americans, Oct. 23/
The Washington Post, 11-1:(A)22.

Edmund S. Muskie
United States Senator, D–Maine

The history of the South during the past decade offers proof that it is possible to achieve fundamental social changes in this country. Customs and practices which seem fixed in concrete have been overturned.

San Francisco Examiner & Chronicle,
(This World), 5-9:2.

(Regarding school busing for racial balance): Busing is an inadequate answer, an answer we don't like. Yet it is an answer that is being used and must be used to make a beginning on this problem . . . I understand the fears of parents. I would hope that the mood of our country would be that of obeying the law of the land and trying to develop the best answers they can for their communities. We know that denial of equal educational opportunity because of race and the color of one's skin is wrong. (But) no one, including the President, has offered a complete substitute for busing dealing with this problem. Busing is an instrument for doing so. I don't think in the long run it is the final answer or the best answer. But until we can begin to get at the task of redrawing school lines, planning new school facilities in a way that will open up educational opportunity and rewrite Federal legislation, we're going to have to rely on busing to some extent to deal with this problem.

News conference, San Francisco, Sept. 7/
Los Angeles Times, 9-8:(1)3.

(Regarding the possibility of his running for President with a black man as his running mate): If I run it would be for the purpose of winning in order to do something about the problems affecting black people in this country. I think that in view of the climate in the country today, if a black man were on the ticket, we would both lose.

Los Angeles/Los Angeles Herald-Examiner,
9-26:(A)15.

Richard M. Nixon
President of the United States

We're going to carry out the law. We're going to open up opportunities for all Americans to move into housing—any housing that they're able to afford. But, on the other hand, for the Federal government to go further than the law, to force integration in the suburbs, I think is unrealistic. I think it would be counterproductive and not in the interest of better race relations.

Television interview, Washington, Jan. 4/
The New York Times, 1-6:42.

When we consider today that . . . 38 per cent of all black children in the South now go to majority white schools, as compared to 28 per cent of all black children in the North going to majority white schools, we can see that a very quiet but significant revolution has taken place in this country. And it's to the great credit of the far-seeing, law-abiding black and white leaders of the South that this has taken place.

News conference, San Clemente, Calif., May 1/
The New York Times, 5-2:(1)66.

I am against busing as that term is commonly used in school desegregation cases. I have consistently opposed the busing of our nation's school children to achieve racial balance, and I am opposed to the busing of children simply for the sake of busing. Further, while the Executive branch will continue to enforce the order of the (Supreme) Court, including court-ordered busing, I have instructed the Attorney General and the Secretary of HEW that they are to work with individual school districts to hold busing to the minimum required by law.

Aug. 3/San Francisco Examiner & Chronicle
(This World), 9-5:10.

I believe that it is frankly a libel on the American people to suggest that the American people . . . would vote against a man because of his religion or his race or his color. Now, having stated that general proposition, there are occasions when that happens, I am sure; but the American people are very fair-minded people and they tend to bend over backwards when they are confronted with this problem. Before the 1960 elections, it was said that America could not elect a Catholic as President, based on the Al Smith case in 1928. 1960 dispelled that (with the election of John Kennedy). . . I think the example of (Senator) Ed Brooke in Massachusetts is eloquent demonstration of the fact that the American people, when confronted with a superior man, will not vote against him because of his race.

News conference, Washington, Sept. 16/
The New York Times, 9-17:27.

Sidney Poitier
Actor

We (blacks) are an integral part of the social fabric of America. Those of us who can afford it, drive Cadillacs and Lincolns. Those of us who can afford it, buy homes in the same suburbs the white folks live in. When we can afford it, we go to Paris and the Bahamas and Mexico for vacations. We wear hot-pants. And that doesn't make us any less black.

Quote, 12-5:529.

Max Rafferty
Dean, School of Education, Troy State University, Alabama; Former California State Superintendent of Public Instruction

A recent poll asked American parents of all races if they favored busing (of school) children to solve problems of racial imbalance. The results were: 86 per cent said "No"; 11% said "Yes"; 3 per cent were undecided. Almost never has a poll registered such near unanimity in regard to one of the major issues of our times. Hardly anyone mentioned race as a factor in their opinion. They want their children where they can keep an eye on them, where they can visit school without having to conduct a cross-country safari, and where close cooperation between parent and teacher is at least possible.

Quote, 10-17:363.

Jean-Francois Revel
French author

The United States is now one of the least racist countries in the world. You were forced to pass through this (civil rights) crisis. Europe didn't have this problem, and look at the racism toward foreign workers in France.

San Francisco Examiner & Chronicle
(This World), 4-18:2.

Abraham A. Ribicoff
United States Senator, D—Conn.

Racial isolation is now just as pervasive in the North as it is in the South . . . We may have been more artful about catering to our biases in the North; but we have been no less ruthless in

(ABRAHAM A. RIBICOFF)

imposing them.

Before the Senate, Washington, March 16/
The New York Times, 3-17:23.

Nixon's entire civil rights record, as President, has been one of temerity. He plays politics right down the middle. He's ducked every de facto integration problem. My feeling is that the American people want leaders to be tough on this issue, even come up with hard solutions.

Interview, Washington/
Los Angeles Times, 5-11:(2)7.

Elliot L. Richardson
Secretary of Health, Education and Welfare of the United States

The pupil desegregation battle in the South has been brought to a point where the only remaining steps are to follow up on the job. But the back (of segregation) has been broken.

News conference, Washington, Jan. 14/
The New York Times, 1-15:12.

The awareness of the indispensable part played by individual understanding and mutual trust is at the heart of Administration policies in the field of civil rights. We are committed to the full enforcement of the requirements of the law. But we are convinced that these requirements can now be fulfilled more effectively by cooperation than by coercion, by persuasion than by force.

Before National Association for the Advancement of Colored People Legal Defense and Educational Fund, New York, April 21/
The New York Times, 4-23:21.

Wilson Riles
California State Superintendent of Public Instruction

Integration is a good concept; but some people have pushed it purely as a way to help minority students. It is never sold on the right basis: To be able to function in a multiracial

society is just as important for the white child as it is for a black child.

Interview/
Life, 2-26:30.

(Regarding school busing for racial balance): We're really not talking about a civil rights issue. We're talking about how we can develop a quality education program with equal opportunity for all. That's the issue—rather than just busing kids all over the place.

Interview, San Francisco/
San Francisco Examiner, 9-13:14.

Bayard Rustin
Executive director,
A. Philip Randolph Institute

The problems of the ghetto will have to be solved by the elite who have come out of the ghetto. The real answers to the immense problems of our time will not be found by young people screaming in the streets, nor by "women libbers," or black people chanting slogans and calling names. Don't get me wrong. I'm for Afro hairdos, for the study of black literature and art, for soul food—even if it has too much grease. (But) eating soul food will not solve a single problem of housing, employment or education.

At Cheyney (Pa.) State College commencement/The New York Times, 6-14:44.

Harold R. Sims
Acting executive director,
National Urban League

The rights of black people are now at a low ebb. The nation is in the grips of not a silent but a selfish majority.

Before National Newspaper Publishers Association, Atlanta, June 17/
The New York Times, 6-18:21.

Stephen G. Spottswood
Chairman, National Association for the Advancement of Colored People

We need clear, positive leadership for civil rights from 1600 Pennsylvania Avenue, Northwest. Twenty-three million black Americans and an unestimated number of white

Americans look to the President to provide this leadership. Civil rights is the fulcrum of democracy, without which the nation will perish.

Minneapolis, July 15/Vital Speeches, 8-15:663.

John C. Stennis
United States Senator, D—Miss.

I am frank to say that I do not believe the parents . . . beyond the South will submit to the total, massive forced integration of their schools of the type that is being forced on *us.* They have sufficient political power and strength to keep it from being done—and no Administration, present or future, will dare undertake to apply the same . . . pattern of desegregation *beyond* the South that is now applied *in* the South.

Before the Senate, Washington, April 14/
The Washington Post, 4-15:(A)5.

Neil V. Sullivan
Massachusetts Commissioner of Education

School integregation is legally, morally and educationally correct. We must stop dodging it. But we should start at the kindergarten level.

At conference sponsored by National Com-
mittee for Support of the Public Schools,
Washington, March 30/
The Washington Post, 3-31:(A)3.

Strom Thurmond
United States Senator, R—S.C.

I've worked around black people all my life and get along real well with them. I don't think anybody living can say I've ever done anything to try to hurt any black person. It's not the color of people that counts but the manner of people that really counts. It kind of hurts me when anyone portrays me as being biased or prejudiced because I'm not . . . Black people are benefiting more under the Nixon Administration and because of my connections with the Nixon Administration than from anything ever done for them. And I'm glad to help them.

Interview/The New York Times, 10-17:(1)46.

George C. Wallace
Governor of Alabama

(Regarding school integration): Our schools are being destroyed, because the South and other sections of the country—who believe in government, and not by bureaucrats—failed to unite against the despotic tyranny of a Federal government.

Inauguration address, Montgomery, Jan. 18/
The New York Times, 1-19:20.

. . . I have always felt and do feel now that the best school systems are those where the policy is determined by local authorities, a local democratic institution. But in 1954 and in 1963, when I attempted to raise the issue, the Constitutional issue, of whether the government of the country could run the schools, or the State of Alabama, the other states, that was pushed aside, and so we now have non-discrimination. We have accepted that, and it should have been accepted and has been accepted. But now (with government ordered school busing) the government comes along and says, "But we are going to destroy free choice." In 1954 they said, "You cannot assign a student because of race to a certain school." And now, that is all they do—racial quotas. So I say to you, we in Alabama have accepted the right of any child to go to any school of their choice. We haven't accepted the closing of schools and the busing of students 40 and 50 and 60 and 100 miles to achieve a racial balance as prohibited in the 1964 Civil Rights Act. The courts themselves are violating the 1964 Civil Rights Act, which says that nothing in this Act empowers any court to bus any child to achieve racial balance; and every judge in the United States that handles these cases violates the law of the land.

TV-radio interview/"Meet the Press," National
Broadcasting Company, Washington, 8-22.

(Regarding his fight against school busing to achieve racial balance): All I'm trying to do is help the President and the Attorney General and his wife—what's her name? Martha?—to do what they say they all want to do, and that's stop busing. That's all I'm trying to do. Just make these judges stop toting our kids all over creation.

The New York Times, 8-22:(4)3.

Earl Warren
Former Chief Justice of the United States

We cannot be content until every American citizen has every freedom every other American has. The progress has been all too slow, but not so slow that I despair.

Interview, Washington, March 18/
The New York Times, 3-19:19.

John Wayne
Actor

With a lot of blacks, there's quite a bit of resentment along with their dissent, and possibly rightfully so. But we can't all of a sudden get down on our knees and turn everything over to the leadership of the blacks. I believe in white supremacy until the blacks are educated to a point of responsibility. I don't believe in giving authority and positions of leadership and judgment to irresponsible people . . . I will say this, though: I think any black who can compete with a white today can get a better break than a white man. I wish they'd tell me where in the world they have it better than right here in America.

Interview/Playboy, May:80.

John C. West
Governor of South Carolina

We pledge to minority groups no special status other than full-fledged responsibility in a government that is totally color-blind . . . The politics of race and divisiveness have fortunately been soundly repudiated in South Carolina. The achievement of these goals can become a reality only if the people of this state unite and work together, putting aside differences of race, politics, generation or other.

Inaugural address, Columbia, Jan. 19/
Los Angeles Times, 1-20:(1)16.

Roy Wilkins
Executive director,
National Association for the
Advancement of Colored People

In the racial situation in which we black people find ourselves in America, there is only one path to be followed. It has been found that integration is the way in which a 10 per cent minority gets along with a 90 per cent majority . . . (The philosophy of Whitney Young, Jr., late executive director of the National Urban League did) not preclude race pride, individuality, the teaching of racial history, the influence of a sense of dignity and equality in the race as a whole and youth in particular. It does not preclude the maximum use of black political power not the building of black economic strengths. It does preclude extravagant rhetoric and suicidal tactics.

Interview, March 12/
The New York Times, 3-13:18.

There has been progress (in civil rights) not as much as the conservatives claim, not as little as the scoffers disdainfully insist, but a foundation has been laid. It is ready now for a superstructure fit for the occupancy of all Americans, whatever their color or race or nationality, in an equality that recognizes the human dignity of men.

Before graduating class,
University of Missouri at St. Louis, June 10/
The Washington Post, 6-12:(A)9.

. . . when you weigh in the Vice President (Agnew), and his off-the-cuff remarks, you have to give the (Nixon) Administration, even though it disavows those remarks, a sort of a black eye (on civil rights)—for Mr. Agnew saying, for example, that black leadership in the United States could learn a lot from the black heads of state in Africa. He ignored completely the fact that black heads of state have armies, treasuries and all that sort of thing at their disposal. And the black leadership in this country has only one Spiro Agnew to fall back upon. That's pretty weak support.

Radio interview, Aug. 11/
The Washington Post, 8-12:(A)2.

(Regarding President Nixon's opposition to school busing for racial balance): Mr. Nixon ignores the fact that about 20 million American children, for one reason or another, are transported to schools each day by bus. What the President is saying in unmistakable language is that busing may be used for any reason under the sun, except to correct racial imbalance in the schools . . . This naked discriminatory nature of this position will not be lost on black Americans and their friends.

Before American Federation of Teachers,
San Francisco, Aug. 17/
San Francisco Examiner, 8-18:9.

We condemn black racism just as we condemn white racism. Racial nationalism is not the way. It just won't work. The Negroes have been here for 350 years. They are more American than most Americans. And they aren't about to go away. They are fighting not for release from this country, but for inclusion in this country—and inclusion in all the benefits that citizens are supposed to enjoy.

Interview/U.S. News & World Report, 8-23:28.

If I didn't believe it was possible for minority groups in this country to achieve equality by using the tools within the system—voting, legislation, court action—I would have given up

long ago. More and more people—principally black—are giving more and more money to the human-rights fight. They believe, with us, that it's possible to make progress within the system.

Los Angeles Herald-Examiner,
9-2:(A)6.

(Referring to proposed flying of a "black liberation" flag at largely Negro schools): Until black people put away (such) childish things and tackle the slow, difficult, frustrating and yet satisfying development of manhood, they will live and die chasing will-o' the-wisps.

Human Events, 12-25:2.

Whitney M. Young, Jr.
Executive director,
National Urban League

We (blacks) have had an excess of callousness in America historically. I am not worried if there is going to be an excess in caring.

The Christian Science Monitor, 1-13:2.

Commerce · Industry · Finance

Walter Adams
Professor of Economics,
Michigan State University

If this voracious appetite (of big corporations) for mergers and acquisitions is to be curbed, and the consequent erosion of the competitive marketplace is to be arrested, new legislation is clearly in order. And such legislation would not . . . require a wholesale restructuring of an oligopoly-dominated economy. It would call for . . . the Federal incorporation of giant corporations on the ground that their operations are so extensive and their impact on the nation's economic life so pervasive that they are "affected with the public interest."

At conference of corporate accountability,
Washington, Oct. 30/
The New York Times, 10-31:(1)63.

Roger S. Ahlbrandt
President, Allegheny Ludlum Industries

There is a pressing imperative for the United States to formulate, as quickly as possible, a strategy and policy for international trade—one that will protect our nation's vital interests, just as the vital interests of competing economies are being protected. Our "monopoly phobia" and our views about present-day antitrust policy will have to be examined and changed. The new competitive factors, such as the fact that steel imports are now the third largest steel "company" in the United States, cannot be ignored in setting antitrust policy for the future. Such a policy must be related to *world industry dynamics* and not merely to the U.S. markets and Americans producing for it.

Before World Affairs Council,
Pittsburgh, May 24/
The New York Times, 6-27:(3)12.

Willis C. Armstrong
President, United States Council,
International Chamber of Commerce

Toward the Russians and the (Communist) Chinese and their allies, we should maintain a position of accepting coexistence, provided there is reciprocity. We should expand trade with both; and we should abolish most of our restrictions on trade and payments. We should not expect political results from expanded economic activity. We should rid our minds of the idea that the United States is a political and economic giant dealing with an enormous number of smaller countries and two big enemies. We should, instead, realize that we are dealing with equals in Western Europe and Japan, and that our enemies and we must coexist. We must remember that a world two-thirds poor is neither safe nor desirable, and that it does not provide an environment in which American business can flourish. Just as business at home today must take full account of the social environment, so must American business take account of the world environment. It is one world, and we can't get off. So we must determine to make the best of it.

Before Greater Philadelphia
Chamber of Commerce, Feb. 22/
Vital Speeches, 3-15:331.

George W. Ball
Former Under Secretary of State
of the United States

. . . it seems fashionable in some quarters to espouse the self-pitying thesis that, because of the ineptitude and flatulence of our (foreign-trade) negotiators, we have been consistently taken advantage of by other less generous and idealistic governments; thus, we now have every right to insist that our trading partners solve our problems for us. I think it significant that, though many American businessmen complain

58

bitterly that the Europeans got far the better of the bargain, I have heard fully as many complaints from European businessmen that Europe gave more than it got in return. Such reciprocal discontent is, I suggest, a good test of a fair negotiation. That we still have some matters to complain about concerning our European partners is, of course, true . . . But the United States is far from innocent. While we have more low tariffs than the Common Market, we also have more high tariffs. We are entrapped in our present unhappy predicament not half so much because of the trading and financial policies of other nations, but because, for a number of years, we have failed to check powerful inflationary forces intensified by—but by no means altogether caused by—an overseas war.

Before Joint Congressional Economic Committee, Washington, Sept. 9/ The New York Times, 10-10:(3)16.

R. F. Barker
Chairman, PPG Industries

What is needed at this point by the U.S. is a clear-cut economic trade policy—embracing domestic as well as international considerations—representing a union of thought, effort and purpose between private enterprise and government that will best serve the interest of the nation. Such a policy should neither promulgate the myth of free trade nor advocate the smothering cloak of protectionism, but instead grant to American industry the chance to compete on a fair and equitable basis.
Before Pennsylvania Chamber of Commerce, Pittsburgh, Nov. 4/ Vital Speeches, 12-15:160.

Lloyd M. Bentsen
United States Senator, D–Tex.

It was a mistake to repeal the seven per cent investment tax credit; and I hope we can restore it, as a justified incentive to the investment which must be made during this decade. America urgently needs a revitalization of the competitive spirit. I think we ought to use the seven per cent tax credit like a shot of adrenalin—put it on when it's needed, as it is obviously needed now with unemployment standing at over six per cent—and remove it when capital investment adds to the inflationary forces.
Before Texas Bankers Association, Dallas, May 3/ The Dallas Times Herald, 5-4:(A)29.

William Bernbach
Chairman,
Doyle Dane Bernbach, Inc., advertising

We're hard-sell, plus being attractive. We say things that stem right from the product—and that's hard-sell—but we try to say them creatively. What's the use of hard-sell that no one listens to—the kind that shouts? How effective can it be? On the other hand, being entertaining without drawing strength from the product itself never was good, either. You need that wonderful combination of both. The advertiser who thinks he has to choose between the straightforward and dull or the beautiful but dumb is mistaken. The trick is to be relevant as well as bright.
Interview, Los Angeles/ Los Angeles Times, 1-11:(3)9.

Fred J. Borch
Chairman and chief executive officer,
General Electric Company

People ask me, "How can you take all the pressure on a job like this?" And I think I can answer for all chief executives: We love it. Any man in the top spot will say things like: "It's tough—tough and hard." But boy, take that pressure away from them, and they burst.
Interview, New York /Nation's Business, February.

Thornton F. Bradshaw
President, Atlantic Richfield Company

The U. S. operates with a huge albatross around its neck, and that is the albatross of its traditions. They are the traditions that brought about our antitrust laws and created the private enterprise system and made it anathema for anyone . . . to talk about the benefits of a corporate state. But that is what Japan is today. I would hope that we will consider . . . what it means to have national goals with industry and government working hand in hand toward those goals.

Panel discussion/Time, 5-10:91.

M. M. Brisco
President, Standard Oil Company (New Jersey)

It would seem obvious that we should develop as many sources of energy as possible to meet the demand situation. Yet . . . petroleum companies have been attacked on "monopoly" grounds for going into uranium, coal and other energy fields. The implication is that this somehow poses a threat to a free economy, that the oil industry is out to control sources of supply so as to stifle competition and, presumably, rig or inflate prices. This is simply not so. So far as my company is concerned, we are actually trying to develop additional sources of supply in these other fields to meet the demand for energy. This obviously results in more competition, not less.

Oklahoma City/
U.S. News & World Report, 4-26:54.

Max E. Brunk
Professor of Marketing, Cornell University

I resent the hypocrisy of the politics behind consumerism—the illusion that someone is doing something for me when, in fact, he is only doing something at my expense to serve his own selfish political interests. Consumer issues gain cheap and appealing headlines for politicians. Only when we realize the cost the consumer pays for his protection—in terms of public administration, in terms of lost productivity, in terms of lost freedom of choice by the consumer, in terms of lost opportunity for improvement in product and service—will consumerism lose much of its illusionary appeal. It seems to me that our responsible public officials should be doing more im-

portant things than writing Federal specifications for panty-hose or the size of lettering on a can of sardines.

Before New York State Agricultural Society,
Albany/The National Observer, 3-1:13.

James L. Buckley
United States Senator, C–N.Y.

(Regarding proposed government-guaranteed loans to Lockheed Aircraft Corporation): If the inefficient or mismanaged firm is insulated from the free-market pressures that other business firms must face, the result will be that scarce economic human resources will be squandered on enterprises whose activities do not meet the standards imposed by the marketplace—standards which have assured us of the efficiency on which our industrial supremacy has been built.

Washington, July 24/The New York
Times, 7-25:(1)22.

Dean Burch
Chairman,
Federal Communications Commission

Children are different. They cannot be treated like any other audience of potential customers. We make this distinction again and again. To give but one example, the main concern of our obscenity laws—correctly in my judgment—is to keep pornography out of the hands of children. And the same distinction must be made with respect to false and deceptive advertising. I believe that, in the case of advertising directed to children, the standards of what is false and deceptive must be judged in light of the crucial fact that the audience is so unsophisticated, so young and trusting. It is, I submit, intolerable to seek to bilk the innocent with shoddy advertising appeals. As some person aptly put it, that is akin to statutory rape.

Before American Advertising Federation/
The Wall Street Journal, 2-16:18.

Arthur F. Burns
Chairman, Federal Reserve Board

. . . our international competitive position appears to have deteriorated. In the first five months of 1971, imports spurted and our normal trade surplus vanished. This is a distressingly poor performance in an economy experiencing substantial underutilization of its resources of labor and capital. The problem is dramatized by the success of foreign manufacturers in capturing a rapidly-expanding share of our automobile market. In the past six months, sales of foreign models have accounted for 16 per cent of total U.S. sales; and, in addition, close to one-tenth of the American models sold were produced in Canada. It may be tempting to react to foreign competition by imposing added restrictions and quotas on imports, but such a policy would not serve our national interests. The constructive course is to bring inflation under control and to stimulate our businessmen to increase their penetration of the expanding markets abroad and to compete more effectively with foreign producers in our domestic markets. I would favor consideration of new government incentives toward this end.

Before Joint Congressional Economic Committee, Washington, July 23/ U.S. News & World Report, 8-9:50.

Earl L. Butz
Secretary of Agriculture-designate of the United States

This trend toward less farms is not bad. From a national point of view, it is good that we have been able to produce an increasing amount of food with the work of a smaller percentage of our population. This releases people to do something else useful in our society. If the goal is to have lots of people on the land, then the ideal would be China or India, with millions mired in subsistence agriculture . . . Agriculture (in the U.S.) is making a transition from being a way of life to a way of making a living.

Interview/The Washington Post, 11-14:(A)10.

To blame the Secretary of Agriculture for the decreasing number of farmers is akin to blaming the Census Bureau for the increase in population. When I said we were going to have upwards of a million fewer farmers by 1980,

that didn't mean necessarily that I approved of that. I simply was reporting what is going to happen. I think it is inevitable.

TV-radio interview/"Meet the Press," National Broadcasting Company, Washington, 12-12;

Edward Carlson
President, United Air Lines

. . . any time you have a big company, you have a problem at being as nimble as a smaller company, which is quicker to respond to changing conditions . . . There are (always) people in business who dislike responsibility, and if they get a tough problem, they buck it upstairs to someone else. Then you get it up into a main office. They've got a lot of other problems, and it gets shoved on someone's desk and, finally, it works its way back down (the company hierarchy). By that time, the problem doesn't exist; some competitor has come in and taken all the stuff away from you, and you've created this bureaucracy for a corporate organization.

Interview/The Washington Post, 10-25:(D)12.

William J. Casey
Chairman, Securities and Exchange Commission of the United States

(Regarding suggestions that the securities laws be used to force corporations to adopt socially-oriented policies): In approaching the role of the SEC, I start off with what I believe to be a deep concern for the environment and for the underprivileged and for America's role in the world. But I must confess to a strong disposition not to confuse the role of the SEC with that of the Environmental Protection Agency, the Department of Health, Education and Welfare or the Department of State.

The New York Times, 6-18:53.

Nello Cellio
Finance Minister of Switzerland

With their easy money policies, the Americans have created sources of inflation throughout the world.

San Francisco Examiner, 5-17:30.

Roy D. Chapin
Chairman, American Motors Corporation

Moralizing will not produce solutions to problems. It will not eliminate poverty; nor cure urban congestion; nor clean up rivers; nor control contaminants in the air. Only enterprise—hard-headed and creative— can accomplish these things. Enterprise flourishes in an atmosphere of personal and economic freedom . . . and only in such an atmosphere. And of the other side of this coin, the encouragement and stimulation of business enterprise creates an atmosphere in which human aspirations can be met and the dimension of freedom expanded. This is a lesson of history. A great contribution of our nation to the forward march of mankind has been in demonstrating that freedom of enterprise is vital if the highest goals of man are to be reached.

Before Society of Automotive Engineers, Detroit/The Christian Science Monitor, 1-20:10.

A. W. Clausen
President, Bank of America

Despite some of the heroic and bold efforts made by individual corporations here and there, we will not see any really substantial and intelligently-directed commitment of private resources to public problems until we have developed an analytical framework by which such a commitment can be justified and monitored . . . We need a system where net output is increased or decreased by the amount that total assets—capital, knowledge, skills, physical and socio-political environment—are augmented or reduced as a consequence of our activities . . . Where economic growth deteriorates the physical environment, a set of accounts should register not only the usual increase in net output resulting from growth in the market sector, but also record any offset to the degree the physical environment assets depreciate, lessening the future flow of benefits.

At National Industrial Conference Board Finance Conference, New York/ The Dallas Times Herald, 2-25:(A)30.

John B. Connally, Jr.
Secretary of the Treasury of the United States

. . . I do think we are going to have to use a different approach—a stronger approach—in dealing with most countries in the world. These countries have grown accustomed to our being relaxed, fairly generous, always forgiving, always easy in our dealings with them. Consequently, they have built up tariff arrangements, they have built up trade restrictions against U.S. goods, they have carved out territorial areas where they now grant preferences. And they expect us to take it and like it, just because in the aftermath of World War II—when we were sitting here with nearly 25 billion dollars in gold, with the only viable economy in the free world—we were generous in our trade agreements. There is not a free country on the face of this earth that, when it ran into economic trouble, did not find us willing to help it. I think it is only fair now for us to ask the same. I am not one of those who treats this whole question of foreign trade with benign neglect. I am worried about it. All I am saying is that if other nations are concerned—as they ultimately will be if we continue to have balance-of-payments deficits of 10 billion dollars a year—they must be fair with us. We don't have reciprocity in our trade agreements. I think we are entitled to it. It is just that simple.

Interview, Washington/ U.S. News & World Report, 4-12:55.

(Supporting government-guaranteed loans for Lockheed Aircraft Corporation): Foremost in my mind is the imperative need to protect and foster the rising confidence that will gradually restore the jobs and growth lost in recent months. The opposite of confidence is fear. Restoration of confidence means, in effect, the elimination of fear. At this time, with the economy moving ahead and unemployment topping out, the failure of the nation's largest defense contractor . . . would, beyond any shadow of doubt, generate deep-seated fears. Workers throughout the aerospace industry . . . would face heightened competition for their own jobs. Thus, a new wave of anxieties would be created. Stockholders throughout American industry . . . might well question the future values of their own investments. The results would be market repercussions that could severely dampen and perhaps thwart business recovery.

Interview, Washington, July 20/
The New York Times, 7-21:45.

(Regarding the recently-instituted 10 per cent surcharge on imports): Removal of the surcharge prior to making substantial progress toward our objectives would accomplish nothing toward correcting the balance of payments deficit . . . If other governments will make tangible progress toward dismantling specific barriers to trade over coming weeks and will be prepared to allow market realities freely to determine exchange rates for their currencies for a transitional period, we, for our part, would be prepared to remove the surcharge.

Before International Monetary Fund,
Washington, Sept. 30/
Los Angeles Herald-Examiner, 9-30:(D)1.

(Regarding the effect of President Nixon's economic program on America's foreign-trade partners): On the international front, a great many prophets of doom say that we have taken steps that our trading partners won't like. We are being castigated by some at home, and we are being criticized by many abroad—and for what? For doing what others have been asking us to do and criticizing us for not doing for the last three years . . . We knew we weren't going to win any popularity contest abroad, and that the goal of a turnaround in our trade balances would not make our trading partners jump up and down with glee.

Before American Bankers Association,
San Francisco, Oct. 20/
Los Angeles Times, 10-21:(3)12.

John T. Connor
Chairman, Allied Chemical Corporation

In the years immediately ahead, we are going to have to develop a workable system of cooperative government-business enterprise going far beyond anything we've achieved up to this point. Business is now being asked to solve,

or to join with government in solving, a whole series of social and other ills that are shaking the foundations of our society. The problems are there to see in any American city; slums and substandard housing; the poverty of great numbers of undereducated, untrained persons adrift in a job market that demands ever more sophisticated skills; the soaring cost of health services; streets being choked with traffic while systems of mass transportation disintegrate; outmoded waste disposal systems; and large-scale pollution of our air and water. But some way must be found, in turning business' attention to these pressing needs, to preserve the profit motive—the essential ingredient of private enterprise. Unless business is to be allowed to seek *business* solutions, these public needs will not be met; because there simply will not be enough taxpayers' dollars available for government alone to finance the solutions.

Lausanne-Ouchy, Switzerland/
The Wall Street Journal,
5-25:14.

Joseph F. Cullman III
Chairman, Philip Morris, Inc.

The head of a corporation has two constituencies. His primary one is the public, upon whom the corporation is dependent for its existence. His second constituency is made up of the stockholders, who place him in office, and the employees, without whom the corporation could not function. It is, therefore, not only correct that the corporation lend its good offices and full support to social involvement for the good of the public; it also happens to be one of the institutions best able to do so, for three simple reasons: Corporations have talented people who are well qualified to make contributions that go beyond immediate day-to-day business affairs; secondly, they are structured and organized in a way which permits effective utilization of their talents; and thirdly, corporations have the means and influence with which to make significant contributions and to inspire others to do likewise.

At University of Virginia,
Graduate School of Business Forum/
The Wall Street Journal, 2-1:10.

Robert A. Dahl
Professor of Political Science,
Yale University

Every large corporation should be thought of as a social enterprise; that is, an entity whose existence and decisions can be justified only insofar as they serve public or social purposes.

At conference on corporate accountability,
Washington, Oct. 30/
The New York Times, 10-31:(1)63.

Archie K. Davis
President, Chamber of Commerce of
the United States

It has been said that Japan is more a corporation than a country. That is another way of saying that Japanese business, labor and government cooperate to advance Japanese interests in world markets. In America, I am afraid the situation is quite the reverse. Labor and management feud, while government actions are frequently inconsistent, and at times even harmful to business.

At Printing Industry of America convention,
Chicago/Quote, 9-5:226.

William T. Dentzer, Jr.
New York State Banking Superintendent

I believe banks should be able to follow their customers from city to suburb. This would allow city-based banks to enter new markets around their cities and vice versa—though I realize there would not be much vice versa.

U. S. News & World Report, 3-29:78.

E. M. de Windt
Chairman, Eaton Yale & Towne, Inc.

The 1970's could be the decade in which American industry prices itself out of business; the time when labor costs transform our nation into a computerized research laboratory and general service center for a world industry with everything from automobiles to zippers being produced beyond our borders; a time in which we abdicate that world leadership that has been ours since World War II.

Or—the 1970s could see a return to the dark ages of trade warfare, through which America will find itself in a position akin to the "splendid isolation" that marked the downfall of Great Britain as the world's ranking leader in trade and commerce. Or—in the next few years, the world company—many with U.S. origins—could emerge as the strongest force for peace, progress and free enterprise in the history of mankind. The world company—owned, managed and operated without regard to the physical, political and philosophical boundaries of nationalism—can well become a reality in this century.

At Mid-America World Trade Conference,
Chicago, Feb. 25/
The Wall Street Journal, 3-30:16.

An American company can no longer be happy in considering its foreign operations as so many puppet shows. There is no room in world business for the home office "expert" who flies into a country with a satchel full of directives and lots of advice. There is no place today for the attitude that what's good in America is good anywhere. For any of us to believe that Americans have a monopoly on intelligence, business judgment, initiative or incentiveness is more than naive—it's foolhardy, and it's a direct denial of the very thing that made this country great: a competitive mixture of many talents, many cultures.

At Mid-America World Trade Conference,
Chicago, Feb. 25/
Vital Speeches, 4-1:366.

The United States must take the lead in developing world peace through world business. No other nation or group of nations has demonstrated the benefits of free enterprise more graphically. Despite our many problems and a seeming mania for self-criticism, we are the most advanced, most affluent and most well-endowed nation on earth. I don't hesitate for a moment to state that we arrived at this position through the steady and fruitful pursuit of profits.

At National Inter-departmental Seminar,
Foreign Service Institute, Washington, July 29/
Vital Speeches, 9-15:727.

Nicholas Diederichs
Finance Minister of South Africa

It is quite clear that the United States is not in the least concerned about its balance of payments deficit. Their attitude is that, if they have a deficit and billions of dollars flow to other states, then those states should revalue their currencies . . . If the choice was whether the mark should be revalued or the dollar devalued, then the answer should have been that the dollar should be devalued, because it is the weaker.

San Francisco Examiner & Chronicle
(This World), 5-16:16.

Earl of Cromer
British Ambassador to the United States

Any drift toward neo-isolationism on either side of the Atlantic would be alarming. Economic protectionism would certainly provoke action and reaction across the Atlantic which would reduce the exports of all of us to each other, not only creating the unemployment that protectionism was originally designed to prevent, but also embittering relations between us.

Interview, Washington/
The Dallas Times Herald, 7-21:(A)16.

F. N. Ekard
President, American Petroleum Institute

We (the oil industry) are accused of a sterile complacency—even though the major, overriding preoccupation throughout the entire industry is to find ways of closing the energy gap, to maintain the quality of American life by maintaining a continuous flow of energy to the homes and factories and means of transportation of the American people. Energy to keep the country going, as well as energy to keep it growing, consistent with ecological requirements. Meanwhile, those who advocate "zero growth"—those who trumpet their concern for the so-called real quality of American life—would have us ignore this responsibility. I say that they are guilty of a callous complacency on a most profound level. I charge them with a cruel indifference to the very real material needs of millions of Americans who have not yet achieved their full share of American affluence—yes, and their intellectual, aesthetic and cultural share as well. Is the job of American industry finished? Shall we now devote ourselves to simply managing the status quo? Ask the 25 million men, women and children who barely subsist in poverty on family incomes of less than $4,000 a year. Ask them in Appalachia. Ask them in the dismal ghettos. Ask any black man . . . If it is, don't tell the Mayor of any major city, whose one most persistent frustration is money—a lack of funds to rebuild, to renovate, to repair the decay of decades. Don't tell any social administrator—whether his job be hospitals, schools, parks. And where will the needed money come from, the surplus wealth to improve the earning power of the disadvantaged, to expand our social programs, to rebuild our cities, to enhance our natural environment in a world of technology that is here to stay? It will come from the steady growth of our economy. It will come from the steady expansion of our industry, especially the petroleum industry—because we supply the energy for the increase in mechanical productivity that makes growth possible. Those who would like to create national policy out of their yearning for a simpler, more rustic way of life—and there aren't many among them who ever got their feet wet in the barnyard—they always look the other way when it comes to the realities of productivity and what those realities mean to American life.

On "Oil Appreciation Day," Snyder, Tex./
The Wall Street Journal, 6-30:10.

Victor Elting, Jr.
Chairman, American Advertising Federation

. . . it is our feeling that poor taste in much of today's advertising is a factor in the public's attitude toward the industry. This cannot be regulated by government. But because it affects the public's attitude toward advertising, it is one of the factors to which any advertising self-regulatory effort must address itself.

At American Advertising Federation
Government Affairs Conference,
Washington, Feb. 1/Daily Variety, 2-2:34.

Raymond C. Firestone
Chairman, Firestone Tire & Rubber Company

The days of having the luxury of people knocking down our (America's) door to buy our goods are at an end. We now must act with that understanding, while at the same time making U.S. products as attractive in price and quality as those flooding us as imports. If we cannot do this, we will not be able to compete in our own country, let alone in other countries.

> *At National Foreign Trade Council*
> *Convention, New York/*
> *Los Angeles Herald-Examiner, 12-12:(C)8.*

John P. Fishwick
President, Norfolk & Western Railway

. . . real progress may lie in the loss of a company unable or unwilling to meet new standards of social responsibility.

> *Before Greater Richmond (Va.) Chamber of*
> *Commerce, Jan. 27/*
> *The Washington Post, 1-29:(B)12.*

Janet Flanner
Writer

The mendaciousness of American advertising is absolutely vomitorious—the gullibility of the American public, which opens its ears like mouths as if they could stretch the whole ear tunnel to listen to more guff.

> *Interview, New York/*
> *The New York Times, 1-30:29.*

Paul Foley
Chairman, McCann-Erickson, Inc., advertising

(1970) was a year in which persuasion that sells was the order of the day, not advertising that bedazzles the award committees.

> *The New York Times, 1-10:(12)19.*

Gaylord A. Freeman, Jr.
Chairman, First National Bank of Chicago;
Member, President's Commission on International Trade and Investment Policy

Our country's position is a little like mine would be if I invited four or five of you in to play poker and got out the cigar box of chips and sold you each $10 worth. If I lost hand after hand for perhaps 20 hands and contin-

ually reached into the box to replenish my own pile of chips, you might begin to wonder whether I would have the cash to redeem all of the chips piling up on the table. Then, after an hour or two of this, if I said that I could no longer redeem all of the chips and asked you not to cash any in, but to just keep on playing, you, as a friend, might say, "Okay, for a while." But as the hour grew later and I continued to lose every hand and constantly put more chips on the table, the time would come when you would say, "We aren't going to play any more unless you can make those chips good—or at least begin to bring some more money into the game." As you know, our country has—with only two exceptions—had a balance of payments deficit in every year since 1950. That is, we have lost 18 hands in the Big Game between nations and have just continued to issue more dollars . . . We will have another balance of payments deficit this year, and again will finance it by issuing more dollar claims—more chips. Since we can't redeem all of those foreign-held dollar claims, we have since early in the 1960s asked Germany and our other foreign friends not to ask for gold for their dollars, but to wait awhile. They have waited and waited and waited. Meanwhile, our position has deteriorated every year. Our time is running out.

> *At Annual Conference of Bank Correspondents/*
> *The Wall Street Journal, 2-17:14.*

Milton Friedman
Professor of Economics, University of Chicago

The official price of gold is of no practical importance so long as the U. S. does not sell gold. The question to ask is what difference does it make to anybody if the U. S. announces to the world we will sell nobody gold at $35 an ounce or if it announces we will sell nobody any gold at $38 an ounce? (However) it was a great mistake (to devalue the dollar) because, from the longer-run point of view, it will raise the question about convertibility, and I think it would be a great mistake for the United States ever again to commit itself to converting the dollar into gold . . . or anything else. (Over the past 20 years, European bankers) have gotten an enormous power over us because we were so foolish as to promise to give an ounce of gold for every $35.

Interview, Dec. 14/The Washington Post,
12-16:(L)12.

Betty Furness
Chairman, New York State Consumer Protection Board

The Consumer Game is tougher than pro football and more conniving than chess. One side (industry) invents the rules, and the other side (consumers) is left to guess what they are . . . The consumer cannot move intelligently without the facts, and the consumer is not given the facts. The Consumer Game has too often been played like a con game.

San Gabriel, Calif./
Los Angeles Times, 3-1:(4)7.

If American industry continues to sow contempt for the consumer, it will reap contempt from the consumer. And from Congress, it will reap statutes. It could be the most spectacular case of statutory reap in history.

At conference on corporate responsibility/
The New York Times, 5-16:(4)4.

I think there is a great deal to be said for the Ralph Nader approach (in consumerism) —(to) stand outside and holler at everybody.

Newsweek, 7-26:44.

I'm beginning to wonder why they even set up this office. Industry in New York does not advise the legislators—it controls them.

Announcing her resignation/
Quote, 8-22:169.

John Kenneth Galbraith
Professor of Economics,
Harvard University

It is very hard for women to do well in business; not because they are unfitted for it, but because there is a secret and invisible barrier—the male world of luncheon clubs, golf, locker rooms and peculiar jokes, in

which they do not participate and where so much business wheeling and dealing is done.

Interview, London/
Los Angeles Times, 5-16:(E)22.

(Regarding a proposed U. S. government-guaranteed loan for Lockheed Aircraft Corp.): If Lockheed is given this loan, it will be proof that, despite recent criticism, the military-industrial complex is alive in Washington and doing well.

Before Senate Banking Committee,
Washington, July 8/
The Boston Globe, 7-9:2.

James M. Gavin
Chairman, Arthur D. Little, Inc.

The American business community is the most highly respected, highly regarded, indeed, highly copied of any in the world. It has been hard-nosed. But when it has had to be, it has proven to be receptive, sensitive and responsive. When it had to be as tender as a kitten in its sensitivity, it could be. I do not use that analogy carelessly. Anthropologists will tell you that the soft, fuzzy animal is the one who has survived; not the animal like the triceratops, which had built heavy bone structures about itself, being constantly reactive and trying to find some way to protect itself, instead of being sensitive, intelligent and adaptable to the future. So, too, the corporation that survives will be not only tough and hard-nosed, but also sensitive to the changes that are swirling about.

New York/
The Wall Street Journal, 4-15:10.

Eli Ginzberg
Chairman,
National Manpower Advisory Committee

I believe that the best way to run an organization is to make sure that all of its work never gets done. Any time a boss tells me that his company gets all its work done, I figure it's a poorly-run organization. You ought always to have more work chasing people than you have people chasing work.

Interview/
U. S. News & World Report, 8-23:55.

Douglas Grymes
President, Koppers Company

. . . in theory, in a free-enterprise system, only the strong companies are supposed to survive. But in the United States, we protect the weak and hamstring the strong through a variety of antitrust laws. It is true, anybody with enough money should be able to open up a business. But unfortunately, if he fails, is inefficient or even though he has some value to a competitor, the competitor is not permitted to buy him out. So they *both suffer*. You and I have been taught that bigness and monopolies are bad—they are taboo in an enterprise-oriented economy. In spite of what our traditions tell us, both bigness and monopolies can have distinct and positive benefits to the consumer at home and to our efforts to enlarge our markets abroad. At home, our government feels that the more competition the better for both the consumer and the producer. This is another anachronism—that unlimited competition is good. Make no mistake, unlimited competition leads directly to marginal operations, lower efficiency and higher prices.

Before Eastern States Blast Furnace and
Coke Oven Association, Pittsburgh/
The National Observer, 3-29:10.

Robert W. Haack
President, New York Stock Exchange

I am fearful many people in the exchange community fail to realize that the (New York) Stock Exchange is in a competitive fight for its life. Its anticompetitive postures have by themselves provided an impetus to fragment this market, because they've given birth to all these competing entities (other securities exchanges) that are worrying us. What I'm talking about is price—commissions; and service—depth, liquidity of markets; and also utilization of high-speed communications and computerization. These are areas where the Exchange has a chance to be competitive, and I'm not sure we're being competitive in all these areas . . . Our share of the market is now at an all-time low—80 per cent; and there's been a decline of 10 per cent in the last two years . . . The dominance of the New York Stock Exchange is being undermined; and my position has been that our anticompetitive stances are fragmenting this market and are a boon to other markets.

The New York Times, 12-12:(3)1.

Clifford M. Hardin
Secretary of Agriculture of
the United States

This is not a prediction, but I hope the housewife can expect higher food prices this year . . . There have to be ways to equalize this situation (inadequate farm income); and one of the ways this can be achieved is some rise in food prices.

News conference, Dallas, Feb. 17/
The Washington Post,
2-19:(A)2.

John D. Harper
Chairman, Aluminum Company of America

We (businessmen) are working to abolish poverty in the only way it can be abolished—by providing jobs. We are fighting racial injustice the best way we can—with fair employment practices. We are not blind to urban blight. Environmental pollution is our frustration, too.

The Dallas Times Herald,
10-19:(A)18.

Fred R. Harris
United States Senator, D—Okla.

I believe we can be far more aggressive in developing foreign markets, particularly in regard to Western Europe and Japan, which have been protectionists against our products while selling rather freely in our markets. I believe the medicine we need is not more protectionism on our part, but less protectionism on their part. And I would move to open up free access of American businessmen to the markets of the Soviet Union, Eastern Europe and (Communist) China. I would turn the Yankee trader loose. He's bound too much by government restriction.

Interview/
Nation's Business, November:63.

Vance Hartke
United States Senator, D–Ind.

I'm not going to be for Lockheed (Aircraft Corp.) loan guarantees unless the corner grocer gets one, too.
San Francisco Examiner, 5-11:28.

Edward Heath
Prime Minister of the United Kingdom

The United States, faced with deep-seated problems at home and abroad, is working—while in contact with its allies—toward direct arrangements with the Soviet Union and Communist China. Even more important, the United States is acting drastically to protect its own balance of payments and its own trading position against the erosions which they suffered. Everyone concerned with trade and finance knows that rough winds are beginning to blow across the world.
San Francisco Examiner & Chronicle
(This World), 10-24:7.

Walter W. Heller
Professor of Economics, University of
Minnesota; Former Chairman, Council of
Economic Advisors to the
President of the United States

I think one of the most dangerous things we have done is to put that 10 per cent import surtax (announced by the President Aug. 15) in; and if we don't take it off rather promptly, we will be overplaying our hand . . . If we follow a "beggar thy neighbor" policy, we will hurt other countries who are already on the brink of recession. Let's remember what that did between the wars: It brought on a Hitler; it brought the rest of the world and ourselves into (depression). When we followed a different policy in the post-war period, we had the most prosperous period the world has ever known. I think we ought to think of it (the surtax) completely as a short-term bargaining instrument, and then get rid of it before we damage not only the world but ourselves.
TV-radio interview/"Meet the Press,"
National Broadcasting Company,
Washington, 10-17.

J. Edgar Hoover
Director, Federal Bureau of Investigation

In today's society, business is not being measured by the specific goods produced or services rendered, but by the totality of its influence and contributions to the whole community. Hence, wild ducks, public parks, ecology, recreation—factors which may seem far afield from operating a business—are now vital parts of decisions being made at the office.
Quote, 6-20:579.

Hendrik S. Houthakker
Member, Council of Economic Advisers to the
President of the United States

I can't be very encouraged by the American steel industry. They (steel firms) have made very large investments in modernization, and have essentially nothing to show for it. Productivity in the industry has been almost flat since 1965. It is something of a mystery.
Interview, Washington/
The Christian Science Monitor,
4-22:10.

John A. Howard
President, Rockford College

There has been, nationwide, a tendency among college personnel to be suspicious of, or hostile to, the private enterprise system and the mechanisms which animate it—competition, the profit motive and the marketplace as the determinant for producing and distributing goods and services. The imperfections of this economic system and the misdeeds of the misdoers seem to be magnified and dwelt upon out of all proportion to the actual benefits produced by the system and without regard to the percentage of its practitioners who do their work honestly and commendably. In all fairness, I think we must apply the grade-on-the-curve concept to our evaluation of private enterprise. Before one adds his bit to the fashionable scorn directed at this whipping boy, he should check the record, and I think he will discover that no other economic arrangement begins to measure up to this one in productivity and in

(JOHN A. HOWARD)

potential for easing man's burdens.

Convocation address,
Rockford College, Sept. 8/
Vital Speeches, 10-15:30.

Lee A. Iacocca
President, Ford Motor Company

In the long run, the key to providing more jobs for American workers, to keeping costs and prices down and to restoring the competitive vitality of American industry in world markets is to increase the rate of growth in productivity. The key to higher productivity is a sustained high level of capital investment. One of the secrets of Japan's success is its very high level of capital investment which, last year, amounted to 40 per cent of its gross national product. In the United States, on the other hand, capital investment amounts to only 14 per cent of GNP. American industry cannot compete with Japanese industry if that difference persists. Restoration of the investment tax credit will serve the dual purpose of stimulating investment and helping industry to absorb rising costs. It will not be a windfall for business, but a way of keeping American jobs in America. We hope that when Congress reconvenes it gives top priority to enacting this proposal.

News conference, Detroit, Aug. 16/
Los Angeles Herald-Examiner, 8-24:(D)5.

I've heard people say really often—I bet once a week—"I wouldn't want your job for all the money in the world." And I never respond to that. I don't know what the hell the response is. I love my job. They look upon it as a position that just grinds you and kills you off. I don't. Maybe that's the difference. In fact, maybe that's why the guys that say things like that will never get my job.

Interview, Dearborn, Mich./
Los Angeles Times, 12-19:(H)7.

Mary Gardiner Jones
Commissioner, Federal Trade Commission

It will no longer do for business to take the attitude that consumers' concerns are based on misinformation, while at the same time refusing to provide the information the consumer seeks in making his market decisions. If business fails to meet consumer needs voluntarily, government must move into the breach to compel it to take the steps necessary to make the market-place competitive, non-deceptive and fair to competitors and consumers.

At Seminar of Illinois Institute for
Continuing Legal Education, March 26/
The Washington Post, 3-27:(E)6.

Henry Kearns
President, Export-Import Bank of
the United States

The only way to get our international payments into balance any time soon is to increase exports. We need a trade surplus of $5-to $7-billion every year, not just an occasional surplus. To achieve a real solution, a long-range program must be followed. We cannot depend on emergency measures that are usually counterproductive . . . I think the additional trade we need can be achieved. The markets are available, if we just generate the sales effort—get our manufacturers to go out and sell, and back them up with adequate financing.

Interview, Washington/
U.S. News & World Report, 7-19:54.

Donald M. Kendall
President, Pepsico, Inc.

. . . the trade battle will continue, dividing us on the home front as well as posing problems of the most serious nature with our trading partners. A significant number of nations have already put this country on notice that if we turn back the international trading clock (by imposing trade quotas, etc.), they will do likewise. I cannot believe that we will repeat the mistakes of the 1930s with a worldwide trade war and depression. Our Atlantic trading partners share with us and the rest of the world the perplexing problem of inflation; but their economies are sound and burgeoning. But one sure result of protectionism is that trade expansion would be halted and set back.

At Mid-America Trade Conference, Chicago, Feb. 24/The New York Times, 2-25:59.

I have no ax to grind, as an advertiser, in choosing any one set of advertising appeals instead of another—"factual," "emotional" or what have you. But I do feel an obligation to "inform" people about what matters to them—that is, the pleasure or enjoyment they can derive from using my product. My commitment is to give the consumer what she wants; and if her "wants" have an emotional component to them, it behooves me to recognize that fact.

At Federal Trade Commission hearing, Washington, Oct. 20/ The New York Times, 10-21:26.

(The current discontent with advertising reflects) a deepening misunderstanding or distrust of the whole American system of free enterprise . . . (Distrust of advertising is) taught often and all too well by men whose intentions for our country are either curious or unknown to me. Advertising offers the highest silhouette, the most convenient aiming point for these people—but I think the ultimate target is free enterprise itself.

At Federal Trade Commission hearing, Washington, Oct. 20/ The New York Times, 10-21:26.

Miles W. Kirkpatrick
Chairman, Federal Trade Commission

(Regarding advertising): I, along with what I am sure are many millions of Americans, am far from happy with a good deal of what I see and hear. Much, quite frankly, repels me as insulting to good judgment and taste. Far from giving even the minimum of information upon which an interested person might make a selection of products among alternatives, the effort appears frequently to obscure the relevant information and to bring other considerations to the foreground . . . the amount of shoddy advertising must be a significant factor

in the average consumer's concept of American business and the American businessman. Sensible people, I believe, are entitled to be somewhat skeptical of the business organizations which are responsible for the tasteless and uninformative ads that are often stock-in-trade today. The problem goes, of course, not only to the advertising itself, but encompasses as well sales and service policies . . . when the consumer is dissatisfied with the product, he is often endlessly shuttled back and forth between the retailer, the wholesaler and the manufacturer. Each of them frequently looks the other way and sends out another form letter. The inevitable result of this state of affairs, it seems to me, is to alienate the consumer from the American business community. His suspicions and mistrust are aroused and fed by those who bombard him with tawdry and calculatedly uninformative messages . . . if the public's image of American business is an increasingly tarnished one, I, for one, attribute that in some measure to business' most visible product—its own advertising.

Before International Newspaper Advertising Executives, New York, Jan. 8/ The Dallas Times Herald, 1-11:(C)6.

Thomas S. Kleppe
Administrator, Small Business Administration of the United States

The business of our country is small business—at least in numbers. Small business is the real exponent of the free-enterprise system that built this country and will sustain it.

The New York Times, 5-16:(3)3.

Virginia H. Knauer
Special Assistant to the President of the United States for Consumer Affairs

As I travel around the country, one question keeps recurring from the housewives I meet. They want to know why so many ads treat women like children, like third-graders.

71

(VIRGINIA H. KNAUER)

Should the American housewife be treated like a moron? Is the best selling appeal one which insults a person's intelligence . . .? You are at the crossroads; because there are those in the advertising world who are not so decent, not so honorable. There are those who believe integrity is something one can sell or buy for a few dollars. This audience—the advertising profession—is at this point right now. The choice is still yours. One road leads to government regulations, the other to self-reform.

Before American Advertising Federation, Washington, Feb. 1/ Los Angeles Times, 2-2:(1)12.

S. E. Knudsen
Chairman, White Motor Company

In the days ahead, the management of any consumer-goods company is going to have only two options: build a trouble-free product, or be ready to fix the product fast.

Before Cleveland Advertising Club and Greater Cleveland Growth Association/ The Wall Street Journal, 10-8:6.

William J. Kuhfuss
President, American Farm Bureau Federation

If agriculture is to be a full partner in America's competitive enterprise system, government farm policies must place greater reliance on the market system instead of requiring farmers and ranchers to depend on Federal subsidies for a substantial part of their income.

Washington, May 6/ The Dallas Times Herald, 5-7:(A)4.

Frederick G. Larkin, Jr.
Chairman, Security Pacific National Bank, Los Angeles

I would very much hope that we (the United States) do not take the path to greater protectionism (in trade). I want to make it clear, however, that I am not suggesting a unilateral dismantling of trade restrictions by the U. S. A. Any move to freer trade by us must be accompanied by similar, meaningful moves in other countries that, at the same time, take into account the legitimate problems of . . . those in a developing stage.

At opening of the bank's European headquarters, Brussels, Feb. 23/ Los Angeles Times, 2-24:(3)9.

R. Heath Larry
Vice chairman, United States Steel Corporation

How unfortunate it is that so many people seem honestly to believe that profit dollars are dollars which pour "into the coffers of corporations" and just lie there, not helping anyone, and which in turn can be taken away without hurting anyone. Yet there never was a profit dollar that didn't go to work, and promptly, whether by flowing out of the business to the investors—who either spend it like any other consumer, or reinvest it—or by flowing through the business itself, for plant and equipment or for something else needed to improve or continue the business as a job-providing entity. Those who are genuinely interested in helping to reduce unemployment had better take a long look at the number of new entrants into the work force expected in the next 10 or 20 years. For jobs just don't come into being without a companion capital formation to provide the facilities on which they can exist. And without an adequate profit opportunity, there is no way by which the necessary capital formation can occur.

Before Economic Club, Chicago, Oct. 14/ Vital Speeches, 11-1:59.

Lee Loevinger
Former Assistant Attorney General, Antitrust Division, Department of Justice of the United States

Under the undefined and undefinable scope of (the) "potentiality theory," the determinations as to where, and how much, business can expand will inevitably get shifted from the numerous markets, executive suites and board rooms to the tight little group comprising the government antitrust enforcement bureaucracy. The power of the public, consumers, management and stockholders over economic development will be decreased, and the power of government will be increased. The ultimate effect will be that of establishing government regulation to control the expansion, through internal growth or acquisition, of every business, large and small. The concentration of such power in government is as dangerous and as contrary to the historical and fundamental spirit of antitrust as the concentration of economic power in private hands.

Before Association for Corporate Growth, New York, Jan. 13/ The New York Times, 1-14:53.

(Arguing against excessive Justice Department control over business): If economic power acquired by merger can be prohibited or broken up because of the potentiality of abuse, there is no logical basis for refusing to reach the same conclusion with respect to economic power acquired by expansion or growth.

Before American Marketing Association, Chicago/Los Angeles Times, 3-4:(3)13.

Joseph Martin, Jr.
General counsel,
Federal Trade Commission

Cases of built-in (product) obsolescence are common. This planned obsolescence is accomplished in several ways: by failing to provide a source of spare parts for the reasonable life of the product, by making frequent style or nonfunctional changes so that the user feels he must turn in his old model for one which gives him better performance, and by including certain components made of materials which have a shorter life than the reasonable life expectancy of the product itself.

At Northwestern University/ The New York Times, 3-28:(1)40.

William McChesney Martin, Jr.
Former Chairman, Federal Reserve Board

I'm a believer in pure competition . . . There should be losses occasionally, as well as

profits, in a free-enterprise society.

Interview/The New York Times, 1-25:33.

What's good for the United States is good for the New York Stock Exchange. But what's good for the New York Stock Exchange might not be good for the United States.

Interview, New York/ The New York Times, 7-4:(3)3.

L. S. Matthews
President, Leo Burnett Company, advertising

I'm . . . convinced of advertising's contributions to the social improvement of the nation. Sure, the American public has been sold a whole raft of products through advertising that aren't necessities. Television sets aren't necessities; neither are air conditioners, nor dishwashers, nor vacuum cleaners, nor a whole range of other products which have enriched the consumer's life. Sure, he or she was stimulated to work harder to get the dough to buy all these things, with the result that our economy is the most productive in the world. The consumer also doesn't *need* cosmetics or mini-skirts or hot-pants or wide ties or striped shirts or a thousand and one things which make the difference between existing and living. The socialist economies of the world are living examples that none of these things are necessities; but what a dull gray world they live in. I ask you, is the consumer king in these countries? You know damn well she's not. These are the places where the government decides what's best for the consumer—in their bureaucratic, infinite wisdom.

Before Chicago Advertising Club, April 15/ Vital Speeches, 6-1:506.

. . . advertising and marketing have never been under more severe attack: by headline-hunters in Congress, who have found consumerism is a big producer of newspaper lineage; by self-styled experts, self-appointed unqualified protectors of the consumer, who

(L. S. MATTHEWS)

blatantly use the technique of half-truths and undocumented claims they accuse advertising of using; by academicians, well versed in economic theory but illiterate in the practical workings of a free marketplace; by bureaucrats in the Federal agencies, who went to Washington as bright young lawyers and who also have never experienced the realities of marketing a product in a competitive economy; and unthinkingly, too, by the press—not just the newspapers but the television and radio newspeople, too; by headlining the undocumented charges of the consumerists and the Congressional headline-hunters, they contribute to an unbalanced presentation of the issues.

Before Chicago Advertising Club, April 15/
Vital Speeches, 6-1:506.

C. Peter McColough
President, Xerox Corporation

It is very difficult to operate around the world with our antitrust laws. We cannot select a foreign partner and say, "We are going to work with you forever." This leads to great difficulty for us, because we have to write agreements that are short-term when we really intend them to be long-term. I don't know any other government that makes companies obey not only the laws of the foreign nations where they operate, but also certain laws of the home country. We are unique in that.

Panel discussion/
Time, 5-10:91.

Richard W. McLaren
Assistant Attorney General,
Antitrust Division,
Department of Justice of the United States

This nation's economic policy favors the competitive rather than the joint industry approach. We would urge that collaboration among competitors be kept to a minimum and that firms be permitted to exchange research and feasibility information only upon a strong showing by the proponents that a collective approach will yield substantial net gains. The antitrust laws and many of this nation's other economic policies are based upon the general assumption that innovation is more likely to flourish through competitive efforts than by collective endeavors.

Before antitrust section, American
Bar Association, Washington, April 1/
The Washington Post, 4-2:(D)11.

George Meany
President, American Federation of Labor-
Congress of Industrial Organizations

(Imports) will have to be limited in some way in order to protect jobs, unless we are going to allow the rest of the world to make all the things that we use and just become a service nation. This is a real problem. It is not foreign competition. Thirty years ago it was referred to as foreign competition. It is not foreign. It is competition from American capital that has been exported from overseas . . . Of course, in the final analysis you could perhaps say, "Well, we've just got to lower our wages to compete with these people." This, of course, would change the whole picture of the United States. We would no longer have this dynamic economy we like to brag about now . . . if we are going to compete with the rest of the world on the basis of who can pay the least wages, then we are going to forget the America that we knew, forget the America that you and I have known in the last 50 years. Forget the America with the dynamic economy that keeps things moving forward; because when you are going to use human misery as an ingredient in competition to see how low people can get, then we are out of that.

TV-radio interview/"Meet the Press,"
National Broadcasting Company,
Washington, 7-11.

Basil J. Mezines
Executive Director, Federal Trade Commission

If businessmen believe that the Commission and other government agencies are becoming more enforcement-oriented, then we begin to hear the suggestion that self-regulation is (a) reasonable alternative to the time-consuming lawsuit. (But) if the consumer is cynically regarded as fair game . . . no amount of moralizing will alter the business climate, and no program of self- regulation will work.

*Before American Society of
Association Executives, Washington/
San Francisco Examiner, 9-7:60.*

Thomas G. Moore
*Professor of Economics,
Michigan State University*

(Arguing against government support for failing firms): The carrot and the stick of profits and losses are the goals that keep business and our economy efficient and productive. It would be a pity if we went down the path that the British followed just when they have learned the hard lesson that the stick of losses is necessary as well as the carrot of profits.

*Before Senate Banking and
Currency Committee, Washington, June 21/
The New York Times, 6-22:45.*

William H. Moore
*Chairman,
Bankers Trust Company, New York*

I believe that we have come along to the time when the government and the private sector, for the good of the United States, are going to have to join hands in many projects. Now this is a rather Boy Scouty statement, but really, I sincerely believe it. Basically, there isn't a private enterprise company or organization that isn't now receiving help or about to get help. The steel and the textile people, for instance, they want help from a point of view of quotas. The farm people have been helped for years. Also, we're not talking about big guys and little guys. We've got SBAs (guarantees by the Small Business Administration) that have

been running for a helluva long time. So I think the concept is nothing that really strikes at the heart of private enterprise at all.

*Interview, New York/
The New York Times, 7-13:43.*

Ralph Nader
Lawyer, Consumer Rights Advocate

. . . I don't think we have a capitalistic system now. There are too many government controls over the market mechanism, too many subsidies and far too much oligopoly and shared monopoly over the market mechanism. It's much better, I think, to call it part capitalistic. The trend is to have increasing interwoveness between large corporations and large government units. This is why it's no longer a surprise for Penn Central to apply to Washington for welfare.

Interview/The New York Times, 1-24:(3)1.

It's more important to love than to want to be loved. What would happen to me if I went out to Jim Roche's (Chairman of General Motors) house to dinner, for instance? Well, pretty soon it's Ralph and Jim, and pretty soon there's a report coming out on GM, and someone says, "You know, you can't do this to Jim. Remember those great dinners at his house. Not to good old Jim." Well, there it is—the most important quality for this kind of work (consumer rights) is to have no anxiety to be loved.

*Interview, Colorado Springs/
Time, 5-10:18.*

I have a consistent rule: The American people should know as much about the Pentagon as the Soviet Union and (Communist) China do, as much about General Motors as Ford does, and as much about (New York's First National) City Bank as Chase Manhattan does.

*At seminar of bank executives,
Washington, June 11/
The New York Times, 6-12:37.*

James J. Needham
*Commissioner, Securities and
Exchange Commission of the United States*

. . . we must leave the ownership of the

(JAMES J. NEEDHAM)

securities industry in private hands. What's more, the regulation of the industry must be left in the private sector, subject only to Federal oversight, as it is today. I do not mean to imply that I consider the self-regulatory system has worked to perfection in the past; I wish it had. And I don't mean to imply that, as presently constituted, it will work to perfection in the future. As a matter of fact, I am completely agreeable to a review of it for the purpose of improving its future effectiveness. What is important is that the concept of self-regulation be maintained. The securities industry, like other industries, may falter and stumble along at times; but again, like other industries, it has its men of vision and ability. Their voices can and will be heard; and, with the assistance of all concerned within and without the government, they will lead the industry to a new era of profitability and fulfillment of its public responsibility.

New York, May 17/
Vital Speeches, 7-1:552.

John J. Nevin
President,
Zenith Radio Corporation

I'm a free trader, and I'm for fair price competition. But our government seems far more exercised about breaking up anything that appears monopolistic. It either doesn't or won't understand the effect of "dumping" from abroad. We've been diddling around for three miserable years over the Japanese dumping of radios and television sets here at prices far below what they charge at home. This is just as unfair to American business as monopoly practices are to American customers.

Interview, Chicago/
The New York Times, 7-25:(3)7.

Richard M. Nixon
President of the United States

Everyone in this audience today has heard some young person—perhaps even his own

son—say something like this: "I don't want to go into business. That nine-to-five rat race is not for me. I want to do something to help people." The simple truth is this: No government agency, no philanthropy, no voluntary organization or foundation has done as much to help people as the private enterprise system. It doesn't get the credit, of course. There is no message stamped on every welfare check that reads "this comes to you from the taxes raised from the private enterprise system." Because a government is the distributor, many recipients make the mistake of thinking government is the producer—and nothing could be further from the truth. We need to take a lot more pride in the system that makes it possible for us to be the most generous and most compassionate nation on the face of the earth. The system that has delivered more self-respect to more human beings than any other system devised by man deserves to be treated with more respect itself.

Before Chamber of Commerce of the
United States, Washington, April 26/
The Washington Post, 4-27:(A)6.

(Regarding possible loan guarantees for Lockheed Aircraft Corporation): . . . Lockheed is one of the nation's great companies. It provides an enormous employment lift to this part of the country. And I'm going to be heavily influenced by the need to see to it that Southern California, after taking the disappointment of not getting the SST—which would, of course, have brought many, many jobs to this part of the country—that California does not have an additional jolt of losing Lockheed. That gives you an indication of where I'm leaning. On the other hand, if the Secretary of the Treasury comes in and gives me strong arguments to the contrary, I will look in the other direction.

News conference, San Clemente, Calif.,
May 1/The New York Times, 5-2:(1)66.

At the end of World War II, the economies of the major industrial nations of Europe and Asia were shattered. To help them get on their feet and to protect their freedom, the United States has provided $143 billion in

76

foreign aid. That was the right thing for us to do. Today, largely with our help, they have regained their vitality and have become strong competitors. Now that other nations are economically strong, the time has come for them to bear their fair share of the burden of defending freedom around the world. The time has come for exchange rates to be set straight and for the major nations to compete as equals. There is no longer any need for the United States to compete with one hand tied behind her back.

TV-radio address, Washington, Aug. 15/
Los Angeles Times, 8-16:(1)15.

Productivity holds the key to America's economic well-being. Only by increasing productivity can we achieve a higher standard of living without rampant inflation at home. And only by increasing productivity can we win a stronger position over the long run in the marketplaces and trading lanes of the world.

Before Associated Milk Producers,
Chicago, Sept. 3/
The Washington Post, 9-4:(A)1.

We cannot remain a great nation if we build a permanent wall of tariffs and quotas around the United States. We cannot live behind a wall that shuts the rest of the world out. The world is too small, and the United States is too important a part of that world. If we were not a great power, we would not be the America we know. If we do not stay a great power, the world will not stay safe for free men. We cannot turn inward, we cannot drop out of competition with the rest of the world, and remain a great nation. Because when a nation ceases to compete, when it ceases to try to do its best, then that nation ceases to be a great nation. America today is Number 1 in the world economically. Let us resolve that we shall stay number 1.

Before Congress, Washington, Sept. 9/
The Washington Post, 9-10:(A)12.

Can American producers compete with others in the world without some subsidy? It may be necessary in some areas that there be subsidy, and we should consider that. We have got to see to it that the American workman—the highest-paid workman in the world—is not driven out of competition because an unfair advantage is obtained by a workman abroad who is paid less because his government subsidizes him and our government doesn't subsidize ours. It is subsidizing only in that area that we would favor.

Before Economic Club of Detroit, Sept. 23/
U.S. News & World Report, 10-4:78.

John E. O'Toole
President,
Foote, Cone & Belding, advertising

. . . I'm afraid I detect some Future Shock in the advertising community lately. In a business (in) which, more than any other, professionals should be looking ahead, pointing the way, preparing themselves and their clients for the future, we still see people trying to sell things clients don't want, defending the outdated, making advertising that assumes the consumer is a jerk and generally facing the future with both feet planted solidly in 1960. It's particularly evident in the response—or lack of response—on the part of advertiser and advertising people to the increasing attacks by consumerism groups and the legislators grabbing for their banners. To assume that we should adopt a low silhouette and wait for all that to pass away is terminal Future Shock. I've been told there are more than 100 pieces of legislation, all affecting advertising, prepared or in preparation for consideration by Congress. If a small proportion is enacted, advertising might never recover. And among the serious losses would be the small, unique body of talent that knows more about the successful use of mass communications than any group in history.

Before Los Angeles Ad Club/
The Wall Street Journal, 3-3:10.

Hugh F. Owens
Commissioner, Securities and Exchange Commission of the United States

Now that it is the security of the United States Treasury that protects customers' accounts, as well as the funds of (stock) exchange members, you can be assured that the Commission will have a far greater voice in determining what action should be taken in regard to ailing firms . . . If there is any

(HUGH F. OWENS)

lesson that has been learned from our experiences of the last few years, it is that the Commission must have plenary power to take whatever action is required in the public interest and should not have to wait and see what action a self-regulatory body will or will not take before it acts.

Before American Society of Corporate Secretaries, Chicago, Jan. 13/ The Washington Post, 1-14:(E)1.

Wright Patman
United States Representative, D—Tex.

No one can match the consistent, unyielding pressure that is supplied by the banking industry. I am convinced that the major banking legislation in this nation is decided on (a) pure dollars-and-cents basis—not on the basis of superior testimony or the public interest. It is pure, raw economic power that decides the issue.

Daily World, 1-15:7;

Herbert P. Patterson
President,
Chase Manhattan Bank, New York

One must not lose those direct, sensitive and trusting personal relationships which are the essentials of managing human beings. A (company) president must resist the solicitous urgings of his staff, who seek to conserve his time and energy by putting him into the traditional ivory tower. Once there, safely isolated from the functioning everyday realities that shape the lives of his employees and the general public, he is well on the way to being neutralized. With the best will in the world, his staff will commandeer his appointment calendar and condense all adversity into easily-swallowed capsules that won't upset his stomach. But without continuous exposure to the challenge and the stimulation of contrary views, an executive will be ill-equipped to guide his company with strength and intelligence.

At Graduate School of Business, Stanford University/The National Observer, 1-11:10.

Thomas P. Phelan
President,
Pacific Coast Stock Exchange

Just because a trade occurs away from the floor of the New York Stock Exchange does not mean the end of the securities industry . . . Fragmentation is not a good description of what has occurred. The trading has broken into different components, and the regionals have become a part of the whole, contributing to the overall trading process and adding to the liquidity.

Before Bond Club, San Francisco, Jan. 20/The New York Times, 1-21:47.

Georges Pompidou
President of France

We cannot keep forever as our basic monetary yardstick a national currency (the American dollar) that constantly loses value as a result of purely internal policies. The rest of the world cannot be expected to regulate its life by a clock which is always slow.

News conference, Brussels, May 26/ The Washington Post, 5-17:(A)27.

William Proxmire
United States Senator, D—Wis.

The freedom to fail may at times appear to be an overly painful solution—particularly to the firm going out of business. But business failures serve a higher public purpose. They are the means by which our economy discards obsolete or inefficient ways of doing business. In this way, the overall efficiency of our economy is improved. Business failures are not tragic events to be prevented; they are the sign of a healthy and productive economy.

Salt Lake City Deseret News, 5-27:(A)22.

Although we've been led to believe that the economy is on the rebound after a long period of marking time, a careful analysis of business profit statistics shows an alarming trend . . . While the Congress and the Administration battle to save jobs and business for Penn-Central, Lockheed, Boeing and the automobile Big Three companies that admittedly have great impact on the economy, smaller firms are finding it ever more difficult to keep their heads above the red ink flood. And these smaller firms simply don't have the visibility or the raw political power to get the type of Federal attention lavished on their big brothers.

Sept. 6/The Washington Post, 9-7:(A)6.

Donald T. Regan
Chairman, Merrill Lynch, Pierce,
Fenner and Smith

If we keep averaging 20 million shares a day (on the New York Stock Exchange), with peaks of 25 million, as we have in February, it seems to me we're going to need some type of slowdown. To avoid that, we need a quota system . . . When the bus is full, the driver shuts the door.

News conference, New York, Feb. 9/
The Washington Post, 2-10:(D)10.

John C. Renner
Director, Office of International
Trade, Department of State of the
United States

Unilateral action by any country to restrict trade changes the balance of concessions arrived at over the years, and is most likely to provoke counteraction to restore equilibrium.

Jan. 30/The Washington Post,
10-24:(L)1.

Hyman G. Rickover
Vice Admiral, United States Navy

If the government has an obligation to rescue the firm (Lockheed Aircraft Corp.), then it must also see that it is properly managed; and this will inevitably lead to government socialism. We are far more Communistic than the Russians when it comes to tolerating failure. When the men in Russia foul up, they are dismissed, sometimes losing their necks. But we protect those who fail and press them to the government bosom.

Before Joint Congressional Economic
Committee, Washington, April 28/
The Washington Post, 4-29:(A)2.

Pierre A. Rinfret
Economist

I'm for protectionism, because we must redress the balance of trade. We've got to stop giving away every competitive advantage in international trade.

At American Iron and Steel Institute
conference/U.S. News & World Report,
7-12:33.

James M. Roche
Chairman, General Motors Corporation

American business is so widely-owned and its benefits so widely-dispersed that when we criticize business, we are, in effect, criticizing ourselves. When business does not do the job expected of it, it is we—all of us—who are both accountable and concerned.

Before Economic Club of New York,
March 10/The New York Times,
3-11:66.

Those critics (of business) whose aim is destructive are following a basic tactic of devisiveness—and with considerable success. They are endeavoring to turn various segments of our society—government, labor, the universities—against business. They are trying to make America in the 1970s a society at war with itself. Their ultimate aim is to alienate the American consumer from business, to tear down long-established relationships which have served both so well. They tell the consumer he is being victimized; new products are being foisted upon him, whether he wants them or not; these products are not as good as they should be—that is, they are less than perfect; businessmen are greedy and uncaring; corporations are beyond reach and above response to the consumer's needs; advertising is false; prices are padded; labels are inaccurate. Therefore, the consumer, many would have us believe, is helpless and unprotected when he shops and is really not responsible for what he buys. This delusion—that the consumer cannot trust his own free choice—strikes at the very heart of our free competitive system. The system is founded on the conviction that in the long run the consumer is the best judge of his own welfare. The entire success of free enterprise can be

(JAMES M. ROCHE)

traced to the vitality it gains by competitive striving to satisfy the discriminating customer. To destroy the concept of consumer supremacy is to destroy free enterprise. If the consumer can be convinced that he really does not know what is good for him—and this is what the critics try to do—then freedom leaves free enterprise. In other words, if the consumer cannot protect his own interest, then someone else must do it. That someone else will then dictate what can be made, what can be sold and at what price. That will surely mark the end of free enterprise. The greatest of our economic freedoms—the freedom to decide our purchases—will be gone. This cannot happen, many will say. To them we should reply, look back. Look back at only the past decade to see how rapidly we have expanded the role of government in the marketplace.

Before Executive Club, Chicago, March 25/
Vital Speeches, 5-1:446.

While I have discussed it in public remarks on many occasions, I never ceased to be amazed that the word (consumerism) has come to connote dissatisfaction, complaint and fraudulent business practices. Consumerism should have a more positive meaning—it should stand for satisfying the customer. In this very real sense, consumerism is what our free-enterprise system is all about. There is only one way a business can earn a profit, and that is to make a product a consumer wants to buy, produce it efficiently, provide good service and treat the consumer honestly and fairly.

Denver/ The National Observer, 10-23:13.

We are losing our competitive position in the world. There are those who would not regret the loss of our leadership. They say this was a role we should not have assumed and should not try to continue. They say the cost is too great, the risks are too many and the rewards are too few. I feel otherwise. A nation dedicated as we are to man's individual dignity and freedom has no alternative but to lead.

Before Fifth Avenue Association, New York,
Oct. 29/The New York Times, 10-30:41.

David Rockefeller
Chairman, Chase Manhattan Bank,
New York

Businesses are leaving the cities for a variety of reasons. Crime, rising taxes and insurance rates and congestion are among the reasons. Also, many feel there is a more plentiful supply of better-quality labor in the suburbs. Others feel they are following their customers. Additional factors sometimes include room for expansion, aesthetics and convenience of commuting. However, the road isn't all one way, for many businesses are still flocking to the city—and others, having tried the suburbs, have come back, for they missed the dynamism, the excitement, the culture and the marketplace for the exchange of ideas that only the large cities provide.

Interview, Washington/
U.S. News & World Report, 6-7:51.

We can increase it (American foreign trade) provided we get inflation under control. This has been the principal deterrent to trade. If you look back less than 10 years, our trade surplus then was running at a level of about $6 billion. Now it has dropped to where there is actually a deficit. People raise questions of foreign competition and lower wages and that kind of thing. Those are factors. But inflation has always been the prime reason. However, I am convinced that if we continue to spend money on research and development, continue to be aggressive in marketing techniques, there is no reason why we can't stay one jump ahead of the others in many areas.

Interview, New York/Nation's
Business, December:37.

John D. Rockefeller III
Philanthropist

Who is competent to deal with the complex social problems of our time—the problems of poverty, race, population growth, environment, urban decay? Is there any reason to believe that government or labor or the universities are any more competent to deal with such problems than business? In these troubled times, the creativity and organizational skill, the energy and resources of the business community are indispensable. It is, therefore, a challenge to business—indeed a responsibility—to harness its competence to the solution of our pressing social problems.

*At Conference on the Individual and
the Corporation in a Changing Society,
Stanford, Calif., March 26/San
Francisco Examiner, 3-26:5.*

H. I. Romnes
*Chairman, American Telephone and
Telegraph Company*

One man can't know the right answers to every problem, because he can't possibly have all the facts or all the considerations involved. That means, of course, that you have to pick people in whom you have confidence, who have gone through the hoops and have a lot of experience and have demonstrated good judgment. And then you have to give them the authority to make decisions. Sometimes you have to bite your tongue after they *do* make decisions and those decisions don't make sense. In those cases, you talk it out and try to learn why they went in a certain direction. But you can't dictate—unless you want to make all the mistakes yourself.

*Interview, New York/
Nation's Business, April.*

William D. Ruckelshaus
*Administrator, Environmental Protection
Agency of the United States*

Industries and businesses that must operate in the market-place of free choice know that they must change, they must adapt, they must accomodate to changes in public attitudes—or they will surely die.

*Before National Industrial
Pollution Control Council,
Washington, Feb. 10/
The New York Times, 2-14:(4)2.*

Paul A. Samuelson
*Professor of Economics
Massachusetts Institute of Technology*

I'd hate to go on a cruise now for 10 years

and say I'd stay 100 per cent invested in common stocks.

*Interview, Cambridge, Mass./
The New York Times, 3-14:(3)18.*

(Regarding the fluctuation on the European money market): (It is) a very good thing . . .not an economic Pearl Harbor. This is not a defeat for the dollar. This is very much in line with what I had hoped would happen. It is good for the dollar, because, in my judgment, that dollar was overvalued. And it is good for the West German mark, because, in my view, the mark was undervalued. Both of them will benefit from the movement toward equilibrium.

*Interview, Cambridge, Mass., May 10/
The Washington Post, 5-11:(A)6.*

President Nixon on August 15 announced the de facto devaluation of the dollar. The moment he instructed Secretary of the Treasury Connally to suspend gold payments, the fixed-exchange system set up in 1944 at Bretton Woods became a part of history. The President had no real choice. His hand was forced by the massive hemorrhage of dollar reserves of recent weeks. Although President Nixon blamed the devaluation on international speculators, they were merely the effect and symptom of an underlying cause. For more than a decade, the American dollar has been overvalued currency.

The Dallas Times Herald, 8-22:(B)10.

Robert W. Sarnoff
Chairman, RCA Corporation

I urge that we stop looking nervously over our shoulders at consumerism as a movement. We should look, instead, at the consumer as an individual who insists upon being dealt with in an honest and straightforward manner. It is not a faceless horde out there to whom we are talking. You and I are consumers, too; and our experience should teach us much about human desires, expectations and reactions. Life styles may differ, but a $5 "lemon" is just as sour as a $5,000 "lemon"; and double-talk is no more welcome in a Main Line home than in a Harlem flat or on a Kansas farm. Young or

WHAT THEY SAID IN 1971

(ROBERT W. SARNOFF)

old, dove or hawk, square or hippie, one tie that binds us all is irritation at getting had.

Before Poor Richard Club,
Philadelphia, Jan. 16/
The Washington Post, 1-23:(A)14.

I expect European multinational business growth in the United States to advance during the 1970's at a rate approaching American industrial growth in Europe in the 1960's . . . I view multinational business as the spearhead of an irreversible drive toward a true world economy. It seeks the most efficient use of resources on a global scale. It encourages economic integration, generates new capital resources and fosters the spread of useful technology and management knowhow.

At dedication of RCA semiconductor plant,
Liege, Belgium/
The Wall Street Journal, 6-4:6.

Pierre-Paul Schweitzer
Managing director,
International Monetary Fund

(Regarding President Nixon's cutting the dollar off from its gold backing): You can keep markets for a week, perhaps, without gold, but not much longer. In my opinion, there is not the slightest chance . . . there will emerge anything to put the U.S. balance of payments in order or which would constitute any satisfactory exchange rate pattern. The only way to achieve this is gold.

TV interview, Aug. 24/
The Washington Post, 8-26:(E)1.

Dan Seymour
President, J. Walter Thompson
Company, advertising

The advertising business always heads in new directions. There is a very real challenge with the consumer movement increasing, and I think there will be more need for news and facts about products. But that doesn't mean that the creative skills will change very much. People are always the same; only the times change.

Interview, Los Angeles/
Los Angeles Times, 3-29:(3)9.

Thomas R. Shepard, Jr.
Publisher, "Look" magazine

. . . the consumerists of our nation and their representatives in government are well-meaning people. They are sincere in their belief that, by eliminating free enterprise and by shifting control of industry into the hands of a beneficent government commission, they will make it possible for the people of America to lead happier lives. They are convinced that, as an intellectual elite, they know what is best for the average consumer . . . what foods he should eat, what cars he should drive, what TV show he should watch, what ads he should read. You see, deep down, the consumerist—although he would deny the allegation most vehemently—is a consummate snob. For it is his belief that the average man is too stupid, too naive and too deficient in most aspects of culture and refinement to be allowed to select his own method of living. He has to be taken by the hand and shown the way. And who is better suited to do the leading than the good old consumerist himself?

Before Rotary Club, Philadelphia/
The Wall Street Journal, 4-23:6.

Members of the "disaster lobby" look back with fond nostalgia to the "good old days" when there weren't any nasty factories to pollute the air and kill the animals and drive people to distraction with misleading advertisements. But what was life really like in America 150 years ago? . . . Whatever American businessmen have done to bring us out of that "paradise" of 150 years ago, I say let's give them a grateful pat on the back—not a knife in it.

Before Soap and Detergent Association/
U.S. News & World Report, 4-26:53.

. . . it is absurd for anyone to believe that an established businessman—whether he is a manufacturer or a retailer—would deliberately cheat his customers. It costs so much money to introduce a new product or to build up a retail clientele, that only an idiot would risk losing that investment by going after a dishonest dollar or two. He might get that dollar once, but his customer will never come back. And there isn't a businessman in the country who can make a go of it on one-time patronage. He simply must have repeat business; and the only way he can get it is by delivering a good product or service at a fair price.

Before Better Business Bureau of Eastern Massachusetts, Boston, May 7/Human Events, 7-10:10.

F. Ritter Shumway
President, Chamber of Commerce of the United States

Consumerism is a force of growing power; and the businessman who ignores it or takes it lightly does so at peril to his very economic survival.

U.S. News & World Report, 1-18:20.

John G. Simon
Professor of Law, Yale University

Although we don't have enough data to say that socially-responsible companies will be more productive in long-term growth, we pretty well think that maximum return and an attempt to correct irresponsible corporate activities won't have a negative effect on returns.

The New York Times, 4-4:(3)14.

Theodore C. Sorensen
Lawyer; Former Special Counsel to the President of the United States

Consumerism is getting more and more business leaders out of their executive suites and into the marketplaces they should have visited before. They are discovering sources of customer dissatisfaction they never knew existed. They are improving communications and customer relations, checking on services and advertising warranties, finding out what makes customers buy—and becoming better chief executives as a result.

Before National Businessmen's Council, New York/The Wall Street Journal, 6-1:12.

Oren Lee Staley
President, National Farmers Organization

(Referring to Secretary of Agriculture-designate Earl Butz): (He is) one of those land-grant college educators who was supposed to assist all farmers in America, but who identified instead with giant agribusiness corporations ... at the very time they were driving thousands of bona-fide family farmers to the wall. Many people regard Mr. Butz as a symbol of the betrayal of agriculture by some of its educational institutions to giant corporate interests.

The Washington Post, 11-14:(A)10.

Maurice H. Stans
Secretary of Commerce of the United States

Business is more than 99.44 per cent pure ... the charlatans, the malefactors, the quick-buck artists represent no more than 1 per cent of the business community, and all of industry must not be penalized for the sins of the few.

San Francisco Examiner & Chronicle (This World), 5-16:2.

In one way or another, American business and American products have been placed in competitive jeopardy over the past decade or less by a wide variety of unpublished regulations, administrative rules, tax discriminations, import restrictions, export subsidies and preferential trading agreements. Using these discriminations, some of our major trading partners are continuing to do business in violation of the rules of GATT. Some of the rules of international trade are not being fairly applied by all the trading nations of the world. We have been expected to put up with restrictions on American products and investments which others do not want us to impose on them. We do not seek special advantages from nations with which we do business. But we do seek and expect the end of these barricades to fair competition, so that our two-way trade with the rest of the world may continue to expand.

U.S. News & World Report, 7-12:32.

If American businessmen can, over a time, develop a better understanding of the Soviet business system, and they (the Soviets), in turn, can develop a better understanding of the American system, I would say there are good potentials for trade in both directions. It is

(MAURICE H. STANS)

wholly logical that the two countries in the world with the largest economies and gross national product could, in a perfectly normal way, increase substantially the amount of trade above what it is now. The barriers up to now have been political differences, numerous obstacles for American firms in the U.S.S.R., the absence of credit facilities and the feeling on the part of the Soviet government that American restrictions are discriminatory. If these difficulties can be reduced, I would say that the possibilities of improved and enlarged commercial relationships are very promising.

Interview, Washington/
U.S. News & World Report, 12-20:60.

Herman E. Talmadge
United States Senator, D–Ga.

The answer to the textile-import problem is not a surcharge. We are not going to solve the problem by relying on so-called self-restraint by the Japanese. The only way to effectively attack the problem is through import quotas. Such action is imperative if we are going to protect the jobs and incomes of American workers . . . As far as Japanese and Oriental textiles are concerned, the 10 per cent surcharge (announced by President Nixon on imported products) is like trying to treat cancer with a Band-aid. These imports are produced for wages and under working conditions that would be illegal in this country. They undersell our American-made products by such a wide margin that the surtax will not even make a dent in the problem.

Before the Senate, Washington,
Sept. 13/San Francisco Examiner,
9-13:10.

Charles B. Thornton
Chairman, Litton Industries

One of the most important things that the Administration can do is to provide business with an investment tax credit. Not only will that create jobs now, but it will improve productivity and help the U.S. maintain an edge over foreign competition. Too many of our

production facilities are not modern enough and desperately need updating.

Interview/Time, 8-16:69.

Nobuhiko Ushiba
Japanese Ambassador to the
United States

It is true that the United States maintains fewer import restrictions than any other major trading nation, except possibly Canada. But it is also true that, from time to time, the United States raises the threat of import quotas or other barriers in order to persuade its trading partners to limit their exports to American markets.

San Francisco, March 15/ San
Francisco Examiner, 3-16:3.

Unfortunately, in recent years there have been heard in America many criticisms of Japanese economic and trade policies. Some criticisms are valid, but most of them are either false or exaggerated. For instance, some believe that the Japanese tariff rate is much higher than American or European tariff rates. That is obviously not correct. Some believe that Japan has more import quotas and other restrictive practices than other countries. They are most outdated now. Some ascribe the present difficulties faced by some of the American industries to the "flood" of Japanese goods. In many cases, imports from Japan are not the cause but the result of changes in American economic life. I must also refer to the contributions we are making to U.S. customers in supplying good products at better prices.

At National Press Club, Washington,
Aug. 11/The Washington Post,
8-13:(A)22.

C. H. von Platen
Swedish envoy to Organization for
European Cooperation and
Development

American industrialists have been, and are, able to plan and act with courage and freedom. They have grown accustomed to trying new methods, new approaches to experimenting, to change and improvement . . . People are not afraid to change profession or line of business. Competition has been keen and on a continental scale. The system of rewards is based on performance and not on seniority. One can still make fortunes, even rapidly. Taxes are high, but not altogether crippling, or . . . confiscatory.

The New York Times, 3-19:37.

Elkins Wetherill
President,
Philadelphia-Baltimore-Washington
Stock Exchange

When (Robert W. Haack, president of the New York Stock Exchange) said in a speech recently that the Big Board doesn't have the only game in town any more, he was right. He thinks this is bad, but I say no. The ultimate function of our business is to deliver the best execution of customers' orders, and competition is the best way to do that. With more markets, you're more sure of getting the best price.

Interview, Los Angeles, Jan. 12/
Los Angeles Times, 1-13:(3)13.

Edward B. Wilson II
Executive vice president,
J. Walter Thompson Company,
advertising

(Advertising) cannot make people buy against their wills. It cannot induce repeated purchases of inferior products. It cannot prolong the life of a product that has outlived its usefulness or which has been outmoded . . . The power of advertising is limited. And the thousands of net product failures are testimony to the fact that, if something does not fill a need, fulfill an aspiration or provide some comfort or solace, real or emotional, it cannot succeed no matter how many dollars are invested in advertising.

Before National Office Products
Association/San Francisco Examiner,
10-27:63.

Crime • Law Enforcement

Spiro T. Agnew
Vice President of the United States

I think it is something more than age that is the real issue in the effort to drive (FBI Director) J. Edgar Hoover out of office. A more likely explanation is the fact that he is anathema to the New Left and extremists of every stripe; and he doesn't mince words in calling attention to them as dangerous to the country. Personally, I have complete confidence in this dedicated, steel-willed public servant with the 20-20 vision into our national security and crime-control problems and the institution that he has made the beacon of law enforcement in America. I am sure they will again triumph over their critics; and the American people will be the winners.

*Before Southern Gas Association,
New Orleans, April 26/The New
York Times, 4-27:17.*

If you took literally some of the more dramatic statements in the news accounts about the FBI controversy, you could only conclude that there is an agent behind every tree and monument in Washington, in the closet of every Congressman's office, in automobiles trailing him from work to home to parties, and in listening posts that monitor his wiretapped conversations . . . Since the FBI has a total of only 8,365 agents throughout the entire nation—and the great majority of those operate outside Washington—the agency would be hard-pressed, indeed, to keep the members of Congress under surveillance.

*Before Southern Gas Association,
New Orleans, April 26/Los Angeles
Times, 4-27:(1)5.*

(Regarding Washington antiwar demonstrations): We have been instructed that when 10,000 persons rage through the streets and neighborhoods of our nation's capital, defacing buildings with their favorite obscenity or Maoist slogan of the moment, disabling automobiles, burning public park benches, strewing garbage and otherwise depriving other citizens of their right of unhindered movement in a free community, the perpetrators of such actions are engaging in "nonviolent dissent." From the vantage point of Jackson (Miss.), these people may look like hoodlums and lawbreakers, to be sure. But given the editorial insight of *The (New York) Times*, *The (Washington) Post* and some national magazines, they undergo a metamorphosis—or should I say "mediamorphosis." And they emerge simply as "kids" who are trying to tell us something if we would only listen.

*At Republican fund-raising dinner,
Jackson, Miss., May 18/The New
York Times, 5-19:30.*

(Regarding the prison revolt at Attica, N.Y.): At some point . . . the full force of the major national news media will be brought to bear as columnists, commentators and the producers of television documentaries descend upon the scene. They will plumb the purported "root causes" of the incident, focus on members of the militant minority and emerge with a verdict that the "tragedy" which occurred could have been avoided had only the legally-constituted authorities not "over-reacted" but instead had shown more sensitivity to the need for change in these difficult times. Along with millions of other Americans, I reject the inversion of values which has enabled the enemies of our society to thus advance their pernicious objectives. I reject the undermining of public confidence in our free institutions. I reject the sowing of seeds of hatred among our people, and I reject the projection of criminals as heroes and heroes as criminals through the constant drumming of leftist propaganda.

*At International Chiefs of Police
conference, Anaheim, Calif., Sept. 27/
Los Angeles Times, 9-28:(1)3.*

When those who protect us (the police) are attacked, we are all attacked. When those who safeguard our institutions are endangered, our institutions are endangered. When those few assigned to uphold our laws give their lives in the conduct of their duty, then we—the many who survive—have a renewed responsibility to see to it that their sacrifice was not in vain, that the government of law for which they died is upheld against those who would destroy it.

At International Chiefs of Police conference, Anaheim, Calif., Sept. 27/San Francisco Examiner, 9-28:4.

Hale Boggs
United States Representative, D–La.

The greatest thing we have in this nation is the Bill of Rights. We are a great country because we are a free country under the Bill of Rights. The way (Director J. Edgar) Hoover is running the FBI today, it is no longer a free country. I was astonished to read in the paper this morning where (Attorney General John) Mitchell says that he is a law-and-order man; therefore, that Mr. Hoover, being a law-and-order man, will stay on. If law and order means the suppression of the Bill of Rights, infiltration of college campuses, the tapping of the telephones of members of Congress of the United States, then I say, "God help us."

Before the House, Washington, April 5/Los Angeles Times, 4-6:(1)18.

(Regarding FBI and government surveillance of individuals): Today, I see what, until now, I did not permit myself to see. Our apathy in this Congress, our silence in the House, our very fear of speaking out in other forums has watered the roots and hastened the growth of a vine of tyranny which is ensnaring that Constitution and Bill of Rights which we are each sworn to defend and uphold . . . What has occurred could not have occurred without our consent and complicity here on Capitol Hill . . . We have established the rule of the dossier.

We have conferred respectability upon the informer. We have sanctioned the use of bribes and payments to citizen to spy on citizen . . . No member of this House knows—or can know with any certainty—what the bureaus and agencies involved with the liberties of the American people may be doing . . . Today, as we in the Congress undertake to recover and restore the people's liberty, we find that it is ourselves who are called to account, ourselves who are under surveillance, ourselves who are prisoners of the power which our silence permitted to come into being.

Before the House, Washington, April 22/The Washington Post, 4-28:(A)22.

McGeorge Bundy
President, Ford Foundation

The weaknesses in American police forces are apparent to any observer. But an institution so central to our society as the police should neither be ignored nor treated with contempt.

March 6/The Washington Post, 3-7:(A)2.

Warren E. Burger
Chief Justice of the United States

Nothing that I can see would suggest to me that we are in danger of oppression at the hands of law-enforcement agencies. In fact, I suspect the general opinion of the American people, including the overwhelming majority of lawyers and judges, would be that it is quite the reverse of that situation—that the law-enforcement agencies simply are not able to cope with the problems of law enforcement.

Interview, June/The New York Times, 7-4:(1)24.

Law enforcement agencies have been the step-children of all governments. They can be fairly described as poorly trained, poorly paid and poorly regarded by society.

Quote, 10-24:385.

The figures on (prisoner) illiteracy alone are enough to make one wish that every sentence imposed could include a provision that would grant release when the prisoner has learned to read and write, to do simple arithmetic, and

(WARREN E. BURGER)

then to develop some basic skill that is salable in the marketplace of the outside world to which he must someday return and in which he must compete. We should develop sentencing techniques to impose a sentence so that an inmate can literally "learn his way" out of prison as we now try to let him earn his way out with "good behavior."

At National Conference on Corrections, Williamsburg, Va., Dec. 7/ Los Angeles Times, 12-8:(1)6.

William Cahn
District Attorney, Nassau County, N.Y.

Many types of criminal cases can rarely be proved except by wiretap evidence. Among these are organized gambling offenses, governmental corruption, labor racketeering and, indeed, all the types of wrongdoing which may be described under the heading of organized crime . . . Experience shows that organized gangsterism cannot be stopped without wiretapping, and that bigtime hoodlums must continue to do business on the telephone even in states permitting official wiretapping, since it is an indispensable aid to wide-ranging illegality.

Before joint session of California State Senate Judiciary Committee and Assembly Committee on Criminal Justice, Sacramento, March 10/ Los Angeles Herald-Examiner, 3-10:(A)4.

Ramsey Clark
Former Attorney General of the United States

The elements of criminal justice have been tragically neglected . . . We have not devoted the necessary talents, initiatives or resources for decades to do a professional job. As a result, the prevention and control of crime and the quality of criminal justice all suffer. I do not believe one serious crime in 50 results in a conviction. If that's true, then the connection between the occurrence of crime and the potential for its correction through the criminal justice processes is extremely limited. Once convicted, we complete the failure, because

corrections do not rehabilitate . . . We manufacture crime at the end.

Interview/ Los Angeles Herald-Examiner, 4-2(A)8.

(Regarding mass arrests at antiwar demonstrations): It is intolerable, in my judgement, in a free society for the police to ever act in excess of the law; and you cannot arrest people except where you have evidence that they have violated the law. You've got to charge them formally; you've got to be prepared to prosecute them. And if this government and this nation permit police to merely pick people up and incarcerate them—detain them because we're frightened—we've lost our freedom, and it's going to be a more violent time ahead—no alternative.

TV-radio interview/"Face the Nation," Columbia Broadcasting System, 5-23.

I don't think penal "reform" is adequate. I think what we're talking about is building a new system. We have to care about criminals as human beings and recognize their and our common humanity.

At conference on prisoners' rights, Chicago, Nov. 5/The New York Times, 11-8:24.

Alvin W. Cohn
Director of correctional programs, Center for Administration of Justice, American University

I don't know of anyone in the field who is willing to state that the prison system materially reduces crime. In fact, it produces embittered people who, for the most part, leave to be bigger and better criminals.

The Washington Post, 3-29:(A)15.

Ronald V. Dellums
United States Representative, D–Calif.

(Regarding antiwar demonstrations in Washington): I see the police venting their frustrations on a small bunch of dogmatic young people who see disruption as the only means of halting our tragic adventurism in Southeast Asia. I disagree with the demonstrators over tactics; but I am more repelled by the force thrown against them by the police and the military.

San Francisco Examiner, 5-4:4.

Bob Dole
United States Senator, R–Kan.

No wonder the extremists had a heyday under the Democrats when they knew that the chief law-enforcement official of the Federal Government was a left-leaning marshmallow like (former Attorney General) Ramsey Clark.

At Republican fund-raising dinner,
Cumberland, Md., March 10/
San Francisco Examiner, 3-11:2.

(Regarding criticism of the FBI by Senator Edmund Muskie and others): What we have here, whether or not those who are leading the attack will admit it, is a concerted and deliberate effort to turn the FBI in the eyes of the American people into an American version of the Gestapo. It has been well said in recent days that the McCarthyism of the Fifties pales by comparison with the Muskieism of the Seventies.

At Republican Governors Conference,
Williamsburg, Va., April 18/
The Washington Post, 4-19:(A)4.

Clinton T. Duffy
Former warden, San Quentin
(Calif.) State Prison

One of the main stumbling blocks in the effort of prisons to remotivate (their) inmates is lack of adequate program financing and adequately-paid personnel. Every prison administrator I've known—and that covers hundreds—wished to have a better-developed program in their institutions ... but most prison budgets are considered toward the bottom rung on the ladder. Idleness and assignment gimcracks that are not meaningful are a cause of much trouble inside the walls. Active minds that are being developed toward a change in their personal lives and future rarely cause trouble ... of those who do return to society, a good many today are as good as you and me and are good

citizens because they had the proper approach to their needs.

San Francisco/Los Angeles Times, 12-9:(7)8.

Sam J. Ervin, Jr.
United States Senator, D–N.C.

I believe the Attorney General is of sufficient intelligence to know that trying to fight crime by preventive detention is about as practical as trying to empty the Atlantic Ocean with a quart cup.

San Francisco Examiner, 6-2:32.

I hate the thoughts of the Black Panthers, Students for a Democratic Society, Fascists and others who adopt violence as a creed. But these people have the same rights to freedom of speech as I do. I will fight for their rights to think the thoughts and speak the words that I hate.

Washington, Aug. 3/
The Washington Post, 8-4:(A)10.

Abe Fortas
Former Associate Justice,
Supreme Court of the United States

I have a fear that the marvelous quality of American life—free, rambunctious, ebullient, sometimes irresponsible—may be disappearing. In Joe McCarthy's day, there was a quiet veto on meaningful conversation. Today, we are concerned with not just the suppression of protest, but fear—the fear that we might be bugged or under surveillance. No amount of reassurance that these things are not being misused will counteract that fear.

Interview/Time, 6-21:42.

It's not worth much of a damn to have First Amendment rights if you're subjected to arbitrary arrest. People don't realize that the basic rules of criminal procedure are laid down to protect the entire population; instead, they regard these rules as a threat to themselves. It's reflected in the turmoil in this country. And it was dramatically illustrated by the recent (anti-

(ABE FORTAS)

war) demonstrations in Washington. The police must operate within certain rules.

Interview/Time, 6-21:42.

Blaming the courts for crime is like blaming a meat chopper for the quality of the hamburger.

San Francisco Examiner, 11-10:38.

Charles R. Gain
Chief of Police of Oakland, Calif.

Police cannot do the job alone. The essential ingredient in reducing crime is to bring a sense of community. What has to happen in America is for the citizens to become aware of how crime affects them and to cooperate with the police. And the long-range solution is to do something about family disorganization and psychological factors and social discrimination and poverty.

U.S. News & World Report, 1-18:16.

If the police do not operate within the rule of the law, and instead are allowed to exercise their own judgment on what's right or wrong without regard to the law, that is the best definition of a police state there is.

Interview/
San Francisco Examiner & Chronicle,
11-28:(A)13.

Kenneth A. Gibson
Mayor of Newark, N.J.

I assume the (government) agencies that watch activists have been watching me for a number of years, because I was an activist. Once they start watching you, they don't stop watching just because you become Mayor. I made a joke of it. I start out my speeches by saying "friends, spies and bugs . . . "

Interview, Newark, July 1/
The Dallas Times Herald, 7-1:(A)5.

Barry Goldwater, Jr.
United States Representative, R–Calif.

I would suggest that any member (of Congress) who feels the (House Internal Security)

Committee's existence is unwarranted take a careful look around him today. Let him look at the offices of those Senators who were invaded by the so-called "peaceful protestors," individuals who shoved around secretaries and threw red paint over office walls and furniture. I would suggest that members take a look at the bomb damage to our Capitol, to hundreds of public facilities around the country, to the headquarters of major corporations and to buildings on campuses of our great universities.

Human Events, 5-8:5.

David Hall
Governor of Oklahoma

The national Administration's rhetoric on crime is hard. The funding is soft.

At Midwestern Governors Conference,
South Sioux City, Neb., July 21/
The Washington Post, 7-22:(A)2.

Philip A. Hart
United States Senator, D–Mich.

Possessing a handgun in the house doesn't increase your security; it diminishes it. We've got an incredible overkill in our bedrooms and living rooms in our country.

News conference, Washington, Oct. 8/
The New York Times, 10-9:9.

James R. Hoffa
Former president, International
Brotherhood of Teamsters

Anyone who tells you prison's not tough just isn't telling the truth. I have spent many days in loneliness.

News conference upon his release
from prison, Lewisburg, Pa.,
Dec. 23/The New York Times, 12-24:12.

Lawrence J. Hogan
United States Representative, R–Md.

(Criticizing Representative Hale Boggs' denunciation of FBI surveillance practices): I am shocked, disgusted and nauseated at the stench of red herring in this chamber.

Before the House, Washington,
April 22/The Washington Post,
4-23:(A)1.

Richard Hongisto
Sheriff-elect of San Francisco County

(During the election campaign) I considered my opponents domestic hawks who try to solve social problems here in the United States in much the same way as we've tried to solve problems in Vietnam—by the use of more guns, more money, more men and more repressive force. It is not working in Vietnam; we have lost more face and political prestige than at any other time in our history. Internally, the domestic hawks are trying to do the same thing with criminal justice. Policemen are losing more face, more prestige, becoming more hated and they're being called pigs. They are using more repressive force than at any other time. More money is being spent. Helicopters are over our heads, and in some cities the police have tanks. The results are the same as in Vietnam—increased taxes, economic chaos in the country and an escalating crime rate that is not being dealt with.

Interview, San Francisco, Nov. 3/
Los Angeles Times, 11-4:(1)3.

J. Edgar Hoover
Director, Federal Bureau of
Investigation

We have exacting standards in the FBI, and we apologize to no one for them. We have no intention of arbitrarily compromising these standards to accommodate kooks, misfits, drunks and slobs . . .

Before Washington chapter,
Society of Former Special Agents of the FBI,
Oct. 22/The Dallas Times Herald, 11-21:(A)34.

Too long we have concerned ourselves with the plight of the criminal. We have coddled him, we have shown him compassion, mercy and leniency; and all too often, he has shown us contempt and non-repentance. It is time we stopped coddling the hoodlums and the hippies who are causing so much serious trouble these days. Let us treat them like the vicious enemies of society they really are, regardless of their age.

Los Angeles Herald-Examiner,
11-25:(B)6.

I have never considered stepping down from my position in the FBI as long as I can be of service to my country and have the health, vigor and enthusiasm to perform my responsibilities in the manner my superiors and the public have a right to expect.

Interview, Washington/
San Francisco Examiner, 12-27:9.

Richard H. Ichord
United States Representative, D–Mo.

There must be a universal awareness throughout our nation of the dangers that threaten us. We cannot operate in a vacuum of indifference; because if we do, we create the mistaken impression that the noisy and rowdy ones in the street speak for the majority of Americans. There are more than 200 million people in our great country, but all too often a small minority, by banding together, can create the impression they speak for the majority simply because they yell louder and are more boisterous . . . Public opinion must be taken into account; but disruptive and obstructive demonstrations designed to turn Washington upside down do not fall in the category of responsible and patriotic expressions of public opinion.

The Austin (Tex.) Statesman,
4-29:(A)10.

Henry M. Jackson
United States Senator, D–Wash.

The very purpose of preventive detention is to permit the jailing of citizens not for crimes they have committed, but for crimes—in the opinion of the authorities—they might commit. Such a power is the first power of tyranny . . . the power to detain citizens for crimes which they might commit is not far-removed from the power to detain citizens for words they might speak or thoughts they might think.

Before Wayne State University
Law School alumni, Detroit, April 17/
San Francisco Examiner & Chronicle,
4-18:(A)14.

(Regarding the use of force by dissident demonstrators): By the use of force, political

(HENRY M. JACKSON)

parties are impeded in their orderly functioning; courts have been disrupted; centers of learning have been torn asunder; public dialogue has been impaired and public agencies have been obstructed. When universities are bombed, when businesses are burned, when public streets are blocked, when speakers are driven from platforms, when tongues are silenced and minds intimidated and free discussion of public issues inhibited, then *that* is repression . . .

Interview, Dallas/
The Dallas Times Herald, 5-16:(A)38.

Americans feel that the crime situation in this country is out of hand. And so do I. It is a scandal. We are the only Western industrial democracy where people are afraid to go out on the streets at night. Talk about civil rights! What about the civil rights and civil liberties of Americans—of all races—who don't feel safe in their own neighborhoods? Yet many politicians wince at the public's demand for law and order. They say law and order is a code word for racism or for repression. I say that until we are prepared to acknowledge that law and order is a real problem, we won't solve it.

News conference, Washington, Nov. 19/
Human Events, 12-4:3.

Leon Jaworski
President-elect,
American Bar Association

(Lack of respect for the law is) spreading like a cancerous growth. If the chaos extends itself unchecked, we shall surely fall victim to the authoritarian rule which the radicals of the left pretend to fear.

Before Law Student Division,
American Bar Association, New York, July 4/
Los Angeles Herald-Examiner, 7-5:(A)7.

Herman Kahn
Director, Hudson Institute

The silliness of American society has become extremely widespread. You can see it in the way the law-and-order issue has been distorted. Law-and-order is supposed to be anti-Negro;

but it was never used in that sense by reasonable people. We have in America a great many cities where it is unsafe to go out at night or even during the hours of daylight. The call for law and order was raised because people wanted to make the cities safe; that's all. There was no backlash against the Negro; in fact, if you look at it closely, the slogan expressed the grave dissatisfaction of the white lower-middle class American with the white upper-middle class American, the white educated class, if you like. Everyone in America had a very clear understanding of this except the intellectual press and the representatives of the foreign press in the U.S. Someone aptly remarked in one of our papers, "Is it true that the U.S. has raised the silliest educated class in history? Not quite, but almost."

Interview, Davos, Switzerland/
The New York Times Magazine, 6-20:24.

Richard G. Kleindienst
Deputy Attorney General of the United States

(Regarding the Nixon Administration's fight against crime): Given a few years, when the full impact of these revisions and these new programs and planning and all this money can be felt all across the land, there's going to be a strong resultant effect on the statistics of crime. These civil libertarian bastards complain about what we are doing, but the fact remains that we are clearing up many of these problems. In all of these (crime) areas, you have to do it with vigor and determination and honest people who don't care for the political consequences but go right ahead and fight crime. You can't do it with weak, opportunistic, chicken-hearted bastards.

Interview/Look, 10-19:50.

Jerris Leonard
Administrator, Law Enforcement Assistance
Administration of the United States

Crime has been slowed. And because of that, there has been a speedup in another activity: criticism of the nationwide crime control program. I suggest that the crime criticism index parallels the crime index—the first goes up as the other goes down.

At conference of law-enforcement officials,
Washington, Sept. 9/
The Washington Post, 9-10:(A)6.

John V. Lindsay
Mayor of New York

We can no more excuse the tactics of terror than we can excuse the appeals to repression. A protester who murders a man in cold blood is a murderer—not a political hero. A worker who bludgeons a war dissident is a thug—not a patriot. And a speaker who urges listeners to destruction is no better—whether he wears a hooded robe, a blue collar or tie-dyed jeans and beads.

At "Peace and New Priorities"
rally, Pittsburgh, Sept. 9/
The New York Times, 9-10:43.

Do we care about crime? Of course it is an issue. Its chief victims are not the comfortable and secure. Its victims are themselves among the poor, old and working people of all creeds and colors. It is not an issue to be waved away—or to be met with the illusion that we can have safe streets and secure shops by ripping up the Bill of Rights . . . Let us insist on two essential truths: first, that a court and prison system which herds men like cattle from the streets to the precincts to prisons to the streets without changing these men is a conduit of crime; that tough talk and timid action accomplishes nothing. And second, let us once and for all demand a law to stop the cancerous spread of handguns into the streets of America. To say we care about crime while fighting the efforts to keep these guns out of the hands of criminals and lunatics is sheer nonsense . . .

Before New York Democratic State
Committee Advisory Council, Sept. 17/
The Washington Post, 9-22:(A)22.

Carl M. Loeb, Jr.
President, National Council
on Crime and Delinquency

Organized crime is by far the greatest danger facing America today. You can forget about the Communists; they don't have the dough.

The New York Times, 2-22:37.

Mike Mansfield
United States Senator, D—Mont.

The point has been reached where we must give consideration to the victim of crime—to the one who suffers because of crime. For him, society has failed miserably . . . Society has an obligation. When the protection of society is not sufficient to prevent a person from being victimized, society then has the obligation to compensate the victim for that failure of protection.

Before the Senate, Washington/
U.S. News & World Report, 4-5:40.

Charles McC. Mathias, Jr.
United States Senator, R—Md.

We are now witnessing a tremendous surge in the development and use of computerized data banks by law-enforcement agencies throughout the nation. Although no single, nationwide Federal-state-local system for collecting and transmitting personal histories has yet been established, all signs show that law-enforcement agencies are hurtling in this direction, fueled largely by Federal funds and unrestrained by any consistent controls. Within the Department of Justice there are several large, active computerized data banks: the FBI's National Crime Information Center on wanted persons; the BNDD files on narcotics users; the FBI's Known Professional Check Passers File; the Organized Crime Intelligence System; a file on offenders based on Federal penitentiary records; and the records of the Immigration and Naturalization Service . . . While each of these data banks is currently separately maintained, the contents of each—with the exception of some intelligence data—is made available when needed not just within the Justice Department, but also to other Federal agencies with even marginal law-enforcement mandates, to state and local agencies, and in some cases to private establishments such as national banks. The Federal stamp, of course, gives all such data the force and validity of gospel. Federal law, in

(CHARLES McC. MATHIAS, JR.)

fact, encourages the collection and exchange of criminal records under the aegis of law enforcement.

Before Senate Judiciary Subcommittee on Constitutional Rights, Washington, March 9/The Washington Post, 3-12:(A)22.

George S. McGovern
United States Senator, D–S.D.

The obvious fact is that (FBI Director J. Edgar) Hoover is retained in office not out of a sense of confidence, but out of fear—out of political fear that the Administration cannot afford to remove this "sacred cow" from the public scene.

At Lewis-St. Francis College, Lockport, Ill., April 19/Daily World, 4-27:7.

There is no doubt in my mind that virtually every political figure, every student activist, every leader for peace and social justice is under the surveillance of the FBI.

Human Events, 5-29:8.

Abner J. Mikva
United States Representative, D–Ill.

(Regarding military surveillance of civilians): Those military officials who would arrogate to themselves the duty to watch peaceful civilians' political activities are the true subversives in our society. If allowed to continue, they will end up creating a climate of fear and suspicion in this country the likes of which would make Joseph McCarthy look like a civil libertarian.

Before Senate Constitutional Rights Subcommittee, Washington, Feb. 24/ The Dallas Times Herald, 2-24:(A)7.

John N. Mitchell
Attorney General of the United States

By reforming criminal justice in America and attacking the environmental roots of crime, we may dare to look forward to an enlightened day when we will need few, rather than more, prisons, police stations and even courthouses.

San Francisco Examiner & Chronicle (This World), 2-28:2.

Our (the Justice Department's) biggest problem is to bring the American system of criminal justice into the twentieth century. At all levels, that system is outmoded and ineffective. I'm talking about every phase of criminal justice: law-enforcement agencies, the courts and our outmoded correctional institutions and techniques. We need new ideas and new approaches all along the line; and our job in the Department of Justice is to provide leadership to our friends in the states and municipalities who deal with these matters . . . it is only through the improvement of our total criminal-justice system that we will have a permanent reduction in crime.

Interview, Washington/ U.S. News & World Report, 3-22:42.

The FBI has not tapped the telephones of any member of the House or Senate—now or in the past.

Before Kentucky Bar Association, Cincinnati, April 23/ The Dallas Times Herald, 4-24:(A)5.

Does a national-security wiretap with court order conflict with the individual's right of privacy, and must it give way before the right? Privacy is a precious right; but it is never absolute to the exclusion of other rights. The Fourth Amendment, which protects privacy, does not prohibit all searches and seizures. It prohibits only unreasonable searches and seizures . . . on the other hand, what about the right . . . of the public to protect itself and to preserve the government it has created? This right is implicit in the Constitution's very existence, and in the political theory on which it is based.

Before Kentucky Bar Association, Cincinnati, April 23/ The Washington Post, 4-24:(A)12.

There is no dividing line between hostile foreign forces seeking to undermine our internal security and hostile domestic groups seeking the overthrow of our government by any means necessary. I don't see how we can separate the two; but if it were possible, I would say that history has shown greater danger from the domestic variety.

*Before Virginia State Bar Association,
Roanoke, June 11/The Washington Post,
6-12:(A)4.*

(Regarding law enforcement's successes a-
gainst organized crime): In New York City,
where there are five organized crime "families,"
four of the five bosses or acting bosses have
either been indicted or convicted. In Chicago,
nine out of the 13 top gangland leaders have
been brought under the processes of justice,
and for months the top spot has gone begging.
In New England, the top leadership is practically decimated. Of the nine leaders who have
been identified, two are on death row and
three—including the boss—are in prison.

*Before Associated Press Managing
Editors Association, Philadelphia,
Oct. 20/The New York Times, 10-21:22.*

It does little good to train and equip our
police forces if our prisons are turning out
criminals faster than they can be rounded up.
Certainly we need firm law enforcement; but
there's more to reducing crime than making
arrests. Until we bring our corrections systems
into the 20th century, all our efforts will be
frustrated.

*At Police Appreciation Day luncheon,
Charlotte, N.C., Nov. 19/
Los Angeles Herald-Examiner, 11-19:(A)5.*

Walter F. Mondale
United States Senator, D—Mo.

We always say, "Crime doesn't pay." But, in
fact, most crimes do.

The Christian Science Monitor, 2-3:7.

Norval Morris
*Director, Center for Studies in Criminal Justice,
University of Chicago*

I regard the political aspect of these uprisings
(prison riots) mainly as a rationalization. But
because they are not real in the beginning
doesn't mean that they will not become real in
the minds of prisoners. What happens is that
the inmate invests ordinary criminal activity
with the idea that he is a part of political

change. That way you end up with the absurdity that killing a policeman or robbing a store is
somehow a political act. The common criminals
have never been on the cutting edge of any
revolutionary movement; nor are they now.
They are being used, and misused, by some
elements of the New Left. But it is important
to understand how blacks come to see all of
this. They see that prisons are disproportion-
ately black and run by whites. They come to
view the American prison system as meaning
simply blacks locked up by whites. This is the
kind of thing that feeds this rhetoric of
revolution, and ultimately the violence. What
we have now in our prisons is the fusing of the
ideology of the political prisoner with the
technology of the common criminal. It is an
explosive mixture.

Interview/Life, 9-24:36.

Daniel P. Moynihan
*Former Counsellor to the
President of the United States*

I think the sooner (FBI Director J. Edgar)
Hoover retires, the better the FBI will be. It has
become a cankered bureaucracy preserving the
unnecessary vanities of a man who has served
too long in office.

*Television broadcast, Dec. 26/
San Francisco Examiner, 12-27:9.*

Patrick V. Murphy
Police Commissioner of New York City

. . . I think the job of the patrolman is just
as important and complex and difficult as the
job of being an FBI agent. Yet, the FBI agent
gets $20,000 a year and the patrolman less than
$11,000. I agree with former Attorney General
Ramsey Clark that patrolmen should get at
least $15,000 a year, that we should be
attracting the kind of men who can make
$15,000 a year.

*Before Council of New York Law
Associates, New York, Jan. 22/
The New York Times, 1-23:16.*

It is unfortunate that it takes a tragedy of
such major proportions as the killing of policemen to force attention on the absurdity of

(PATRICK V. MURPHY)

allowing large numbers of private citizens to possess firearms. Any policeman at any time has become the target for a killer, and this is plainly intolerable. No officer can be expected to perform his duty at the high level which the public properly expects if he must be continuously apprehensive that even his most routine assignment will bring him face to face with a senseless killer.

Before International Association of Police Chiefs, Anaheim, Calif./ The New York Times, 10-3:(1)72.

(Addressing his men regarding current hearings on police corruption on the force): There is no reason to be ashamed because one or another traitor to the uniform that you wear so proudly seeks to justify his own dishonesty by pretending that none of you is honest. That is not true. There are bad policemen. I ask you to help me rid this department of them. The dishonest cop is not our brother.

New York, Oct. 21/ The New York Times, 10-22:44.

A police administrator should never say this, I suppose, but it may be that the police get too large a share of the criminal justice dollar. Correction and rehabilitation are the most neglected parts of the system, and this is doubtless why there are so many habitual offenders.

The New York Times Magazine, 12-19:47.

There is more crime today than ever before. But too many criminals are not going to jail; and their victims scream that the criminal-justice system has broken down, and they are right. The victims scream that the police are at fault, but this is not right and it is not fair. We, the police, are far from perfect, but we have shouldered the entire blame long enough. We, the police, are more efficient today than ever. We pour arrested criminals into the wide end of the criminal-justice funnel, and they choke it up until they spill over the top—and when I say spill over, they spill over into the street and commit more crime. So we arrest them again,

pour them into the funnel as far as the court system again, and they spill out again. And the cycle repeats itself day after day. (The idea that imprisonment is a deterrent to crime) has become a farce. Professional stickup men, narcotics pushers, gamblers, laugh at it. Not only are we not jailing them, but each arrest that they walk away from leads to an increased disrespect of the law, not only by the persons arrested, but also by young criminals, amateur criminals, would-be criminals who would emulate them.

Before Association of the Bar of the City of New York, Dec. 20/ The New York Times, 12-21:32.

Edmund S. Muskie
United States Senator, D—Maine

Surveillance is more than excessive zeal by the FBI. It is a threat to our freedom. Surveillance leads to fear. Secret surveillance which produces secret files to be used by unknown persons—these are the ingredients for fear. Every dictator knows that elementary rule.

Before the Senate, Washington, April 14/ Los Angeles Herald-Examiner, 4-14:(A)3.

If there was widespread surveillance of Earth Day last year, is there any political activity in the country which the FBI doesn't consider a legitimate subject for watching? If antipollution rallies are a subject of intelligence concern, is anything immune? Is there any citizen involved in politics who is not a potential subject for an FBI dossier?

Before the Senate, Washington, April 14/ Los Angeles Herald-Examiner, 4-14:(A)3.

In recent years, men who should surely know better have turned to repression as an answer to crime. The prediction is that their strategy will expand their political support; and it very well might. The prediction is that anyone who opposes them will endanger his own support; and that, too, may be true. But the more important truth is that cold words cannot build law and order.

At Washington and Jefferson College commencement, May 29/ The Washington Post, 5-30:(A)2.

Louis Nelson
Warden, San Quentin (Calif.)
State Prison

(Concerning current interest in prison reforms): The once sordid and repellent world of the con and ex-con has suddenly become as chic and piquant as the opera season at Monte Carlo . . . Prison people are a little tired of having amateurs—and that includes many so-called experts—tell them how to run their institutions from the depths of what is often profound naivete and boundless inexperience. Even some of the top-level authorities—within quotation marks—seem to have moved into some penal Disneyland.

Interview, Dec. 18/
San Francisco Examiner & Chronicle,
12-19:(A)24.

Richard M. Nixon
President of the United States

We must make it possible for each community to train its police to carry out their duties, using the most modern methods of detection and crime prevention. We must make it possible for the convicted criminal to receive constructive training while in confinement, instead of what he receives now: an advanced course in crime. The time has come to repudiate, once and for all, the idea that prisons are warehouses for human rubbish. Our correctional systems must be changed to make them places that will correct and educate.

At National Conference on the Judiciary,
Williamsburg, Va., March 11/
The New York Times, 1-12:18.

We live in a time when headlines are being made by those few who want to tear down our institutions, by those who say they defy the law. But we also live in a time when history is being made by those who are willing to reform and rebuild our institutions—and that can only be accomplished by those who respect the law.

San Francisco Examiner & Chronicle,
4-11:(B)2.

Today, right today, at this moment, there are one half as many (wire) taps as there were in 1961, '62 and '63, and 10 times as many news stories about them. There wasn't a police state in 1961, '62 and '63, in my opinion, because even then there were less than 100 taps; and there are less than 50 today; and there is none now, at the present time. All of this hysteria— and it is hysteria; and much of it, of course, is political demagoguery to the effect that the FBI is tapping my telephone and the rest— simply doesn't serve the public purpose.

News conference, San Clemente, Calif. May 1/
The Dallas Times Herald, 5-2:(A)1.

The right to demonstrate for peace abroad does not carry with it the right to break the peace at home.

Los Angeles Herald-Examiner, 5-5:(A)12.

(Regarding antiwar demonstrations in Washington): The right to demonstrate is recognized and protected by the Washington Police. Thousands of demonstrators have come down here peacefully and have not been, of course, bothered. They've been protected in that right. But when people come in and slice tires, when they block traffic, when they make a trash-bin out of Georgetown and other areas of the city, and when they terrorize innocent bystanders, they are not demonstrators, they are vandals and hoodlums and lawbreakers, and they should be treated as lawbreakers . . . and that kind of activity, which is not demonstration but vandalism, lawbreaking, is not going to be tolerated in this capital.

News conference, Washington, June 1/
The New York Times, 6-2:24.

I have stated categorically, and I state it again here today, that, in this Administration, the era of permissiveness in law enforcement has come to an end. We are going to continue to support strong laws dealing with criminal elements, to support law-enforcement officials up and down this land, and continue to have a program that will reduce the rising crime and eventually reverse it.

Before newspaper, TV and radio executives,
Kansas City/The National Observer, 7-12:2.

Richard B. Ogilvie
Governor of Illinois

The permanent goal of our correctional system is to secure the safety and well-being of the overwhelming majority of law-abiding citizens who will never see the inside of a prison. But I submit we do not serve that end by operating inhuman institutions which lock men up in despair and indignity for an appointed period of time and then return them to the streets more incorrigible than ever with little preparation for the responsibilities of citizenship.

San Francisco Examiner & Chronicle,
11-28:(B)2.

Carl Parsell
President, International Conference
of Police Associations

If police killings are to end, it looks like the only people who are interested in stopping the slaughter are the police officers themselves. Shotguns must be in every patrol car and be ready to use every minute of every day. If these radical extremists want war, then the police of our country stand ready. Police killers will be eliminated one way or another.

Before Police Officers Association
of Michigan, Lansing, May 25/
Los Angeles Herald-Examiner, 5-26:(A)13.

William H. Rehnquist
Assistant Attorney General,
Office of Legal Council,
Department of Justice of the United States

It is of little consolation to a woman who is mugged on the street of a large city to be told that the person who mugged her grew up in an urban ghetto . . . We must not only do our best to reduce the disposition to commit criminal acts in future generations, but we must also strive to curtail—indeed, if you will, "repress"—criminal acts committed today.

Before Senate subcommittee, Washington,
March/Newsweek, 11-1:19.

Is the invasion of privacy entailed by wiretapping too high a price to pay for a successful method of attacking this (organized) and similar types of crime? I think not, given the safeguards which attend its use in the United States. The Attorney General must report to Congress the total number of Federal applications for wiretapping made each year; and the report he furnished indicated that last year the Federal government sought 183 wiretap warrants. This is not a "pervasive" use of wiretapping, using that adjective in its narrowest possible sense. It is, instead, a restrained and careful use of that technique which has led to a series of genuinely significant arrests and convictions in the field of organized crime in the past three years.

Before American Bar Association, London,
July 15/U.S. News & World Report, 11-8:42.

Elliot L. Richardson
Secretary of Health, Education and Welfare
of the United States

As with most human rights, privacy is not an absolute right. A balance must be struck between society's need for information and the individual's right of privacy.

Before Senate Constitutional Rights
Subcommittee, Washington, March 15/
Los Angeles Times, 3-16:(1)4.

Frank Rizzo
Mayor-elect and former Police Commissioner
of Philadelphia

I've patrolled this town for 28 years. I talked with the merchants and senior citizens, the housewives and school kids. Jewish, Christian, it doesn't make any difference. They are petrified by crime and disgusted by the permissiveness and coddling that encourage it left and right.

Human Events, 11-13:5.

Nelson A. Rockefeller
Governor of New York

(The failures of the criminal justice system) stem as much from the failure of our society and government, in terms of the individual, as from the actions of those small groups which would exploit legitimate grievances not because they want to correct them but because they try to use them for the overthrow of our society. We can no longer delay in making radical reforms in our whole system of criminal justice—from the problem of protecting the rights and dignity of innocent citizens on the streets and in their homes to protecting alike the rights and dignity of both prison inmates and correction officers.

Before New York State Bar Association,
Albany, Sept. 24/
The New York Times, 9-25:16.

Theodore L. Sendak
Attorney General of Indiana

There have been many sentimental journeys into the psychological realm of the criminals who are to be executed; I think there should be more sympathetic concern expressed for the thousands of innocent victims of those criminals. Opponents of the death penalty may rejoice that in 1968 there were 47 fewer murderers executed in this country than was the case in 1962. But do they say anything of the fact that some 5,250 more innocent persons died by criminal violence in 1968 than was the case in 1962? In the question of human suffering, this is a staggering loss of more than 5,000 individual innocent lives. What about the human rights and civil rights of the individual victim? Are not those 5,000 persons entitled to the dignity and sacredness of life? Is that a result of which humanitarians can be proud? I think not. Only misguided emotionalism, and not facts, disputes the truth that the death penalty is a deterrent of capital crime.

At Law Enforcement Luncheon Meeting
of Officials of Northern Indiana,
Wabash, May 12/Human Events, 6-5:19.

Whitney N. Seymour, Jr.
United States Attorney for the
Southern District of New York

It is sad but true that the public generally accepts the notion that there is extensive local police corruption.

Before New York State District Attorneys
Association, New York, Jan. 30/
The New York Times, 1-31:(1)67.

Fred Speaker
Attorney General of Pennsylvania

I believe deeply that our practice of killing criminals is both a disgusting indecency and demeaning to the society that tolerates it.

The Washington Post, 1-22:(A)6.

James V. Stanton
United States Representative, D—Ohio

The crime rate and crime totals around the country keep rising, with crimes of violence setting the pace. This is obvious to our constituents, who, of course, are not fooled by Justice Department attempts to assure them with phony communiques that juggle statistics and suggest "progress" in the war against crime.

News conference, Washington, Nov. 17/
The New York Times, 11-18:19.

Carl B. Stokes
Mayor of Cleveland

It is an established, historical fact that when injustice and oppression exist, the people turn to the only recourse left—violence.

Cleveland, April 18/
San Francisco Examiner, 4-19:6.

John V. Tunney
United States Senator, D—Calif.

I have no sympathy for those who set out deliberately to disrupt our government. Violence may be justified in those ossified autocracies where orderly change is impossible; but it is not justified and it cannot be tolerated in our nation's capital, itself a worldwide symbol of orderly change, of due process, of democracy.

Before Women's Democratic Club,
Washington, May/
The New York Times Magazine, 12-26:10.

Sam Tyler
Director, Massachusetts Council
on Crime and Correction

The way we responded to the ghettos in the 1960s is the kind of thing we must do for

(SAM TYLER)

prisons in the 1970s. We must develop "con power" in much the same way we developed black power and brown power and student power.

San Francisco Examiner & Chronicle
(This World), 1-24:2.

Wesley C. Uhlman
Mayor of Seattle

. . . the proper community attitude is more important (in controlling crime) than hanging a nightstick in your cummerbund.

The National Observer, 4-5:3.

Richard W. Velde
Associate Administrator, Law Enforcement
Assistance Administration of the United States

If a youth is a criminal at 18, the chances are overwhelming that he will be a criminal—and a much more adept one—at 24 or 28. I think it is clear to everybody that the juvenile justice system is not fulfilling its mandate. It does not correct. It does not rehabilitate. Sadly, it does not even meet ordinary standards of human decency in some cases.

Before Senate Juvenile Delinquency
Subcommittee, Washington, March 31/
San Antonio Express, 4-1:(A)3.

Henry Wade
District Attorney, Dallas County, Texas

(Regarding the U.S. Supreme Court's upholding the death penalty): There are three deterrents to crime. First, the fear of being arrested; second, the fear of swift and sure punishment; and third, the fear of the severity of the punishment. That third fear, knowing the possibility of the death penalty, will help law enforcement.

The Dallas Times Herald, 5-4:(A)21.

George C. Wallace
Governor of Alabama

. . . what I want to see is strong law enforcement. The time has come to make a

man fearful. When you go to arrest a man, show him you mean business. If it takes a good slap on the head sometimes, go ahead and do it.

Before law enforcement officers, Montgomery,
Feb. 4/San Francisco Examiner, 2-5:16.

(Regarding the recent revolt at Attica State Prison in New York State): I'll tell you why there is an Attica. It's the permissive attitude of the bleeding hearts and the courts who tell prisoners anything they do is right.

San Francisco Examiner & Chronicle
(This World), 10-3:2.

Fred T. Wilkinson
Director, Missouri State Department
of Corrections

We're reaping a harvest of the cult of permissiveness. Disciplines and controls in communities have been destroyed. And this has now reached our prisons, where so many militants and violence-oriented people from outside have been confined within the last year or two. They have carried with them hostility against any kind of law enforcement and order. You must have reasonable discipline—the kind of discipline we impose on ourselves in a community. A prison is a community.

Interview/
U.S. News & World Report, 9-27:22.

Jerry V. Wilson
Chief of Police of the District of Columbia

Policemen make decisions in the middle of the night within the space of five seconds. In the brightness and safety of the next morning, their activities are examined in ivory towers, in offices, courts and newspapers. If a chief is going to keep control of his men, he has to convince them that he will back them and tolerate honest errors.

Interview, Washington/Los Angeles Times,
9-6:(2)7.

There appears to be a growing attitude that prisons are too inhuman to hold anybody, even criminals. While I sympathize with this view, until we find some satisfactory alternative to the prison system, I have to listen to the victims, not the convicts.

Interview, Washington/
Los Angeles Times, 9-6:(2)7.

Samuel W. Yorty
Mayor of Los Angeles

I like the FBI. They can tap my line any time they want to.

Bedford, N.H., April 27/
Los Angeles Herald-Examiner, 4-27:(A)3.

Evelle J. Younger
Attorney General of California

Some policemen are dishonest, some are brutal and many are ill-trained. But the overwhelming majority are sincere representatives of justice . . . They are imperfect, but they are on society's side. Criminals are the enemy.

Before American Legionnaires, Los Angeles,
June 24/Los Angeles Times, 6-25:(2)2.

The revolutionaries (in prison) want to use the desperate, violent men that make up a large part of the prison population, and these prisoners want very much to be used . . . Once a prisoner believes that he is in prison not because he held up a bank and shot a teller but because of his radical political views, he begins to act like a martyr and is less responsive to reasonable discipline.

Before Rotary Clubs, Whittier, Calif., Oct. 22/
Los Angeles Times, 10-23:(1)19.

Prisons should be smaller, better designed and not located out in the sticks but in metropolitan areas where the inmates' family contacts could be easily maintained and where psychiatrists, ministers and other volunteers are available and willing to perform needed services.

Before California Grand Lodge of Masons,
San Francisco/The Dallas Times Herald,
10-24:(B)12.

Rehabilitation (of prisoners) is an ideal to which everyone can subscribe and for which everyone hopes, but is much overplayed in describing the role of a prison. The fact is no man can be rehabilitated against his will. The most sophisticated techniques of persuasion, the most rigidly applied principles of psychiatry, or the most appealing training or vocational programs are absolutely worthless for a man who isn't interested in changing himself.

Before Town Hall, Los Angeles, Oct. 26/
Los Angeles Herald-Examiner, 10-26:(A)13.

Education

James E. Allen, Jr.
Former Commissioner of Education
of the United States

For generations, we have assumed that the proper place for education to take place is in the school, in formal classroom settings—all framed with a fixed schedule of hours, days, months and years. Now we are beginning to recognize that the school is only a part, not the whole, and that the arena for educational planning and operation is as broad as the community, the environment and the total experience of the individual. While I am certainly not prepared to abandon the school altogether, as some would have us do, it is increasingly clear that the school, as we have known it, has not been a productive place for learning for large numbers of the age group it was developed to serve. Indeed, evidence abounds that for children who enter school with the disabilities caused by poverty and prejudice, the school has been a miserable failure; and for large numbers of others, there is the feeling that the school is not the best place for preparing youthful citizens for the society of tomorrow.

At Columbia University, July 5/
Vital Speeches, 8-15:655.

William R. Allen
Professor of Economics,
University of California at Los Angeles

Research is to teaching what sin is to confession: Without the one, you have nothing to say in the other.

Plainview (Tex.) Daily Herald, 7-23:6.

William B. Arthur
Editor, "Look" magazine

We live in an atmosphere . . . in which our President (Nixon) finds the dissenting col-

legiate young so distasteful that he calls them "bums"; and his Vice President (Agnew) finds the protesting youths to be "rotten apples" to be ruthlessly plucked from the barrel. It is a malignant atmosphere. And I believe that the present Administration nurtures and inflames it.

Before northeastern region members of Sigma
Delta Chi, Windsor, Conn., April 24/
San Francisco Examiner & Chronicle,
4-25:(A)24.

Norman P. Auburn
President, University of Akron (Ohio)

(Regarding the office of university president): If the job is impossible, why are there always so many applicants whenever a presidency is vacant? If the job is untenable, why are there thousands of ambitious academicians and college administrators who want to wear the presidential hat and believe that, for them at least, it will not turn out to be a crown of thorns?

Plainview (Tex.) Daily Herald, 7-28:8.

Stephen K. Bailey
Chairman, Policy Institute,
Syracuse University Research Corporation

There are massive numbers of bored individuals in our secondary schools. They watch a Jacques Cousteau show on television on Sunday night and then go to school Monday morning for dull, gray periods of teaching.

Before House subcommittee, Washington,
Feb. 24/The Washington Post, 2-25:(A)2.

Helen Pate Bain
President, National Education Association

I have visited no country that does not have a minister of education or department of education. We are asking the President, in restructuring the administrative branch, to take the "E" out of HEW. We do not want to see education further buried.

Before Town Hall, Los Angeles, March 2/
Los Angeles Herald-Examiner, 3-3:(A)9.

Edward J. Bloustein
President, Rutgers University

The contemporary university is threatened with losing its soul, not because it serves society, but because for too long it has served too narrow a range of social interest. The paymasters of government and industry have distorted the life of the university by luring too much of its intellectual capital into enterprises of war, barren technology and commercialism.

At his inauguration, Rutgers University,
Nov. 10/The New York Times, 11-11:52.

Derek C. Bok
President-elect, Harvard University

The last several years should have taught us that universities should be rather modest in their capacity to solve a great many problems of the world. Their major responsibility must be teaching and scholarship. That does not preclude social action; but we must understand our priorities.

At his election, Cambridge, Mass., Jan. 11/
The New York Times, 1-12:1.

The idea of a three-year college education is becoming increasingly popular. For one thing, it would cost the student a lot less money. Another reason is that, on the whole, our students now get a better high school education, so they can start at a higher level. There is also a growing feeling among students that an exclusive diet of classroom work is not the best way of achieving the classic goals of a college education, which include finding oneself and developing attitudes on major personal, moral and social issues. If one could cut down a bit on the length of education and substitute some direct practical experience, you might get a much better educational mix. In fact, one could push the idea a lot further. I'm not sure that those four years when you

can study the culture and learning of the world, free from all outside pressure, should be compressed into four years between the ages of 17 and 21. It might do a lot to close the gulf that separates the generations if people returned to the university for a sabbatical year later in their lives to mingle with a new generation of students.

Interview/Life, 1-22:36.

One reason they (students) remain students is that they don't see what there is of real value to do afterward. They hold out against a life of routine work or meaningless money-making . . . It is up to society to provide a way for students to go on expressing their idealism in life.

Interview, Cambridge, Mass./
The New York Times, 3-27:29.

Albert H. Bowker
Chancellor-elect,
University of California at Berkeley

I think the move among students generally . . . is away from confrontation and violence. For one thing, communications is better now between faculty and students . . . I think the 18-year-old vote, the increasing activity of students in politics, the success of minority communities in electing public officials—all are good signs. Also, I think, President Nixon has at least reduced the divisiveness of the Vietnam war by committing himself to the withdrawal of troops and actually withdrawing them. I know that many young people continue to criticize him; but overall, I think that issue—the most divisive of all issues—is on its way to resolution.

Interview, New York/
Los Angeles Times, 4-26:(1)19.

I think there's a certain sense of humility now in higher education. Fifteen years ago, we thought we could run laboratories, hospitals, cities, governments and everything else. Now, in the past five or six years, we're led to believe we have to learn how to run ourselves first of all. I think the main function of the university . . . is teaching and scholarship and

(ALBERT H. BOWKER)

not changing the world, no matter how desirable that may be.

News conference, Berkeley, May 6/
Los Angeles Times, 5-7:(1)3.

William B. Boyd
President, Central Michigan University

A specter that has been haunting higher education—the specter of collective bargaining—is now a living presence. The unthinkable became thinkable, then bearable, and soon may be taken for granted. While I have no crystal ball, my hunch is that we are more apt to see the emergence of unions for (college) presidents and deans than to see a reversal in the movement of faculties toward unions.

The New York Times, 11-14:(1)1.

Kingman Brewster, Jr.
President, Yale University

The student generation is not "radical" in the sense of being captivated by any simple, single, sweeping social prescription. To the well established, they may seem radical because they are skeptical of authority. They suspect the tendency of authority to be self-serving and self-perpetuating. They are impatient with any argument which begins and ends with "because that is the way we have always done it."

Weil Lecture, University of North Carolina/
The Washington Post, 5-24:(A)20.

George Hay Brown
Director, Bureau of the Census
of the United States

If anyone ever asks you, "What ever happened to the old-fashioned student who worked his way through college?" you can quote me as saying, "He's still here; and there are more of him than ever before."

Before Economic Club, Detroit/
Quote, 4-4:316.

John Anthony Brown
President, The Lindenwood Colleges,
St. Charles, Mo.

To outward appearance, today's student seems to be mad at something or somebody—the (college) administration and the president more often than not. If he chooses ridiculous issues and far-fetched excuses over which to rebel, is it his sometimes outrageous choice of weapons which should concern us or his mood? For the mood is one that can be used to advantage if we understand it. And the mood can be very destructive if we ignore it or misread it or misuse it. It is a mood that grasps for meaning, that seeks human freedom, that distrusts the pressures that come from modern technology to standardize everything, even the quality of life itself. It is a mood in rebellion against the multiversity, a mood opposed to mass culture with common forms of expression and majority-imposed standards for creativity, a mood that questions the family as it now functions and even marriage as it now appears. It is a mood highly critical of the past, and a mood which sweepingly threatens to discard everything good in its rejection of everything bad.

At St. Louis University commencement,
Feb. 7/Vital Speeches, 4-15:399.

James L. Buckley
United States Senator-elect, C–N.Y.

I think we've probably done a great disservice to an awful lot of people by this emphasis on the sheepskin for the sake of the sheepskin, as opposed to the emphasis on the dignity of work. Somebody who chooses—or ends up—working with his hands is entitled to the same respect, I believe, as somebody who sits in an office with a B.A. degree and files papers all day.

Interview/The Washington Post, 1-10:(B)2.

McGeorge Bundy
President, Ford Foundation

In the long run, in the next run, economics will be a more significant element in the process of university decision-making than student unrest has been in the last five years.

The New York Times, 1-11:67.

John Bunzel
President, San Jose (Calif.) State College

A college president is a faculty leader, chief psychiatrist, crisis leader, chief communicator, rider of storms, principal mediator, ambassador and diplomat, chief justice, commander-in-chief of the armed forces, and manager of the apocalypse.

Interview/San Francisco Examiner, 8-30:42.

Otto Butz
President, Golden Gate College,
San Francisco

For too long, public education has been like a public dairy. The dairy foreman says, "Here's how we package the milk, fellas. We hope you like it. But if you don't, it's too bad." Students are now finding they can have another choice. They can go somewhere else.

San Francisco Examiner & Chronicle
(This World), 8-22:2.

Matthew Byrne, Jr.
Executive Director,
President's Commission on Campus Unrest

The majority of the American people don't really look at you (educators) with great favor. The public is very anxious to gain control of universities.

Panel discussion before American Association
for Higher Education, Chicago/
Los Angeles Times, 3-31:(1)21.

Robert Christin
President, St. Norbert College, Wisconsin

(Regarding fiscal belt-tightening by colleges): The faculties are the big problem. But they're going to have to go along with this kind of management—or they're going to be arguing about it not in the faculty lounge but in some unemployment line somewhere.

Interview, Harriman, N.Y./
The New York Times, 3-15:33.

Harold R. Collier
United States Representative, R–Ill.

There is no such thing as "free education."

Education is very expensive, whether it is paid for through property taxes, income taxes, bond issues, tuition payments or endowments. It costs a lot of money, whether the funds are provided by local, state and Federal governments, or by students, parents or philanthropists.

Quote, 11-28:509.

Forrest E. Conner
Executive secretary, American
Association of School Administrators

It's our general philosophy that a good administrator is one who knows what chalk dust smells like—a person who has had experience at other levels in the school system. With rare exceptions, there's no substitute for experience at the classroom level.

The New York Times, 1-11:69.

Sidney M. B. Coulling
Professor of English,
Washington and Lee University;
President, Gamma of Virginia chapter of
Phi Beta Kappa

Of all the threats to Phi Beta Kappa, as it has been traditionally conceived, probably none is more pervasive than that of the so-called counter-culture, with its elevation of instinct over intellect, mysticism over reason, consciousness over scholarship, sensitivity over discipline. The signs of this new movement are everywhere around us, and they have already made their presence known within the society. While one would be hesitant to say that (the University of California at) Berkeley is the bellwether of American academic life, it is nevertheless true that trends there often anticipate larger trends across the nation. There is reason to pause, consequently, on the reflection that last year some of the students at California who were elected to membership (in Phi Beta Kappa) declined to accept because of the conviction that education by "sensing" was more important than education by learning . . .

At Washington and Lee University's
Phi Beta Kappa banquet/
The Wall Street Journal, 5-7:8.

Frederick R. Cyphert
Dean, School of Education,
University of Virginia

Many of today's teachers are able to talk better lessons than teach. They are artists at best, unimaginative and anti-intellectual pedants at worst and scientists almost never. They reflect accurately the professional programs which produced them.

The Austin (Tex.) Statesman, 4-21:(A)16.

Edward D. Eddy
President, Chatham College

Genuine liberal education is not a cram course for life's cultural quiz on which a job may depend. It is, instead, the preparation for enjoying life irrespective of one's particular livelihood.

At Agnes Scott College, Decatur, Ga./
The National Observer, 11-20:15.

Robert L. Ewigleben
President, Ferris State College,
Big Rapids, Mich.

I think there's nothing more tragic to education than turning out students who understand all about their culture but nothing about making a living.

Plainview (Tex.) Daily Herald, 12-10:8.

Lawrence Fertig
Economic affairs columnist

. . . in many departments of American universities—such as economics, sociology, history and the other so-called social sciences—the ideological content taught to students is entirely one-sided. It is of the modern liberal persuasion, and often does not even make a bow to the old traditional liberalism or the modern conservative viewpoint. As an example, there are cases I personally know of where capable students have received their Doctorate of Philosophy degree in Economics from a major university although they had never even heard of, or been taught about, such distinguished free-market economists as Ludwig von Mises,

Frederick Hayek or Wilhelm Roepke—three world famous economists. Imagine that for a Ph.D. in Economics!

Before Society of the Four Arts, Palm Beach,
Fla., March 2/Vital Speeches, 5-15:458.

Buckminster Fuller
Engineer, Author, Designer

Our whole university and educational experience is quite wrong. Kids are still being baby-sat. I would like to know why it is that we have disregarded all children's significantly spontaneous and comprehensive curiosity and in our formal education have deliberately instituted processes leading only to narrow specialization.

Los Angeles Times, 10-24:A.

Richard C. Gilman
President, Occidental College

. . . the campus is, and must remain, a place of lively discussion and earnest debate, of intellectual freedom and social concern . . . We must be wary if a campus be too tranquil, too quiet, lest that quietude reflect an attitude of apathy and unconcern.

At Occidental College commencement, June 13/
Los Angeles Herald-Examiner, 6-14:(A)16.

Robert F. Goheen
President, Princeton University

I met the other night with the University Council, which includes 15 undergraduate and eight graduate student representatives. Ten years ago, perhaps even five years ago, the students would have been spruced up, clean shaven, wearing neckties. But let me say this: Once you get over the shock of the hair, the beards, the dirty blue jeans, they are as fine as any young people I've ever known. I believe in them, in their future.

Interview, Princeton, N.J./
The Washington Post, 2-15:(A)19.

On a number of occasions extending back some time, I have expressed my conviction that, in times like these when the pace of change is marked, the term of a university president should normally run 10 to 15 years.

Announcing his resignation, Princeton, N.J., March 25/The Washington Post, 3-26:(A)2.

Paul Goodman
Author, Educator

The very worst thing you can do for people is to help them. That is precisely why I think the whole school and education do is a lot of bunk. They continually *create* learning situations. The *world* is the learning situation. Just give people the autonomy, the freedom to develop themselves in their own way.

Quote, 12-12:565.

Milton S. Gould
Lawyer

Somewhere in the secondary schools, maybe in the primary schools, they (current law-school students) have not been exposed as we were to as broad a panorama of the substance of human experience. They don't know as much about history; they don't know as much about literature. They're mostly insensitive to the heritage of literature. If you quote Wordsworth to them, they're not sure who Wordsworth was. They don't have the same degree of language skills that we have, in English and in foreign languages. They don't know anything about punctuation. They don't know anything about grammar. They don't know how to phrase a sentence. To suggest to them that, as a matter of style, we don't split infinitives—not with just one word, but split them so you can drive a truck through them—they don't know what you're talking about.

The Wall Street Journal, 12-28:6.

Samuel B. Gould
Chairman, Commission on Non-Traditional Study; Former chancellor, State University of New York

. . . our boys and girls become men and women far earlier than ever before; yet we keep them bound in the traditional straitjackets of the past: 12 years of elementary and secondary school, the four years of college, the intermin-

able years of graduate and professional study. They are over-supervised until they rebel, or they are undersupervised to such a point of permissiveness that they bend and often break at every pressure upon them. There is good reason to believe that the present elementary, secondary and collegiate years could be cut by as much as a third with beneficial results to youth.

Before Education Commission of the States/ The Wall Street Journal, 11-24:10.

Edith Green
United States Representative, D—Ore.

(Advocating an upgrading in status of technical skills and vocational training): I've always argued that it is just as desirable, just as possible, to have philosopher plumbers as philosopher kings. There's no reason why a plumber can't enjoy a Beethoven symphony, can't take courses in South African literature or anything else he wants to. (The exaltation of colleges and college students) led a generation of parents and a generation of students to believe that the only road to success and happiness is by the acquisition of that degree from a four-year institution all tied up in blue ribbon.

Interview, Washington, Aug. 1/ The Dallas Times Herald, 8-2:(A)10.

Fred R. Harris
United States Senator, D—Okla.

Right now, only 3 per cent of the colleges in this country have students as voting members of their boards of trustees. The redistribution of power in our schools and colleges should be an important priority for all of us concerned about higher education. I believe the government can promote this by requiring all colleges and universities receiving Federal funds to have significant student representation on their boards of trustees—not control, but representation.

Before Association of Student Governments, Washington/The Dallas Times Herald, 10-7:(A)22.

Theodore M. Hesburgh
President, University of Notre Dame

If our lives in education have any meaning or significance, it will be in our reading the signs of the times and in educating the young of our times in the visions and values that will civilize and make for reasonable human progress and lasting peace on earth.

Before National Catholic Educational Association, Minneapolis, April 12/ Los Angeles Herald-Examiner, 4-13:(A)7.

Roger W. Heyns
Chancellor, University of California at Berkeley

If it is not to be lost catastrophically, all of us must reassert our faith in the educational process and in the fundamental integrity of our institutions . . . This does not mean blind or uncritical support; but it does mean a positive faith and confidence in the university—confidence in its student body, its administration and its faculty . . . The university is a truly remarkable achievement and a great asset, one that must be appreciated, supported and cher-ished.

McEnerney Lecture, University of California at Berkeley, May 26/ San Francisco Examiner, 5-27:3.

Linwood Holton
Governor of Virginia

What we need among our faculties today is less dedication to tenure and more to teaching, less emphasis on research and more on relevance.

Before Virginia chapter, American Association of University Professors, Richmond, March 20/ The Washington Post, 3-21:(D)5.

Sidney Hook
Professor of Philosophy, New York University

The future (of education) depends primarily on the intelligence and courage of the faculties. The dangers (to) higher education lie not only in the erosion of the principles of academic freedom but also the debasement of educational standards.

At San Francisco State College, April 16/ San Francisco Examiner, 4-17:5.

Stephen Horn
President, California State College at Long Beach

Too many students are not in college to prepare for their future . . . but because their parents want them to have a degree. Perhaps we should award the bachelor's degree upon enrollment and then invite the students who want an education to stick around another four years.

News conference, Beverly Hills, Calif., March 17/ Los Angeles Herald-Examiner, 3-18:(A)8.

John A. Howard
President, Rockford College

We have had an uncritical faith in the educational process in this country. We have had the idea that everything would be fine if we could shove all the young people through an educational machine that is characterized by high salaries and small classes, a proper racial mix, plenty of books in the library and plenty of equipment in the laboratory. This is naive. These mechanics of education are important; as we improve the mechanics, we can improve the efficiency of the educational vehicle. But if we haven't identified the destination, it makes no difference how fast the vehicle is traveling.

Interview, Washington/ U.S. News & World Report, 9-6:43.

Charles G. Hurst, Jr.
President, Malcolm X College, Chicago

College courses are overrated. There is nothing in college that the average person cannot learn if given time and the proper motivation. Here, we deal in motivation, and we give them time.

Time, 8-16:50.

Hans H. Jenny
Vice president, College of Wooster, Ohio

When an entire educational system approaches the stage of perennial deficits and financial doom, the incentive for corrective action may not be so strong. After all, misery will have good company and plenty of it.

Newsweek, 3-22:64.

Howard W. Johnson
President,
Massachusetts Institute of Technology

To many observers, the university today appears to be the most fragile, the most troubled and least-certain of its goals among all institutions. At the same time, it has the chance to become the strongest, the surest-footed and the pace-setter for the next great social advance. It has this chance because it contains the human resources of intelligence, energy and vitality that can make of the university an inspiration for all society. There is no question that the university has had these resources, the autonomy and the know-how to be an exemplary institution. Yet at this moment, the universities are far from being an inspiration—a city on the hill—for the people of our time. Some university must take the lead, for its own preservation and the preservation of all universities.

At MIT commencement/
The Boston Globe, 6-14:11.

William J. Johnston
Superintendent,
Los Angeles Public School System

Too often, we tend to think that education consists only of programs, projects, curriculum. They are valuable parts—but only parts—of a whole. Education, to me, is what happens between teacher and pupil—the spark that ignites challenge, the key that unlocks the desire for learning, the hunger for discovery.

Upon taking office, Los Angeles, Jan. 11/
Los Angeles Times, 1-12:(2)1.

Albert R. Jonsen
President, University of San Francisco

Education is a search for the common word that people with outward differences can speak to each other. It is a search for understanding, the key that unlocks diversity.

San Francisco, Sept. 21/
San Francisco Examiner, 9-22:22.

Kenneth Keniston
Professor of Psychiatry,
Yale University

In explaining the silence this year (in the student activist movement), the sense of discouragement and despair, the feeling of embarrassment and shame, are indeed important. But underlying these feelings has been the increasing realization that a movement and a new culture dedicated above all to peace, justice, democracy and equality was moving toward the systematic violation of these very principles. The members of the student movement gradually came to realize that, if they allowed themselves to be led by their most rigid and destructive factions, dogmatism and death lay at the end of their road. In a peculiar way, then, the silence, the introspectiveness, the self-criticism and self-examination that has characterized activist students this year testify to the ultimate sanity and decency of most student activists.

At University of Notre Dame
commencement/The New York Times,
6-14:44.

Clark Kerr
Former president,
University of California

. . . contrary to the impression given by many reports of campus disturbances, faculty members, graduate students and undergraduates tend to be in strong agreement that disruptions by activists are inimical to academic freedom and the educational process. They are probably inclined to support policies that are designed to prevent campus violence or disruption and to support punishment for those who violate such policies.

San Francisco Examiner, 1-15:1.

Robert J. Kibbee
President, Pittsburgh Board of Education;
Chancellor-designate,
City University of New York.

The quality of a university is measured more by the kind of student it turns out than the kind of (student) it takes in.

Interview, New York, July 27/
The New York Times, 7-28:39.

Jerzy Kosinski
*Author; Professor of Dramatic Prose
and Criticism, Yale University School of Drama*

The dominant trait of the students of today is their short span of attention—their inability to know or believe anything for more than half-an-hour.

*Television interview/"Comment,"
National Broadcasting Company, 2-28.*

Charles LeMaistre
*Chancellor,
University of Texas system*

There are . . . increasing pressures from the minority and culturally-deprived groups seeking special consideration for admission to the process of higher education. How are we to deal with this dilemma? Obviously, I cannot face the general public or the Legislature with a quota system—a percentage for white Anglo-Saxon Protestants and a percentage for others . . . And obviously, I cannot defend the admission of an academically-unqualified minority student and the rejection of an otherwise academically-qualified student . . . I submit to you that those of us who are involved and concerned with higher education have just begun to hear the outraged cries of the disadvantaged . . . Unless we "tool up" the educational system to meet this challenge, the urgency of their demand will overwhelm us in a few short years.

*At College Entrance Examination
Board Meeting, Dallas, Feb. 25/
The Dallas Times Herald, 2-26:(A)4.*

John V. Lindsay
Mayor of New York

When a teacher is shouted down or beaten up, peaceful students are robbed of a crucial chance to learn and discuss. And when that happens, the student's hope for a better life dies at an early age. He is diminished—and so is our society and all the rest of us.

*Before United Parent-Teachers Association,
New York, Jan. 16/The New York Times,
1-17:(1)76.*

Sol M. Linowitz
*Chairman, Commission on Campus Unrest,
American Council on Education*

There is such a thing as succeeding too well in quelling dissent. With all the problems this nation has, a campus which is not troubled today is not worth its salt.

*Panel discussion before American Council
for Higher Education, Chicago/
Los Angeles Times, 3-31:(1)21.*

Henry Cabot Lodge
*Former United States Ambassador
to the United Nations*

(Regarding demonstrators whose shouting prevented him from speaking at Stanford University): Those children kept shouting "power to the people." But I don't see how you're going to have power if you don't know anything. And I could have told them some interesting things.

Plainview (Tex.) Daily Herald, 2-7:(A)4.

Louis B. Lundborg
Chairman, Bank of America

I think it is time that we face squarely one of the touchy issues and challenge the whole concept of a college degree as a status symbol . . . Collectively, we have fallen for a mass production, mass marketing, Madison Avenue-selling kind of approach that has said, "Everybody has got to have a college degree just like everybody else—or else you're not "in."

*San Francisco Examiner & Chronicle
(This World), 3-28:2.*

Richard W. Lyman
President, Stanford University

. . . universities do not exist for the purpose of saving souls or single-mindedly remodeling the world. They exist to help people, in the ways that education *can* help, to decide whether their souls need saving and how to do it; whether the world needs remodeling and how to do it. They exist to enable men and women of all ages and all races and all economic and social conditions to examine the mysteries of human existence, and of the physical universe around us, and find their ways to such answers as may be reached by mortal beings. Universities exist to question everything, and to persecute nothing.

Before Stanford Alumni Association, May 22/
Vital Speeches, 10-1:759.

Fritz Machlup
Professor of Economics, Princeton University

I define higher education as the level of scholarly teaching, learning and researching that is accessible to only a small fraction of the people. Any level of education that is designed for a larger portion of the population is, if extended beyond the age of completing high school, in fact only continuing second-level education. An affluent society can offer continuing education to as many people as may want to take it. But we should not kid them, and still less ourselves, by the fake assertion that this is higher education . . . I firmly believe that higher education should be open to all who want it and can take it. But we cannot change the fact that perhaps 80 per cent of the people find it "not relevant" to their interests and capabilities.

At Educational Testing Service conference/
The Washington Post, 2-28:(B)1.

Sidney P. Marland, Jr.
Commissioner of Education
of the United States

. . . we must blend our curricula and our students into a single strong secondary school system. Let the academic preparation be balanced with the vocational or career program. Let one student take strength from another. And for the future hope of education, let us end the divisive, snobbish, destructive distinctions in learning that do no service to the cause of knowledge, and do no honor to the name of American enterprise. It is terribly important to teach a youngster the skills he needs to live, whether we call them academic or vocational, whether he intends to make his living with a wrench, or a slide-rule, or folio editions of Shakespeare.

Before National Association
of Secondary School Principals, Houston,
Jan. 23/Vital Speeches, 3-15:335.

The "general curriculum" (in high school education) for those . . . not familiar with it, is a fallacious compromise between the true academic liberal arts and the true vocational offerings. It is made up, as its name suggests, of generalized courses, possessing neither the practicality and reality of vocational courses nor the quality of college-preparatory offerings. Watered-down mathematics, nonspecific science, "easier" English—such is the bland diet offered in the name of the "general curriculum"; not much to chew on, not much to swallow.

The Christian Science Monitor, 8-7:11.

We are so preoccupied with higher education that it has become a national fetish. High schools measure their success by the number of their students who go on to college. People view vocational education as a great thing for the neighbor's children.

Interview, Washington/
The New York Times, 8-8:(1)1.

School finance is a complex, complicated subject, entangled in governmental, organizational and legal technicalities that most of our citizens are likely to find baffling. In the long run, however, it is their understanding and their support that will decide the issue . . . The growing evidence of inequity, erosion, inadequacy and ineffectiveness in the ways by which education is supported is clear and persuasive. From district to district and state to state, the record shows that the present system of raising and allocating funds for the schools adds up to a rigged lottery that cheats students and taxpayers alike. The need for reform in school financing is crucial and urgent.

Before National Association of State Boards
of Education, Atlanta, Oct. 12/
Vital Speeches, 12-1:125.

. . . our society has developed a kind of folklore that says to be good you must go to college; to be somebody you must have at least a BA degree. For many years, that was a very appropriate goal, and it served as a world model to increase the intellectual, social and economic level of our country. But we have come to the point where a kind of self-hypnosis has set in.

(SIDNEY P. MARLAND, JR.)

People are convinced that this is the only way to glory. And I hold that it is not true. I'm not talking only about differences in intellect. I'm talking about differences in aspiration, in goals; differences in human needs and what people want to do with their lives. I think there is a false set of values surrounding the whole theme of vocational-technical education that says, "That's for the other people, but my children are going to go to college" . . . I'm not trying to discourage young people from going to college—quite the contrary. What we must do is create social value and prestige in a wholly different kind of education for the nearly 50 per cent of young people who choose not to enter college, and for the much larger percentage which includes those who enter but soon exit. I want to give exposure to what the world of work is all about to all children.

Interview, Washington/
U.S. News & World Report, 11-1:81.

William J. McGill
President, Columbia University

All of us need to recognize that the campus rhetoric of the last several years is a form of verbal pollution as destructive to the environment as smog, boiling sea water and jet noise.

San Francisco Examiner & Chronicle
(This World), 4-4:2.

There's a definite rate at which the chief administrator of a major university runs out of gas. It's about five years under current, almost revolutionary, conditions of change. The job just eats you up; even the toughest administrative hide becomes penetrated.

Interview, New York/
The New York Times, 8-22:(1)47.

Years of student unrest, followed by serious fiscal problems, have produced a crisis of the spirit in our universities. While campus disorders have eroded public support for higher education somewhat, our financial troubles are far more complicated and far more serious.

Before American Council on Education,
Washington, Oct. 7/
The Washington Post, 10-8:(A)2.

We are proceeding toward the fall term in a campus climate so outwardly serene as to make one wonder whether the last several years (of student unrest) might not have been just a nightmare.

September/
U.S. News & World Report, 10-25:41.

Edward J. Meade, Jr.
Director of public education programs,
Ford Foundation

What the kids are saying is that schools and teachers can no longer divorce reality from what they teach and the way they teach it. Mass communications have had such a dominant effect on their lives. They watch the Vietnam war or a bit on pollution for supper and go back to school the next day to study Chaucer or the Industrial Revolution. I'm not putting Chaucer or the Revolution down—it's just that the kids are so much more mature and sensitized today that they're relating more closely to current social issues and trends.

Interview, New York/
The New York Times, 1-11:73.

Martin Meyerson
President, University of Pennsylvania

Most colleges' and universities' faculties and administrations are like men's clubs: courteous to women, served by women, but denying them full privileges. Just as boys at elementary schools are cheated by knowing only women teachers, so women, and men as well, in college are cheated by knowing only men professors.

Philadelphia, Jan. 15/
The New York Times, 1-17:(1)61.

William G. Milliken
Governor of Michigan

The important thing is quality education for all children . . . the tragedy is that the schools fail so often precisely where they should be attaining the greatest success—where people are poor and education is the only hope for ending their poverty.

Los Angeles Herald-Examiner, 9-1:(A)3.

John N. Mitchell
Attorney General of the United States

. . . I would say that, even if you defuse the (Vietnam) war issue entirely, there will always be some other issue that will generate a great deal of enthusiasm on the campuses. Whether it be the war, the environment or civil rights, students are going to have some issue. They are in somewhat of a foment and wanting to be heard; and I think this is always healthy.

Interview, Washington/
U.S. News & World Report, 3-22:42.

(Regarding the shooting of four students by National Guardsmen at Kent State University, Ohio, in May, 1970): A sense of tragedy over the events which took place at Kent is as common to everyone in the Department (of Justice) as it is to the American people; but this incident cannot be undone. I am satisfied that the Department has taken every possible action to serve justice. I have communicated this decision to the parents of the four students who died and restated my sympathy with the full knowledge that nothing can be said to mitigate their sorrow and remorse. We can only hope that any type of recurrence can be avoided by this experience and (that) incidents like this will never again be a part of our national life.

Washington, Aug. 13/
The New York Times, 8-14:9.

Robert Moses
Government planner and builder

I have long since abandoned the notion that higher education is essential to either success or happiness. Hothouses of learning do not always grow anything edible.

At Queensboro (N.Y.) Community College
commencement, June 10/
The New York Times, 6-11:41.

Julian Nava
President, Los Angeles Board of Education

To say a child doesn't want to learn is to say he doesn't want to live.

Los Angeles Times, 2-25:(1)28.

Calvin C. Nolan
President, North Texas State University

I think (as a university president) you have to have some understanding, whether by experience or study, of the nature of a university as a complex institution in a complex world and yet with roots that go back to 1000 A.D. There is something different about the university as an institution. It's not just a manufacturing plant. It's hard to articulate this, but I think you have to have an abiding faith in the idea of a university—that there must be a place that can harness the ideas of young people to grow, develop and learn from the past so they can correct mistakes in the future and, hopefully, develop their individual personalities so they can come to grips with problems of the world.

The Dallas Times Herald
(Sunday magazine), 11-28:31.

Ewald Nyquist
New York State Commissioner of Education

The cry for relevance has echoed through our compartmentalized schools, with their lock-step programs, standardized schedules, prescribed curriculums and other rigidities. Instead of being man-centered, idea-centered, experience-centered, problem-oriented and interdisciplinary, present education is too frequently an experience characterized by information-gathering, with its fact-centered, course-centered, subject-centered, grade-getting, bell-interrupted activities, and fragmentation in terms of time, space objects and teachers. I am reminded of the three R's: rote, restraint and regurgitation.

At Superintendents Work Conference,
Columbia University, July 15/
Vital Speeches, 8-15:646.

Allan W. Ostar
Executive director, American Association
of State Colleges and Universities

For some reason, the American people have an outmoded idea that academic careers offer more status and economic security than occupational or technical careers. We know this

(ALLAN W. OSTAR)

isn't true. All work merits dignity and status, and all work should provide economic security. Quality should determine status, not occupation. I would rather be known as a good engineering technician than a poor philosopher.

At Kansas State College commencement/
The Wall Street Journal, 7-6:16.

Roman C. Pucinski
United States Representative, D—Ill.

(Referring to America's basic school system): With all its faults and shortcomings, it still offers America's youngsters a broad preparation for life in a very complicated world. And certainly, the things that children have to learn today are vastly more than their parents had to learn, or their grandparents had to learn. It is a much tougher job to teach today. There are many factors involved. But . . . I think that, on total, we have one of the finest educational systems in the history of mankind. But what is happening is that, because of the cost-push forces at play against the existing system . . . the system is deteriorating—as in the examples when a school has to drop 14 teachers; when a school has to drop a counselor; when a school has to drop a librarian; when a system like the one in New York City has to lay off 10,000 teachers; when a system like that at Chicago is faced with curtailing the services of 4,000 teachers; when you bring down the statutory requirement of 178 days of school year down to 150 school days; when you have to increase the size of classes in the classrooms beyond the capacity of the teacher to handle a class like that. When you have all of these forces brought to play, then we are deteriorating what has been the finest educational system in the world. You cannot indict the system, because America has made more progress in every single field of human endeavor than any other nation in the world; and that progress has been made possible by our educational institutions. Those institutions, I believe, have done very well in a

complex society. But . . . the system is now at the breaking point; the system is at the crash point; the system is at the point of no return. I am really amazed at the ingenuity of our educators in keeping the system going under these fantastic social pressures that have beset the system in the last decade, and I think that we owe our educators a mandate of gratitude.

Before the House, Washington, March 16/
Congressional Record, 3-16:(H)1600.

Nathan M. Pusey
President, Harvard University

In recent years, campus revolutionaries, here and elsewhere, have held that a debilitating and dehumanizing contagion, allegedly springing from the interests and arrangements of the world outside, has so deeply penetrated and widely infected the activities and structures of academic societies, and has so controlled them—has made them so thoroughly deceitful and corrupt—that the only acceptable attitude toward them must also be one of hatred, denigration and attack. This has disturbed me more than any other development during recent years. If they are to be believed, the world, unready as yet to be set right by them, is totally corrupt—governed, controlled and manipulated by schemers, of whom, I suppose, at least in the minor way, I must be considered one.

At Harvard University baccalaureate service,
June 15/The New York Times, 6-16:29.

Universities are no longer universally admired. Indeed, some people have even come to look upon them less as saviors than as the source of evils from which society must be saved. The general public evidences less esteem for university faculties. Even the professors themselves have come to have doubts about what they are doing; or perhaps, rather, about their chances of gaining wider public appreciation and support of the significance of the work they care about so deeply. A growing number of students are less readily impressed by what professors have to offer and less ready to devote sustained attention to their teaching. These sharply critical students are also less convinced of the integrity and validity of society's institutions, including its colleges and universities; and they are less ready to work in and for them, on established terms, than were the young who for the most part were happy to be attending and serving these same institutions just a few years ago. The aims and methods of universities have come into question—fundamentally. Again they stand in need of articulation and of redefinition. There can be no doubt that we are entering a new, very different and, it appears, a very troubled period in higher education. The goals which meant so much to us a generation ago have lost much of their appeal. The public's gaze is now shifting back from the big world to the domestic scene. Prejudice, poverty, urban blight, injustices at home, disturbances and thefts in our own neighborhoods, increasing delinquency—things of this kind force their way to the forefront of attention. They of course deserve attention. But now there is much less certainty that answers will be found in knowledge. At least not quickly. There is also less confidence that universities can, or will want to, produce the requisite knowledge. And there is even less confidence that, if they knew how and wanted to produce the knowledge, they could also produce the people with the stamina and character to put it to work to accomplish the constructive ends.

Before Associated Harvard Alumni,
Cambridge, Mass., June 17/
The Boston Globe, 6-18:21.

Max Rafferty
Dean, School of Education,
Troy State University, Alabama

(Regarding today's student compared with those of the past): The visible segment of the student is noticeably dirtier in every respect—physically, morally and every other way. They are also visibly more interested. The articulate portion of this generation is more involved. But they are far more inclined to turn people off . . . they are incredibly slovenly, arrogant and violent.

Interview, Troy, Ala./
The Washington Post, 4-1:(F)6.

Ronald Reagan
Governor of California

The original and legitimate reasons for tenure no longer exist. Tenure has become a haven for the incompetent teacher. It should be altered to include a system of merit pay which provides real incentives for quality teaching. This should not be precipitous; a judicious sensible phase-out would be a real service to all concerned—the student, the public and the teaching profession.

State of the State address,
Sacramento, Jan. 12/
Los Angeles Herald-Examiner, 1-12:(A)2.

Many of our young people, on and off campus, are forcing a critical examination of obsolete social values based on the false premise that the only good education is one capped by four years of college. They are challenging and rejecting as unrealistic and snobbish the social pressures which imply that the highly-skilled electronics technician or mechanic is somehow less important or less of a valued member of society than the accountant or junior executive . . . We must strike a more equitable balance between meeting the educational needs of the 20 per cent of students who start and finish 4-year college programs and providing occupational training for the 80 per cent of our young people who will enter the job market without a four-year degree.

At Los Angeles Trade-Technical College,
March 24/Los Angeles Times, 3-25:(1)3.

(Guarantees he would give to students): The right to be taught by a faculty which includes teaching as one of its highest priorities. The right to continue their education without interruptions, without threats of violence or disorder. The right to hear and digest all sides of all major issues; to weigh alternatives which include the whole spectrum of America's values

(RONALD REAGAN)

and political opinions, from the middle out to, and including, the extremes. An opportunity, regardless of economic status, to continue their education to the maximum of their ability and interest.

Before Commonwealth Club, San Francisco, June 22/Los Angeles Times, 6-23:(1)25.

James F. Redmond
Chicago Superintendent of Schools

It seems there is always some other activity or service that pushes education from top priority for funds. Last year it was new roads. This year it was welfare. Some day it must be education.

Chicago/The New York Times, 12-12:(4)7.

Wilson Riles
California State Superintendent of Public Instruction

We ought to think of the last year of high school as being the first year of college or the jump-off point for a trade. A youngster should be able to get off the ladder, take a job, get some experience and, if he chooses, come back and pick up where he left off. We have to build some kind of flexibility into our educational system.

Interview/Life, 2-26:31.

Harold Saperstein
President, New York Board of Rabbis

For many years, the Jewish community has been virtually unanimous in opposition to any form of government aid to religious education. But now, there is need for an intensified search for means by which . . . aid can be given within the framework of our Constitution and without violating the principle of separation of church and state . . . The insistence that those involved (in such schools) carry the full financial burden themselves has become increasingly unrealistic in the contemporary economy.

Before New York Board of Rabbis, Jan. 27/ The New York Times, 1-28:1,2.

Charles I. Schottland
President, Brandeis University

Never before in our history has Federal assistance to the private university been so important. Because never before have so many millions been attending colleges, and never before have we had such insistent demands for educated youth to man our public and private enterprises.

Inaugural address, Brandeis University, June 13/ The Boston Globe, 6-14:1.

Harvey B. Scribner
Chancellor, New York City School System

The schools of America nurture a climate of protest when they overly constrain the life of the student, when they perpetuate policies which serve to harass and antagonize them, when they unduly limit his decisions, when they offer him too little responsibility, and they fail to offer a real possibility and a legitimate means by which the student can influence those school policies which directly affect his education and his life within the school through democratic participation in his school.

Before Council of (School) Supervisors and Administrators, Freeport, Bahamas, Feb. 14/The New York Times, 2-15:33.

The public schools, in my opinion, cannot be reshaped in a creative and elementary way unless and until the education of teachers is drastically changed. Reform of the schools and reform of teacher education are inseparable.

Before Association of Teacher Educators, Chicago, Feb. 25/ The New York Times, 2-26:24.

(Regarding his job): It's been something like flying in a plane. One minute the sun looks beautiful. The next minute you're in a cloud, and you can't see a thing. Then, there's the sun again, looking more beautiful than ever.

Interview, New York/ The New York Times, 3-1:27.

. . . the "program approach" to school reform—so popular in the decade just passed—is obsolete. It is no longer enough to speak of educational reform solely in terms of the new math and the new physics; solely in the context of more books for the library and new equipment for the language laboratory; solely in terms of special programs for special groups of students; solely on the premise that a new school building equals better education; solely in the belief that more money would solve everything; exclusively on the assumption that the basic structure of American schooling is essentially sound, and that what is needed at most is some fresh plaster and new paint. It won't wash. We have traveled that route before and changed little truly basic in the nature of schooling.

At Superintendents Work Conference,
Columbia University, July 16/
Vital Speeches, 8-15:670.

Any government, at whatever level, that decides priorities so as to sacrifice public educational opportunities for children and youth is likely to preside over the beginnings of social disintegration.

New York, Dec. 8/
The New York Times, 12-9:33.

Milton J. Shapp
Governor of Pennsylvania

Education is whatever prepares the mind, the spirit and the body for a life of competence and joy. Education can and does take place in homes, on streets and playgrounds and at work; it also takes place—sometimes—in schools. Schooling, on the other hand, is what takes place only within the walls of a school. It is probably true that "the more education, the better"; it is clearly *not* true that "the more schooling, the better."

Before Pennsylvania Education Congress,
Harrisburg, Sept. 23/Vital Speeches, 11-1:50.

Mark R. Shedd
Philadelphia Superintendent of Schools

I'm asking . . . that the Federal government nationalize the big-city school systems of this country, that their operation and their funding be taken over by the government. I realize only too well that this is a drastic step, and I recommend it only after four years of fiscal

agony in Philadelphia and a good deal of soul-searching during the past several months. The job of rescuing the nation's urban schools from disaster simply has become too big for the limited resources of the state and local governments to accomplish . . . I see a national school system in the big cities, totally Federally funded, as the only solution. When a hurricane devastates the Gulf Coast, the government immediately declares a national disaster and steps in with great sums of money to rebuild what the storm has torn down. When the Mississippi overflows its banks and ravages the countryside, a national disaster is declared, and the government steps in to help restore what has been swept away . . . I contend that urban education today is a national disaster, and nothing short of massive Federal intervention will save it.

Before Senate Select Committee on Equal
Educational Opportunity, Washington/
The Washington Post, 11-3:(A)14.

John R. Silber
President, Boston University

Right now, the United States educational system justifies the most appallingly boring, incoherent, irrational sequence of courses in the freshman year (of college) that nobody in his right mind would take except that he's forced to take them to get to the sophomore year. And in the sophomore year, he has to put up with a great deal that is essentially degrading both to the human spirit and to intelligence in order to get to the third year. He may not get any sense of what he's about until seven or eight years down the line when somebody hands him a degree which is nothing more than a union card entitling him to practice. There's got to be something better than that. I'm not disparaging the union card. I think that vocational orientation is not merely all right, it's highly desirable. But we have got to introduce a coherent, meaningful educational program in every year of the student's involvement . . .

Interview, Boston/
The Christian Science Monitor, 11-22:13.

Alan Simpson
President, Vassar College

Coeducation adds to the variety of the whole

117

(ALAN SIMPSON)

educational experience. It is a lift to morale and everyone's spirits.

Parade, 1-17:9.

J. Carlyle Sitterson
Chancellor, University of
North Carolina at Chapel Hill

. . . once the university claims for itself the right to establish a right and a wrong position on the political issues of our time, it has, in fact, entered the political arena as an active participant. The university cannot escape the consequences of such action.

At University of North Carolina
at Chapel Hill Commencement/
The New York Times, 6-14:44.

Ed Stewart
Deputy Minister of Education
of Ontario, Canada

Education was previously seen as the answer to all problems. But people aren't sure now that the world's a better place. "Students are raising a rumpus; they're not even grateful," they say. So what kinds of programs should we have? It all adds up to a lack of confidence in educational leadership.

Interview, Toronto/
The Christian Science Monitor, 10-23:9.

Willis M. Tate
President, Southern Methodist University

We say "student unrest" when we are talking about student disruption, student disrespect, student violence. Student unrest is something different. I'm all for student unrest, because all progress came from people who were restless . . . Columbus was one of the most restless men in history.

Before Woman's Auxiliary, Dallas (Tex.)
County Medical Society, Jan. 6/
The Dallas Times Herald, 1-7:(B)3.

Harold Taylor
Former president,
Sarah Lawrence College

There is deep irony in the fact that the educational reform on the campuses has had its main thrust in the agitation and criticism of students; and they have been met with a mixture of sympathy, skepticism, aloofness, opposition and repression. Faculty members and educators should at least be as interested in education as students, their parents, politicians and government officials.

At Southern Methodist University,
March 5/The Dallas Times Herald, 3-6:(A)7.

Martin Trow
Professor of Sociology, University
of California at Berkeley

There are two things that fuel campus unrest. The war (in Vietnam) is one; it is immensely unpopular. The second factor is that no one makes proper allowance for the power of a few people. Most of us aren't aware that 20 or 30 activists can prevent (Henry) Cabot Lodge from speaking, or burn down a Bank of America. Campus unrest is not a function of an enraged populace. It's a highly organized business.

Newsweek, 2-22:62.

Jack Vaughn
President, National Urban Coalition

The university should be very careful about getting into the field of problem-solving. To solve problems, you must be willing to throw out your theories and models and deal with "facts." You have to be "relevant." You have to have "power." Now, the more the universities do that, the more they become part of the problem. They become indistinguishable from what every other political group is doing. No better. No worse.

Before New England district, American
College Public Relations Association,
Hartford, Conn./The Wall Street Journal,
5-19:14.

Eric A. Walker
Former president,
Pennsylvania State University

Educators rarely ask how much money can be saved and how costs can be lowered, how the system can become more efficient, how it can deliver more education per dollar spent.

The key is efficiency—efficiency in education, efficiency in teaching, and the reduction of costs which modern technology makes possible. But in a university community, "efficiency" is almost a dirty word.

U.S. News & World Report, 5-10:29.

W. Allen Wallis
Chancellor, University of Rochester

Most people outside universities seem to believe that the root of the Great Campus Craze (of 1965 through 1970) was what they call, all in one word, the "radicalfaculty." There is a sense in which faculty were the root of the trouble; but it is not the sense that the outsiders have in mind. Very few faculty members were overt inciters and active participants, though the outside public seems to think that most were. Far more faculty sought to prevent disruption than sought to create it. By far, the most important way that faculties shared the responsibility for the Great Campus Craze was by failing to impart to students and young colleagues an understanding of, much less respect and reverence for, the central moral and intellectual ideals of a university. Too often, they betrayed those ideals themselves, by subordinating them to passing issues asserted to be of surpassing importance.

At University of Rochester Trustees'
Dinner for the Faculties/
The Wall Street Journal, 2-26:8.

Jacqueline Grennan Wexler
President, Hunter College

When a Cabinet wife (Martha Mitchell, wife of the Attorney General) can be quoted as saying, "The academic society is responsible for all our troubles in the country," we are getting the kind of random firing of a sniper gone amok.

Interview/Los Angeles Times, 3-23:(1)2.

Robert I. White
President, Kent State University, Ohio

The presidency is now totally consuming and has been for some time. Its unending confiscation of all time and thought destroys home and

personal life . . . At the same time, the rewards and satisfactions are far less than they used to be; and new demands cascade in torrents.

Announcing his intention to resign/
Plainview (Tex.) Daily Herald, 3-9:12.

Jack K. Williams
President, Texas A&M University

We may continue to have in some parts of our country disruption and violence by the ragtag of student and nonstudent activists, together with their camp followers and ego trippers. But . . . we will witness a quicker reaction to episodes involving these indefensible maneuevers. Police in strength will be called without hesitation; those identified as leaders of felonious conduct and as inciters of riots will be moved off campus. (Such action) will be openly and soundly supported by students themselves . . . I believe that all who have interest in the welfare of education are demanding that these malcontents not be allowed to interfere further with the educational process.

Inauguration address, College Station, Tex.,
April 16/The Dallas Times Herald, 4-16:(A)9.

Harris L. Wofford, Jr.
President, Bryn Mawr College

Education should free man. In the classical definition of liberal education, man should be able to be his own teacher. Education should develop man's intellectual capacity to do what he wants to do; to option for what he puts his hands and mind to. It should enable him to live an effective life. Education should be a preparation for life-long freedom.

Interview, Bryn Mawr, Pa./
The Christian Science Monitor, 1-16:(B)8.

Bernard Wolfman
Dean, University of Pennsylvania
Law School

A professor is really much more in control of what he does than a dean is. A professor is as close to being a free man in American society as anyone can come.

Interview/The New York Times, 1-22:37.

Charles E. Young
Chancellor, University
of California at Los Angeles

The university serves best by attempting in a very broad way to see that we have the necessary knowledge, that we have people who are properly educated to use that knowledge and that the problems which confront us are sufficiently well identified and understood to be dealt with appropriately. All of us associated with the university must strive to see to it that we ourselves develop a proper understanding of this role in principle, that we make such an understanding operational and that we communicate this understanding to the public at large. If we succeed in that task, I believe we will have come a long way toward re-establishing the level of support—both tangible and intangible—which the university must have if it is to succeed in its several missions.

At UCLA commencement/
Los Angeles Times, 6-27:(H)3.

Paul E. Zinner
Professor of Political Science,
University of California at Davis

Education is the most precious possession that people can have; and the university has traditionally provided it. At this stage of our societal development, there is increasing premium on quality and quantity of education. All people should have an opportunity for well-being, and for that a university is vital. The new horizons won't be overcome by pioneers with guts and courage alone. I look at education as the front line for advancement of society toward dignity and happiness.

Interview/San Francisco Examiner, 7-19:12.

The Environment

I. W. Abel
President, United Steelworkers of America

We are increasingly being confronted by claims from industry that the demands made on it by citizens and government will not control pollution but rather will bring complete stoppage of plant operations. This is a throwback to the antiquated escape route of "smoke means jobs." It is environmental blackmail of the worst sort.

Plainview (Tex.) Daily Herald, 9-3:6.

Spiro T. Agnew
Vice President of the United States

The damage caused by the air pollution from sulfur oxides alone has been estimated at more than $8 billion annually. And the total damage done by all forms of pollution to property, crops, wild life and human health is beyond practical estimate. Compared to those unrecorded but very real costs, the price of pollution control will be low.

Before National Pollution Control Conference, Detroit, April 14/The Washington Post, 4-15:(A)2.

William G. Agnew
Director of emissions research,
General Motors Corporation

(Regarding the cost of reducing automobile air pollution): Critics say take it out of profits. Well, what are profits? Profits are return on investment to the stockholders. When you say take it out of profits, you're saying take it out of the stockholders' pockets. It's the people who are going to have to pay; it is not some inanimate corporation somewhere.

The New York Times, 1-17:(4)7.

Wendell R. Anderson
Governor of Minnesota

The greatest political barrier to effective pollution control is the threat of our worst polluters to move their factories out of any state that seriously tries to protect the environment.

Before House Public Works Committee, Washington, Dec. 9/ The Washington Post, 12-10:(A)8.

Ben Barnes
Lieutenant Governor of Texas

There is tyranny in modern civilization as well as promise. There is tyranny of ugliness, of pollution, of the loss of individual liberty, of the waste of human resources, of government ineptitude and financial paralysis. (There are days when) smog covers our major cities and oil blackens our sandy beaches. Where there were rolling hills and open spaces, there is urban sprawl and traffic jams. We must control civilization and make it work for us. We must be its masters rather than its slaves.

Inauguration address, Austin, Jan. 19/ The Dallas Times-Herald, 1-20:(AA)1.

Earle B. Barnes
President, Dow Chemical U.S.A.

Not all countries are as conscious of the environment as the U.S. There is at least a short-range advantage for some countries to produce more cheaply because manufacturers are not being pressed as fast or as hard to clean up their plants. Personally, I think this advantage is very short-ranged. This world of ours is very small. For the country that sleeps now on the need for rigid environmental control, there will be a large future bill for delayed action.

Before Synthetic Organic Chemicals Manufacturers Association, New York/ The Wall Street Journal, 11-8:10.

Birch Bayh
United States Senator, D–Ind.

Beautification is not at the top of everyone's list of priorities, but it is symbolic of a need to change attitudes if we are to solve our problems too. We all sing, talk and think "America the beautiful," but too few are willing to have pride in the way their neighborhoods and highways look.

> *At Outdoor Advertising Association*
> *of America convention, New York/*
> *The New York Times, 11-3:54.*

Karl R. Bendetsen
Chairman, U.S. Plywood-Champion Papers, Inc.

With a few noteworthy exceptions, American industry has opposed almost every Federal legislative proposal having to do with the control of water pollution that has been advanced in the last 15 years. Despite industry's opposition, most of these proposals found their way into law. When this happened, we rationalized that industry's opposition at least resulted in "laws that we can live with." It has also resulted, in the eyes of some, in laws so slow and cumbersome in their operation that they cannot control pollution.

> *Before American Paper Institute Open Forum,*
> *New York/The Wall Street Journal, 4-27:18.*

Mario Biaggi
United States Representative, D–N.Y.

The theatricals of riding bikes or banning cars for a few hours on Madison Avenue (New York) by our city fathers to dramatize Earth Week is a safe one-shot gimmick. The real test between promise and performance would be for the city fathers to jump into and swim in both the Hudson and East Rivers, where 325 million gallons of totally untreated filthy raw sewage is discharged each day by the city.

> *The New York Times, 4-19:30.*

Daniel J. Boorstin
*Director, National Museum of Science
and Technology, Washington*

We sputter against the polluted environment as if it was invented in the age of the automobile. We compare our smoggy air not with the odor of horse dung and the plague of flies and the smell of garbage which filled cities in the past, but with the honeysuckle perfumes of some non-existent City Beautiful. We forget that, even though the water in many cities today is not as spring-pure nor as palatable as we would like, for most of history the water of the cities—and of the countrysides—was undrinkable.

> *San Francisco Examiner, 2-1:34.*

Norman E. Borlaug
Nobel Prize-winning agronomist

I have dedicated myself to finding better methods of feeding the world's starving populations. Without DDT and other important agricultural chemicals, our goals are simply unattainable, and starvation and world chaos will result. I have spent my life working with the nations of the world to help them feed themselves. I know how they will react if we terminate uses of DDT in this country and, in effect, label it "poison." "If it is not good enough for your purposes," they will reason, "then it shouldn't be used in our countries." The impact will be catastrophic . . . There has not been one shred of reliable evidence that DDT has put any species of wildlife in danger . . . the argument that pesticides are upsetting the balance of nature is utter nonsense.

> *News conference, Washington, Oct. 7/*
> *Los Angeles Herald-Examiner, 10-8:(A)4.*

Thornton F. Bradshaw
President, Atlantic Richfield Company

There is a school of environmentalists that believes we have to slow down our economy, we have to change our way of life—not only because we are wasting resources for the future, but because it isn't a very good way to live and because we are polluting the atmosphere and we are getting ourselves crowded into cities and the quality of life has deteriorated. Now, there is a lot in that which is very difficult to disagree with. But on the other hand, in the short run, no nation changes its form of life except through repressive government action. We have about 30 million people below the poverty level in this country; and they are not going to be satisfied if the spigots are turned off before they get a taste of prosperity. And in addition to poverty, we have enormous unsolved social problems—education, medicine, racism and so on. Solving these problems requires wealth —wealth in the economic sense of the word. A poor nation can't tackle and solve these problems. So I don't want to see America slow down, frankly. I want to see us devote more and more of our national wealth to the solution of these social problems. If we slow down, the pie is going to get smaller; and the slice that we can devote to the solution of environmental problems and the solution of social problems will be that much smaller.

Interview/U.S. News & World Report, 5-10:91.

Andrew F. Brimmer
Member, Federal Reserve Board

We must face squarely an inescapable fact: There is a fundamental conflict between our efforts to maximize the growth of our gross national product as traditionally defined and our effort to devote a substantial share of our real resources to pollution control . . . The rate of growth of real output in the U.S. depends heavily on the pace of investment in plant and equipment to expand productive capacity. With much more of our net investment being channeled into pollution abatement, the rate of expansion of the American economy as a whole will probably slow down perceptibly. The fundamental question that must be asked is this: Are we prepared to pay these real costs? Only the American people as a whole can answer.

U.S. News & World Report, 8-23:49.

David Brower
Environmentalist;
Former executive director, Sierra Club

There is no more than $25 million a year being spent in the whole area of conservation. General Motors spills that much.

Quote, 1-31:97.

We cannot maintain our standard of living unless we sharply curtail our use of all forms of energy except, perhaps, wind. The search for

energy fuel, its development, its transportation and its eventual use all combine to cost the earth too much. Until now, we've never had to consider how deeply we've dug into the earth's environmental capital to fuel the industrial revolution. We've just gone merrily on, doubling our demands every decade or so. I think we're now traveling at a speed where the next doubling will be fatal to mankind. History won't help us, because there is no history of anyone's traveling so fast. If we define the standard of living as the number of energy-consuming conveniences we have, then that standard really must drop. I go along with the biologist Les Pengelly of Montana, who says: "Forget the standard of living. I want to live a better life." Let me put it this way: If it takes war to make jobs, then we don't want jobs that badly. And if it requires pollution to make the economy go fast, we don't need that much speed. If we knock out this planet's life-support system, then we'll all be below the poverty level.

Interview/U.S. News & World Report, 7-5:64.

Earl L. Butz
Secretary of Agriculture of the United States

Without the modern input of chemicals, of pesticides, of antibiotics, of herbicides, we simply couldn't do the job (of feeding 206 million Americans). Before we go back to an organic agriculture in this country, somebody must decide which 50 million Americans we are going to let starve or go hungry; and I don't want to make that decision.

TV-radio interview/"Meet the Press," National Broadcasting Company, Washington, 12-12.

J. Phil Campbell
Under Secretary of Agriculture of the United States

There is a popular myth that is widespread in this country that farmers are well-heeled millionaires who need pesticides only to help buy the accessories for their luxurious limousines. Nothing could be further from the truth; and we believe that the public and decision-makers in government need to have a clearer picture of the facts. It is true that a few agricultural

(J. PHIL CAMPBELL)

producers have very high incomes. It is true that 30 per cent of the farmers, those with sales over $10,000, produce 80 per cent of cash receipts from agricultural products. The average net income per farm operator from farming in 1970 was about $5,400. We believe the livelihood of these people—their need to earn a living—the inability of many of them to earn it in any other way—should be the criterion, second in importance to public health, in the consideration of pesticide benefits and hazards. To do otherwise—to put the deleterious effects of pesticides on a few species of esthetically-desirable birds ahead of the needs of people —would be a perversion of human values. We hear no demands to tear down apartments, to rip up existing superhighways, to close the public parks and swimming beaches, to eliminate cities and suburbs, all of which have encroached and threatened the existence of birds more than all our pesticides.

Before House Committee on Agriculture, Washington/The National Observer, 3-15:11.

Lord Caradon
Chairman, Family Planning Association International; Former British Ambassador to the United Nations

If we bring children into the world without giving them some reasonable expectation of survival and some hope of human dignity, it will be a waste, a criminal waste, an utterly unforgiveable waste, of the most precious thing in the world—the potentiality of the human personality. Some still maintain that numbers alone make strength. I heard a Nigerian recently boast that in a few more decades Nigeria will have a hundred million people, and that consequently Nigeria will be the strongest nation in Africa. Not so, I fear . . . Strength comes from the conservation of resources and constructive development, not from spreading limited resources ever thinner to meet the widening and insatiable demand. The conception of strength by numbers is a delusion and a deception.

The Christian Science Monitor, 8-11:14

F. J. Clarke
Lieutenant General and Chief of Engineers, United States Army

When Theodore Roosevelt became President in 1901, things were in some ways as bad as some people describe them to be today. About four-fifths of America's primeval forest had been levelled. Soil fertility was becoming exhausted in some areas and, in others, prairie soil had been exposed to wind and rain erosion. An estimated one-third of the wild bird population had been destroyed. Some native wildlife species had been exterminated; others, like the buffalo, beaver and seal, were endangered. Many rivers were in far worse shape than they are today. Sewage, sanitation and disease control were major problems; the accumulations of manure in city streets and alleys were subjects of outcry and alarm . . . Under Theodore Roosevelt's leadership, a brand new idea in world history was hammered out and brought into workable shape—an idea that has been called America's foremost truly original contribution to human thought: the Conservation concept . . . Today, we have more and bigger and better-managed forests than we had then . . . Whole major rivers, which formerly knew only rough fish if any, have been transformed into prime fish habitat. We have more game preserves. The buffalo population has increased. Endangered species have been rescued. Soil and watershed and grassland management programs extend across the nation. We have hundreds more lakes, and have them in regions where lakes were unknown before . . And we have all these things despite the fact that during that time our population has more than doubled, our productivity has multiplied many times (and) our standard of living risen to the highest ever known to any nation.

Before Red River Valley Association, Shreveport, La., April 12/ The Washington Post, 4-13:(A)18.

Barry Commoner
Professor of Biology, Washington University, St. Louis

We now know the (pollution) problem stems from the development of new production technologies which ignore ecology and which are driven by profit. The problem is fundamentally economic, and it's not going to get cured simply by calling for re-cycling and cleaning up.

Interview/The New York Times, 9-20:27.

Jacques-Yves Cousteau
Underwater explorer

The sea is the universal sewer where all kinds of pollution wind up.

Before science and technology panel of House Science and Astronautics Committee/ The Dallas Times Herald, 1-29:(A)2.

We must plant the sea and herd its animals. We must use the sea as farmers instead of hunters. That is what civilization is all about —farming replacing hunting. Fishing as we do it is hunting, and in the sea we act as barbarians . . . Until now, we have had the excuse of ignorance. Now ignorance is vanishing. If we go on the way we have, the fault is our greed. To take care of this will cost money. If we are not willing, we will disappear from the face of the globe, to be replaced by the insect.

Interview, New York/ Los Angeles Times, 7-18:(A)20.

W. Donham Crawford
President, Edison Electric Institute

The fact is, we need more power to do the very re-cycling of waste that is so desirable. We need it to operate the vastly-expanded sewage-treatment plants that a growing population demands. We need it for the immeasurably-developed system of mass transportation that our metropolitan areas must have if the automobile is not to make the human lung outmoded. We need it for the Herculean clean-up of the nation's lakes and rivers. And, not least, we need it if all who are just emerging from dire poverty are to enjoy a standard of living we have so come to take for granted that many now hold it in scorn—or pretend to. Those who have yet to enjoy it understandably prefer not to knock it till they've tried it.

Washington, February/ The Christian Science Monitor, 3-20:7.

Walter Cunningham
American astronaut

Putting a man on the moon was child's play compared to solving the environmental problems we face here on earth. But space flight has an important part in solving these problems. Before we can manage the world's resources, we must have a continuing inventory of those resources. Space is the place to conduct that inventory.

Before Natural History Museum Alliance, Los Angeles/ Los Angeles Herald-Examiner, 5-25:(A)6.

Alexander de Seversky
Aerospace consultant

The stupidity of the ecologist lies in his solution. He says the automobile pollutes; abolish the automobile. The plane pollutes; abandon the airplane. So we are pushed back to the horse-and-buggy age. Billions of horses. And we are buried in manure. That solves pollution?

Interview, San Francisco, Aug. 10/ San Francisco Examiner, 8-11:10.

Hedley Donovan
Editor-in-chief, Time, Inc.

I would make a distinction . . . between, say, a wildlife species literally facing extinction—there is a finality about that—and some of the desperate accounts of broader environmental dangers, where we occasionally read that vast bodies of water are being irretrievably ruined, or great blankets of foul air are threatening tens of million of lives, etc. I think it is fair to say that much of this talk is at least somewhat exaggerated. In terms of getting things accomplished and making people feel it is worthwhile to work at these things, I think is useful when journalists and people who get interviewed by journalists discuss some of the specific improvements and victories that have been achieved, along with the many menaces and uglinesses remaining and still growing.

At International World Wildlife Congress, London/The National Observer, 3-29:10.

B. R. Dorsey
President, Gulf Oil Corporation

The concept of a growing economy and the energy sources it needs seems to be on a collision course with the ecology of our environment. If it is, then something has to give; and it better be the growing economy, or we'll be committing mass suicide. I'm one of those eternal optimists who believes we can avoid a collision. We'll have to be careful. And we'll need all the knowledge we can get. The cavalry is not going to come galloping to the rescue. It is going to be the engineers.

At University of Texas at Austin/
The National Observer, 6-14:9.

Rene Dubos
Professor of Microbiology,
Rockefeller University

Should present technologic and ecologic trends continue for but a few decades, man indeed would be doomed—not doomed to extinction, but doomed to despicable ways of life.

Before American Association of School
Administrators, Atlantic City, N.J./
The Dallas Times Herald, 2-25:(A)3.

Some believe the ultimate danger is atomic warfare; but I won't even speak of that because if it happens, we're all done for. Several ecologists believe we're going to be poisoned or starved in the very near future. But I don't believe either will happen. I think the greatest danger is that we will continue to accept worsening conditions without realizing that, little by little, we are spoiling the very quality of life.

Interview/Modern Maturity, Aug.-Sept.:58.

Paul R. Ehrlich
Professor of Biology, Stanford University

. . . today roughly 37 per cent of the people of the world are under 15 and, in the developing countries, some 40 to 45 per cent are. This means that the parents are already born who are going to produce the next great spurt of population growth . . . Even if there were an instantaneous miracle in the area of population control, and the average family size worldwide dropped to, say, between two and three children per couple, we would still face rapid population growth until well into the next century. Therefore, unless the Green Revolution is capable of keeping up with population growth for at least five or six decades, we will in the future still face an enormous gap between the number of mouths to feed and the amount of food available.

San Francisco Examiner & Chronicle,
1-10:(B)2.

Henry Ford II
Chairman, Ford Motor Company

One of the troubles with the moralistic approach to problems is that it doesn't lend itself to rational solutions. If something is identified as a sin, like vehicle air pollution, then obviously it should be stopped 100 per cent right now. And if 100 per cent right now is impossible, the "bad guy" approach doesn't help you decide what's best. If you have to compromise with sin, you might as well compromise on a nice round number like 90 per cent on some nice round date like January 1, 1975. This is just what the Senate did when it passed its version of the new Clean Air Act by a vote of 73 to 0. After all, if air pollution is a moral issue, not a practical one, then there's no need to consider what's necessary, what's possible or how the benefits compare with the costs. One arbitrary compromise is as good as another. And as for the 73-0 vote, no politician can afford to vote for sin. Another trouble with the moralistic approach is that it keeps us from listening to each other. If the other guy is the "bad guy," then obviously he speaks for the Devil, and you should shut your ears.

Chicago/The National Observer, 2-15:13.

Donald Garrett
Director of research,
Occidental Petroleum Company

When we consider the resources of the country and the world, we come to the realization that many of the resources are vanishing. If, on the other hand, we look at municipal trash as a commodity and try to assess its potential recoverable value, it's really quite startling . . . perhaps $20 a ton. And this exceeds the value of most of the ores that are currently being processed. Solid wastes do represent really urban ore, a potentially attractive material for economic recovery.

San Francisco Examiner & Chronicle
(Datebook), 3-28:15.

William R. Gianelli
Director, California Department
of Water Resources

As a political ploy, the environment has surpassed motherhood, apple pie and the American flag . . . Yet just the use of the word can provide a cloak of right to the wildest of accusations. As a product, it has been researched, packaged, advertised and sold to the public with the type of enthusiasm that is usually only used for a new detergent.

San Francisco Examiner & Chronicle
(This World), 11-14:2.

Stanley Greenfield
Assistant Administrator, Environmental
Protection Agency of the United States

Organized citizens' groups remain strong, but the general public responsiveness (to the environment issue) peaked about a year ago. The intense drive is gone now . . . What we must do is build deep interest and concern about the environment into the very subconsciousness of Americans, and try to solve our problems over the long haul.

Interview, Palm Springs, Calif., April 22/
Los Angeles Times, 4-23:(3)13.

Philip Handler
President, National Academy of Sciences

Those who, in my view, exaggerate the nature or magnitude of the pollution problem nevertheless are on the side of the angels. They want a clean, healthy United States. To argue with that is nonsense. And they have generated a climate in which effective action should be possible. Our problems are to accurately assess environmental hazards, learn the processes which are involved and reach realistic public

decisions about their management. Public panic is as completely unwarranted as concern is justified.

Interview/Nation's Business, April.

Clifford M. Hardin
Secretary of Agriculture of the United States

Given our agricultural ability (for food abundance) and enough determination to help build a better environment, we can have both. With the right sense of priority, and with the support and involvement of the public, we will have both.

Washington, Jan. 6/
The New York Times, 1-10:(1)35.

George B. Hartzog, Jr.
Director, National Park Service
of the United States

As we become more urbanized, parks become more urgent. The parks really can become the links and roots by which an urban society can find some stability. They can give us a sense of place in a mobile country. For tens of millions of Americans, national parks and historic monuments take the place of local roots . . . The parks, the outdoors contribute to one's understanding of who he is, where he came from and where he might be going. He has something he can identify with. I find that people are coming more and more to appreciate this. There are many families that go to these areas today not necessarily for the outdoor experience, but because it is a deep emotional experience with them.

The Dallas Times Herald, 12-15:(A)17.

Thor Heyerdahl
Explorer

We can't go on as we are now (polluting the world). Laws must be passed immediately by international agreement. For thousands of years we've been fighting nature, but nature was strong enough to win. Now, during the last decade, man is winning his fight against nature—and it's a catastrophe.

Interview, New York, Sept. 9/
San Francisco Examiner, 9-10:5.

James D. Hodgson
Secretary of Labor of the United States

He (Malthus, in *Essay on Population*) was saying exactly the same thing then as people are saying today: that there are going to be too many people and that the world won't be able to accommodate everybody who is coming along. I really haven't found it in my heart to worry about this problem, in recognition of the fact that, 200 or more years ago, they were worrying about the same thing.

*Interview/The Washington Post
(Book World), 1-3:2.*

Hubert H. Humphrey
United States Senator, D–Minn.

More than 30 million people have abandoned the small farms and towns for the cities, so that 75 per cent of our people are crowded onto less than two per cent of the land. The result of all this movement has been a national crisis of the environment, which in many respects lies at the heart of today's focus on ecology.

*Before World Farm Foundation, Anaheim,
Calif., Dec. 8/
Los Angeles Herald-Examiner, 12-8:(A)7.*

Henry M. Jackson
United States Senator, D–Wash.

. . . as strongly as I feel about the environment, I will never subscribe to the idea that we have to slow down our economy in order to clean the environment.

*News conference, Washington, Nov. 19/
San Francisco Examiner, 11-19:16.*

Jerome Kretchmer
*Environmental Protection Administrator,
City of New York*

We will have to change our life-style so we don't demand as much out of the environment as we do now. A good example is garbage. We collect garbage in 1971 the same way the Romans collected it in 2000 B.C. They had a chariot that was made of wood, with a horse that made the streets dirty. And the Romans walked behind it in their togas and they dumped their garbage in it. We have a steel truck, with a gasoline engine that makes the air dirty, and the guys wear uniforms instead of togas. But they're still dumping it in the back of the same trucks in the same way.

*New York/
The New York Times Magazine, 4-25:38.*

William P. Lear
Industrialist

I had hoped that the government would come forth with some assistance (for development of his automobile steam engine) commensurate with their big mouth—which, of course, has been that they're going to spend billions cleaning up the atmosphere. And if they've done anything, they've just expanded their bureaucracy . . .

*Interview, Reno, Nev./
The Washington Post, 3-28:(B)5.*

David E. Lilienthal
*Former Chairman, Atomic Energy Commission
of the United States*

There is general disillusionment about what government bodies can do to protect people against the hazards of pollution, whether it's nuclear or out of smokestacks or in its effect on waters. And so we critics have helped to stir up one of the most important political movements since the Populist days; that is the organization of citizen's committees—of housewives—concerned with the environment. It should not be discounted. This is not a fad. This is a grassroots movement. What it has done is to repudiate, with very serious consequences, the government bodies as the source of protection in this field.

Interview/Modern Maturity, December:54.

Charles A. Lindbergh
Aviator

It seems to me that our ideals, laws and customs should be based on the proposition that each generation, in turn, becomes the custodian rather than the absolute owner of our resources—and each generation has the obligation to pass this inheritance on to the future. It is the mission of government in this connection to see that no individual or organization seriously or inadvisably depletes or destroys it. Few people value individual freedom more than I; but with respect to the use of our resources, I have to say, reluctantly, that government must step in and control—no, I don't like "control"—to monitor and guide how we use our environment. Individual volunteer action is grand—it should be encouraged—but it is not sufficient to meet national needs.

The New York Times Magazine, 5-23:29.

P. D. McTaggart-Cowan
Executive director,
Science Council of Canada

Lake Erie will not die in the next five years as pessimists predict; because while mankind is appallingly stupid, nature is exceedingly forgiving.

Plainview (Tex.) Daily Herald, 8-2:3.

Margaret Mead
Anthropologist

A baby born in the United States is 95 times the drain on resources of the planet as a baby born in India. It is absolutely essential to check population growth. If it is to be done, it must start with the United States. We must be willing to set the style for the world—and stick with it. We are endangering the whole planet. We will wreck the quality of life everywhere in the world.

News conference, San Francisco/
San Francisco Examiner, 10-1:26.

Arthur Miller
Author, Playwright

(Regarding a proposal to install 70 miles of transmission lines across western Connecticut): The question, I think, is how much landscape you are ready to destroy for how much progress. The hills of Connecticut, the soil and trees, took many hundreds of millions of years for nature to create. Is it too much to ask that more than four months be set aside to consider before we irrevocably destroy what took millenia to build? It is bad enough to see the ruin of beauty when the life of the people makes it necessary. But it is unpardonable when it is done because not enough time and money and passion went into its avoidance. Let planning take on the vision of Emerson's most practical observation. "The sky," he wrote, "is the daily bread of the eyes."

Sports Illustrated, 3-22:57.

Edgar D. Mitchell
American astronaut

It's so incredibly impressive when you look back at our planet from out there in space, and you realize so forcibly that it's a closed system—that we don't have any unlimited resources, that there's only so much air and so much water. You realize, as you look at that little spaceship, how important it is to start learning to use the resources properly, as we've been prone to avoid doing.

Interview, San Francisco/
Los Angeles Herald-Examiner, 4-11:(A)16.

Rogers C. B. Morton
Secretary of the Interior of the United States

Ecology is the most important thing in the world—until the lights go out. I am very understanding, but not altogether sympathetic, to the oil industry's beliefs that outspoken conservationists are contributing to a worldwide energy shortage. There are, however, some people expressing totally unrealistic opposition to progress . . . To go so far as to shut this important source of energy down or restrict it from developing would be so unrealistic that it would become an Alice in Wonderland-type of rhetoric.

At International Petroleum Exposition,
Tulsa, May 15/
The Washington Post, 5-16:(A)20.

(Regarding impurities in the Colorado River): The day will come when the President of Mexico is going to walk into the White House and say, "This stuff you're sending me is no longer water."

At Lake Powell, Ariz., Aug. 15/
The Dallas Times Herald, 8-16:(A)4.

As I look ahead, it seems to me that the country that is going to umpire the ballgame in

(ROGERS C. B. MORTON)

this world is not necessarily the one that has the most military hardware. It is more likely to be the nation that does the best job of managing its environment and extending the life of its finite resources.

San Francisco Examiner & Chronicle,
10-10:(B)2.

Edmund S. Muskie
United States Senator, D—Maine

The President (Nixon) talks a good game on the environment. But he has not acted—to enforce laws vigorously, to fund programs fully and to lead in making tough but essential choices. The signs of a sham attack on pollution are everywhere in the record of the Nixon Administration.

At Democratic dinner, Phoenix, Nov. 6/
San Francisco Examiner & Chronicle,
11-7:(A)8.

Today, the rivers of this country serve as little more than sewers to the sea.

San Francisco Examiner, 12-13:36.

Ralph Nader
Lawyer; Consumer rights advocate

Earth Day 1970 was an important event. It played a key role in raising the level of environmental consciousness. In 1971, however, it is necessary to switch the focus from educational activities to action strategies calculated to effect change. The large corporations have embarked on an advertising campaign to desensitize public concern over these crucial problems confronting the people. Corporate advertisements carry the message that the public need not be concerned about the environment, that oil refineries are good for ducks, that timber-cutting preserves forests and that gasoline can keep the air clean. The time has come to blow the whistle on those who would lay waste the earth.

San Francisco Examiner & Chronicle
(This World), 2-28:22.

It's interesting that the Justice Department has a list of the 10 Most-Wanted Criminals, but they don't have a list called "The 10 Most-Wanted Corporate Polluters." If it is unpatriotic to tear down the American flag, why isn't it 1,000 times more unpatriotic to pollute, contaminate the air, land, water and environment that make up the United States of America?

Cleveland, April 19/
Los Angeles Times, 4-20:(1)19.

There is no way of getting away from air pollution, unless you develop a technique of not inhaling.

Quote, 4-25:408.

John N. Nassikas
Chairman, Federal Power Commission

Every major industrial and economic decision that results in a change in our land, water and air resources cannot be condemned out of hand without sacrificing decades of important advances in our standard of living . . . (The challenge becomes balancing) sound environmental planning (with) national needs in order to maintain and enhance economic progress while preserving the ecology of our land . . .

The Christian Science Monitor, 3-20:7.

Richard M. Nixon
President of the United States

To subdue the land is one thing. To destroy it is another. And we've been destroying it. And now we must undo what we have done. You (young people) must help in this venture. It will require all the dedication you can bring to it—your brains, your energy, your imagination, those special qualities you possess in such abundance—idealism, impatience and faith. To preserve the good earth is a great goal.

At University of Nebraska, Jan. 14/
The New York Times, 1-15:12.

I have proposed to Congress a sweeping and comprehensive program . . . to end the plunder of America's natural heritage. A nation's history is written in the book of its words, the book of its deeds, the book of its art. A people's history is also written in what they do with the natural beauty Providence bestowed upon them.

Washington, Feb. 8/
The New York Times, 2-9:1.

I do not see the problem of cleaning up the environment as being one of the people versus business or government versus business. I am not among those who believe the United States would be just (a) wonderful place in which to live if we could just get rid of all this industrial progress that has made us the richest and strongest nation in the world.

Before National Industrial Pollution
Control Council, Washington, Feb. 10/
The Washington Post, 2-11:(A)24.

J. Allen Overton, Jr.
Executive vice president,
American Mining Congress

Make no mistake about it—the mining industry of the United States could be seriously crippled, if not put out of business, by simultaneous across-the-board demands to do everything yesterday . . . Unless the environmental requirements imposed on the mining industry are appropriate and equitable, it is safe to say that much of the future exploration and development of minerals will not be in this country but in foreign countries.

Human Events, 12-25:4.

Bob Packwood
United States Senator, R—Ore.

I would consider it a mark of progress if we had no more people in this country 10 years from now than we have today.

Quote, 8-1:97.

William A. Pate
Director, Maryland Division
of Economic Development

Let's face it. There has been a lot of unalloyed nonsense served up to us, without shame or apology, during the last few years (about degradation of the environment) . . . What is so distressing about such inanities is not

so much that they are uttered—and uttered seriously—but that they are not challenged. Environmentalism has assumed the sacrosanct status of patriotism and motherhood . . . Try to remember when you last heard of a responsible leader categorically rejecting as unworthy of serious consideration an environmentalist protest—no matter how illogical, impractical or downright silly it might be.

Before American Gas Association,
Washington, April 6/
U.S. News & World Report, 4-26:53.

Jacques Piccard
Underwater explorer

We are living more and more with the sea, and we are depending completely on the sea not only for food but also for breathing. About two-thirds of the atmosphere's oxygen comes from the sea, produced directly by phytoplankton or algae . . . If by pollution we destroy these algae, it is a real possibility that all life on earth could suffocate.

Interview, Rome, Jan. 22/
Los Angeles Herald-Examiner, 1-22:(A)3.

W. R. Poage
United States Representative, D—Tex.

Myths and distorted facts characterize much of the information disseminated these days about pesticides, especially DDT; and unless reason and sound judgment dispel the current emotional jag on the subject, Americans may be victims, rather than beneficiaries, of actions prompted by well-meaning conservation-minded individuals and organizations.

The New York Times, 2-20:27.

James T. Ramey
Commissioner, Atomic Energy
Commission of the United States

Some people have been questioning whether the rates of electrical growth can and should continue, and have been calling for a drastic slowing down or curtailment. In my opinion, this course of action is neither practical nor necessary. The continuing availability of abundant and low-cost electrical energy is critical to

(JAMES T. RAMEY)

the well-being and growth of our society. Our problem will not be solved by cutting back on the use of power, as some have advocated. Rather, we must learn to do a better job of producing the power while minimizing the impact on the environment.

Before California State Environment Quality Council, Sacramento/ The National Observer, 5-24:9.

William D. Ruckelshaus
Administrator, Environmental Protection Agency of the United States

Business sometimes says they want to be told more clearly what is expected of them so they can invest in pollution-control measures with assurance that their investments will not be lost. They deserve clearer answers than they sometimes receive. Nevertheless, the businessman who initiates control measures in consonance with the best available technology can be certain that no one will blame him or tell him to stop controlling pollution.

At National Press Club, Washington, Jan. 12/The New York Times, 1-13:65

I am going to insist, with all the authority I have and with all the powers of persuasion at my command, that all existing means of controlling pollution be applied, across the board, in every city and town and on every industry in this country—starting right now.

Before National Press Club, Washington/ The Dallas Times Herald, 1-13:(A)2.

Industries and businessmen that must operate in the marketplace of free choice know that they must change, they must adapt, they must accommodate to changes in public attitudes—or they will surely die.

Before National Industrial Pollution Control Council, Washington, Feb. 10/ The New York Times, 2-11:80.

The most important first step (in fighting environmental pollution) in this country is to stop pointing the finger of guilt at each other. None of us in government or industry or as private individuals is without sin. None of us has done enough soon enough to protect our resources and living space. It's clearly time to pull together and do the job that needs to be done to restore and enhance the quality of our air, water and soil. Pollution isn't industry's problem or government's problem. It is society's problem. It's a useless exercise to look for guilty parties.

Interview, Washington/ U.S. News & World Report, 3-29:75.

There are some who call environmental protection a luxury the poor can't afford. They argue that a loaf of bread is more important to a starving man than a little fresh air. If this were the only choice, they would be right. But the fact is that man should and can have both.

At World Wildlife Fund anniversary dinner, New York/ The Christian Science Monitor, 11-30:13.

James R. Schlesinger
Chairman, Atomic Energy Commission of the United States

(Regarding some environmentalists' objection to nuclear power plants): Environmentalists have raised many legitimate questions. A number have bad manners, but I believe that broadside diatribes against environmentalists to be not only in bad taste but wrong . . . the responsible environmentalists are keenly aware that the present situation can boomerang. If there are power interruptions, brownouts and blackouts, the environmental movement may pay a severe price along with the rest of us.

Before meeting of Atomic Industrial Forum and American Nuclear Society, Bal Harbour, Fla., Oct. 20/ The New York Times, 10-21:23.

Thomas R. Shepard, Jr.
Publisher, "Look" magazine

Our Disaster Group opponents have the most cockeyed set of priorities I have ever encountered. To save a few trees, they would prevent construction of a power plant that could provide essential electricity to scores of hospitals and schools. To protect some birds, they would deprive mankind of food. To keep fish healthy, they would allow human beings to become sick . . . Immaturity is also a characteristic of Disaster Man. His favorite question is, "Why can't we have everything? Why can't we have simon-pure air and plentiful electricity and low utility rates, all at the same time? Why can't we have ample food and a ban on pesticides?" I recommend the same answer you would give a not-too-intelligent 5-year-old who asks, "Why can't I eat that cookie and still have it?" You explain that you just can't under our present technology. This inability of the Disaster People to accept reality is reflected in their frequent complaint that mankind interferes with nature. Such a thing is patently impossible. Man is part of nature. We didn't come here from some other planet. Anything we do, we do as card-carrying instruments of nature. You don't accuse a beaver of interfering with nature when it chops down a tree to build a dam. Then why condemn human beings for chopping down a lot of trees to build a lot of dams . . . or to do anything else that will make their lives safer or longer or more enjoyable? When it comes to a choice between saving human lives and saving some fish, I will sacrifice the fish without a whimper. It's not that I'm antifish; it's just that I am pro-people.

Before Soap and Detergent Association,
New York/The National Observer, 6-14:9.

Anthony Wayne Smith
President, National Parks and
Conservation Association

American factories . . . are still belching forth intolerable quantities of poisonous gases and dust. The power plants are doing the same thing . . . Much of this pollution can be eliminated, and some of it can be converted to useful by-products. Regulation is coming, be-cause human beings do not intend to be smothered.

U.S. News & World Report, 11-22:60.

Athelstan Spilhaus
President, American Association
for the Advancement of Science

We are running out of an "away" to throw things away.

Reader's Digest, February:135.

Maurice H. Stans
Secretary of Commerce
of the United States

Understandable as the public's interest is for immediate solutions (to environmental problems), and justified as the impatience of the public may be, we have the obligation to see the problem in the whole, not just piecemeal. We cannot have single-track minds, in which the environmental issue overrides everything. But that is how some of the people would have us look at our problems. If we settle for quick, immediate solutions to one set of problems, we can catapult ourselves into others that are much more serious; and we are beginning to find that out. So we have to begin to look a little farther down the road. I think it is high time for the entire nation to weigh the needs against the demands and say: "Wait a minute. What are our priorities?" We need to weigh the requirements against our resources and say: "Wait a minute. Which can we afford? Which can we achieve?" We need to weigh technological capabilities against the timetables and the options and say: "How can we get there from here?" We need to weigh environmental goals against economic reality and say: "Wait a minute. How do the benefits compare with the costs?" In other words, the problem is: How do we develop public and private policies in which economics and technology are factored into every environmental assessment?

Before National Petroleum Council,
Washington, July 15/Vital Speeches, 9-1:690.

Edward Durell Stone
Architect

Everybody wants his own house on his own 50-by-100-foot lot. This is a mistake. Instead, we should build wall-to-wall townhouses facing

(EDWARD DURELL STONE)

on cul de sacs or courtyards, with several buildings having their own park in the center, well removed from cars. You can say that I prophesy that this is all coming in the not too distant future. The single family house is ultimately doomed.

Interview, San Diego, Dec. 13/
San Francisco Examiner & Chronicle
(Sunday Homes), 12-19:Page A.

Conrad F. Taeuber
Associate Director,
United States Bureau of the Census

The population problems of the United States are and will be much more a matter of geographic distribution and the way we use our resources than of the rate of increase in our total numbers . . . Changing standards and habits, in activities, technology and the style of life have much more to do with the accumulation and disposition of waste materials and pollutants than does the number of persons involved.

At Mount Holyoke College, Jan. 13/
Newsweek, 1-25:78.

William P. Tavoulareas
President, Mobil Oil Corporation

The people and government should keep an eye on what business is doing. Constant criticism of pollution is a definite good; because there is a tendency, when you are trying to make a profit, to forget other values.

Interview, New York/
The New York Times, 1-17:(3)5.

Stuart G. Tipton
President, Air Transport Association
of America

The tragedy of the slam-bang approach to environmental improvement is that it will turn a meaningful environmental crusade into a momentary fad. The economic toll will be so great that disillusionment will set in, and society will abandon the crusade before accomplishing necessary and obtainable environ-

mental objectives. The more desirable alternative is that environmental progress move forward at a measured pace, in accordance with the public's ability to pay the bill. And make no mistake about it: Environmental improvement is not paid for by faceless corporations or governments; it is the consumers and taxpayers who pay.

Miami/The National Observer, 1-18:18.

Russell E. Train
Chairman, President's Council
on Environmental Quality

I absolutely do not think that what we are dealing with is a confrontation between environment and economy. That's ridiculous. The costs that we see involved in meeting air and water pollution standards, for example, while very significant, are far less than the annual wage increases that the American people take as a matter of course. Far less. The American economy has adjusted successfully to a high level of wages, high level of worker security, protection and safety. I see absolutely no reason whatever why the economy can't adjust just as successfully to the requirements of a decent environment.

Interview, Washington/
Los Angeles Times, 8-6:(2)9.

There are those who see environmental policies as a threat to economic growth and to jobs. There are those who charge environmentalists with responsibility for stopping technological progress, with blocking important projects and generally retarding progress. Like most such generalizations, this is nonsense.

Before National Soft Drink Association,
Houston, Nov. 17/
Los Angeles Times, 11-18:(1)25.

Dow Votaw
Professor of Business Administration,
University of California at Berkeley

Americans have been raised on the growth idea. Recall those signs on the outskirts of small towns saying "Watch Us Grow." We are now discovering there are certain costs to this growth.

The Christian Science Monitor, 4-10:(B)13.

Lowell P. Weicker, Jr.
United States Senator, R—Conn.

Those who use the environment as packaging for national self-chastisement in all fields of endeavor deny a better life to their children just as surely as did the whole-hog polluters and despoilers of our environment. Let's make decisions on the best answers, not on the best monologues. If we concede to each other some good and decide intelligently, is that not better than condemning out of hand and deciding emotionally? In other words, let's get excellence back into both the package and its contents. The U.S. was built on building better mouse traps, not speaking derogatorily about mice.

Before American Management Association
Packaging Conference/
The Wall Street Journal, 5-11:18.

Jack D. Westman
Professor of Psychiatry,
University of Wisconsin

(Regarding noise pollution): In the home, a loud voice, a dishwasher, running faucet or washing machine can produce sufficient sound to mobilize bodily responses that cause narrowing of the arteries, an increase in diastolic blood pressure and a decrease in blood supply to the heart. The sound levels produced by shouting, intense arguing, a range-vent fan, a garbage disposal, an electric knife, a blender or a knife sharpener cause dilation of the pupils, drying of the mouth, loss of skin color, muscular contraction, reduction in flow of gastric juices and an increase in heart rate. The combination of any of these sources of noise, augmented by the background sound of a television set, clearly can cause or aggravate a state of heightened body arousal and general nervous tension.

Before Senate Environment Subcommittee,
Washington, June 28/
San Francisco Examiner, 6-29:5.

Samuel W. Yorty
Mayor of Los Angeles

(Environmentalists) cannot expect immediate solutions to problems that have taken many years to develop. They must realize that we know the dimensions of our problems and that we are correcting them as rapidly as possible. But I must warn the environmentalists that, unless reason prevails and harassment ceases, the entire economy of this nation will grind to a halt. I do not feel that the silent majority of this country wants to forego a paycheck or to pay exhorbitant taxes to further some of the "far-out" environmental proposals.

At dedication of Palmdale (Calif.)
Air Terminal, June 29/
Los Angeles Times, 6-30:(2)4.

Foreign Affairs

Spiro T. Agnew
Vice President of the United States

I have said that the "doves" of the Senate and House are well-motivated. However, good motivations and intentions do not keep these Congressional doves from being absolutely wrong in the policies which they urge upon the nation. Who doubts, for example, that in the late 1930s Neville Chamberlain was every bit as patriotic and concerned with the future of his country as was Winston Churchill? No one questions Chamberlain's love of country or his good intentions. But in his judgment of events —of what was right for England and right for the cause of lasting peace in the world—Chamberlain was wrong.

At Republican fund-raising dinner, Jackson, Miss., May 18/The New York Times, 5-19:30.

I don't think we can say that the Nixon Doctrine is a withdrawal from our role in the world. I think it's a reasonable reassessment of how that role is to be carried out; whether it's to be carried out with American troops every time there's a flare-up in the world, to act in a policing fashion, or whether it's a role to make certain that governments retain the capability to defend themselves against this. And, of course, the key to the Nixon Doctrine is the recognition that with the growing prosperity of a nation comes the ability to defend itself. So I think we're continuing to recognize that we must play a catalytic role in assisting these nations to get the capability to defend themselves.

Interview, Washington/ The Christian Science Monitor, 8-11:3.

I find these fellows on the (Capitol) Hill very disturbing, particularly the attitude of the Senate Foreign Relations Committee. Of course, (Senator J. William) Fulbright is going to get away free. Events will never catch up with him. He'll be dead by the time the results of what he advocates afflict this country. We're talking now about our grandchildren, or at least about the next generation. Then is when the blow will come from the Soviets. By that time, we will be so weak that we will not be able to respond unless we are willing to launch a massive retaliation that could blow up the world; they have been extremely clever in never forcing a crisis. Their method is to work around us and weaken us on every side without forcing a confrontation. Again I say it scares me, because these fellows in the Senate and in the House who oppose our foreign policy are doing things to this country which cannot possibly be reversed unless we start soon to do them. They will soon be irreversible.

Interview, Washington/Look, 10-19:39.

I am very much disturbed by the trend of American policy under which, prodded on by the press and the liberals, we are steadily withdrawing from commitments around the world. It is not so much that this reduces our power militarily to a dangerous level as it is that it erodes the faith other nations have that we are strong enough to do something should a crisis arise. When I went to Asia, I found that they said, "You can't do anything, really, if a pinch comes, because you are withdrawing." In the same way, when we sometimes appear to be retreating before the Soviets in some other areas, this erodes the world's confidence that the United States will really do what it says it will do. Frankly, it scares me.

Interview, Washington/Look, 10-19:39.

George D. Aiken
United States Senator, R–Vt.

I am convinced that neither the Senate nor the American people are of an isolationist mind; for we all know that the self-righteousness of isolationism is as dangerous to our security and prosperity as is the self-righteousness of misguided intervention.

Quote, 3-14:248.

The Nixon Doctrine ought to work. Nations ought to do more for themselves, particularly those countries which have grown so strong economically. They are long past needing any help from us. But what is good in the Pacific ought to be good for other parts of the world—such as Europe . . . Our low profile should extend there, too.

Interview, Washington/
U.S. News & World Report, 6-28:27.

Carl Albert
United States Representative, D–Okla.

Harry Truman saved the Western world with the containment policy, which was essential when the Communists were knocking on the doors of Greece and Turkey . . . But the doctrine of containment has become a little outworn. We need new Harry Trumans with the initiatives to meet the issues of the day and the changing conditions of time.

Interview/Los Angeles Times, 7-25:(F)2.

Georgi A. Arbatov
Director, Institute of the U.S.A., Moscow

On the one hand, the (Nixon) Administration well understands that within the country there is a growing unhappiness with foreign policy adventures, heavy commitments and the participation of the United States in aggressive wars. The government cannot but take account of this unhappiness. It tries to show that it is responsible to the mood of public opinion. On the other hand, the Administration demonstrates a noticeable nervousness that some powers, particularly those whom the United States confronts in the world arena, will notice the complicated domestic situation in America and recognize that this limits the freedom of Washington's actions. This nervousness apparently pushes some American leaders to adventurist actions in order to demonstrate that the United States government, as before, has full freedom of action and, in case of necessity, is prepared for any worsening of the situation, and can proceed everywhere.

Panel discussion, Moscow/
The New York Times, 3-22:10.

John M. Ashbrook
United States Representative, R–Ohio

If the President's (Nixon) domestic performance is bad, the foreign-policy record, save possibly for Vietnam, is far from what we had a right to expect in 1968. The principal impact of the President's Cold War conduct has been to confirm and deepen the illusion of detente . . . in direct defiance of his statements across the years and many specific pledges made when running for the Presidency three years ago. Considering the fact that his public reputation was made as a tough and knowledgeable anti-Communist, this has been his principal apostasy; and, because it involves the question of our national survival, it is also the most frightening.

Before the House, Washington, Dec. 15/
Human Events, 1-8('72)8.

Anthony Barber
Chancellor of the Exchequer
of the United Kingdom

The problems faced by the United States Administration, both as to the balance of payments and as to the domestic American economy, are immense. Here is a nation which over the years has shown a generosity unparalleled in history; a people who have been prepared to back one Administration after another in their actions to fortify the industrial world and to aid the developing world. They are entitled now to look to their friends and to call for a common solution to a common problem. And if some of us have been urging upon the U.S. Administration—as I have—some modification of the position they took on August 15 (President Nixon's new economic

(ANTHONY BARBER)

program), that does not detract from the responsibility of the rest of us; a responsibility not merely to record our gratitude but to act together with the United States to work out a solution of the immediate problem, and a responsibility, working through the IMF, to evolve a new international monetary system to meet the demands of the 1970s and beyond.

Before International Monetary Fund, Washington, Sept. 28/Vital Speeches, 11-1:62.

Joseph H. Blatchford
Director of the Peace Corps

The shame and terror of the Vietnamese war are bound to dampen our national ego for years to come. We are disenchanted. We no longer see ourselves as possessing magic spells by which we can make the world right . . . In our world dealings we seek today the voice of an equal, not a superpower. After being punched about the head for half a dozen years in Southeast Asia, we have gotten the message.

At American University School of International Service commencement, Washington/Los Angeles Times, 6-21:(2)7.

Chester A. Bowles
Former Under Secretary of State of the United States

(Regarding U.S. arms sales to foreign nations): It's a little bit like selling heroin. You say everybody's selling it, so we might as well get in on it ourselves.

The New York Times, 1-24:(4)10.

Willy Brandt
Chancellor of West Germany

The United States, in view of its trade and other interests, cannot be inward-looking. Or let me put it another way: A world power—there are not many world powers nowadays—cannot be an isolationist power in the old sense. If you reach the level of world power, a certain kind of commitment and world responsibility results from it. I think this makes isolationism impossible.

Interview, Bonn/ U.S. News & World Report, 6-14:41.

Leonid I. Brezhnev
General Secretary, Communist Party of the Soviet Union

(U.S. imperialism) seeks to dominate everywhere, interferes in the affairs of other peoples, high-handedly tramples on their legitimate rights and sovereignty, and seeks by force, bribery and economic penetration to impose its will on states and whole areas of the world.

At Soviet Communist Party Congress, Moscow, March 30/ The Washington Post, 3-31:(A)16.

William E. Brock III
United States Senator, R—Tenn.

We were all indignant, I think, and rightly so with the United Nations action in expelling Taiwan (Nationalist China) last Monday night. But have we honestly explored why this happened, the fact that there was a political circus on that floor that particular night, as members of the United Nations engaged in dances and slapped each other on the backs and traded opportunities to insult the United States and stepped on the heel of the big boy? I wonder if anybody really thought about whether this could happen in one night, or whether it has been coming for 10 or 15 years, and why. Maybe the why is because people do not have confidence in this country any more, and maybe the why is because we keep retreating; we have allowed ourselves to be patsies time and time again by nations that abuse our good hospitality and friendship, by people who take our largess with one hand and stab us with the other . . .

Before the Senate, Washington/ The Washington Post, 11-3:(A)14.

Edward W. Brooke
United States Senator, R—Mass.

(President Nixon is) beginning to assemble a mosaic of foreign policy that is pragmatic in style but virtually prophetic in substance. In his quest for peace, President Nixon's foreign policy entitles him to the trust and support of every American.

Before World Affairs Council, Boston, Aug. 17/The Washington Post, 8-18:(B)4.

James L. Buckley
United States Senator-elect, C–N.Y.

I, for one, am not prepared to turn my back on the rest of the world. I just don't think we have the option, given today's armaments, of being isolationists, as this was an option that I think was available in the 1930s.

Interview/The Washington Post, 1-10:(B)2.

If our compulsive anti-militarism is not soon brought to heel, we will find that American foreign policy objectives will have become irrelevant because we will be without the means of implementing them. It will be irrelevant that the United States is committed to the survival of the state of Israel, or that the United States opposes a Russian hegemony in the Middle East; because, in a showdown, the United States will have no choice but to back down. And once we begin backing down under pressure here and there around the globe, we will court the disaster of a third world war; because aggressive nations seem inevitably to overestimate the readiness of free men to back down. This was the lesson of the first and second world wars. It is a lesson which we will forget at our mortal peril.

At National Press Club, Washington,
July 14/Human Events, 7-24:5.

Robert C. Byrd
United States Senator, D–W.Va.

. . . I am constrained to say that our foreign-aid program has actually contributed to our own economic difficulties. We have lavishly poured funds into projects in foreign lands while withholding funds from urgently-needed projects at home—funds which could have provided the stimulant to make our economy soar. And our largess has strengthened those abroad who now compete with us . . . I do not want to see a vote against this (foreign-aid) bill as in any way a vote for repudiation of American commitments, promised or implied. I see it, instead, as recognition of the fact that we have reached a point of diminishing returns in what we have sought to do abroad. I see it as recognition of the fact that programs do outlive their usefulness. A vote against $3 billion more

for foreign aid means to me a vote for a return to hard-headed Yankee realism where America's interests are concerned—a realism that has almost been lost in the fuzzy thinking which has, too long, kept this program alive . . .

Before the Senate, Washington/
The Washington Post, 11-3:(A)14.

Chou En-lai
Premier of Communist China

Even (U.S. President) Nixon recognized, on 6 July 1971 in a press conference, that 25 years ago it would have been impossible even to imagine that U.S. prestige would have fallen as low as it is now. As he contemplates the 20 years since the end of World War II, the United States has suffered such loss of prestige throughout the world that even the President indicates his surprise. The origin of these problems, the lack of prestige, we know well: It is due to the attempt of the United States to dominate the world.

Interview/Los Angeles Times, 9-15:(2)7.

Frank Church
United States Senator, D–Idaho

We continue to see ourselves as the benevolent sentinel of what we still call the "free world"—when, in truth, it is mainly composed, like the Communistic world, of despotic governments that are the very antithesis of all we stand for as a nation.

At College and University Conference and
Exposition, Atlantic City, N.J.,
March 26/San Francisco Examiner, 3-27:2.

This country simply cannot afford to sustain such an outlay (U.S. foreign aid) out of habit, especially when in terms of its stated objectives—the containment of Communism, the promotion of economic development and the advancement of freedom—the program is on the whole a proven failure, whose termination is warranted on these empirical grounds alone.

Before the Senate, Washington, Oct. 29/
Los Angeles Times, 10-30:(1)9.

If we learn nothing else from the experience of the '60s, it will profit us immeasurably to

(FRANK CHURCH)

have learned that being richer and stronger than everybody else has not made us wiser. When it comes to wisdom, we are part of the pack; just knowing that will be wisdom enough.

Before the Senate, Washington, Oct. 29/
Los Angeles Times, 10-30:(1)9.

The major preoccupation of the present foreign-aid program is the massive disbursement of munitions, which we either give away or make available at bargain-basement prices. We ply half a hundred foreign governments with our weaponry. Most of the world has become a dumping ground for ships, tanks and planes, which we label as excess to our needs. Easy credit is available at interest rates well below the cost of money to the U.S. government. The military assistance program has become a preposterous scandal. It should be drastically curtailed, not enlarged . . .

Before the Senate, Washington/
The Washington Post, 11-3:(A)14.

Henry Steele Commager
Professor of History, Amherst College

(On five occasions in the past 10 years, U.S. Presidents) have mounted major military interventions in foreign nations without prior consultation with the Congress (the Bay of Pigs in Cuba, the invasion of the Dominican Republic and attacks on North Vietnam, Cambodia and Laos). None of these now appear to have represented a genuine emergency. None were in response to attacks upon the United States which implacably required immediate military reaction. None, therefore, appear to meet the requirements for the exercise of war powers by the President formulated by the makers of the Constitution . . . (All of the gestures to limit Presidential warmaking ability) address themselves to symptoms rather than to the fundamental disease. That disease is the psychology of the cold war. That disease is our obsession with power. That disease is our assumption that the great problems that glare upon us so hideously from every corner of the horizon can be solved by force. Abuse of power by Presidents is a reflection—and perhaps a consequence—of abuse of power by the American people and nation. For two decades now we have misused our prodigious power.

Before Senate Foreign Relations
Committee, Washington, March 8/
Los Angeles Times, 3-9:(1)6.

Almost every instance of the use of Presidential force in the past has been against small, backward or distraught peoples—just the situation today. Call the roll of the victims of Presidential application of force in the past: Spanish Florida, Honduras, Santo Domingo, Nicaragua, Panama, Haiti, Guatemala, a China torn by civil war, a Mexico distraught by civil war, a Russia and a Vietnam riven by war. It is a sobering fact that Presidents do not thus rush in with the weapons of war to bring Britain, France, Italy, Russia or Japan to heel. Would we have bombarded Southampton to collect a debt? Would we have sent an expedition into Rome to protect Americans against a threat from a Fascist government? Would we have precipitated a war with Britain over a boundary dispute in Maine? Would we land Marines in France if customs collectors did not behave themselves? Would we bomb Siberia for years if shots were fired—without any hits—at an American vessel? And does it really comport with the honor and dignity of a great nation to indulge its Chief Executive in one standard of conduct for the strong and another for the weak?

Before Senate Foreign Relations Committee,
Washington, March 8/
Congressional Record, 3-16:(S)3357.

As we have greater power than any other nation, so we should display greater moderation in using it, greater humility in justifying it and greater magnanimity in withholding it.

Before Senate Foreign Relations Committee,
Washington, March 8/
Congressional Record, 3-16:(S)3357.

John B. Connally, Jr.
Secretary of the Treasury of the United States

. . . I am afraid that we are heading, in the short run at least, to a wave of isolationism.

Perhaps it would be better expressed as a rejection of responsibility, as a flight from leadership. The vote on the SST (defeating its continued development) may reflect such a trend—a retreat in the field of commercial aviation. We're retreating in space. The war in Vietnam is winding down, and that's fine. But as a result of all this retrenchment, we are going to retreat in research. We may reduce research and development in many areas, including medicines and foods—many other things—as well as weaponry. Frankly, all this worries me. Too many people want to withdraw into a shell. They don't understand the responsibility of world leadership, the value of it. If the attitudes you see among many people in Washington prevail, then they signify a vast change in the structure of our country. It would mean an entirely different world for us.

Interview, Washington/
U.S. News & World Report, 4-12:57.

Alan Cranston
United States Senator, D—Calif.

We keep making the same mistakes over and over. We endanger American lives by getting involved in wars we should stay out of. Then, to protect them, we endanger still more American lives.

The Dallas Times Herald, 2-27:(A)1.

Rodger P. Davies
Deputy Assistant Secretary for Near
Eastern and South Asian Affairs,
Department of State of the United States

We have to come to recognize that withholding military or economic assistance is an ineffective tactic in persuading foreign governments to move in directions we consider desirable.

Before House Foreign Affairs Subcommittee,
Washington, July 12/
The Washington Post, 7-13:(A)3.

Ebenezer Moses Debrah
Ambassador to the United States from Ghana

What is (diplomatic) protocol? Not putting on a shirt and top hat; that doesn't win you

friends. It's the art of being decent—that is all.

The Washington Post, 12-5:(D)3.

Peter H. Dominick
United States Senator, R—Colo.

Survival of the world may depend upon the ability, education, training and intelligence of the men and women charged with the responsibilities relating to the foreign affairs of the United States.

The Dallas Times Herald, 1-29:(A)2.

J. William Fulbright
United States Senator, D—Ark.

Many years ago, a Senate colleague of mine said that we have laws enough to last 10,000 years, and what was now required was the wisdom that comes from deliberation. Something of the same might now be said about our foreign military commitments; we suffer from no lack of them; and what is now required is the wisdom to sort them out and determine which are in our interests and which are not.

At South Florida University, Feb. 4/
Vital Speeches, 3-1:294.

Russia plays for some of our people the role that we played for Castro and that we've played for Mao. We're their foreign devil, and Russia's our foreign devil. Candidates can get up and denounce Russia. At appropriation time, every year about this time, we always discover some tremendous new development in Russia that threatens our security. It's a ritual.

Interview, Washington/
The Christian Science Monitor, 3-19:3.

When it comes to anti-Communism, as we have noted in Vietnam and elsewhere, the United States is highly susceptible—rather like a drug addict; and the world is full of ideological "pushers." It is a fine thing to respect a small country's independence and to abstain from interference in its internal affairs. It is quite another matter when in the name of these worthy principles—but really because of our continuing obsession with Communism—we permit client states like Israel and South Viet-

(J. WILLIAM FULBRIGHT)

nam to manipulate American policy toward purposes contrary to our interest, and probably to theirs as well.

Before Yale Political Union,
New Haven, Conn., April 4/
The New York Times, 4-5:3.

Thirty years of war, cold war and crisis have propelled the American political system far along the road to an Executive despotism, at least in the conduct of foreign relations and the making of war.

Before American Society
of Newspaper Editors,
April 16/Daily World, 4-28:7.

The United States has over 2,000 major and minor bases spread across more than 30 foreign countries and areas, and virtually surrounding the Soviet Union and mainland (Communist) China. The extent of these installations is instructive. We maintain some 50 major bases in Japan and Okinawa, where we have invested $843 million in facilities. We have 4 in Taiwan, 41 in Korea, 7 in the Philippines and 8 in the Marianas. We have 12 major bases in the Canal Zone. I am referring only to major bases—the places where we have smaller installations and stations reads like a geography book . . . Unless we manage to bring under some kind of public control the enormous military bureaucracy abroad, we will end up as did the Roman Empire, which became so much of a slave to its foreign commitments that it died at home.

Before the Senate, Washington, May 18/
U.S. News & World Report, 6-21:35.

Most treaties have provisions for abrogation. But my judgment is that they often outlive their usefulness. Actually, it might be a healthy thing to review treaties every few years, like cleaning off your desk. Times change, and treaty requirements change with them.

Interview, Washington/
U.S. News & World Report, 6-28:26.

No foreign policy can be successful unless it has the support of the American people. Both

foreign aid and the war in Vietnam are prime examples. Foreign aid squeaked through Congress each year only because it was constantly being sweetened up with something for everybody—exports for business and labor, investment guarantees for the bankers, fighting Communism with arms aid for the conservatives, building schools and hospitals for the liberals and so on down the list. Foreign-aid bills have become a grab bag for everybody but the American people, who pay the bills.

Before the Senate, Washington, Nov. 9/
The New York Times, 11-10:9.

Arthur J. Goldberg
Former Associate Justice,
Supreme Court of the United States

Let the President not make further wars without seeking Congressional approval. Let Congress face up to its responsibilities in this area and insist upon being adequately informed before sanctioning a war. And let Congress not pass the buck to the President by ratifying undeclared wars through appropriations to wage them.

Before Senate Foreign Relations Committee,
Washington, Oct. 6/
The New York Times, 10-7:3.

Barry M. Goldwater
United States Senator, R—Ariz.

Let me tell you that if the new isolationists in the Senate and House succeed in forcing U.S. withdrawal from world affairs on a massive scale, the ballgame will be over by default.

San Francisco Examiner & Chronicle
(This World), 3-28:2.

Henry B. Gonzalez
United States Representative, D—Tex.

In Korea . . . we unwisely allowed men to be conscripted and sent to war without Congress ever having acted to declare war. The people soon became divided, and it was not long before politicians started calling it "Truman's war." And it was not long before political witch hunts began. Then we had Vietnam, and again we allowed men to be drafted and sent into combat without declaring war. And that became known as "Johnson's war." And now "Nixon's war." And it was not long before the country was beset by deep and tragic divisions that are with us yet. When will we learn? When will we learn the folly of Presidential wars? How long does it take us to realize the wisdom of our forefathers? When will we learn that only Congress can commit this country to war, and that if we fail in that responsibility, the result can only be division, confusion and invitation to chaos?

Before the House, Washington, April 1/
Congressional Record, 4-1:(H)2362.

H. R. Gross
United States Representative, R—Iowa

(Regarding the United Nations vote which expelled Nationalist China, while admitting Communist China): The United States, if it now has an inch of backbone left, should withdraw from the United Nations, lift its economic boycott of Rhodesia and do what it should have done long ago—assist only those few countries around the world that have demonstrated evidence of fair play and friendship.

Human Events, 11-6:12.

John A. Hannah
Administrator, Agency for International Development, Department of State of the United States

(Concerning American foreign aid): The U.S. is not going to be an isolated island in this shrinking world. You just cannot have a large part of the world's people violent, unhappy and prey to social unrest. We are either going to pay our fair share in the world or it simply isn't going to be a world worth living in.

Newsweek, 11-15:41.

W. Averell Harriman
Former United States Ambassador-at-Large

. . . you must always look at the best the other side has to offer, rather than looking at the worst.

News conference, New York, Jan. 5/
The New York Times, 1-6:38.

Summitry has become more or less standard practice nowadays. It is accepted as a normal form of diplomacy. But it can accomplish very little except for creating good will. It makes the peoples of different countries feel good. They are full of spectacle, and they allow the peoples of the involved countries to know each other better. Sometimes, when the heads of government get together, they can smooth over the rough edges; but in a brief time they can't carry on a protracted negotiation of a technical nature. On balance, they have value; but the idea that heads of government can go to another country and negotiate in a few days very complicated and previously unexplored, in-depth issues is really an unreality. The dangers inherent are that you put in all your reserves. There isn't anybody the President can refer to. On a matter of yes or no, a lesser official could delay by saying he had to refer to his government; but with heads of government, there is no one in the background.

Interview, Washington/
The Dallas Times Herald, 10-17:(B)10.

Fred R. Harris
United States Senator, D—Okla.

If I were President of the United States, I would seek to dramatize in several ways our new determination to normalize relations with the East in a way that would tend to draw affirmative reaction from each of the other countries . . . I would agree to return to Czechoslovakia their $20 million in gold bullion which we captured from the Germans at the end of World War II. I would go to Budapest and personally return to the people of Hungary the Holy Crown of St. Stephen (another national treasure captured in the war). I would issue an executive order agreeing to stretch out Poland's repayments to us for commodities we furnished them (under the Food for Peace program).

Before Town Hall, Los Angeles, July 6/
Los Angeles Times, 7-7:(2)2.

Mark O. Hatfield
United States Senator, R—Ore.

I trust that the Nixon Doctrine means something other than supplying the American

(MARK O. HATFIELD)

arms and the money, rather than the American lives, for the regimes we want to survive. I am most deeply disturbed by the thought that we are relying more on military hardware given to other countries as a primary means for pursuing our foreign-policy objectives and working for some kind of peace in the world. Further, it is the moral insensitivity of this approach that I cannot accept. It is suggested that our hardware, our ammunition, our planes, our bombs and our ships can all be used as long as it is not our men—but rather theirs—that will have to sacrifice their lives . . .

Before the Senate, Washington/
The Washington Post, 11-3:(A)14.

F. Edward Hebert
United States Representative, D—La.

I think we're trying to cover too many spots in the world. I think the butter is getting pretty thin on that slice of bread. I don't think the role of America is to save the world.

Interview, Washington/
Los Angeles Times, 1-3:(1)7.

Richard Helms
Director, Central Intelligence Agency
of the United States

On the one hand, I can assure you that the quality of foreign intelligence available to the United States government in 1971 is better than it has ever been before. On the other hand, at a time when it seems to me to be self-evident that our government must be kept fully informed on foreign developments, there is a persistent and growing body of criticism which questions the need and the propriety for a democratic society to have a Central Intelligence Agency. I am not referring to the occasional criticism of CIA's performance—the question of whether we gave advance warning of this coup or that revolt, or how accurately we forecast the outcome of an election or a military operation. By necessity, intelligence organizations do not publish the extent of their knowledge, and we neither confirm nor deny challenges of this nature. We answer to those

we serve in government. What I *am* referring to are the assertions that the Central Intelligence Agency is an "invisible government"—a law unto itself, engaged in provocative covert activities repugnant to a democratic society, and subject to no controls. This is an outgrowth, I suppose, of an inherent American distaste for the peacetime gathering of intelligence. Our mission, in the eyes of many thoughtful Americans, may appear to be in conflict with some of the traditions and ideals of a free society. It is difficult for me to agree with this view, but I respect it. It is quite another matter when some of our critics—taking advantage of the traditional silence of those engaged in intelligence—say things that are either vicious, or just plain silly . . . The nation must, to a degree, take it on faith that we, too, are honorable men devoted to her service . . . I can assure you that what I have asked you to take on faith, the elected officials of the United States government watch over extensively, intensively and continuously . . . In short, the Central Intelligence Agency is not and cannot be its own master. It is the servant of the United States government, undertaking what the government asks it to do, under the directives and controls the government has established. We make no foreign policy . . . We are, after all, a part of this democracy, and we believe in it. We would not want to see our work distort its values and its principles. We propose to adapt intelligence to American society—not vice versa.

Before American Society
of Newspaper Editors, Washington,
April 14/The National Observer, 4-19:3.

Hubert H. Humphrey
United States Senator, D—Minn.

Peace or war depends on how we get along with the Soviet Union. It doesn't mean we have to accept their philosophy. But we have to get along . . .

San Francisco, May 17/
San Francisco Examiner, 5-18:12.

. . . the time is at hand when we can make some systematic reductions in American troop commitments around the world. I would like to negotiate those rather than do it unilaterally; that's the sensible way. But the first thing we need is a total re-evaluation of our commitments—not with the objective of abandoning willy-nilly, but of finding which are really vital now.

Interview/Nation's Business, November:65.

Henry M. Jackson
United States Senator, D—Wash.

(If the balance of power continues to tilt in Moscow's favor) we could expect Soviet intransigence in negotiations and efforts at blackmail and intimidation across a broad range of foreign-policy issues, with a consequent rise in the incidence of dangerous situations. Beyond that, if present trends in the strategic balance continue, we could find ourselves in a situation that encouraged Soviet brinkmanship, with a resulting risk of accident, miscalculation and nuclear war. The motto of the Kremlin today is very likely: "No more Cubas." The Soviets may relish the prospect that, in future crisis encounters, we, and not they, will back down and accept diplomatic defeat.

*Before American Society
of Newspaper Editors, Washington,
April 15/The Washington Post, 4-16:(A)17.*

Jacob K. Javits
United States Senator, R—N.Y.

(Regarding the Senate's vote to cut off foreign aid): It has been a black day for the United States. By this vote it is indicated that the United States would propose to end its role of responsibility in the world commensurate with its size, importance and productivity . . . It is inconceivable that we will not have such a program and totally inconsistent with our will for a peaceful and prosperous world.

*Washington, Oct. 29/
Los Angeles Times, 10-30:(1)11.*

Lyndon B. Johnson
Former President of the United States

Let us never forget: We remain—and will remain for a long time—critically important to the world's security and its prosperity. We alone cannot bring stable peace in Asia. But

there will be no stable peace in Asia unless there is a strong and steady American interest there. We alone cannot bring peace to the Middle East. But without us, the prospects of peace in that sensitive region will be dim indeed. We cannot guarantee the security of Western Europe . . . but without America's presence and participation and interest, Europe will not enjoy much stability and security.

*At New York University, Nov. 15/
Los Angeles Times, 11-16:(1)4.*

Herman Kahn
Director, Hudson Institute

In American society, there is a lack of reality-testing, which can get us into trouble. Our people just aren't careful enough in foreign policy. They can allow situations to arise which should never have arisen. How does this come about? Well, there is a refusal to face problems in time. There is a lack of seriousness. But there is no law in any of this; there is no mechanism that I know of. Perhaps it is in the nature of democracy that foresight is at a discount, especially when the things foreseen demand unpleasant and unpopular measures in the short term.

*Interview, Davos, Switzerland/
The New York Times Magazine, 6-20:20.*

The United States is still the largest power, but not the overwhelming one it once was. It will still play the role of the world policeman for the next 10 or 20 years, but it will be doing it less and liking it less. In fact, the United States will probably only intervene in case of a flagrant violation.

*Before Women's Group of Dallas
Council on World Affairs, Oct. 19/
The Dallas Times Herald, 10-20:(C)1.*

Edward M. Kennedy
United States Senator, D—Mass.

The unfettered power of the President to draft young men has become a central factor in the loss of Congressional influence in the design and execution of American foreign policy.

The New York Times, 6-10:16.

Thanat Khoman
Former Foreign Minister of Thailand

I doubt that the Americans have the necessary moral fiber for world leadership.

Interview/The Washington Post, 12-27:(A)16.

Alexei N. Kosygin
Premier of the Soviet Union

The barbarity committed (by the United States) in Indochina, the disregard for other peoples, the rude flouting of their lawful rights and interests, and such action by the United States as actual support for Israel's expansion in the Middle East and opposition to a relaxation of tensions in Europe cannot but have a negative influence on Soviet-American relations. There arises the legitimate question: Where does the United States government intend to direct developments—to the preservation and intensification of international tensions or to a search for mutually-acceptable solutions of real problems? There is no doubt that, given a realistic approach to the present state of affairs in the world, the choice must be made unhesitatingly in favor of the second road. We are also convinced that such a choice would have the support of the American people.

Moscow, June 9/The New York Times, 6-10:3.

Walter Lippmann
Former political columnist

The United States is so big and so rich that no particular event in some small, weak country is of vital importance to it. Inconvenient, yes; but not vitally important.

*Interview, Seal Harbor, Me./
The Washington Post, 10-10:(C)5.*

In 1968, when I decided that I had to be for Nixon (for President), it was because I had come to the conclusion that we were at the end of a period of probably 40 years of inflation of foreign policy commitments; we had promised too much and committed ourselves to too much. There had to be a big deflation, and a man who wasn't popular couldn't lose much by doing such a deflation, which is always an

unpopular thing to do. And I think on the whole he's proving to be a deflationist.

*Interview, Seal Harbor, Me./
The Washington Post, 10-17:(C)5.*

Andre Malraux
*Author; Former Minister of State
for Culture of France*

Historically speaking, there has never been an American foreign policy. Of course, the U.S. has lived moments of great historical importance, such as its entry into the last two world wars. What is lacking is a sense of destiny. A great country subordinates its domestic policy to its foreign policy. President Nixon maneuvers as if he were the President of Luxembourg.

*Interview, Verrieres-le-Buisson, France/
Time, 11-15:43.*

Mike Mansfield
United States Senator, D—Mont.

There is no escape by national isolation from the complexities of our times. We will have to live with these complexities and work with them, and do so in cooperation with other nations of the world or in conflict with other nations. There is no shell of sky large enough to shut out the rest of the globe. There is no sweep of ocean. There is no electronic shield, no insulating web of missiles. Isolation is no answer to the nation's needs. But neither is internationalism some sort of incantation against the ills of international life. We will search in vain to safeguard our security and well-being by an internationalism which leads us to project military forces into the farthest reaches of the globe and to maintain them there without the comprehension of the people of this nation and without the understanding and cooperation of the rest of the world's people. That reality ought not be overlooked in an excess of concern in the Executive Branch that the American people will "retreat to isolation" at any suggestion of an adjustment in the present course of foreign policy. We would do well, instead, to note carefully the danger of persisting in a course which has already alienated many people at home and abroad and has led the nation a long way down the road to an isolated internationalism.

At Olivet College, Michigan, March 29/
Vital Speeches, 5-1:418.

I wouldn't say the country is making any turn toward isolation at all. That is an overworked word, a figment of the past. The world is just too small for isolationism. Communications and transportation have reached the point where we couldn't be isolated if we chose to. As for the Senate, I'd say we are facing up to our responsibilities in foreign policy. We realize that we might have to disagree with policies which might have been good 10 or 20 years ago. But this is certainly not any move to isolationism, but rather a facing up to the reality of the present and an overview analysis of the past.

Interview, Washington/
U.S. News & World Report, 6-28:24.

I think we ought to return to the old concept of foreign aid, which could best be described, I think, in what used to be known as the Point Four Program—people-to-people assistance rather than government-to-government; because I think much of the government assistance stays in the hands of the government and doesn't get down to the people. Aid in the true sense is worthwhile; but aid the way it's been spread out and misinterpreted and used in late years, I think, has gone contrary to the basic tenets of the Marshall Plan and its immediate successors. The ill and the hungry and the poor—those people ought to be helped. The underdeveloped countries should be given some assistance, but we have to change our methods and our procedures.

Interview, Washington/
U.S. News & World Report, 12-6:58.

Ferdinand E. Marcos
President of the Philippines

Even Americans seem prone to forget the good things they have done since the end of World War II. When I have gotten into debate here, I have said: "For an alleged imperialist nation, the U.S. has certainly been most generous.

Interview, Manila/
Los Angeles Herald-Examiner, 11-17:(A)8.

George S. McGovern
United States Senator, D—S.D.

Vietnam is just the most grievous manifestation of a world view that is based on what we're afraid of rather than what we stand for. I was a bomber pilot in World War II. I'm not a pacifist. I think we've now lost sight of the absolutely essential need for coexistence, even with countries with whom we don't agree.

Interview/Time, 1-25:21.

Wilbur D. Mills
United States Representative, D—Ark.

We need to be more cognizant, frankly, of the economic consequences of foreign policy than we have been for the last 40 years. We have made decisions that involved economic matters on our part too often in return for some political favor such as a vote in the UN, or something of that sort. We have given up far more on the economic side than we ever received in return. We must return to the old doctrine of "Yankee trader."

Interview/Nation's Business, November:71.

Daniel P. Moynihan
Former Counsellor to the President
of the United States

I don't think we're (the U.S.) good at ideological argument. Nuance and subtlety and quiet thrust are not taught at American universities, and it's not what we learn in American government . . . We have a lot of experience about how you run a decent country, but surprisingly little experience at describing the process. This is a weakness of our foreign policy and the strength of our democracy.

Interview, New York/
The New York Times, 11-10:16.

Edmund S. Muskie
United States Senator, D—Maine

Our military power is at a peak and our influence at a low. Power alone doesn't bring prestige, doesn't buy us friends and doesn't intimidate enemies.

At New York University, Nov. 14/
The New York Times, 11-15:24.

Richard M. Nixon
President of the United States

. . . when we talk about an era of negotiation rather than confrontation, we must remember that negotiation means exactly that. It means that you have two parties that have very great differences with regard to their vital interests, and the negotiation process will sometimes be very, very extended . . . Negotiation does not necessarily mean agreement.
Television interview, Jan. 4/
The New York Times, 1-6:42.

We have learned in recent years the dangers of overinvolvement. The other danger—a grave risk we are equally determined to avoid—is underinvolvement. After a long and unpopular war, there is a temptation to turn inward—to withdraw from the world, to back away from our commitments. That deceptively smooth road of the new isolationism is surely the road to war. Our foreign policy today steers a steady course between the past danger of overinvolvement and the new temptation of underinvolvement.
State of the World address, Feb. 25/
The New York Times, 2-26:13.

In carrying out what is referred to as the Nixon Doctrine, we recognize that we cannot transfer burdens too swiftly. We must strike a balance between doing too much and preventing self-reliance and suddenly doing too little and undermining self-confidence. We intend to give our friends the time and the means to adjust, materially and psychologically, to a new form of American participation in the world.
State of the World address, Feb. 25/
The New York Times, 2-26:13.

In all our relations with the Soviets, we shall make the most progress by recognizing that in many cases our national interests are not the same. It serves no purpose to pretend they are. Our differences are not matters of mood; they are matters of substance.
State of the World address, Feb. 25/
U.S. News & World Report, 3-8:52.

In past times, the No. 1 nation was always in that position because of military conquests. But the mantle of leadership fell on American shoulders not by our desire and not for the purposes of conquest. But we have that position today; and how we handle ourselves will determine the chances for world peace. Do you know, in all my travels, not one leader I have talked to ever said to me in private that he feared the United States as a nation bent on conquest. And I have met many Communist leaders, as you know. Whatever some of them may pretend in public, they understand our true troubles, and they are also thankful that the United States wants nothing—nothing but the right of everyone to live and let live.
Interview, Washington, March 8/
The New York Times, 3-10:14.

Our responsibilities are not limited to this great continent but include Europe, the Middle East, Southeast Asia, East Asia, many areas whose fate affects the peace of the world. We must, above all, tend to our national obligations. We must not forget our alliances or our interests. Other nations must know that the United States has both the capability and the will to defend these allies and protect these interests. Unless people understand this and understand it well, the United States will simply retreat into isolationism, both politically and diplomatically. We would, of course, continue to be an economic giant; but that is not enough.
Interview, Washington, March 8/
The New York Times, 3-10:14.

The day the United States quits playing a responsible role in the world—in Europe or Asia or the Middle East—or gives up or recedes from its efforts to maintain an adequate defense force—on that day, this will become a very unsafe world to live in.
Interview, Washington, March 8/
The New York Times, 3-10:14.

Our goal is no American fighting and dying anyplace in the world. Every decision I have made in the past and every decision I make in the future will have the purpose of achieving that goal.

Television address, Washington, April 7/
Los Angeles Herald-Examiner, 4-8:(A)2.

In today's world, declarations of statesman-like intent are not difficult; but instances of statesmanlike reactions are few.

Washington, June 30/The Boston Globe, 7-1:2.

We have been in four wars in this century, and four times young Americans have gone abroad. We have done so without any idea of conquest or domination. We have lost hundreds of thousands of lives, and we have not gotten a thing out of any of it; and we have helped each of our enemies, after each of the wars, get on his feet again. We made our mistakes; we make them now, for example, as we made them in previous wars. Let me say this: Think for a moment. What other nation in the world would you like to have in the position of pre-eminent power? What other nation in the world that has what it takes would have the attitude that the United States has, as far as its foreign policy is concerned? Here is a nation that did not seek the pre-eminent world position. It came to us because of what had happened in World War II.

Before Midwestern newspaper executives,
Kansas City, July 6/Vital Speeches, 8-1:614.

We presently provide military and/or economic aid to 91 countries in the world. I checked these various countries as far as their heads of government are concerned, and in only 30 of those countries do they have leaders who are there as a result of a contested election by any standard that we would consider fair. In fact, we would have to cut off aid to two-thirds of the nations of the world—in Africa, in Latin America, in Asia—to whom we are presently giving aid if we apply the standards that some suggest we apply to South Vietnam.

News conference, Washington, Sept. 16/
The New York Times, 9-17:27.

(Referring to the Senate's vote against foreign aid): If the United States at this particular time should determine that it will discontinue its programs of mutual assistance for countries

abroad—helping them so they can help themselves—it can only mean that the world will become more unstable, that the dangers of war will greatly increase and that the United States will no longer be a world power respected in the world.

At Republican dinner, New York, Nov. 9/
The Christian Science Monitor, 11-11:6.

I am confident that the United States right now is on the brink of exercising its power to do good in the world—such good as never has been done in the history of civilization; because we now can, muster our moral force, our economic force, and we, of course, have the military power to back up our words. Our aim is to build a structure of peace such as we could not dream of after World War II. We couldn't dream of this when Eisenhower was President; it wasn't the right time. It wasn't the right time when Kennedy was there. But now the time may have come, and we must seize the moment—seize the moment in our relationships with the superpowers.

Interview, Washington, December/
Time, 1-3('72):15.

Otto E. Passman
United States Representative, D—La.

. . . we are violating everything that made our country great, and all this started a few years ago with this misguided foreign-aid program. We have to dabble in everybody's business everywhere. We have no way of knowing whether or not these people (recipients of foreign aid) would have subscribed to our philosophy, whether or not anything that we stand for would be supported by them in reality; because as long as Uncle Sam is there with this black grab bag playing Santa Claus, you will never know, in all probability, their real intention.

June 21/Los Angeles Times, 12-12:(I)2.

William Proxmire
United States Senator, D—Wis.

Most of us in Washington have seen a lot of mismanagement in government programs. But military-assistance is the first program I have

(WILLIAM PROXMIRE)

come across that appears to be characterized by "unmanagement." The problem here seems to be that no one is in charge. In some respects, the United States has been transformed from the "arsenal of democracy" to a gigantic discount supermarket, with no check-out counters, no cash registers, no store managers—only clerks who blithely deliver to foreign governments of practically any political persuasion whatever they happen to see and like. For most of the stuff, there is no charge and no return.

Before Joint Congressional
Economic Subcommittee, Washington,
Jan. 6/The New York Times, 1-7:11.

. . . to give foreign military aid mindlessly, without either knowing the total amounts or considering the consequences, is incredible. To shove out billions of dollars in weapons of destruction without questioning the amounts or the purposes for which they are used is for the citizens of this country and the lawmakers of the land to abdicate their responsibilities and to cede power to the military which it should not be theirs to exercise except through the deliberate action of the people—and, I should say, the representatives of the people. We have given arms to two or more countries which have been used to fight each other rather than to defend against some common enemy. Weapons have been used to undermine political democracy and to keep reactionary governments in power. And more often than not, the decisions to do so have been made secretly and surreptitiously without proper questioning or debate as to whether they really defend the vital interests of the people of the United States, or whether they do not in fact undermine our efforts for peace in the world.

Before the Senate, Washington, March 8/
Congressional Record, 3-8:(S)2567.

John R. Rarick
United States Representative, D–La.

What has happened to America that we will not stand up to the Soviet threat? Are we a nation of pusillanimous sheep or of valiant and courageous men? Are we still the land of the free and the home of the brave, or have we become the land of the subdued and the home of the cowardly? Are we going to be blackmailed into selling our children into collectivistic bondage by the Soviet threat of a nuclear holocaust? The Russians have always backed down when their bluff was called . . . Will we go on allowing our fighting men to die in no-win undeclared treaty wars under United Nations auspices, or are we going to declare our wars and end them with victory? Are we going to keep on talking about the "peace," or are we going to end the war with a victory? Whoever heard of negotiating peace with Communists from a position of weakness? If America continues to pursue the present policy of seeking to win a nebulous "peace" through unending conflict instead of ending wars with victory, I fear for the future of our children; for the issue is not peace or war, but rather freedom or slavery.

Before the House, Washington, Feb. 26/
Congressional Record, 2-26:E1222.

Abraham A. Ribicoff
United States Senator, D–Conn.

We must reorder our priorities in foreign affairs, elevating the international economic problems to the high level of attention they deserve . . . American diplomacy in the 1960s toward Europe, (for) example, concentrated on NATO political-military issues; but these issues were of declining interest to Europeans. While we concerned ourselves with the NATO order of battle, the Germans were more concerned over orders for Volkswagens.

Before Senate Finance Committee,
Washington, March 5/
The Washington Post, 3-6:(C)7.

Hyman G. Rickover
Vice Admiral, United States Navy

(Regarding the U.S. becoming a second-rate power): For the first time in history, a great power is deliberately throwing away its inescapable obligations of leadership to adopt deliberate weakness as a national policy. This nation is well on the road to withdrawal from the facts of life—the long-ago discredited vision by which the old isolationists very nearly allowed Hitler and imperial Japan to destroy the world.

Before House Appropriations Committee,
Washington, May/
The New York Times, 9-27:16.

Chalmers M. Roberts
Diplomatic correspondent,
"The Washington Post"

. . . we have a terrible problem in the United States, what I call the baseball syndrome. We think that we ought to be able to get up at the end of the ninth inning, know who won and go home and have dinner. It doesn't work that way with the Soviet Union. The Russians make agreements with us when it is in their interest; but those agreements are pieces of a much larger framework. They don't make agreements to resolve once and forever, for the rest of human history, differences between these two countries . . . And we've got to get it out of our heads here that, somehow or other, a SALT agreement, a Berlin agreement, a Middle East agreement or any other single agreement is going to bring things into a nice status-quo framework. We as a status-quo power want that; they as a non-status-quo power don't want that. So that when the President (Nixon) says he hopes to move from an era of confrontation to an era of negotiation, it is a nonsense statement.

The Washington Post, 1-31:(B)5.

William P. Rogers
Secretary of State of the United States

Scientific and technological cooperation is not a one-way street. We have as much to gain as anybody from cooperation. Thus, it is the general policy of this Administration—and I'm sure it is not known publicly—to permit the exchange of unclassified scientific and technical information with the scientists and institutions of any country, regardless of the state of our diplomatic relations with that country.

Before House Science and Astronautics
Committee, Washington, Jan. 26/
The New York Times, 1-27:6.

America needed a new perception of its place in the world, a new unity and sense of purpose in its foreign affairs. That is what we are undertaking to achieve . . . By ending our involvement (in Vietnam) . . . we will restore perspective. By altering the character of our involvement in the world, we hope we will re-establish a balance in the conduct of our relations . . . My greatest hope is that the path we are now taking can help create among Americans a new national unity and purpose in our foreign policy; a policy no longer haunted by the past, but committed freshly to the opportunities of the future.

Washington, March 27/
The Washington Post, 3-28:(A)1.

In Richard Nixon, the American people have a representative who is idealistic enough to believe that a generation of peace is possible, and who is realistic enough to know that the only way it can come about is for a strong America to take the lead in achieving it . . . If ever there was a man with an open mind and a tough mind, it is the man who now serves as President of the United States. He will protect your interests wherever he goes and whomever he sees.

At American Legion convention, Houston,
Aug. 31/The Washington Post, 9-1:(A)10.

In order to continue to be effective in today's world, American foreign policy must maintain the principles which have brought our nation to its position of leadership: strength, a competitive spirit, a sense of fair play, a drive to excel, loyalty to country and pride in achievement.

At American Legion convention, Houston,
Aug. 31/The New York Times, 9-1:3.

The foreseeable future cannot be expected to bring an end to the differences between the Soviet and American political systems or to the competition between us. But it can bring important and beneficial changes in our relations. Many agreements have been achieved in recent years between us. The success of those agreements has stimulated the efforts to negotiate still others. Collectively they could promote

(WILLIAM P. ROGERS)

not just co-existence but, if we proceed to build on durable foundations, cooperation as well.

At United Nations, New York, Oct. 4/
U.S. News & World Report, 10-18:104.

We can't become an isolated nation. It would be a catastrophe for us to become isolated. We have conducted foreign affairs in a responsible and commendable manner since World War II. We have helped to restore Germany and Japan to strong positions in the world. We have alliances that have provided stability ever since World War II. We have by far the greatest investment abroad of any nation—almost as much as the rest of the world put together. Isolationism would be self-defeating. We benefit from world trade. If trade is free and fair, everyone benefits from world trade. After all, the great advantage that a free society has is our mobility and willingness to compete in the world. We thus demonstrate the success of our social system. Furthermore, we benefit from our willingness to share the successes we have with the less fortunate in the world. And certainly, the security of the United States is involved, because if one part of the world is at war, we get involved one way or another, whether we like it or not. We learned that lesson in both World War I and World War II. So for security reasons we can't be isolated; for commercial reasons we must not be isolated; and for humanitarian reasons we would not want to be isolated. For example, every time there's a catastrophe anywhere in the world, Americans respond—not just the government, all Americans. We have got to continue our involvement in the world. We have no choice. After all, we're natural explorers. We like to travel, we like to explore, we like to compete, we like to help—and we can't change our character as a nation.

Interview, Washington/
U.S. News & World Report, 11-22:34.

We have been undertaking extensive change in American foreign policy. We believe these are constructive and necessary changes. But in that process of change, America's partnership with Western Europe, America's support for its unity and America's commitment to its defense have not been diminished.

Before North Atlantic Treaty Organization
ministerial council, Brussels, Dec. 9/
The New York Times, 12-10:6.

Dean Rusk
Former Secretary of State of the United States

. . . we haven't become the world's policeman. Hundreds of situations of violence have developed since World War II, and I think we've been involved in about six or seven of them. We don't go around looking for business, places to intervene. But in those areas which we, by formal Constitutional arrangement, have decided, or did decide, were vital to our own interests and to the possibilities of peace—that means basically in Western Europe, this hemisphere and certain spots on the other side of the Pacific—then it is not only the immediate situation that is involved, it is the reliability and the status of our other security agreements and the judgments that might be made in the minds of some other capitals as to what might happen if they take one or another move. Now, it's unfashionable these days to talk about such things, but I myself believe that one of the principal pillars of peace in the world is the feeling on the part of certain capitals that we better be just a little careful because those crazy Americans might just do something about it. And if that question is ever transformed into a certainty that we will not do something about it, then I think we're headed for periods of very great danger.

Television Interview,
The New York Times, 7-14:33.

I feel in some ways the world has passed me by. An entire generation in foreign affairs—Truman, McCloy, Stimson, Marshall, Lovett, Acheson and others—is leaving the scene. It is a generation that, in my judgment, has written a record of progress, generosity and restraint. While it is passing, however, the younger generation has not yet focused on what their answers will be. When you say "no war," that doesn't necessarily mean an end to war. That might invite war. Remember the moves that

Stalin made when we hastily demobilized our forces after the Second World War. Half our population today has no memories of those events. World War II to them is just a chapter, like the War of the Roses. You can't blame people who have no chance to remember. But the difficulty is that my generation is getting old and tired of the burdens we bore. We are forgetting. Hence, we have a dialog between those who are beginning to forget and those who have no chance to remember. This gap can produce a period of aimlessness and indecision and unpredictability. It could be a dangerous period because of the possibility of miscalculation in foreign capitals.

Interview, Washington/
Los Angeles Times, 8-1:(I)7.

Terry Sanford
President, Duke University

Like other nations through history, ours has always relied on military strength . . . we have never felt the need to find, develop and proclaim an alternative to a foreign policy based on force and military power. But now, history demands that some great and good nation must be the first of all time to find such an alternative. The United States of America is . . . at this moment capable of leading the world into a new era of international relations based on moral posture and moral suasion. The height of the challenge now facing us, however, is the question of whether we have the nerve and the guts to apply our faith in moral strength and moral suasion to our international relations. Clearly, it will require immeasurably greater strength as a nation to assert a moral posture than a military one . . . if we had only abandoned our military draft—not out of weariness but as part of a new national policy of implementing moral rather than military force —we would have inspired the faith of peoples of other nations in the sincerity of our political rhetoric about seeking world peace . . . Risk is always inherent in leadership. And the risk both to individual life and to national survival is small compared to the far greater risk we run by continuing to drift, stumble and stampede along our present militaristic course of foreign policy.

At University of Texas at
Austin commencement/
The Dallas Times Herald, 5-17:(C)8.

William B. Saxbe
United States Senator, R—Ohio

The hatred of the military and the opposition we have to the war in Vietnam should not be so strong that it blinds us to the world role that we in this country play . . . What is that role? Is it to pull back until we have nothing but a garrison force, or are we going to have a world front? If we are going to have the former, let us not fool anybody; let us trim our sails, let us pull back in; let us take the second-rate seat we would deserve under such conditions, and turn Germany and Japan loose . . . then hope that our grandchildren will not have to deal with that problem.

The National Observer, 5-17:6.

Helmut Schmidt
Minister of Defense of West Germany

We Germans look upon the United States as our most important friend and ally. We share your concern and anxieties about peace in our time, and we also share your aspirations and efforts in this regard. We hope wholeheartedly that your government will find the way to disentangle your country from the war in Southeast Asia; for this is a matter of urgent interest not only to you but to us as well. We, too, hope that your government will be able to bring about a SALT agreement and further limitations of the arms race; and we will assist you in this respect to the best of our abilities. We know that in your own interest you will not let us down over Berlin. We share your government's belief in the necessity of bringing about peace in the Middle East and especially of satisfying Israel's legitimate security requirements. We know of the American concern about possible future quarrels between the EEC and the United States on foreign trade regulations and economic regulations; and we fully share your government's belief that such disputes ought to be avoided. We will do our best

(HELMUT SCHMIDT)

to evade such clashes of interest, because we are pretty certain that, in the long run, it is in our common interest not to let them arise.

At Princeton University, April 21/
Vital Speeches, 5-15:462.

Margaret Chase Smith
United States Senator, R—Maine

For decades, our foreign policy has been one oriented on containment of Communism through economic aid to try to win friends and woo nations away from the wiles of Soviet Russia, and to intervene militarily in defense of our friends. At the cost of billions of dollars, we have learned that we can't buy friendship, as we experience the economic warfare our own allies—like Western European nations, West Germany and Japan—wage against us in foreign trade and finance in their attack on the American dollar and gold position and their pirating of our markets. We see no real support from our allies in defense against Communist aggression in Korea and Vietnam—and fat and rich Western European allies we rebuilt with Marshall Plan aid not even carrying their proper share of the NATO that was created and exists for their defense and security. The catalyst and rallying point for public support of the foreign policy of containment of Communism has been the credibility of the threat of international Communism to our own security. The fear is gone. The threat no longer has the great credibility it once had. The once external threat no longer preoccupies the American people.

Interview, Washington/
U.S. News & World Report, 6-28:27.

Yes, the U.S. is turning toward isolationism; but few want to admit it—especially the liberal-Presidential-aspirant critics of President Nixon . . . Behind the turn is weariness on the part of the American public to carry the continued heavy sacrifice of lives, blood and high taxes—(and) the concurrent loss of funds and application of resources for internal improvement—that being big brother, world po-

liceman and good Samaritan have cost.

Interview, Washington/
U.S. News & World Report, 6-28:27.

Will the Nixon Doctrine work? No American is qualified to say whether or not it will work. The question is more properly and accurately posed to those nations with whom we have treaties. The question is whether they are willing to fight for their own defense. One thing is reasonably sure—that we are not going to carry the major part of the burden of the defense of another country in the foreseeable future. To that extent, the Nixon Doctrine has already constituted in a degree an "abrogation," "revision" or "renegotiation" of our present treaties.

Interview, Washington/
U.S. News & World Report, 6-28:28.

John C. Stennis
United States Senator, D—Miss.

We are making a turn in the direction of isolation; but I don't believe isolationism is exactly what we will adopt. I certainly do not think we will revert to the position we took following World War I, when we reduced our strength to a dangerously low level, declared ourselves against war in almost all circumstances, and even sank our own battleships. We realized in part the inadequacy of this posture when World War II began. After that war, we swept over to the other extreme and undertook to underwrite the protection of all nations of the free world through agreements . . . These positions are two extremes. We have to seek a more practical, realistic middle ground. We cannot abandon our commitments. But we have to bring our obligations more in line with our capabilities. We cannot underwrite the protection of the entire free world. We cannot help nations whose people are not willing to fight to the death themselves. That is not isolationism. I want us to keep our obligations as a world power and world leader and have the strength to back up that policy. But it cannot be an all-inclusive policy. We do not have the manpower nor the wealth to do it all alone.

Interview, Washington/
U.S. News & World Report, 6-28:25.

(Regarding restriction of the President's war-making powers): I believe we can begin to re-establish the balance required by the Constitution in the field of war powers. But I want to point out that more important than legislation is a commitment by the people that they must decide in the future whether or not to go to war. The most important balance to be restored is the balance in the minds of the nation's citizens—both those who are inclined to surrender their own responsibilities of decision to the Executive, as too many in Congress have too often done, and those who believe that no cause is worth fighting for. For, as with most things, the truth lies somewhere between these extremes, and the people of the United States must understand that the health of our constitutional system depends upon their own willingness to help make the difficult choice of peace or war, if and when the question arises for us again. We of the Congress are nothing more than their representatives; and without their support, no balance can be restored.

The Wall Street Journal, 10-19:22.

Stuart Symington
United States Senator, D—Mo.

Most disturbing is the concentration of foreign policy decision-making power in the White House, with a resultant obvious decline in the prestige and position of the Secretary of State and his Department. Presidential Adviser Henry Kissinger emerges as clearly the most powerful man in the Nixon Administration next to the President himself. Under the present concept of executive privilege, however, he has never appeared before the proper committees of the Congress to justify any of his decisions . . . How can those of us who are elected to represent the people, and in whose hands is the sole authority to appropriate those funds necessary for the Executive Branch to carry out policy, perform properly our Constitutional function if we are barred from knowledge of the true reasons for said policy or policies? This development is of particular concern in the field of foreign affairs. In that field, the people are forced to rely more on the wisdom of their elected representatives—primarily because of

national security considerations—than is the case with respect to domestic affairs. Nevertheless, it is in the former area that Congress is now being asked to appropriate increasing amounts of money so as to carry out policies and programs about which they have been receiving increasingly less knowledge.

Before the Senate, Washington/
The National Observer, 3-15:11.

No, the U.S. is not turning toward isolation. The move toward trade with the People's Republic of (Communist) China is a sign of less, as against more, isolation. The possible favorable development in the SALT arms-control talks with Russia is a sign of less, not more, isolation. The fact that some of us don't agree the U.S. has a self-appointed mission to both defend and finance the free world does not make us isolationists. That deduction is one of the absurdities of our time.

Interview, Washington/
U.S. News & World Report, 6-28:28.

John G. Tower
United States Senator, R.—Tex.

Overseas there is a crisis of confidence in America. Our friends think that we are shaky allies. Every time a resolution like Senator (Mike) Mansfield's comes—aimed at reducing our troops in Europe—it diminishes our influence. There is no substitute for American presence. It relates to our total world influence—economic and political.

Interview, Washington/
U.S. News & World Report, 6-28:29.

Barbara Tuchman
Author, Historian

I'm as strongly in favor of containing Communism from our shores as (California Governor Ronald) Reagan. I'm perfectly sure that under any Communist regime I'll be one of the first shot; I can't take being dictated to. But our foreign affairs are not going to be on a firm basis unless we get rid of our obsessive fear of it (Communism). It's a tragedy that, with world power, we have become a status quo power. We have become an ancient regime, dedicated to

(BARBARA TUCHMAN)

holding on, not to allow any changes because they scare us.

Interview/Los Angeles Times, 11-25:(6)8.

Peregrine Worsthorne
Political commentator,
"The Sunday Telegraph," London

I don't see the troubles at home drawing American resources, imagination and dynamism from abroad. On the contrary, I see Americans looking abroad for an outlet for this imagination and dynamism that is not to be found at home. Also remember: When governments don't know how to solve internal problems, they tend to compensate by pretending to themselves that they know what to do with the rest of the world.

Interview/U.S. News & World Report, 5-3:69.

Bella S. Abzug
United States Representative, D–N.Y.

The House of Representatives has the distinction of being the most unrepresentative body in the West. Both houses (of Congress) are dominated by a male, white, middle-aged, middle-and upper-middle-class power elite that stand with their backs turned to the needs and demands of our people for realistic change.
Time, 8-16:16.

I would like to see new people running for Congress all over the country—more women, more young people, more people who are other than lawyers. I'm a lawyer, myself; but I don't think that's the whole of America. Congress has nice men in it and many of good will. But they really represent a rather limited grouping of people. It's got to be more diverse.
Interview/The New York Times, 10-11:37.

Eva Adams
Former Director, United States Mint

(Regarding women in government): You're supposed to think like a man, dress like a queen, speak like a lady and work like a dog.
Reno, Nev./The New York Times, 10-16:31.

Spiro T. Agnew
Vice President of the United States

(President Nixon's revenue-sharing plan is) a program conceived by the best bipartisan talent of all levels of government, supported by just about everyone except a high-handed clique of powerful Congressmen temporarily aground on the shoals of militant intransigent political ambition.
Before National League of Cities, Honolulu, Nov. 30/ Los Angeles Herald-Examiner, 12-1:(A)16.

Carl Albert
United States Representative, D–Okla.

I look upon (the seniority system) as Churchill looked on democracy: It's the worst system ever devised, except for every other one suggested to take its place.
Interview, Washington/ The Washington Post, 1-10:(B)3.

(Regarding his position as Speaker of the House): Most people think of me as the presiding officer of the House and nothing else. Yet I'm also the political leader in the House. I'm the House chief executive officer. I appoint lots of committees and commissions. I am the House's chief administrative officer. Everyone I see working in this building is working for me.
Interview, Washington/ The Christian Science Monitor, 4-15:3.

William R. Anderson
United States Representative, D–Tenn.

I think there has been a loss of confidence in the Federal government. There's a growing tendency to have a relationship with the public that's something less than humble and candid. It's the failure of bureaucracy to respond to the needs of the citizens; but more important, the feeling of people that they cannot believe what the government tells them. These people are frustrated. I feel a little frustrated myself.
Look, 4-20:48.

John M. Ashbrook
United States Representative, R–Ohio

I have been an advocate of direct revenue-sharing for the past 10 years. Our government has become far too centralized, with a finger in every pie; and I think our state and local governments are certainly in a better

(JOHN M. ASHBROOK)

position to know what the local problems are and to deal with them effectively . . . Reducing the grip of Washington on state, county and city matters would have deep implications for the future of state and local governments, which historically have been more responsive to public needs and are now direly in need of strengthening.

Human Events, 2-6:1.

Birch Bayh
United States Senator, D–Ind.

Whether a man is eligible to be President can't be determined by his voting record (in Congress). He needs the quality to stimulate people . . . to challenge them to be bigger than they are.

News conference, Sacramento, Jan. 24/
Los Angeles Herald-Examiner, 1-25:(A)9.

Daniel Bell
Professor of Sociology, Harvard University

The whole administrative structure of our society is out of whack. It makes no sense to have 50 states that were created out of accidents of history. An organization of 13 or 15 regional commonwealths might provide a far better base from which to manage our affairs.

Before American Jewish Committee,
New York/The Wall Street Journal, 6-16:12.

Lloyd M. Bentsen
United States Senator, D–Tex.

The Senate owes the country all the care and attention of due deliberation; but we cannot afford the luxury of unlimited debate by using it to obstruct the majority will.

The Dallas Times Herald, 2-1:(A)26.

Winton M. Blount
Postmaster General and Chairman,
United States Postal Service

President Nixon announced, 15 days after coming into office in 1969, that we were going to take politics out of the Post Office; and since

that time, patronage politics has been removed from the postal service. I think that you will always have, in an organization as large as this, instances where internal politics is a problem. We are going to work very hard at that. This now has become a performance-oriented organization, and you have got to remember that over the past 200 years it hasn't been a performance-oriented organization. It has been one oriented toward patronage politics. We have removed that. We are now on the road to providing an efficient, effective nationwide utility; and I think that if you look five years downstream, that that is what the United States Postal Service will be.

TV-radio interview/"Meet the Press,"
National Broadcasting Company,
Washington, 7-4.

Hale Boggs
United States Representative, D–La.

. . . when you look at Congress today compared with earlier years, the job is so much more demanding. Ten years ago, we didn't have to worry about an argument over the SST, for instance. Twenty years ago, no one thought that the environment would be one of the great issues confronting Congress. Twenty years ago, no one dreamed of a space program, or of intercontinental ballistic missiles and nuclear submarines and spaceships. In times past, no one dreamed of cities absolutely jam-packed full of people who had migrated from other parts of the country without any skills or training or education. No one dreamed of the millions and millions of automobiles jamming and packing the streets of every community in the country. No one dreamed of the decline of railroads and the rise of aviation. These are all problems we are confronted with now. They are difficult problems. There are no easy solutions. And Congress works on these things all day long—every day. If you could sit in some of the closed sessions of committees and see how these members are working and seeking information, your respect for Congress would increase considerably.

Interview/U.S. News & World Report, 3-22:80.

I am totally opposed to it (revenue-sharing). The idea of members of Congress being responsible for raising the revenue and then having no responsibility for its expenditure is obviously wrong and obviously cannot really happen. Looking down the road, let's say you have revenue-sharing. Let's say it was $20 billion, and you had a scandal in a given city. It happens. We had one in Newark. Congress would, of course, immediately legislate all types of control. And that impact would be that hundreds and thousands of local governments would actually come under the control of the national government. It's a very dangerous act.

Interview, Washington/
The Christian Science Monitor, 4-14:3.

David Brinkley
News commentator,
National Broadcasting Company

The Washington establishment does not serve the American people's real needs and real wants; it serves its own. (The government) resists change because, in the process of change, it might lose some money and some power. The American people continue to see plans and programs they do not like and do not want; yet they find themselves powerless to change them . . . It is simply the nature of a power center of a bureaucracy that has gone its own way. Ours has gone its own way for so long, it is out of control of the people, of Congress and even of the President.

Before National Association of Elementary
School Principals, Cleveland, April 18/
San Francisco Examiner, 4-19:7.

James L. Buckley
United States Senator, C–N.Y.

Government has had a talent for creating as many problems as it set out to solve.

Before Buffalo (N.Y.) Area
Chamber of Commerce, March 15/
The New York Times, 3-16:27.

I am particularly enthusiastic about the special revenue-sharing proposals because they signal a conscious, historic decision to reverse the flow of power to Washington. If these proposals are enacted by the Congress, we can expect to see state and local governments revitalized as they are weaned of their growing dependence on Washington. And because the voters will know where the buck stops, they will be able to hold their elected officials directly accountable for the manner in which they discharge their responsibilities.

Before the Senate, Washington, April 20/
Human Events, 5-22:8.

The majority of Americans have come to understand, if the Congress has not, the bureaucratic paralysis which sets in as Washington tries to mastermind and plan every detail of responsibilities which can be far more flexibly, or more efficiently, handled at state and local levels of government.

At New York State Conservative Party dinner,
New York, Oct. 8/
The New York Times, 10-9:51.

Warren E. Burger
Chief Justice of the United States

I think a very good case can be made for some outer limits of age for all people in public service—courts, the Executive branch and the Legislative branch. There comes a time when people can't function at their full peak of efficiency and power. The military has recognized this; it mandatorily retires Army officers, I believe, at age 64. All industries do this. Other professions do it.

Interview, June/
The New York Times, 7-4:(1)24.

James MacGregor Burns
Author; Political scientist

. . . I believe Presidents are men of exceptional power, who should be held to exceptionally-high standards. To what extent historians wish to apply their own standards to Presidents is a decision for each historian to make and for each reader to judge . . . I believe that Presidents—all Presidents—should be held to account. If a President promises peace, he should be held to that promise. If he does not fulfill his promise, it may be because of forces outside his control; but this is a question that historians

159

(JAMES MacGREGOR BURNS)

must explore, and that, inevitably, in one way or another, they judge. The Presidency is potentially the most beneficial—and potentially the most disastrous—governmental institution that we have. I think that most Presidents come to the White House with a sense of history, and, once in the White House, become keenly concerned with what will be the verdict of history. Actually, there are many verdicts of history and many jurors casting ballots. But one constraint on the President may be his realization that obscure historians, burrowing into the records, will, in their own way, hold him accountable for word and deed, and the relation between word and deed.

Receiving 1971 National Book Award in History and Biography, New York, March 2/The Wall Street Journal, 4-12:10.

John W. Byrnes
United States Representative, R—Wis.

Federal revenue-sharing would be great for state and local legislators, but bad for the taxpayers who must pay the bill . . . Maybe I'm old-fashioned, but I most sincerely believe that with the pleasure of spending public funds there should also be the odium of collecting them. It is the one protection we have—even though not always effective—that there will be some restraint and prudence in the spending of public funds.

The National Observer, 1-25:14.

Let's remember that all government spending eventually focuses at one spot—the American taxpayer. He is the one who must pay the bill . . . Too often, I get the feeling—as I hear Mayors and Governors and Federal officials discussing revenue-sharing—that I am witnessing a gathering of Robin Hoods planning a robbery, with the participants trying to figure out how the loot is to be divided. I suggest to you as taxpayers that it's your money they are talking about taking and dividing among them.

At National Public Affairs Conference of American Bankers Association, Washington/Human Events, 4-3:3.

(Regarding revenue-sharing): If we will be just a little realistic, we must recognize that there is no revenue to share. The only thing the Federal government has to share today is debt.

The Austin (Tex.) American-Statesman, 5-1:5.

Homer E. Capehart
Former United States Senator, R—Ind.

Legislators today don't approach problems realistically. They want to blame everything on everybody who went before.

Newsweek, 1-25:8.

Barber B. Conable, Jr.
United States Representative, R—N.Y.

I am getting pretty distressed at having the Congress judged by the performance of the other body (the Senate). If we rely on the other end of the Capitol to set the image of our Legislative Branch, we can be certain only of capriciousness, posturing, a high absentee rate and an insensitivity to the public mood.

Before the House, Washington, Nov. 3/ San Francisco Examiner & Chronicle (This World), 11-21:21.

John B. Connally, Jr.
Secretary of the Treasury-designate of the United States

Without in any sense appearing to be arrogant, as long as I am Secretary of the Treasury, I shall be Secretary of the Treasury.

Before Senate Finance Committee hearing on his nomination, Washington, Jan. 28/San Francisco Examiner, 1-29:2.

John B. Connally, Jr.
Secretary of the Treasury of the United States

Everybody says we're not going to get revenue-sharing, but it depends on how you define the term. We have revenue-sharing now, by my definition. Twenty-five per cent of our budget in Texas came from the Federal government; so you have revenue-sharing. The question is the manner in which it comes.

Interview, Washington, Feb. 18/ The Washington Post, 2-19:(A)4.

John T. Connor
Chairman, Allied Chemical Corporation

Practically speaking—and this may sound strange coming from a businessman—don't we have to have a freeze on any further tax cuts so that the Federal government can pay its bills, instead of continuing this deficit-financing practice with its pernicious inflationary effects?
Cleveland/The Wall Street Journal, 11-11:18.

Silvio O. Conte
United States Representative, R—Mass.

(After a telecast of a House Appropriations Committee session): If they televise a few more of these hearings, the revolution will come real fast.
The Dallas Times Herald, 2-25:(A)2.

Alan Cranston
United States Senator, D—Calif.

The Vice Presidency is one of the worst jobs in the country, and being a Senator is the best. The Vice President has only one boss, the President. I have 20 million bosses, the people of California. I like that much better.
Interview, Washington/San Francisco Examiner & Chronicle, 3-21:(A)10.

Carl T. Curtis
United States Senator, R—Neb.

(Regarding secret Pentagon papers on U.S. involvement in Vietnam published by several newspapers): Judging by what I have read and heard about these Vietnam war documents, the government tends to stamp a "secret" or "top secret" classification on too many documents and too much information in an attempt to hide it from the public. The classification system should never be used to cover up a lie or a documented case of public deceit by the officials of any agency of government.
Before the Senate, Washington/ The Dallas Times Herald, 6-18:(AA)1.

Ronald V. Dellums
United States Representative, D—Calif.

As I get closer and closer to the leadership in this country, I begin to see, not its superhuman qualities, but its incredible level of mediocrity.
The National Observer, 2-1:2.

William O. Douglas
Associate Justice,
Supreme Court of the United States

The Federal bureaucracy isn't dishonest. It's heavy; it's remote; it's impossible to reach.
At University of Kansas, March 17/ The Washington Post, 3-19:(A)21.

Thomas F. Eagleton
United States Senator, D—Mo.

I am Chairman of the District of Columbia Committee—not the most coveted position in the U.S. Senate, I assure my colleagues. In my normal routine day, after trying to dispose and contemplate those matters that I think have some direct bearing on the people who sent me here—and I hope will keep me here—and then considering such matters as are before committees of the Senate that have some national scope insofar as jurisdiction is concerned, and after, perhaps, attending to personal chores, if I have 5 minutes, or perhaps 10 minutes, then I can contemplate and guess at what might be good for 750,000 people that I do not know and to whom I am not accountable. They cannot elect me, and they cannot defeat me. And if I have time, if I want to give it some time, that is what they get from me. That is what they get from other members of the District of Columbia Committee; and I daresay they get even less from the other 93 members of the Senate who do not serve on the District of Columbia Committee.
Before the Senate, Washington/ The Washington Post, 3-13:(A)14.

Some would argue that decades of Congressional acquiescence, plus our performance during the Vietnam war, constitute a persuasive case for *formally* restructuring the Constitution so as to give the President a broader, more unilateral war-making authority. I, for one, would oppose any such formal abdication of Congressional authority, as I oppose its further erosion. To me, the tragic Presidential miscalculations on Vietnam—almost destroying that

(THOMAS F. EAGLETON)

country while seriously dividing this one—are an even more compelling argument for returning to the principles of collective judgment and deliberations.

Before Senate Foreign Relations Committee,
Washington, March 24/
The Washington Post, 3-25:(A)20.

Cyrus S. Eaton
Industrialist

I am a capitalist. I believe in our system. In the long run, I think it's probably the best yet devised. But it's far from perfect; it often goes wrong. The final answers to any of the great problems in economics or politics or government have not yet been found; so I've ceased to be dogmatic. If you've got a different system, try it out. If you're highly successful in it, fine and dandy. I don't think there's anything sacred about any system of government or economics; so I've an open mind.

Parade, 12-5:6.

Sam J. Ervin, Jr.
United States Senator, D–N.C.

When people fear (government) surveillance—whether it exists or not—when they grow afraid to speak their minds and hearts freely to their government or to any one else—then we shall cease to be a free society.

Before Senate Judiciary Subcommittee
on Constitutional Rights, Washington,
Feb. 23/Los Angeles Times, 2-24:(1)13.

(Regarding government classification of information): When the people do not know what their government is doing, those who govern are not accountable for their actions. And accountability is basic to the democratic system.

Before Senate Judiciary Subcommittee,
Washington, July 27/
The Dallas Times Herald, 7-27:(A)10.

Walter E. Fauntroy
Delegate to United States House
of Representatives, D–D.C.

I want to stress that the 92nd Congress must be the one to recognize self-determination for the people of this city (Washington). We have seen the ground begin to give way—my presence here is evidence of that—and we will not relent. We will not be handed any more hollow promises or offered cosmetic changes in the District government that do not shift power to the people.

Before Senate District of Columbia
Committee, Washington, April 26/
The Washington Post, 4-27:(C)2.

J. William Fulbright
United States Senator, D–Ark.

The major virtue of legislatures . . . is neither wisdom nor prescience—and certainly not charisma—but a basic inability to threaten the liberties of the people. The ancient Egyptians spent themselves into penury to give their mummified Pharoahs glorious sendoffs to heaven; humble folk were rewarded by vicarious participation in the ascent. We, in turn, build great monuments to revered departed Presidents, perhaps for similar reasons. But who would dream of mummifying or deifying a legislature? The plodding workaday character of Congress, its lack of dash and mystery, its closeness to ordinary people with ordinary problems, even its much-reviled "parochialism," make of our national legislature an object entirely unsuitable for deification. That is why Congress is incapable of threatening our democratic liberties; that, too, is why an assertive, independent Congress is the first line of defense against an expanding Executive—which can and does threaten our liberties.

At South Florida University, Feb. 4/
The Wall Street Journal, 2-23:14.

(Regarding President Nixon): I can't recall a President who has gone as far in the Commander-in-Chief's role as this one. He invades countries to protect troops. He supports the repeal of the Tonkin resolution because he feels he has full powers to make war without any Congressional approval. And he builds enormous power into the National Security Council, with Dr. Henry Kissinger and his staff of 110. There must be 500 people in the White House now; and there weren't 50 in Ike's (Dwight D. Eisenhower) day.

Interview, Washington/
Los Angeles Times, 2-15:(2)6.

In those days (the 1940s, '50s and early '60s), when the magic glow of F.D.R. (Franklin D. Roosevelt) still flickered in our memories, when (Dwight D.) Eisenhower reigned with paternal benignancy and the Kennedys appeared on white chargers with promises of Camelot, it was possible to forget the wisdom of the founding fathers, who had taught us to mistrust power, to check and balance it and never to yield up the means of thwarting it. Now, after bitter experience, we are having to learn all over again that no single man or institution can ever be counted upon as a reliable or predictable repository of wisdom or benevolence, that the possession of great power can impair a man's judgment and cloud his perception of reality, and that our only protection against the misuse of power is the institutionalized interaction of diversity of independent opinions. To arrest and reverse the decline of democratic government in America, we are going to have to recover our mistrust of power—in the Presidency and wherever else it is found.

At Yale Law Journal annual banquet,
New Haven, Conn., April 3/
The New York Times, 4-4:(1)27.

I cannot emphasize too strongly my belief that a legislative body's accomplishments consist as much in what it prevents as in what it enacts.

Before American Society
of Newspaper Editors, Washington,
April 16/The Washington Post, 4-17:(A)2.

John W. Gardner
Chairman, Common Cause

Americans from all levels of society . . . are increasingly skeptical of the great institutions that dominate their lives. These doubts, as expressed by ordinary, law-abiding citizens, don't sound very alarming; but to a thinking observer, they are a fireball in the night.

Before Senate committee on reform of the
seniority system, Washington, Jan. 18/
The New York Times, 1-19:19.

Most of the work of the Congress is done in committees; and the committee chairmen constitute the power structure in Congress. They determine what legislation will come before Congress, whether or not hearings will be held, how $200 billion in appropriations will be allocated . . . The word "dictatorial" is not too strong to describe the power they wield. The chairman dominates his committee. By giving or withholding favors, he can effectively discipline committee members. He may, and often does, defy the elected leadership of the chamber . . . One might suppose that men who enjoy such enormous power would be chosen with great care by fellow members of Congress on the basis of well-accepted criteria—wisdom, experience, intelligence, integrity or leadership. But . . . in fact, they gain their chairmanship by one criterion only—length of continuous service on the committee.

Washington, Jan. 18/
The Washington Post, 1-19:(A)2.

The American people, who once seemed endlessly tolerant of official bumbling, are losing their patience; not just with Congress, but with the quality of our public life generally. They are fed to the teeth with power-hungry politicians. They are weary of self-serving administrators. They are sick of being bilked and manipulated. They are tired of the sense of powerless(ness) that afflicts them. They want to know what's going on. They want to have their say. They resent the unresponsiveness of their government institutions.

Before Senate Committee, Washington/
The Christian Science Monitor, 1-23:12.

People have a wholly unrealistic notion of the power of the President or of any elected official. If you replaced 10 per cent of the officials with the best people in the country,

(JOHN W. GARDNER)

which would change a lot, and got the very best possible President, it would still make very little difference toward fixing the things that are wrong. By the time they are elected, they've had to make their deals, and the man is molded to the system.

Interview/The Washington Post, 5-11:(A)18.

Most Americans simply haven't the faintest idea where or how the decisions are made that govern their lives, and this is not an accident. We must ask that our institutions be responsive, accountable, and that the people have access to them, and they don't have now. Ninety-five per cent of the American people are victimized by institutions which are poorly designed for contemporary purposes; they do not serve the people, and I'm sorry to say that all too many of them are corrupt. The word is corruption. In the city councils, the state boards of supervisors, the state legislatures, too many public officials are bought and paid for.

*TV-radio interview/"Face the Nation,"
Columbia Broadcasting System, 8-15.*

Leonard Garment
*Special Consultant to the President
of the United States*

The nation needs coolness more than clarion calls; intelligence more than charisma; a sense of history more than a sense of humor. It's not important that a President be loved or lovely or charming—but only that he have the constitutional toughness, discipline and flexibility needed to discharge his Constitutional duties in an impossibly difficult time.

*Before Federal City Club, Washington/
Los Angeles Times, 4-2:(2)9.*

John J. Gilligan
Governor of Ohio

All Governors and all Mayors are for revenue-sharing as a concept. It's like true love. The problem is defining it.

The Austin (Tex.) Statesman, 4-22:(A)4.

Arthur J. Goldberg
*Former Associate Justice,
Supreme Court of the United States*

The present system whereby the Executive branch itself determines the rules for disclosure (to the public) of its own documents has proved inadequate in keeping Congress and citizens informed. Our constitutional system requires that the people be adequately informed about the great issues that affect their lives and welfare. If this means that government must, by and large, be conducted in a goldfish bowl, so be it; for in no other way can it retain the consent of the governed.

*Before House Foreign Operations and
Government Information Subcommittee,
Washington, June 23/Parade, 8-32:5.*

. . . I have read and prepared countless thousands of classified documents and participated in classifying some of them. In my experience, 75 per cent of these never should have been classified in the first place; another 15 per cent quickly outlived the need for secrecy; and only about 10 per cent genuinely required restricted access over any significant period of time.

*Before House Foreign Operations
and Government Information Subcommittee,
Washington, June 23/Parade, 8-22:5.*

Barry Goldwater, Jr.
United States Representative, R—Calif.

You can't be effective (in government) until you've been here five or six terms, until you've gained a certain amount of seniority. To me, that's wrong. It's frustrating going to a committee meeting and sitting on the end of the bench, not even given a small amount of responsibility.

*Washington/San Francisco Examiner
& Chronicle, 5-30:(A)12.*

W. Averell Harriman
Former United States Ambassador-at-Large

Congress is entitled to more information than it has sometimes received. Clearly, the President does have the right, indeed the duty, to protect his Constitutional responsibility by withholding information from Congress which he considers may impair the functioning of the Executive or the interests of our nation. Striking a balance between these two conflicting requirements is difficult; and I do not see how it can be done by definitive rules.

Before Senate Judiciary Subcommittee,
Washington, July 29/
The New York Times, 7-30:3.

Fred R. Harris
United States Senator, D–Okla.

Around this town, what people respect is power; and everybody knows the Vice President has no power. He has no responsibility for the administration of any program. He doesn't have anything much to do that anyone thinks is very important. I think that's a waste of the talents of a man chosen for that high office who has nothing to do much but wait around until he may become President.

Interview, Washington, Oct. 9/
The Dallas Times Herald, 10-10:(A)12.

Richard G. Hatcher
Mayor of Gary, Ind.

We have learned through painful experience that (the) seeming transferral of power from those who rule to those who are ruled has been more myth than fact. The "new federalism" and the proposed revenue-sharing plan could eliminate what little fact there is, unless we are careful.

Airlie, Va., Feb. 22/
The Washington Post, 2-23:(A)7.

Mark O. Hatfield
United States Senator, R–Ore.

I've worked within the system all my life, and I believe in our system. But when I look at what we need to do, and I see how much time it takes, how hard you have to shove to get the slightest response, I have to agree some days with the kids who say it may not be enough. It may not be enough . . .

The Washington Post, 2-11:(A)20.

It is in the interests of keeping the government responsive to the people that we should require members of Congress to reacquaint themselves with their state, their district and their constituents, and to be removed periodically from the daily pressures of Congressional life, gaining new perspectives and ideas.

Before the Senate, Washington, April 27/
The New York Times, 4-28:20.

F. Edward Hebert
United States Representative, D–La.

I don't think you could keep a secret in Washington if you told it to your mirror.

San Francisco Examiner & Chronicle,
7-4:(B)2.

Walter J. Hickel
Former Secretary of the Interior
of the United States

There might be too many people in government; I won't argue with that. It may be misdirected; I won't argue with that. But I'll argue until I die that there is not enough government in the areas which are choking the living of life in modern America—areas such as transportation, the environment and the urban crisis.

Receiving Ripon Society Man of the Year
award, Seattle, April 21/
Los Angeles Times, 4-22:(1)25.

I think what America needs in government today—more than management—is conscience and compassion—compassion for everyone. That will solve more problems than billions of dollars.

Interview, Anchorage, Alaska, Sept. 28/
The Washington Post, 9-30:(F)3.

Bob Hope
Entertainer

I heard his (President Nixon's) State of the Union address. I thought it was great when he said the country's in fine shape. It's wonderful

(BOB HOPE)

when he asks Congress to give up its power. I wish I could get laughs like that.

At White House dinner, Washington, Feb. 23/
San Francisco Examiner, 2-24:2.

Hubert H. Humphrey
United States Senator, D–Minn.

Government on all levels is facing a moment of truth . . . can our governmental and political institutions cope with the new demands, as well as with the age-old problems of a highly-mobile, urbanized, industrialized and heterogeneous society? . . . Government on all levels seems to be muscle-bound, unresponsive and ineffective. It is big and costly, yet seemingly unable to assure the citizens of the most elemental of government services—the security and protection of life and property.

At Downtown Jaycees' Arthur S. Flemming
Awards Luncheon, Washington, Feb. 18/
The Washington Post, 2-19:(D)8.

I don't care whether they call it "revenue-sharing," the "Nixon Doctrine" or the "Humphrey blooper," just so it gets passed. Cities need hard cash and they need it now.

At United States Conference of Mayors,
Philadelphia, June 14/
Los Angeles Herald-Examiner, 6-15:(A)6.

The Congress can do a very good service for the country by conducting a high-level study . . . and setting rules for the declassification of sensitive documents . . . It is my judgment that there is an excessive amount of over-classification. Often it is just bureaucratic political arterial sclerosis.

News conference, Beverly Hills, Calif., June 28/
Los Angeles Herald-Examiner, 6-28:(A)2.

Daniel K. Inouye
United States Senator, D–Hawaii

(Regarding government spending for the District of Columbia): The people of the District and the nation are entitled to get their dollar's worth. And that's why I'm continuing to prod, harass and, at times, nitpick.

Television interview, Washington/
The Washington Post, 3-29:(A)18.

Jacob K. Javits
United States Senator, R–N.Y.

Our tragic experience in Indochina shows that the pendulum has swung too far in the direction of Presidential war-making power. To those who would argue that the President's powers as Commander-in-Chief, in the absence of a declaration of war, are whatever the President defines them to be, I would reply that nothing could be further from the spirit and letter of the Constitution—and nothing could be more hazardous to our constitutional form of government.

Washington, Feb. 10/
The New York Times, 2-11:17.

Nicholas Johnson
Commissioner,
Federal Communications Commission

. . . some people have been kind of bothering me about the moustache and asking about it, so I thought I'd just explain. You see, so many public officials act like bandits but want to look like public servants that I thought, just for fun, there ought to be one that would act like a public official and look like a bandit.

Los Angeles/
The New York Times, 6-13:(2)19.

James C. Kirby, Jr.
Dean, Ohio State University Law School

Fifty or 100 years ago, cynicism about public officials was limited to an informed minority which constituted such reform efforts as those of the populists and the progressives. Today, it is the average citizen who is the cynic. One Gallup poll taken in the spring of 1967 revealed that 6 of 10 Americans believed shady conduct among Congressmen was "fairly common"; and a Harris survey in the same period noted that over half the citizenry felt that at least some Congressmen were "receiving money personally for voting a certain way" on bills that come up in Congress. Another Harris report published only last February was even more disturbing. It revealed that in a brief 6-year period—from 1965 to 1971—the percentage of the public which gave Congress a positive rating declined from 64 per cent to 26 per cent.

Before Senate Subcommittee on Privileges and Elections, Washington/ The Christian Science Monitor, 11-17:3.

Henry A. Kissinger
Assistant to the President of the United States for National Security Affairs

The trouble is that so many people, so many students, simply don't understand my job, which is one of presenting various options to the President, of presenting all the halfway reasonable points of view which exist . . . It would be preposterous to say that somebody in my position is not asked which course he prefers. Of course I have convictions, and when the President asks me what I think—and he often does—I tell him. And then the last thing that usually happens is that he withdraws for a day or two with all the papers and then makes his decision.

Interview/Parade, 10-24:5.

Herbert G. Klein
Director of Communications for the President of the United States

Revenue-sharing follows a direction which has fitted the President's (Nixon) own philosophy for many years—and that's the need to start decentralizing the Federal power and giving more power in the hands of local communities and the states. This is the first major change in the direction of power in the Federal government since the early 1930s. And government reorganization is the first major reorganization of the Federal structure in almost 200 years of the republic.

Interview, Washington/ The National Observer, 4-12:5.

Dan H. Kuykendall
United States Representative, R—Tenn.

(Advocating Federal handling of revenue-sharing): I hate to admit ever that the Federal government does anything better than anybody else; but there's one thing they can do—collect taxes—honestly, more efficiently than anyone else.

News conference, Sacramento, Calif., July 22/ Los Angeles Herald-Examiner, 7-23:(A)16.

J. Bracken Lee
Mayor of Salt Lake City, Former Governor of Utah

Unless some miracle happens to stop it, the Federal government is going to be running everything. I believe if you give anyone too much power, it's going to be abused. I don't care if he's an angel, and I don't think there are any angels in the human race.

Interview, Salt Lake City/ Los Angeles Times, 12-1:(6)2.

John V. Lindsay
Mayor of New York

Revenue-sharing for states, counties and cities is no revenue-sharing at all if it is financed, even in part, on the backs of the cities. Any proposal of this kind will add to urban tensions and will, therefore, be unacceptable.

At United States Conference of Mayors meeting, Washington, Jan. 21/ Los Angeles Times, 1-22:(1)5.

Revenue-sharing is not a substitute for categorical grants-in-aid in areas where Congress has indicated its rightful concern, but rather a device to enable the functioning of local governments.

News conference, San Francisco, Feb. 11/ The New York Times, 2-12:18.

I am saddened by the reduction of the Secretary of State to a position of lesser influence. This is evident in a thousand different ways. Ever since I have been in elective office—which is now 13 years—the influence of the State Department has been reduced. The result has been that the United States has become too defense-and Pentagon-minded.

Interview, New York/ San Francisco Examiner, 12-22:12.

Richard G. Lugar
Mayor of Indianapolis

A few U.S. Congressmen seek to maintain the illusion that Congress can establish national priorities, pass laws to alleviate discovered needs, raise revenues and appropriate monies to meet these needs, formulate organizational structures to implement the spending, review the results by conducting public hearings and reading reports from the field, and thus respond to the national will and achieve the public good. In truth, the Congress of the United States, as a body, reacts very sluggishly, if at all, to current needs . . . State and local governments stand between the Congress and sheer anarchy.

At International Conference of Cities,
Indianapolis/The Wall Street Journal, 6-2:12.

We are contending that we in the cities are a very important part of the fabric of government in America, that it is one whole cloth, and that there is no more important way in which $5 billion could be spent than through a revenue-sharing bill. In other words, we are contending that there isn't going to be a great deal of Federal government or a great deal of federalism at all in this country unless there are strong cities and local governments. This is a very high-priority item, so we would suggest if there is a budget deficit, that in fact other programs will have to be eliminated in favor of aid for local governments. By that I mean states, counties and cities.

TV-radio interview/"Meet the Press,"
National Broadcasting Company,
Philadelphia, 7-13.

Warren G. Magnuson
United States Senator, D–Wash.

You know, there are times now when they've been up there on the Senate floor changing a poverty program . . . while we've been in an Appropriations Committee meeting appropriating money for the old program.

Interview/
The Dallas Times Herald, 1-4:(A)2.

William S. Mailliard
United States Representative, R–Calif.

Fifty years ago, the individual citizen had practically no dealings with the Federal government, and could go through life in touch with no Federal official except the postman. Now being Congressman has evolved into a two-part job—a legislator and an errand boy for constituents frustrated by their government.

San Francisco Examiner & Chronicle
(This World), 11-21:2.

Robert C. Mardian
Assistant Attorney General,
Internal Security Division,
Department of Justice of the United States

The vast majority of Americans would . . . agree that persons who are knowing members (of subversive groups) should not be employed in even non-sensitive (government) positions; not simply because they are disloyal, but because such people are not likely to improve the delivery of governmental services of a government system they are trying to destroy.

At Atomic Energy Commission
security conference, Washington/
San Francisco Examiner, 10-28:2.

Charles McC. Mathias, Jr.
United States Senator, R–Md.

The reason we have become a nation of demonstration, protest and violent debate is that there has been no balance, because someone somewhere has not been responding to the needs and wants of the people. And the reason that there has often been little or no response is that for too long people have sat by without questioning what their leaders and elected representatives were doing. They seemed to listen only at election time. They would read the newspapers and make judgments, often without examining particular situations in depth, as an educated society should . . . Now that we have the 18-year-old vote, the nation's political process is going to be forced to be more responsive and our institutions are going to have to respond to the needs of the people, for the young will have it no other way.

At Baltimore Polytechnic Institute, May 21/
The Washington Post, 6-4:(A)20.

Eugene J. McCarthy
Former United States Senator, D—Minn.

(Regarding the increase of Presidential power): We are now in the position the colonists were when they protested taxation without representation. It was not taxation they protested but lack of representation; and I say government without representation, if it is not tyranny, it may soon become such.

Before Boston Lawyers' Vietnam Committee,
Feb. 22/The New York Times, 2-23:8.

John L. McClellan
United States Senator, D—Ark.

Any time you try to abolish or consolidate an established agency of government, you run into trouble.

The New York Times, 1-24:(1)46.

John W. McCormack
United States Representative, D—Mass.

Next to God and Mrs. McCormack, I love most the House of Representatives.

On retiring after 42 years in Congress,
Washington, Jan. 2/The Washington Post,
1-3:(A)2.

Gale W. McGee
United States Senator, D—Wyo.

Remembering the political explosions which persuaded President (Lyndon) Johnson not to run again and the current speculation in regard to President Nixon's dropping political stance, I think we ought to give serious thought to the wisdom of one-term Presidents, but lengthening that term to seven years. Most political scientists would agree that a single four-year term does not really give a new President, once he was elected, enough time to launch his program or live up to his commitments before he has to shift political gears to try for a second term. What would be the consequences if a President knew he had only one term, but would have

seven years in which to put his programs into action? I think we ought to be discussing very seriously such a prospect.

At Austin College, Sherman, Tex./
The Washington Post, 3-26:(A)27.

George S. McGovern
United States Senator, D—S.D.

(Revenue-sharing) just tends to put more power into the hands of those who already have power—those whose priorities are often far different from the urgent priorities of those who are still powerless and so remain poor.

Before National Federation of Settlement
and Neighborhood Centers, Washington,
Feb. 11/The Washington Post, 2-12:(A)2.

John L. McMillan
United States Representative, D—S.C.

I don't think any (committee) chairman in the Congress who has any sense would appoint subcommittee chairmen who wouldn't back him.

Washington, Feb. 25/
The Washington Post, 2-26:(A)18.

Jack Miller
United States Senator, R—Iowa

One of the simplest but most effective reforms we can make (for improving the efficiency of Congress and the Federal Judiciary) is to set a mandatory retirement age of 72. Unfortunately, old age does not bring with it increased capacity for work. Clogged legislative and court calendars are a deterrent to the best functioning of our system of government. Also, younger voices need to be heard in this system as the proportion of young voters grows larger in our country.

Washington, June 14/
Los Angeles Herald-Examiner, 6-14:(A)6.

Wilbur D. Mills
United States Representative, D—Ark.

I've told the states I'll make a deal with them: We'll share our revenue, if they'll share our deficit.

The Christian Science Monitor, 1-12:1.

(WILBUR D. MILLS)

In my view, we already have too little restraint on spending programs at the present time. If the revenue-sharing machine is to be cranked up, I fear we will lose much of what restraint we now have. I am not at all sure that this was not really the intent of some of the originators of the idea of revenue-sharing . . .

Before the House, Washington/
The National Observer, 2-1:4.

(Regarding the post of Speaker of the House): The Speaker is a presiding officer, not a legislator. I like to legislate. I like to apply my mind against the minds of others. I like to get up on that floor and handle a bill and be ready for the questions of 430 other members.

Interview, Washington/
Los Angeles Times, 3-1:(1)16.

Wholly apart from the welfare payments, I am opposed to revenue-sharing in principle. We have only deficits at the Federal level. We are almost in a pauperized position ourselves, as far as Federal funds are concerned. Our Federal debt subject to the debt ceiling is now about 400 billion dollars. Some states and localities have very little, if any, debt. For us to be granting largess to state and local governments, when we have to borrow or finance our own responsibilities, just adds more flames to inflation.

Interview/
U.S. News & World Report, 3-15:46.

(Regarding the possibility of his running for the Presidency): I think I know too much . . . about the problems of a President. I don't know why anybody, knowing as I do what you are walking into, would want that job . . . I frankly wonder whether any one person anymore has the capacity, mentally and physically, to handle this most onerous job.

TV-radio interview/"Meet the Press,"
National Broadcasting Company,
Washington, 6-6.

I don't like being in the position of being flatly against revenue-sharing, but I think there is a responsibility on the legislative body that has the authority to tax constituents to see to it, too, that it has some authority over the spending of the money that it raises . . . As I told the President (Nixon) when I went to the White House for a briefing on revenue-sharing last January, "I've been against this since before you ever thought about running for President, and that's a long time ago."

Interview/The Washington Post, 9-12:(B)5.

John N. Mitchell
Attorney General of the United States

(Regarding the life of top Administration officials): You're always faced with decisions. You have to have a strong back, a weak mind and a cast-iron stomach.

Quote, 7-4:626.

Arch A. Moore, Jr.
Governor of West Virginia

An important plus in strengthening the hands of the states is what I see as a change in the type of individuals who are being elected Governors. We probably have a group of chief executives who have more ability and more capacity than in the past. That might sound disrespectful to some of our predecessors, but it isn't meant in that light. I think today's Governors are more alert to the necessity for maintaining the state role in the Federal system. They are somewhat younger men. So from the standpoint of the quality of leadership, the states are in a stronger position. But having said that, I still don't believe we, as state officials, have reached the point where the Federal government trusts us. There is a general tendency in the Federal bureaucracy—those officials who stay in office regardless of who is President—to think that Governors are operating in a purely political manner in whatever they do. They don't look with much favor on doing business with the Governors.

Interview/Nation's Business, December:27.

Daniel P. Moynihan
Former Counsellor to the President
of the United States

The thing I learned most (while serving in

government) is the powerful continuity of American government. I know this is a time when there is a feeling that the country has slipped its moorings, that things have changed for the worse. Yet, if you have had the experience of being in the Kennedy and Johnson subcabinets and then in the Cabinet of Mr. Nixon, the most powerful impression is how steady has been the national purpose in both domestic and foreign affairs.

Interview/
The New York Times Magazine, 6-27:10.

Ralph Nader
Lawyer; Consumer rights advocate

A civil servant should be forced to make the law work; and if he won't do it, he should be censured or expelled from the government.

Interview/The New York Times, 3-21:16.

Congress has been a continuous under-achiever. It would be difficult to overstate the extent of abdication to which Congress has been driven by external and internal forces. Contrary to its pre-eminent Constitutional authority and Constitutional stature as the branch of government closest to the people, it has been reduced to a puny twig through which flows the allocation of a massive taxpayer treasure chest of over $200 billion in appropriations, largely at the beck and call of Executive-branch and special-interest advocacy and pressure. It reacts to the Executive far more than it initiates.

Washington/
The New York Times, 12-23:25.

Richard M. Nixon
President of the United States

When you come into office, the Presidency, one has ideas as to what he can accomplish; and he believes he can accomplish a great deal, even though he may have a Congress that is not of his own party. And then, after he gets in, he finds that what he had hoped, in terms of achieving goals, will not be as great as the actual performance turns out to be. So I would say that in terms of how I have changed, it is in realizing that, while we must set high goals and always seek them, that we must not become

impatient and we must plow forward, recognizing that, in the end, we're going to make some progress, if not all the progress that we hoped. I would say, in other words, at this time, I'm not disappointed in the record of the last two years, in terms of some of the things that we accomplished. But I have great hopes for the next two years. Because I think I know better how to do the job. I think I know better how to deal with the Congress. I think I know better how to work with the Cabinet. This is perhaps how I have changed. I know more. I'm better, more experienced. I hope I do better.

Television interview, Washington, Jan. 4/
The New York Times, 1-6-:42.

(Regarding the 18-year-old vote): . . . in the year 1970, we have taken a step which could have a very dramatic effect on your (young people's) future and the future of America. We have provided you with the most powerful means the citizen has of making himself felt in a free and democratic society—you now have the right to vote. Today, in a new and exciting and dramatically-promising way, you—each of you 18 or over—has a voice in the future of America. The whole history of democracy in this country is a chronicle of the constant broadening of the power to participate. Each new group receiving the franchise has had a beneficial effect on the course of America. Each new group has given freshness and vitality to the purposes of government. And now, it's your turn to do the same. So much is in your hands now. To those who have believed the system would not be moved, I say try it. To those who have thought that the system was impenetrable, I say there's no longer a need to penetrate—that door is open.

At University of Nebraska, Jan. 14/
The New York Times, 1-15:12.

Based on a long and intensive study with the aid of the best advice obtainable, I have concluded that a sweeping reorganization of the Executive branch is needed if the government is to keep up with the times and with the needs of the people. I propose that we reduce the present 12 Cabinet Departments to eight. I propose that the Departments of State, Treas-

(RICHARD M. NIXON)

ury, Defense and Justice remain, but that all the other Departments be consolidated into four: Human Resources, Community Development, Natural Resources and Economic Development . . . Under this plan, rather than dividing up our Departments by narrow subjects, we would organize them around the great purposes of government. Rather than scattering responsibility by adding new levels of bureaucracy, we would focus and concentrate the responsibility for getting problems solved.

State of the Union address, Washington, Jan. 22/The Washington Post, 1-23:(A)12.

I reject the patronizing idea that government in Washington is inevitably more wise, more honest and more efficient than government at the local or state level. The honesty and efficiency of government depends on people. Government at all levels has good people and bad people.

State of the Union address, Washington, Jan. 22/The Washington Post, 1-23:(A)12.

The time has come to reverse the flow of power and resources from the states and communities to Washington, and start power and resources flowing back from Washington to the states and communities—and more important, to the people, all across America. The time has come for a new partnership between the Federal government and the states and localities—a partnership in which we entrust the states and localities with a larger share of the nation's responsibilities, and in which we share our revenues with them so they can meet those responsibilities.

State of the Union address, Washington, Jan. 22/The Washington Post, 1-23:(A)12.

The further away government is from people, the stronger government becomes and the weaker people become. And a nation with a strong government and a weak people is an empty shell.

State of the Union address, Washington, Jan. 22/The Washington Post, 1-23:(A)12.

(Opposition to revenue-sharing) is what is happening at the summit (in Washington). Down in the valleys, where the people live, you will find there that the people in the front lines, the leaders in the front lines, the Governors, the Mayors, the county officials, an overwhelming majority of them are for revenue-sharing . . . and also an overwhelming majority of the people of this country are for revenue-sharing. Eventually, then, it will be approved. I am not suggesting exactly in the form we have submitted it; but it will be approved, because those of us who are in Washington have to reflect, eventually, what the majority of the people of this country feel.

News conference, Washington, Feb. 17/ The New York Times, 2-18:14.

I am certain a Gallup poll would show that the great majority of the people would want to pull out of Vietnam. But a Gallup poll would also show that a great majority of the people would want to pull three or more divisions out of Europe. And it would also show that a great majority of the people would cut our defense budget. Polls are not the answer. You must look at the facts.

Interview, Washington, March 8/ The New York Times, 3-10:14.

The watchword of my Administration has been "reform." As we have undertaken it in many fields, this is what we have found: "Reform" as an abstraction is something that everybody is for; but "reform" as a specific is something that a lot of people are against.

At National Conference on the Judiciary, Williamsburg, Va., March 11/ The New York Times, 3-12:18.

Sometimes, the question is how is that man (the President) going to feel when he alone has to sit there and make a real tough decision? Does he have around him people who aren't panicking, people who aren't throwing up their hands about what they heard on television that night, the lousy column or the terrible cartoon . . . somebody that brings serenity, calmness or strength into the room that makes the difference? . . . I imagine that, when Harry Truman had to handle some of the hard, hard ones, he would go home and I am sure Bess Truman stood there like a rock with him.

News conference, Washington, March 11/
The Dallas Times Herald, 3-14:(A)1.

The President, with the enormous responsibilities that he has, must not be constantly preening in front of a mirror, wondering whether or not he is getting across as this kind of individual or that. He has got to be sure that he . . . does the very best possible job he can for this country . . . I don't worry about polls. I don't worry about images . . . If I had, I wouldn't be sitting here now; someone else would . . These public-relations experts always come in and are constantly riding me—or they used to in the campaign and they do now. "You have got to do this, that and the other thing to change your image." I am not going to change my image. I am just going to do a good job for this country. I really wonder, you know . . . what Lincoln, TR (Theodore Roosevelt), Wilson, FDR (Franklin D. Roosevelt) . . . if they had been constantly worrying about their image, what kind of leaders they would have been. I don't think nearly as good.

Television interview, Washington/
"Today" show,
National Broadcasting Company, 3-15.

. . . the government is just like a person. Once it acquires something, it never likes to give it up.

San Onofre Beach, Calif., March 31/
Los Angeles Times, 4-1:(1)3.

. . . with regard to the (antiwar) demonstrators, when I say that I will not be intimidated, and the Congress will not be intimidated, I am simply stating the American principle that, while everybody has a right to protest peacefully . . . policy in this country is not made by protests . . .

News conference, San Clemente, Calif.,
May 1/The Dallas Times Herald, 5-2:(A)1.

You cannot have jawboning that is effective without teeth.

News conference, Washington, Sept. 16/
The New York Times, 9-17:1.

Wright Patman
United States Representative, D—Tex.

Instead of taxing the banks, the corporations, the corporations, the foundations and other holders of great wealth, local governments are turning to gambling devices in an attempt to extract money by trickery from those who can least afford to pay. Three states—New Hampshire, New York and New Jersey—actually operate full-scale lotteries, and Connecticut has just joined the parade. New York City, of course, now has its city-operated horse parlors . . . This is a dangerous trend, and it is one which the Congress must carefully watch. If necessary, the Congress should consider legislation which will control, if not stop, some of these more outlandish schemes to raise public monies through gambling.

Before the House, Washington/
The Dallas Times Herald, 7-13:(C)7.

Otis G. Pike
United States Representative, D—N.Y.

(Regarding Congress' midsummer vacation): Sometimes one wonders if anything would really change if Congress just went home and never came back at all.

San Francisco Examiner & Chronicle
(This World), 8-22:2.

Robert D. Price
United States Representative, R—Tex.

Instead of trying to solve our (governmental) financial woes by spending more money, let us, just for once, take a serious stab at attempting to solve our financial woes by spending less money. I say it is time, indeed it is way past time, to recognize a fundamental law of economics: namely, you cannot spend or give away more than that which you *have* to spend or give away. I realize this simple precept might shock a highly-paid bureaucrat who is more comfortable dealing with abstract facts and na-

(ROBERT D. PRICE)

tional-debt account figures, but I am confident every last wage earner, every last taxpayer who has to make out and stick to a budget will know full well what I am saying and will accept it for the basic truth it is. You simply cannot spend more than you have . . . The "go now, pay later" boys have overspent the real resources of this nation to the point that U.S. gold reserves have shrunk from almost $24 billion to under $11 billion at the same time short-term U.S. dollar claims held by foreign interests have climbed to more than $42 billion. Yet in the face of this financial crunch, what do we hear from the free spenders? We hear, "The heck with reality, the heck with financial stability; open the doors of the nation's Treasury and full speed ahead" . . . Now is the time to say, "Enough is enough." Now is the time to say, "This far and no further." Now is the time to say "tonstaffl"—"There is no free lunch." Somebody pays for it sometime. In the case of the national debt, that "somebody" is the taxpayer, and the "sometime" is, I am afraid, soon.

Before the House, Washington, March 3/
Congressional Record, 3-8:(E)1580.

William Proxmire
United States Senator, D—Wis.

Federal spending policies are promoting the fat, the lazy and the inefficient. Too many groups and institutions are rushing to Washington to get both feet and their nose in the Federal trough through tax loopholes, big subsidies, grants, gifts or special privileges.

Before Milwaukee Press Club, Feb. 16/
The New York Times, 2-21:(1)23.

Instead of sneering and whining at mistaken Presidential proposals while surrendering meekly to White House and Cabinet blandishments, Congress should stand on its own two feet and rebuff mistaken requests . . . While many members of Congress have talked a good line on cutting military waste, ending the draft, putting a date certain to withdraw from Vietnam, and cutting back on the excessive number of troops in Europe, far too many have either voted

wrong, been absent when the votes were cast or folded under White House, Pentagon or narrow-interest pressures.

Midland, Mich., Oct. 25/
The Washington Post, 10-26:(A)2.

Ronald Reagan
Governor of California

When those who are governed do too little, those who govern can—and often will—do too much.

Inauguration address, Sacramento, Jan. 4/
Los Angeles Herald-Examiner, 1-4:(A)3.

If government curbs its normal appetite and curtails some less-than-vital activities, who knows—we might discover some of those activities are so less than vital they won't even be missed.

State of the State address, Sacramento,
Jan. 12/Los Angeles Times, 1-13:(1)18.

Hyman G. Rickover
Vice Admiral, United States Navy

One of the most surprising and ubiquitous aspects of rule in our governmental bureaucracies is the assumption of superior knowledge and wisdom by appointed officials. Generally, these are men who are active, but not too much given to contemplation. They appear to be uneasy unless they can indulge in making frequent decisions. No matter how complex the issue or problem, no matter how little their knowledge or experience, they have readymade views and do not hesitate to put them into effect. Advice from knowledgeable and experienced subordinates is often disregarded. I have pondered over this phenomenon for many years. The only rationale I can come to is that everything in life has been easy for these officials. They have been carried along by family, by wealth, by friends, possibly by political considerations. In a position requiring technical expertise for the first time in their lives, they believe themselves capable of solving these problems by using the "personality" methods that have previously gotten them by.

They make the fatal error of equating authority with knowledge.

Congressional testimony, Washington/
The New York Times, 10-12:43.

Nelson A. Rockefeller
Governor of New York

The year now before us will be a testing time; not alone for our state, but for our entire system of Federalism. Many local governments—particularly in our great cities—verge on actual financial collapse. And now, for the first time, the states also find their backs to the financial wall. Yet, while state and local governments bear most of the nation's domestic burdens, the Federal government collects most of the taxes. Our Federal system has reached a crucial point. We recognize, realistically, that we, as a single state, can no longer realize our future hopes alone. It is a time of testing for our national government. Only through the effective joint action of all levels of government, working together on a coordinated basis, can we effectively meet people's needs and shape our future.

State of the State address, Albany,
Jan. 6/The New York Times, 1-7:26.

Given the breakdown in local services, the Federal government must either provide the needed money or take over these vital services. But the prospect of the Interior Department cleaning the streets of our cities, for example, is inconceivable. Revenue-sharing and less-rigid Federal grants are the right answers.

At National Urban Coalition conference,
Warrenton, Va., Feb. 21/
The New York Times, 2-22:33.

Donald Rumsfeld
Counsellor to the
President of the United States

The best policy as a Counsellor to the President . . . is to counsel the President and not to counsel about how he counsels the President.

Interview, Washington/
The Christian Science Monitor, 10-21:8.

Dean Rusk
Former Secretary of State of the United States

(Regarding government's right to privacy and secrecy in certain circumstances): . . . in a democratic society the public does have a right to know. But the public also has a right to have its public business transacted in a responsible fashion, and the problem is where do you draw the line? . . . For example, the President and a Secretary of State must have an opportunity to hold private conversations with their principal advisors; must have an opportunity to talk privately with other governments. Senators and Congressmen must have the right to talk things over privately with their own staff, or to talk with their friends about how to plan their campaigns . . . Now, this does not mean that there is a great conspiracy. I mean, there are many things that are secret. The press has its own secrets . . .

Television interview,
National Broadcasting Company/
The New York Times, 7-14:33.

Hugh Scott
United States Senator, R–Pa.

I think the people always give a sigh of relief whenever Congress goes home. I do not suppose it is all that bad, but there comes a time when the members need to go home. They need to refresh themselves and, like Antaeus, increase their strength tenfold by touching the earth of their home constituencies.

The Wall Street Journal, 10-6:12.

Milton J. Shapp
Governor of Pennsylvania

As a Governor, I would be derelict in my duty if I did not take any money you might hand out as general revenue-sharing. But that is the wrong way to do it—to proliferate funds without any control on how they are spent.

Before House Ways and Means Committee,
Washington, June 23/
The Washington Post, 6-24:(A)4.

Howard K. Smith
News commentator,
American Broadcasting Company

The "chief of state" is like the flag—you have

(HOWARD K. SMITH)

to be deferential. The "head of government" is nothing but a politician—and you can be rough and relentless with him. We (in the United States) combine the two in one person—the President—and suffer all the psychological stresses usual when you adopt two contradictory attitudes. (In the British system) you bow and scrape to the monarch—but you raise hell with the Prime Minister.

Time, 1-18:36.

Margaret Chase Smith
United States Senator, R—Maine

The United States Senate is in trouble. It is because growing numbers of its members no longer regard it as a high institution for dedicated and honorable service, but rather only as a means to an end. It has become a mere springboard to those who would use it—even abuse it—for their selfish interests—whether such interests be commercializing their position and title with the acquisition of high-price lecture fees or running for President. I have no criticism of Presidential aspirations as long as those Presidential aspirations do not result in dereliction of Senate duties in representation of state and national constituencies . . . A greater cause of Senate debilitation comes from the Senate "moonlighters," who regard the Senate as strictly secondary to their money-making activities in being offered high-paid lecture fees simply because they are Senators. As the Republican dean of the Senate recently said, "being paid $2,500 for $50 speeches . . ."

Before the Senate, Washington,
Dec. 20/The National Observer, 1-1('72):2.

. . . the Senate is a club of prima donnas, intensely self-oriented—99 kings and 1 queen—dedicated to their own personal accommodation. Consequently, the Senate is simply incapable of disciplining its members, whether it be violation of Senate rules of order and conduct, breach of national security, improper use or abuse of authority, or absenteeism. In the 23 years I have been a member of the Senate, only twice has the Senate reprimanded a member.

Before the Senate, Washington, Dec. 20/
Los Angeles Times, 12-26:(H)3.

William B. Spong, Jr.
United States Senator, D—Va.

Because of the enormous power it represents, the modern Presidency has become an intensely political office; and this can only detract from the kind of leadership we must have to cope with today's problems. (Limiting Presidents to a single term would) free the incumbent to base his decisions on what he thinks is best for the country, rather than what is best for his chances of re-election.

Before Rotary Club, Portsmouth, Va.,
April 8/The Washington Post, 4-9:(A)12.

Charles Stenvig
Mayor of Minneapolis

Government *for* the people has been around a long time. What we need is more government *by* the people.

Interview, Minneapolis/
The Christian Science Monitor, 2-3:11.

Adlai E. Stevenson III
United States Senator, D—Ill.

There isn't time (in the Senate) for many of the things that are most important. You aren't doing what we expect our Senators to be doing—to think and reflect upon all the great issues, to catch their breath every so often, to maintain their equilibrium, to give the country some sensible, long-term direction . . . I don't think it's quite fair to call us zombies. But there isn't enough time—and I don't think there ever will be—to become the whole individual which we should be as policy-makers for the nation.

Interview, Washington/
San Francisco Examiner, 11-22:6.

Maxwell D. Taylor
Former United States Ambassador
to South Vietnam

(Regarding government classification of information): . . . I would say that, as a general principle, the public has a right to know those things it is interested in, needs to know and wants to know; but not those things which, if revealed, would work against the public interest. And the public unfortunately, or inevitably, doesn't know many times those things which really should be held back.

TV-radio interview/"Issues and Answers,"
American Broadcasting Company, 7-4.

Jerome R. Waldie
United States Representative, D—Calif.

I flatly state, with regret and some despair, that the U.S. Congress has become irrelevant to America of the '70s. The attitudes reflected and the solutions proposed to the critical and desperate condition of America of the '70s are generally unrelated to those problems and consist more of rhetoric than commitment.

Before Town Hall, Los Angeles, Feb. 16/
Los Angeles Times, 2-17:(2)3.

John J. Williams
United States Senator, R—Del.

I've been here (in the Senate) 24 years, and I've seen bills delayed that were supposed to hold life or death for the country. But I've never seen a piece of legislation yet that was kept off the books when the people wanted it.

It may be a year or two later, but it always comes to pass.

Interview, Washington/
The National Observer, 1-11:12.

Ralph W. Yarborough
Former United States Senator, D—Tex.

There is too much bureaucracy in the Federal government, because only 537 of its employees are elected. You have the President and the Vice President, 100 Senators and 435 Congressmen; and then you have 2.5 million employees who are not elected by the people. The people elected by the people are close to the people.

Before County and District Clerks'
Association of Texas, Dallas, June 18/
The Dallas Times Herald, 6-19:(A)5.

Ronald L. Zeigler
Press Secretary to the
President of the United States

I have seen in the last few years here that occasionally the bureaucracy is not as responsive to the White House as some may suspect. But let me assure you that those who work within the government in various departments are going to be responsive, and those who are not responsive to the policies set forth by the President will find themselves involved in other assignments, and quite possibly not assignments within the Federal government.

Washington, Aug. 11/
The Washington Post, 8-15:(B)6.

Labor · The Economy

I. W. Abel
President, United Steelworkers of America

. . . why is it that all of a sudden, when we (the steelworkers) come up for bargaining, it's we who have jawboning? Where in the hell was (the President) in the GM thing? Where was he in the building-trades negotiations last year? Where was he in the truck situation? Where was his jawboning in railroads? Why is it that it is always appropriate to jawbone when it comes to steel?

Interview/Newsweek, 2-1:51.

I think the record of the AFL-CIO has been quite clear for some time. We have said not once but many, many times that we of labor are prepared to make our sacrifices with all other segments of the economy. When the time comes that the President of the United States thinks that it is necessary for us to have some kind of (wage-price) controls or regulations, the labor movement stands prepared to make its sacrifices, just so long as business and all other segments are asked to do the same thing.

TV-radio interview/"Meet the Press," National Broadcasting Company, Washington, 6-27.

Spiro T. Agnew
Vice President of the United States

(Regarding Democratic Presidential hopefuls' criticism of President Nixon's new economic program announced Aug. 15): Pettifogging delays, nitpicking for the sake of political advantage, senseless pride of authorship, jockeying for position at the expense of the unified sense of national purpose—all of these must be set firmly aside in the American people's move to a new prosperity without war.

Before American Society of Association Executives, Miami Beach, Aug. 25/ Los Angeles Times, 8-26:(1)25.

Let me say the unsayable: Rising corporate profits are good for the average man and are needed more than ever by the poor. If corporate profits were to rise next year to the level of the average of the past 20 years, as part of a full-employment economy, the Federal government tax receipts would increase by more than $8 billion . . . that's the kind of money that could go toward helping a great many people who could use the help. That's why we don't want to freeze profits. We want to increase profits that generate jobs, profits that generate tax revenues, profits that help to raise the average American's standard of living.

At National Governors Conference, San Juan, P.R., Sept. 13/ Los Angeles Times, 9-14:(1)4.

Carl Albert
United States Representative, D—Okla.

I welcome Republican conversion to Keynesian economy a full generation after it was accepted by the Democrats.

Washington, Jan. 29/ The New York Times, 1-30:12.

This is the 1970s and not the 1930s. To control inflation, it is necessary to have a direct intervention by the President through the use of standby credit controls and wage and price controls, use of the moral power of the Presidency, jawboning and antitrust enforcement.

San Francisco Examiner, 1-30:4.

All of the economic indicators now available suggest that we are still in the throes of the 1970 recession. While the art of the optimistic forecast has been developed to new levels of ingenuity, a look behind the rhetoric discloses that our economy is continuing to set new records—all of them bad. I find nowhere in the statistics any prospect for recovery, much less the boom predicted by the Administration.

News conference, Washington, April 8/
The New York Times, 4-9:13.

Joseph W. Barr
Former Secretary of the Treasury
of the United States

I do not believe that any government in any industrial nation today has enough clout to control an economy by raising taxes or monkeying around with their budgets.

Before Institute of Internal Auditors,
Chicago, June 28/
The Washington Post, 6-29:(D)7.

Joseph A. Beirne
President, Communications Workers of America

(Regarding President Nixon's new economic program announced Aug. 15): Overall, we'd certainly agree the President's program is as bold and sweeping as they say. However, as far as the wage-price freeze is concerned, this does not appear to be nearly as well thought out as other parts of the program. If it means that progressive wage increases now due will not go into effect, it just won't work. It would create consternation in our industry.

Aug. 16/The New York Times, 8-17:21.

Hale Boggs
United States Representative, D–La.

The people are concerned. They're worried. Six million people are unemployed. This is a tremendous waste of resources. Thirty per cent of the industrial capacity of the country is unused. These resources are desperately needed—the resources of men and the resources of machines. Then there is the human disaster: when a man goes home and tells his wife he doesn't have a job anymore, and he starts pounding the pavement. This is something that shouldn't happen in America.

Interview, Washington/
The Christian Science Monitor, 4-14:3.

George H. Bolt
Chairman, Pay Board,
Federal Cost of Living Council

Every American, however sophisticated, knows that inflation, by whatever name you

call it, is a very bad thing, and that somehow or other we must find ways to control it. If we do not, disaster will certainly follow, in perhaps forms that we cannot presently understand or contemplate. Thus, I think the American people almost unanimously will find some way of arresting at least the rate of inflation.

News conference, Washington, Oct. 22/
The New York Times, 10-23:15.

William F. Buckley, Jr.
Political columnist; Editor, "National Review"

The requirement that an individual pay dues to a private organization (labor union) in order to work is a modern writ of indenture; the requirement that he do the same in order to express an opinion over the public airways (such as Buckley does on his television program) involves an act of coercion by a private organization operating under government sanction. What is involved here is a fundamental civil and human right. And unless this country has lost hold of its reason, the Supreme Court will acknowledge, as I am confident it will, the right of the individual to exercise his rights as guaranteed under the First Amendment, even if he declines to join a union. Many of the people in the country, labeled as "liberals," eloquently object to any compromise of the individual rights of the citizen against the government—particularly free speech and privacy. I think it is time they join me in demanding that the individual have a right to join or not join, to pay dues or not pay dues to a private organization without surrendering his right to speak.

News conference, New York, Jan. 12/
National Review, 1-26:73.

John R. Bunting
President, First Pennsylvania Corporation

The economic program announced by President Nixon 45 days ago (Aug. 15) is a watershed in American economic history, with promise to lead the economy out of its current malaise. In large measure, the new program is less important for what was said than who said it. That a Republican President has suspended the competitive market system capitalism for three months and that he will,

(JOHN R. BUNTING)

in all probability, lead us into an era of far greater economic planning is significant because it unifies the vast majority of both conservative and liberal economists on the issue of planning prices and wages. For the rest of our active business careers, we will work in an economy in which, to some extent, wages and prices will be planned by a government board or boards.

Before Executive Club, Chicago, Sept. 24/
Vital Speeches, 11-1:53.

Arthur F. Burns
Chairman, Federal Reserve Board

The Federal Reserve will not stand idly by and let the American economy stagnate for want of money and credit. But we also intend to guard against the confusion—which sometimes exists even in intellectual circles—between a shortage of confidence to use abundantly-available money and credit, on the one hand, and an actual shortage of money and credit, on the other. I wish to reaffirm the assurance that I gave this Committee and the nation a year ago—namely, that the Federal Reserve will not become the architect of a new wave of inflation.

Before Joint Congressional Economic
Committee, Washington, Feb. 19/
The New York Times, 2-20:33.

I think we may be approaching an (economic) emergency in our country. I must confess that at times, in the dead of night, I find myself thinking about a wage-price freeze. But when I arise and have a cup of coffee, I forget it.

Before Joint Congressional Economic
Committee, Washington, Feb. 19/
The Dallas Times Herald, 2-20:(A)7.

Economic developments since (President Nixon's economic program was announced on) August 15 have, on the whole, been heartening. The new stabilization program has received widespread public support, and recent data on prices and wage rates made it clear that the freeze has been extremely effective. Consumer buying has picked up materially,

and demand for labor has risen sufficiently to begin reducing unemployment. Interest rates have come down substantially as the inflationary premium has been squeezed out.

San Francisco Examiner & Chronicle,
11-14:(A)7.

Shirley Chisholm
United States Representative, D–N.Y.

If you attend labor conventions these days, the union leaders, with few exceptions, are all dressed in fine suits and have generous expense accounts. Some of the charges of exclusivity and status-quo-ism which labor has aimed at management can now be aimed at parts of the labor movement.

Before House Education and Labor
Committee, Washington, March 18/
Daily World, 3-19:3.

John B. Connally, Jr.
Secretary of the Treasury-designate
of the United States

Everybody ought to pay some tax. It is wrong to have a democracy in which all the people don't contribute.

At his confirmation hearing before Senate
Finance Committee, Washington, Jan. 28/
The New York Times, 1-29:12.

John B. Connally, Jr.
Secretary of the Treasury of the United States

When you freeze wages and prices in one industry, people all over the country will say, "You froze it for them, why not for us? Our industry has 12 per cent inflation, and we can't take it." Then if you freeze it for that industry, too, another one will come in to complain. Once you start a freeze, how do you stop? That is why I am against freezes.

Interview, Washington/
U.S. News & World Report, 4-12:54.

You don't turn around an economy that is generating a gross national product in excess of a trillion dollars a year and affecting over 200 million people. You just don't turn it around. It is not like a yo-yo.

Washington, June 29/
The New York Times, 6-30:22.

(Regarding President Nixon's 90-day wage-price freeze announced Aug. 15): I think it's highly unlikely, it still remains a possibility, but I think it's highly unlikely (that all controls will be lifted after the 90 days). I would think there would have to be more than that. What it will be, how intensive it will be, how pervasive it will be, what it will be called, I don't know. One of the principal advantages, it seems to me, of the wage-price freeze is to cause the American people to halt for a moment and think about what they are doing to themselves with this constant stair-stepping of wages and costs and price increases . . .

Interview, Washington, Aug. 23/
The Dallas Times Herald, 8-24:(A)1.

(Regarding President Nixon's 90-day wage-price freeze): We are at the end of an era in our economic policy. It will be the disposition of the American people to have as few constraints as possible after the 90-day freeze period, and if we can get voluntary compliance now, we can avoid stringent controls later. But it would be unwise to think we can go back to where we were before. American business and labor may have to get used to the idea of living within certain parameters.

Interview, Washington/
The New York Times, 8-29:(1)1.

We must make abundantly clear that we cannot permit one man (AFL-CIO President George Meany) to put himself above the interest of all the working people of this country. There are 80 million working people in the United States. He does not represent all of these people.

News conference, Washington, Nov. 22/
The New York Times, 11-23:1.

Carl T. Curtis
United States Senator, R—Neb.

I do not exaggerate when I state that I believe that unbridled spending by our Federal government carries the seeds of destruction for our republic. The United States will never be conquered by a foreign foe. Our citizens are too patriotic to permit the subversive elements within to take over our government. Our danger lies in excessive spending and the resulting depreciation of the value of our money, and ruinous inflation.

Before the Senate, Washington, April 5/
Vital Speeches, 4-5:488.

Archie K. Davis
President, Chamber of Commerce
of the United States

Our society owes a great debt to labor. Generally speaking, the American worker is the best in the world. Beyond that, it was the American labor movement which proved that workers in a capitalistic system can create for themselves a far higher standard of living than socialist workers. But labor is just as subject to human failings as business, government, education or any other human institution. Labor can become set in its ways and inflexible. Labor can become too greedy. Labor power, like all power, can be misused . . . Labor can be terrifyingly blind to the fact that the power to compel capitulation to its demands is infinitely greater than are the means to meet those demands. Yet, the (labor) unions at times appear willing to kill off an entire industry—to kill off jobs—rather than moderate their position. A "good" contract with a company that is forced to close is hardly an economic victory . . . Labor did not bring on inflation. It came as the result of government fiscal irresponsibility and a belief that we could have both guns and butter without some degree of sacrifice. But labor can easily sabotage efforts to halt it. "Catch-up" wage demands are understandable. However, wage increases that go far beyond that, and consistently exceed productivity gains, merely feed the fires of inflation and leave no one better off, not even the workers who receive them. The whole process is self-defeating; and the continuing escalation of our wage and price structure is steadily but surely pricing American goods out of world markets, just as surely as wage increases in the construction

(ARCHIE K. DAVIS)

industry are pricing the average American out of the housing market.

At Printing Industry of America convention, Chicago, June 30/Vital Speeches, 8-1:633.

To halt inflation, Federal government spending must be frozen—better yet, cut—and the money supply restrained. Economic controls deal with the results of inflation. Frozen or reduced spending is one sure way to reduce inflationary pressures. As wage and price increases are deferred, so too should spending for new Federal programs be deferred.

Dallas, Nov. 4/ The Dallas Times Herald, 11-4:(A)1.

John H. Dent
United States Representative, D–Pa.

The inflation that we have and the trouble we are in is because high-wage workers are able to buy low-wage products.

Quote, 4-25:386.

Arthur A. Fletcher
Assistant Secretary of Labor of the United States

The era of arrogance and discrimination by some trade unions has ended . . . The unions have lost public support because of their outrageous abuse of their power, both in terms of demands for heavy wage increases and in the effort which they made to preserve the segregated character of some of the unions.

Before Associated Builders and Contractors, March 12/The Washington Post, 3-13:(A)4.

Milton Friedman
Professor of Economics, University of Chicago

(Regarding President Nixon's wage-price freeze announced Aug. 15): The effect will be to conceal price and wage increases, not prevent them. Our experience from World War II and other times proves that people will find ways to evade the freeze.

The Dallas Times Herald, 8-22:(B)10.

When men do not regard governmental measures as just and right, they will find a

way around them. The effects extend beyond the original source, generate widespread disrespect for the law, and promote corruption and violence. We found this out to our cost in the 1920s with Prohibition; in World War II with price control and rationing; today with drug laws. We shall experience it yet again with price and wage controls if they are ever more than a paper facade.

San Francisco Examiner & Chronicle (This World), 11-7:2.

John Kenneth Galbraith
Professor of Economics, Harvard University

(Regarding Nixon Administration attempts to improve the U.S. economy): (Lamentable is) the effort to convert failure into success by resort to psychological measures—by the use of faith, hope, prediction and appeal for positive thought as instruments of policy. Statistics that seemed to suggest progress have been brightly featured; any retrograde tendencies have been passed over in dull and heavy silence. One is tempted to suppose that part of this policy derives from the President's unquestionably very wholesome interest in spectator sports. The football fan has always attached a somewhat exaggerated importance to the impact of the cheering section on the outcome of the game . . .

Before Joint Congressional Economic Committee, Washington, July 20/ The Washington Post, 7-21:(A)2.

As long as one has strong unions and strong corporations, one is going to have competition between the unions and corporations that can shove up the prices. So there is going to be a continuing need for some kind of wage-price restraint. Those who think otherwise are fooling themselves.

Interview, Townshend, Vt., Aug. 17/ Los Angeles Herald-Examiner, 8-18:(D)11.

We've been approaching the whole subject of wage and price control (in) somewhat the same fashion that a conservative clergyman approaches an erotic statue. He knows he must look at it, but he doesn't want anyone to see him do it.

Interview, Townshend, Vt., Aug. 17/
San Francisco Examiner, 8-18:5.

Barry M. Goldwater
United States Senator, R—Ariz.

I am and always have been and always will be a disciple of the balanced budget.

Quote, 8-15:145.

If a man earns $5 an hour, pay him $5 an hour; but don't take the $1.50 man and give *him* $5 an hour. When I drive my car into the garage, I want it fixed within a week. When I call the plumber to my house, I expect him to fix the faucet before the day is out. Craftsmen will have to be craftsmen again.

Before National Office Products Association,
Chicago, Oct. 20/
The New York Times, 10-21:32.

C. Jackson Grayson
Chairman, Price Commission,
Federal Cost of Living Council

Sometimes there comes a point where someone (in management) must make a firm decision that may result in a (labor) strike. And in the long run, it may be better than continuing what has been happening—that is, no strikes in order to pass through higher prices to the consumer at all costs. In fact, there is a greater cost, and it's called inflation.

Interview/Newsweek, 12-20:71.

W. P. Gullander
President,
National Association of Manufacturers

There is a need for (labor) union officials to recognize that they do not do their members a service by getting them fantastic wage increases which are beyond productivity. But I'll defend the union's right to make demands without government interference just as strongly as management's right to try to settle without government interference.

Before Rotary Club, Los Angeles, Sept. 17/
Los Angeles Herald-Examiner, 9-18:(A)3.

Walter W. Heller
Professor of Economics, University of
Minnesota; Former Chairman, Council of
Economic Advisers to the President of
the United States

When we come out of this shock treatment (President Nixon's 90-day wage-price freeze), will we have to put the patient (the economy) in a strait jacket of wage-price controls, or can we develop some tranquilizers, such as a wage-price review board? Long-term wage and price controls would amount to the Sovietization of the economy. We'll have a bunch of bureaucrats trying to play economic gods.

Austin, Tex., Aug. 18/
Los Angeles Times, 8-19:(1)23.

I welcome the President's (Nixon) shift from a do-nothing to a do-something policy; but tax breaks of $9 billion for industry and some $2 billion for individual taxpayers represent a very lopsided program in pursuit of very laudable goals. That's raw meat for big business, while the consumer gets little more than a soup bone.

Quote, 9-12:241.

James D. Hodgson
Secretary of Labor of the United States

Industry-wide strikes have become something like an industrial H-bomb. And I just wonder how long the nation is going to tolerate this kind of bizarre brinksmanship.

News conference, Washington, Jan. 4/
The New York Times, 1-6:41.

The fight against inflation is not only a matter of keeping wage and price increases at reasonable levels but also of increasing our nation's productivity. Our productivity growth-rate started dropping in the late 1960s. It picked up hearteningly in the second and third quarters of last year, but dropped again the last quarter because of the auto strike. In any case, greater productivity is an absolute essential if we are to undertake successfully all the jobs we see ahead—combatting foreign competition, meeting all the large social and environmental goals we have set for ourselves

(JAMES D. HODGSON)

and increasing real wages. We need to learn that the only way a nation can improve its real wages is to improve its productivity.

Before Associated Industries of the Quad-Cities, Moline, Ill., Feb. 24/Vital Speeches, 4-1:384.

(Regarding AFL-CIO president George Meany's criticism of President Nixon's new economic program announced Aug. 15): Mr. Meany has advocated an increase in employment opportunities for American working men. The President's program has done just that. Mr. Meany has advocated price stabilization and, in fact, wage and price controls. The President's (wage-price) freeze is a forthright step to protect the workers' earnings. Indeed, the whole purpose of the President's initiative is to create jobs, halt the vicious cycle of inflation and strengthen our competitive position. All of these objectives benefit the American worker. I really doubt that George Meany could oppose those goals. I can only conclude that Mr. Meany will revise his views with more study of the program. I am confident that the vast majority of working men and women across America wholeheartedly endorse our efforts to create more jobs to keep America competitive in a competitive world, to improve the market for America's products and, most importantly, to protect the purchasing power of the American worker's dollar.

Aug. 17/The Christian Science Monitor, 8-20:6.

Hendrik S. Houthakker
Member, Council of Economic Advisers to the President of the United States

This particular nostrum (wage and price controls) is far worse than the disease it is supposed to cure. Even if it were effective in stabilizing prices, a freeze or a system of controls would do lasting damage to our free economic institutions . . . In addition to suitable fiscal and monetary policies, the key to better price behavior lies in the very essence of a properly-working decentralized economy—namely, in competition.

March 11/ The Christian Science Monitor, 3-15:11.

Hubert H. Humphrey
United States Senator, D—Minn.

How can he, (President) Nixon, be for a *full*-employment budget in 1972 when we are in an *un*employment budget in 1971?

Hampton, Va., March 14/ The Washington Post, 3-16:(A)17.

The issue is the economy. The people are worried about the economy, and they have a right to worry. (President) Nixon has no more control over the economy than a baby has over the rising and setting of the sun.

News conference, Washington, Aug. 5/ The New York Times, 8-6:35.

The (Nixon) Administration is still applying quack remedies to our economy. It is prescribing simultaneous doses of "uppers" and "downers"—persistent inflation and high unemployment, side by side for the first time in the history of our nation.

At Texas AFL-CIO convention, Dallas, Aug. 13/Los Angeles Times, 8-14:(1)4.

(Regarding President Nixon's new economic program announced Aug. 15): Thank goodness the President has acted; but the fact is that, for two years, he has refused to act . . . President Nixon's long-awaited, long-needed bold action comes at a time when the economic landscape is strewn with economic wreckage.

Los Angeles Times, 8-17:(1)20.

Unemployment is America's Number 1 hypocrisy. We've got 250,000 aerospace scientists out of work, and we can't get mass transit built. As important as it is, Mr. Nixon, for you to go to Moscow and Peking, how about going to the employment offices and see all the people looking for jobs? You don't get any withholding tax out of welfare checks.

Los Angeles Times, 11-5:(2)7.

Lee A. Iacocca
President, Ford Motor Company

The country cannot hope to have a sustained economic recovery without a strong increase in investment. It is disquieting that the outlook for capital spending is so weak. We would urge Congress to restore the investment tax credit permanently. Changes that promote investment are in the best interests of everyone.

Interview/Time, 8-16:69.

As businessmen, you know as well as I do that there is no way to absorb an 11% increase in labor costs with a 3%, 4% or even 5% gain in productivity. Either prices go up and you have inflation, or profits disappear—and with them go jobs, tax revenues and just about everything else we need to keep this country strong and prosperous.

At Los Angeles area Chamber of Commerce 1972 Business Outlook Conference, Nov. 3/ Los Angeles Times, 11-4:(3)15.

Henry M. Jackson
United States Senator, D–Wash.

After almost 1,000 consecutive months of economic expansion, this Republican Administration took little more than 100 days to plunge us down the slopes of another Republican recession . . . We are being brought together in bankruptcy courts, food stamp lines and unemployment offices all over America. We are witnessing an American tragedy.

News conference, Los Angeles, April 26/ Los Angeles Times, 4-27:(1)21.

The nation's number one priority is jobs. To talk simply of six per cent unemployment is misleading. There are thousands of Americans out of work, looking for work, hoping for work who never show up in that statistic. We simply cannot tolerate an economic performance that assumes and accepts this kind of employment as inevitable. And we cannot indulge in pious speeches about the homely virtues of honest labor when we are failing to provide large numbers of men and women with basic job opportunities.

At Nevada State Democratic Party's Jefferson-Jackson Day dinner, Las Vegas, May 24/Las Vegas Sun, 5-25:4.

There are some people in the Democratic Party who, intentionally or not, have turned their backs on the working man. They are either indifferent to him or downright hostile. Their cocktail parties abound with snide jokes about "hardhats" and "ethnics." They mouth fashionable cliches about how workers have grown fat and conservative with affluence, and how their unions are reactionary or racist. They ignore the fact that, in the last two decades, unions have been at the forefront of everything decent in this country—from civil rights to education to national health insurance. In fact, if it were not for the labor movement, many of these so-called liberals would not enjoy the affluence they now take for granted.

At New York State AFL-CIO convention, New York, Aug. 10/ The New York Times, 8-11:1.

. . . I think the central issue (in the 1972 Presidential election) is the economy, because unless you can make this economic system work, you can't generate the revenues to do the things you need to do at home. That's why, when people ask me, "Senator, what is your list of priorities?" I point out that you can't talk about your list of priorities unless you talk about Priority One, and that's the economy. Every time you lose a billion dollars of the national product, you lose over $300 million in Federal revenue. And thanks to the mismanagement of our economy, we lost over $30 billion in revenue last year—last fiscal year ending June 30. We lost over $4 billion in revenue at the state and local level. That's why I have made it my little hobby to spend a lot of time in the economic area and talk to a lot of people that I think are wise and shrewd. And so, unless you make this economic system work, you can't do these things that we need to do. And that involves, of course, the quality of American life. I mean, you've got to end discrimination, you've got to end poverty, you have to rebuild your cities, you're going to have to build new cities, you're going to have to demonstrate—and we can, if we are willing to do it—that we can have economic growth and

(HENRY M. JACKSON)

have quality life—clean air, clean water and clean land. But to me, you start with the economy, and from there you really move out logically and talk about the things you can do.

Interview, Washington/
The Washington Post, 11-21:(C)4.

Eliot Janeway
Economist

(Regarding "Phase Two" of President Nixon's economic program, announced Aug. 15): It's Operation Tanglefoot; an exercise in stimulative restraint—that's self-contradictory. The most important question about Phase Two is how quickly Phase Three will start.

Interview, New York/
The New York Times, 11-1:69.

Albert W. Johnson
United States Representative, R—Pa.

I think that, beyond any question, the polls would show that a majority of people would favor it (wage and price controls). If they really realized what they were saying, I question that they would be in favor of it . . . Now, if they thought they had to go through rationing, if they thought they couldn't get a wage increase, couldn't get a salary increase, couldn't raise the price of anything they sold without going through a board somewhere, I think you would get an entirely different answer. Everybody has forgotten what living under OPA is like. It is kind of like everybody favored Prohibition, but it just didn't work. Everybody thought they wanted it—but they didn't want it . . . It is like everybody says they want to live: "I wish I could live in the good old days." Well, when they start thinking about how it is to travel by covered wagon as opposed to a jet airplane, they really don't mean that.

Before House Banking and Currency
Committee, Washington, Feb. 23/
U.S. News & World Report, 3-8:77.

Clarence D. Long
United States Representative, D—Md.

(Wage and price) controls would create

mountains of red tape for business and labor. A standard joke during World War II was that Lincoln took only 267 words for his Gettysburg Address, but it took the OPA 22,000 words to establish the price of a head of cabbage.

Quote, 6-13:567.

Paul W. McCracken
Chairman, Council of Economic Advisers
to the President of the United States

. . . one of the things that's very important in this business is to resist the temptation to think that whatever is will never change. In an inflationary boom, it is hard for people to believe there could be anything other than ebullience forever. If the thing moves the other way, there will be a period when people can't believe that it'll ever get any better.

Interview, Washington/
The Christian Science Monitor, 5-1:14.

Congress has given the President authority to impose mandatory price and wage controls; but when faced with the opportunity to do so, the House of Representatives voted overwhelmingly against imposing such controls on its own initiative. Why this great reluctance to impose mandatory controls? It is because the element of control makes clear that what is involved is forcibly preventing workers, businessmen, lenders and other individuals from doing what they want to do, which they regard as equitable, and which may be equitable by a more objective standard, and which may be in the general economic interest. Naturally, there is reluctance to adopt measures which have this transparent result. But still being determined to find a less difficult solution, many resort to willing the end without willing the means—calling for the results of control without the controls. This is what is meant nowadays by an effective incomes policy—a policy that compels without being compulsory and operates by force of government without legislation.

Before Joint Congressional Economic
Committee, Washington, July 8/
U.S. News & World Report, 7-26:59.

(Regarding criticism that President Nixon's new economic program, announced August 15, favors business rather than ordinary people): Is it bad for workers if we expand the economy and create more new job opportunities? Is it bad for ordinary people if we have strong measures for safeguarding the buying power of their pay envelopes? Is it bad for employees if we have measures to enable U.S. industry to compete internationally on more even terms, thereby enlarging employment here? Is it bad for people to have programs to encourage things that give us the rising productivity which is the only source of higher real incomes? That charge, to use a word not in the textbook, is bunk.

Interview, Washington/
U.S. News & World Report, 8-30:50.

James P. McFarland
Chairman, General Mills, Inc.

Our forecasters foresee a rise in gross national product to about $2 trillion in 1980. I don't imagine any of us can really grasp how much $2 trillion is, but I do know it will buy a lot of cake mix.

At Newspaper Food Editors Conference,
Chicago/The Dallas Times Herald, 10-7:(B)2.

George S. McGovern
United States Senator, D–S.D.

(Advocating a six-month wage and price freeze): I paid $94 last week to a man who came out to fix my refrigerator. He was there about 20 minutes. Now that's an outrage.

TV-radio interview/
The Wall Street Journal, 7-2:6.

(Regarding President Nixon's new economic program announced Aug. 15): What was the new Nixon game plan? It was a bonanza for the rich and no help at all for those really being hurt by inflation . . . Mr. Nixon gave the nation's corporations a $5 billion bonanza in investment tax credits, and he took away from labor the gains won in collective bargaining and the just compensation due because of past inflation. He gave the corporations in-

centive to use all the old tax loopholes and a couple of new ones, and he tried to take away from the working man and the hourly wage earner the right to strike. He gave the corporations and big business what may be the biggest free ride in the history of this country, and he did nothing for the working man, the small merchant or the farmer. So what we have is the most unfair economic package ever designed by a President of the United States. I called it economic madness, and I still believe that is exactly what it is.

At United Automobile Workers Region 2
Labor Day picnic, Cleveland, Sept. 6/
Los Angeles Times, 9-7:(1)7.

Before the President (Nixon) acted (by imposing a wage-price freeze) in August, I had long advocated a wage-price freeze of at least six months to break the inflation spiral. Then I suggested we assess the situation at the end of that time to determine whether restraints ought to be retained. But that freeze must be accompanied by similar limits on windfall profits, dividends and interest. It is unfair to make the working man and woman, the small businessman and farmer bear the burden of sacrifice. Instead, I favor the concept of equality of sacrifice.

Interview/Nation's Business, November:68.

George Meany
President, American Federation of
Labor-Congress of Industrial Organizations

We want our fair share of the economic pie, and we will not be intimidated, frightened or stopped. And we won't relinquish the right to bargain collectively any more than we will surrender the right to strike. If it takes strikes to achieve economic justice, we won't hesitate to withhold our labor.

May 26/The New York Times, 5-27:52.

We have an inflationary psychology in this country. We have people raising prices when there is just no reason. They just raise them because it is in the air; this is the thing you

(GEORGE MEANY)

do. You know, according to all of the rules that the economists live by, according to the book, when you cause more unemployment, when you tighten up on the money supply and you keep business from expanding and thereby cause more and more people to become unemployed, prices should go down according to all the rules. Prices should have started to come down at least two years ago in the early spring of 1969. But what has happened? Prices have gone up . . . So this is running contrary to all of the economic rules. You have unemployment, you have the purchasing power which is down. It is a rather strange situation, because—as I say—I am not an economist, I don't fully understand, but during all this period the savings of the American people have been going up. I'd like to have some economist . . . put all these together; unemployment going up, inflation, people out of work, and more savings, and so on and so forth. I don't understand.

TV-radio interview/"Meet the Press,"
National Broadcasting Company,
Washington, 7-11.

He (Treasury Secretary John Connally) is a proven expert at Texas politics and knows quite a bit about the oil companies and their needs and the banks and the insurance companies and what they want. I'm not sure he knows much about the national economy, and I am certain he doesn't understand the problems of American workers . . . His shocking lack of faith in the ability of the American people and the American system to reach and maintain full employment . . . sounds like acceptance of Communist propaganda . . . Secretary Connally needs lessons in the ingenuity of the American people and some understanding of the American economy. He needs faith in America.

Washington, July 12/
Los Angeles Times, 7-13:(1)5.

We are prepared to cooperate with mandatory government (wage-price) controls, if the President decides they are necessary, provided such controls are even-handed and across-the-board. The one way I know to stop inflation at this time is by imposition of controls.

News conference, San Francisco, Aug. 10/
Los Angeles Herald-Examiner, 8-10:(C)1.

I don't pay much attention to the Secretary of Labor. After all, if you have a problem with the landlord, you don't discuss it with the janitor.

News conference, Washington, Aug. 19/
Los Angeles Herald-Examiner, 8-19:(A)1.

(What President Nixon could have said on Aug. 15 when announcing his new economic program was) "We are freezing wages and prices for the next 90 days or less, and we are immediately going to call all interested parties—labor, business and so on—to try to work out some system for a short time—a year or so—to keep prices somewhere within range." If he had done that . . we would have said "Amen," because this was on the record. This is what we said we'd do. We'd cooperate. But when he comes out with a whole package and it's so completely biased *against* the worker and *for* business, we couldn't buy it.

News conference, Washington/
San Francisco Examiner, 9-5:(A)6.

What is proposed here (in President Nixon's economic program) is a radical distribution of the nation's income and wealth in favor of the rich and at the expense of the public interest. Altogether, the President's program would give big business $70 billion over the next 10 years. This would be the biggest tax bonanza in corporate history and would severely lessen tax responsibility of corporations, shifting it to wage and salary earners. For those who have much, the President proposes more. For those who have little, the President proposes less. The $70 billion the President would give big business over the next 10 years—$37 billion in already ordered depreciation allowances and the balance in his new proposals—should be used to meet the needs that actually exist. What are these needs? America needs schools and hospitals. America needs a vast expansion of medical facilities and medical personnel. America needs 25 million new housing units. America needs new, efficient, low-cost transit systems in every major city. America needs new waste-disposal systems, new technology and new hardware to extract poisons from the air, the water and the soil. Public investment, in short, is precisely what America needs in order to strengthen the economy and provide millions of much-needed jobs. With 6.1 per cent of the labor force jobless—5.1 million workers without employment—the United States needs incomes and purchasing power to put these people back in the marketplace to buy the goods of plants now idle. The President's program does not go to these needs. Instead, he proposes to hand over the people's money to industry in order, he says, to stimulate industrial investment. But at this very hour, industry can find no use for 27 per cent of the industrial capacity that already exists. The President labels this scheme a "job development program," but he knows well that much of industry's investment in new machinery and equipment will eliminate jobs. When all of the economic proposals are examined closely— who will be the recipients, who will be the losers, who will have to pay more out in taxes, and who will pay less in taxes—it is clear that the President's proposal is a form of socialism for big business.

Before House Ways and Means Committee,
Washington, Sept. 13/
I. F. Stone's Bi-weekly, 10-4:3.

(Generally), I think as time goes on, there is going to be more and more thought given to some substitute for strikes. This is something that has certainly got to be explored, because strikes today are too expensive.

The Christian Science Monitor, 9-15:2.

We are really at a historic moment in the life of this nation, whether for good or evil only time will tell. This is the first time in the history of America that any President ever set out to control the economic life of the nation in peacetime. It is no disrespect to the President (Nixon) to say that, on the basis of his track record, we don't have very much confidence . . . But it is obvious that if the present program doesn't work—and there is no sure indication that it will work—the next step would be more stringent and oppressive measures that could destroy our American institutions. If Phase II (of the President's economic program) fails, political expediency demands a scapegoat. The man in the White House never says, "It is my fault." No politician ever says it is his fault. It demands the scapegoat, and we have no doubt as to who that scapegoat will be . . . There will be no explanations and no apology if Phase II happens to fail. Harsher measures will be promulgated, surely—directed against the nation's workers and their unions; and we can expect anti-strike edicts and injunctions and all the other harassments that have been the lot of labor in the authoritarian countries in recent history.

At AFL-CIO convention, Bal Harbour, Fla.,
Nov. 18/The Washington Post, 11-20:(A)13.

(On the reception accorded a speech by President Nixon at the AFL-CIO convention Nov. 19): He came here to contrive a situation under which he could claim he had been unfairly treated. We were not discourteous. There was no booing and there was no jeering, (but there was some) derisive laughter . . . I'm willing to concede that this laughter was of a type that indicated disagreement with the President. I still think we have a constitutional right to laugh. This isn't a monarchy.

Bal Harbour, Fla., Nov. 22/San Francisco
Examiner & Chronicle (This World), 11-28:8.

There's a complete lack of confidence in (President) Nixon today on the part of the American people—even on the part of business people who have been busy applauding Mr. Nixon and all of his actions. They show very little confidence in his ability to manage the economy. I say this advisedly, and there's nothing disrespectful about it. It's just a question of fact. President Nixon has nothing in his experience to indicate that he has the ability or the intelligence or the knowledge to

(GEORGE MEANY)

control the economy of this country.

At AFL-CIO convention, Bal Harbour, Fla., Nov. 22/The Dallas Times Herald, 11-23:(A)14.

Wilbur D. Mills
United States Representative, D—Ark.

This (Nixon) Administration has managed to impale this nation on the horns of a distressing and dangerous dilemma—serious inflation accompanied by high unemployment. Inflation is a problem which the present Administration inherited. (But the recession) is clearly of the present Administration's own making.

Ogden, Utah, July 18/
Los Angeles Herald-Examiner, 7-18:(A)2.

(It is hoped the Nixon Administration) will get back on base with its new economic policy, and I will continue to do all that I can to help it do so. But the fact remains that American business, American labor, the American people generally have been paying an exhorbitant and tragic price for a total lack of economic performance. Like Washington baseball fans, we have been forced to pay too much for too little for too long. The need is obvious for a new team in this country, but, more particularly, for new front-office management.

Before National Press Club, Washington, Oct. 20/The Washington Post, 10-21:(A)2.

How in the world can business continue to be competitive, how in the world can wage-earners continue to be competitive, if they are going to be the enemy of each other? I think it is highly important that we get away from this constant fight between management and labor. Each must realize it cannot do the job alone. If we can get them to work together, they can constitute a greater force in the world for the preservation of their own opportunities than government ever could. Somehow, we must get them together. I, frankly, at this point don't know how.

Interview, Nation's Business, November:71

Edmund S. Muskie
United States Senator, D—Maine

For 27 months, this (Nixon) Administration has watched millions of Americans lose the right to earn a decent living. For 27 months, this Administration has let millions more fall on hard times because of rising costs. (President Nixon claims to) have a game plan for the economy; but the only ones who can do any scoring are the bankers. We must tell this Administration in plain language: "Stop playing games. Stop putting all the blame for inflation on the backs of construction workers. Stop making organized labor the scapegoat for the failures of this Administration."

At Louisiana AFL-CIO convention, Baton Rouge, April 15/ Austin (Tex.) Statesman, 4-16:24.

Those of us who are negotiating for prosperity cannot accept more years of an Administration (Nixon's) which pledges recovery, produces recession and then pronounces its failure a smashing success.

At Texas AFL-CIO convention, Dallas, Aug. 11/ The Washington Post, 8-12:(A)8.

Richard M. Nixon
President of the United States

1971 is going to be a year of an expanding economy, in which inflation . . . the rise in inflation, is going to continue to go down; in which unemployment, which is presently too high, will finally come under control and begin to recede. 1971, in essence, will be a good year. And 1972 will be a very good year. Now, having made that prediction, I will say that the purpose of this Administration will be to have an activist economic policy designed to control inflation, but, at the same time, to expand the economy so that we can reduce unemployment, and to have what this country has not had for 20 years—and that is a situation where we can have full employment in peacetime, without the cost of war and without the cost of excessive inflation.

Television interview, Washington, Jan 4/The New York Times, 1-6:42.

I am now a Keynesian in economics.
Television interview,
Washington, Jan. 4/
The New York Times, 1-10:(4)1.

I will forever be amazed at those who cry "repression of freedom" at the drop of a hat, but who—in the next breath—advocate total repression of the economic freedom of businessmen and workingmen. I have been to countries whose leaders thought they could legislate economic growth. They drew up their plans, they passed the laws, they pushed the button—nothing happened. They discovered, in time, that no law that they passed could repeal the law of supply and demand; and no social motive, no matter how high-sounding, could replace the impetus of the profit motive.
Before Chamber of Commerce of the
United States, Washington, April 26/
The Washington Post, 4-27:(A)6.

Twenty years ago, when I was a Senator from California, the United States produced 50 per cent of all steel in the world. Today, we produce 20 per cent. Last year, for example, steel profits were 2.5 per cent. That's the lowest of any major industry, looking at it from a competitive standpoint. Japan 20 years ago produced five million tons of steel, last year produced 100 million tons of steel and by 1974 will produce more steel than the United States of America. Now, what does all this mean to us? It means that this (upcoming steel) settlement, a wage-price settlement, must reflect the competitive realities in the world or we're going to find . . . that the United States steel industry, which has been the backbone of our economy and is the backbone of any strong industrial economy, is going to be noncompetitive in the world . . .
News conference, San Clemente, Calif.,
May 1/The New York Times. 5-2:(1)66.

Last month, I met at the White House with leaders of several organizations; and I was particularly struck to learn from them that approximately 70 per cent of Americans over 65 own their own homes. This means that the growing burden of property taxes falls on their shoulders with special weight. When a person retires, his income goes down—and so do most of his tax bills. But his property taxes keep right on climbing, and he may even be forced out of the home he has paid for. This is one reason I want revenue-sharing: to ease the pressure on property taxes, for older Americans and for all Americans.
At National Retired Teachers
Association-American Association of
Retired Persons joint convention, Chicago,
June 25/The New York Times, 6-26:11.

In terms of our economy, when we talk about how we can change it and how we can deal, for example, with problems like the wage-price escalation, it of course has not gone unnoticed that many at this time tend to throw up their hands and conclude that the only answer to the problem is to go to wage and price controls. Some nibble at it at the edges and say, "Well, we ought to have a wage-price board"; or others go all the way and say, "Why not wage and price controls?" When you talk to management, however, they want wage controls. When you talk to labor, they want price controls. When you talk to government, they recognize, as we recognize, that you cannot have wage controls without price controls and . . . you cannot have wage and price controls without rationing . . . So despite the fact that a majority of the American people, when asked do you believe there should be wage and price controls, they say yes; if they had them for a while, they would say no with a vengeance; one, because they do not work in peacetime in controlling the problem, and two, because the cost in terms of snuffing out (the) dynamism and strength of the American economy would be a cost much too high to pay.
Before Midwestern newspaper executives,
Kansas City, July 6/
Vital Speeches, 8-1:613.

WHAT THEY SAID IN 1971

(RICHARD M. NIXON)

I am today ordering a freeze on all prices and wages throughout the United States for a period of 90 days. In addition, I call upon corporations to extend the wage-price freeze to all dividends. I have today appointed a Cost of Living Council within the government. I have directed this Council to work with leaders of labor and business to set up the proper mechanism for achieving continued price and wage stability after the 90-day freeze is over. Let me emphasize two characteristics to this action: One, it is temporary; to put the strong, vigorous American economy into a permanent strait jacket would lock in unfairness and stifle the expansion of our free-enterprise system. Two, while the wage-price freeze will be backed by government sanctions if necessary, it will not be accompanied by the establishment of a huge price-control bureaucracy. I am relying (on) the voluntary cooperation of all Americans—workers, employers, consumers—to make this freeze work. Working together, we will break the back of inflation. And we will do it without the mandatory wage and price controls that crush economic and personal freedom.

TV-radio address to the nation,
Washington, Aug. 15/
San Francisco Examiner, 8-16:5.

(Regarding his wage-price freeze order announced Aug. 15): It's not easy for a workingman to forego for a while the wage increase he deserves. It's not easy for a businessman to hold the line on prices when his costs are high and profits are slim. It's not easy for Federal employees to cover the same amount of work with less personnel because of a cut in Federal spending. It's not easy for investors—more than 30 million of them—to forego an increase in dividends. But if the temporary sacrifice of each of these Americans will result in stopping the rise in the cost of living for all Americans, this is a great deal worth sacrificing for.

Before Knights of Columbus, New York,
Aug. 17/The New York Times, 8-18:23.

The one great ingredient (determining whether his economic policies succeed) is the spirit of the American people. The spirit to which I refer is the spirit which thrives on competition, which rises to meet adversity, which endures great burdens, because it can envision even greater rewards.

Before Associated Milk Producers
members, Chicago, Sept. 3/
Los Angeles Times, 9-4:(1)8.

In the coming year, the Congress will face many temptations to raise spending and to cut taxes in addition to the recommendations I have made. In the short run, these always are popular measures. But as we look at the realities of the budget at this time, we must face up to this hard fact: Any additional spending increases not accompanied by tax increases—and any additional tax cuts not accompanied by spending cuts—will be certain to start us again on a spiral of higher prices. To spend more than we can afford or to tax less than we can afford is the sure route to prices higher than we can afford.

Before Congress, Washington, Sept. 9/
The Washington Post, 9-10:(A)12.

I am announcing tonight that when the 90-day (wage-price) freeze is over on November 13, we shall continue our program of wage and price restraint. We began this battle against inflation for the purpose of winning it. We are going to stay in it until we do win it.

TV-radio address, Washington, Oct. 7/
The New York Times, 10-8:39.

Many of my good friends have advised me that the only politically popular position to take is to be against profits. But let us recognize an unassailable fact of economic life: All Americans will benefit from more profits. More profits fuel the expansion that generates more jobs; it means more investment that will make our goods more competitive; it also means there will be more tax revenues to pay for the programs that help people in need. That's why higher profits in the American economy would be good for every person in America.

TV-radio address, Washington, Oct. 7/
The Washington Post, 10-8:(A)11.

I would strongly advise anybody who invests (in the stock market) to invest on the long term, not the short term. On the long term, 1972 is going to be a good year. When we see, for example, inflation cut in half—which is our goal—when we see employment beginning to rise—it rose over a million during the period of the (wage-price) freeze—and when we see something else, when we see our economy now being built on the basis of peace rather than war, this is a time when people looking to the future . . . could, it seems to me, well invest in America with the hope that their investments will prove well.

News conference, Washington, Nov. 12/
The Washington Post, 11-13:(A)6.

In order to stop the rise in the cost of living, we want the participation of business, we want the participation of labor, we want the participation of consumers and all the other areas of the society. We hope we get it. But whether we get that participation or not, it is my obligation as President of the United States to make this program of stopping the rise in the cost of living succeed. And to the extent that my powers allow it, I shall do exactly that.

At AFL-CIO convention, Bal Harbour,
Fla., Nov. 19/
The New York Times, 11-20:16.

I think we should all be pleased that the American people so generally have supported the wage-price freeze and controls. However, there is a warning note to be sounded here. A great number of Americans might say, "Let's continue to have the controls." I don't want that; because if our people and this economy get used to that crutch, we will never throw it away.

Interview, Washington, December/
Time, 1-3:('72):14.

Lawrence F. O'Brien
Chairman,
Democratic National Committee

No amount of statistical juggling can hide the fact that unemployment is at its worst

level since late 1961, when a Democratic Administration was reducing the record unemployment rates inherited from the last Republican Administration.

Los Angeles Herald-Examiner, 2-7:(A)2.

(Concerning President Nixon's economic program announced August 15): Unemployment still hovers near 6 per cent. Industrial production has not rebounded strongly. Uncertainty and chaos surround the implementation of Phase II of the anti-inflation program. The inequities of the freeze period have not been corrected. Consumer confidence is still low. The inflation psychology has not been broken. The stock market continues to fall.

San Francisco Examiner & Chronicle,
11-14:(A)7.

Arthur M. Okun
Senior fellow, Brookings Institution;
Former Chairman, Council of Economic
Advisers to the President
of the United States

(Regarding President Nixon's 90-day wage-price freeze announced Aug. 15): . . . the experience of the 90-day freeze should demonstrate that across-the-board, rigid wage-price control is not appropriate business for the government. It may even help to teach people why most economists have been so unenthusiastic about such a system. It is a sad spectacle to view high government officials drawing arbitrary dividing lines between old and new pro-football agreements, between 10-month and 12-month teacher contracts, and between pickles and cucumbers. It is upsetting to witness the use of Presidential power to abrogate lawful contracts freely arrived at by the participants. It may well have been necessary given where we were at mid-August. All of us can and should accept the costs of the 90-day freeze; but the nation should not and will not accept stifling controls for long.

Before Joint Congressional Economic
Committee, Washington, Sept. 1/
The Wall Street Journal, 9-7:12.

Wright Patman
United States Representative, D–Tex.

I think we are getting closer to a depression by the day and by the hour. As long as we are losing on unemployment and inflation, it is a dangerous situation. The signs are similar to 1932. When you see sheriffs' sales and bankruptcies, when the largest firms in America are going bankrupt, that is a matter of concern.

> *Interview, Las Vegas, Nev., Aug. 30/*
> *Los Angeles Herald-Examiner, 8-31:(A)7.*

Thomas M. Pelly
United States Representative, R–Wash.

I venture to say America will not halt its inflation and restore prosperity until in this country production per man-hour is in balance with the cost per man-hour. Rising costs have priced U.S. goods out of the marketplace both abroad and at home, and U.S. capital has fled to foreign countries to meet this situation. I do not blame labor for seeking more for its services. I do blame management for yielding on wages without gaining assurances of increased production. Collective bargaining seems to be failing, and the strike weapon seems neither to benefit the worker nor management, but instead penalizes the consumer and the public. As I see it today, this country must seek alternatives in labor-management relations, and greater production should be the basis of increased wages if we are going to curb inflation and reduce unemployment.

> *Before the House, Washington/*
> *Los Angeles Herald-Examiner, 10-8:(A)10.*

William H. Peterson
Economist

Today our trade unions not only insist on a wage increase to cover productivity improvement, whether achieved or not. They also insist on another (increase) to cover "cost of living," frequently with a guaranteed minimum amount, whether experienced in cost-of-living terms or not. But a wage increase for cost of living, in addition to one for productivity, becomes a case for the price cat chasing its cost tail. Sooner or later, such an increase is translated into higher unit labor costs and has to be covered by price increases or layoffs, or by both layoffs and price increases—a "stagflationary" combination which has been dogging us for some two years along with economy-paralyzing strikes and balance-of-payments difficulties. In short, wage rates are the thing. This nice country has overpriced labor—to labor's and the whole economy's detriment.

> *At The Conference Board forum,*
> *New York, Nov. 23/*
> *U.S. News & World Report, 1-10('72):38.*

Ronald Reagan
Governor of California

A few in our midst have raised the haunting spectre of panic and depression. It is time we inoculated ourselves against the contagion of fear they would spread.

> *Inauguration address, Sacramento, Jan. 4/*
> *Los Angeles Herald-Examiner, 1-4:(A)3.*

John S. Reed
President, Atchison, Topeka
& Santa Fe Railway

The answer of some (labor) unions to the work rules problem is to nationalize the railroads—telling the public that, if we cannot pay their bills, just let the government do it! Without having my tongue too far in cheek, I suggest that there may be another course which I have not heard anyone propose yet. Why not consider nationalizing the unions? Maybe they should have some Federal management. It would cost next to nothing and would be immeasurably easier than nationalizing the railroads. If this sounds far-fetched, think about it a minute. The courts have already painted the unions as, in effect, quasi-governmental organizations enjoying by the leave of Congress an array of unique powers.

Why not make them a little more "quasi" by attaching some meaningful responsibilities which would take into account the possible inflationary impact of demands, and which would make it possible for us to get genuine relief from make-work rules and practices? I believe this could be done.

Before Traffic Club, Chicago/
The Wall Street Journal, 6-10:12.

Donald Rumsfeld
Director,
Federal Cost of Living Council

It's very natural for people to look at the (wage-price) controls and equate them with the nation's effort to achieve price stability. To do so would be inaccurate, because the controls constitute only one part of the nation's over-all effort to achieve price stability. There are other important elements involved beyond the restraints on wages and prices; for instance, fiscal policy, monetary policy and such factors as productivity which are beyond government control also affect price stability. The controls should be taken off, in my judgment, at that point where they have done their part of the job. They should not be maintained beyond that point. The danger with controls is that tendons and muscles tend to grow around them, so to speak, and some people could get to like them and want to keep controls as a crutch.

Interview, Washington/
U.S. News & World Report, 12-13:42.

Paul A. Samuelson
Professor of Economics,
Massachusetts Institute of Technology

I'm in favor of a much more activist incomes policy than President Nixon has been willing to take, but I stop short of mandatory price controls. I'm for jawboning, for moral suasion. To hold down prices, I would let in more imports, and I would use government procurement policies.

Interview/Time, 8-16:69.

It's an inadmissible alibi to say that, because of the winding down of the (Viet-nam) war, we have unemployment. It's the business of the modern economy to make sure those swords are not turned into bread lines. Can a modern economy afford peace? My answer is yes.

At Allied Social Science Association
convention, New Orleans, Dec. 27/
The Washington Post, 12-29:(C)6.

Raymond J. Saulnier
Former Chairman, Council of
Economic Advisers to the
President of the United States

I'm afraid that wage inflation has gone so far now that it requires much more direct intervention by government. I'm not talking about freezes or mandatory controls. But I am talking about a much more direct, determined and explicit government intervention. I come to this conclusion sadly and reluctantly.

Interview/Time, 8-16:69.

George P. Shultz
Director, Office of Management
and the Budget of the United States

There is a school of thought that our economy has changed to such an extent that the free-market economy will no longer work well enough. In order to achieve stability, this school says, government must do much more to manage the private sector. Some members of this school believe that more government management is needed not only temporarily to cure our current inflation but indefinitely . . . Government does have the responsibility to remove artificial props to wages and prices when the free-market system is abused. And in selective cases, in a critical industry, or in an especially flagrant situation, government should be willing to be the catalyst in achieving voluntary stabilization and, when necessary, to help restructure the bargaining process. But we will not be drawn into a series of steps that will lead to wage and price controls, rationing, black markets and a loss of the effectiveness of the free economic system.

April 22/
The Christian Science Monitor, 4-29:10.

Robert M. Solow
Professor of Economics,
Massachusetts Institute of Technology

So many people feel that the consequences of inflation are fatal, and that the choice is merely between indications of tempo—creeping, crawling, running or galloping. All these words may be frightening; but there's no evidence that the consequences are fatal, or that one pace necessarily entails the next. Inflation characterizes almost every economy one can think of that operates with markets. The British have it more than we do; they have a wage explosion and have had high unemployment since 1968. All the Scandinavians have wage controls because of their wage explosions. Even Yugoslavia, which runs its system with markets, has inflation.

Interview, Cambridge, Mass./
The New York Times, 2-7:(3)3.

Maurice H. Stans
Secretary of Commerce of the United States

Other nations are gaining on us in productivity but not in wages—and this is a major factor in the decline of our competitive position in the world . . . The time has come for productivity in American life to become an honored concept once more. In no area is there a greater opportunity for business and labor leaders to bury the old antagonisms and go forward together.

Before West Side Association
of Commerce, New York, Nov. 16/
The New York Times, 11-17:75.

Sam Steiger
United States Representative, R—Ariz.

It seems amazing to me that we in the United States, who are so protective and concerned with individual liberties, have so long tolerated such flagrant abuse of individual liberties as compulsory unionism.

Washington, Nov. 17/
San Francisco Examiner, 11-18:54.

Herbert Stein
Member, Council of Economic Advisers
to the President of the United States

The Federal government had a deficit in fiscal year 1970; it will have a large deficit in fiscal year 1971, the current year; it will have another deficit in fiscal 1972. The Federal government had a deficit in fiscal year 1970; it will have a large deficit in fiscal year 1971, the current year; it will have another deficit in fiscal 1972. The Federal government had a deficit in fiscal year 1970; it will have a large deficit in fiscal year 1971, the current year; it will have another deficit in fiscal 1972. You may ask why I repeat these simple statements three times, and I will tell you. I am trying to demonstrate that the Administration is not ashamed of the fact that we had, have and will have deficits and is not trying to conceal the fact. We do not talk about the full-employment budget in order to deny the existence of deficits.

At Finance Outlook Conference,
New York/Los Angeles Times, 3-26:(2)15.

I suspect there will be no heroes of Phase II (of President Nixon's economic program). Phase II bears about the same relation to the (Phase I wage-price) freeze as an occupation bears to a war. The occupation has to hold and pacify ground won during the war and possibly prepare for its maintenance over a long period. It is less glamorous and dramatic, more irritating, political and controversial than the earlier phase. But if it generates no heroes, it may nonetheless have an honorable and useful role in our history.

Washington/The National Observer, 11-27:2.

Louis Stulberg
President, International Ladies
Garment Workers Union

We are for trade among nations; but we are for trade among equals. And it is not trade among equals when an American or Canadian garment worker earning $2.50 or $3.50 an hour has to compete with 9 cents an hour in Korea, 15 cents in Taiwan, 23 cents in the

Philippines, 25 cents in Spain, 30 cents in Mexico, 39 cents in Japan. And these hourly earnings don't even begin to approximate the hourly cost of our fringe benefits. That's not trade—that's cutting each other's throat.

At ILGWU convention, Miami Beach, May 6/
The New York Times, 5-7:42.

John G. Tower
United States Senator, R–Tex.

Labor operates from behind a statutory wall of protection that gives it more political and economic power than any other segment of our society. There are strictures on business, as there should be. But there are virtually no strictures on labor. And at a time when the economy is sluggish and there is high unemployment, where there is no perceptible increase in man-hour productivity, organized labor is able to ask for and to get wage contracts that are very, very inflationary, far beyond any advance in the cost-of-living index. To me, it seems this power has got to be brought under control. Our labor laws are antiquated. They were designed for a time when labor was abused. Labor then had some catching up to do. But these laws are now obsolete.

Dallas, Oct. 18/
The Dallas Times Herald, 10-19:(A)21.

George C. Wallace
Governor of Alabama

I might tell the parties, both Democrat and Republican, that the great thing that exists in the air today is the unfair tax structure, and you had better give tax relief to the average man in this country and put it on the filthy rich on Wall Street, or you might wind up short at the next election period in the United States.

Inauguration address, Montgomery,
Jan. 18/The New York Times, 1-19:20.

The Democrats sometimes blame big business, and the Republicans sometimes blame labor, as has been in the past; but the blame

for inflation is on the government of the United States. They have brought about inflation, running these multibillion-dollar deficits, putting this money into circulation that devalues the dollar in a man's wallet and in his bank account, giving this money overseas by the billions and billions of dollars—and the day of reckoning is here.

TV-radio interview/"Meet the Press,"
National Broadcasting Company,
Washington, 8-22.

Leonard Woodcock
President, United Automobile
Workers of America

(Regarding President Nixon's new economic program announced Aug. 15): If this Administration thinks that just by issuing an edict, by the stroke of a pen, they can tear up (labor) contracts, they are saying to us they want war. If they want war, they can have war.

Aug. 18/The New York Times, 8-19:1.

We have long urged, and I would hope the Congress would enact, and I would hope the (Nixon) Administration would sponsor, a wage-price review board on a permanent basis—not necessarily to have controls, but to take the dominant price leaders in the various industries, and if they propose to increase prices, to require them to come forward under powers of subpoena to lay all the economic facts on the line; and if their allegation is that the union—or unions—involved is causing the push toward having to increase the price, that the union, too, be required to come forward, under the power of subpoena, to lay all of its facts on the line, and to let the power of public opinion into what are really now closed off areas of our national life.

TV-radio interview/"Meet the Press,"
National Broadcasting Company,
Washington, 8-29.

Labor has been the victim of social snobbery by the Democratic Party and by liberals and intellectuals generally. Read any story involving a blue-collar worker in the high-

(LEONARD WOODCOCK)

flown monthly and weekly magazines and other publications, and the worker invariably shows up as a stupid clod and, more frequently than not, very close to an alcoholic.

Human Events, 11-13:7.

Jerry Wurf
President, American Federation of State,
County and Municipal Employees

This (Nixon) Administration opposes almost every measure designed to ease the economic and social woes in America today. "Just die a little longer," they tell us, "and we'll be better prepared to try to save your life." They hold our heads under water and tell us to breathe.

The Washington Post, 7-13:(A)8.

Samuel W. Yorty
Mayor of Los Angeles

(President) Nixon is fueling the fires of inflation at the same time he's putting his hand on the boiling pot. If Nixon takes his hand off, the inflationary pressure will be enormous. But if he keeps his hand on, he'll ruin the American economy. I don't think he really knows much about economics.

News conference, New York, Oct. 25/
Los Angeles Herald-Examiner, 10-25:(A)4.

David L. Bazelon
Chief Judge, United States Court of
Appeals for the District of Columbia

Today, the practice of "plea bargaining" is widely regarded as indispensable for the operation of our system of criminal justice . . . In order to speed people through the system . . . we are running a bargain counter that may tempt even innocent people to plead guilty; for any defendant, innocent or guilty, must pay a high price for asserting the right to go to trial. We may be confident that not many innocent defendants are convicted; but we know that imperfections in the factfinding process must mean that some are. And one ironic quirk of the "plea bargaining" process is that it gives the heaviest sentences to the group most likely to include some innocent people—the group with close cases; for an innocent defendant is more likely to resist the pressure to plead guilty and insist on going to trial. Some of these people will be convicted—after all, no system of justice is perfect—and those innocent people will get the heavy sentences reserved for people who insist on trials.

At New York University School of Law/
The Washington Post, 4-25:(B)4.

Lloyd M. Bentsen
United States Senator, D–Tex.

I am tired of seeing criminals, found guilty beyond a reasonable doubt, go free on some insignificant technicality . . . We simply cannot allow our system of criminal justice to become a game in which the slickest stratagems can save the most blatantly guilty individual.

Before the Senate, Washington/
The Dallas Times Herald, 10-10:(A)38.

Alexander M. Bickel
Professor of Law, Yale University

(Regarding William Rehnquist, nominee for the U.S. Supreme Court): He is a very, very conservative gentleman who is going to startle the country. We've got someone here who is going to make us all sit up. This man is a thinking conservative, and we have not seen his like on the Court in decades. He is not just a conservative in judicial philosophy. He is a man with a well-thought-out deeply conservative political philosophy.

The National Observer, 10-30:4.

Hugo L. Black
Associate Justice, Supreme Court
of the United States

The layman's Constitutional view is that what he likes is Constitutional and that which he doesn't like is un-Constitutional. That about measures up the Constitutional acumen of the average person.

News conference, Washington, Feb. 25/
The New York Times, 2-26:38.

Harry A. Blackmun
Associate Justice, Supreme Court
of the United States

It's easier to be cynical than to be correct. I know that from the judging business. It's easier to write a stinging dissent than a persuasive majority opinion.

San Francisco Examiner, 7-12:30.

199

James L. Buckley
United States Senator-elect, C–N.Y.

One of the first things I was taught when I went through law school was that we should have predictability in our laws. What has happened is that the Supreme Court has too often destroyed predictability, with awesome consequences to all kinds of arrangements, because of its assumption of the legislative authority. I would prefer to see legislative bodies legislate and the amendatory procedures used to amend the Constitution.

Interview/The Washington Post, 1-10:(B)2.

Warren E. Burger
Chief Justice of the United States

For a long time we have talked of the need for a closer exchange and closer co-operation among the states and between the states and the Federal courts on judicial problems. No state is without grave problems in the administration of justice . . . The time has come . . . to bring into being some kind of national clearinghouse or center to serve all the states and to cooperate with all the agencies seeking to improve justice.

At National Conference on the Judiciary,
Williamsburg, Va., March 12/
U.S. News & World Report, 3-22:37.

I have said before, but I hope it will bear repeating, that, with reference to methods and procedure (in the judicial system), we may be carrying continuity and tradition too far when we see that John Adams, Hamilton or Burr, Jefferson or Marshall, reincarnated, could step into any court today and, after a minimal briefing on procedure and updating in certain areas of law, try a case with the best of today's lawyers. Those great lawyers of the 18th and 19th centuries would need no more than a hurried briefing and a Brooks Brothers suit. They would not even need a haircut, given the styles of our day.

At National Conference on the Judiciary,
Williamsburg, Va., March 12/
Vital Speeches, 4-15:386.

We are rapidly approaching the point (where) piet and patient Americans will totally lose patience with the cumbersome system that makes people wait two, three, four or more years to dispose of an ordinary civil claim, while, at the same time, they witness flagrant defiance of law by a growing number of law-breakers who jeopardize cities and towns and life and property of law-abiding people, and monopolize the courts in the process.

At National Conference on the Judiciary,
Williamsburg, Va., March 12/
The Washington Post, 3-13:(A)1.

With all deference, I submit that lawyers who know how to think but have not learned how to behave are a menace and a liability, not an asset, to the administration of justice. And without undue deference, I say in all frankness that when insolence and arrogance are confused with zealous advocacy, we are in the same trouble the courts of England suffered through more than a century ago. Today, English barristers are the most tightly-regulated and disciplined in the world, and nowhere is there more zealous advocacy. I suggest the necessity for civility is relevant to lawyers because they are the living exemplars—and thus teachers—every day in every case, and in every court; and their worst conduct will be emulated perhaps more readily than their best. When a lawyer flouts the standards of professional conduct once, his conduct will be echoed in multiples and for years to come and long after he leaves the scene. Finally, civility is relevant to judges, and especially trial judges because they are under greater stress than other judges, and subject to the temptation to respond in kind to the insolence and bad manners of lawyers. Every judge must remember that, no matter what the provocation, the judicial response must be judicious response and that no one more surely sets the tone and the pattern for courtroom conduct than the presider . . . I urge that we never forget the necessity for civility as an indispensable part—the lubri-

cant—that keeps our adversary system functioning. If we want to protect that system, we must firmly insist on the lubricant.
Before American Law Institute, Washington/
The National Observer, 5-24:2.

In my conception of it, the primary role of the (U.S. Supreme) Court is to decide cases. From the decision of cases, of course, some changes develop. But to try to create or substantially change civil or criminal procedure, for example, by judicial decision is the worst possible way to do it. The Supreme Court is simply not equipped to do that job properly.
Interview, June/
The New York Times, 7-4:(1)24.

We cannot keep up with the volume of work and maintain a quality historically expected from the Supreme Court. Either the quantity or the quality of the work of the Supreme Court must soon yield to the realities.
State of the Judiciary address, before
American Bar Association, New York,
July 5/The Boston Globe, 7-6:5.

To a large extent, what people think (of the courts) is shaped by what we do or fail to do with less than two per cent of the criminal cases in the Federal system. What is desperately needed is to have . . . the serious cases brought on for trial in 60 days after indictment and the appeal disposed of in another 60 days. It can be done. Every large district court should have a procedure by which the chief judge, or possibly a committee designated by the chief judge, will have the power to identify cases in which delays should not be tolerated—the two per cent group—and then make certain that these cases are not allowed to take the pace that the lawyers want . . . Not all of the two per cent are newsworthy; but within that two per cent are those few cases that drag on for two, three, four and more years and are often the "notorious" and the "spectacular" cases because

of the crime factor involved, the identity of the accused or his counsel, or all three factors. Also within the two per cent are the cases in which delays give rise to public anxiety and concern and even anger. These are the cases that undermine public confidence in the system.
San Francisco Examiner, 9-15:36.

Ramsey Clark
Former Attorney General of the United States

. . . isn't it a fact that the overwhelming majority of people accused of crimes plead guilty and never have a lawyer? If it takes a little longer in a trial to have justice, which should be sacrificed, speed or justice? The question is, what does this society want? What do we really believe? Do we think a poor man should have a lawyer, too? And . . . the poor man can't appeal unless somebody helps him pay for it. Are we going to say we can't afford that? Then we can't afford equal justice.
Interview, Washington/San Francisco
Examiner & Chronicle, 3-28:(A)19.

Tom Clark
Former Associate Justice, Supreme Court
of the United States

Any President who thinks he can mold the (Supreme) Court through appointments doesn't know the Court. They've tried again and again. That was one of the reasons Theodore Roosevelt got mad at (Justice Oliver Wendell) Holmes. I'm sure Roosevelt Number 2 (Franklin) was disappointed in some of the actions of (Justice Felix) Frankfurter. And some of the people were disappointed in some of the actions of (Justice Hugo) Black. President Eisenhower told me himself he was disappointed with some of the actions of (Chief Justice Earl) Warren. So, if a President thinks that by appointing a certain person he is going to change the trend of the Court, he is mistaken, entirely mistaken.
Interview, San Francisco/
The Dallas Times Herald, 1-10:(A)7.

Thomas T. Curtin
Judge, United States District Court
for the Western District of New York

The court should be a place where anybody can come—whatever they have in their pocket—and be able to file a complaint in simple fashion and at least have somebody give consideration to it and give them an opportunity to be heard.

The New York Times, 10-7:54.

Edward J. Ennis
Chairman, American Civil Liberties Union

We know (Supreme Court nominee) William Rehnquist as an advocate of dragnet arrests, as an opponent of racial integration, as a champion of executive authority to engage in electronic eavesdropping and political surveillance, as a campaigner for pretrial incarceration and as an engineer of the Justice Department's programs to abrogate the rights of persons accused of crimes.

News conference/
San Francisco Examiner, 12-6:2.

Gerald R. Ford
United States Representative, R–Mich.

We have heard often that "the Constitution is what the Supreme Court says it is." But the Constitution belongs to the American people and not to the Supreme Court. When there is overwhelming opposition to a significant Supreme Court decision, the Congress owes it to the American people to examine that decision and to give the people an opportunity to pass on its merits.

Before the House, Washington/
Human Events, 11-20:4.

Paul A. Freund
Professor of Law, Harvard University

I certainly don't believe there ought to be a Jewish seat (on the Supreme Court) or a Catholic seat or a black seat or a Southern seat. At the same time, to put an extreme case, if we had a Court of nine New Yorkers, I think there would be legitimate cause for complaint. I look on a Court of nine as an opportunity for diversity—not a mandate, but an opportunity for diversity.

Interview, Cambridge, Mass./
The New York Times, 11-26:23.

Charles W. Halleck
Judge, Superior Court
of the District of Columbia

You only have so many options when you sentence. You can put a defendant on probation, order him to be put on work-release and go to a half-way house, or send him to an institution. But what it comes right down to is that there's no alternative that's any good. That's a hell of a note. I guess you could call it a judge's dilemma.

Interview, Washington, Oct. 8/
The Washington Post, 10-9:(B)1.

Roman L. Hruska
United States Senator, R–Neb.

For 30 years we have been holding hearings on (Supreme Court) nominees, and for 30 years they have been of liberal bent. As a conservative, I sat here sometimes in agony and sometimes in frustration. Now we are getting men with a philosophy on the other side. We should take advantage of this happy circumstance.

At Senate hearing on Supreme Court
nominations of Lewis F. Powell and
William H. Rehnquist, Washington/
The Christian Science Monitor, 11-9:15.

Henry M. Jackson
United States Senator, D–Wash.

(The concept of) one law, one standard, one justice for all has been honored more in the breach than in the observance. We are tolerating not only one law for the poor and one law for the rich; we are as well accepting submissively one law for the young and one law for their elders; one law for the dissident and one law for the conformist; one law (for the military and) one law for the civilian; one law for the uneducated and one law for the college graduate; one law for the small taxpayer and one law for the large tax-avoider;

one law for the ordinary voter and one law for the big contributor; one law for the buyer and one law for the seller; one law for the borrower and one law for the lender. This is wrong. We know it is wrong. Yet among those who have chosen . . . to serve as custodians of the law, there remains all too often a curious passivity toward these wrongs.

Before Wayne State University Law School alumni, Detroit, April 17/San Francisco Examiner & Chronicle, 4-18:(A)14.

Jacob K. Javits
United States Senator, R–N.Y.

I have heard it said that the Senate ought to confirm a (Supreme Court) nominee unless we find the nominee either lacking in integrity or basically incompetent, and that otherwise the choice is for the President. I thoroughly disagree, for both historical and practical reasons . . . Whatever may be the traditions of the Senate when it comes to advice and consent to the appointment of Cabinet and similar officials, judicial appointments are altogether different in kind. I have been quite prepared to vote to confirm, subject to substantiality and integrity, Presidential nominations of Cabinet or similar officials chosen by the President precisely *because* these appointees are loyal to the President, share his views and will work *with him* and *for him.* But I do *not* apply that view to Supreme Court justices. The Court is an independent coordinate branch of the government. Its justices are appointed not for the duration of any Administration or a limited term of years, but for life.

Before the Senate, Washington, 10-20:(A)26.

Leon Jaworski
President-elect, American Bar Association

The task of law is to maintain an ever-re-adjusted balance between the needful restraint on the powers of government and the needful exercise of the powers of government.

Before law student division, American Bar Association, New York, July 4/ The Boston Globe, 7-5:10.

Edward M. Kennedy
United States Senator, D–Mass.

(Regarding President Nixon's list of possible nominees for the U.S. Supreme Court): (In submitting the list) the President reveals himself as a radical in the true sense of the word, as a man who seeks to undermine the basic and vital institutions of our nation—the Supreme Court as an equal partner of government under the Constitution and as the ultimate guardian of our fundamental rights as free people.

Washington, Oct. 15/ Los Angeles Times, 10-16:(1)18.

Robert A. Leflar
Former Justice, Supreme Court of Arkansas; Former dean, University of Arkansas Law School

The law does not exist just for the lawyers, though there are some of us who seem to think that it does. The law is for all the people, and the lawyers are only its ministers. As the law's ministers, we have the professional responsibility, more than anyone else has, of seeing to it that our law and its administration are good enough to keep a civilized society operating not only in 1984 and in the year 2000, which is day after tomorrow, but even in the years beyond 2000.

Before American Judicature Society/ The Wall Street Journal, 5-27:12.

John V. Lindsay
Mayor of New York

I hope all of us, as lawyers, will demonstrate to our children and to the larger communities we serve that lawyers are right to seek social progress, that judges are right to break new legal ground and that it remains the historic role of the legal profession not only to preserve our heritage but also to promote reform, liberty and justice in this troubled country of ours.

Before American Bar Association, New York, July 7/ The Dallas Times Herald, 7-8:(A)10.

Robert Mark
*Deputy Commissioner and
Commissioner-designate,
London (England) Metropolitan Police*

The criminal trial (in Britain) today is less a
test of guilt or innocence than a competition
in which the knowledge of the rules, games-
manship and, above all, self-control, is likely
to decide the outcome; a kind of show-
jumping contest in which the rider for the
prosecution must clear every obstacle to succeed.

The Washington Post, 11-23:(A)16.

George S. McGovern
United States Senator, D–S.D.

For 200 years, the highest court in the land
(the U.S. Supreme Court) has been an exclusive all-male club. While Justice is female, all
the justices have been male. I'd put an end to
that, first chance I got.

*Before Women's National Democratic Club,
Washington, June 17/
The Washington Post, 6-18:(B)3.*

John N. Mitchell
Attorney General of the United States

If our justice system is going to deter
crime, each case must have a predictable time
when it can be said with finality, "The man is
innocent or guilty"; and if he is guilty, "This
man must now pay the penalty."

*At Republican fund-raising dinner,
Millburn, N.J., March 12/
The New York Times, 3-14:(1)10.*

Too often, judicial delays, rehearings, appeals and almost endless collateral attacks
after conviction—all these convince the criminal that he will "beat the rap." And too
often he does!

*At Republican fund-raising dinner,
Millburn, N.J., March 12/
The Washington Post, 3-13:(A)1.*

Thirty-seven years ago, Mr. Justice Benja-
min Cardozo wrote an opinion which contained a memorable warning: "Justice," he
said, "though due to the accused, is due to
the accuser also. The concept of fairness must
not be strained till it is narrowed to a fila-
ment. We are to keep the balance true." Had
this warning been more widely heeded, we
would not be facing today a serious imbalance
in the scales of justice . . . A preoccupation
with fairness for the accused has done violence to fairness for the accuser. In the process, fairness as a concept has often been
strained to a meaningless shred . . . In our
adversary court system, the prosecutor already
has an inherent disadvantage. He has to show
proof beyond a reasonable doubt. Is justice
served now by shackling the prosecutor and
giving more weapons to the defense? I refer to
the extravagant means by which evidence is
often disallowed. I refer to the over-weening
attention to proceduralisms, far beyond the
meaning of the Constitution—almost all of it
benefiting the accused. I refer to the astonish-
ing extremities that some courts have reached
in demanding proof of guilt. I refer to the
fatuous argument that, because Americans
read the newspapers and watch television, it is
impossible for us to get impartial juries. And
I refer to the interminable post-trial devices
which rob justice of any finality.
Little wonder that, as the record tells us, only
one crime in a hundred is actually punished.
Little wonder that, as we often hear, the
public is losing confidence in the ability of
the courts to dispense justice.

*Before National District Attorneys
Association, Washington, June 9/
Human Events, 6-26:9.*

The history of man's progress has been
measured by his willingness to accept the
world of law, rather than of brute force
unrestrained by law.

*San Francisco Examiner & Chronicle
(This World), 11-28:2.*

Richard M. Nixon
President of the United States

Our courts are overloaded for the best of
reasons: Because our society found the courts
willing—and partially able—to assume the bur-

den of its gravest problems. Throughout a tumultuous generation, our system of justice has helped America improve herself. There is an urgent need now for America to help the courts improve our system of justice. But if we limit ourselves to calling for more judges, more police, more lawyers—operating in the same system—we will produce more backlogs, more delays, more litigation, more jails and more criminals. "More of the same" is not the answer. What is needed now is genuine reform—the kind of change that requires imagination and daring, that demands a focus on ultimate goals.

At National Conference on the Judiciary, Williamsburg, Va., March 11/ The New York Times, 3-12:18.

Justice delayed is not only justice denied—it is also justice circumvented, justice mocked and the system of justice undermined.

At National Conference on the Judiciary, Williamsburg, Va., March 11/ The New York Times, 3-12:18.

. . . is it a requirement, and should it be a requirement, that the judge or the nominee (for the Supreme Court) be one who has judicial experience? The answer is no. Mr. Justice Frankfurter was a teacher. He was one of the great judges; whether you agreed or not with his philosophy, he was a great judge. Mr. Justice Brandeis, who was one of my heroes when I was in law school, one of the great dissenters along with Holmes, was a man who was a great practicing lawyer, a labor lawyer primarily, fighting great causes; but that did not mean that he did not become one of the great judges. So teachers, legislators, for example, with great experience in the Judiciary Committee or the House or Senate, they are also good possibilities.

The Washington Post, 10-14:(A)18.

Over the past few years, many cases have come before the (Supreme) Court involving that delicate balance between the rights of society and the rights of defendants accused

of crimes against society. And honest and dedicated constitutional lawyers have disagreed as to where and how to maintain that balance. As a judicial conservative, I believe some court decisions have gone too far in the past in weakening the peace forces as against the criminal forces in our society. In maintaining, as it must be maintained, the delicate balance between the rights of society and defendants accused of crimes, I believe the peace forces must not be denied the legal tools they need to protect the innocent from criminal elements. And I believe we can strengthen the hand of the peace forces without compromising our precious principle that the rights of individuals accused of crimes must always be protected.

TV-radio address, Washington, Oct. 21/ Los Angeles Times, 10-22:(1)16.

We have had many historic, and even sometimes violent, debates throughout our history about the role of the Supreme Court in our government. But let us never forget that respect for the Court as the final interpreter of the law is indispensable if America is to remain a free society.

TV-radio address, Washington, Oct. 21/ Los Angeles Times, 10-22:(1)16.

Lewis F. Powell, Jr.
Lawyer; United States Supreme Court nominee

I go onto the Court with deep personal misgivings about whether I will like it. In fact, I rather suppose I won't . . . (However) if you're asked by the President of the United States to go on the Supreme Court, one doesn't say no. But there are reasons for my acceptance that go beyond that. I might have said no to an appointment on almost any other agency or commission at this time in my life. But the Supreme Court has a very special place in the life and attitude of any lawyer my age. I don't know what the younger generation of lawyers thinks of the Supreme Court, but, for those of my generation,

(LEWIS F. POWELL, JR.)

it is a revered institution, the pinnacle of our profession.

Interview, Richmond, Va./
The Washington Post, 10-24:(A)4.

Ronald Reagan
Governor of California

The self-proclaimed revolutionaries and their legal champions denounce the "system" . . . yet they wrap themselves in the Constitution at every step in legal proceedings that involve them. To accept their idea of "justice" is to accept tyranny and anarchy. If Moses himself stood on Nob Hill (in San Francisco) and solemnly intoned the Ten Commandments, he probably would be denounced as a reactionary seeking to impose a repressive and outmoded life-style on the multitude.

Los Angeles Herald-Examiner, 12-2:(A)12.

Whitney N. Seymour, Jr.
United States Attorney for the
Southern District of New York

Why does it make sense . . . to suppress evidence which clearly establishes a defendant's guilt because an over-zealous law enforcement officer has failed to comply with the latest technical requirements for a search warrant? What is our objective? Is it to let the guilty man go free, or is it to educate police officers on the need to respect the rights of suspects? If it is the latter, then there are much more practical ways of achieving the result than by forcing the dismissal of the charges against the defendant.

Before Academy of Police Science, New York,
Sept. 29/The New York Times, 9-30:40.

George C. Wallace
Governor of Alabama

I have nothing but utter contempt for the courts of this land.

Plainview (Tex.) Daily Herald, 9-24:2.

Earl Warren
Former Chief Justice of the United States

The (Supreme) Court is the creature of the litigation the lawyers bring to it.

Interview/The Washington Post, 3-15:(A)2.

In my opinion, the greatest weakness of our judicial system is that it has become clogged, and does not function in a fluent fashion resulting in prompt determination of the guilt or innocence of those charged with crime. Today, in many communities in the nation, it takes from three to four years to have a jury trial in a civil case; and, in many of those same jurisdictions, it will take a year or even more to have a jury trial in a criminal case . . . If an innocent man is required to wait two years for a jury trial, even though acquitted by the jury, he has lost those two years of his life by reason of the cloud which has been hanging over him. On the other hand, if a man is guilty and has been out on bail for two years between the time of his arrest and his conviction, there is no way of knowing how many crimes he may have committed in the meantime. Under no circumstances can that be justice to the people of the community.

At Milton S. Eisenhower Symposium/
The Wall Street Journal, 3-19:6.

Byron R. White
Associate Justice,
Supreme Court of the United States

Law is no longer accepted by lawyers or others as irrefutable pronouncements from on high. (For that reason, lawyers) can no longer view their profession in isolation. Science, economics and the behavioral disciplines become major determinants in the lawyer's work.

At University of Southern California/
The Christian Science Monitor, 2-24:3.

Ernest L. Wilkinson
President, Brigham Young University

(Most of the "failing" welfare programs as well as the high cost of government and public debt have been made possible) by a Supreme Court—appointed not because of their judicial experience or reverence for past decisions, but because of their liberal political views—which has overruled over 150 prior Supreme Court decisions, many of which relate to the limitations which the Constitution imposed upon government. This, in my judgment, is the most significant change that has occurred in our history as a nation and which has permitted our becoming a welfare state.

At Brigham Young University commencement, May 28/The Salt Lake Tribune, 5-29:2.

Edward Bennett Williams
Lawyer

The time has come to eliminate slow-motion justice in America. Nothing is more difficult to explain about American institutions to the intelligent inquiring layman than why a man accused of robbing a fellow citizen at the point of a gun can stall the process for two years before facing the day of punishment. We worry about increasing episodes of contempt of court by political defendants. We must worry equally over whether the criminal-justice system is not forfeiting its right to respect by its anachronistic delays and its failure to respond to the needs of society in the 1970s.

At National Conference on the Judiciary/ Los Angeles Times, 7-18:(G)1.

Edward L. Wright
President, American Bar Association

The law will never move as rapidly as a bullet, nor will its dispositions ever be as demolishing as a bomb. Justice should be reasoned, and reasoning takes a certain length of time.

Plainview (Tex.) Daily Herald, 7-13:6.

Evelle J. Younger
Attorney General of California

An incompetent attorney can delay a trial for years or months. A competent attorney can delay one even longer.

Before Women's Division, Los Angeles Chamber of Commerce/ Los Angeles Times, 3-3:(4)1.

National Defense • The Military

Bella S. Abzug
United States Representative, D–N.Y.

I am unalterably opposed to military conscription and believe it should be dismantled. Changes in a system of involuntary servitude can never correct the basic injustices perpetrated by a form of slavery.

> *Before House Armed Services*
> *Committee, Washington, March 1/*
> *San Francisco Examiner, 3-1:11.*

Spiro T. Agnew
Vice President of the United States

Totally eliminated in the current critical assessment (of the armed forces) is the positive—the complete dedication of America's military services to the security of the country, including protection for their harshest critics to rant and rave. We are one of the few countries in the world that doesn't have to fear a military takeover of the civilian government. I wonder sometimes if our people appreciate this fact.

> *Before Los Angeles Chamber of Commerce,*
> *San Francisco Examiner, 4-7:15.*

To say that we are drifting toward imminent peril, to say that our national survival is at stake, is no exaggeration . . . We cannot allow a small but influential minority of neo--isolationists—in and out of Congress—to cripple our defense capability . . . nor can we countenance the false pretense that dismantling our defense establishment is an intelligent way to provide the funds to cover all of our social ills.

> *Sept. 23/The Washington Post, 9-30:(A)18.*

William R. Anderson
United States Representative, D–Tenn.

While the United States has poured some $150 billion into Vietnam, the U.S.S.R. has built the most modern navy in the world, a completely modern merchant marine and a fishing fleet that dwarfs our own . . . We have not been out-fought, we have been out-thought.

> *Portsmouth, N.H., June 26/*
> *The Washington Post, 6-27:(A)2.*

Leslie C. Arends
United States Representative, R–Ill.

(We) are now in the winter of discontent insofar as our national defense is concerned. We simply cannot let Soviet Russia control the seas. We simply cannot let the Russians move into a position of strategic superiority. Our strategic offense forces are not only the principal deterrent to global war, they are the principal deterrent to the kind of nuclear blackmail that a superior Soviet Russia could carry out—nuclear blackmail which would endanger freedom in our own country and destroy it in other parts of the world.

> *Before Veterans of Foreign Wars/*
> *Human Events, 3-27:4.*

Magne Braadland
Rear Admiral, Norwegian Navy

(Concerning the build-up of the Soviet Navy): The threat to the U.S. is not coming from Vietnam and not from Central Europe, either. It is sailing from Murmansk.

> *Time, 10-18:39.*

Leonid I. Brezhnev
General Secretary, Communist
Party of the Soviet Union

We have never thought, and do not think now, that it is an ideal situation when the navies of great powers are sailing for a long time at the other end of the world, away from their native coasts. We are ready to solve this problem, but to make an equal bargain.

> *Moscow, June 11/*
> *The Washington Post, 6-12:(A)1.*

In the United States . . . hue and cry are raised time and again about Soviet defense programs, particularly on the eve of adopting a new military budget in Washington. The measures we take to strengthen our defenses are depicted at the same time as something well nigh treachery, a direct threat to the success of the (SALT) talks. But (on) what grounds, we are entitled to ask, has Washington to expect from us renunciation of the already-adopted programs if the American Administration itself, during the period of the talks, has taken several very big decisions of building up its strategic forces? It is high time to discard this double standard.

Moscow, June 11/
The Washington Post, 6-12:(A)14.

Edward W. Brooke
United States Senator, R—Mass.

I remain convinced that the mutual deterrence on which American and Soviet security depends can best be preserved by avoiding a major deployment of antiballistic missiles by either country. In my judgment, mutual security would best be reinforced by a "zero level" limit on the two countries' ABM deployments, coupled with decided restraint in offensive weapons, especially MIRV systems. The vital goal, however, is to move from the competitive, strategic relationship in which we and the Soviet Union have been trapped into a more cooperative strategic environment, in which the two superpowers recognize their overriding common interest in preventing war. That transformation, it seems to me, is the fundamental objective and magnificent promise of the Strategic Arms Limitation Talks.

Before World Affairs Council, Boston/
The Christian Science Monitor, 9-1:16.

George S. Brown
General, United States Air Force;
Commander, Air Force Systems Command

. . . the so-called military-industrial complex is what has helped the United States to survive and to grow and prosper in a world that has been steadily growing increasingly dangerous. But the very essence of any art is to hide the labor that went into its creation. And I think, perhaps, we have hidden it a little too well. Maybe we have made it seem as if there is no threat, or that we are somehow immune from threats no matter what we do, or fail to do. How else could you explain the seeming indifference of some of the American people to the fantastic growth of Soviet global military power? What can they possibly imagine those huge SS-9 missiles—able to throw 25-megaton warheads halfway around the earth—are for? Or the new ICBM construction recently discovered that may foreshadow an even newer generation of missile? Or the large, ultra-modern navy sailing with greater frequency all the oceans of the world, including nuclear submarines armed with ballistic missiles? Or the exceedingly ambitious modernization of their armies and air forces, with more prototype aircraft developed in a year than we undertake in a decade? In this harsh world . . . it is always very foolish not to be prepared for people eventually doing what they are visibly preparing to do. Certainly the Soviets are being as visible about these things as it is possible to be.

Before Washington chapter, American
Ordnance Association, Washington,
April 12/Vital Speeches, 6-15:514.

James L. Buckley
United States Senator, C—N.Y.

. . . there is no inherent virtue in maintaining extensive and costly military forces or in developing increasingly sophisticated weapons. No nation with peaceful intentions requires or can justify a defense establishment which is larger than that which is necessary to meet the needs of her own security. But the adequacy or inadequacy of a nation's defenses is not determined by considerations of domestic priorities, but by the power relationships within which it must operate. We must keep in mind that, in the real world, no country can conduct an effective foreign policy without a military capability which is appropriate to its responsibilities.

At National Press Club, Washington,
July 14/Human Events, 7-24:1.

J. Herbert Burke
United States Representative, R—Fla.

Why must we delude ourselves with the idealist belief that all is well in the world and that it is a world of brotherly love? I wish this was true, but unfortunately it is not. The path to world peace is not by weakness—but through strength. Our military strength has been our salvation and our willingness to accept this fact has made our country great.

Before the House, Washington, April 1/
Congressional Record, 4-1:(H)2376.

John H. Chafee
Secretary of the Navy of the United States

I don't see why some people think the world is coming to an end just because the Russians decide to build 43 missile submarines when we have 41.

Interview/The Washington Post, 11-26:(A)22.

Leonard F. Chapman, Jr.
General and Commandant,
United States Marine Corps

We are not going to change anything (in the Marine Corps) just for the sake of change; because we know that change does not always mean progress, and progress is what we are seeking . . . We are not abandoning the old Marine Corps. It's true, we are tradition-minded . . . If our training is traditionally tough, it's because the application of our purpose is tough—in combat and in being constantly ready for combat. If our discipline is traditionally exacting, it is because discipline is the key to winning and surviving in battle.

At Navy League symposium, March 17/
The Washington Post, 3-18:(A)3.

The basic secret of the Marine Corps is that every Marine is trained as a rifleman or a platoon leader in a stern tradition of tough discipline. The Marine Corps is a com-bat-ready, top-quality fighting force. It is tough, hard, lean and professional, with highly disciplined, motivated and trained fighting men . . . We are not relaxing. If anything, we are trying to tighten up and get tougher.

The Washington Post, 12-19:(G)1.

Frank Church
United States Senator, D—Idaho

With all the money we're spending on the military, if the Russians are still outstripping us on technology, we're sure wasting a hell of a lot of money.

Los Angeles Times, 11-22:(1)9.

John B. Connally, Jr.
Secretary of the Treasury of the United States

We today spend nearly nine per cent of our gross national product on defense—nearly $5 billion of that overseas, and much of it in Western Europe and Japan. Financing a military shield is part of the burden of leadership. But 25 years after World War II, legitimate questions arise over how the cost of these responsibilities should be allocated among the free-world allies who benefit from that shield.

At International Banking Conference,
Munich, May 28/
Los Angeles-Examiner, 5-28:(D)1.

Alan Cranston
United States Senator, D—Calif.

It was the easy availability of virtually unlimited numbers of men who could be pressed into military service merely by raising the draft call that enabled President (Lyndon) Johnson to escalate the fighting in Southeast Asia without having to ask the permission of Congress . . . Since World War II, the draft has become a bad habit of political convenience that needs to be broken before it further jeopardizes our freedom.

Santa Cruz, Calif., March 27/San Francisco
Examiner & Chronicle, 3-28:(A)29.

Edward E. David, Jr.
Science Adviser to the
President of the United States

The United States hopes to obtain from these (SALT) talks limitations on both offensive and defensive missile systems. (But) should the Soviet Union agree to an enforceable limit, the time may well come when a land-based retaliatory force, either missiles or aircraft, will not be able to survive a first strike by the opposing force. The alternative to land-basing, of course, is to send the missiles to sea, as we and the Soviets have already done in part. It is the survivability of sea-based missiles in submarines which could turn out to be the last refuge for a survivable force. Should sea-based submarine forces become the major deterrent to a nuclear war, underwater sound and submarine warfare will assume a much more important role in national and world security than presently.

Before Acoustical Society of America,
Washington, April 21/
The Dallas Times Herald, 4-22:(A)6.

Michael S. Davison
General and Commander-in-Chief/Europe,
United States Army

One of the myths now circulating among younger people is that the Army is really a collection of brutalized guys who've been taught nothing but to kill, kill, kill. It's going to be difficult to break through that and present the Army as a constructive institution which is a very necessary and useful part of the overall national fabric. That's going to be very, very difficult to do. But I think once you make that breakthrough, we ought to be able to present to the young people that the Army is a profession within which there are certain ethical standards that anyone should be willing to subscribe to and live by. Indeed, it represents a set of ethical values that idealistically-inclined young people can work for—the duty, honor, country thing. I think these ethical values are salable values.

Interview/The Washington Post, 9-12:(A)16.

David W. Dennis
United States Representative, R–Ind.

It seems to me that a soldier pretty much has to be a soldier, an army has to be pretty much an army, and I rather doubt whether you can really run an army with two different classes of soldiers (conscriptees and volunteers), some of whom are liable to certain duties and others of whom are liable to other duties. The thing is, we have a basic feeling in this country—and I share it—that you should not have to be a soldier and do all these things a soldier has to do except in the case of a national emergency. What we need to do, it seems to me, is to get back to where we used to be, where the fellow who does these things is a soldier, he intends to be a soldier, he expects to be a soldier and he expects to do the duty of a soldier. That is where we need the volunteer force, and that is why we ought to get there. But until we do get there, I very much doubt whether we can have an armed force with soldiers of two different classes included.

Before the House, Washington, April 1/
Congressional Record, 4-1:(H)2369.

Bob Dole
United States Senator, R–Kan.

It may seem only the puffing and huffing of a few misguided idealists, but there is a concerted campaign against America's system of national defense which, carried to its logical conclusion, could be suicidal.

At American Medical Association workshop,
Washington, March 14/
The Dallas Times Herald, 3-15:(A)16.

John G. Dow
United States Representative, D–N.Y.

. . . there are two kinds of war that we should contemplate in the future. One of them is a nuclear war; and in that kind of war there will be no need for numbers in the Army. Grandma will be in the trenches. Grandma is in the trenches today, with poised projectiles only a half-hour away from her and everybody else right now. So we do not need numbers to fight a nuclear war. Now, turning to the other kind of war, an infantry war, it seems to me that we should have learned from Vietnam to fight no more brush fires. We should end the concept of a *pax americana* and close some of the hundreds of bases that we have; they are only provocative of more Vietnams. So I see no need whatsoever for large numbers of men, greater than either the Chinese or the Russians now muster. It should not be hard to strike a balance between the diminished enlistments under a volunteer system and our true manpower needs under a concept of restraint in our numbers of men, in our numbers of bases, in our outlays of defense dollars and in our posture generally.

Before the House, Washington, April 1/
Congressional Record, 4-1:(H)2375.

Thomas F. Eagleton
United States Senator, D—Mo.

Let us not fool ourselves . . . An all-volunteer Army will be a poor boys' Army. It will be composed of young men from the lower end of the socio-economic scale who, because of lack of formal education, lack of training, lack of opportunity and lack of money, accept military service as a means of economic survival. In this era in which succeeding Presidents—Truman, Eisenhower, Kennedy, Johnson and Nixon—have all expanded upon the theory of the Commander-in-Chief's power to the point where it is viewed in the White House as being almost totally without limits, an all-volunteer poor boys' Army of 2,400,000 is an awesome juggernaut at one man's disposal or one man's whim. Who will complain when a poor boys' Army continues to fight in Vietnam or when, years later, in a different era, a different President, perceiving a different "threat," sends an army of the well-paid poor to yet another foreign land to fight yet another mistaken war? Certainly, poor mothers and fathers will complain. But . . . Congress has a rather immaculate record of not deeply concerning itself with the pleas of the poor. The poor are numerous, but the voices of the poor are seldom heard in the halls of Congress . . . In the light of past Congressional performance—and absent any new check on the unrestrained Commander-in-Chief power—the only leash this nation can have on future military adventures is the pragmatic fact that Presidents and Congresses will be held accountable by affluent and middle America. Both the President and Congress must know that the lives that are lost and the blood that is spilled will come not only from the vast plains of Kansas and the ghettos. It will also be the blood of Chevy Chase, Md. and Ladue, Mo., and Exeter and Groton.

Before the Senate, Washington/
The Wall Street Journal, 6-11:6.

Gerald R. Ford
United States Representative, R—Mich.

Most Americans are not fully aware of the extent to which the Vietnam war effort was financed at the expense of other essential U.S. defense programs. I am concerned that Congress and the American people, in their disillusionment and war weariness of the present moment, will so restrict future funds . . . that the Soviet momentum, which has moved forward on all fronts while we were bogged down in Vietnam, will gain such a lead that we can never catch up.

At Zionist Organization of America
convention, Pittsburgh, Sept. 4/
The Washington Post, 9-6:(A)4.

John S. Foster, Jr.
Director of Research and Engineering,
Department of Defense of the United States

(Regarding Soviet defense research): It stands to reason that a capital investment in R&D (research and development), exceeding our own by several billion dollars a year will yield the Russians important, perhaps even decisive, discoveries. By 1975, if the present disparity in investment should continue, I would fully expect to find the Russians with major new weapons systems deployed, or ready for deployment, which will represent a technological surprise to us; systems we do not now see, or may not know about or even suspect, but which may be in intense development.

(Soviet Premier) Kosygin's successor will have more choices in weapons and strategy than (President) Nixon's will have.

Reader's Digest, February:97.

Carl A. Gerstacker
Chairman, Dow Chemical Company

I am violently against a professional Army, and violently for the draft. Unless the wealthiest people's children, or the smartest people's children or the politicians' children are drafted along with the poorest people's children, we are sowing the seeds of our own destruction.

Interview/Nation's Business, July:44.

Barry M. Goldwater
United States Senator, R—Ariz.

(Regarding the military draft): As a conservative, I believe that the most precious and fundamental right of man is the right to live his own life. When force is used to tell a young man how he shall spend several years of his life, I consider this to invade his basic personal liberty.

The National Observer, 3-8:7.

Antagonism toward the Defense Department is all part of the (Senators) Fulbright-Proxmire thrust. It is nothing new in history. The military runs a cycle from extreme popularity to extreme unpopularity. Earlier, there was the attack on the "military-industrial complex." Before the detractors started their fire, it was known as the "arsenal of democracy." The present attack is hurting badly. Morale is at an all-time low in the armed services. If we give up our world leadership, that would be the signal for World War III—as Russia and China oppose each other in trying to take over the leadership.

*Interview, Washington/
U.S. News & World Report, 6-28:27.*

Andrew J. Goodpaster
*General, United States Army;
Supreme Allied Commander/Europe*

For young officers and enlisted men on whom our services depend today and who must be the leaders of tomorrow, the anti-military sentiment is deeply disturbing. Indeed, it is causing the loss of men we need very badly. This could affect the morale of our armed forces in many ways. It would be a sad thing if, in preoccupation with domestic problems, serious as they may be, we were to cast away our own security. Without this security, how can the country dedicate itself to the task of solving its internal problems?

*Interview, Shape, Belgium/
Los Angeles Times, 9-28:(2)7.*

Mike Gravel
United States Senator, D—Alaska

(Regarding filibustering the military draft): If I can get 34 Senators to hang tough until June 30 (the expiration of the current draft law), we will have no more draft. If we succeed, it will be the first victory for peace this country has had.

*Interview, Washington/
Los Angeles Herald-Examiner, 5-8:(A)3.*

(Regarding the military draft): Where is there virtue, freedom, justice, or for that matter security, in a system that rests its defense upon force, upon sheer brute force, upon the involuntary servitude toward whose abolition this land was supposed to be a beacon? A nation in peacetime employing the draft is the practitioner of involuntary servitude . . . Let the draft end, and lift this cursed system of forced conscription which daily washes away the foundation of our republic. Let the draft end, and once more the lives of our young men will be our most precious coin and not some commodity in surplus to be spent recklessly under the cover of conscription. Let the draft end, and simply ask the Commander-in-Chief to speak of America's cause in terms that free men will not reject. Let the draft end, and you do not comfort enemies—you simply serve notice upon the entire world that, henceforth, America is prepared to trust in freedom explicitly.

*Before the Senate, Washington/
The Wall Street Journal, 6-24:8.*

Vance Hartke
United States Senator, D–Ind.

Our continuing deployment of MIRV missiles in silos and submarines, plus the implementation of *Safeguard* ABM, has not prompted the Soviet Union to seek a negotiated arms settlement. It has, instead, caused them to interpret our actions as being designed to acquire a first-strike capability. The American negotiating strategy, that of attempting to bargain from a position of strength, has simply provoked the U.S.S.R. to place greater dependence upon an increased rather than decreased SS-9 missile capability . . . A concession, such as the reduction in the number of our fighter-bombers in Europe, could help get the (SALT) talks off dead center and evoke a reciprocal positive response from the U.S.S.R. . . . By deciding what military capabilities we really need to serve our national security, by tempering our provocative statements concerning Soviet military capabilities so as to reflect a more conciliatory attitude in negotiations, and to respond—cautiously but constructively—to Soviet initiatives, by these changes we may achieve the progress at the talks we profess to seek.

At University of Virginia commencement,
June 6/Los Angeles Times, 6-7:(3)9.

Mark O. Hatfield
United States Senator, R–Ore.

There is no institution of our government more contrary to our democratic ideals, more limiting of our freedom and more disruptive to the lives of our youth than the (military) draft.
The National Observer, 3-8:7.

F. Edward Hebert
United States Representative, D–La.

(Regarding the "new Army"): I'm shaking in my boots. I am scared to death. When you turn the military into a country club, discipline goes out the window. The military is not a democracy. Are we going to have miniskirts in the mess halls? Will the commanding officer and the enlisted men pass each other and give a wave and say, "Hi, toots?" They'll get so soft they won't get dirt on their hands.
Washington/Time, 1-11:11.

In our present situation, I think the only way to get an all-volunteer Army is to draft it.
Before House Armed Services Committee,
Washington, Feb. 23/
The Washington Post, 2-24:(A)14.

The day we lose control of the seas, the security of our nation is a myth.
Quote, 9-5:217.

Lewis B. Hershey
Former Director, Selective Service
System of the United States

. . . employment recently hasn't been all that it has been in the past. I certainly don't want to be quoted as saying I want a depression; but if the economy gets worse, it makes sense that (military) recruiting will go better. If the Army is the only place a man can get a job, he'll probably go into the Army. I'd say, if we get out of Vietnam, and the Arabs and Israelis embrace, and war doesn't break out in any of the half-dozen other possible places, we can have a volunteer Army by 1973.
At University of Florida/Parade, 3-14:20.

Bruce K. Holloway
General, United States Air Force;
Commander-in-Chief, Strategic Air Command

The actual physical threat to the existence of the United States is greater now in the 1970s than at any time in our history since the 1770s . . . Not since that time has there been a military power arrayed against us by an antagonist which could immediately destroy us as a nation. That power is under the single control of the U.S.S.R.—not the entire Communist bloc, but one country—a country which has been amassing military power of all types at forced draft since the early 1960s.
Before Commonwealth Club, San Francisco,
Aug. 27/San Francisco Examiner, 8-28:5.

A great many Americans—to include some of the so-called silent majority—simply do not understand that weapons modernization is a mandate for survival of the United States as a free country. It is unequivocally necessary if we are to have a sufficiency of strategic forces —which the President and Secretary of Defense have declared our paramount military requirement and responsibility. This is so whether we are concerned with being blown to bits or being coerced or blackmailed to bits—and it could happen either way if we were to fail to keep strong through modernization and a healthy research-and-development base.

Interview, Washington/
U.S. News & World Report, 12-27:54.

Hubert H. Humphrey
United States Senator, D—Minn.

Do the Russians intend to build a first-strike capability sufficient to destroy our *Minuteman* (missile) force? I believe that this possibility is too fanciful to merit our serious concern. It ignores the political development of a decade in our relations with the Soviet Union. It ignores the certainty that the Russians would face a continued, all-out nuclear arms race with us—a race they could not win. We would never stand idly by and permit that. But most important, the case for believing in a Soviet first-strike capability against *Minuteman* ignores totally the existence of our powerful *Polaris* submarine force. Today that force on its own—and without MIRV—is capable of utterly destroying the Soviet Union, if this brings any comfort to anyone. We cannot continue to assert, without convincing evidence, that the Soviet Union is bent upon the destruction of our land-based missiles; and we must not undertake programs based upon that assertion. If we do, we stand to forfeit the possibility that the arms race itself can be brought to an end. Overinsurance, and the hysteria which breeds it, may only help to bring into being the very offensive threat that is the object of the *Safeguard* (antimissile) defense.

Before the Senate, Washington, March 25/
The Washington Post, 4-6:(A)16.

We should be generous—but we must not be foolhardy. I am proud of my advocacy over the years of international disarmament—but I have never advocated unilateral disarmament. Therein lies the road not to peace, but to possible disaster.

The New York Times, 10-6:45.

Henry M. Jackson
United States Senator, D—Wash.

It will come as a shock to a lot of Americans—after much discussion that they (the Soviet Union) have leveled off the deployment of SS-9s (missiles)—to know that the Russians are now in the process of deploying a new generation, an advanced generation, of offensive systems contrary to the position earlier indicated with the so-called leveling off of the number of SS-9 sites . . . These are huge new missiles that, from a qualitative point of view, certainly present a different problem for the United States to face in the 1970s.

Radio-TV interview, Washington/
"Face the Nation,"
Columbia Broadcasting System, 3-7.

I'm not a hawk or a dove. I just don't want my country to be a pigeon.

Time, 3-22:14.

It is remarkable to me that, in the face of Soviet refusal to limit its offensive missile force—a position that must raise doubts about their intentions—some Americans are arguing that we should assume their good will and move to limit our defenses. How would an agreement on our part to leave our deterrent unprotected increase the Soviets' interest in doing later what they are evidently unprepared to do now: halt their offensive build-up? An agreement limited to defense only, far from slowing the arms race, would actually accelerate it. To believe otherwise requires one to place his faith in nothing more tangible than a dream of Soviet self-restraint.

Before American Society of Newspaper
Editors, Washington, April 15/
Vital Speeches, 6-1:485.

Morris A. Kaplan
Professor of Political Science,
University of Chicago

In the real world, the Soviet Union is a tough customer that may not actually start a war with us—but the myth of "harmony" is ours, not theirs. "Peaceful coexistence" means they intend to beat us. We mistakenly separate political doctrines of Communists and Nazis; whereas the true alignment would combine them as "Commu-Nazis." We are very unwise to let Russia acquire first-strike capability against us; but we are determined to erase our "big, bad military image" . . . We under-estimate Russian strength. We assumed they would stop at parity—but they didn't. Now they're ahead of us; but it's hard for Americans to realize or admit that.

Los Angeles, May 4/
Los Angeles Herald-Examiner, 5-5:(A)7.

Melvin R. Laird
Secretary of Defense of the United States

We need a strategy for the 1970s that can effectively deter not only nuclear war but all levels of armed conflict. It was that need, coupled with an awareness of the realities we face, that led to the adoption of what we call the Strategy of Realistic Deterrence. We call it realistic because it is designed to take account of the major realities facing America and the rest of the world in these difficult times. It recognizes that there cannot be any instant solutions to the problems that simultaneously confront us. And it underscores the fact that the United States by itself cannot provide realistic deterrence on a global scale. The four basic realities which led to the new strategy are: a strategic reality; a fiscal reality; a manpower reality; and a political reality. The strategic reality includes, most notably, the tremendous growth in Soviet military strength from a position of clear inferiority in the early 1960s to near parity today; it also includes an emerging nuclear capability on the part of the People's Republic of China (Communist China). The fiscal reality involves not only the heavy pressure in Congress for reduced defense spending but the upward pressure of inflation on the cost of everything we need to buy to maintain adequate military forces. The manpower reality is not yet fully understood. People constitute the single biggest cost in the defense budget. Pay and related costs in (fiscal) 1972 will claim some 52 per cent of the total defense budget, based on the pay increases we have recommended. It will cost us almost $18 billion more than it did in 1964 for 133,000 fewer people . . . The political reality severely complicates the other three—whether you look at it from the standpoint of the political and psychological effects of Soviet policy and growing presence around the world, such as in the Mediterranean and the Middle East; whether you look at it from the standpoint of political pressures from our allies to maintain forward-deployed U.S. forces; whether you look at it from the standpoint of Congressional pressure to reduce those forces; or whether you look at it from the standpoint of gaining broad political support here at home for doing all the things we have to do to assure our national-security interests while continuing to reorder our national priorities. The most pressing reality remains the strategic reality. The most essential requirement in terms of national survival remains assuring the adequacy of our strategic deterrent . . .

Before American Newspaper Publishers
Association, New York, April 21/
The National Observer, 4-26:3.

We have been in a period of almost moratorium since 1967 on new strategic weapons deployment. That was the time that the last *Polaris* (missile) went forward; that was the time that the last of the *Minutemen* (missile) deployments were approved. We have not come forward with any new bombers. I think we can characterize the Soviet activity as momentum; our activity has been almost moratorium.

News conference/Human Events, 5-22:3.

Next to lack of definitive progress in negotiations (around the world), I suppose my greatest frustration is the manner in which the military is looked upon in this country. So much is being done to downgrade the military. Most of the military men I've come into contact with during the last 20 or so years in Washington have been pretty good people . . . People in the military are beginning to think that maybe they should be looking someplace else.

Interview, Washington/
The New York Times Magazine, 6-13:33.

Anyone with any political ambitions doesn't go anywhere from Secretary of Defense. I'm getting out of this job after four years, whatever happens. (Former Defense Secretary) Bob McNamara told me the first mistake he made was staying in the job too long. After four years, I'm getting out. I guarantee it.

Interview, Washington/
The New York Times Magazine, 6-13:33.

My objective (as Secretary of Defense) is to see that United States military forces are in a position where they provide a realistic deterrent; at the end of my term of service, that we be at peace and that no American is being shot at in any part of the world or is shooting in any part of the world.

News conference, Washington, Sept. 1/
The New York Times, 9-2:8.

Thomas A. Lane
Major General, United States Army (Ret.);
Former Professor of Military History,
United States Military Academy, West Point

False alarms about military usurpation of civil authority seem especially contrived in an era when President (Lyndon) Johnson could boast that (in the Vietnam war) not a chicken shed was bombed without his permission . . . The era of Napoleon is long dead. We live in an age of civilian dictatorships, all socialist, all modeled on the examples of Lenin, Mussolini and Hitler.

San Francisco Examiner, 2-16:32.

Stanley R. Larson
Lieutenant General, United States Army;
Commanding General, Sixth Army

The disadvantages of a volunteer Army are

that it is more expensive to maintain, it usually does not represent a cross-section of the population and it tends to isolate itself from the local society; consequently, its loyalties are more easily turned toward its leaders than toward its government.

'Before Res Publica, Los Angeles/
Los Angeles Herald-Examiner, 1-24:(A)15.

John V. Lindsay
Mayor of New York

If the United States would make domestic and internal well-being its first priority, it would achieve far greater strength than it has achieved by putting such a massive amount of its resources into defense mechanisms. The way things are going, we will fall apart internally. We will do to ourselves what no enemy can do to us.

Interview, New York/
Los Angeles Herald-Examiner, 12-26:(A)14.

Mike Mansfield
United States Senator, D—Mont.

The 92nd Congress, I believe, would . . . be performing a necessary public service by continuing to seek to cut expenditures for exotic weapons which are of dubious utility or are already in excessive supply.

At Senate Democratic caucus, Washington,
Jan. 21/The New York Times, 1-22:12.

Charles McC. Mathias, Jr.
United States Senator, R—Md.

(Arguing against a "blank check" for military expenditures): Congress has to see that providing for the common defense—as is our duty under the Constitution—is a 365-degree problem. It is providing for defense in a military sense with adequate weapons systems. It is providing for defense in the economic field so that you don't let your concentration on weapons systems totally debilitate the economy. And it is providing for the common defense in the area of the kind of morale and the kind of confidence and the kind of steadiness in the population which—as we have been observing in the Vietnam war—is an essential ingredient to any kind of defense policy. If

(CHARLES McC. MATHIAS, JR.)

there is any function given to the Federal government and to the Congress, it is to provide for the common defense. And if we delegate that authority and just shrug our shoulders and say, "We don't know—go ahead and buy it," what is there left really within our Constitutional scope of duty?

The Washington Post, 10-25:(A)19.

Paul N. McCloskey, Jr.
United States Representative, R–Calif.

Do any of us know any reasonable young men today who are willing to serve as combat infantrymen in a cause in which we have admittedly given up the will to win? In years to come, the United States will be in desperate need of professional military men who are the equivalent of our best minds in science, the professions and the business community. Our military establishment will need the pride and esprit de corps that have characterized it since Lexington and Concord. By turning away from the pleas of our young people to end this war now, we may be depriving our future military forces of the ability to attract men of the necessary dedication and abilities . . .

Feb. 18/The National Observer, 3-22:5.

(Arguing in support of the military draft): If reasonable men will not volunteer for combat infantry duty in peacetime, I suspect there is little benefit in seeking to attract unreasonable men to volunteer. There are men who love to kill; but it seems to me the nation is far safer when its army is made up of reluctant citizen-soldiers than by men who take pride in being professional killers.

Before House Armed Services Committee,
Washington, March 3/
The Washington Post, 3-4:(A)4.

. . . I believe that the arguments over the continuation of the (military) draft are distorted by reason of the current unpopularity of our Vietnam war policy. It is understandable that young men asked to kill a people

whom they do not hate, in a cause in which they do not believe, might focus their hostility against the law which requires their service. I suspect, however, that the young men of deep sensitivity who have gone to Sweden or Canada or sought conscientious objector status or willingly undergone jail sentences, would be the same men who, 30 years ago, memorized eye charts and traveled to Canada to enlist in Canadian forces rather than wait for American involvement in the war against Nazi Germany. In brief, I believe that it is the Vietnam war policy which causes today's protest against mandatory military service, not a sudden abandonment of the principle that a young man should serve his country for a short time during his youth. It may be that I am biased in this regard, but it has always seemed to me that the privileges and freedoms of being an American citizen justify two years of service in times of war or threat to the national security.

Before the House, Washington, April 1/
Congressional Record, 4-1:(H)2379.

(Regarding an all-volunteer army): What reasonable young man is going to give up a life of drinking beer with his friends, enjoying drive-in movies with his girl and sleeping late on weekends in order to volunteer for the hard and rigorous life of running 20 miles a day, standing watch half the night, crawling through jungles and generally being miserable?

The New York Times, 4-4:(4)3.

George S. McGovern
United States Senator, D–S.D.

Needless war and military waste contribute to the economic crisis, not only through inflation, but by the dissipation of labor and resources in nonproductive enterprise. For too long the taxes of our citizens and revenues desperately needed by our cities and states have been drawn into Washington and wasted on senseless war and unnecessary military gadgets. Each month, Washington wastes enough on military folly to rebuild an American city or give new life to a rural area. A major task of the 1970s is the conversion of our economy from the excesses of war to the works of peace.

> *Announcing his candidacy for 1972*
> *Presidential election, Jan. 18/*
> *The New York Times, 1-19:18.*

John C. Meyer
General and Vice Chief of Staff,
United States Air Force

As we move toward (a) more productive Air Force . . . we cannot neglect the importance of sheer numbers of men and machines—especially in the context of Soviet military expansion. The best fighter in the world, with the best fighter pilot in the world, won't give us air superiority unless we have *enough* of them, *where* we need them. Neither will the most advanced bomber deter an attack if we don't have enough of them. And the same goes for all of our other weapons and the people to operate them. So as we look out into the next decade—indeed, into the next budget—we must be alert to the danger of cutting our forces too thin. To err on the short side of men and machines for today's Air Force can be every bit as disastrous as foregoing the technology of tomorrow's . . . And where the price of liberty is oft-quoted as eternal vigilance, I would point out that it also has a price tag in men, machines and money—and with the world as it is, it is a price we Americans dare not fail to pay.

> *Before Air Force Association,*
> *Alamo Chapter, San Antonio, Tex.,*
> *Sept. 29/Vital Speeches, 11-1:58.*

James Michener
Author

The new life cycle can find no place for patriotism in the old sense, while respect for the military has been replaced by contempt. These are the direct consequences of the Vietnam war and the draft (that) was needed to support it. A generation of young men have had to grapple with one of the most confusing draft systems ever devised by a democracy, and they have grown to hate it and everything associated with it.

> *At Kent State University, Ohio/*
> *The National Observer, 1-11:10.*

Abner J. Mikva
United States Representative, D–Ill.

We have far more men under arms than we need and probably than is wise. There is an obvious risk that, in order to keep all these excess numbers of armed men busy, the Pentagon will be tempted to promote military adventures.

> *News conference, Washington/*
> *The Dallas Times Herald, 7-12:(A)23.*

Thomas H. Moorer
Admiral, United States Navy;
Chairman, Joint Chiefs of Staff

Our (military) lead has now all but vanished; and, within the next five or six years, we could actually find ourselves in a position of over-all strategic inferiority, certainly as far as numbers of offensive delivery vehicles and megatons and air-defense systems are concerned . . . We will pay a very high price in the effectiveness of our diplomacy if we permit the Soviet Union to achieve a clearly-evident over-all strategic superiority, even were the superiority to have no practical effect on the outcome of an all-out nuclear exchange.

> *Before House Armed Services Committee,*
> *Washington/Human Events, 3-20:4.*

. . . today we have an attitude in this country against military services in general, which I think is very unfortunate. The American people can't have it both ways. They can't, on one hand, insist on an adequate defense against this build-up of capabilities on the part of potential enemies and, on the other hand, demean and degrade those in uniform. I know of several cases, for instance, where young men have been discouraged from going to West Point, Annapolis or the Air Force Academy. We've had cases where some of the leading colleges have removed the ROTCs. People responsible should realize that they could be undermining the security of their sons and grandsons. If we're going to have a volunteer force, young people have got to volunteer for it, and the American people have got to support it. Right now is a difficult time for the volunteer; because a youngster

(THOMAS H. MOORER)

wants to feel that when he joins an organization it's respected and that his mother and father and his friends don't say, "Well, what in hell are you doing that for?" They ought to tell him, "Son, we're proud of you for what you're doing for your country."

Interview, Washington/
U.S. News & World Report, 4-5:47.

Let me try to place the defense budget in perspective. Defense outlays for the current fiscal year are projected at $76 billion—a sum so large it has meaning for most of us only in relative terms. In terms of gross national product, we are spending 6.8 per cent for defense . . . the lowest level in 20 years.

Before Wings Club, New York/San Francisco
Examiner & Chronicle, 11-28:(B)3.

Will is absolutely essential to deterrence. It makes no difference how powerful a nation may be militarily; if the will to use that power is lacking—or even if others believe such will is lacking—then a strategy based on deterrence loses credibility.

Before Wings Club, New York/San Francisco
Examiner & Chronicle, 11-28:(B)3.

Edmund S. Muskie
United States Senator, D–Maine

If we deploy new weapons, knowing full well that Soviet deployment of similar weapons will follow, will the result be more or less security for our nation?

The Albuquerque Tribune, 6-1:(B)5.

Richard M. Nixon
President of the United States

Until the United States obtains an arms-control limitation between the great superpowers—one which we and they can rely upon—it is essential for the United States to maintain adequate armed forces. Not because we want war; but because, in the truest sense of the word, in peace time the armed forces of the United States are peace forces.

Before American Legion,
Washington, Feb. 16/
Los Angeles Herald-Examiner, 2-17:(A)12.

The United States will deal, as it must, from strength. We will not reduce our defenses below the level I consider essential to our national security. A strong America is essential to the cause of peace today. Until we have the kind of agreements we can rely on, we shall remain strong. But America's power will always be used for building a peace, never for breaking it—only for defending freedom, never for destroying it. America's strength will be, as it must be, second to none. But the strength that this nation is proudest of is the strength of our determination to create a peaceful world.

State of the World address, Washington,
Feb. 25/U.S. News & World Report, 3-8:52.

(Regarding the arguments of the "new isolationists"): Though we cut defense spending, we cannot cut it enough. Though we greatly increase domestic spending in proportion to defense spending, we cannot increase it enough . . . I understand these arguments. I understand the cost of weakness, too. This question of what is enough is not academic—it is crucial to the survival of this nation. If we have the most extensive urban-renewal programs and the most far-reaching medical-care provisions and the finest highways and the most comprehensive education assistance efforts and the most effective antipoverty programs—if we have all this and more, and we have it all at the expense of our ability to defend ourselves, then we would soon enjoy none of the fruits of our efforts; and the only peace we would know would be that terrible peace imposed upon those who are the victims of their own lack of vigilance.

At Naval Officer Candidate School,
Newport, R.I., March 12/
The New York Times, 3-13:(1).

To those who speak of American might as something arrogant, something ominous, you need only ask one question: "In the world today, a world which permits no vacuum of power, what other nation would you trust more with that power than America?"

At United States Military Academy,
West Point, N.Y., May 29/
The New York Times, 5-30:(1)1.

Wolfgang Panofsky
Physicist; Director, Stanford
Linear Accelerator Center

Strategic arms constitute only about 10 per cent of the present U.S. military budget. But nuclear weapons are by far the cheapest way to kill; so budget pressures may actually push us back into increased reliance on nuclear armaments to counter threats that might best be answered by other means.

At National Academy of Sciences seminar,
Washington/San Francisco Examiner
& Chronicle (Sunday Punch), 2-28:4.

William Proxmire
United States Senator, D—Wis.

The nation should be told why the military budget is going up while the Vietnam war is being wound down. The cruel fact is that there is no peace dividend. It is the only time in American history that we will spend more for the military at the end of a war than while the war was still going strong.

Before the Senate, Washington, Feb. 3/
Los Angeles Times, 2-4:(1)24.

. . . if the military fails to reform, it may so endanger its own credibility as to bring about the very neo-isolationism it claims to oppose. By reforming procurement, by reviewing our commitments, by taking a realistic view of the Russian and Chinese threat, by doing away with unneeded and overlapping weapons and by limiting the expansion of our nuclear strategic terror, we could make great savings in the defense budget without endangering our security . . . We must soon end the all-this-and-heaven-too military weapons policy in order that we can produce those weapons we need most and which may be vital to our security.

Before Coalition on National Priorities
and Military Policy, Washington, April 12/
The Dallas Times Herald, 4-12:(A)10.

We have just witnessed the shortest missile gap in history. In mid-April, Secretary (of Defense) Laird and Senator (Henry M.) Jackson issued a series of "scare 'em" statements based on the fact that the Russians had dug forty new holes. On the wholly unproven assumption that these holes were designed for the huge new 25-megaton SS-9 missiles, Secretary Laird told us that the "U.S. may be moving toward a second-rate strategic position." Senator Jackson charged that ". . . the overall strategic balance may be tilting in Moscow's favor." I said at the time that these were highly exaggerated and even semi-hysterical conclusions. I said that, every year, just when the crocusus push through the winter soil and the forsythia and dogwood burst into bloom, one can predict a new round of speeches based on selected intelligence data telling us that the Russians are ten feet tall. Now the facts are out. *The New York Times* reports today that ". . . the Central Intelligence Agency concluded that at least two-thirds of the large new silo holes recently detected in the Soviet Union were intended for the relatively small SS-11 intercontinental ballistic missile and not for a large new weapon, as the Defense Department has suggested" . . . The strategic balance did not "tilt." We have not become a "second rate" power. In a month, without the U.S. lifting a finger or spending a dime, this missile gap was closed. The lesson is clear. Congress and the public should not be swept off their feet by leaks designed merely to propagandize for a fatter military budget.

Before the Senate, Washington, May 26/
I. F. Stone's Bi-Weekly, 6-14:2.

(Concerning a report that the Soviet Union now has the initiative in weapons development): Good God, what's happening to all the money we're spending (on the military), nearly $80 billion a year? What do we have to show for it in new weapons? Practically none.

Los Angeles Times, 11-22:(1)9.

Stanley R. Resor
Secretary of the Army of the United States

Conventional forces are particularly essential today, because we now live in an age of nuclear parity. Since the Soviets now have less fear of nuclear retaliation, we can expect them to test our will at lower levels of conflict. In this changed environment, conventional forces emerge as an increasingly effective means for exerting either military or diplomatic pressure. The continued Soviet emphasis on such forces indicates their awareness of this trend.

Interview/The Washington Post, 1-25:(A)17.

Hyman G. Rickover
Vice Admiral, United States Navy

I believe the real danger lies in our allowing the capability of our general-purpose forces for conventional warfare to deteriorate relative to the rapidly-expanding Soviet capability for conventional warfare. They already have an army far superior to ours. If they now succeed in building a navy which can prevent our own Navy from supporting overseas military operations, they can have their way over any issue for which we are not willing to risk nuclear war. They then could whittle away at us, and there would be no need for them to resort to nuclear war.

Before House Appropriations Committee, Washington, May/ The New York Times, 9-27:16.

The blunt situation facing us is that Soviet Russia is doing all the things a nation would do if it wanted to be the number one military power with clear unequivocal superiority. The U.S. Navy has not taken any further steps to increase its strategic offensive force. There has not been an arms race; the Soviets have been running at full speed all by themselves.

On receiving Gold Medal Award from American Ordnance Association, New York/San Francisco Examiner & Chronicle, 11-28:(B)3.

Matthew B. Ridgway
General (Ret.) and former Chief of Staff, United States Army

Not before in my lifetime—and I was born into the Army in the nineteenth century—has the Army's public image suffered so many grievous blows and fallen to such low esteem in such wide areas of our society.

San Francisco Examiner & Chronicle (This World), 4-11:2.

Richard S. Schweiker
United States Senator, R–Pa.

The Pharaohs of Egypt, the Caesars of Rome, the kings of Europe paid their soldiers proportionately far more than we pay our own GIs.

Quote, 7-11:25.

John C. Stennis
United States Senator, D–Miss.

I totally reject the concept advocated from time to time that the President has certain inherent powers as Commander-in-Chief which enable him to extensively commit major forces to combat without Congressional consent. As one Senator, I am striving to help perfect a more realistic method that Congress shall use in providing explicit authority for the President to repel an attack, but requiring Congressional authorization before hostilities can be extended for an appreciable time. This is an area that must have clarification.

Jackson, Miss., Jan. 11/ The Washington Post, 1-14:(A)8.

(If the cost increases of military weapons are) not sharply reversed, then even significant increases in the Defense budget may not insure the force levels required for our national security. It seems absolutely clear to me that we reduce and even endanger our national security by developing and procuring costly and ineffective weapons systems. If the weapons we develop are so costly that we cannot afford enough of them, and if they are so technically complex that they are unreliable and difficult to maintain, we have done the nation a disservice by developing and procuring them.

Washington, Dec. 3/
The Dallas Times Herald, 12-3:(AA)1.

Stuart Symington
United States Senator, D–Mo.

The tendency of the military in any country—especially in a country which won the last war—is to operate on tradition as against modernity. Militarily, the need for bases abroad was sound. But with intercontinental ballistic missiles, long-range bombers, and now—probably most important—*Polaris* submarines leading into *Poseidons*, I don't see why we need for our security nearly as many bases in the future as we have needed in the past. And these occupations hurt us from a diplomatic standpoint. No one likes to be occupied. I wouldn't want to see foreign troops walking down the streets of our cities. There's already much resentment toward our troops in such proud countries as Germany and Japan. And it's all mighty expensive from the standpoint of the taxpayers of this country.

Interview, Washington/
U.S. News & World Report, 6-28:29.

O. C. Talbott
Major General, United States Army;
Commander, Fort Benning, Ga.

In the long run, our Army cannot exist without the good will of the people. Draft or not draft, volunteer or not volunteer, it just cannot exist, because it is the people themselves who are coming to it. They will come to it bitterly and with distaste, or with pride and willingness to perform—based upon the national attitude of the people as a whole. And that has to be wrapped in. It is not a simple military question.

Interview/The Washington Post, 9-15:(A)8.

Curtis W. Tarr
Director, Selective Service System
of the United States

I talked with some protestors who said that if you did away with the armed services you wouldn't lose that much. That's not realistic. Fly the B-52s into the ocean? Make duds out of *Minuteman* (missiles)? Our relations with Russia would change drastically and quickly. When a fellow says we can junk it all out and be better off, I say he's not being intellectually honest.

Interview/Life, 6-11:58.

John V. Tunney
United States Senator, D–Calif.

We must dissent from the policies of a government that spends more on guns and useless military hardware than it does on housing.

Columbia, S.C., April 5/
San Francisco Examiner, 4-5:11.

George C. Wallace
Governor of Alabama

We've talked of unilateral disarmament. We've tried to grovel. I know one thing for sure: The best way to have World War III is to have parity with the Soviet Union.

The Washington Post, 8-30:(A)16.

An Alabaman sitting on a tractor or on the courthouse steps can tell you we got to be so strong that the Communists will want to talk to us. But while we're talking disarmament, the Soviets double the number of ICBMs they have. (President) Nixon's own blue-ribbon report called on the nation to regain—not retain, but regain—our nuclear superiority. Parity won't work. This country is a second-rate military power. When the people find out, they will deliver swift political vengeance.

Interview, Montgomery, Ala./
Los Angeles Times, 12-19:(H)6.

Lewis W. Walt
General and Assistant Commandant,
United States Marine Corps

We need to educate our children why we need strong armed forces. Neutrality is a great thing; but who is going to enforce neutrality?

Washington, Jan. 4/
The Washington Post, 1-5:(A)7.

William C. Westmoreland
General and Chief of Staff,
United States Army

We cannot expect to achieve our goal of a zero draft volunteer force when the Army is maligned by some, directly attacked by others and half-heartedly supported by many.

Williamsburg, Va./
The Dallas Times Herald, 1-15:(A)2.

If the military is continually made the scapegoat for national problems and short-comings—if the military is continually demeaned within the country—this can only have an undesirable effect over the long run . . . Your Army has never been a threat to our country. And it has never compromised its sacred oath to support the Constitution of the United States. Through 13 wars and 157 campaigns, the Army has never failed the nation on the battlefield. What concerns many people is that America will turn inward and away from her international obligations. America must always be able to deal from a position of strength. Only from such a position can she face squarely her responsibilities as a free nation. It is unfortunate that public hostility toward the military is at a dangerously high level.

Before China, Burma, India Veterans
Association, Dallas, Aug. 7/
The Dallas Times Herald, 8-8:(A)33.

Elmo R. Zumwalt, Jr.
Admiral, United States Navy;
Chief of Naval Operations

I think it's terribly important for all of us in positions of responsibility to insure that the American people understand that we are again going through one of those phases that democracies tend to go through—where they are lulled into a sense of security.

Interview/The Washington Post, 1-17:(A)12.

I've yet to be shown how beards and sideburns or neat haircuts detract from a ship's ability to carry out its functions.

Quote, 3-14:241.

Just as the Soviets have been rational and back down in the face of our (military) superiority, they will expect us to be rational and back down if they gain that superiority—and I think that we would have to.

Washington, July 27/
Los Angeles Times, 7-29:(1)7.

I think there is a significant minority who feels that the military services and military personnel are simply no longer relevant in the modern world. Fortunately, I believe that a respectable majority still continues to understand that, as the President has suggested, you can only have a generation of peace by maintaining the necessary military strength.

Interview, Washington/
U.S. News & World Report, 9-13:77.

The biggest single problem in the Navy today is people: the problem of retaining after a single tour—and attracting for that first tour—motivated individuals, in face of the very imminent loss of draft authority. This No. 1 problem is compounded by the fact that the military service at the present time is not considered a popular place in which to serve by a large body of our young people. We've got the job of trying to turn that around in the months and years ahead.

Interview/The Washington Post, 12-26:(A)2.

Spiro T. Agnew
Vice President of the United States

I suppose I'm the foremost articulator of the destruction of liberal dogma at the moment, and there are very few people on the public scene who attack the sacrosanct institutions . . . And when you do that, when you imply that it's entirely possible that these predispositions on the part of the liberal community are not necessarily accurate, you immediately trigger a Pavlovian reaction.

San Francisco Examiner & Chronicle
(This World), 1-10:2.

If I were a Southerner, I would be irritated by this constant wail of "Southern strategy." It's as if being in favor of equal treatment to the South—a section of the country that has been subjected to undue harassment over a long period of time—were some sort of crime. Apparently, the "liberal" political machine does not like the idea of evenhandedness in dealing with the various regions of the country. What these so-called liberals have embarked on, therefore, is a Southern strategy of their own—a strategy that can best be described in this fashion: Keep kicking the South, because it's easy to sell to the people in the rest of the country; it makes them feel good and clean and pure. So you see, the people who practice the real Southern strategy are those who talk so much about it—not those they accuse of practicing it. It's a trick political tactic of our opposition.

Interview/U.S. News & World Report, 4-19:62.

(President Nixon) must cope each day not only with the crises inherited as a result of the foreign and domestic policy errors of his predecessors, but must also cope with the politically-oriented criticism and carping of many of the very men who urged the decisions that created those crises.

At Republican fund-raising dinner,
Jackson, Miss., May 18/
The Washington Post, 5-19:(A)2.

A President must select the most potent and powerful Vice President that he can find. I expect that President Nixon will do this, and I believe he will make that decision no earlier than the first of next year. Until he decides, it would be fruitless for me to make any decision (about running again). Whatever he decides, I will be with him in his corner strongly; and should he select another running mate, I will support that person, too.

TV-radio interview/"Issues and Answers,"
American Broadcasting Company, 8-22.

So that there can be no misunderstanding about my feelings on this subject (divisiveness), I not only plead guilty to this charge, but I am somewhat flattered by it. If division is caused by a forthright definition of positions on issues facing the American people, I think such division must occur before a solution to those points in dispute can be reached . . .

At dinner honoring Senator John Tower,
El Paso, Tex., Oct. 5/
Los Angeles Times, 10-6:(1)12.

Carl Albert
United States Representative, D–Okla.

I guess you'd say that the main element in my climb to the leadership (Speaker of the House) is in the fact that I've heard more speeches than anyone else and called more people by their first names . . . I got so that I could guess within a few votes how they'd vote on any given issue.

Interview, Washington/
The Washington Post, 1-10:(B)3.

Joseph L. Alioto
Mayor of San Francisco

If you have a crony who is eminently qualified for public office, what is the harm in appointing him? You know, I have this rule: you look for high-qualified friends. If you exhaust that category, then you look for qualified neutrals. If you exhaust that category, then you look for qualified enemies. Well, it so happens I have a great many friends, so I've never been compelled to dip into the other two categories.

San Francisco Examiner, 11-4:6.

George Andrews
United States Representative, D–Ala.

History will record that whoever robs Peter to pay Paul will always get the vote of Paul.

San Francisco Examiner, 8-11:32.

John M. Ashbrook
United States Representative, R–Ohio

A conservative, as distinguished from a liberal, is one who believes first of all in more individual freedom and stresses limited government, which would include less Federal expenditures. And he believes in free enterprise and a strong national posture on defense and foreign policy, particularly vis-a-vis Communism. I think that is a key distinction. Liberals tend to feel that Communism is not a very big problem.

Interview, Washington/
Los Angeles Herald-Examiner, 12-12:(A)19.

Ben Barnes
Lieutenant Governor of Texas

In 1970, we made Richard Nixon a better President by sending him a Democratic Senator and 20 Democratic Representatives from Texas. I want us to start right now by making plans to make Richard Nixon an even better President in 1972 by making him an ex-President in 1973.

At Texas Democratic 1970 election
victory party, Austin, Jan. 18/
The Dallas Times Herald, 1-19:(A)3.

Birch Bayh
United States Senator, D–Ind.

(President Nixon two years ago) urged us to lower our voices. (And yet this is the same man who) sent (Vice President) Spiro Agnew across the land to articulate suspicion, create division, magnify distrust—a sort of sinister Johnny Appleseed sowing hatred, prejudice and fear wherever he passed.

Before California Democratic State
Central Committee, Sacramento, Jan. 24/
Los Angeles Times, 1-25:(1)3.

I've asked myself whether or not I should be President. Sometimes, I think that nobody from Shirkeyville, Ind., should be President; but then, that's the quality of the United States . . If I can become President without too much compromise, I will. If not, I like being a Senator. I have a feeling of inner peace. I don't think it is humanly possible for anybody to be as good a President as he would like. But the people of the heartland of America like good common sense, not liberal rhetoric. Something may be a liberal idea, but if it makes sense to "Middle America," they'll buy it. If I were in the White House, I would put aside rhetoric and political double talk and say, "These are the facts." The people want someone who can tell it to them straight.

Interview, Washington/
The Washington Post, 6-20:(G)8.

Kingman Brewster, Jr.
President, Yale University

. . . the enfranchising of the student generation will have a tremendous impact on the direction, focus and quality of political life in the United States. I would compound the risk of such prediction further by also asserting that this impact will be demonstrably for the better. Even if their total numbers are modest . . . even if their energy is not overwhelmingly political in its motivation, even if they will not in large numbers avail themselves of their relative freedom to schedule their own lives around political action, the voters between the ages of 18 and 25 are a large enough group so that few politicians in the future will be able to afford the luxury of ignoring them. However lazy, apathetic, impertinent, scornful of the process the new voters may be, politicians will have to try to appeal to them.

At University of North Carolina,
April 28/The Boston Globe, 6-13:68.

Politics requires not only the manipulation of the media but it certainly requires disciplined organization. This is not just the discipline of hard work, grubby work, tedious work . . . But as a mentor of mine once warned me, politics requires the willingness to go along with all kinds of things you don't believe in. Even at the highest level of political leadership, there is great truth in the saying that you have to pretend to be a hundred per cent for things that you are really only fifty-one per cent for.

Weil Lecture, University of North Carolina/
The Washington Post, 5-24:(A)20.

Art Buchwald
Columnist, Humorist

People keep asking me if I have ever met President Nixon. My answer is: "I don't remember."

At "The Washington Post" Book and
Author Luncheon, Washington,
Oct. 20/The Washington Post, 10-21:(C)2.

James L. Buckley
United States Senator, C–N.Y.

I believe we stand at a turning point. There is a fluidity in the political scene, a regrouping going on as Americans search for more realistic, more effective approaches to government. And if New York is any indication, Americans are showing a new predisposition to listen to the conservative analysis and a new willingness to become directly involved in the political process. This is a willingness born of a sense of urgency, and founded on a continuing faith in the essential soundness of the American system. This is the authentic "new politics" which I had in mind when I proclaimed myself the voice of that politics. It is a politics structured on reality and a new understanding of what reality is. We have a significant opportunity to reshape the politics of this country precisely because the people are searching for new answers, honest answers —answers which substitute common sense for theory and toughness for soft-headedness. And it is because of this new mood and understanding that we who have labored in the vineyard of conservatism have cause for hope.

At Conservative Awards Dinner, Washington,
Feb. 4/Congressional Record, 2-26:E1208.

Joseph A. Califano, Jr.
General counsel,
Democratic National Committee

The continuing erosion of trust in government, our increased concern with the appearance of corruption and the American crisis of political confidence has led us to the conclusion that it is time for radical surgery. It is time to take private wealth out of politics; it is time to make it a criminal offense to contribute or receive private funds for the public purpose of election to Federal office.

Before Senate Communications Subcommittee,
Washington, March 3/
The New York Times, 3-4:25.

Maria Callas
Opera singer

Politics is the opposite of music: It promises everything—and delivers nothing.

San Francisco Examiner, 3-23:26.

Abram Chayes
Professor of Law, Harvard University

The charisma problem (of Presidential candidates) is really not a problem. The people of the United States are getting sick and tired of charisma, in the sense that it offers expectation of quick and magic solutions and that the problems will go away . . . We may be ready for a quieter, much less hectic Presidential candidate.

The National Observer, 5-17:5.

227

Richard Childs
Chairman, executive committee,
National Municipal League

My arguments as a reformer have always returned to the thesis that people's minds aren't too short, but the ballot is too long. Today, it's better but not good. Try to trim it and politicians yell it's undemocratic. For instance, here in New York there are 250 elected judges, the names of which are supplied by political parties. Do the people know them all? No. Nor do they know all 100 officials they can vote for within a four-year political cycle.

Interview, New York/
The Christian Science Montitor, 1-26:15.

Shirley Chisholm
United States Representative, D–N.Y.

The number of women in politics is declining, which is bad. We need the voices of women in the political arena specifically. Women can address themselves to issues that concern the family and home—education, welfare, nutrition, for instance—with more feeling, intuition and know-how. It's not that the gentlemen are ignoring these issues. It's just that they're more concerned with banking, defense weapons, trade, insurance.

Interview, Washington/
The Christian Science Monitor, 1-7:13.

(Regarding her possible candidacy for President in the 1972 election): I'm doing it to shake the system up. This country is run by old, old men from the South, and I want to make the people at the national convention know they will have to deal with me.

Interview, New York/
Los Angeles Times, 9-16:(1)4.

People who used to think Shirley Chisholm was half-crazy, half-cocked, are going to see that she's got one of the shrewdest, canniest political brains in this country.

Life, 11-5:81.

John B. Connally, Jr.
Secretary of the Treasury
of the United States

I told the President (Nixon) that I would come in (to the Cabinet) as a Democrat and I expected to leave as a Democrat—and that was our whole understanding.

Interview, Washington, Feb. 18/
The Washington Post, 2-19:(A)1.

. . . if I had political ambitions, I probably would not have agreed to become Secretary of the Treasury as a Democrat in a Republican Adminsitration. It tends to infuriate the Republicans and anger the Democrats, and you lose on both sides. From a political standpoint, I don't think it is very wise. I don't have any political ambition; it is just that simple.

TV-radio interview/"Meet the Press,"
National Broadcasting Company,
Washington, 3-14.

The prospect of a realignment, of polarization, into two quite different (political) parties is entirely possible, particularly at a time when people are seeking security and stability. But the danger there is that the militants among the conservatives and the militants among the radicals will tend to dominate. I would like to see two parties survive, but two parties as we now know them, each one including a broad spectrum of views. This insures in advance that the men who emerge as candidates for the Presidency will be centrists, tempered by the divergent views within their organizations.

Interview, Washington/
The New York Times, 8-29:(1)44.

(Concerning whether he would reject an offer to become the Vice Presidential candidate with President Nixon in the 1972 election): Things have happened in my life to convince me that a man should never make a flat unequivocal statement of that character.

TV interview, Nov. 20/
The Washington Post, 11-21:(A)11.

Richard J. Daley
Mayor of Chicago

The (Democratic) Party ought to be doing a lot of things. We have an obligation to let the people know this is a party, with party programs and real concerns for the people. There is no justification for waiting for the Executive wing to propose everything and then dealing with that. Sometimes the Executive does not propose, or it proposes the wrong things.

Los Angeles Times, 4-2:(2)8.

Edward M. Davis
Chief of Police of Los Angeles

(Regarding the American Civil Liberties Union): I'm not saying they're Communists. But I've noticed that when the Communist Party takes a deep breath, the ACLU's chest goes out.

Newsweek, 4-26:32.

Ronald V. Dellums
United States Representative, D—Calif.

I am not going to back away from being called a "radical." If being an advocate of peace, justice and humanity toward all human beings is radical, then I'm glad to be called a radical. And if it is radical to oppose the use of 70 per cent of Federal monies for destruction and war, then I am a radical.

Interview/Daily World, 2-6:10.

Harry S. Dent
*Counsellor to
the President of the United States*

Conservative Republicanism should never mean inflexibility. The voters must view us as being capable of encompassing the needs and aspirations of all the people of our state (South Carolina). This is true whether all or only part choose to join our cause. Let us show, in word and deed, that we South

Carolina Republicans are conservative in our political tone; but the music we play is in harmony with the times in which we are called to live and lead.

*Columbia, S.C., January/
Los Angeles Times, 2-8:(2)6.*

Bob Dole
*United States Senator, R—Kans.; Chairman,
Republican National Committee*

Those of us who speak out for the President and his policies are put in some special category. According to the press, we're the "bad guys" and the "hatchet men." But those Democrats and Republicans who attack the President and Vice President—they're fine fellows, they're progressive. Around Washington, you don't get attention from the news media by supporting your President. You get it by attacking the President. I've never been able to see what is so bad about supporting your President. I'm convinced that if you support the President, he will appreciate it, and the country will be better off.

Interview/U.S. News & World Report, 2-1:14.

The new slant of the Democratic Party has given aid and comfort to assaults on the fundamental processes of our political, judicial and social institutions. If I could write a prescription for American politics in 1971, it would be a strong dose of awareness and activism—to be administered by the people, the voters of this country, to the Democratic Party.

*Before American Medical Association,
Washington, March 14/
The New York Times, 3-15:37.*

Charges thrown recklessly by Richard Nixon's enemies and reported too casually by some members of the news media . . . simply are not true . . . Those of us who support the President . . . from time to time try to correct the misconceptions about Richard

(BOB DOLE)

Nixon—misconceptions that he is an expedient man, that he is a man who changes with the mood of the times or to meet the needs of the moment. Richard Nixon is a consistent man—more consistent than most politicians and pundits . . . (a) man of well-thought-out views and opinions, which he changes only as he finds them to be wrong or outdated, or when a better idea comes along.

> *At Pepperdine University Distinguished*
> *Citizen Award banquet, Los Angeles, May 4/*
> *Los Angeles Herald-Examiner, 5-5:(A)7.*

Helen Gahagan Douglas
Former United States Representative, D—Calif.

What is disheartening and self-defeating are campaigns waged in a way to avoid issues, to annihilate the opponent. If fear is the basis on which they ask us for votes, it creates an atmosphere where people can't think, and that in itself is self-defeating. The issues are so great that candidates should take every opportunity to elucidate them. The alienation of the voter from the representative is very great and very serious.

> *Interview/The New York Times, 1-5:30.*

Bob Eckhardt
United States Representative, D—Tex.

Even though liberals are frequently much maligned, nevertheless they are the ones who think about change and ponder its results.

> *Before National YWCA Institute*
> *on Racism, Dallas, May 15/*
> *The Dallas Times Herald, 5-16:(A)39.*

Allen J. Ellender
United States Senator, D—La.

(Explaining why, at 81, he intends to seek re-election in 1972): The people of Louisiana made it possible for me to become President Pro Tempore of the Senate and Chairman of the Senate Appropriations Committee. I do not intend to desert them now when I am in a position to represent them better than ever. That is why I am seeking re-election. Besides, doctors say my health is excellent, my col-

leagues congratulate me on my workload, and there are some problems up here I believe I can help to solve.

> *Washington/*
> *The Dallas Times Herald, 10-28:(A)28.*

Sam J. Ervin, Jr.
United States Senator, D—N.C.

There are some things which are not proper functions for the government . . . and one is financing the campaigns of any candidate or any political party, directly or indirectly, out of the Federal Treasury.

> *Before the Senate, Washington/*
> *U.S. News & World Report, 12-6:16.*

Amital W. Etzioni
Professor of Sociology, Columbia University

Demonstrations of one kind or another can be expected to continue as an integral part of the American political system so long as there is protest to express and television to communicate.

> *U.S. News & World Report, 4-19:92.*

Robert M. Flanigan
Chairman, program planning committee,
1972 Republican National Convention

(At the convention) we're going to try to cut down on demonstrations, awards of gavels, presentations of orange blossoms, and the speeches, the endless speeches.

> *Washington, Dec. 10/*
> *The Washington Post, 12-11:(A)2.*

Reuven Frank
President,
National Broadcasting Company News

We stand here today at the threshhold of another American quadrennial election—to the despair of our foreign friends, to the joy of our millions momentarily relieved of a sense of passivity in the face of great events, to the patronizing scorn of the scholarly and to the raucous contempt of the disaffected. Americans who elect to take part will choose their governors by methods which will again seem to the supercilious to be irrelevant, outmoded and frivolous, insulting the sensibilities of every bluenose and pecksniff on the face of the globe, including some candidates. It will once more be a year in which candidates by the hundreds will demand more attention for what interests them and less for what interests the voters about them. "Get that hot and uncomfortable spotlight out of my opponent's eyes," they will say to us. "You are demeaning the democratic process." There will be thousands of candidates kneeing and gouging each other for a share of attention—more than a dozen now identifiable for the office of President alone—each claiming unique dedication to continuing unharmed the integrity of our Constitution and the intentions of our Founding Fathers. And afterwards, the losers will say they lost because we (the press) cheated them out of the attention they deserved; and the winners will say they won despite our twisted reporting, our inattention to what they really meant.

At Sigma Delta Chi convention,
Washington, Nov. 11/
Vital Speeches, 12-1:126.

John W. Gardner
Chairman, Common Cause

If one examines the world of politics and government—local political machines, city government, counties, states, the Congress of the United States, regulatory agencies, the courts—it appears at first glance that most of these institutions are merely inefficient. A second glance reveals that all too many of them are corrupt. Most of the political process has become—behind the scenes—a vast game of barter and purchase involving campaign contributions, appointments to high office, business favors, favorable legal decisions, favorable location of defense installations. It is a game that is going on all the time at every level of government. And it is paid for, ultimately, by you and me. There are many honest and decent men and women in politics, and we must honor them. But it is hard for them to survive. No one would be so foolish as to suggest that we can rid politics of the trading of favors or the rewarding of one's most loyal associates. But we have gone

far, far beyond normal considerations of loyalty, party cohesion and representation of one's constituency. Armed with the power and money we give them with our votes and our tax dollars, politicians are well equipped to play their part in the cycle of favors and obligations. There isn't any end to the ways they can favor their friends and allies . . . The time has come to do something about it. The time has come to stem the tidal wave of political flim-flam. Perhaps at a less critical time in our history we could tolerate ubiquitous rascality. But not now. We cannot tolerate the dominance of courthouse politics, the shady deal and the crass payoff.

Before American Association of Sunday and
Feature Editors, Portland, Ore./
Los Angeles Times, 10-24:(G)3.

Kenneth A. Gibson
Mayor of Newark, N.J.

Too many decisions by politicians are based on what's good for them and their careers, and not on the basis of what's good for their constituents.

San Francisco, Feb. 12/
The New York Times, 2-13:22.

Barry M. Goldwater
United States Senator, R—Ariz.

. . . (Vice President) Agnew is more popular than Dick Nixon across the country, especially with Republicans. There will be an open revolution if the President tries to get rid of him.

Newsweek, 3-22:23.

Clifford P. Hansen
United States Senator, R—Wyo.

About every two years, the liberals of the Senate make a concerted effort to abolish, alter or cripple Rule XXII. The conservatives vote for retaining the two-thirds vote required for cloture, and the liberals oppose the retention. What is ironic is that the liberals like to claim they are protectors of the minorities of the nation. But when it comes to extended debate on an issue of great importance, it is

(CLIFFORD P. HANSEN)

almost without fail the liberals who want to shut off the freedom of speech for the minority. So this is a pretty good test for determining the philosophical makeup of each Congress. Look for the vote on Rule XXII. The conservatives will vote for the retention of freedom of speech for minorities, and the liberals generally will oppose this freedom.

At Conservative Awards Dinner,
Washington, Feb. 4/
Human Events, 2-20:12.

W. Averell Harriman
Former United States Ambassador-at-Large

(Regarding New York Mayor John Lindsay's switch to the Democratic Party): I did the same thing over 40 years ago, and I found it a heck of a lot more fun after I left the Republican Party.

Newsweek, 8-23:19.

Fred R. Harris
United States Senator, D—Okla.

Inordinate economic power usually translates into inordinate political power.

At "Money in Politics" seminar,
University of Southern California, Nov. 8/
The Christian Science Monitor, 11-15:3.

Ernest F. Hollings
United States Senator, D—S.C.

The best way to run for Vice President is to run for President.

Interview/Los Angeles Times, 2-26:(1)21.

Hubert H. Humphrey
United States Senator, D—Minn.

The Nixon Administration is telling the press how they are to report and outlining the limits of freedom of the press; telling college authorities how to operate the universities; and using the issue of law and order for hopeful political advantage—while the nation slips deeper and deeper into economic recession; while the jobless rate continues to mount; while family income shrinks; while

prices rise and business conditions continue to worsen. The Administration postures and poses and conducts its own version of the *Tonight Show* on national television—while the nation is dissolving into a sea of red tape and red ink.

Before Women's National Democratic
Club, Washington, Jan. 15/
The Washington Post, 1-16:(A)4.

There is today yet another "new Nixon" —the Richard Nixon "leveling" with the American people through a series of restricted and insulated network and newspaper interviews. We are told by unnamed White House assistants that this, finally, is the real Nixon, the Nixon who truly understands the terribly complicated foreign and domestic problems that challenge this nation. Well, I respectfully disagree.

At Democratic conference on the issues
of 1972, Washington, March 24/
The Dallas Times Herald, 3-24:(A)6.

(Regarding the Nixon Administration): Never have the American people encountered a national Administration that relied so heavily upon a unique mixture of Executive arrogance, public relations gimmickry and the blatant intimidation of the news media.

At Democratic conference on the issues
of 1972, Washington, March 24/
The New York Times, 3-25:32.

(Regarding the 1972 Presidential election) . . . it is important that we (Democrats) win. I think it is also important that we know what we are doing when we win—what we are trying to do for our country, what it is that we have in mind. I don't want us to win by default, simply because the current Administration becomes so unpopular that anybody can win. I want to be sure that the Democratic Party wins with someone who has the qualities to lead the country, a program to lead the country, who speaks to the future, who can instill some confidence in this country.

Interview, Washington/
The Christian Science Monitor, 4-29:4.

This (Nixon) Administration is not only apathetic. It is questionable if it is alive.
Interview, Washington/Time, 5-17:7.

There are some in politics who appeal to the worst in us, to the beast that's in us; who appeal to our hatreds and fears. And they sometimes get elected.
At Texas AFL-CIO convention, Dallas, Aug. 13/The Washington Post, 8-15:(A)2.

Henry M. Jackson
United States Senator, D—Wash.

The real national majority is practical, principled and patriotic. It is not attracted by radical chic or reactionary vogue, or by . . . appeals that seem so precious and precocious.
Before Democratic Party state chairmen, Washington, March 26/
The Washington Post, 3-27(A)2.

This Republican Administration has given the American worker money without value, jobs without security—or no jobs at all—and promises without performance. The one pledge that President Nixon has kept to the American people is the one he made on Inauguration Day. "Bring Us Together," he said; and he has: He has brought Americans together in bankruptcy courts, in unemployment offices and in food stamp lines all over the country.
At Nevada State Democratic Party's Jefferson-Jackson Day dinner, Las Vegas, May 24/
Las Vegas Review-Journal, 5-25:1.

(The Democratic Party) can listen to the siren song of the radical fringe, cater to it, condone it, apologize for it—and gain the scorn of the majority of Americans for leading the country and the Party into a sick and dangerous era. Or we can look to our roots . . . to those Americans who understand we have a role to play in the affairs of the world, to those Americans who are weary of listening to those who scorn this nation. In their seeming zeal to avoid the wrath of those who have come to despise America, some Democratic leaders have bent over backwards to pay

homage to the fringe elements of this Party. In doing so . . . they have come dangerously close to establishing themselves as Democrats of Dejection and Despair, when in fact what this Party needs are Democrats of Confidence and Hope.
At Nevada State Democratic Party's Jefferson-Jackson Day dinner, Las Vegas, May 24/
Las Vegas Sun, 5-25:4.

(Regarding New York Mayor John Lindsay's switch to the Democratic Party and his chances of swift promotion to a position of Party leadership): We believe in the right of redemption. But if you join the church on one Sunday, you can't expect to be chairman of the board of deacons the following Sunday.
News conference, Dallas, Aug. 11/
The Washington Post, 8-12:(A)4.

I'm a liberal, but I'm no damn fool.
The National Observer, 10-23:5.

It's obvious that whether you're a conservative or a liberal depends on your stand on defense and foreign policy. All other matters are exclusionary, and that is the sole test. And if you applied those tests retroactively, John F. Kennedy and Harry Truman and Franklin Roosevelt would be arch reactionaries . . .
News conference, Washington/
San Francisco Examiner & Chronicle (This World), 11-28:9.

I call myself a liberal. Some people say I'm too liberal; some say I'm too conservative. If that makes me a middle-of-the-roader, that's all right with me.
San Francisco Examiner & Chronicle (This World), 11-28:2.

Jacob K. Javits
United States Senator, R—N.Y.

What the Conservative Party fails to understand, and what our (Republican) Party is in danger of forgetting, is that while many middle-class New Yorkers are very disturbed by and negatively reacting to crime and violence, they are still not reactionaries on the bread and butter issues—the great social reforms that have characterized the last 40 years.

San Francisco Examiner & Chronicle
(This World), 12-5:2.

Perhaps the most important element of 1971, as I see it, has been the dramatic movement by President Nixon away from the conservative course of the first two-and-a-half years of his Administration which threatened to make him a one-term President.

News conference, New York, Dec. 21/
The New York Times, 12-22:22.

Lyndon B. Johnson
Former President of the United States

I can't think of a single—not a single—distinguished service that I performed in 1970. In fact, the last distinguished service I can recall performing was more than two years ago, when I turned over to the new Administration a balanced budget.

Before Texas Press Association,
San Antonio, Jan. 23/
The Dallas Times Herald, 1-24:(A)22.

The people are always better off during a Democratic Administration, because the Democratic Party is for the majority of the people.

Greenville, Tex., Nov. 19/
The Dallas Times Herald, 11-20:(A)8.

I don't want to do anything to make (President) Nixon's job harder. I've had my game, and it's over, and I did the best I could. This is his game. You get your try, and you come up and play. When they blow the whistle, the game's over; and if you haven't made your touchdown by then, that's too bad.

Interview, Nov. 29/
Los Angeles Times, 11-30:(1)5.

Edward M. Kennedy
United States Senator, D-Mass.

I think when you lose (in politics), you

lose. If you don't know how to lose, you don't deserve to win.

News conference after being defeated for
Senate Whip, Washington, Jan. 21/
Los Angeles Herald-Examiner, 1-21:(A)2.

(Regarding the possibility of his running for President in 1972): I don't believe you can do one job well while thinking of another. I have important work to do in the Senate. It is a real opportunity for service. There's a lot wrong in this country, and it's a terrible thing if you are in a position to do something about it and don't . . . Sure, I know the Presidency is the real power for bringing about change. But that isn't the whole story. A lifetime in the Senate can be damned fruitful, in the sense of accomplishing things.

Interview, McLean, Va./Look, 8-10:20.

(Addressing Harvard students): Richard Nixon was elected in 1968 because people like you sat on their hands. They did not work in the campaign because their own candidates had been lost (at the political conventions) in Los Angeles and Chicago . . . And so we have (Chief Justice) Warren Burger instead of Earl Warren. And so we almost had George Harrold Carswell. And so we have Otto Otepka. And we have John Mitchell and Richard Kleindienst and Will Wilson and Robert Mardian and a host of defeated Republican office-seekers sitting where John Doar and Ramsey Clark and John Douglas and Burke Marshall once sat. And we have a return to trickle-down economics and trickle-up unemployment. We have the Southern strategy and benign neglect, the dismantling of the anti-poverty program and political tests for Federal employment. We have vetoes on housing and health and employment legislation. We have the Commander-in-Chief going out of his way to support William Calley at Mylai and Nelson Rockefeller at Attica. And we have Spiro Agnew. Your own apathy will surely nourish the forces that alienate you. Richard Nixon lives in a Skinner box. He responds only to your rewards and punishments that his senses can appreciate. Your silence is not neutral in his environment; it counts distinctly as pleasure. And this reinforces the rewards he gets from his own narrow constituency whenever he appeals to their basest instincts and panders to their prejudices.

At Harvard Law School Forum/
The National Observer, 10-9:2.

For generations, we have blindly accepted the principle of private financing (of political campaigns), long after the principle had become twisted and distorted in a way that no democracy worthy of the name could tolerate . . .

Before the Senate, Washington, Nov. 17/
The Dallas Times Herald, 11-18:(A)1.

J. Bracken Lee
Mayor of Salt Lake City; Former Governor of Utah

It's (politics) no longer any fun. People are getting more critical and more unreasonable; and I don't blame them, because I feel the same way about my government. I don't think the people are properly represented or have been for many years. I'm disgusted with politicians as a rule, and politics in particular. I'm ashamed of the profession, ashamed of the people who are running and misleading people to get elected.

Interview, Salt Lake City/
Los Angeles Times, 12-1:(6)2.

John V. Lindsay
Mayor of New York

(Regarding the possibility of his running for President in 1972): I am not a candidate for any office, will not accept the nomination, and if elected—well, we'll cross that bridge when we get there.

At St. Anselm's College, Manchester, N.H.
June 6/The New York Times, 6-7:24.

(Announcing his switch from the Republican to the Democratic Party): I was born into a Republican family. Lincoln, Theodore Roosevelt and LaGuardia were my political heroes. As a Republican, I worked for progressive goals through seven years in Congress and almost six years as Mayor. And those

times when I thought my Party wrong, I followed an independent course. From battle to battle, that course became more necessary. Today, the Republican Party has moved so far from what I perceive as necessary policies for our city and for the country that I can no longer try to work within it. It has become clear that the Republican Party and its controlling leaders in Washington have finally abandoned the fight for a government that will respond to the real needs of most of our people—and of those most in need. I join the Democratic Party today because it offers the best hope for a change in national direction and national leadership in the 1972 election.

New York, Aug. 11/
The Washington Post, 8-12:(A)4

I know of no free democracy in the Western world that puts its (political) candidates through so much for so long. To some extent, it's a test of endurance.

Before Florida State Democratic Party
Rules Committee, Tallahassee, Oct. 25/
The Washington Post, 10-26:(A)2.

(On whether he would accept the Vice Presidential nomination in the 1972 election): I have the second toughest job in the nation. Why should I be interested in the third?

TV-radio interview/"Issues and Answers,"
American Broadcasting Company, 11-21.

(Announcing his candidacy for the Democratic Presidential nomination): I am here because I share in common with hundreds of Mayors and millions of citizens an overwhelming sense of exclusion from the power centers of Washington—a sense that how we live, what we care about, what we need for a chance at a better life simply does not matter to those who run this country. And in 1972, someone must speak for the America that Washington has ignored.

News conference, Miami, Dec. 28/
Los Angeles Times, 12-29:(1)11.

Walter Lippmann
Former political columnist

I think that a country as big as this one could

235

(WALTER LIPPMANN)

not be governed by a party system in which the two parties were diametrically opposed. I think you'd get a civil war. If all the extremists of one side were united in one party and all the other extremists in another, I think it would be bad. You can't keep 200 million people in the same political system unless you have a very strong center.

Interview, Seal Harbor, Me./
The Washington Post, 10-17:(C)1.

Lester G. Maddox
Governor of Georgia

Even a liberal can find the truth if you give him enough time.

The New York Times, 1-11:19.

William M. Magruder
Director, Office of Supersonic Transport Development, Department of Transportation of the United States

To be successful in Washington, you have to be able to lay a firm foundation with the bricks others throw at you.

Plainview (Tex.) Daily Herald, 8-30:3.

Mike Mansfield
United States Senator, D—Mont.

To be sure, there are differences among us—differences between Democrats, between the parties and between the Senate and the President. Differences notwithstanding, we have—all of us—a great deal in common. There is a far higher stake than the political fortunes of any one of us. There is the stake in the future of America and our individual responsibilities to that future. Insofar as the Senate is concerned, therefore, it would be my hope that the politics of 1972 will be left to November, 1972. It would be my hope that the concern of Congress—no less than the Administration—will be with the needs of the nation now and in the years ahead. That is what the people ask of us. That is what they have a right to expect. That is what the majority leadership sets as its single purpose in

this Senate of the 92nd Congress.

At Senate Democratic caucus, Washington,
Jan. 21/The New York Times, 1-22:12.

Eugene J. McCarthy
Former United States Senator, D—Minn.

The third party is beginning to look like a good risk, especially as it now appears that the Democrats and the Republicans are again going to come to the people, as they did in 1968, without offering any real choice and without raising the important issues for public examination.

At Center for the Study of Democratic
Institutions, Santa Barbara, Calif./
The New York Times, 3-14:(1)52.

He (Democratic National Chairman Lawrence F. O'Brien) campaigned against me in 1968 on the grounds that my success would give aid and comfort to the enemy (in Vietnam). Later in that campaign, he supported Senator Robert Kennedy, who was also opposed to our military policy; and then still later reappeared as a quasi-hawk in support of Hubert H. Humphrey; and then still later reappeared within a few days after the Nixon inauguration as fully committed against the war. That takes versatility.

Bloomington, Minn., May 23/
The New York Times, 5-24:19.

The central and overriding issue of the politics of today is beginning to take shape. That issue is not the war or militarism. It is not ecology or what we do about our cities . . . The real issue is the integrity of the democratic process.

Minneapolis, May 23/
Los Angeles Times, 5-24:(1)5.

The center of the Republican Party is still Main Street, the chamber of commerce, the small owners. The center of the Democratic Party now is the labor union men, who are also property owners. All around these centers you have the young, the poor, the blacks, the professional people, the business managers out of jobs, the people who want change but feel politically impotent. These are the groups in both Parties ready to whirl off from the center. What we have shaping up is a revolt of the insecure against the secure—security being measured in both economic and political terms.

At University of Colorado at Boulder/Los Angeles Times, 8-8:(G)2.

Paul N. McCloskey, Jr.
United States Representative, R–Calif.

Republicans have a right to disagree with the leadership. This whole idea that somehow Republicans have to march together in lock step is going to kill the Republican Party. You can't get a person under 30 to register as a Republican these days because of this kind of leadership . . . This is a fairly broad party, just like the Democrats. It embraces a divergence of philosophy.

Washington/ Los Angeles Times (West), 5-23:27.

. . . I think some of the best Republicans in America today aren't even in politics. I think some of our business leaders, our great lawyers, people that have stayed behind the scenes . . . these are men that are competent to serve as President of the United States; and I hope that party politics will change . . . so that we have a chance not always to elect a person that appears to be the most prominent politician.

TV-radio interview/"Meet the Press," National Broadcasting Company, Washington, 7-18.

There is an incredible arrogance on the part of the government. The deceit, deception and the news management of this (Nixon) Administration is difficult to believe. I don't think the (Lyndon) Johnson Administration came close to this one in its paranoia about anything getting out that will embarrass the White House.

News conference, San Francisco, Nov. 19/ San Francisco Examiner, 11-20:3.

George S. McGovern
United States Senator, D–S.D.

I think that there's a different mood in the Democratic Party since the 1968 Chicago (convention) experience. (Candidates for Party nomination are) going to have to demonstrate strength in the primaries. It's not going to be settled in the back rooms.

Interview/Time, 1-25:21.

I can't conceive of (New York Mayor John) Lindsay's ever being nominated by a Democratic convention. I think he'd be much better advised to stay in the party (Republican) that he's lived off for the last 20 or 25 years. I think it will be a real test of his guts and integrity if he decides not to jump ship now just because the ship is sinking.

San Francisco Examiner & Chronicle (This World), 3-21:2.

No man should advocate a course in private that he's ashamed to admit in public.

LaCrosse, Wis., July 31/ The New York Times, 8-1:27.

My greatest single asset is truth-telling. I don't duck the issues, and I'm not capable of deception. I'm open, honest, Midwestern and rural in background. People think I come across like a Sunday school teacher, that I'm not an effective communicator. I think a lot of the American people are tired of flash and charisma and show business spectacles or candidates getting special instruction in television techniques and image-changing. I think truthfulness and trustworthiness are more important than flash appeal and charisma.

Parade, 8-1:5.

On the political level, I think what this nation needs more than anything else are leaders who will tell the truth and stop trying to con the American public into accepting policies that are not in the national interest . . . We have to stop lying to each other in this country if we want to restore confidence in our system and in each other.

Interview/Nation's Business, November:69.

George Meany
*President, American Federation
of Labor-Congress of
Industrial Organizations*

Do you want to make some money? Next time (President) Nixon decides he is going to make a speech on economic policy or foreign policy, you buy, because the stock market is going to go up. But sell within 48 hours; get the hell out . . . The stock market goes up. But then the people—and this includes your big business tycoons . . . they say, "What the hell did he say?" and they get to reading and analyzing . . He didn't say anything. So then the stock market goes down. That is the time to get out and wait until he announces that he is going to speak again, and then get in.
Washington/The Wall Street Journal, 11-19:8.

Arthur Miller
Author, Playwright

Liberalism today is a wandering spirit looking for a body.
The Washington Post, 1-16:(C)2.

William G. Milliken
Governor of Michigan

Whether we're talking about youth or blacks or other voters, perhaps the biggest lesson of the 1970 elections was that voters have arrived at a new level of sophistication and discrimination. Millions in every state split their tickets, proving they weren't voting for parties, but for individuals.
*San Francisco Examiner & Chronicle
(This World), 1-17:2.*

Daniel P. Moynihan
*Former Counsellor to the
President of the United States*

Unless we (the Democratic Party) can be more open about what we presided over (in the 1960s), I fear we will have learned nothing when the Party returns to power, as soon or late it will. I can't conceive any reason for having lived through the 1960s if it is not to have learned how mistakes are made in government. There is a story about one of

Roosevelt's campaigns. He made a speech or had a press conference or something in Pittsburgh, and in the course of it, by common agreement of his advisers, dropped some remark that was a bad mistake. They got back to New York and huddled together to plan how to recoup. Finally, someone said, "I think the best thing is to deny you have ever been in Pittsburgh." Too many people I can think of are, in effect, denying they ever were in Washington in the 1960s.
*Interview/
The New York Times Magazine, 6-27:11.*

Edmund S. Muskie
United States Senator, D—Maine

. . . I think that the Democratic Party, whatever difficulties we've had in the past, over its history has demonstrated a concern for values which are more clearly linked to the thrust for change today than the Republican Party. Indeed, the fact that we lost in 1968 perhaps puts us in a better mood for change . . . The party that wins is likely to like the status quo. Because we lost in ('68) . . . (we) are most sensitive, and I think more receptive and responsive, to the need for change . . .
*Television interview/
The Washington Post, 1-29:(A)18.*

I am glad to discover that a poor boy can become President of this country if he can pick up $20 million for expenses on the way.
Los Angeles Times, 3-21:(C)3.

I'm a human being, with quite a range of emotions . . . I can get angry, you know—sometimes with reason and sometimes without reason . . . but I hope I'm capable of love as well, and compassion and sympathy. I have virtues and I have weaknesses; and I'm sure that both of them will be fully explored in the next two years (before the 1972 Presidential election).
*Interview/"The David Frost Show,"
Metromedia Television, 3-31.*

The blunt truth is that liberals have achieved virtually no fundamental changes in our society since the end of the New Deal.

Before New York State Liberal Party/
The Dallas Times Herald, 10-13:(A)28.

Richard M. Nixon
President of the United States

. . . the young people of America are a very volatile group . . . they are a group that both parties are going to have to go out and have to try to win. I think that we (Republicans) have just as good a shot at them as others do. But we don't have the confidence of young people that some in the other party have, which they have at this time, because we have all of the problems and we are responsible for them. But if we can end the war (in Vietnam), if we can end the draft, if we can bring jobs and equal opportunity without the cost of war and without the cost of a rising inflation, I believe that young people, as they see our very imaginative programs for reforming government, for the environment and the rest, they will be attracted to our party, not as a party, but to our principles beyond party.

Television interview, Washington, Jan. 4/
U.S. News & World Report, 1-18:68.

When I am the candidate, I run the campaign.

San Clemente, Calif./
Los Angeles Herald-Examiner, 1-7:(A)3.

I know that there are those who scorn the political life; and I can assure you that politics attracts its share of bad people, but so do all the other professions. This does not reflect on the political system. For politics is a process, not an end in itself; and the process can be as good or as bad as the people that are part of it.

At University of Nebraska, Jan. 14/
The New York Times, 1-15:12.

By itself, neither political party in this country can win an election. In order to win, it is necessary to pick up enough independents and enough members of the other party to get a majority.

At dedication of Dwight D. Eisenhower
Center (Republican national headquarters
building), Washington, Jan. 15/
The New York Times, 1-16:18.

Those who think Vietnam is going to be a good political issue (during the U.S. Presidential election) next year are making a grave miscalculation. Now, I am not applying our policy there for political reasons, but for reasons of national security. Nevertheless, those who are counting on Vietnam as a political issue in this country next year are going to have the rug jerked from under them . . . I can tell you that, if I were running as a political candidate, I wouldn't select as an issue something that is likely to become a nonissue.

Interview, Washington, March 8/
Los Angeles Herald-Examiner, 5-10:(A)2.

Lawrence F. O'Brien
Chairman,
Democratic National Committee

We must prove that the other major political entity in the United States (the Democratic Party) has something else to offer—something so much better that the choice is vividly, unmistakably clear. Only then will we have proved our right to national leadership.

Before Democratic National Committee,
Washington, Feb. 19/
The Dallas Times Herald, 2-19:(A)6.

I read the newspapers as soon as they come out, hoping that none of the potential (Democratic Presidential) candidates will "cut up" any of the others and start an internecine war. It's a little like trying to guide a group of speeding cars, encouraging all of them equally and praying there is no crack-up.

Interview, Washington/
Los Angeles Times, 10-15:(1-A)2.

(Advocating Federal financing of Presidential election campaigns): Some of my colleagues say I've got a hangup on this, but I believe in it down in my guts, overriding any considerations for 1972. Sure, the Democratic Party is burdened with debts. A party with a $9.3 million debt,

239

(LAWRENCE F. O'BRIEN)

threatened by creditors orchestrated by the White House, is obviously in trouble. Obviously, we are going to be drained in the primaries. Obviously, the Republicans will be able to outspend us. But beyond all that, I am concerned about the two-party system. Until funding of Presidential elections is taken out of the private sector, we do not have built-in controls to challenge the influence of money in politics. And wealth does have a voice.

San Francisco Examiner & Chronicle,
12-5:(A)20.

John O. Pastore
United States Senator, D–R.I.

To run for the Presidency of the United States today requires a barrel of money. Either you have that money or you have to go out and get it . . . The whole process is demeaning to the Presidency.

Before the Senate, Washington/
U.S. News & World Report, 12-6:16.

James B. Pearson
United States Senator, R–Kan.

The continuing spectacle of millions upon millions of dollars being spent on political advertising has aroused both the citizenry and public officials alike as never before in my memory. Thus, I am more optimistic about the chances for success (of election campaign reform) in this session of the Congress than in any previous session in which I have participated.

Los Angeles Times, 2-11:(7)5.

William Proxmire
United States Senator, D–Wis.

I think it is good to have (New York) Mayor (John) Lindsay as a Democrat. I think it is great to have him. He is the Mayor of the biggest city in the country. It means we have a big Democrat in New York State. We haven't had that before. That's helpful. But I think the prospects of Mayor Lindsay successfully running for the Presidency are very, very limited, because he is

a recent Rupublican, because he enters in an ideological area where he would share the support of people like George McGovern who have already worked very hard, and possibly Senator Harris and other candidates; Ted Kennedy, if he decided to get into it. I think the prospects of his winning the nomination are not great, and his prospect of being a Vice Presidential selection is even less the case. I think the reason he got into it . . . is because he had to do that to get re-elected Mayor of New York. He had to do that to have any future as possible Governor of New York, and he is looking to the future. He is a young man; he is 49 years old. He could run in '76 or '80, and I think he would be in a much stronger position at that time than he would be in '72.

TV-radio interview/"Meet the Press,"
National Broadcasting Company,
Washington, 8-15.

Max Rafferty
Dean, School of Education,
Troy State University, Alabama;
Former California State Superintendent
of Public Instruction

California's a frivolous state. California voters are frivolous in the classic sense of the word. They react to appearances that are ephemeral and essentially superficial. They like labels . . . if a face or a name becomes too familiar to Californians—regardless of experience or service or excellence—then Californians will turn to a new face, regardless of whether he's conservative or liberal. Take (California Governor Ronald) Reagan. He did what he promised. He cut government expenses, refused to hire new employees into vacancies and opposed the withholding tax. There never was an elected candidate who did more of what he promised. His reward for keeping his word was having his plurality halved last year. What a reward for keeping your word!

Interview, Troy, Ala./
Los Angeles Times, 3-28:(A)1.

Ronald Reagan
Governor of California

Most young people, if I understand their

complaints, are against a great big government that is unresponsive to their needs, that is impossible for them to contact, regimentation, interference with personal freedom. All of these things can be laid to the some 37 years out of the last 39 that the Democrats as a party have actually been in control of government in America . . . If the students would really engage in a search for truth, they'd find that the Republicans have been campaigning for and asking for the same things that the students are now asking for. And here they (the students) seem to be throwing their lot in with the very people that caused what they don't like.

News conference, Sacramento, May 25/
Los Angeles Times, 5-26:(1)25.

Two-and-a-half years ago, we put a new captain (President Nixon) on the barnacle-encrusted ship of state. And now, the people who allowed that ship to become encrusted and swerve off course blame the captain for not providing an instant moonlight cruise.

At Republican fund-raising dinner,
Framingham, Mass., June 14/
San Francisco Examiner, 6-15:10.

Nelson A. Rockefeller
Governor of New York

The biggest challenge facing us (Republicans) today as a Party is the 18-year-old vote which the President and I have advocated for a long time. We need the idealism, the faith and the perception of the young people in our Party. They are the future of America, and let's encourage them to help us shape the future through the Republican Party.

Before Republican National
Committee, Denver, July 23/
The Dallas Times Herald, 7-25:(A)43.

Winthrop Rockefeller
Former Governor of Arkansas

(Regarding his defeat for re-election last year): It's really damned foolishness for you taxpayers to train a man like me four years for something, and then, poof!

Interview, Winrock Farm, Ark./
The New York Times, 7-22:19.

Richard Scammon
Political analyst

(Regarding the new voting rights of young people): Youth isn't going to vote in any homogeneous way. What is it about young people that differs from the rest of the country? The fact of the matter is, there isn't much.

Interview/Los Angeles
Herald-Examiner, 4-15:(A)3.

William J. Scherle
United States Representative, R—Iowa

Farmers are going to be very vindictive in (the elections in) 1972, but we can't seem to reach these Administration people about the seriousness of the situation. I would think the '70 election would have been a lesson. (President) Nixon can make all the trips to China and Moscow he wants to, but the greatest impact on the voter is mood. If a farmer goes to the polls with a jingle in his pocket and the weather is right and he can pay for his new equipment, he'll vote for the incumbent. If not, he'll go to vote with vengeance in his heart, and the people in power will be out by 8 o'clock that night.

Interview/Time, 11-22:21.

Hugh Scott
United States Senator, R—Pa.

I think the Vice President (Agnew) and I know the President (Nixon) is aware of the fact that overly-belligerent campaigning—of which we had illustrations in 1970—are counterproductive. They won't bring you as many people as they turn off. I don't expect that kind of campaign in 1972. I think the partisanship is going to be more confined to the Democratic and Republican National Committees; and the President will commit himself on the issues; and the Vice President will be on his guard, and I don't expect the Vice President to carry forward this sort of thing. There will be a tendency in 1972 to rely on the record.

Interview, Washington/San Francisco
Examiner & Chronicle, 3-14:(A)8.

John V. Tunney
United States Senator, D–Calif.

I am probably one of the few members of the Senate who is not a candidate for the Presidency.

Quote, 3-28:289.

Morris K. Udall
United States Representative, D–Ariz.

It may seem presumptuous for a Congressman to stand up here tonight and talk about politics and morality. There are a lot of people who think the two concepts are mutually exclusive. But I suppose most people, when they hear the two terms linked, are inclined to think in terms of monetary morality, of kickbacks and money passed under the table, of fat contracts negotiated under a kind of most-favored-brother-in-law agreement . . . One of our fundamental mistakes, I think, has been to confine our concern for morality in politics to narrow pecuniary terms. Too often, we have been satisfied if our leaders just didn't steal from us, or at least didn't get caught at it. And too often, we've gotten just what we demanded: conventionally honest men who were content to devote their public lives to the maintenance of their comfortable positions.

The Washington Post, 6-17:(A)18.

George C. Wallace
Governor of Alabama

The only thing that would keep me out (of the 1972 Presidential race) is a meaningful change of direction in the Nixon Administration or the Democratic Party. I have no realistic hopes that such miracles will come to pass. I will be running to win. Some people think I just like to run just to run; but I'll be a serious candidate in 1972 because I believe that a victory for me is quite possible.

Interview, Montgomery, Aug. 4/
The New York Times, 8-6:1.

Murray L. Weidenbaum
Former Assistant Secretary of the
Treasury of the United States

. . . I know that it is fashionable to lambaste the upper reaches of the Nixon Administration. Now certainly, the cast of characters does not exclusively consist of lovable or self-effacing men and women. However, I must bear witness to the fact that the dominant impressions that I bring back with me after more than two years of working with them, sometimes in very close relationships, are positive—an abiding loyalty, intelligence, industry and dedication to the public interest—of course as they see it.

Lecture, Washington University, St. Louis,
Nov. 3/The Washington Post, 11-7:(L)1.

Robert Welch
President, John Birch Society

The record seems to me to indicate quite clearly that, since at least 1960, Richard Nixon has had the all-pervading ambition and unshakable determination to use the Presidency of the United States as a stepping stone from which to become the first ruler of the world.

San Francisco Examiner & Chronicle
(This World), 10-17:2.

John Joseph Cardinal Wright
Prefect of the Sacred Congregation
of the Clergy, The Vatican

We were once told that where there is no vision, the people perish. The warning applies to our times and to our country as much as it has ever done anywhere. On the Right, we find confusion born of fear. On the Left, we find confusion born of contempt. In the center—to the extent that there remains anything like a vital center—we find confusion born of indecision and of the tension between the defensiveness of the Right and the defiance of the Left.

Interview, Rome/
Los Angeles Herald-Examiner, 3-20:(A)9.

Samuel W. Yorty
Mayor of Los Angeles

In the West, you don't get publicity. (New York Mayor John) Lindsay wipes his eyebrow and he gets publicity.

Los Angeles Times, 4-11:(A)21.

Ralph D. Abernathy
President, Southern Christian
Leadership Conference

As I look out onto the horizon, I do not see things bettering. The whole nation is on welfare, including Penn Central, Lockheed Corporation and TWA. Calculated genocide is being practiced on blacks and poor people alike. These and more are symbols of repression.

New York, March 11/Daily World, 3-13:5.

Spiro T. Agnew
Vice President of the United States

I have a theory that these (welfare) problems will never be subject to complete solution until somebody in public life is willing to take on the hard social judgments that, very frankly, no one that I know in elective office is willing to even think about. If a woman has not taken care of her children properly, who is going to say to that woman, "We are going to take that child from you—the natural mother—and put that child somewhere (where) it will receive the proper care"? Who is going to say to a welfare mother who has had three or four illegitimate children who are now charges of the state, "We're very sorry, but we will not be able to allow you to have any more children"?

Sacramento, Calif., Jan. 14/
The New York Times, 1-15:15.

. . . pumping more money into programs that have been tried and have proved worthless in the ghettos of the big cities is not the way to national greatness, or even to national happiness.

Before Los Angeles Chamber
of Commerce, April 7/
The New York Times, 4-8:12.

Joseph L. Alioto
Mayor of San Francisco

I know it is intoxicating to blame some hippie goldbricking on welfare. But I tell you this: There is more graft in government and in business than in the entire welfare program.

Before Homeowners Tax Control
Association, San Francisco, April 26/
Los Angeles Times, 4-28:(2)2.

Hugh L. Carey
United States Representative, D–N.Y.

This Committee (House Ways and Means) is sick and tired of welfare protestors and sick and tired of the poor who come to city hall because their children have no shoes to wear to school. A Judeo-Christian concern for the poor is very hard to find in this Committee at this time. We're using the excuse of reform to write a penny ante (welfare) bill with regressive and repressive measures. We'll show those shirkers—that's the attitude.

The Washington Post, 3-27:(A)17.

Ramsey Clark
Former Attorney General
of the United States

We just "tinkered" with the problems of health, education, jobs and housing. You get justice when you really have a passion for it; you get equality when you really work for it.

Plainview (Tex.) Daily Herald, 7-6:(A)12.

John T. Connor
Chairman, Allied Chemical Corporation

When making a case for elimination of some social ill, it is easy to say that we must find the money. It is a lot harder to say how, and even more difficult to predict whether or not in our democracy the people will agree to

(JOHN T. CONNOR)

foot the bill. We must remind ourselves that the final decisions are not going to be made just by the so-called elite who are prominent among the proposers of the changes, or even by the beneficiaries, but by the common garden variety types of American citizens who as taxpayers are called upon to modify their personal plans in order to pay the higher taxes that are required.

Cleveland, Oct. 28/
Vital Speeches, 12-1:106.

Archie K. Davis
President, Chamber of Commerce
of the United States

No matter how hard Congress tries to "abolish poverty by 1976," poverty cannot be abolished by legislation; it can only be abolished by intelligent use of our resources to raise people's real incomes by economic growth and a stable dollar. Abolishing poverty by legislative fiat is a tragic and deceptive shell game to buy off the poor, while taxes and inflation eat away at their incomes and at the vital center of our confidence in intelligent economic advance . . . We need in this country to open, not close, the door to job opportunity. We can guarantee opportunity for the poor and the non-poor, for business and labor, not by more subsidies that swell the size of an already surfeited welfare state, but by getting our government fiscal house in order, winning the battle against inflation, which has been bleeding poor and non-poor alike, and providing conditions for stable, non-inflationary economic growth and high employment.

Before West Virginia Chamber of Commerce,
White Sulphur Springs, W.Va., Sept. 3/
Vital Speeches, 10-1:768.

Deane C. Davis
Governor of Vermont

A high-quality education is part of the long-range solution (to the welfare problem); but the tragedy is, a long-term solution is of little help to a child who is hungry, sick or cold this winter.

The New York Times, 8-16:36.

Ronald V. Dellums
United States Representative, D–Calif.

One of the most devastating questions that needs to be dealt with in America, where we desperately need to redirect our energies and our economic resources, is the critical problem of the lack of equity in the distribution of wealth in America. Forty per cent of the labor force earns between $5,000 and $10,000 a year. They work 40 hours a week for the privilege of being poor. That problem needs to be solved. Fifteen to twenty per cent of America earns below $4,000 a year. Millions of American people are welfare recipients in this country. The present Administration has advocated $1,600 a year as an adequate income for a family of four. This is an absurdity. The Department of Labor, through its own statistics, has pointed out that $6,500 a year for a family of four is what is necessary for the family to sustain themselves with pride and dignity in the present economic climate of this country. And anything less, it seems to me, is a shame. As long as we can spend money building bombs, it seems to me that we could spend money building the dignity and the worth of human beings in this country.

Daily World, 6-25:6.

Mitchell I. Ginsberg
Dean, Columbia University
Graduate School of Social Work

Most jobs offered to welfare clients are not useful jobs. One could feel somewhat differently if society were getting something out of it. Work relief is a means of punishment . . . Most things I am hesitant about predicting, but I am completely confident that, in a year or two, we will have passed through this stage. We'll have found again that it doesn't work. But in five years, we will start it up again.

Interview, New York/The Christian
Science Monitor, 11-29:5.

Billy Graham
Evangelist

As a boy, I lived in poverty; except we didn't know we were poor. We didn't have sociologists, educators and newscasters constantly reminding us of how poor we were.

On "Billy Graham Day," Charlotte, N.C./
The Dallas Times Herald, 10-27:(A)32.

Paul Harvey
News commentator,
American Broadcasting Company

The very idea that we have 8,700,000 Americans on welfare, with newspapers bulging with jobs waiting for people, just makes no sense, no sense at all. Part of my poor-boy philosophy is, when you're hungry, you aren't choosy.

Interview, Chicago/TV Guide, 2-20:22.

Hubert H. Humphrey
United States Senator, D–Minn.

. . . I'd like to see him (President Nixon) look at the unemployment lines in this state and in this nation. I'd like to see him come to a labor meeting here to talk about the wage-price freeze. When is the last time he went into the inner city? When did he last see a welfare recipient or an elderly person trying to survive inflation on a fixed income? Yes, and when did he last visit a college campus?

Before San Mateo (Calif.) County
Central Labor Council's Committee on
Political Education/
San Francisco Examiner, 11-6:3.

Jacob K. Javits
United States Senator, R–N.Y.

It is true today that those who live in the ghettos, barrios and rural poverty pockets of our nation are more distant from the Mayor's office than from the Federal establishment.

The New York Times, 1-31:(4)1.

Edward M. Kennedy
United States Senator, D–Mass.

(Regarding the welfare system): I don't be-
lieve there ought to be required work for the mothers of dependent children. I don't know what it is about our society and culture. There's something wrong with our thinking to say we must pay people to care for other people's children so they must work, even if it ends up costing the government more. Mothers should be permitted to care for their own children, if they would prefer to do this.

Interview, Washington/
The Washington Post, 7-27:(A)6.

John V. Lindsay
Mayor of New York

For the first time in a decade, the trend in this nation is toward more people living in poverty, not less. This is a tragedy far too deep for a one-day headline. This is the statistical footprint of economic inaction on a scale unknown since the Depression.

At Urban Affairs Institute Seminar,
Colorado College, Colorado Springs,
July 28/The New York Times, 7-29:20.

. . . to those of you who are part of the college generation, there exists a whole class of Americans who may be almost invisible to you, a contemporary of yours virtually unseen by the media and the self-proclaimed youth experts. He is the young worker—seemingly unafflicted by discrimination, hopelessness, poverty or disease. Yet, consider for a moment his life. This worker reads that he is part of an affluent society—and compared with the jobless, so he may be. But he earns $1,000 less than the government says he needs for a moderate standard of living. And in the last five years, his real pay has dropped by almost $1 a week. He is in debt all of his life. And any sudden reversal—from a layoff to a medical catastrophe—may plunge him from uneasy subsistence into bankruptcy. His reality is a kind of indentured servitude.

At "Peace and New Priorities" rally,
Pittsburgh, Sept. 9/
The Washington Post, 9-10:(A)7.

(JOHN V. LINDSAY)

We know the key to poverty: jobs. Can one look around America and say there is not work to be done—in our schools and hospitals and streets and parks? Can anyone deny that this is the single most insistent demand of the poor—not to be given handouts and promises, but jobs? To those who tell us to trust in the ultimate good of rising corporate profits, let us say: open the day-care centers to let mothers work while their children are cared for; hire those without jobs to do work that needs doing. And stop shutting out of view the fact that families without work will still need food and shelter—and not lectures on self-reliance.

Before New York Democratic State Committee Advisory Council, Sept. 17/ The Washington Post, 9-22(A)22.

George S. McGovern
United States Senator, D–S.D.

There's a man like the Governor of California (Ronald Reagan) who will take $25,000 to give a speech, who lives in a house provided by the State of California and drives around in big limousines, but somehow can't see his way clear to pay any state taxes. And this man—who apparently is chiseling at the expense of his state—complains about welfare chiselers. It's really a little hard to understand.

At National Welfare Rights Organization convention, Brown University, July 29/ The New York Times, 7-30:55.

Charles W. V. Meares
Chairman, New York Life Insurance Company

Significantly, in this era of bigness, the concept of greater participation by the individual is closely linked to the revival of local government and local leadership. The elder Henry Ford used to say, no job is too big to master if it is broken down into small enough pieces. So, since we must begin somewhere, why not in our own back yards? As one community leader put it recently—if you can't move the world, at least nudge a neighborhood. If we want to bridge the generation gap, we must not only communicate with our children, we must demonstrate to them and others our support of high-quality schools and recreational facilities. If we care about the millions who remain poor in our affluent land, we must change personal attitudes as well as local and state laws to provide decent housing and proper education for those still crippled by poverty. If we believe our prisons are brutalizing inmates instead of rehabilitating them, we must be prepared to pay the high price of reform.

Before Rotary Club, New York/ The National Observer, 6-28:15.

Lloyd Meeds
United States Representative, D–Wash.

. . . we're going to have to spend money—money for jobs, for schools, for housing, for medical care, for welfare reform, for law enforcement. Let's face up to reality. You don't get the money simply by firing half the Pentagon. You don't get the funds by telling the farmers to feed their kids without crop subsidies. Where you get it from is taxes. The starkest truth today is that we can't defeat or even win a skirmish with our problems unless those who have it pay more taxes to help those who don't. It means, J. Paul Getty, that the oil companies are going to have to give up the depletion allowance so that Dallas can have a better school system. It means, David Rockefeller, that the banks and insurance companies are going to have to forsake a few loopholes so your servants can buy enough protein. It means, George Wallace, that you are going to have to pay additional taxes to help your black brother in the South Bronx get off the needle and onto a payroll. It means, Ronald Reagan, that you and your agri-barons are going to have to pay more taxes to support the California Rural Legal Assistance Program. It means, Mrs. Average Housewife in Dayton, that you and your husband are going to have to help put Cleveland back together. If we choose to ignore this reality, then we're going to face another one: This country will self-destruct in 50 years.

Before National Coordinating Council on Drug Abuse Education and Information, Washington, June 14/The Washington Post, 6-19:(A)20.

Wilbur D. Mills
United States Representative, D–Ark.

The only way in the world that these people (on welfare) will ever get out of this vicious cycle is for us to do what we have been doing since the beginning of this great Republic, since the beginning of this great nation of ours: by lending the hand of those who *have*—either individually or through the government—downward to grasp the hand of the fellow below; by giving that fellow the strength and the financial help he needs to pull him up to help himself to a greater life and to a more abundant life and to know that dignity that comes, as all of us know, at the end of the day when we feel that we have rendered a service to our people, to our country and to our God.

Washington, June/
The Washington Post, 9-12:(B)5.

Walter F. Mondale
United States Senator, D–Minn.

I wish he'd (President Nixon) stop this cheap line that implies welfare recipients are basically chiselers.

Washington, Sept. 9/
The Washington Post, 9-10:(A)12.

There are about 6,000,000 pre-school children whose mothers work; yet there are only 700,000 government-certified day care slots in the whole country. We don't know what happens to many of these children. But we know that hundreds of thousands are "latch key" children, cared for by nobody. Many are in overcrowded, custodial care that is damaging children. In a country in which more and more mothers are working, we better start worrying about what is happening to their children.

The Washington Post, 11-1:(A)20.

Daniel P. Moynihan
Former Counsellor to the
President of the United States

What Family Assistance does is provide income as a matter of right, not as a matter of judgment, of whether you are worthy of get-ting it. It does not mean that a county commissioner of welfare likes the Wierzynskis and thinks that they are good Polish stock and they can be depended on, and does not like the Moynihans and thinks that they are a bunch of drunken Irish. It is nobody's business. Your income comes as a matter of right; and therefore, it enhances your dignity.

Interview, Cambridge, Mass./Time, 2-8:23.

(Regarding the current welfare system): It presents these awful sudden-death situations. You earn an extra dollar and you're out of public housing; earn an extra dollar and you're out of Medicaid; earn an extra dollar and you're out of food stamps. This is really an insane kind of arrangement.

Interview/Newsweek, 2-8:26.

Richard M. Nixon
President of the United States

. . . I think the greatest disappointment (during his first two years in office), legislatively, was the failure to get welfare reform. I believe this would have done more than anything else to deal with the problems of poverty in this country, the problems that many of our cities have and our states have, the problems of minority groups who have particular difficulties insofar as welfare is concerned.

Television interview, Washington,
Jan. 4/The New York Times, 1-6:42.

The present welfare system has become a monstrous, consuming outrage—an outrage against the community, against the taxpayer and particularly against the children it is supposed to help. We may honestly disagree on what to do about it. But we can all agree that we must meet the challenge not by pouring more money into the old system, but by abolishing it and adopting a new one . . . Let us generously help those who are not able to help themselves. But let us stop helping those who are able to help themselves but refuse to do so.

State of the Union address,
Washington, Jan. 22/
The Washington Post, 1-23:(A)12.

(RICHARD M. NIXON)

I advocate a (welfare) system that will encourage people to take work—and that means whatever work is available. It does not mean the attitude expressed not long ago . . . when a lady got up at a welfare hearing and screamed: "Don't talk to us about any of those menial jobs." I am not sure what she considers a menial job, but I probably have done quite a few in my lifetime. I never thought they were demeaning. If a job puts bread on the table, if it gives you the satisfaction of providing for your children and lets you look everyone else in the eye, I don't think that it is menial. But it is just this attitude that makes others, particularly low-income workers, feel somehow that certain kinds of work are demeaning—scrubbing floors, emptying bedpans. My mother used to do that. It is not enjoyable work, but a lot of people do it—and there is as much dignity in that as there is in any other work to be done in this country, including my own.

At Republican Governors Conference,
Williamsburg, Va., April 19/
U.S. News & World Report, 5-3:67.

(The welfare system) makes the taxpayer furious; it makes the welfare recipient bitter; and it inflicts the distillation of all this anger and bitterness on the children who inherit this land. It is a disgrace to the American spirit.

San Francisco Examiner & Chronicle
(This World), 4-25:2.

I believe that human welfare is too important to be left to the "welfare-staters." This is a nation with a conscience, and that conscience demands that we see to it the handicapped and the dependent are given what they need to lead lives of decency and self-respect. Because I believe in human dignity, I am fighting for a total overhaul of the demeaning welfare system—to provide a floor of income under every dependent family with children in the United States. And for that very same reason—because I believe in human dignity—I am against a guaranteed annual wage, and I am against any scheme that makes it more profitable for an able-

bodied person to sit at home rather than to go to work. When you make it possible for able-bodied men and women to get welfare, you make it impossible for those people to get ahead in life. If we were to underwrite everybody's income, we would be undermining everybody's character.

Before Chamber of Commerce of the
United States, Washington, April 26/
The Washington Post, 4-27:(A)6.

As we consider your (older people's) suggestions, we will be guided by this conviction: Any action which enhances the dignity of older Americans enhances the dignity of all Americans. For unless the American dream comes true for our older generation, it cannot be complete for any generation. This country will have to be at its best if we are to meet the challenge of competition in the world in the 1970s. And we cannot be at our best if we keep our most experienced players on the bench.

At White House Conference on Aging,
Washington, Dec. 2/
Los Angeles Herald-Examiner, 12-2:(A)3.

Lawrence F. O'Brien
Chairman,
Democratic National Committee

What priority does air pollution have to a mother in the core city whose baby has been bitten by a rat? What priority does a polluted lake have to a family whose main recreation area is a littered alley? If we cannot solve the problems of poverty and squalor and racial bigotry that have created our slums, it will do us no good to solve the problems of water and air pollution and contamination that are despoiling our countryside.

At Wheeling (W.Va.) College commencement,
May 15/The Washington Post, 5-16:(A)4.

Herbert P. Patterson
President, Chase Manhattan
Bank, New York

If anyone thinks that business and banking are complacently rolling along on the theory of "business-as-usual," totally unaffected by the social currents now running in our country, let me tell you about a day I had recently . . . At 8:45 a.m., I had my weekly briefing on the status of legislation in Congress. At 9 a.m., I and a group of senior officers met with our Urban Affairs Task Force—a group of officers, none of whom has been out of college more than five years—to discuss pioneering approaches for our community-improvement programs. In the course of the discussion, we authorized more high-risk loans to small businessmen in depressed areas of the city and assigned another bank officer to work full-time as a job developer for the New York Urban Coalition. At 10 a.m., I left the bank and went uptown for a meeting at the National Council on Crime and Delinquency, of which I am a trustee. The purpose of the meeting was to discuss what position, if any, the council should take on the legalization of marijuana. By 11:30 a.m., I was back at my desk to be briefed by our loan review officer on the latest developments on some of our stickier loans. Then, lunch with one of our customers—a large Wall Street investment firm—who had just moved into new quarters in our new operations building. At an afternoon meeting of the Chase Manhattan Bank Foundation, various grants to urban groups were approved, including one for a mobile information center to distribute bilingual consumer guidance to disadvantaged communities. Before leaving that day, I spoke briefly at graduation ceremonies for one of our manpower training classes—composed mostly of high school drop-outs.

The Wall Street Journal, 2-18:12.

James A. Perkins
Chairman, International Council
for Educational Development;
Former president, Cornell University

I find the idea of the "retired person's haven"—be it in Florida or Arizona—frankly a horror. Just a horror, those havens where no young voices are heard, where infirmity is the order of the day, where we just put our old people in warm storage—not cold storage but warm, because they all go to a warm climate. I consider Florida the greatest scene of displaced persons in the United States, or the world may-

be. I think that it is a vicious thing for older people to be with no one but their own age group . . . I guess if I wanted to describe the two greatest agonies in our society, I would list our postponing adulthood—the source of so much student unrest—and hastening discharge from the system at the other end.

Interview/The Washington Post, 12-26:(K)5.

William Proxmire
United States Senator, D—Wis.

If we do not set priorities within (social) programs, they too will generate excessive spending and become huge engines of inflation which will threaten our ability to fund those programs we need. We must weed out the wasteful, inefficient and unnecessary social programs as well as wasteful, inefficient and unnecessary military programs.

At Bowdoin College, May 8/San Francisco Examiner & Chronicle, 5-9:(A)25.

Charles B. Rangel
United States Representative, D—N.Y.

(Regarding his Harlem constituency): I wish I had the luxury of talking about clearing up the air and harbors. But when you represent people concerned with heat and hot water, ecology to them means do they collect the damn garbage.

Interview, Washington/
San Francisco Examiner, 2-17:12.

Ronald Reagan
Governor of California

Mandated by statute and Federal regulation, welfare has proliferated and grown into a leviathan of unsupportable dimensions. We have economized and even stripped essential public services to feed its appetite.

Inauguration address, Sacramento,
Jan. 4/The Washington Post, 1-5:(A)4.

The welfare program in this country is adrift without rudder or compass. It basically has no goal. To simply say we're going to keep on feeding and providing a livelihood for an ever-increasing number of people is not a goal. My

(RONALD REAGAN)

own idea of a goal for welfare—and I know this is contrary to the whole philosophy and ideology of the so-called professional welfare worker—would be to eliminate the need for it.

Interview/U.S. News & World Report, 3-1:36.

We must assure that no one in this state will perish from want. I've already had a bellyfull of people who think tinkering with the welfare system is lacking in compassion. But the majority of the poor have been herded into a great big government feed lot and told to just raise hell until you get a larger trough.

San Francisco Examiner & Chronicle (This World), 3-28:2.

We have created a segment of society which looks upon poverty as a perfectly acceptable career. I do not share that view . . . Nothing could be more destructive to our society than to subsidize a permanent and growing poverty population that must be indefinitely supported at public expense. We want to begin measuring welfare's progress, not by how many people are added to the rolls each year, but by how many we restore to economic self-sufficiency.

Before American Association of University Women, Fresno, Calif., May 1/ Los Angeles Herald-Examiner, 5-1:(A)2.

Elliot L. Richardson
Secretary of Health, Education and Welfare of the United States

We are at a critical stage. We (at HEW) have promised so much and built up expectations so high that we have really contributed to a cumulative sense of frustration. To overcome this, we have to bring expectations into scale with reality. We have been scattering our resources. We have been doing too little over a wide front to get much of anything done on any one line.

Interview, McLean, Va./ The Washington Post, 1-3:(F)7.

I'm sick of hearing this (Nixon) Administration attacked for lack of sufficient concern for the poor and disadvantaged. Our most urgent domestic priority is to break the hopeless cycle which traps generation after generation in a treadmill of despair, degradation and dependency. This is why the Administration is seeking to help local school systems prevent the educational handicaps caused by segregation, to assure that no qualified student is prevented by lack of funds from benefiting from a higher education, and to enable welfare mothers to obtain day care for their children.

News conference, Washington, Nov. 2/ The Dallas Times Herald, 11-3:(A)22.

Charles I. Schottland
President, Brandeis University; Former Commissioner of Social Security of the United States

(Advocating Federalization of public assistance): There's no reason a person in California should get twice as much as a person in Nevada. States aren't allowed now to decide who shall vote—why should we let them decide who shall eat?

San Francisco, Nov. 18/ San Francisco Examiner, 11-19:20.

Strom Thurmond
United States Senator, R—S.C.

(The food stamp) program is, of course, supported by the taxpayers who, I am sure, do not mind their tax dollars being used to help those who are genuinely in need. However, taxpayers should not be required to put food on the table of those (on strike) who have jobs and voluntarily refuse to work.

Human Events, 3-27:5.

William Walker
Director, Equal Opportunity Division, Department of Housing and Urban Development of the United States

I suggest . . . that many of us who are advantaged have a vested interest in keeping the disadvantaged exactly where they are. Our economic and political strategies are clearly designed to keep a segment of our population poor and powerless. I suggest that many of our social welfare programs have failed and are failing to help the poor and oppressed among us because they were never intended to help them.

Before Population Commission, Little Rock, Ark./The National Observer, 6-21:7.

George Wiley
Director, National Welfare
Rights Organization

The Nixon (welfare-reform) plan is an attempt to stem the tide of rising benefits. This so-called welfare reform will be more punitive than the present system. The welfare department will be a new employment agency for substandard industry, agriculture, laundries, sweatshops.

The Washington Post, 2-9:(A)7.

Roy Wilkins
Executive director, National Association
for the Advancement of Colored People

. . . I agree with the basic principle that there should be a floor under welfare. I think this would be a step forward. And I think the President (Nixon) in advocating it is really taking a step forward for which he deserves brownie points. I don't agree that the $2,400 floor is an adequate one. It's ridiculous.

Radio interview/
The Washington Post, 8-12:(A)2.

George K. Wyman
New York State
Commissioner of Welfare

The presence of employable adults on welfare in New York reflects not only the present economic climate but a growing unwillingness on the part of assistance recipients to accept what have traditionally been the entrance-level jobs for unskilled and untrained workers. The result is a growing trend for the public assistance rolls to become the permanent home of many individuals who can and should work.

September/
The Dallas Times Herald, 11-26:(A)10.

Transportation

Spiro T. Agnew
Vice President of the United States

(Regarding the termination of the American SST project): We have invested $1 billion over the past 10 years in a plane that will never fly. We have ended direct employment for some 15,000 highly-skilled workers and eliminated, the potential future employment of an estimated 250,000 to 500,000 in the airframe and aviation industry. Even more important, we may have forfeited our leadership in this field.

Before Los Angeles Area Chamber of Commerce, April 7/ Los Angeles Herald-Examiner, 4-7:(A)2.

I believe we have now learned in this country that transportation is not a matter of either good highways or a good urban transit system. We need both, one tying in with the other, if it is to be an effective system and really move people. And moving people is what it is all about . . . We should concentrate on the individual and how to best get him from his home to school or to work or to the store or to the sports stadium or theatre—at a price he can afford and without taking all day—whether he drives his own car or rides a bus or train. For too long, we thought in terms of having either rapid transit or automobiles and trucks as the backbone of a city's transportation. We now know, as our friends overseas have accepted all along, that it is a combination of both. We cannot eliminate the motor vehicle. But we can reduce the dependence on it by enhancing the attractiveness of other forms of transportation.

Pittsburgh/The Washington Post, 9-12:(B)6.

William D. Bachman
President, American Automobile Association

It would seem from (consumer advocate Ralph) Nader's press releases that cars cause highway accidents or that highway deaths can be eliminated by making safer cars. We know that the car is a relatively minor factor . . . The single-minded focus on cars promoted by Mr. Nader is taking the public's eye off the real culprits—the driver and the highway.

At American Automobile Association annual meeting, New York, Sept. 20/ San Francisco Examiner, 9-21:4.

B. F. Biaggini
President, Southern Pacific (Railway) Company

. . . American railroad transportation, for a long time now, has been our most economical type of wheeled transport, and it continues to hold this advantage against newer and more flexible forms. At the same time, we recognize that it is not as productive as it could be. It is not as productive as it must become if it is to continue to be the privately-owned backbone of our national transportation system. And it is not as productive as, in my opinion, it will become in the reasonably near future. If my prediction proves correct, the principal reason will be that more attention finally has been given to creating a healthy regulatory climate for efficient transportation. For too many years, not nearly enough attention has been paid to this, despite the fact that transportation figures heavily in the cost of almost everything produced, bought and sold and is an important foundation of our dynamic national economy.

Before National Forest Products Association, San Francisco, Nov. 8/ Vital Speeches, 12-15:130.

Secor D. Browne
Chairman, Civil Aeronautics Board
of the United States

My responsibility, in short, is to see that the public convenience and necessity are served by (an) available, healthy, efficient civil air industry.

Interview/The New York Times, 2-13:33.

Silvio O. Conte
United States Representative, R—Mass.

I find it incredible that some of my colleagues, who yesterday voted to deny the release of the District of Columbia's $34.2 million share of the Metro's (subway) fiscal 1971 construction program, today are supporting an $85 million effort to reinstate and reinvigorate and bring back to life funding for the SST prototypes. I find it shocking that the fancies of a tiny elite of jet-setters are being catered to, while the legitimate needs of the millions of District of Columbia area residents are being flouted and ignored. On no scale of values can the whim of arriving overseas two or three hours faster outweigh the just desire to reach one's job or residence without suffering the anger and frustration of being suffocated in an endless stream of bumper-to-bumper traffic. It would be nothing short of hypocritical for this body to turn around and fund the SST project today in the name of technological progress after so cruelly rejecting the subway project yesterday. We face a mass transit crisis in this country of alarming proportions. To bury our head in the sand, to ignore this situation and casually vote government funds for a program that will benefit only a few—a select coterie of bon vivants—is justly to invite upon us derision and scorn. I, for one, will have no part of such a contemptuous and irresponsible action.

Before the House, Washington, May 12/
The Washington Post, 5-16:(B)6.

Maurice Doublet
Mayor of Paris, France

If they brought New York's subway to Paris, I assure you, there would be a revolution.

News conference, Paris/
The New York Times, 3-28:(1)58.

Barry M. Goldwater
United States Senator, R—Ariz.

American cars are made shoddily. The doors don't work. The tires don't go beyond 10,000 miles. The brakes don't work. Cars made overseas are far superior.

Before National Office Products
Association, Chicago, Oct. 20/
The New York Times, 10-21:32.

H. R. Gross
United States Representative, R—Iowa

Let the promoters of this SST organize some type of Comsat Corporation; and those of you who feel that this is such a good deal then would have the opportunity to step up and put some of your capital to work by buying stock in this corporation. Let private risk capital take over from here and produce this plane if it is so good. It is time to quit hornswoggling the taxpayers.

Before the House, Washington/
The National Observer, 3-22:2.

William Haddon, Jr.
President, Insurance Institute
for Highway Safety

The largely cosmetic, eggshell front and rear end of new automobiles remain with us in showrooms and on the streets, insuring . . . the continued operation of a highly remunerative market in replacement parts sales, most of which automobile design has made certain will be made by the maker of the automobile itself.

Before Senate Commerce Committee,
Washington, March 10/
Los Angeles Times, 3-11:(1)6.

253

Karl G. Harr, Jr.
President, Aerospace Industries Association

It's strange to hear critics (of the SST) voice foolish charges in the name of environmental protection and economy, and then demand an end to the research program designed to insure environmental protection and economic health in a project of vital importance to the nation . . . If these people really believe their own charges, I should think they would welcome the opportunity to prove them. Instead, they want (SST) research halted and the building of the test prototypes forbidden. Knowledge is not advanced by refusing to research the facts. Any advocate of environmental protection who will look at the facts of the SST and not let himself be blinded by emotional rhetoric will become a supporter of the program.

Princeton, N.J., Feb. 23/
Los Angeles Times, 2-24:(3)13.

Philip A. Hart
United States Senator, D–Mich.

The only kind of competition open to airlines (involves) the frequency of costume changes of the stewardesses, the kind of dessert (served on planes) and the color of the plane.

At Senate Subcommittee on Aviation
hearing, Washington, Feb. 10/
The Washington Post, 2-11:(H)1.

Walter W. Heller
Professor of Economics, University of
Minnesota; Former Chairman, Council of
Economic Advisers to the President
of the United States

If the SST is such a profitable undertaking, why does the U.S. government, i.e. the taxpayer, have to put up 80-90 per cent of the development costs? As of March 30, the U.S. government has put up $864 million of the $1,009 million thus far invested in this program. If private industry can't even take it from here . . . one can only conclude that the SST dismally fails the fundamental test of the market place . . . The SST approach to job creation seems to say that no matter how questionable the priority of this project, let's push

ahead with it, because it preserves jobs in areas where aerospace unemployment is high. That's a little like saying that, as Vietnam winds down, we should start another war to restore employment in the defense industries and the Pentagon . . .

The New York Times, 3-17:41.

Samuel L. Higginbottom
President, Eastern Airlines

Last year, more than half of the country's 12 major air carriers . . . lost money, real money —over $100 million. And losses so far this year make last year's look like a gold mine by comparison.

Before Professional Air Traffic
Controllers' Organization, Atlanta/
The Christian Science Monitor, 5-1:14.

Lee A. Iacocca
President, Ford Motor Company

With all the congestion and problems, there is nobody, on average, driving less. Nobody has given up driving, including the kids who are talking about ecology. They still are driving. You see, most people really have no option. It's difficult to switch to the bus or the railroad, because often there isn't any. That's why, in some cities, there has to be more of an attempt made for doing something with the bus lines or even so-called rapid-transit lines. Something has to happen. We've always felt that, in some cities, you have to have a means of transportation to complement the car. We've said that for years. We may not agree with how they finance the thing; but we've agreed you can't say "ever and onward" with cars and cars alone. You can't get to or from an airport without a car; you can't get to or from a boat without a car; you can't get to or from a train without a car. I didn't create that. When I walked into this business 25 years ago, the American public had already made up its mind on that. That's the love affair. But it's not just a love affair—it's a way of life.

Interview, Washington/
U.S. News & World Report, 3-8:32.

Our industry employs more people than any other single industry in this country, and this is a car-related economy. So—let's give in to the hysterical outbursts from the radicals and ban cars. Let's do it for just one week. We'd have a chaotic depression the likes of which we've never dreamed.

Interview, Detroit/
San Francisco Examiner, 8-14:11.

I've often said this to government people: "You look at me like (I'm) some ogre who looks out the window at automobiles and says, 'Ah, good—the traffic's rolling and they're polluting the air, and that means money.' " I said: "you never look at my side, that I am a family man with children, and I worry about their future. I worry about it every time they're in a car; if they don't have their seat belts on, I worry like hell. I have the same problems you do; but don't castigate my role, which I enjoy; but I think it's been a good one, providing transportation for people, safe as we know how to make it." People don't believe that, you know. They don't believe that the things that are saving lives today in cars—we can prove this—are threefold: seat belts, the new laminated glass and the collapsible steering column; not the headrests, not the shoulder harness. The three I mentioned are the big three. Ah, but those three were all on American cars before we knew who (consumer advocate) Ralph Nader was. Now they say, "Well, you mean to say that he and others—the consumer advocates—didn't prod you?" Oh yeah, I give everybody their due; they create a hell of an awareness. It's when they go beyond it and say: Lick that problem in five years that took 50 to create. Some of them are social problems. If we took 100 years to create them, I'm not saying we need 100 years to solve them. But don't put in an 18-month schedule, 'cause I got news for you—it ain't gonna work.

Interview, Dearborn, Mich./
Los Angeles Times, 12-19:(H)7.

Henry M. Jackson
United States Senator, D—Wash.

If the SST is shown to damage the environ-

ment, then it ought to be banned from the entire planet, not just the United States. But first, let's build two prototypes and find out.

Parade, 3-7:7.

(Regarding the Senate defeat of the SST): The know-nothings are taking over.

The National Observer, 3-29:3.

Nicholas Johnson
Commissioner,
Federal Communications Commission

I don't ride a bicycle because I hate General Motors but don't have the courage to bomb an auto plant. I don't do it as a gesture of great stoicism and personal sacrifice. I am not even engaged, necessarily, in an act of political protest over the company's responsibility for most of the air pollution by tonnage in the United States. It's like finally giving up cigarettes. You just wake up one morning and realize you don't want to start the day with another automobile. You ride a bicycle because it feels good. The air feels good on your body; even the rain feels good. The blood starts moving around your body, and pretty soon it gets to your head and, glory be, your head feels good. You start noticing things. You look until you really see. You hear things and smell smells you never knew were there. You start whistling nice little original tunes to suit the moment. Words start getting caught in the web of poetry in your mind. And there's a nice feeling, too, in knowing you're doing a fundamental life thing for yourself: transportation. You got a little bit of your life back!

Testifying in favor of designating certain
Washington streets as bicycle pathways/
The Wall Street Journal, 6-2:12.

David M. Kendall
Chairman, National Passenger
Railroad Corporation

We believe that this (the new Railpax system) is one of the most significant developments in the history of American transportation—one that offers great promise not only to provide modern, attractive, efficient rail transportation, but also to provide an offset to the

(DAVID M. KENDALL)

mounting problems of pollution and congestion afflicting our urban areas.

News conference, Washington, March 22/
Los Angeles Times, 3-23:(1)1.

James Kerrigan
President, Greyhound (Bus) Lines

Air, rail and bus have to work together to get people out of the automobile. If we took 25 per cent of the airline business, it wouldn't be 1 per cent of the people in cars.

The Washington Post, 3-17:(E)11.

Charles A. Lindbergh
Aviator

One of the troubles with us today is that our cars are too powerful and too big. Who needs 300 horsepower and eight cylinders? Why, that's a lot more horsepower than I had in "The Spirit of St. Louis!" We could easily get along with less power and use unleaded gasoline, and really cut down on exhaust pollutants. I haven't used high-octane fuels in my own cars for more than a quarter-century. But our system is such that when there's affluence, people want bigger and more powerful cars, and Detroit responds. Power and speed—these are false gods. If we worship them, they're going to destroy us.

Interview/
The New York Times Magazine, 5-23:44.

Warren G. Magnuson
United States Senator, D—Wash.

If you're talking about no SST, you're talking about no *American* SST. (By stopping work on the American SST) you will be leading America down the road toward becoming a third-rate nation in aviation. We'll be running into a technological Appalachia around here if we're not careful.

Before the Senate, Washington/Time, 4-5:11.

William M. Magruder
Director, Office of Supersonic Transport
Development, Department of Transportation
of the United States

I am frequently challenged by the opponents of the SST program who ask how I can advocate a new airplane when there are so many "human needs" going unmet. I'm not sure how stopping the SST program would do anything to advance the cause of health or education or urban problems, but I would like to submit that aviation also serves uniquely "human" needs. The airplane transports medicines and missionaries; it carries bereaved relatives as well as businessmen; it speeds (the) mail and provides mobility for the masses. Overall, the aerospace industry has been a significant contributor to the quality of life and—given a chance—it can make even greater contributions in the times ahead.

Before Economic Club, Detroit, Feb.1/
Vital Speeches, 4-1:361.

If the United States fails to build an SST, then for the first time in your lifetime and mine we will have announced that we no longer are going to be the supplier of the most-wanted civil air transports of the world. The free world's 173 airlines buy 85 per cent of their equipment today from the United States. Aircraft manufacturing creates employment for three quarters of a million people and has produced almost 20 billion dollars in favorable trade balance in the last 10 years. If we let the SST slip away to the Russians and the French and the British—who, incidentally, are already flying their SSTs—it would strengthen their hand in manufacturing all kinds of aircraft; and we would lose our leadership and all the economic benefits that go with it.

Interview/U.S. News & World Report, 3-15:68.

In the case of the SST, I believe all-time records were set for misinforming the public. As a result of this rampant misinformation, members of Congress and some Senators became party to, and even endorsed, theories and presumptions SST opponents put forth in the guise of fact. All of these opinions received nationwide coverage. What did not receive coverage was that in most cases authors of these ideas were not, and did not claim to be, experts in any areas about which they offered SST opinions.

At Air Line Pilots Association's Air Safety Forum banquet, Dallas, July 22/ The Dallas Times Herald, 7-23:(A)29.

M. S. McLaughlin
President, Ford (Motor Company) Marketing Corporation

. . . the total and massive effect of continually one-sided criticism of the automobile and the automobile industry has been to sow unwarranted seeds of distrust, dissatisfaction and depression among a discriminating, knowledgeable and highly pragmatic American motoring public. The end result has been to create unfair suspicion of American business integrity and to imply that owning and driving a car is sort of anti-social or anti-environmental behavior. Add to this the increasing competition for every consumer dollar from travel, recreation, education, country homes, boats and stocks, and it becomes crystal clear that all of us in the automobile business have a tremendous job to do in preventing the erosions of consumer enthusiasm and confidence in the buying, owning and using of a car.

The Dallas Times Herald, 1-24:(D)7.

George Meany
President, American Federation of Labor-Congress of Industrial Organizations

(Regarding saving the American SST project): We're not fighting merely for 42,000 jobs now and 150,000 more in the future. We're fighting to conserve one of America's most important industries. We're asking Congress to fund a program that will not only keep people off unemployment and welfare rolls, but that will create billions of dollars worth of new revenue.

Before Senate Appropriations Subcommittee, Washington, March 10/ San Francisco Examiner, 3-10:2.

William H. Moore
President, Penn Central Transportation Company

One of the prime causes of railroad illness is starvation—a denial by the government of enough income to stay healthy. Railroads must have greater freedom to regulate their freight rates. Costs should be the controlling factor in setting rates—as they are for practically every other business in the country. When our costs decrease, we should have the power to immediately decrease our charges to shippers—not have to wade through a series of Interstate Commerce Commission hearings and, meanwhile, watch some of our competitors take advantage of our total lack of mobility in a free-enterprise system. This same attitude should prevail toward increasing costs. We should be allowed to increase our rates immediately to meet such costs, and not have to dig ourselves a deeper and deeper monetary hole and wend our way through an endless maze of regulatory procedures. Railroads cannot survive in this restrictive atmosphere. It's a minor miracle that the industry has done as well as it has.

Before Ohio Grain, Feed and Fertilizer Association/The Wall Street Journal, 3-2:14.

Ralph Nader
Lawyer; Consumer rights advocate

(Regarding AMTRAK): Congress, in its haste to avoid the industry's threats of massive passenger discontinuances and widespread bankruptcies, has created an SST on rails, a form of private socialism that is inimical to worthy American traditions.

The Austin (Tex.) Statesman, 4-27:4.

Gaylord Nelson
United States Senator, D—Wis.

. . . the American SST is expected to cost about 50 million dollars per airplane if it ever goes into production—twice as much as either the (British-French) *Concorde* or the 747. The airlines will then be expected to pay an enormous amount of money for a plane that costs substantially more to carry each passenger. It is a high-cost, high-fare plane being built to serve a small constituency that may be willing to pay a substantial extra fee to save three hours' travel time to Europe. These people are flying on expense accounts or fat pocketbooks. If

(GAYLORD NELSON)

there is sufficient demand to support such a plane, it should stand on its own and be built without subsidy. The economics of this plane involve a basic national-priority question. With Federal funds in short supply, where should they be spent first? It is ironic that with mass transportation within our major cities and across the nation in a state of collapse, we should be spending more to solve the travel problems for a few than we are spending to solve the transportation problems of 200 million Americans.

Interview/U.S. News & World Report, 3-15:69.

Arthur M. Okun
Senior fellow, Brookings Institution;
Former Chairman, Council of Economic
Advisers to the President
of the United States

(The SST) promises no enormous gains to others in the community who do not choose to ride airplanes. Why should they pay the bill? Why should the government underwrite this project? What criterion makes SST different from color television or flip-top cans? Try as I may, I can't find a reason.

Before Senate Appropriations
Committee, Washington, March 10/
The New York Times, 3-11:70.

Georges Pompidou
President of France

It (the British-French *Concorde* SST) was indeed a gamble; and today it is still, to some extent, a gamble. But the gamble was taken on, and it has been and will be kept. On the technical level, the results are in and the plane meets the most ambitious hopes. On the financial level, the French government has decided to pursue the effort to its conclusion . . . Everything that is great is criticized; everything that is great is difficult. But the important thing is to do it; and France will have done it.

Toulouse, France, May 7/
The New York Times, 5-8:46.

William Proxmire
United States Senator, D—Wis.

I have received some letters from State of Washington residents telling me they intend to boycott Wisconsin cheese and other products because of my opposition to SST. That is their loss, not ours.

Quote, 4-11:338.

John S. Reed
President, Atchison, Topeka
& Santa Fe Railway

If American (rail)roads operated on the basis of the nationalized railroads of foreign countries, the U.S. taxpayers' bill would be more than $2 billion a year to cover operating losses alone. And if our government—in the same hypothetical situation—spent as much for capital improvements as American railroads now spend, the bill imposed on the public could reach $4 billion a year. There would also be a huge loss of tax revenue—paid today by the nation's railroads to Federal, state and local governments—and this tax load would have to be shifted to the already over-burdened American taxpayer. And could shippers of freight expect lower freight rates? This can best be answered by referring . . . to the comparison with nationalized operation in other countries, which shows that the average freight revenue per ton-mile on American railroads was substantially less than on any of the nationalized systems in the comparison. Perhaps the biggest financial question of all—in considering whether the public can afford a Federal take-over—is the initial cost of acquisition. Estimates of this run as high as $60 billion—no one really knows what the cost would be or how it would be accomplished—and if government bonds were issued to present holders of railroad securities, additional billions of dollars would be required for interest payments. Let's face it. Neither management, labor, the government, nor you or I as a taxpayer can afford nationalization.

Before Traffic Club, Chicago,
May 20/Vital Speeches, 7-1:570.

Frank Reynolds
News commentator,
American Broadcasting Company

We need transit more than planes—why can't
Boeing make streetcars?
Interview/Los Angeles Times, 1-13:(4)16.

James M. Roche
Chairman, General Motors Corporation

We're working in our industry . . . You
can't argue about safety and pollution. We've
made steady progress in safety. We've got to do
more with licensing of drivers, auto inspection
and drunk drivers. We're learning about the
chemistry of pollution and are well on the way
to solving it. We've made mistakes. There was
inadequate planning on traffic congestion. We
didn't understand the demand for smaller cars,
and responded too much to demand for performance. But weigh the great benefits of the
automobile—the greatest mobility for people
and goods on a cost basis unequaled in the
world. Automobiles make for the highest standard of living, one we really enjoy.
Interview, Detroit/
Los Angeles Times, 9-10:(2)7.

Some people are referring to the end of the
"love affair" between Americans and the automobile. I don't think that the public's love affair with the automobile is over. But I do think
it has matured to the point where the utility
value (of the auto) is given more consideration
today perhaps than any time in the past, primarily because of the many different uses to
which the automobile is being put today. The
fact remains that the average American likes the
personal mobility of an automobile. We're going to have to find different ways of handling
some phases of the problem; for example, the
parking facilities, the flow of traffic, things like
that. But I think the automobile is going to be
with us for a long time.
The New York Times Magazine, 9-12:124.

William J. Ronan
Chairman, New York State Metropolitan
Transportation Authority

Rarely, in recent years, have we seen mass

transportation developed in anticipation of the
inevitable.
Before Institute of Rapid Transit,
Mexico City, June 9/
The New York Times, 6-10:78.

Paul A. Samuelson
Professor of Economics,
Massachusetts Institute of Technology

If as many as six of those *Concordes* (Brit-
ish-French SSTs) are sold, it will be only by
miscalculation.
Before Senate Appropriations
Committee, Washington, March 11/
The New York Times, 3-12:62.

John H. Shaffer
Administrator,
Federal Aviation Administration

The supersonic plane is an absolute necessity
. . . The SST is so fast that fewer of them can
do the same work as a larger number of slower
planes. Look at it this way: If we were still
using DC-3s, it would take 50,000 of them to
do what we are now doing in the United States
with 3000 planes. Why, if we were still depending on stage coaches, I have not checked the
figures, but I am sure there is not enough graz-
ing land in France to feed all the horses we
would need. And we would be up to our ears in
pollution—literally.
Paris, June 5/San Francisco
Examiner & Chronicle, 6-6:(A)11.

Robert F. Six
President, Continental Airlines

(Regarding new airports): Cities throughout
the country are building monuments that are
concrete wastelands. It's costing a fortune, and
we can't afford it. What people really want is
fast check-in and better baggage handling.
They're disgusted with the miserably-long hike
between airport ticket counters and debarka-
tion point.
The Christian Science Monitor, 4-24:12.

Russell V. Stephenson
President, Mohawk Airlines

Unless solutions are found to the problems

(RUSSELL V. STEPHENSON)

plaguing airlines today, scores of communities throughout the United States are in danger of losing even more of their scheduled air transportation services during the early 1970s than they have lost in the past or will lose in the immediate present. We can no longer continue to operate an airline service that costs more than the public pays in fares and the government pays in subsidy . . . We find ourselves with several bad years behind us, with an ominous 1971 ahead and with a public which has grown to regard overabundant air service as a Constitutional right. It is not. Air service is important. But someone has to pay for it—all of it.

Binghamton, N.Y./
The New York Times, 1-31:(1)66.

John W. R. Taylor
Editor, "Jane's All the World's Aircraft"

Once people are accustomed to the British-French *Concorde,* and the Soviet *Tupolev* TN-144 supersonics—which are smaller and not so fast as the American project—the Americans will feel impelled to build their own SST.

Plainview (Tex.) Daily Herald, 4-16:6.

Charles C. Tillinghast
Chairman, Trans World Airlines

In the maritime field, you've seen almost a complete disappearance of United States shipping. One of the fundamental questions one has to ask himself today is whether that also can happen to the airlines or whether there's a possibility, if we are to have flag representation on the Atlantic, that there will have to be some sort of subsidization of it. Suffice to say that many of the foreign carriers with whom we compete are subsidized, despite the fact that they also have the benefit of lower labor costs and more favorable credit terms on their equipment purchases. I think the only thing you can say is that competition on the North Atlantic is very rough, and it is difficult to predict the future with any certainty. I think the only thing one can say with full conviction is that one cannot be complacent and take for granted

that the next 10 years are going to be like the last 10, because it is quite clear that they are going to be different.

Interview, New York/
The New York Times, 8-15:(3)5.

John V. Tunney
United States Senator, D–Calif.

Our claim to world leadership is going to be validated right here at ground-zero in our country—on our city streets, along the waterways and throughout the countryside. Squadrons of SSTs are not going to preserve our prestige if we fritter it away through continued disorder in our streets and further pollution of our air and water.

Before the Senate, Washington,
March 23/Los Angeles Times, 3-24:(1)15.

Francis C. Turner
Administrator,
Federal Highway Administration

Highways are the very lifelines of the cities. They are the conduits that keep cities viable. Without them, cities inevitably would stagnate and die. It is as simple as that. Practically every service in a city depends on highways. And city dwellers, when they go to the supermarket, or a drug store, or to the theatre or the movies, or a concert or a sporting event or to visit friends—how do they generally travel? By highway transportation, of course.

Sept. 23/The Washington Post, 11-29:(C)5.

Planners must face squarely the unassailable fact that people want personal mobility and freedom of movement. People use the best mode (of transportation) available, and the best today for the most happens to be the automobile. Nothing better has come along and, until it does, we must build our backbone transportation around the street and the automobile and its cousins, trucks and buses.

Before American Transit Association,
Dallas, Oct. 7/
The Dallas Times Herald, 10-7:(A)28.

Stewart L. Udall
Former Secretary of the Interior
of the United States

I have talked with high-placed airline officials in recent weeks. Most of them will not appear here; and the few who do will come out of duty, having foolishly pledged their support to the pro-SST coalition several years ago. These officials are privately appalled at the prospect of having to sign solid contracts for these aircraft. They are already in deep financial trouble trying to meet their obligations for the current generation of jet aircraft.

Before House Appropriations
Subcommittee, Washington, March 2/
Los Angeles Times, 3-3:(3)16.

John A. Volpe
Secretary of Transportation
of the United States

If prototype testing shows that the SST will do irreparable harm to our environment, I will do everything possible—and the President has asked me to say this—to ensure that a United States SST does not fly in commercial service.

Washington, March 1/
The Dallas Times Herald, 3-2:(A)12.

(AMTRAK will bring) a new era in intercity railroad passenger service throughout the United States. For the first time, a single corporation will hold itself responsible for the total travel experience of passengers on trains and in stations throughout the nation.

May 1/The Dallas Times Herald, 5-2:(A)26.

Samuel W. Yorty
Mayor of Los Angeles

California's two U.S. Senators, in voting against the SST, have turned their backs on one of the most important industries in our state, as well as on all the people working in aerospace, most of whom were asked by their labor leaders to vote for and help finance the misleading campaigns of these two unreliable Senators. The Russian Communists are already trying to push us out of our aerospace lead by advertising their own SST for sale in the world market. The Senate action (voting down the American SST) gives our foreign competition a clear field. This is shocking beyond belief.

Los Angeles, March 25/
Los Angeles Herald-Examiner, 3-25:(A)1.

Urban Affairs

Spiro T. Agnew
Vice President of the United States

I find it almost irresistible to avoid commenting on the suggestion that a very well known American Mayor made that cities should become city-states with a special relationship to the Federal government in Washington. I want to let you know how unproductive I think that would be. I have always taken the view that it is extremely urgent that we bring into being the sense of shared problems between state, county and city governments. I can think of no way worse to achieve that objective than attempting to place the American city in some insulated provincial posture that would make the people of the counties and states turn their backs on city problems.

At International Conference of Cities,
Indianapolis, May 28/
The New York Times, 5-29:27.

(Advocating President Nixon's revenue-sharing plan): (The cities' problems) will never be solved as long as the Mayor has to go to Washington—or to the state capital—with cup in hand like a mendicant on the street begging for a handout to help him through another day.

Before National League of Cities,
Honolulu, Nov. 30/
Los Angeles Herald-Examiner, 12-1:(A)16.

Joseph L. Alioto
Mayor of San Francisco

I'll be frank . . . The sky's falling in on us in the cities; it really is. We've had six cops killed in San Francisco since I took office. We need jobs and money for the poor and haven't money for either. Our people are trying to put a Maginot Line around the suburbs and

zoning them. We can't go on like this. Even the capitalistic system's not going to survive the way we're going.

Washington, March 23/
The New York Times, 3-24:39.

Birch Bayh
United States Senator, D—Ind.

If we can put footsteps on the moon, we should be able to put a new face on downtown U.S.A.

Quote, 7-25:73.

Richard J. Daley
Mayor of Chicago

The experts are all saying that our big cities have become ungovernable. What the hell do the experts know?

Newsweek, 4-5:80.

Clay Felker
Editor, "New York" magazine

Let's not forget that so often when we talk about the city's problems—say, traffic congestion—we overlook the fact that they are also evidence of the city's vitality. Cities work, despite all prophecies of chaos and doom.

Interview/
The Christian Science Monitor, 3-22:13.

Peter Flaherty
Mayor of Pittsburgh

You can't understand how lonely a Mayor feels with his problems. The people in the suburbs use our facilities but won't help pay for them. The Pittsburgh Zoo costs us $1 million a year. Three out of four people who go there come from outside the city. But when I ask the county commissioners for help, they look out the window.

Washington, March 23/
The New York Times, 3-24:39.

Kenneth A. Gibson
Mayor of Newark, N.J.

The toughest aspect of being Mayor is not being able to make the changes in the cities as rapidly as you'd like. You can develop programs; but there's always reasons you can't implement them right away. The basic problems are money, local and state legislative bodies and an inherited bureaucracy that can't seem to shift gears fast enough.

New York, April 21/
The Dallas Times Herald, 4-22:(A)8.

The city was, is and always will be the single most important source of economic, social, educational, cultural and political innovation and vitality. With all the difficulties we have today, we are this country's heartbeat, and it strangles us at its own peril.

At Jersey City State College commencement/
The New York Times, 6-14:44.

Harry G. Haskell
Mayor of Wilmington, Del.

A city doesn't go bankrupt with a bang—it just shrivels up. I'm afraid it is going to be the same old story in America: Until the situation gets really bad, no one will look for a solution.

New York/
The Austin (Tex.) Statesman, 4-28:12.

Hubert H. Humphrey
United States Senator, D–Minn.

This is one of the areas—urban problems—where the (Nixon) Administration is very weak. They're doing it on a hit-and-miss basis. They come up with a Federal revenue-sharing plan as if this is the whole thing. It's pathetic.

Interview, Washington, Jan. 20/
The New York Times, 1-21:18.

Moon Landrieu
Mayor of New Orleans

(In New Orleans) we've taxed everything that moves and everything that stands still; and if anything moves again, we tax that, too. So we're inclined to get frustrated and angry.

It's not that we don't have enough money to rebuild; we don't have enough to give things even a new coat of paint. The cities are going down the pipe; and if we're going to save them, we'd better do it now. Three years from now will be too late.

Washington, March 23/
The New York Times, 3-24:39.

Our population (in New Orleans) is 593,000; but we provide the transportation facilities, every major park, the zoo, cultural facilities and the airport for a metropolitan area of 1.1 million. And we get nothing back from the suburbs; they contribute nothing. We don't even get the sales tax, because of shopping centers in the suburbs. All we get is the poor and an eroding tax base . . . The trend is frightening . . . We tax anything that moves. I might go to suburbia myself.

New York, April 21/
The New York Times, 4-22:48.

Years ago, all the Mayor had to concern himself with was housekeeping chores. But that isn't where it's at today. No Mayor can survive just as a housekeeper. Now he has to be a salesman, an innovator and a negotiator.

New York/
The Austin (Tex.) Statesman, 4-28:12.

Patience Latting
Mayor of Oklahoma City

We have been building cities for industries, business, automobiles too long. We have built cities for everybody but people. Now let's build cities for human beings.

At Southern Methodist University,
April 23/
The Dallas Times Herald, 4-23:(B)2.

John V. Lindsay
Mayor of New York

If we cannot move forward in the cities, we will move backward in America. If we fail now, the cost will far outweigh today's financial deficits. They will be measured in despair, in hatred, in bitterness and in strife.

Time, 1-11:14.

(JOHN V. LINDSAY)

We have heard repeated reports that urban programs may be shortchanged as part of a sleight-of-hand play to finance a general revenue-sharing program with a minimum of new money. (Such cuts) will add to urban tensions and urban deterioration and will, therefore, be unacceptable. The plight of the cities is too ominous to be made part of a budgetary and political shell game.

News conference, Washington, Jan. 21/
The Washington Post, 1-22:(A)1.

Mayors do not create distorted priorities or a declining national economy. And Mayors cannot veto a destructive state budget. They are just left to manage the local agony that results.

Before United Federation of
Teachers, New York, April 24/
The New York Times, 4-25:(1)69.

Washington responds more vigorously to the threatened bankruptcy of a single corporation than it does to the devastation of 50 Brownsvilles across the country. This is not only the shame of our nation; it is the single greatest threat to our economic stability . . . It reflects both a distortion of national priorities and a double standard for Federal policy.

Before American Insurance
Association, New York, May 19/
The New York Times, 5-20:45.

What do I like most about it (his job)? I'd say the drama, the pace, which is tremendous. I like New Yorkers. I like the people; especially the little people who are all by themselves and whom you run into in the shops and on the streets. There are other aspects about the job which I don't like. I'm talking about the heartbreaks—the wounded policeman, the hurt fireman, the poor person without a job, the family paying too much for bad housing.

Interview, New York/
Los Angeles Times, 5-23:(A)2.

We (the cities) do not plead for charity. We don't look for a hand-out. We don't even ask Washington to bail us out. We simply seek the return of our own money to our own cities where the problems are. We seek assistance based on desperate need, proven effort and demonstrated ability to manage our own affairs.

Before House Ways and Means Committee,
Washington, June 11/
The New York Times, 6-12:14.

It's got to come together in 1972 for the cities, it's got to; and if the cities go, so will the suburbs—that's the one domino theory I believe in.

Interview, New York, Aug. 27/
The New York Times, 8-29:(1)31.

. . . a government which can spend $12 billion on an antiballistic missile system, $5 billion on a single airplane (the SST), a quarter of a billion dollars to prop up an aerospace giant (Lockheed), cannot claim a lack of money to save our cities. It may not care to make the city an equal partner in America—but to say it cannot do so is hypocrisy.

Before New York Democratic State
Committee Advisory Council, Sept. 17/
The Washington Post, 9-22:(A)22.

Richard G. Lugar
Mayor of Indianapolis

If I leave my office and walk two blocks, I'll have 12 conversations. When I'm ready to drive off the third tee at the golf course, I'll see somebody heading across the fairway toward me with a problem or something they want to talk about. When I take my four boys to a basketball game, it sometimes gets to be an open house for people who want to talk to me about almost anything—a better job or a complex business proposal for the city. Some of the basic decisions a Mayor of a city this size has to make are on allocation of time, on who to see and what invitations to accept, on how to structure your staff to maximum advantage—and how to give every attention to human problems in the midst of everything else. Dealing with widely dissimilar subjects is another aspect of the job. You find yourself discussing real estate taxes, then the drug problem, then tertiary treatment of sewage; then speaking to a veterans' convention and then meeting with students. You have to be able to maintain your equilibrium, your sense of humor and your common sense in a myriad of situations.

Nation's Business, June:25.

Henry W. Maier
Mayor of Milwaukee

We (Mayors) continuously have crises in resources and authority, and if you're going to be a Mayor with vision, you're going to have to carry the water on both shoulders. It's hard. You lack statutory powers for some action and there is an inability to move other governments at other times. Plus the property taxes need to be considered; they were never built to carry the loads they do.

New York/
The Austin (Tex.) Statesman, 4-28:12.

Edmund S. Muskie
United States Senator, D–Maine

As we approach the 200th anniversary of our nation's beginnings, we must make a new beginning in urban government. That may even require that we take another lead from our forefathers by calling a multitude of "urban constitutional conventions"—conventions where Governors and Mayors, legislators and community leaders can raise and resolve some of the hardest problems our cities and suburbs face. With a little luck and a lot of reform, we might end up with government subunits in every city and a government superunit in every metropolitan area.

Before American Jewish Committee,
New York, May 14/
The Washington Post, 5-15:(A)5.

Richard M. Nixon
President of the United States

Through time, cities have been centers of culture and commerce, and nowhere has this

been more true than in America. But today, many of our great cities are dying. We must not let this happen. We can do better than this. We must do better than this. Only if the American city can prosper can the American dream really prevail.

At University of Nebraska, Jan. 14/
The New York Times, 1-15:12.

As one indication of the rising cost of local government, I discovered the other day that my home town of Whittier, California—with a population of only 67,000—has a budget for 1971 bigger than the entire Federal budget in 1791.

State of the Union address,
Washington, Jan. 22/
The Washington Post, 1-23:(A)12.

John Portman, Jr.
Architect

The city has developed with very little concern for people amenities. You look at cities today and you find there's no place for people. There are places for buildings, places for automobiles, for trucks and taxicabs; but there's no nature left, there's no tranquility, there's nothing for the human spirit except dejection.

Interview, Atlanta/
The Dallas Times Herald, 8-25:(A)16.

George W. Romney
Secretary of Housing and Urban
Development of the United States

The flight of the affluent from the city to the suburbs, together with the influx of the poor into the central city, has created a white suburb noose around an impoverished black central core.

At United States Conference of Mayors,
Philadelphia, June 14/
Los Angeles Herald-Examiner, 6-15:(A)6.

George S. Sternlieb
Director, Center for Urban Policy
Research, Rutgers University

The problem of the city is a crisis of func-

(GEORGE S. STERNLIEB)

tion. What is left to the city that it does better than someplace else? In our free market we have considerable fluidity of mortgaging and debt structure. We have people who can vote with their feet or with their automobile —and they are voting for the suburbs. What actually does the city have to offer to keep people? The answer today is: very little.

Interview, Washington/
U.S. News & World Report, 7-26:42.

Carl B. Stokes
Mayor of Cleveland

When I talk around the country, I hear black people rejoice in the number of black Mayors, rejoice in black political power. But what kind of power is it? To preside over disease, poverty and pestilence? Ken Gibson has the honor of sitting in that Mayor's chair in Newark. But what kind of honor is it to govern over the highest rate of venereal disease, illegitimacy, crime or infant mortality? What is there to rejoice in?

Interview, Cleveland/
The New York Times, 5-1:22.

One of the most vexing problems in the inner city is the suburbanite who expects police protection, bright street lights, clean streets and all the rest. Meanwhile, he is unwilling to contribute to the city that is the source of his income. The city must pay for these services demanded by this eight-hour-a-day population.

Boston/
The Christian Science Monitor, 10-13:5.

David Susskind
Motion picture-stage-television producer

New York (City) isn't sick; it's cancerous, living on borrowed time. I am appalled, frightened and amazed at the number of people who are fed up with New York. It isn't just cocktail talk; they genuinely want to get out of New York. Fear is rampant. People are being mugged, raped and beaten on Fifth Avenue. The subways aren't fit for animals, and five million people have to use them.

There is rape and robbery in the subways. Anybody with half a buck spends that half a buck to send his child to a private school. If it sounds despairing, it is despairing. The middle class will not come back to New York. There is nothing there to bring them back. Nothing is being done to bring them back. It's a city of the desperately poor and a few rich.

San Francisco, June 29/
San Francisco Examiner, 6-30:18.

Wesley C. Uhlman
Mayor of Seattle

We are suffering from a real sickness, a kind of schizophrenia. The people say they love the cities, but wouldn't want to live there.

Washington, March 23/
The New York Times, 3-24:39.

I love to see other Mayors; misery loves company.

New York, April 21/
The New York Times, 4-22:48.

Walter E. Washington
Mayor of Washington, D. C.

We (city and suburban governments) can plan air pollution, water pollution, sewer problems together. But when it comes to *sharing* the substantive needs of the city and suburban ring, there is a reluctance to get together.

Before American Society of Newspaper
Editors, Washington, April 16/
The Washington Post, 4-17:(A)2.

Kevin White
Mayor of Boston

I don't know what kind of clout Mayors have in Presidential politics any more; but whatever it is, we're going to use it—as a group—for our cities. We are up for grabs, and we're letting everyone know it.

Washington/
The Washington Post, 3-30:(A)15.

Boston is a tinderbox . . . The fact is, it's an armed camp. One out of every five people in Boston is on welfare. Look, we raise 70 per cent of our money with the property tax, but half our property is untaxable and 20 per cent of our people are bankrupt. Could you run a business that way?

The New York Times, 4-23:35.

Even if you're a drowning man, you don't believe you're going to drown. It's just you don't believe it. And you don't, if you're a Mayor, accept the fact that your city is going to die. I'm no Cassandra. I'm almost an incurable optimist. But the fact of the matter is I don't see any chance for it (the American city) to survive. I don't see it coming back. I don't see anything happening to it. I really don't. I mean that sincerely.

Interview, Boston/
Los Angeles Times, 6-20:(A)4.

PART TWO

International Affairs

John J. Akar
*Ambassador to the United States
from Sierra Leone*

If Sierra Leone goes Communist with Guinea, they pose a great danger to all of West Africa, and Communist subversion will become a political phenomenon in that contiguous region. Russia has a massive presence in the Mediterranean. If it can establish another massive presence in the West of Africa, all of that area will be exposed to a Communist threat.

*Interview/The Washington Post,
4-23:(B)1.*

Idi Amin
*Commander of the armed forces and
leader of the military
government of Uganda*

(Regarding the military takeover of the government): I can tell you without any doubt whatsoever that the new government is firmly in control of the entire republic of Uganda. My government will, at the right time, make arrangements for honest, fair, completely free general elections . . . and I shall go back to the barracks and take orders from whoever is elected President.

*Before foreign diplomats,
Kampala, Jan. 29/
Los Angeles Times, 1-30:(1)4.*

Charles Onana Awana
Planning Minister of Cameroon

We are trying to take Cameroon out of underdevelopment. We haven't been able to fulfill all of our hopes. I ask, though, that you look at what we have achieved in 10 years and compare it to what was achieved before 1960 by the colonial powers that were here for 40 years.

*Interview, Yaounde, Cameroon/
The Washington Post, 3-15:(D)9.*

Hastings Kamuzu Banda
President of Malawi

. . . this country is supposed to be poor—no mines, no gold; but people are far better off here than they are in many African countries. They are not starving, whereas in other African countries people are starving. Why? Difference in leadership. Other leaders are . . . busy shouting against South Africa whites . . . busy serving the poor Africans in South Africa, when their own people right at home are starving, are going about naked. To me, charity begins at home.

The Washington Post, 8-15:(A)17.

Christiaan Barnard
Surgeon

I love my country (South Africa). But it is my personal opinion that there is no future for South Africa, for you or for me or for our children, unless we adopt a progressive outlook (toward racial integration).

Los Angeles Times, 2-25:(1)2.

Houari Boumedienne
President of Algeria

We wish to build a socialist society adjusted to realities and suitable to our traditions. It cannot be atheist because we are religious Moslems, and we will not impose socialism by force. Moreover, we wish to keep certain private sectors. We want foreign capital to help, and we will pay acceptable profits. During this phase of our development, there is coexistence between the socialist, nationalized sectors and the private sectors, and we definitely encourage capital investment.

*Interview, Algiers/
The New York Times, 2-26:31.*

. . . in the long term, we would like to see the Mediterranean demilitarized. We don't want

271

(HOUARI BOUMEDIENNE)

to see this region transformed into a zone of tension between the superpowers. But this is not merely a question for the Arab states; it is for all the riverine states who should work together so that we no longer need the presence of superpower fleets. We are not a cake to be sliced up by the superpowers. We want nobody to partition our area.

Interview, Algiers/
The New York Times, 2-28:(4)13.

Habib Bourguiba
President of Tunisia

(Regarding his country's high 3 per cent annual population growth): This is a veritable calamity. Our situation will be similar to that of a rower who finds himself carried two meters backward by the current every time he advances one meter.

The New York Times, 1-9:14.

Theo Gerdener
Minister of the Interior
of South Africa

Throughout history it has been proved that such gigantic differences in living standards as we have (between whites and non-whites) in South Africa can convert neighborliness into enmity. It can be more serious. It can lead to murder and violence because the less-privileged of the two can no longer tolerate the apparent wealth, ease and prosperity of his neighbor.

Johannesburg/
The New York Times, 11-13:3.

Hassan II
King of Morocco

I don't think I have had retrogressive economic and social ideas in the past. On the contrary. No. But you know there may sometimes be a gap between theory and practice. The only man who managed to reconcile theory and practice was Beethoven; he was deaf and he made beautiful music. In life, often the sentiments are good but the application is not good.

And it is there that the most important changes must occur.

Interview, Skhirat, Morocco,
July 26/
The New York Times, 7-29:3.

We have often said that our policy and our socialism is aimed to enrich the poor without beggaring the rich. Unfortunately, we have noted that the poor have not become rich, while the rich have increased their fortunes.

San Francisco Examiner, 8-7:4.

Felix Houphouet-Boigny
President of the Ivory Coast

(Regarding apartheid in South Africa): What must be decided is whether bellicose verbalism—the disastrous consequences of which are known to all—or a carefully thought-out approach, conducted with serenity, realism and modesty, would serve more faithfully the dignity, the pride and the best interests of our continent. I, too, could howl with the wolves. (Instead) we have to persuade the South Africans. Who would have thought 10 years ago of all the progress blacks have made in the United States. But blacks had confidence in the United States and made it aware; and now they are solving this problem. Why shouldn't we make the same effort here?

Abidjan, April 28/
The New York Times, 4-29:15.

E. Bolaji Idowu
Professor,
University of Ibaden, Nigeria

The African is a person who, on the whole, accepts life as it comes. This is something that modern sophistication has frequently destroyed elsewhere.

The New York Times, 3-12:10.

Leabua Jonathan
Prime Minister of Lesotho

I favor a nonracial society with equal opportunity for all. South Africa's policy of apartheid cannot possibly work. I am certain it will fail, both for moral and practical reasons.

The New York Times, 4-21:43.

Joe Kachingwe
Ambassador to South Africa
from Malawi

Some people say we are cooperating with South Africa because we are a poor country. It is true that we get economic aid from South Africa; but we also get economic aid from Britain, the United States and West Germany. Economic aid and contact are two quite different things. Other African states are demanding the isolation of South Africa. We say that is not the way to go about it. Isolation is not the way to get South Africa to change its (racial) policies.

News conference, Pretoria,
July 29/
The New York Times, 7-30:7.

Mansur Khalid
Foreign Minister of Sudan

The Sudan is now matching word and deed as far as nonalignment is concerned. Previously, it was nonaligned more toward the East . . . The Sudan is now trying to improve relations with the non-socialist world . . .

Interview/The Washington Post,
12-16:(G)8.

Seretse Khama
President of Botswana

It's not enough to say we are building a nation. We must ask ourselves what kind of a nation. The answer is that we are building a Botswana which relies on its own resources and which refuses to divide its people by income or occupation, just as it refuses to divide them by tribe or race.

Gaborone, Botswana/
The Washington Post, 2-14:(H)6.

I see few signs that the peoples and governments of Asia and Latin America—much less the great powers and their allies—are more committed to our (Africa's) cause than they were 10 years ago, even though more is now known about conditions in Southern Africa. Indeed, it may be the case that greater knowledge has led to pessimism about the prospects of change. Behind the screen of words, international activity has been directed toward areas where the dangers of great-power confrontation and the risks of starting a Third World War are much more immediate. I find this understandable. Although I and my countrymen have first-hand experience of the inhumanities and indignities of apartheid and white supremacy, I cannot regard Africa, as some of my colleagues do, as the world's unhappiest continent.

At Africana-American Dialogues
conference, Lagos, Nigeria, March/
Vital Speeches, 9-1:680.

Wanume Kibedi
Foreign Minister of Uganda

We think it's important to establish relations with as many countries as possible. We want to insure that Uganda's case—that is, the revolutionary changes going on here—may be understood by the whole world . . . We are not at all worried about the question of recognition. Many countries have informed us that their policy is to recognize states, not governments.

Interview, Nairobi, Kenya/
The Christian Science Monitor,
3-18:2.

Jaafar al Nimeiry
President of Sudan

(I pledge to) crush the Communists and dismiss Party members from their jobs . . . You must destroy anyone who claims there is a Sudanese Communist Party.

Address to the Sudanese people,
Feb. 12/
The Washington Post, 2-13:(A)13.

Our revolution has caused the Sudanese people to do an about-face, to turn its back on a blind alley and to move forward in a new avenue . . . We have offered the Third World the example of revolution through the armed forces. An army as an organized body, strong and united, can cause change.

Interview/The Washington Post,
5-25:(A)20.

Apparently some of the Communist countries have beliefs, strong beliefs, that our

(JAAFAR AL NIMEIRY)

friendship with them means we accept their ideology and doctrine . . . We learned that we must be very cautious in our relations with foreign countries, especially with superpowers . . . and we cannot accept any interference from any quarter in our internal affairs.

Interview, Khartoum/
The Christian Science Monitor,
8-16:1.

(Regarding the recent attempted Communist coup in Sudan): We found out that some countries, which pretended to be friendly toward us, were leading figures in the conspiracy. The European Communist countries, with the exception of Yugoslavia, colluded in the conspiracy. Those countries, led by Moscow, conspired to bring their hirelings in the Sudan to power. They were as stupid as the Sudanese Communists . . . We have committed a mistake by seeking friendship with Moscow and by inviting them to our country.

Al Gereef Sharg, Sudan,
Sept. 9/Los Angeles Times, 10-3:(I)1.

Julius K. Nyerere
President of Tanzania

If any of us compromise with racialism (such as in South Africa) under any circumstances except the direct and most obvious urgent necessity of national survival, then either we have to leave the (British) Commonwealth or we destroy the Commonwealth by denying its meaning.

At British Commonwealth conference,
Singapore, Jan. 20/
The New York Times, 1-21:7.

Harry Oppenheimer
South African industrialist

If you don't give people a chance to struggle legally for what they want, it creates a climate for illegality . . . What we are doing in my country burns me up. The long-term future of South Africa is bleak. I will do what I can to influence our rulers to make black and white equal. I realize I am living in a

country which politically is a failure; but somehow we are surviving. It's a nasty sort of survivial, and I often wonder what will happen in 10 years. South Africa could be wiped out.

San Francisco Examiner & Chronicle,
3-21:(A)12.

Gerard Kango Ouedraogo
Prime Minister of Upper Volta

We are absolutely determined to prove to the world that real democracy can exist in Africa.

The New York Times, 8-16:6.

Alan Paton
South African writer

It's not really Communism they (South Africa's leaders) fear; it's change. They—these good Calvinists—fear change much more than they fear God.

The Austin (Tex.) Statesman, 4-14:5.

Ian Smith
Prime Minister of Rhodesia

There is available to the government evidence which shows that, in certain areas, racial harmony is being prejudiced by infiltration. I am sorry to have to add that there is evidence which shows that some of this is stimulated by certain European agitators.

Jan. 1/
The Christian Science Monitor, 1-6:2.

I doubt whether there is any country more dedicated than Rhodesia to opposing the evils of Communism.

Before Parliament, Salisbury, Nov. 25/
The New York Times, 11-26:2.

(If Rhodesians dedicate themselves to the ideals of economic advancement and human dignity), then I believe that, we the people, will match up to Rhodesia, the land, and together this combination will succeed in retaining for us here a haven of peace and sanity in a world which is becoming notorious for its wars, its riots, pestilence, starvation, rebellion, massacre and general anarchy.

Before Parliament, Salisbury, Nov. 25/
The New York Times, 11-28:(4)2.

I would not claim that there is an immediate, imminent threat here from Communism. But we are very conscious of the fact that they are concentrating on Africa to the north of us—that Tanzania today, with the Tanzam railway line well on its way to completion, is virtually a Chinese Communist satellite. So while there is no immediate danger, there is a problem looming on the horizon. We intend to be prepared to meet and deal with this problem when the time comes.

Interview, Salisbury/
U.S. News & World Report, 11-29:41.

Sekou Toure
President of Guinea

(Regarding the recent attempted invasion of the country): Slit the throats of the enemies. Kill the mercenaries first and report later to the authorities. Power is not in the hands of the head of state or the government. It is not even in the hands of this assembly. It is in the hands of the people. Let the people slaughter, cut into pieces and burn their enemies wherever they find them.

Before National Assembly, Conakry/
The Washington Post, 1-27:(A)14.

Of the 13 French colonial territories in Africa, Guinea was the only one that emerged from the French colonial empire to build a really sovereign and revolutionary state, in no form of union with or alliance to any European country. Since then, the young Guinean nation has worked to change its structures and mentality, to completely free itself from the ideological, military, economic, political and cultural influences of all foreign countries.

Before National Assembly, Conakry/
The Washington Post, 1-27:(A)14.

Pierre Elliott Trudeau
Prime Minister of Canada

(Arguing against British arms sales to South

Africa): The threat (in the Indian Ocean area), if it exists, certainly is not immediate. It seems to me that in any kind of major war, it (the Indian Ocean) wouldn't be a telling factor in the destinies of mankind. If there is a real war between the major powers, I suspect that atom bombs would be going off in other parts of the world, and not too many will be wasted in the Indian Ocean.

New Delhi, Jan. 11/
The Washington Post, 1-13:(A)18.

John Vorster
Prime Minister of South Africa

The ideal position would be if the U.S. said (to South Africa), "We don't like your domestic policy, but that's your business." There must be scores of countries with whose domestic policy the U.S. doesn't agree, and yet you cooperate. We ask nothing more than that. Apartheid is not for export, and we don't expect the U.S. to subscribe to it.

Interview, Cape Town/
The New York Times, 4-25:(4)15.

We view Israel's position and problems with understanding and sympathy. Like us, they have to deal with terrorist infiltration across the border; and like us, they have enemies bent on their destruction.

The New York Times, 4-30:37.

(Regarding a World Court ruling that South Africa should surrender its administration of South-West Africa): An advisory opinion by its very nature has no binding force and in the present case is totally unconvincing. It is our duty to administer South-West Africa so as to promote the well-being and progress of its inhabitants. We have guided and administered the peoples of South-West Africa for more than half a century in a manner which has earned their full-hearted confidence. We have set them on the way of peace, prosperity and self-determination, and we do not intend to fail that trust.

Radio broadcast, Pretoria, June 21/
The Washington Post, 6-22:(A)15.

Harold Wilson
Leader, British Labor Party;
Former Prime Minister of the
United Kingdom

(Arguing against Britain selling helicopters to South Africa because of that country's policy of apartheid): What does it profit a man or government to gain control through three or four helicopters of a few more square miles of the Indian Ocean—and it is not more than that—and to lose the battle for the hundreds of millions of hearts and minds on continents washed by that ocean?

Before House of Commons,
London, March 3/
The New York Times, 3-4:16.

Salvador Allende (Gossens)
President of Chile

I am not the hypocrite to say I am President of all Chileans, although all merit respect under the law. I am the Comrade President of Popular Unity, and my obligation is to carry out its program. There are some Chileans who would like to see me fried in oil.

News conference/
The New York Times, 2-15:1.

The United States should recognize that our democracy here is authentic democracy, and that we will never do anything against the United States or contribute to injuring its sovereignty. For example, we will never provide a military base that might be used against the United States. Chile will never permit her territory to be used for a military base by any foreign power—by anybody.

Interview, Santiago, March 23/
The New York Times, 3-28:(1)1.

What we are doing in internal reform is simply to improve our own country and our own society and standard of living. The United States should understand that, if we nationalize copper installations in which there have been United States interests and United States investment, it is because we need to do so because it is vital in the interests of the Chilean nation and the Chilean people. It would have been just the same had the copper mines been in the hands of investors or companies from Japan or the Soviet Union or France. We are doing this to develop our property for the benefit of our country. I simply cannot imagine that the United States government would make common cause with private enterprise on an issue like this and

frame policy accordingly. Unfortunately, history does teach that, on occasion in the past, this has been the case.

Interview, Santiago, March 23/
The New York Times, 3-28:(1)24.

I want to be a man of Chile. We are a small country, but we have national feelings, and we will never be at the service of any great power. Chile will never be a base for the U.S. nor China nor Russia, and that should be enough for you (the United States). Your problems are Russia and China. These are not my problems. My troubles are milk, bread and work.

Interview/Time, 4-19:26.

There are many differences between (Cuban Prime Minister Fidel) Castro and me, although we are friends. He took power by force of arms, and I won a free election. He has never had any elections, and Chile has just completed municipal elections. He has no political party, and I have been Socialist all my life. He spends money on armaments, and I do not. What is good for Cuba or for the Soviet Union or mainland (Communist) China is not necessarily what is good for Chile.

Interview, Santiago/
The Boston Globe, 6-13:28.

We are not taking over the American copper companies outright. We are paying for them. And we will pay them indemnities that we think are legitimate, according to our laws. And if they don't approve, they have the right to appeal to our courts of justice. It is all legal. And yet, if in spite of this legal nationalization we are denied international credits, great difficulties would be created for us. The only thing we want is that our principles be respected. I would just like it to be understood

(SALVADOR ALLENDE [GOSSENS])

that a country's dignity should not be measured by its per capita income.

Interview/Life, 7-16:40.

It is imperative to understand that in this country the President of the republic is the one who has the utmost power; and I exercise that power. When all is said and done, the one who resolves the problems about which there is no unanimity is me. And the one who gives the orders is me.

Interview/Life, 7-16:40.

It's all right for (Communist Chinese) Chairman Mao to call imperialism a paper tiger. He's got 600 million Chinese and he's a long way away. We're smaller and closer, and we know imperialism is tough.

Bogota, Colombia/
The New York Times, 9-2:3.

The government of Chile is not a Marxist government. Marxism—and any halfway intelligent man knows this . . . is one way of interpreting history. This is not a recipe or prescription for running the government. Furthermore, in my country there is a people's government, a people's national revolutionary government of which the Marxist parties are two and the non-Marxist parties are four . . . There is pluralism in the government, and this is why the Chilean phenomenon is important; because it is a government in which for the first time—and hear this well, and I would like to have the people of the United States understand this—both the believers and nonbelievers, Marxist and laymen, Christians—in short, seldom has a country demonstrated that it seeks its own road, its own path, in accordance with its history, its traditions and its customs; and further, a revolutionary government, because we are a revolutionary government. We have reached power through voting, through suffrage, and we are carrying out these changes and transformations within the legal channels established by a minority, which was in power, and we are going to transform these laws or revamp these laws within the channels which the Chilean Constitution allows us.

TV-radio interview/"Meet the Press,"
National Broadcasting Company,
Washington and Santiago, 10-31.

Miguel Aranguren
Deputy director of public information,
Organization of American States

. . . Latin America is not all hungry people covered with lice. It is emerging very fast and is getting ready to compete in the American market.

Washington, April 13/
The Washington Post, 4-14:(D)7.

Hugo Banzer (Suarez)
President of Bolivia

We are going to re-establish the principle of authority, of respect for the law. I am not interested in being liked by anyone—our ultimate objective is the happiness of the people.

News conference two days after seizing
power by revolt, La Paz, Aug. 24/
Los Angeles Times, 8-25:(1)19.

Leonid I. Brezhnev
General Secretary,
Communist Party of the Soviet Union

The victory of the popular-unity forces in Chile (the election of Marxist Salvador Allende to the Presidency in 1970) was a most important event. There, for the first time in the history of the continent, the people have secured, by constitutional means, the installation of a government they want and trust. This has incensed domestic reaction and Yankee imperialism, which seek to deprive the Chilean people of their gains. However, the people of Chile are fully determined to advance along their chosen path. The working people of other Latin American countries have come out in support of Chile's progressive line. The governments of Peru and Bolivia are fighting against enslavement of the U.S. monopolies.

At Soviet Communist Party Congress,
Moscow, March 30/
The New York Times, 3-31:14.

Over (the) years, the Central Committee (of the Soviet Communist Party) has devoted constant attention to strengthening cooperation with the Republic of Cuba and the Communist Party of Cuba. As a result of joint efforts, considerable successes have been achieved in developing Soviet-Cuban relations. The peoples of the Soviet Union and of Cuba are comrades in arms in a common struggle, and their friendship is firm.

At Soviet Communist Party Congress,
Moscow, March 30/
The New York Times, 3-31:14.

Fidel Castro (Ruz)
Premier of Cuba

Some Latin American governments have brought up in the Organization of American States their condemnation of the aggression against Cuba (the 1961 Bay of Pigs invasion). This is clearly Chile's position. Others have suggested that the (OAS) sanctions (against Cuba) be suspended. Sanctions against whom? Who, indeed, is under censure? Who should the sanctions be against? The Yankee imperialists and the puppet governments which were their accomplices in the aggression against Cuba! We may have been censured by that court of bandits, but morally we have never felt under censure. Morally, historically, *they* are the ones under censure and, naturally, we have no intention of lifting—nor can anyone lift—these moral and historic sanctions against the imperialists and their cohorts. That is our position . . . We do not have to account to the imperialists, nor to the OAS. We feel better outside than inside the OAS. We feel more honored, lighter, satisfied and freer outside the OAS. Furthermore, how are they going to allow us into the OAS when we say we are on the side of the revolutionary governments? How, when we say that the OAS is a filthy, rotten bilge with no honor? How, when we say that the OAS causes fits of

vomiting in our country—the name of the OAS, that is? Furthermore, we say publicly that we have supported, we still support and we shall continue to support the revolutionary movements of Latin America!

At 10th anniversary of the defeat
of the Bay of Pigs invasion, April 20/
The Washington Post, 4-28:(A)22.

We . . . reiterate that there is no rapprochement (between Cuba and the United States) and that there never will be one . . . This should be enough for the intriguers and gossip-mongers. We will not make the least concession to imperialists; we will not give up any of the revolutionary positions which our country has maintained until now.

Aug. 29/The New York Times, 9-5:(4)5.

The imperialists should remember that we have never pinned medals on any (airplane) hijackers (to Cuba). But to those encouraging illegality here, let them know we shall encourage illegality there.

Radio address, Havana, Sept. 28/
Los Angeles Times, 9-29:(1)6.

I'm not telling anyone to follow our methods. Our revolution solved problems that were particular to Cuba. Today we have eradicated gambling, prostitution, begging and illiteracy. Today in our country no child goes without shoes or without a chance to attend school. But we don't intend to prescribe solutions to any other country.

News conference, Iquique, Chile, Nov. 16/
The Washington Post, 11-17:(A)21.

There is a new state of consciousness in the world. Things are changing. Some day Cuba will get Guantanamo (the U.S. base in Cuba) back from the United States. We can't get them out now because they're stronger than we are. But the day will come. Cuba will have to fire only one shot, or maybe no shots, and they'll leave.

Punta Arenas, Chile, Nov. 22/
Los Angeles Times, 11-23:(1)5.

(FIDEL CASTRO [RUZ])

The United States government has sent hundreds of invasion groups to Cuba and dropped tons of arms into the island to support counter-revolutionary groups, which we have crushed. The others (Latin American countries) tried to blockade and ruin us. How can they accuse us of being interventionist? The day that interventions cease, Cuba is prepared to respect norms of international cooperation.

Santa Cruz, Chile, Nov. 25/
The New York Times, 11-26:13.

We are steadily losing ground in our struggle to create a true Marxist state (in Cuba). The innumerable problems and immense demands facing us are overwhelming. There is virtually no likelihood of improving our economy and social structure in the foreseeable future. We will be doing well if we merely hold our own.

Human Events, 11-27:10.

Brian Crozier
Director, Institute for the
Study of Conflict, London

In my view, Latin America is now one of the most dangerous spots of all—perhaps the most dangerous. Chile is emerging as the great subversive center in that region—even more important than Cuba, which lately has lost a lot of momentum as a center for subversion. The Communists in Chile, who are disciplined and loyal to Moscow, are working to a pre-ordained plan to take over. What we are witnessing is a new model for a Communist take-over. In 1948, we had the Prague model: the seizure of power under the protection of the Red Army. In 1949, we had the Peking model: the seizure of power after a civil war. What we have in Chile is the Santiago model: There is no Red Army present and there's been no civil war; but the Communists, a minority party who have never had more than 16 per cent of the popular vote—are following

280

a clear plan to take power, and they are moving very, very fast.

Interview, London/
U.S. News & World Report, 3-1:75.

Leon Dion
Professor of Political Science,
Laval University, Quebec, Canada

I see only one principle that would be capable not only of rallying the Canadians but also serving as a foundation stone for the political reality of the future; that is the principle of self-determination for Quebec, and for any other province that might want to invoke it. The solemn proclamation of the principle of self-determination would not signify, for Quebec, automatic separation from the rest of the country; probably that possibility cannot be excluded. Equally well, it could be that—all things considered and in view of the spirit that would not fail to make itself felt in the rest of the country—Quebec would decide by itself to remain, under certain conditions, within a renewed confederation. The proclamation of the principle of self-determination will require, nevertheless, a serious and systematic approach to radical reform of the conditions which hold the Quebecois in a condition of inferiority which they consider abrasive and intolerable. My diagnosis: The Canadian crisis has reached its most critical stage. Conditions can hardly become worse without causing the breakup of the confederation. Any remedy that attempts to soothe the sickness without truly attacking the causes would only poison the situation by increasing the disappointments and exasperations. That is why the proposed remedies must be radical.

Before Canadian Parliamentary Committee
on the Constitution, March 30/
The Washington Post, 4-18:(C)4.

Jean-Claude Duvalier
President of Haiti

People of Haiti, I am the heir to the political philosophy, the doctrine and the revolution which my father (the late Francois

Duvalier) incarnated as President-for-life . . . I have decided to continue his work with the same fierce energy and the same intransigence for the well-being and the future of our immortal fatherland. May God aid me in my high function.

Radio address upon assuming the Presidency, Port-au-Prince, April 22/ The Washington Post, 4-23:(A)20.

The United States was not always cognizant of the facts and did not always deal with Haiti on the basis of equality. But now, all dealings are on the basis of mutual respect. The United States will always find Haiti at its side in the struggle against Communism.

Before National Assembly, Port-au-Prince, April 29/ Los Angeles Herald-Examiner, 4-30:(A)13.

Luis Echeverria (Alvarez)
President of Mexico

(Relations with the United States) have continued with cordiality, which we hope will remain constant through an attitude of mutual fairness and respect. We do not try to ignore the difficulties that spring from the vast economic differences between our respective countries. But as in the past, we aspire only to preserve our political sovereignty and to develop our cultural personality over and above material gain or progress.

State of the Union address, Mexico City, Sept. 1/ Los Angeles Herald-Examiner, 9-1:(A)7.

Jorge Fernandez (Maldonado)
Minister of Energy and Mines of Peru

Nobody seems to want to believe us when we say we are neither capitalist nor Communist. We are building a new relationship between capital and labor, eliminating the traditional battle between the two, making capital recognize labor as human and putting the two together in cooperative enterprises.

Interview/The New York Times, 7-28:10.

Luis A. Ferre
Governor of Puerto Rico

It's important for us to get back into the mainstream of U.S. life . . . We want to be equal politically, but different culturally. We understand the mechanics of American democracy. That's the important thing.

Interview/ The Christian Science Monitor, 1-23:12.

I am revolutionary in my ideas. I am liberal in my objectives. And I am conservative in my methods.

Interview, San Juan/ The Dallas Times Herald, 1-29:(A)16.

When we succeed here, the United States succeeds in Latin America. If we fail and Cuba succeeds, then Russia succeeds in Latin America.

Interview, San Juan, March 13/ The New York Times, 3-15:22.

Luis Guillermo Ferrero (Tamayo)
Brigadier General and Chief of the War Staff, Venezuelan Army

Look at these volumes on military tactics. Worthless. Military men are sworn to defend their countries. Previously, that meant the protection of the fatherland's physical integrity and the established institutions. I say these books are worthless because the nature of our defense has changed. What army is going to invade us? And if established institutions are threatened anywhere in Latin America today, it is only by social, racial and economic disaster and chaos.

Interview, Caracas/ The New York Times, 1-25:51.

Jose Figueres (Ferrer)
President of Costa Rica

(Regarding his country's plan to renew diplomatic relations with the Soviet Union): This diplomatic recognition in no way shakes our loyalty to the United States or to the democratic cause. People everywhere are tired of

(JOSE FIGUERES [FERRER])

the cold war. Russia controls half of Europe; and we want to make the Russians drink coffee instead of tea.

Interview, Feb. 9/
The New York Times, 2-11:2.

Eduardo Frei (Montalva)
Former President of Chile

I have no doubt that the influence of Marxism, in one form or another, is important and growing (in Latin America). This influence is especially strong among intellectual groups, in the universities, in the cultural world of Latin America, in the communications media and among certain groups of skilled industrial workers. The problem of Communism and Marxism, I believe, is not one that can be resolved by force. It is part of an ideological war that is taking place in the minds of Latin Americans. My conviction is that the democratic way will definitely prevail, but with one condition: We cannot defeat Communism by talking of the need to preserve an old form of democracy that only paid lip service to human rights and social justice. In the ideological war with Communism-Marxism, there is only one road for governments in Latin America to take, in my opinion. That is to carry out, while there is still time, the fundamental reforms that will lead to effective economic and social development. And the people in each country must be allowed to play a real part in this transformation—not only in carrying it out but in the distribution of its benefits. It is not only a problem of economic development but also, and fundamentally, of social justice.

Interview/
U.S. News & World Report, 12-20:79.

Paul Hellyer
Former Minister of National Defense
of Canada

More and more, our government is moving in the direction of closer relations and working alliances with the Communist dictatorships.

U.S. News & World Report, 7-19:66.

John Holmes
Director general, Canadian Institute
of International Affairs

Our problem as Canadians is that we cannot pursue logical conclusions too far. Logic often seems to point in the direction of integration (with the United States); but integration is what we want to avoid.

U.S. News & World Report, 7-19:67.

John Irwin
Under Secretary of State
of the United States

In suspending military sales to Ecuador, the United States has in no way adopted coercive measures designed to force the sovereign will of Ecuador and to obtain advantages from it of any kind. The facts show that it is Ecuador which had used economic coercion and force in seizing (American) fishing boats and fining them, thus seeking unilaterally to enforce its claims to territorial seas.

Jan. 30/The Washington Post, 1-31:(A)21.

Jacob K. Javits
United States Senator, R–N.Y.

The role of private foreign investment in Latin America is one of the most pressing questions of the day, and one that must move toward resolution. It is a primary area where the lack of a logical, coherent policy works to the detriment of Latin American growth objectives . . . As is well known, uncertainty is anathema to private capital flows—be these flows to the New York Stock Exchange or to productive investments in Latin America. The figures on private investment in Latin America are beginning to reflect this uncertainty . . . I would suggest that it would be of mutual interest to Latin America and the United States to convene a high-level meeting that would look toward the evolution of a continent-wide foreign investment policy which must safeguard, of course, the sovereign rights of each country.

Mexico City, April 4/
The Washington Post, 4-14:(A)14.

Edward M. Kennedy
United States Senator, D–Mass.

(The buildup of Soviet forces in the Western Hemisphere) culminating in the Cuban missile crisis . . . and (Cuban Premier) Fidel Castro's call for revolution were the reasons why the United States took a policy of isolation toward Cuba. Yet the times have changed . . . There is no longer a Soviet strategic danger on Cuba which can excuse our current policies toward that nation.

Before Chicago Council on Foreign Relations, Oct. 12/
The Dallas Times Herald, 10-13:(A)18.

For 2½ years, this (Nixon) Administration has treated the other nations of this hemisphere with neglect—neglect more malign than benign. It has adopted a policy devoid of rhetoric and a policy devoid of substance as well.

Before Chicago Council on Foreign Relations, Oct. 12/
San Francisco Examiner, 10-13:12.

Melvin R. Laird
Secretary of Defense of the United States

We have a clear preference for free and democratic processes, but we deal with governments as they are . . . I think it is important for us to bear in mind that the military is the only cohesive group in many of the countries of Latin America and that they are very important. No part of the U.S. training given Latin American officers is in any way related to overthrow of governments, but on the contrary is aimed at maintaining internal security and stability in order that economic progress can be achieved.

Before House Appropriations Committee, Washington, March/
The Dallas Times Herald, 9-7:(A)2.

Orlando Letelier
Chilean Ambassador to the United States

I know the Americans are openminded and have no prejudices against Chile. There are no real problems between our countries. (Abraham) Lincoln once said that a nation cannot live half slave and half free. Well, we say a country cannot go on in which the few have a great deal and the many have nothing.

Washington, Feb. 15/
The Washington Post, 2-26:(A)22.

There is no anti-Americanism in Chile. It simply doesn't exist . . . Chile has had important commercial and financial relations with the United States, and it doesn't want them closed . . . What Chile wants is to open a dialogue with the United States and with all the world.

Washington, Feb. 15/
The Washington Post, 2-26:(A)22.

Roberto Marcelo Levingston
President of Argentina

The past illusion that only international generosity and foreign ideas could solve Latin America's problems has proved just that—an illusion. For one thing, the external aid has been insufficient. We must not only look to our own resources, but continue the fight against foreign subversive ideologies.

Before Inter-American Development Bank members, Buenos Aires, March 1/
The New York Times, 3-2:15.

Kari Levitt
Economist, McGill University, Montreal

The problem with Canada in some ways is just that we've been too blasted rich. We have a pile of resources, and we have the sort of sense that we can always sell them off to make a fast buck. But if a country is serious about insuring for its future viability and its future prosperity, you just don't sell off everything for a fast buck. And I think this has been the mentality of Canadian business and Canadian government. Canadian business sells out anything for a fast dollar; and Canadian government really (is) not too much different.

Interview/The New York Times, 2-7:(3)14.

Eugene J. McCarthy
Former United States Senator, D–Minn.

It seems to me quite evident that we

(EUGENE J. McCARTHY)

haven't gained anything over the past 10 years by not moving to recognize (Communist) China. We're finally moving in that direction now. It seems to me that no good has been served by our pretending that Cuba isn't there, at least for the past five years. I see it as a country to which we ought to make a decision—not so much because of the importance of Cuba itself, but it would indicate a mature and responsible approach to general international problems.

Television interview, Miami/
San Francisco Examiner, 12-27:8.

Robert J. McCloskey
Special Assistant to the Secretary
of State of the United States

In clear violation of international law, the Cuban government in the last two weeks has attacked and seized two unarmed vessels in the Caribbean. In one case, the captain of the vessel was an American citizen who was wounded in the attack and who is at present unlawfully detained in Cuba. (The U.S.) considers these attacks upon commercial vessels, and the statement that Cuba intends to continue such attacks, to constitute a clear and present threat to the freedom of navigation and international commerce in the Caribbean and a threat to American citizens. Such threats are intolerable.

Dec. 17/
Los Angeles Herald-Examiner, 12-18:(A)2.

Emilio G. Medici
President of Brazil

I have taken the people's word, expressed at the polls, as approval by Brazilians of the direction, in all sectors, that is guiding the third government of the revolution. I do not see, thus, any reason for even thinking of changing, either in the administrative or the political sphere, the lines along which the nation is being led. I consider that any change in course would gravely compromise the atmosphere of peace and tranquility that Brazil needs to sustain the rhythm of progress that

now distinguishes her.

Brasilia, Feb. 1/
The New York Times, 2-5:2.

Charles A. Meyer
Assistant Secretary for Inter-American
Affairs, Department of State
of the United States

I can see very little reason for us to seek to change our Cuban policy, particularly since (Cuban Premier) Fidel Castro clearly knows that all he has to do to wipe the slate clean is say, "I will no longer export revolution."

The Dallas Times Herald, 8-8:(A)34.

The United States is dedicated to bringing about a new equilibrium in our relations with Latin America by loosening our long-held paternal grip on the other nations of the hemisphere. Tutelary leadership would be—and has been—replaced by a balanced relationship, including discreet leadership, that respects the sovereign rights of our Latin American partners. This policy is confirmed by our continuing support of Latin America's drive for economic and social development—but increasingly only in response to Latin America's initiatives.

Before Inter-American Press Association,
Chicago, Oct. 25/Vital Speeches, 12-1:109.

Richard M. Nixon
President of the United States

. . . what happened in Chile (election of a Marxist President) is not something that we welcomed, although . . . we were very careful to point out that that was the decision of the people of Chile and that, therefore, we accepted that decision and that our programs with Chile—we still recognize the government; we still have our People-to-People program; we still have our Peace Corps program—those programs would continue as long as Chile's foreign policy was not antagonistic to our interests . . . We can only say that, for the United States to have intervened, intervened in a free election, and to have turned it around, I think would have had repercussions all over Latin America that would have been far worse than what has happened in Chile.

And I would say, finally, just as I've told the Chilean Ambassador when he paid his farewell call on me, I told him to tell the new President (Salvador Allende) that, as far as the United States was concerned, we recognized the right of any country to have internal policies and an internal government different from what we might approve of. What we were interested in was their policy toward us in the foreign policy field. So, I haven't given up on Chile or on the Chilean people, and we're going to keep our contact with them.

Television interview, Washington, Jan. 4/
The New York Times, 1-6:42.

President (John F.) Kennedy worked out an understanding in 1962 that the Russians would not put any offensive missiles into Cuba. That understanding was expanded on October 11 (1970) by the Russians when they said it would include a military base in Cuba and a military naval base. They, in effect, said that they would not put a military naval base into Cuba on October the 11th. Now, in the event that nuclear submarines were serviced either in Cuba or from Cuba, that would be a violation of the understanding. That has not happened yet. We are watching the situation closely. The Soviet Union is aware of the fact that we are watching closely. We expect them to abide by the understanding. I believe they will. I don't believe that they want a crisis in the Caribbean, and I don't believe that one is going to occur—particularly since the understanding has been clearly laid out and has been so clearly relied on by us . . .

Television interview, Washington,
Jan. 4/The New York Times, 1-6:42.

He's (Cuban Prime Minister Fidel Castro) exporting revolution all over the hemisphere . . . As long as Castro is adopting an antagonistic, anti-American line, we are certainly not going to normalize our relations with Castro. As soon as he changes his line toward us, we might consider it. But it's his move.

Radio interview/
The National Observer, 4-26:7.

Misael Pastrana (Borrero)
President of Colombia

The greatest failure (in Colombia) is in the field of trade—and above all in coffee, our principal export. What we receive from (the United States) in aid—loans, which, although on favorable terms, must be repaid—we often lose in a single year by falling prices and deteriorating exchange rates. It would be helpful if Washington took Latin-American policy out of the basement, to which it has again been relegated, and moved it to the ground floor.

Interview, Bogota/
The New York Times, 3-24:39.

I believe that Latin America cannot continue mistaking the similarity of governments for a basic unity of the peoples behind them. A continent that should have been very cohesive on account of its identities of languages, and of races, of traditions and of the styles of life, has been one of the most disintegrated of continents, because its countries have been moved by the caprices of ideological rivalries.

Interview, Bogota/
The New York Times, 9-6:2.

Thomas M. Pelly
United States Representative, R—Wash.

(Regarding the seizure of American fishing boats): No wonder these small Latin American countries take such brazen action against United States fishermen. It is a profitable business for them to kidnap Americans off the high seas when they know the United States (State) Department won't enforce the laws passed by Congress.

The New York Times, 1-20:10.

Galo Plaza (Lasso)
Secretary-General,
Organization of American States

(Latin American countries) are becoming increasingly disillusioned in their relations with the wealthy industrial countries, and particularly with the United States. (This is attributable to) the declining flow of financial cooperation, lending conditions that are adding greatly to the external debt, restrictions on market expansion and difficulties in utilizing techno-

(GALO PLAZA [LASSO])

logy from the advanced countries. What is called for is large-scale multilateral financial cooperation from the community of developed countries, together with a trade policy that encourages development.

Before General Assembly of Organization of American States, San Jose, Costa Rica, April 14/The New York Times, 4-15:15.

Stanley J. Randall
Minister of Trade and Development,
Province of Ontario, Canada

Even my detractors would find it hard to deny that just 10 years ago conventional wisdom held that Canada was an underdeveloped country . . . that foreign capital was needed to supplement domestic savings for economic growth . . . and that the potential political implications were not serious, because the major lender was the U.S., our friendly cousins to the south. Today, the conventional wisdom preached by some economic nationalists holds that the U.S. is a racist and imperialist nation bent on subverting Canada by controlling its economy . . . that U.S. corporations are being used as the instruments of U.S. imperialism . . . and that Canada is a developed country that doesn't need foreign capital. The economic nationalists would have us swallow their new-found conventional wisdom; but it keeps going down the wrong way! Their instant wisdom proves they're never too old to learn new mistakes. It also demonstrates that the shortest distance between two points is going from the real to the ridiculous.

Before Rotary Club, Toronto/
The Wall Street Journal, 4-5:12.

Pedro E. Real
Argentine Ambassador to the United States

The United States has a deep world commitment. Many problems call for the presence of the United States in various continents. Those problems are subjected to an order of priorities based on a selective criteria which the United States applies in accordance with

its own interests. It is evident that the subject "Latin America" does not attract the interest of the mass media, government and Congress (of the United States). What we ask of the United States is to determine, once and for all, the place assigned to Latin America on its foreign policy priority scale.

The Dallas Times Herald, 2-28:(A)4.

William P. Rogers
Secretary of State of the United States

Let me state categorically (that) the commitment of the United States to assistance for Latin America is undiminished. Our reorganization of foreign assistance, far from lessening that commitment, is intended to make it possible for us to fulfill it more effectively.

Before General Assembly, Organization of American States, San Jose, Costa Rica, April 15/
The Christian Science Monitor, 4-19:8.

Mitchell Sharp
Secretary of State
for External Affairs of Canada

(Regarding United States President Nixon's institution of a 10% surtax on foreign imports): . . . we in Canada are asking some pretty fundamental questions about the future. We have proceeded in the postwar period on the assumption of freer trade and stable trading relationships between Canada and the United States, relationships which have been profitable to both countries. The announcement of August 15 could not help but shake that assumption, and as a government responsible for the security and prosperity of more than 20 million Canadians, we have to look at the alternatives.

New York, Sept. 21/
The Washington Post, 10-24:(C)6.

It is childish and, I suggest, very immature to suggest the tentative and the positive Canadian moves toward better and more rewarding relations with (Communist) China, the Soviet Union and other Communist nations are an act of defiance toward the United States.

The Wall Street Journal, 11-12:10.

Omar Torrijos (Herrera)
Head of Government of Panama

We receive $1.9 million every year from the United States for the 500 square miles (of the Panama Canal Zone), when the Empire State Building brings in $13 million a year in rentals. This shows how mean the United States is to us.

> *At rally celebrating his third year in office, Panama, Oct. 11/*
> *Los Angeles Herald-Examiner, 10-12:(A)4.*

Pierre Elliott Trudeau
Prime Minister of Canada

Canada is not only a close friend and neighbor of the United States of America, but also an ally in NATO and NORAD. But Canada has found it increasingly important to diversify its channels of communications because of the overpowering presence of the United States of America. This is reflected in the growing consciousness among Canadians of a danger to our national identity.

> *News conference after signing friendship pact with Soviet Union, Moscow, May 20/*
> *The New York Times, 5-21:3.*

Americans are not only our neighbors and allies, but they are even our friends.

> *Addressing Soviet Communist Party leader Leonid Brezhnev, Moscow/*
> *Plainview (Tex.) Daily Herald, 6-24:(A)8.*

. . . (if) it becomes apparent that they (the U.S.) just want us to be sellers of natural resources to them and buyers of their manufactured products, we will have to reassess fundamentally our relations with them—trading, political and otherwise . . . We have a whole gamut of choices, from integration with the U.S. to total war with the U.S., and everything in between.

> *Interview, Sept. 23/*
> *U.S. News & World Report, 10-25:59.*

(Concerning the United States' economic and trade policies toward Canada): I am absolutely certain that the Americans don't want to create instability and unrest in Canada deliberately. I am absolutely certain that they don't want to have on their northern border an unfriendly hostile people. No. (But) they may achieve that result through clumsiness or through lack of our explaining to them what is happening.

> *Interview/*
> *The Christian Science Monitor, 11-4:2.*

Juan Velasco (Alvarado)
President of Peru

The social order we are building will be based on the overall concept of participatory democracy. That means a democracy in which freely-organized men take part in all spheres of decision and exercise directly, or with a minimum of intermediaries, all forms of power—economic, social and political.

> *State of the Nation address, Lima, July 28/The New York Times, 7-29:4.*

Our revolution is aimed at breaking the capitalist yoke; it doesn't want to be subjected to the imperialist boss. And on the other hand, it doesn't want to be subjected to the Communist yoke either. This does not mean that it is the enemy either of capitalism or of Communism, but rather that Peru doesn't want to be subjected to any regime of domination. The Peruvian revolution wants to bring about a society in which men and women live in liberty, in justice and with full and free participation in the important decisions that affect them.

> *News conference, Lima/*
> *The Christian Science Monitor, 11-30:7.*

Asia and the Pacific

Spiro T. Agnew
Vice President of the United States

(South) Korea's inspiring progress in every area of political, economic and social life is a source of pride to all men who value freedom. Much of the credit for this progress, and for Korea's emergence as a vital force in international affairs, belongs to President Park (Chung Hee).

Seoul, June 29/
The Dallas Times Herald, 6-29:(A)3.

I was 100 per cent in favor of the initiative (Communist China's inviting a U.S. table-tennis team to visit China) then, and of course still am. But I am distressed with the euphoria with which the initiative was received. There was an immediate assumption that this meant an end to all tensions between the United States and mainland China and a resolution of all our ideological difficulties. This, of course, is not realistic. We've got a long way to go. But at least we've made a step toward discussing these matters. I don't think we should become so optimistic (about President Nixon's planned trip to Communist China) that people would feel that in case these discussions don't bring about an immediate resolution of all difficulties, they should be discouraged.

Interview/The Washington Post, 8-7:(A)3.

Kiichi Aichi
Foreign Minister of Japan

As long as the determination of our country to remain a peaceful country is firm, and as long as the United States' determination to stand by its security commitments abroad is clear, a situation such as a power vacuum will never occur in Asia; and, therefore, there should be no necessity for our country to acquire an excessive military capability.

Before Foreign Correspondents Club, Tokyo,
Jan. 20/Los Angeles Times, 1-21:(1)7.

The situation in Asia seems to be undergoing a change for the better, and it appears that the external posture of the People's Republic of (Communist) China, as part of this favorable trend, has become more moderate.

At United Nations, New York, Oct. 19/
Los Angeles Times, 10-20:(1)4.

Carl Albert
United States Representative, D–Okla.

We hope there can be a lessening of tension everywhere in the world during this decade. Particularly is it the earnest wish of my country that this be so on the Korean peninsula. We trust that the recent reductions in our force levels in Korea will be a step in this direction. But we have no illusions about the difficulties which stand in the way. We are well aware of the hostile nature of the forces on the other side of the demilitarized zone.

Before National Assembly, Seoul, Aug. 10/
The Washington Post, 8-11:(A)4.

We have learned to live in a world in which the nuclear stand-off between ourselves and Russia has created not a reign of terror but rather a strange sort of stability. The same could be true with (Communist) China. We must look behind the revolutionary rhetoric to determine what this backward nation's real needs are. And I predict—or at least I hope—that this evident eagerness to join the world organization (United Nations) foreshadows that it will be a considerably less belligerent member than expected.

Before American Petroleum Institute,
San Francisco, Nov. 15/
The New York Times, 11-16:76.

Sirimavo Bandaranaike
Prime Minister of Ceylon

(Regarding the revolutionary terrorism in Ceylon): My government will fight these terrorists in the remote areas, will fight them in the provinces and will fight them everywhere—but (I) will not surrender my right to govern.

San Francisco Examiner & Chronicle
(This World), 4-18:16.

Robert W. Barnett
Director, Washington Center of the Asia Society

(Nationalist Chinese President) Chiang Kai-shek lives among people who have mixed and conflicting views about the future of Taiwan (Nationalist China). Madame Chiang, for example, speaks year after year about return to the mainland as a practical prospect, with what happens to be total sincerity. The leadership of the Formosan independence movement, largely underground in Taiwan but quite articulate in places like Tokyo, Hong Kong, New York, San Francisco and St. Louis, rejects the notion of "homeland" at all. Senior officers in Chiang's military establishment will embroider plans for defending Taiwan with preparations of targets of opportunity on their "homeland." However, the rank and file of Chiang's military establishment is now largely Taiwan-born, and for them such operations would be an invasion of a foreign country. These particular anomalies in mainland-Taiwanese attitudes are largely absent in the community of businessmen and bureaucrats, industrialists and farmers who, collectively, have been responsible for the so-called Taiwan success story.

St. Louis/The Washington Post, 4-25:(B)2.

David Ben-Gurion
Former Prime Minister of Israel

Several years ago, the last Russian Ambassador to Israel said to me, "(Communist) China is the greatest danger to the world." I know what he meant. Russia fears China. A professor at the Hebrew University was invited to Communist China, and he came back and told me he had never seen such an able, capable people as the Chinese. Their main aim is to catch up with Russia. It was a great mistake for the United States not to recognize them and keep them out of the United Nations . . . We recognized Communist China in 1950 but . . . we could not follow through. There was American pressure on us against it.

Interview, Tel Aviv/
The Christian Science Monitor, 2-22:2.

Zulifikar Ali Bhutto
Former Foreign Minister of Pakistan

(Regarding the conflict between East and West Pakistan): Naturally, we would like to see a political solution to the problem facing Pakistan. We made every effort to find a political solution, and once the situation comes under control, I am certain that the threads will be picked up and renewed efforts will be made to arrive at a political settlement—for only a political settlement can be a lasting settlement. The present crisis is a legacy of past blunders. We must willingly give the people of East Pakistan their legitimate rights.

News conference, Karachi, April 14/
The New York Times, 4-15:4.

Zulfikar Ali Bhutto
Foreign Minister of Pakistan

(Addressing the UN Security Council on its inability to settle the India-Pakistan conflict): Mr. President, I am not a rat. I've never ratted in my life. I have faced assassination attempts, I've faced imprisonment . . . Today I am not ratting, but I am leaving your Security Council. I find it disgraceful to my person and to my country to remain here a moment longer . . . Impose any decision, have a treaty worse than Versailles, legalize aggression, legalize occupation . . . I will not be a party to it. We will fight . . . My country harkens to me. Why should I waste my time here, in the Security Council? I will not be a party to the ignominious surrender of part of my country. You can take your Security Council—here you are. I am going.

At United Nations, New York, Dec. 15/
San Francisco Chronicle, 12-16:1.

Pakistan is one single thing. The nation's unity must be safeguarded. India has forcefully occupied Pakistani territories (East Pakistan), and a lasting peace cannot be achieved if New Delhi fails to give back what it conquered with its tanks. We do not want to be involved in a war every five or ten years.

News conference, Rome, Dec. 19/
The Dallas Times Herald, 12-20:(A)1.

Zulfikar Ali Bhutto
President of Pakistan

(Concerning the loss of East Pakistan during the recent India-Pakistan war): We will fight and continue to fight for the integrity of Pakistan. We will take revenge so as to undo the temporary humiliation.

Radio broadcast, Dec. 20/
Los Angeles Herald-Examiner, 12-20:(A)1.

(Concerning his country's recent conflict with India and the resultant loss of East Pakistan): Now, as in 1947 (when Pakistan was carved from India), we are engaged in a concerted struggle for preservation of our national identity. Now, as then, we find ourselves pitted against powerful forces which seek to destroy us as a nation.

The Washington Post, 12-26:(A)1.

Leonid I. Brezhnev
General Secretary,
Communist Party of the Soviet Union

. . . our Party and the Soviet government are deeply convinced that an improvement of relations between the Soviet Union and the People's Republic of (Communist) China would be in line with the fundamental long-term interests of both countries, the interests of socialism, the freedom of the peoples and stronger peace. That is why we are prepared in every way to help not only to normalize relations but also to restore neighborliness and friendship between the Soviet Union and the People's Republic of China. And we express the confidence that this will eventually be achieved.

At Soviet Communist Party Congress,
Moscow, March 30/
The New York Times, 3-31:14.

James L. Buckley
United States Senator, C–N.Y.

(Regarding President Nixon's announced plans to visit Communist China): I am deeply concerned over the implications which the President's extraordinary announcement will have both here and abroad. At home, it will inevitably strengthen the hands of those seeking accommodations with the Communist world at almost any price; and in Asia, the grand scale of this overture to Peking will be anything but reassuring to those who have to live with the aggressive reality of mainland China. We have no knowledge, of course, as to what may be the President's real objectives and motivations in this extraordinary move; but until we can be satisfied that there are overriding benefits to the free world to be gained from the proposed meeting in Peking, we can only judge the announcement by its probable effects on the morale of those countries which have had to rely for their security on the steadfastness of America's commitment to her alliances. Given the growing pressures at home for a disengagement from the world, this seems hardly an appropriate time for the President of the United States to add to the doubts of our friends.

Human Events, 7-24:3.

William F. Buckley, Jr.
Political columnist; Editor, "National Review"

. . . we must cherish Taiwan (Nationalist China), which is the West Berlin of China. It was to that island that a tired, bedraggled, dispirited group of refugees, under the leadership of a man already old but of flinty spirit, fled from a shipwrecked nation and addressed themselves to the enterprise of bringing order and a measure of freedom to fifteen million people. We in America helped them. Nowhere was our help more productive. In twenty years, they contrived a standard of living second only, in Asia, to Japan's. They did this while nourishing the culture of their ancestors, adapting it, stressing those qualities in it of patience and fortitude, of stoicism and resignation, of emphasis on the spirit, which have given Taiwan that special presence which will survive (President) Chiang Kai-shek. That small country is abloom with promise. We are bound to it by a treaty which the gates of the United Nations shall not prevail against. It is a far cry from becoming the capital province of all China. But it is the respository of the hopes and dreams of those Chinese in whose breast lingers the seed of resistance to the furies of Maoism—which is

290

to say, in every Chinese, because it is given to man, without exception, to be attracted to that which distinguishes him from other species; to love and compassion, to idealism, to freedom and dignity.

> At China Conference, New York, Oct. 29/
> National Review, 11-19:1318.

Leslie Bury
Foreign Minister of Australia

To those of us who are more nearly (Communist) China's neighbors, there is as yet little to inspire confidence that Peking has in fact abandoned those policies which have prevented her from being regarded as a responsible member of the family of nations and, even more so, as a friendly neighboring country.

> Before Southeast Asia Treaty
> Organization, London, April 27/
> The Washington Post, 4-28:(A)1.

(Arguing against United States President Nixon's planned visit to Communist China): I hate to see the far-reaching interests of Australia and our friends and allies to the near north dragged by the chariot wheels of American political processes and perhaps scattered by an overall deal between two men (Nixon and Chinese Premier Chou En-lai) who may not even be aware of them. It is deplorable, indeed, when foreign policy, which runs to the very root of national security, is allowed to become the plaything of party politics.

> At Liberal Party seminar, Melbourne, Aug. 1/
> The Washington Post, 8-2:(A)16.

Ely R. Callaway, Jr.
President, Burlington Industries

I cannot think of any major industry in America that is not subject to great invasion or attack by the Japanese. The problem is that the Japanese system is the most effective monopoly that has ever been developed in the economic history of the world. The Japanese will do whatever they need to do to take over whatever part of the richest markets in the world that they want to take.

> Panel discussion/Time, 5-10:91.

Lord Caradon
Former British Ambassador
to the United Nations

(Regarding United States President Nixon's announced plans to visit Communist China): This is a turning point in world history. I cannot remember anything in my lifetime more exciting or more encouraging.

> Time, 7-26:11.

Lord Carrington
Defense Secretary of the United Kingdom

This (Russian) naval power has recently been extending to the Indian Ocean, where five years ago there were no Soviet vessels at all. We rely on our shipping lanes across the Indian Ocean and can only watch this expansion with growing concern . . . To allow their presence to go completely unmarked would give them material as well as strategic benefit.

> Before House of Lords, London, Feb. 24/
> Los Angeles Herald-Examiner, 2-25:(A)4.

Theodore H. E. Chen
Director, East Asian Studies Center,
University of Southern California

People under the Nationalist (Chinese) government are enjoying a better life, higher standards of living and more conveniences than ever before. In the past two decades, Taiwan has gained considerably in stability and has made tremendous advances in economic and material reconstruction . . . Taiwan has made this outstanding progress on their own, not under Communism. Anyone would be impressed with the evidence of progress in every direction, the stability under the Nationalist government. We must, by all means, preserve the stability and progress that is underway in Taiwan today.

> Interview, Los Angeles/
> Los Angeles Herald-Examiner, 1-24:(B)8.

Chiang Kai-shek
President of Nationalist China

Due to the perpetuation of the Chinese culture, I have full confidence that the Chinese mainland shall be and will be recovered

(CHIANG KAI-SHEK)

(from the Communists). My confidence has nevered waivered a bit.

Television interview/"60 Minutes,"
Columbia Broadcasting System, 4-27.

The greatness of our nation is not to be measured by the attitudes of other nations but by whether we respect ourselves enough, and by our spirit to struggle to rise again through adversity and difficulty.

Annual National Day message,
Taipei, Oct. 9/
The New York Times, 10-10:(1)10.

We shall never coexist with the traitorous Maoists (of Communist China). There are rumors abroad of secret contacts between us and the enemy. The only contacts between us and the enemy are those of blood and steel in the operations in front of and behind the enemy's lines. Our compatriots, military and civilian alike, will never be deceived by such rumors. Patriotic movements toward unification of the Chinese people can only be achieved through our national revolution, which is aimed at the recovery of the mainland, the termination of tyranny and the restoration of human rights to our people.

New Year's Day message, Taipei, Dec. 31/
Los Angeles Herald-Examiner, 1-1('72):(A)4.

Chiao Kuan-hua
Deputy Foreign Minister of the People's
Republic of (Communist) China

The Chinese people are determined to liberate Taiwan (Nationalist China), and no force on earth can stop us from doing so.

At United Nations, New York, Nov. 15/
Los Angeles Times, 11-16:(1)8.

To date, Korea still remains divided. The Chinese People's volunteers have long since withdrawn from Korea, but up to now the U.S. troops still remain in South Korea. The peaceful unification of their fatherland is the common aspiration of the entire Korean people. The Chinese government and people firmly support the eight-point program for the peaceful unification of the fatherland put forward by the Democratic People's Republic of (North) Korea in April this year, and firmly support its just demand that all the illegal resolutions adopted by the United Nations on the Korean question be annulled and the United Nations Commission for the Unification and Rehabilitation of Korea be dissolved.

At United Nations, New York, Nov. 15/
The New York Times, 11-16:16.

The superpowers want to be superior to others and lord it over others. At no time, neither today nor ever in the future, will China be a superpower, subjecting others to its aggression, subversion, control, interference or bullying.

At United Nations, New York, Nov. 15/
The New York Times, 11-16:16.

Chou En-lai
Premier of the People's Republic
of (Communist) China

Even the United States finally has come to refer to the "People's Republic of China" by its proper name.

Before Japanese trade delegation,
Peking/The New York Times, 3-10:2.

As for (U.S.) President Nixon, he has made several gestures (toward China). He says he wants to go to China and wants his daughter to come to China on her honeymoon . . . isn't that something in the air? . . . It cannot be said there has been a thaw between the governments of China and the United States. It should be said that exchanges between the people of the United States and China have been renewed.

Interview, Peking/
San Francisco Examiner, 5-21:7.

(Communist China is) a weak, underdeveloped nation with no ambitions, now or in the future, to be an expansionist superpower.

Interview/The Washington Post, 5-27:(A)1.

(Nationalist Chinese President) Chiang Kai-shek is opposed to the so-called two Chinas and is also opposed to one China and one independent Taiwan. In the past, we have been allied with Chiang Kai-shek, and we became hostile to him. But on this question, we have our common point. There can be only one China . . .

Peking, June 21/
The New York Times, 6-23:2.

My personal views are: First, China is big in territory and population, but not in terms of real strength; second, we are still in the experimental stage in the field of nuclear weapons, so we aren't a big nuclear power; third, each time we conduct tests we issue a statement that we will at no time and under no circumstances be the first to use nuclear weapons—never; fourth, we believe all countries, regardless of size, should get together and discuss and solve the problem of complete prohibition and destruction of all nuclear weapons. Why, then, do we test these weapons? Precisely to break down the nuclear monopoly and nuclear blackmail and bring about a solution to this problem.

Peking, June 21/
The Washington Post, 6-26:(A)16.

If Taiwan (Nationalist China) returns to the motherland, then its people would be making a contribution to the motherland for which we should give them a reward. Far from exacting revenge on them, we will reward them.

Peking, June 21/
The New York Times, 6-23:2.

It is . . . a correct proposition that the people of all countries should be allowed to solve their problems themselves, and foreign interference should not be permitted. That is why we are in favor of the withdrawal of all United States forces, first of all from the Far East and then from all those places where they committed aggression—South Korea, Japan, China's Taiwan province, the Philippines, the three countries of Indochina, Thailand and so on. Of course, when we say that, we do not mean to limit it only to American forces, but all foreign forces.

Peking, July 5/
Los Angeles Times, 7-7:(1)2.

What are the obstructions in the improvement of the relations between China and the United States? The first point, that is if state relations are to be established with China, then it must be recognized that the government of the People's Republic of China is the sole legitimate government representing the Chinese people. Second, Taiwan is a province of China, and it is an inalienable part of China's territory . . . Third, the so-called theory that the status of Taiwan is yet unsettled, which is the theory that is going about—some people in the world are spreading it—is absurd . . . Fourth point: We oppose any advocacy of a two-China policy, a one-China-one-Taiwan policy, or any similar policy. And if such a situation continues in the United Nations, we will not go there. Fifth point: We are resolutely opposed to the so-called Taiwan Independence Movement, because the people in Taiwan are Chinese . . . The sixth point: The United States should withdraw all of their present military strength and military installations from Taiwan and the Taiwan Straits; and the defense treaty, which was concluded between the United States and Chiang Kai-shek in 1954 about the so-called Defense of Taiwan and Penghu, is illegal and null and void, and the Chinese people do not recognize that treaty. This is our stand; and we stick to our stand. And our stand has not changed from the beginning of the ambassadorial talks between China and the United States that began on the first of August, 1955, first in Geneva and later on in Warsaw. They began after the Bandung Conference. And our stand has not changed from that time up to the present time. And it shall not change.

Peking, July 19/
U.S. News & World Report, 8-9:22.

(Regarding United States President Nixon's announced plans to visit Communist China): China is a country which was blockaded by the United States for more than 20 years.

(CHOU EN-LAI)

Now, since there is a desire to come and look at China, it's all right. And since there is a desire to talk, we are also ready to talk. Of course, it goes without saying that the positions of our two sides are different. And there are a lot of differences between our points of view. To achieve relaxation, there must be a common desire for it; so various questions must be studied, and all these questions may be placed on the table for discussion. We do not expect a settlement of all questions at one stroke. That is not possible. That would not be practicable. But by contacting each other, we may be able to find out from where we should start in solving these questions.

Interview, Peking, Aug. 5/
The New York Times, 8-10:15.

As for us, we do not like armed struggle and we do not provoke others. Not only have we not come to Long Island, we have not gone to Honolulu. Even with the U.S. Navy in the Taiwan Strait, we are for negotiations.

Peking, Oct. 5/
San Francisco Examiner, 10-6:8.

(Regarding United States President Nixon's planned visit to Peking): For us, it is all right if the talks succeed, and it is all right if they fail.

Peking, Oct. 5/
Los Angeles Times, 10-7:(1)8.

(For his country and Japan to have diplomatic relations) it is necessary for the Japanese government to outline a clear-cut attitude on the Taiwan question. The Japanese government must confirm that the People's Republic of (Communist) China is the sole legitimate government of China, that Taiwan is an integral part of the sacred territory of the People's Republic of China and that the Japan-Taiwan treaty is illegal and must be abrogated without fail.

Interview, Peking, Oct. 28/
Los Angeles Herald-Examiner, 11-10:(A)4.

Chow Shu-kai
Nationalist Chinese Ambassador
to the United States

There is a wide gap between Washington and Taiwan on the assessment of the mainland (Communist China) situation. We violently disagree that the mainland has achieved stability and is a unified entity. From our point of view, the situation on the mainland is still obscure and fluid.

The Dallas Times Herald, 2-28:(A)4.

(Regarding current U.S. overtures for better relations with Communist China): I hope the American people will not be fooled by the Communists' psychological warfare. And I hope the steps the United States has taken do not represent a drastic change in policy . . . The purpose (of the Communist Chinese invitation to the U.S. table tennis team to play in China) is to create the illusion that they are moderate and reasonable. But it is all propaganda, and I hope the American people will have better wisdom and judgment than to be fooled by it.

Interview, Washington, April 12/
The New York Times, 4-13:1.

Chow Shu-kai
Foreign Minister of Nationalist China

(Regarding Communist Chinese overtures for better relations with the United States): If we keep cool, if the U.S. and everybody else keeps cool, it will blow away like the many typhoons that sweep over Taiwan each year.

Quote, 8-29:194.

Below the surface of seeming docility (of the people in Communist China), there is a boiling and ultimately irrepressible mass of resentments and suicidal despairs. No one should give them up as irretrievably lost to the Mao regime. Despite a Communist news blackout, bloody anti-Communist and anti-Maoist uprisings are still going on in many parts of the mainland. The Chinese Communist Party, whose total membership represents only about 2 per cent of the population, is torn by dissension and factional strife (and) faces an uncertain future. Obviously, something must be basically wrong with the Chinese Communist Party. It seems that the cancer of fear is gnawing at its vitals.

At United Nations, New York, Oct. 8/
The New York Times, 10-9:10.

There is nothing to suggest that the Chinese Communist regime is ready to give up its policy of world domination. It continues to promote violence and war. It continues to make a fetish of force. It continues to foment armed insurrection in neighboring countries. It continues to supply arms and ammunition to rebel bands in Thailand, Burma, Malaysia and Indonesia. It continues to train, equip and finance guerrillas on a global scale. Rhetoric and friendly gestures notwithstanding, there is no evidence that the regime now intends to pursue a course of action consistent with the United Nations Charter. Indeed, all signs point the other way.

At United Nations, New York, Oct. 8/
The New York Times, 10-9:10.

Frank Church
United States Senator, D–Idaho

We keep shipping arms, ammunition and spare parts to (Pakistan). And although the United States bureaucracy has advised against the filling of the arms' export licenses still outstanding, the President (Nixon) has said to go ahead anyway. If the Nixon Administration were really concerned about the principles of self-determination in Asia, the United States would do all it possibly could to end the gruesome tragedy (civil war) in East Pakistan. At the very least, our policy would be one of total abstention.

Before the Senate, Washington, July 7/
The New York Times, 7-8:7.

Brian Crozier
Director, Institute for the
Study of Conflict, London

If—as seems likely—the Americans withdraw from South Vietnam and maintain only a token presence in Thailand, I think that the (Communist) Chinese and North Vietnamese

will step up their pressure on Thailand. There already are two subversive movements there: one in the northeastern provinces and another in the south on the border with Malaysia. Now, the Thai, with their long history of surviving between rival powers, might decide to come to terms with China; in that event, there would be no need for revolutionary war. But if the Thai dig their heels in on the assumption that America still will protect them, then the Chinese and North Vietnamese will undoubtedly step up the pressure. And I can't imagine the U.S. sending in a large military force to meet that threat. So in the wake of an American withdrawal from Vietnam, there is a real danger that China will establish a direct line of communications through Thailand to the guerrillas on the border of the Malay Peninsula—and that, in turn, would lead to pressure on Malaysia. In short, the "domino theory" would come true.

Interview, London/
U.S. News & World Report, 3-1:78.

D. P. Dhar
Head, Policy Planning Commission,
Foreign Ministry of India

Extremist parties may try to stir up the ethnic, racial and religious tensions created by the (Pakistan) refugee situation . . . Every day that passes increases the dangers the refugees pose to our own social and political stability. If one thinks in terms of timing, I should say that by the end of January (1972) the strains and stresses of the social, political and economic factors involved will be felt acutely by all of the people of India.

The Washington Post, 11-11:(A)27.

Dalai Lama
Former Chief of State of Tibet

The Tibetan peoples' uprising in Lhasa (in 1959) was crushed brutally by the Red Chinese Army. So why do we commemorate this day—a day of defeat when thousands of our people died and when Communist China proved her utter ruthlessness and her total disregard for human values? (Because) it was also a day of victory. For it was on this day

(DALAI LAMA)

that the failure of the oppressive system of Red China in Tibet became apparent and that the Chinese, in their frustration to cover up their deficiencies, had to use violence to promulgate what is essentially the reverse to Communist ideals—namely, colonialism. A thousand more uprisings may take place and a thousand times may the Chinese crush them; but they will never be able to break the spirit of liberty that resides in each one of us. My people will carry on the struggle till we see Tibet once again in its rightful place among the independent nations of the world. I believe in this even though I know that millions march in the Chinese Army. She now even possesses mighty nuclear weapons that make her feared by the most powerful nations of the world. But history is unpredictable. Many great empires, whose glory knew no bounds, have crumbled and passed away. And although never in her history has China been so powerful as she is today, yet there is a weakness in this colossus. Her very foundations are based on fear; like primitive beings, each person in China lives perpetually in fear of retribution for the slightest mistake. Can such an institution hope to remain? I say no. Nearly every totalitarian regime in history has this in common: they never lasted long. Eventually, China has to give way or break. Truth and justice will ultimately triumph. And the time will come when my people will fling away the yoke of Communist China's oppression and rise up to build a new Tibetan nation.

> *On 12th anniversary of Tibetan National Uprising, March/ Human Events, 7-31:10.*

Peter H. Dominick
United States Senator, R—Colo.

. . . which is the *real* Communist China? The smiling welcome of (Chinese Premier) Chou En-lai to an American table-tennis team visiting mainland China in mid-April? Or anti-American slogans shouted in the streets of dozens of Chinese cities on May Day, only two weeks later? A hint by Mao Tse-tung to

journalist Edgar Snow last December that he favored a visit by President Nixon to mainland China? Or an editorial in the *Peking Review* of April 16, 1971, vilifying President Nixon as an "arch-criminal," "arch-murderer" and "chief butcher"? Suggestions from Peking that it wants to negotiate its differences with the United States? Or its insistence in every Chinese Communist propaganda organ that "U.S. imperialism is the common enemy"? Interpretations by various so-called "experts" in this country that the People's Republic of China is ready and willing to enter the United Nations? Or Peking's own declaration that it will reject a seat in the UN unless the Republic of China (Nationalist China) is expelled? During our consideration of these factors, keep in mind the record of Mao's China which (1) has brutally subjugated the Chinese people for 22 years, (2) has been and still is branded by the UN as the "aggressor" in the Korean War, (3) has been accused of "genocide" in Tibet by the International Commission of Jurists in Geneva, (4) continues to supply most of the small arms and ammunition to North Vietnam and (5) has fostered and encouraged insurrection, subversion and "wars of national liberation" in Asia, Africa, Europe and even the United States . . . Which is the real Communist China? The "winsome" China which wines and dines visiting athletes and journalists? Or the brutal China of the Cultural Revolution which tortures its citizens and lets their bodies float down the rivers to the South China Sea? Hundreds of dead bodies found floating in the bay of Hong Kong tell us far more than ping-pong does about the real nature of the Chinese Communist government.

> *Before the Senate, Washington, June 10/Vital Speeches, 7-15:578,579*

Indira Gandhi
Prime Minister of India

Every person has advantages and disadvantages in this job. Some people say a woman hasn't as much stamina as a man; I can't tell, never having been a man. But I certainly have more physical stamina than anyone else around here.

Parade, 2-7:5.

We've made no official move to resume friendly relations with (Communist) China. But, of course, friendship between countries, especially countries which are neighbors, is very important . . . Nothing is achieved by hate. Of course, it can't be friendship at all costs; it has to be in accordance with national self-respect and dignity. But I think the Chinese realize that they have only made enemies so far by their tough stance.

Interview, New Delhi/
The New York Times Magazine, 2-14:58.

Democracy can't be real without socialism. Socialism aims at lessening of economic disparities among the people; and we have no greater cause for discontentment than the disparities between the rich and the poor. Our aim today is to give real meaning to democracy and freedom and see that the fruits of our development are spread throughout the country and not in a very few hands. We want to have change in a democratic manner, in which the bad is removed and the good is retained.

Los Angeles Times, 2-15:(1)24.

We are friends with Russia; but we are also friends with other countries, including the United States and the United Kingdom. Nevertheless, Russia does agree with us on many international issues and supports us at the United Nations, for instance on the issue of racialism. It is not we who support them but they who support us.

Los Angeles Times, 2-15:(1)24.

. . . neither I am a dictator nor is my party a dictator. If at all there is dictatorship, it will be of the people. The elections have proved that the path of socialism is the only way (by) which this country can march ahead, by taking all sections of society along. But the object of our socialism is not to take away everything from the rich and give it to the poor. The idea is to reduce economic disparities and bridge the gap between the one and the other.

After her Congress Party's election
victory, New Delhi, March 14/
The Washington Post, 3-15:(A)1.

Somehow, during our struggle for independence from British rule, we came to use terms like "socialism" to express our feeling and determination that the traditional poverty of the majority of the Indian people must be ameliorated persistently when political power passed into our hands. National independence was not to be merely the substitution of a few Indian rulers and masters for the British rulers and masters, but genuine self-rule of the people themselves.

Interview, New Delhi/
Los Angeles Herald-Examiner, 4-18:(A)8.

More than nine million East Bengalis have come into our country (as a result of the Pakastani conflict). Do they not have the right to live and work in their own homeland? We cannot absorb them. We have problems enough of our own, and we certainly do not need to add to our vast population. This is not an Indo-Pakistani dispute. The problem is an international one. But the weight of it has fallen on India, stretching our resources, financial and otherwise, to the limit. The international response has fallen short of the scale which a grim tragedy of this magnitude demands.

Moscow, Sept. 28/
The New York Times, 9-29:9.

We certainly will do nothing to provoke an attack (from Pakistan) or to start any hostilities; but we have to be alive to our interests and safeguard our security. Unfortunately, Pakistan's record has been one of hatred and desperation. The military regime has let loose a war on its own people, and there is no knowing what it will do next.

Interview, New Dehli/
The New York Times, 10-19:1.

(INDIRA GANDHI)

We have the greatest friendship for America and the American people. But one of the reasons (for deteriorating relations), so far as the Indian public is concerned, is this idea that the U.S. has of always balancing India and Pakistan . . . We don't support the Soviet Union any more than we support America—or we support both equally, whichever way you like to look at it, negatively or positively. The point is that the Soviet Union supports us in basic things for which we have stood and for which we have fought earlier on.

Interview, New Delhi/
The New York Times, 10-19:6.

(Regarding a reported offer by Pakistan President Yahya Kahn for mutual troop withdrawals from their common border): You cannot shake hands with a clenched fist.

News conference, New Delhi, Oct. 19/
The New York Times, 10-20:45.

(Regarding the conflict in Pakistan): This is not a civil war in the conventional sense. It is a genocidal program of civilians, merely because they voted democratically. It is a cynical use of helpless human beings as a weapon against a neighbor nation. They have been terrorized and persecuted by the military rulers of Pakistan and pushed inside our territory, jeopardizing our normal life and our plans for the future.

Before Royal Institute of International
Relations, Brussels, Oct. 25/
Los Angeles Herald-Examiner, 10-26:(A)7.

It has not been easy to get away at a time when India is beleaguered. To the natural calamities of drought, flood and cyclone has been added a man-made tragedy of vast proportions (the Pakistan conflict). I am haunted by the tormented faces in our overcrowded refugee camps reflecting the grim events which have compelled the exodus of those millions from East Bengal (East Pakistan). I have come here looking for a deeper understanding of the situation in our part of the world, in search of some wise impulse which, as history tells us,

has sometimes worked to save humanity from despair.

Washington, Nov. 4/Time, 11-15:34.

(Concerning possible war with Pakistan): India is determined to safeguard her interests. India is united as never before. We want your (the United States') help; we want your support; we want your sympathy. But India is prepared to fight alone for what it thinks is worth fighting for.

At Columbia University, New York, Nov. 6/
The New York Times, 11-7:(1)1.

(Pakistani President Agha Mohammad Yahya Kahn is) one man who could not get elected in his own country if there were a fair election. I would say he would not even get elected in his province if there were a fair election.

Interview/Newsweek, 11-15:53.

Even though Pakistan has declared an emergency, we shall refrain from taking a similar step, unless further aggressive action by Pakistan compels us to do so in the interest of national security. In the meantime, the country should remain unruffled. Our brave armed forces and our people will insure that any adventurism on the part of the military regime of Pakistan meets with adequate rebuff. The rulers of Pakistan must realize that the path of peace —of peaceful negotiation and reconciliation—is more rewarding than that of war and the suppression of liberty and democracy.

Before Parliament, New Delhi, Nov. 24/
The New York Times, 11-25:16.

(Referring to the India-Pakistan conflict): I would certainly welcome a withdrawal of troops, and I think the troops to be withdrawn are the Pakistani troops in Bangla Desh (East Pakistan). They are very far from their homes and they are also suffering. I think they should be taken back to rejoin their families and friends in West Pakistan. The very presence of Pakistani troops in Bangla Desh is a threat to our security.

Before Parliament, New Delhi, Nov. 30/
The Washington Post, 12-1:(A)1.

As for the legitimacy of the government of Bangla Desh (independent East Pakistan), the whole world is now aware that it reflects the will of the overwhelming majority of the people, which not many governments can claim to represent.

Before Parliament, New Delhi, Dec. 6/
The Washington Post, 12-7:(A)12.

V. V. Giri
President of India

We (India) are too many. Today, we are roughly 537 million. On the average, we add about 13 million people to the existing population every year. At the current rate of increase, our population will reach the figure of around 1 billion before the turn of this century. Unless we devise concrete methods of checking the rate of population growth, it is difficult for us to assure even a minimum economic wherewithall to our population.

Interview, New Delhi/
San Francisco Examiner, 4-26:17.

Barry M. Goldwater
United States Senator, R–Ariz.

(Regarding President Nixon's announced plans to visit Communist China): . . . I would certainly caution my Party members to remember that this nation's policy has not been immediately changed by President Nixon's dramatic announcement . . . The passage of time alone has not altered the need for the brutal government of Mao Tse-tung to change many of its attitudes and actions and policies. But I do not oppose efforts by the Nixon Administration to improve the dialogue and the channels of communication through which some of our ideas can be placed realistically before Peking's rulers. In other words, if there is any chance that our President can persuade Peking to mend its ways and to stop exporting aggression and violence and war, then I say more power to him.

Before Republican National Committee,
Denver, July 23/
The Dallas Times Herald, 7-23:(A)7.

(Japan will build) the world's most modern military system—far, far better than ours and far better than the Russians, who are even now better than we are . . . The biggest problems that we face in the far Pacific in the coming years rest neither with (Communist) China nor with the Soviets. They rest with Japan.

At Republican fund-raising dinner,
Kansas City, Oct. 4/
Los Angeles Herald-Examiner, 10-5:(A)4.

Marshall Green
Assistant Secretary for East Asia
and Pacific Affairs, Department of State
of the United States

We are faced with a mainland (Communist) China which, whatever its latest welcome degree of seemingly greater flexibility in international affairs, has presumably not abandoned its basic objectives of greater domination over free Asian countries.

San Francisco Examiner, 5-10:34.

The Japanese see themselves as weak and poor and us as rich and powerful, while we see the Japanese as prosperous 10-foot giants.

The New York Times, 12-5:(4)5.

Andrei A. Gromyko
Foreign Minister of the Soviet Union

There has been much talk lately of the contemplated normalization of relations between the United States of America and the Chinese People's Republic (Communist China). In principle, we regard this as a natural development. Normal relations should exist between all states. As to the position of the Soviet Union, our country has always invariably been against all unlawful actions with respect to the Chinese People's Republic, of its lawful rights in the United Nations, against the two-China concept and against any concepts of a "dual representation of China." This is our fundamental position . . . But the Soviet Union has always been, and is, opposed to policies directed against the legitimate interests and the security of other states, including the Soviet Union,

299

(ANDREI A. GROMYKO)

regardless of the dressing that such policies are served with.

At United Nations, New York, Sept. 28/
The New York Times, 9-29:2.

W. Averell Harriman
Former United States Ambassador-at-Large

(Regarding President Nixon's announced plans to visit Communist China): Historically, foreign potentates have made journeys to the capital of what the Chinese call the Middle Kingdom in order to kowtow—that's the expression the Chinese use—and I don't know why Mr. Nixon is going. He's got a very good Secretary of State, Bill Rogers, and I don't know why he can't send him. Mr. Nixon said he's going in order to get peace in our generation. But we have a war going on in Vietnam, and the war can be settled only with Hanoi and the NLF in Paris. It cannot be settled in Peking.

News conference, Los Angeles, July 22/
Los Angeles Times, 7-23:(2)1.

Keith J. Holyoake
Foreign Minister of New Zealand

Our concern for collective security is as relevant today as it was in 1954 (when SEATO was formed). The realities of that time remain the realities of today. We cannot ignore them . . . We would do so at our own peril and at the peril . . . of the whole region.

Before Southeast Asia Treaty Organization,
London, April 27/
The Washington Post, 4-28:(A)16.

Townsend Hoopes
Former Deputy Assistant Secretary
of Defense of the United States

The Nixon Administration appears to be fashioning a policy (in Asia) in which insubstantial fringe states are expected to become the principal agents of (Communist) containment. United States military assistance, whatever its magnitude, cannot make giants out of pigmies; it cannot determine the military bal-

ance of Asia; it cannot serve as a substitute for the United States presence.

Before Joint Congressional Subcommittee
on Economy in Government, Washington,
Jan. 5/The New York Times, 1-6:24.

Huang Kuo-shu
President, Nationalist Chinese Parliament

(Regarding United States President Nixon's announced plans to visit Communist China): (The United States has been) unable to withstand the pressure of international appeasement and the inducements of the Peking regime, and now has come to a crossroads. We hope that President Nixon, so clever as he is, will not be fooled as the result of his trip to the Chinese mainland. We swear we will fight the Communists until their total defeat and our total victory.

San Francisco Examiner, 8-14:4.

Hubert H. Humphrey
United States Senator, D—Minn.

(Regarding President Nixon's announced plans to visit Communist China): Such a visit could be of immense importance in bringing about a speedy end to the war in Vietnam and in laying the groundwork for an extended period of peace and development throughout all the world and especially Asia.

Los Angeles Herald-Examiner, 7-16:(A)1.

Junius Richard Jayewardene
Leader, United National Party of Ceylon

Democracy is finished in this country. You have to have peace and stability to have democracy; and Ceylon has neither.

Interview/The New York Times, 4-25:(1)2.

U. Alexis Johnson
Under Secretary for Political Affairs,
Department of State of the United States

Japan must recognize that we no longer can accept a double standard in our economic relations around the world. Japan cannot expect to continue to enjoy unfettered access to world markets and resources, especially in the

United States, without similar treatment to foreign enterprises doing business in and with Japan.

Los Angeles, Oct. 18/
The New York Times, 10-19:71.

Walter H. Judd
Former United States Representative;
Authority on Asian Affairs

What has she (Britain) gotten in return (for recognizing Communist China)? Imprisonments, beatings, storming of British Embassies and people and no increase in trade. (The late French President Charles) de Gaulle showed his defiance of us by recognizing Red China. And it was the Chinese Communists who organized the great (Paris) riots in the spring of '68, a major factor in overthrowing de Gaulle. Israel made overtures way back 20 years ago toward Red China. And it was the Communists from China who organized and trained the Palestinian guerrillas which almost blew up into an all-out war against Israel last fall. I would think people would see what's happened when folks have followed these policies of softness toward Communism, and be wary.

Human Events, 5-8:5.

Herman Kahn
Director, Hudson Institute

I would say there are several reasons why the U.S. should stay in Asia—primarily, as a basic stabilizing force in the region. This does not necessarily mean that we should interfere in every minor issue that comes up. But it does mean that we should maintain or have available sufficient forces to react to any sufficiently great and sufficiently stark aggression—and if we decide not to resist, then to be able to contain the results of the aggression. Incidentally, I don't think our presence there—or anywhere outside the U.S., for that matter—can be justified on any narrow economic or strategic calculation of U.S. interests. In other words, one must argue that our continued presence in Asia is mainly in the world's interest and in the U.S.'s mostly because we are part of the world. And if one asks why the U.S. represents the world's interest, the answer is: if not us, then

who? In other words, if there is a real world interest in stabilizing Asia, if we don't do it, who is going to do it? That has to be the basic argument.

Interview, Washington/
U.S. News & World Report, 2-8:60.

My estimate is that, some time in the (19)80s, the Japanese will pass the Russians and become the second largest economic power in the world. This will be a very great shock to the Russian Communists, intellectuals and the managerial class. It was interesting to see that, when Japan passed West Germany about three or four years ago and Britain even before that, nobody got upset. I think they will get very upset in the Soviet Union.

Interview, Davos, Switzerland/
The New York Times Magazine, 6-20:20.

Edward M. Kennedy
United States Senator, D—Mass.

Since very early in April, I have been assured repeatedly—in private conversations and official correspondence—that our government was not supplying arms to Pakistan. I know that other Senators had similar assurances. Whether it is double-talk, incompetence, or both, the shipment of United States arms to Pakistan is a violation of policy. And even worse, it will continue to fuel military actions which have already been the primary cause of over six million refugees (in the West-East Pakistan war) and countless civilian dead.

Before the Senate, Washington, June 22/
The New York Times, 6-23:8.

(Regarding President Nixon's announced plans to visit Communist China): Rarely, I think, has the action of any President so captured the imagination and support of the American people as President Nixon's magnificent gesture last week of improvement in our relations with China.

The New York Times, 7-20:4.

It is argued that the continuation of (U.S.) military aid to West Pakistan somehow gives us "leverage" to constructively influence the Paki-

WHAT THEY SAID IN 1971

(EDWARD M. KENNEDY)

stan military's policy in East Bengal (East Pakistan). Well, where is that leverage? Where is the leverage to stop the use of U.S. arms which produce the refugees and civilian victims that we then must help support in India? Where is the leverage to halt the secret trial of Sheikh Mujib whose only crime is that he won a free election? Where is the leverage to prevent our humanitarian aid from being turned into military equipment when American relief boats are transformed into American gun boats? Why, if we have the leverage to influence the government of Pakistan, must our great nation assist this shabby and shameful enterprise? It is time for Americans to ask their leaders: "Just what kind of government is it that we seek to influence—and for what purpose?"

Before National Press Club, Washington,
Aug. 26/Vital Speeches, 10-1:739.

This war (between India and Pakistan) began not last week with military border-crossings, nor last month with the escalating cross-fire of artillery between India and Pakistan. This war began on the bloody night of March 25 with the brutal suppression by the Pakistan Army of the results of a free election it held in East Bengal . . . The problem in South Asia is today and has been from the very beginning a political problem between the ruling military elite in West Pakistan and the Bengali opposition elected in East Bengal (East Pakistan) . . . Now the (U.S.) Administration tells us—eight months after March 25—that we should condemn, not the repression of the Pakistan Army, but the response of India toward an increasingly desperate situation on its eastern borders—a situation which our nation calculatedly ignored. Certainly, condemnation is justified, but what should we condemn? We should condemn . . . the silence of our leadership. Are we so insensitive to what our country stands for that our government can actually support as well as apologize for a military regime's brutal suppression of democracy? Are we so blind that we can ignore a government that jails a political leader (Mujibur Rahman) whose only crime was the winning of a free election? . . . And

now—in sharp contrast to our deference to Pakistani sensibilities over these past months of violence in East Bengal—our national leadership suddenly denounces India . . . This (Nixon) Administration has rightly taken pride in its efforts to re-establish contact with one-fifth of mankind's population in (Communist) China. But are we going to simultaneously alienate one-sixth of mankind in India—a democratic nation with whom we have had years of productive relations? . . . Our government and the United Nations must come to understand that the actions of the Pakistan Army on the night of March 25 unleashed the forces in South Asia that have led to war.

Before the Senate, Washington, Dec. 7/
U.S. News & World Report, 12-20:68,69.

Kim Il Sung
Premier of North Korea

Despite the blockade and isolation policy of U.S. imperialism, the People's Republic of (Communist) China, far from being suffocated, has grown in strength with each passing day as a socialist power standing imposingly in Asia as a mighty anti-imperialist revolutionary force. So (U.S. President) Nixon is, in the end, going to turn up in Peking (on his planned trip there) with a white flag . . . Nixon's visit to China will not be a march of a victor but a trip of the defeated; and it fully reflects the destiny of U.S. imperialism, which is like a sun sinking in the western sky.

Pyongyang, North Korea, Aug. 6/
The Washington Post, 8-9:(A)18.

Kim Yong Shik
Foreign Minister of South Korea

(Regarding the possibility of discussions on a Korean settlement during United States President Nixon's planned visit to Communist China): I prefer they don't discuss this matter. No conclusion can be reached by them alone. Always the fate of this country has been decided by the big countries without us, and as a result our people suffer. This country was divided in 1945 without our consent.

The New York Times, 10-23:7.

302

Henry A. Kissinger
Assistant to the President of the United States for National Security Affairs

. . . the minimum we expect to get out of this trip (President Nixon's planned visit to Communist China) is a better understanding by both sides of each other's positions and a continuing means of remaining informed about these positions so that one is not so dependent on these very dramatic setpiece encounters. Second, we hope out of this visit could grow at least a beginning of some exchanges in other than political fields that would permit the two peoples to get to know each other better. Again, we are not sentimental about this. We recognize that the People's Republic is led by highly principled men whose principles are diametrically opposed to ours. But . . . it is in our mutual interest that . . . on those matters that are not ideologically controversial in the cultural and intellectual field, we can find cooperative means of effort.

News conference, Washington, Nov. 30/
Los Angeles Times, 12-1:(1)8.

Victor H. Krulak
Lieutenant General (Ret.) and former Pacific Commander, United States Marine Corps

(Regarding United States relations with Communist China): What Senators (J. William) Fulbright and (George S.) McGovern and our "meaningful dialog" proponents are really contending is that there is some benefit to be found in intercourse, not with the men in the fields and factories, but with a tiny hard core of men—Mao and his threadbare satellites. And just who are they? They are a band of nihilistic Marxist brigands, who have survived literally by killing off the opposition wherever they found it. Their murders have numbered 15,000,000 since 1949. They are a group of arrogant and frightened men who have failed in every one of their social experiments, who inspire no loyalty among their people, who really have less popular mandate than Attila

the Hun. Dialog with them? We might as well get in bed with a nest of rattlesnakes.

Before World Affairs Council, San Diego/
The National Observer, 5-3:13.

Melvin R. Laird
Secretary of Defense of the United States

To say that we would not have a presence in Asia (after Vietnam) under the strategy of realistic deterrence . . . would certainly be misleading. I would envision that U.S. presence in Asia—as far as naval forces are concerned, as far as air power is concerned—that this would be a part of the realistic deterrent we would maintain in Asia.

News conference, Washington, April 13/
Los Angeles Herald-Examiner, 4-13:(A)2.

(Regarding President Nixon's announced plans to visit Communist China): He will not repeat the mistakes that have so often flawed our negotiations in the past. He will not be deluded by words that paper over disagreement on substance. He will not make premature or unilateral concessions. He will not conclude agreements that weaken our security. He will not bargain away the rights of any other people. He will not abandon any friends.

At Veterans of Foreign Wars convention,
Dallas, Aug. 16/Los Angeles Times, 8-17:(2)4.

Lee Kuan Yew
Prime Minister of Singapore

Great changes are now in the offing. The American government has set out to thaw their relations with (Communist) China. They are also committed to wind up their military involvement in Vietnam as soon as possible. For a new geopolitical equilibrium to be established, there may have to be trade-offs across the board. New demarcations of spheres of influence may become part of the Asian political landscape. Some countries may be allowed to go neutral. Some may become pro-Communist.

Singapore, Aug. 8/
The Washington Post, 8-9:(A)9.

Li Hsien-nien
Vice Premier of the People's
Republic of (Communist) China

The Chinese government and people are greatly concerned over the present Indo-Pakistan situation. We maintain that disputes between states should be settled by the two parties concerned through peaceful consultation and absolutely not by resorting to force . . . The Chinese government and people resolutely support the Pakistan government and people in their just struggle against foreign aggression and in defense of their state sovereignty and national independence.

Peking, Nov. 29/
The New York Times, 11-30:3.

The U.S. President (Nixon) expressed a desire to raise the level of negotiations . . . through the visit he asked to make to China. On our side, it was not possible to say no to this desire. In accordance with the teachings of Chairman Mao Tse-tung, we could not find anything preventing the U.S. President from making his visit and conducting the talks he wishes—talks which may succeed or may fail. Such a visit by a chief of a state which regards itself as one of the two superpowers in the world requires many arrangements . . . they consider important. With these imperialists, it is difficult to find any common language.

News conference, Cairo, Egypt/
U.S. News & World Report, 12-20:42.

Walter Lippmann
Former political columnist

(Regarding United States President Nixon's plans to visit Communist China): The mere going to China, the willingness to accept the invitation, is in itself an acknowledgment of a colossal error that the United States made at the beginning of the Cold War. That's when we departed from the old American doctrine that the government we recognized—whether we liked it or not—was the one that governed the country. That error has had enormous consequences; because having made the decision to treat the People's Republic of (Communist) China as an enemy, we then made a great number of promises and commitments to carry out that decision—such as the policy with Taiwan and the various treaties and guarantees we scattered around the eastern side of the Pacific. Those commitments were made in good faith and can't be thrown aside lightly, even though we now admit the premise was an error. It will probably take a generation to correct the consequences of having made such a big mistake. My view is that it is better to have made the mistake and to correct it than to persist in it. It's a mistake that can be corrected by a strong power, without humiliation necessarily, and with a certain amount of good faith. The willingness to admit the mistake and adjust to it, to make decisions quietly, to reverse the policy slowly, with due consultation and notice to everybody tactfully—that's what diplomacy is all about.

Interview, Seal Harbor, Me./
The Washington Post, 10-10:(C)1.

Andre Malraux
Author; Former Minister of State
for Culture of France

(Communist Chinese Chairman) Mao understands that the U.S. should believe in a consumer society because America is a capitalist country, but that Russia, the great socialist sister, should have the same values is incomprehensible to him and a betrayal of their common cause. If (Soviet Premier) Kosygin succeeds in giving every Russian a small motorcycle, then that's the end of Mao's spartan Chinese Communism.

Interview, Verrieres-le-Buisson, France/
Time, 11-15:43.

Mike Mansfield
United States Senator, D—Mont.

The time has come . . . to work harder in an attempt to get the President (Nixon) to continue the policy which he is now undertaking and to speed up the withdrawal of U.S. troops from all of Southeast Asia, all of

Indochina and Thailand, and to withdraw lock, stock and barrel.

Television interview, Jan. 26/
U.S. News & World Report, 2-8:37.

(Regarding President Nixon's easing of trade restrictions with Communist China): The change is long overdue. For 20 years, this government has persisted in the treatment of China trade as though the importation of silk, rattan, chopsticks or whatever from the mainland of China would somehow undermine the strength of the nation or contaminate its inhabitants.

Before the Senate, Washington, April 15/
The Washington Post, 4-16:(A)22.

Ferdinand E. Marcos
President of the Philippines

The opening of (Philippine) trade and diplomatic relations with the U.S.S.R. and with other Soviet bloc countries is only a matter of time. On the other hand, we are now engaged in a review of our relations with the United States of America to make them serve more fully the mutual interest of the two countries. The principal aim of Philippine foreign policy in 1971 is to seek an accommodation with reality.

State of the Nation address, Manila,
Jan. 25/The New York Times, 1-26:3.

If we do not reform our society, if we do not make government more responsive to the needs of our people, if we do not narrow the cleavage between rich and poor, there will be no need for the Communists to mount a rebellion. They will just take over.

State of the Nation address, Manila,
Jan. 25/U.S. News & World Report, 3-29:56.

The Communists call me "tutang Amerikano," meaning the running dog of the Americans. This is because I have said repeatedly, "We need the United States now, and we will need them for the next several years." We cannot protect ourselves from external aggression. While there is no such threat now, there would soon be one if the United States was

not here. And the time may come when there will be such a threat.

Interview, Manila/
San Francisco Examiner, 6-22:18.

The greatest challenge that confronts us today is the challenge of the Communist ideology which has placed upon our shoulders the burden to prove that freedom and democracy, as principles of human society, will work for the Filipino people and secure for them better living conditions. The Communist elements in our country try to foster upon the masses the false belief that the ultimate solution to our basic national problems is an armed revolution. They cry to everyone that reform and change is possible only by armed revolution. We need reform and we need change, but we can attain it without violence. For the use of violence totally negates the essential value of human life regardless of the cause under which it is waged.

Interview, Manila/
San Francisco Examiner, 7-5:17.

I don't want to continue (as President) unless it's absolutely necessary to protect the Republic . . . If, by 1973, some damn Communist tries to take over the Presidency of the Republic and I have it within my power to stop him, then I will stop him.

Interview, Manila, Sept. 16/
The New York Times, 9-17:12.

George S. McGovern
United States Senator, D–S.D.

Fog and myths for the past 20 years have befuddled our attitudes and our actions toward mainland (Communist) China. These myths and fears may be the most costly and dangerous untruths in all of American public policy. They have isolated a population of 800 million, more than one-fourth of the world's people. They have isolated the United States position from a large and growing body of world opinion and practice; from trade, from diplomatic recognition and from other forms of contact which should characterize relations between mature societies. They have

(GEORGE S. McGOVERN)

pushed Chinese leadership into belligerence and suspicion toward the United States, creating enormous obstacles to the normalized relations which even the Nixon Administration, led by an architect of our distorted vision, seems now to recognize must ultimately come. They have placed us on the wrong side of nationalistic aspirations throughout Asia, and have forced our alliance with governments which degrade the very principles of democracy, liberty and independence upon which our nation is founded. And they have brought us twice into major wars, with a toll of 100,000 Americans dead in Korea and Vietnam—and the total still rising in seemingly endless devastation. We must begin immediately to escape the tyranny of the untruths which have shackled our thinking for so long and to such ill effect.

At University of the Pacific,
Stockton, Calif., Jan. 24/
The New York Times, 2-5:31.

Where is the evidence that (Communist) China is about to engulf her neighbors? Notwithstanding bellicose rhetoric, Chinese troops have operated beyond Chinese borders rarely in the past 21 years. They entered Korea only when the forces of General (Douglas) MacArthur were racing toward their borders . . . Chinese troops have fought in India and Tibet; but the objectives were to claim disputed territory, not to elevate new ideology.

At University of the Pacific,
Stockton, Calif., Jan. 24/
The Washington Post, 1-25:(A)1.

It's been the height of folly to pretend that the government of China is on that little island of Formosa (Nationalist China). The government of China is in Peking (Communist China). I am delighted that the President (Nixon) has finally recognized that, at least to the point where he's going to visit Peking. We ought to follow that up with an official recognition of that government for admission to the United Nations. We ought to be pressing for trade relations with China. China can be a

great customer of the United States and vice versa. We need each other economically.

Interview/Nation's Business, November:69.

William McMahon
Prime Minister of Australia

(Regarding his new position as Prime Minister): I don't feel the slightest bit excited or emotional. I've seen Prime Ministers come and go.

News conference after assuming office,
Canberra, March 10/
Los Angeles Times, 3-11:(1)21.

George Meany
President, American Federation of Labor-Congress of Industrial Organizations

(Commenting on President Nixon's planned trip to Communist China): The Number 1 stunt of the Number 1 stuntman of our time.

Quote, 9-26:289.

The President (Nixon) is going all-out to cultivate Communist China and almost any other place in the world where freedom no longer exists. There are a lot of American businessmen who have an idea that there's some profit to be made by dealing with Red China on a commercial basis. Well, if I know anything about Red China, the only way Red China can buy anything we produce is if we first lend them the money.

Miami Beach, Nov. 15/
Los Angeles Times, 11-16:(1)13.

Robert Menzies
Former Prime Minister of Australia

Some years ago, most of us would have taken our relations with Great Britain for granted. For most of us they were established in the blood and in our most profound emotions. But in recent times, the nature of the Commonwealth, and the possible or probable entry of Great Britain into the European Community (Common Market), have led in our country to an apparent weakening of the old instinctive ties. I believe in my heart that some of the most enduring elements we have in our nation we derive from Britain and must, with Britain, preserve.

At founding dinner of Australia-Britain Society, Sydney/The New York Times, 8-30:8.

Wayne L. Morse
Former United States Senator, D—Ore.

Anybody (who) thinks that the United States is getting militarily out of Asia—they've never analyzed the Nixon Doctrine. You can't find a single speech today in the pages of the *Congressional Record*, by any member of Congress, that's analyzed the Nixon Doctrine. You can't find a single speech today in the pages of the *Congressional Record*, by any member of Congress, that's analyzed the illegality and un-Constitutionality of the Nixon Doctrine. They've missed it. We're not getting out of Asia . . .

Interview, Eugene, Ore./ The Washington Post, 11-29:(A)11.

Edmund S. Muskie
United States Senator, D—Maine

(Regarding President Nixon's announcement of his plans to visit Communist China): (The failure to give Japan advance notice of the announcement) humiliated the Japanese government in the eyes of the world and its own people. A passion for secrecy and the theatrics of surprise may have turned a political profit here at home. But they have also inflicted terrible damage on our closest friend in Asia. And any President who can make such judgments deserves to be called a one-term President.

At Democratic Party dinner, Phoenix, Nov. 5/ Los Angeles Herald-Examiner, 11-6:(A)5.

Nesti Nase
Foreign Minister of Albania

Of late, the inevitable process of the recognition of the People's Republic of (Communist) China and the re-establishment of diplomatic relations with it has grown more rapidly and has created panic among the enemies of the People's Republic of China, mainly in the United States of America. The People's Republic of China is now recognized even by those who not so long ago did hesitate to do so for various reasons, including, of course, the pressure and the blackmail of the United States. This proves that the traditional policy of the American government to isolate the People's Republic of China in the international arena has failed not only on the political level but also on the diplomatic one.

At United Nations, New York, Oct. 18/ The New York Times, 10-19:12.

Pham Kim Ngoc
Economic Minister of South Vietnam

It's very strange. Everybody would like to see Japan play a more important position in helping us to recover from the war. When I was in the United States, everybody said we have leverage with the Japanese. We don't. We think here in Saigon that the United States has leverage with the Japanese. They don't, either. The Japanese just go their own way.

Interview, Saigon, July 1/ The Washington Post, 7-2:(A)20.

Naomi Nishimura
Director, Self-Defense Forces of Japan

The Japanese people will not support a defense program based on the old classic theory of a military balance, seeking to counter a threat with a comparable military build-up. Our country is simply too exposed and too vulnerable strategically to play the useless nuclear game. I believe this attitude will not change in the foreseeable future.

Before Foreign Correspondents Club of Japan, Tokyo, Oct. 11/ The Washington Post, 10-12:(A)12.

Richard M. Nixon
President of the United States

When considering Asia, the great problem is that everyone overlooks the fact that non-Communist Asia—excluding India and Pakistan—produces three times as much as (Communist)

WHAT THEY SAID IN 1971

(RICHARD M. NIXON)

China. Why, Japan alone produces twice as much as China. What is going to happen if we ignore such basic facts? The United States . . . *is* a Pacific Power.

Interview, Washington, March 8/
The New York Times, 3-10:14.

. . . the long-range goal of this Administration is a normalization of our relationships with mainland (Communist) China—the People's Republic of China—and the ending of its isolation from the other nations of the world. That's a long-range goal . . . We have made some progress toward that goal. We have moved in the field of travel; we have moved in the field of trade. There will be more progress made. For example, at the present time I am circulating among the departments the items which may be released as possible trade items in the future . . . But now, when we move from the field of travel and trade to the field of recognition of the government, to its admission to the United Nations, I am not going to discuss those matters, because it's premature to speculate about that.

News conference, Washington, April 29/
U.S. News & World Report, 5-10:27.

There has been speculation to the effect that the purpose of our . . . attempting to normalize our relations with mainland (Communist) China is to, in some way, irritate the Soviet Union. Nothing could be further from the truth . . . . We seek good relations with the Soviet Union. We are seeking good relations with Communist China. And the interests of world peace require good relations between the Soviet Union and Communist China. It would make no sense for the United States, interested in world peace, to try to get the two to get at each other's throats, because we would be embroiled in the controversy ourselves.

News conference, Washington, April 29/
U.S. News & World Report, 5-10:27.

(Announcing his planned visit to Communist China): Our action in seeking a new relationship with the People's Republic of China will not be at the expense of our old friends. It is not directed against any other nation. We seek friendly relations with all nations. Any nation can be our friend without being any other nation's enemy. I have taken this action because of my profound conviction that all nations will gain from a reduction of tensions and a better relationship between the United States and the People's Republic of China. It is in this spirit that I will undertake what I deeply hope will become a journey for peace—peace not just for our generation but for future generations on this earth we share together.

TV-radio address, Los Angeles, July 15/
The Dallas Times Herald, 7-16:(A)11.

(His announced plan to visit Communist China) does not mean that we go into these meetings on either side with any illusions about the wide differences that we have. Our interests are very different, and both sides recognize this . . . We do not expect that these talks will settle all of those differences. What is important is that we will have opened communication to see, where our differences are irreconcilable, that they can be settled peacefully, and to find those areas where the United States, which today is the most powerful nation in the world, can find an agreement with the most populous nation in the world which potentially in the future could become the most powerful nation in the world.

News conference, Washington, Aug. 4/
The Washington Post, 8-5:(A)10.

The most important decision that I made this year was the decision to open communications with (Communist) China . . . I believe that it will make a greater contribution to the next generation, to peace in the world, than anything else we have done . . . I think we would be less than candid were we not to admit that what really matters here is not the fact that the trip to China is announced . . . but how (it) works. Our people have become accustomed to the spectaculars. It is exciting. A trip to China is like going to the moon. On the other hand, the American people are very volatile. They can be caught up emotionally with a big move; but if it fails, they can turn away just as fast. That is why it is so important that the China trip not be just cosmetics, that it be cast in terms of building to the long-term future. It may well benefit not the present occupant of this office, but somebody five, 10 or 15 years from now.

Interview, Washington, December/
Time, 1-3('72):14.

Park Chung Hee
President of South Korea

Gone are the days when we used to say that we cannot live or defend ourselves without help from others. We can say that we will enjoy abundant life and defend our country through our own efforts. Gone is the cloud of dependence now; instead, the sun of independence and self-reliance has risen high in our sky.

March 17/Los Angeles Times, 4-18:(A)2.

I will devote all my efforts to the realization of national harmony and the build-up of our democratic strength to overwhelm Communist North Korea. Externally, I will carry out a positive and pragmatic diplomacy on the basis of accurate judgment and assessment of the rapidly-changing international situation in order to firmly safeguard (the) peace and freedom of the nation.

After winning re-election, May 1/
The New York Times, 5-2:(1)15.

If the North Korean Communists should even now awaken from their illusions, discarding their avowed militant policy and dogmatic attitude, and if they are willing to join in the new international current, it would not only serve as a significant turning point in the building of world peace, but indeed provide a great hope for the peaceful unification of the country. On our part, I declare once again that we shall continue to pursue national unification solely through peaceful means. I would also like to offer the assurance that a forum for peaceful unification can be arranged at any time, if and when the North Korean Communists genuinely renounce their policy

of force and violence and assume a sincere attitude concerning (peaceful) unification.

On 26th anniversary of Korea's liberation
from Japanese rule, Seoul, Aug. 15/
The New York Times, 8-15:(1)4.

Charles H. Percy
United States Senator, R–Ill.

(Regarding the effects on Japan of U.S. President Nixon's new economic program announced Aug. 15, which includes a 10% surtax on imports and which may affect the value of the yen): They're getting it right between the eyes, and they've had it coming to them. Out of one side of the mouth they talk like the most powerful economic unit in the world, and out of the other side talk like a developing nation—that they need to protect imports, protect capital coming in. They can't have it both ways, and they've tried to. They are selling Toyotas in the United States for $2,200, and $3,000 in Tokyo—the same car. They ship an unlimited amount of steel to us, and yet they won't let us take that steel and put it in an American automobile and ship that automobile to Japan. There are all sorts of restrictions and quotas and limitations and taxes, and they are ingenious at finding ways to do it.

News conference, New Dehli, India, Aug. 28/
The Washington Post, 8-29:(A)3.

S. J. Perelman
Author

I'm forced to report that I found the subcontinent of India just as hysterical, scatterbrained, shrill and bureaucracy-ridden as it ever was. I have been forced to conclude that, deep down, no matter how placid the surface, there's a screw loose in the Indian mentality.

Hong Kong, April 23/
Los Angeles Times, 4-24:(1)15.

Mujibur Rahman
President, Awami League (East
Pakistan independence movement)

Our people have already proclaimed to the world that they shall no longer allow them-

(MUJIBUR RAHMAN)

selves to be exploited as a colony and a market. I pledge to lead the people to emancipation. I am prepared to shed my blood for freedom. This is a fight for freedom, liberty and self-determination. Everyone must be prepared for sacrifice, even death.

The New York Times Magazine, 5-2:92.

Ronald Reagan
Governor of California

I think some conservatives who are perturbed about his (President Nixon's) announcement of wanting to talk to (Communist) China have been frightened over the years by American representatives who have tended to appease and give away too much of America—at Potsdam and Yalta and in subsequent dealings with the totalitarian states. But I think that when the President said he wanted to talk, he made it plain that he was going to stand by our old ally, Chiang Kai-shek. He has made no announcement or indicated that he is going to go and appease or give anything away. All I have cautioned is that those conservatives who, having been burned before, now jump to the conclusion that a simple talk is going to cause us trouble, are forgetting that this is the man who stood in the Soviet Union, in Moscow, and told (Soviet Premier Nikita) Khrushchev when he (Nixon) was Vice President . . . that if they did some of the things Khrushchev was threatening, we would—forgive the expression, but his exact words were, "We will kick the hell out of you."

Television interview/"Meet the Press,"
National Broadcasting Company,
San Juan, P.R., 9-12.

Edwin O. Reischauer
Former United States Ambassador to Japan

It is inconsistent with our basic principles to continue pretending that Taiwan is China. This is a lie, and for a great nation honesty is a necessity.

Newsweek, 2-8:34.

(Regarding President Nixon's announced plans to visit Communist China): The American people must not expect too much too fast. We are still too hung up on China—either we hate her or we love her; we respond either with hostility or excitement.

Time, 7-26:12.

Today, we view the rapprochement with (Communist) China as being perhaps the most important thing in Asia. I think it's a highly desirable thing; but it isn't anywhere near as important as our relationship with Japan. And if we play up to Chinese fears of Japan in seeming to make a deal with the Chinese behind the backs of the Japanese, then we're playing a very dangerous game indeed, and one that could be extremely detrimental to America's real interests.

Interview/Newsweek, 10-4:36.

James Reston
Vice president and columnist,
"The New York Times"

(Regarding his recent trip to Communist China): I'm a Scotch Calvinist. I believe in redemption of the human spirit and the improvement of man. Maybe it's because I believe that or I want to believe it that I was struck by the tremendous effort (in Communist China) to bring out what is best in man, what makes them good, what makes them cooperate with one another and be considerate and not beastly to one another. They are trying that.

Television interview, Tokyo, Aug. 30/
The New York Times, 9-2:16.

William P. Rogers
Secretary of State of the United States

(Regarding Communist China's bid for more friendly relations with the United States): Many motives have been assigned to the move. Some say it is part of a general diplomatic campaign for international recognition, others that it was mainly a reaction to Peking's differences with the Soviet Union, or to an effort, as a Soviet journal has charged . . . to become the world's main superpower. Whatever the motive, we welcome the Chinese move.

Before Southeast Asia Treaty Organization, London, April 27/ The Washington Post, 4-28:(A)1.

In our interdependent world, no significant segment of the world's population and of the world's power should be isolated. It was this consideration which led President Nixon to alter the China policy of the United States. To pursue a policy which did not respond to present realities would risk the future for the sake of the past. On the other hand, to seek to improve relations with the People's Republic of (Communist) China and to contribute to its greater contact with the international community could foster prospects for a stable peace in years to come.

At United Nations, New York, Oct. 4/ U.S. News & World Report, 10-18:104.

(Concerning the tension between India and Pakistan): Diplomatically we are going to do everything we can to prevent war from breaking out. (But) if war breaks out, we intend to stay out. We are not going to get involved in another war.

At Sigma Delta Chi convention, Washington, Nov. 12/ Los Angeles Herald-Examiner, 11-13:(A)4.

Carlos P. Romulo
Foreign Minister of the Philippines

One of the most important (developments in this part of the world) is the development of regional organizations among the free nations of Southeast Asia. We have succeeded in establishing regional groupments that are achieving cooperation in the economic, educational, cultural and political fields. This is a new development in Asia that is generally unbeknown to the public of the world . . . If Europe, a continent riven for centuries by wars, jealousies and intrigues, can have a Common Market and begin to move toward a united Europe, why shouldn't we, who have no deep-rooted hatred or suspicion of our

neighbors, not succeed in creating common regional policies?

Interview, Manila/ San Francisco Examiner, 7-6:12.

Walt W. Rostow
Former Special Assistant to the President of the United States

What would happen if the U.S. walked away from its commitments in Asia? We would soon have at least three nuclear powers in Asia (Communist China, India and Japan) —not just one. China inevitably would be tempted to fill the vacuum left by American withdrawal. The nations of Southeast Asia— including Singapore and possibly Indonesia— could lose their independence or be forced into a fight with externally-supported rebels that would divert them from their promising paths of economic and social progress. Burma, a strategic country for South Asia, would either fall under Communist domination or become the battleground for an Indian-Chinese struggle. I believe that the balance of power in Asia, and the existence of an Asia which is not dominated by a potentially hostile power, is as important to the U.S. as the balance of power in Europe. And it will become increasingly so. We must remember that the last time an aspiring but relatively poor Asian nation tried to upset the balance of power, the result was Pearl Harbor—and that was in a pre-nuclear age.

Interview, Washington/ U.S. News & World Report, 11-8:81.

Dean Rusk
Former Secretary of State of the United States

. . . when I left office, (there were) large numbers of North Vietnamese troops in Laos, South Vietnam and Cambodia, North Vietnamese-trained guerrillas operating in Thailand, men in arms coming across the northeastern frontier of Burma out of China, every week men in arms coming across the 38th parallel from North Korea into South Korea. Now, you don't need dominoes. You look at what is happening, and you feel that there is

(DEAN RUSK)

not going to be peace in Asia until this sort of thing stops, or they simply conquer it and you have that kind of peace of the concentration camp.

Television interview/
National Broadcasting Company, 7-2.

Eisaku Sato
Prime Minister of Japan

Japan should not be hasty in jumping on the bandwagon to recognize (Communist China). We must be sure that it is safe to board, and we must drive carefully.

News conference, Tokyo, Jan. 1/
The Washington Post, 1-2:(A)5.

(Regarding United States President Nixon's new economic program announced Aug. 15, which includes a 10% surtax on imports): One can certainly not deny that repercussions will be far-reaching . . . but Japan and the United States are in the same ship together. If the United States is shipwrecked, so is Japan.

Interview, Tokyo, Aug. 31/
Los Angeles Herald-Examiner, 9-2:(A)4.

Even if we say that we abide by a peace constitution, that we abide by our three non-nuclear principles—that is, not to possess, make or introduce nuclear weapons into Japan—I suppose that people might have some doubt concerning our intentions; they may feel that a country with our economic capacity could sweep all that aside and turn to militarism. But let me say that, from the viewpoint of the Japanese people, it would be far from easy, almost impossible really, to amend the Constitution in view of the present psychology of the nation. Even to change one law, the self-defense law, which forbids the dispatch of troops overseas, would be very difficult. As far as Japan's security is concerned, this is based on the U.S.-Japan security treaty; and the Japanese people have confidence in America, that America would never unilaterally abrogate that treaty; nor would this be possible from the Japanese side. And

so I think that, as far as we are concerned, our safety is guaranteed by the security treaty; and as long as we have that treaty, we also have our three non-nuclear principles. So I feel there is no fear in this respect of any change coming from us.

Interview, Tokyo, Aug. 31/
The New York Times, 9-2:23.

I don't think there will be a total withdrawal of the U.S. from Asia. Things are not as simple as that . . . President Nixon said he will observe U.S. commitments to its friends, and we trust he will observe his commitments to this country (Japan). I trust in his personality, in his character; I trust his words. So I believe what is important for Mr. Nixon is to live up to the expectations of the Asian people.

Interview, Tokyo/Newsweek, 9-20:38.

(Regarding the reversion of Okinawa to Japan by the United States): We are about to achieve the return of an island with one million people. That is a lot of people. Just think how many countries there are in the United Nations with less than a million people. To do that without war, through peaceful talks, is quite an achievement. It should be valued very highly.

Interview, Tokyo/
The Washington Post, 10-14:(A)19.

Haile Selassie
Emperor of Ethiopia

(Referring to Communist China): Never in modern history has a nation successfully made such a determined and massive effort to achieve progress for so many millions of people within such a short span of time.

Peking/
The Christian Science Monitor,
10-9:2.

James C. H. Shen
Nationalist Chinese Ambassador
to the United States

(Regarding United States President Nixon's announced plans to visit Communist China):

Mutual trust is the basis of good relations between any two countries. The Republic of China (Nationalist China) and the U.S. are allies. We have a mutual-defense pact under which we have pledged to help each other in case of armed aggression; and the source of threat is the Chinese Communist regime. Now, without prior consultations with us, the U.S. has suddenly turned around to establish high-level contact with Peking. This is somewhat like when you are in a war and your ally leaves you to make a separate peace with your common enemy.

Interview, Washington/
U.S. News & World Report, 8-2:42.

. . . the successes we have had in developing Taiwan—not just as a military fortress, but as a place for people to live, to work, to raise children in security and peace—that's something the (Chinese) Communists cannot accept. They will regard us as a thorn in their side so long as we exist. They know our position is getting stronger. They know our economic situation is better than ever before. And they also know that the people are more united than ever before in their determination to defend their freedom and their way of life.

Interview, Washington/
U.S. News & World Report, 8-2:44.

Marshall D. Shulman
Director, Russian Institute,
Columbia University

The two-week war (between India and Pakistan) has been a major setback for us (the U.S.), largely as a consequence of our insensitivity and our ineptitude and our misplaced values. The net effect has been to give the Soviet Union a predominance of influence on the subcontinent instead of a healthy balance of external influences, which would have served the interests of the Indians and Pakistanis as well as ourselves. Our excessive reliance on Pakistan as a military bulwark made us silent and impotent in the face of human tragedy on the most massive scale this decade has witnessed. If anyone asks what the United States stands for in the light of the way we

behaved toward events on the subcontinent in this period, the answer would and should make us all ashamed.

Interview, New York/
Los Angeles Times, 12-28:(2)7.

Norodom Sihanouk
Exiled Former Chief of State
of Cambodia

Where do you find any Chinese soldiers outside the frontiers of China? Hong Kong, Macao, Taiwan—these are Chinese territory, but China has not taken them. But where do you find soldiers from the United States? Was the Bay of Pigs not a true symbol of American policy? China wants the liberation of the peoples; but the Chinese are not interested after the liberation in taking over from the banished tyrants.

Interview, Peking/
The New York Times, 2-4:35.

Swaran Singh
Foreign Minister of India

(Regarding the signing of a friendship treaty between India and the Soviet Union): This should act as a deterrent to any powers that may have aggressive designs on our territorial integrity and sovereignty. It is, therefore, in essence, a treaty of peace against war.

Before Parliament, New Delhi,
Aug. 9/San Francisco Examiner, 8-9:8.

International law recognizes that where a mother state (such as Pakistan) has irrevocably lost the allegiance of such a large section of its people, as represented by Bangla Desh (East Pakistan), and cannot bring them under its sway, conditions for the separate existence for such a state come into being. It is India's assessment that this is precisely what has happened in Bangla Desh.

At United Nations, New York,
Dec. 12/Los Angeles Times, 12-13:(1)10.

Edgar Snow
Writer; Authority on Chinese affairs

(Regarding United States President Nixon's announced plans to visit Communist China):

(EDGAR SNOW)

We are witnessing the liquidation of two decades of a U.S. East Asian policy dominated by the ghost of John Foster Dulles. Nixon has now pre-empted a major issue of foreign policy from exploitation by the opposition in the 1972 Presidential race. A new era of Far Eastern and world politics has begun. China stands to gain much from her new stature; but she will not abandon Mao Tse-tung's basic view of the world.

Geneva, July 16/
The New York Times, 7-17:2.

John C. Stennis
United States Senator, D–Miss.

The limitation of our manpower and resources will not permit us to aid every Asian nation any time it is confronted with a Communist threat both from within and without. Moreover, we must make certain that a preponderant proportion of the people in a country must be willing to adhere to the principles of freedom and be united in their willingness to defend their freedoms to the death if necessary.

Jackson, Miss., Jan. 11/
The Washington Post, 1-14:(A)8.

T. N. J. Suharto
President of Indonesia

Our ability to put our household in order, our ability to realize stability and political stability, our ability to overcome difficulties placed before us, our ability to carry out development, remain the basic capital that can increase the degree of foreign confidence in us.

Before Parliament, Jakarta, Aug. 16/
The Washington Post, 8-17:(A)13.

Thanat Khoman
Foreign Minister of Thailand

(Regarding United States President Nixon's announced plans to visit Communist China): This change means that all nations in Asia, including Thailand, are at a historical turning point. Thailand is in a hazardous position. We must be very cautious. We must think about the subjects Nixon will discuss with (Chinese) Premier Chou En-lai. We must guess and estimate—what will be the bargain?

Bangkok, July 20/
The Washington Post, 7-21:(A)12.

(Concerning Prime Minister Thanom Kittikachorn's assumption, that day, of total power): This is a revolution not like revolutions in other parts of the world. This is not an event to bring people into the streets. It is an event to bring calm, decency, order and dedication to the national interest of the country. Basic institutions of government have not changed.

At Foreign Correspondents Club,
Bangkok, Nov. 17/
The New York Times, 11-18:14.

John G. Tower
United States Senator, R–Tex.

(Regarding President Nixon's announced plans to visit Communist China): In view of the irrational attitudes of the present government in Peking; in view of their international banditry and their exportation of the most dogmatic, virulent and bellicose brand of Communism; in view of our long alliance with Nationalist China, I am disturbed by the President's announcement of last evening . . . I do not know what has motivated the President in this move. Perhaps it is our steadily diminishing capability to cope with Soviet expansionism and growing Soviet military might. Perhaps it is from a feeling that mounting isolationism here at home no longer permits an effective American presence throughout the world. Perhaps the President has been led to believe that the establishment of liaison with Peking might lead to Chinese intervention with Hanoi to stop the war. Whatever it is, the President owes the American people an explanation. I hope it will be forthcoming soon.

July 16/Human Events, 7-24:3.

ASIA AND THE PACIFIC

Barbara Tuchman
Author, Historian

(Communist) China is in everybody's future. (China and the United States) are both major powers, and sooner or later—and sooner rather than later—we will have to establish a connection . . . (Recognition) is not too far off. China is gradually being recognized; the great barrier in our case is Vietnam.

Interview, Los Angeles/
Los Angeles Times, 2-11:(4)3.

Nobuhiko Ushiba
Japanese Ambassador to the
United States

The United States is the chief guarantor of the security in the Pacific area; and Japan and the United States are closely tied by the U.S.-Japan Security Treaty. From these simple facts, it is clear that the main political and economic load for the peace and prosperity of Asia will have to be carried by our two countries. And the stakes are enormous. So great, indeed, that in the perspective of history, our transitory differences over whether too many Japanese-knit sweaters are entering the U.S. market, or whether we are liberalizing foreign investment in Japan fast enough, will seem like rather minor considerations indeed. We both have a common interest in placing such differences in their proper perspective. They are not negligible problems, and they need our mutual understanding and cooperation, which Japan is trying wholeheartedly to give them. But they are, if I may say so, secondary.

At The Opening Door symposium,
San Francisco, March 15/
Vital Speeches, 4-15:391.

The Japanese economy will continue to grow at current high rates, at least until 1975. However, it is rapidly becoming an open economy, competing on even terms with its principal partners and undertaking wider responsibilities in trade and economic development. And by devoting greater attention to improving the quality of Japanese life, it will finally close the "quality gap" between Japan and the West. Higher wages and living standards

throughout Japan should permanently put to rest the myth of cheap labor, while at the same time making Japan an increasingly profitable market for foreign goods and capital.

At American Management Association
conference on Japan, New York, March 23/
The New York Times, 3-24:57.

It is quite true that the stability of Southeast Asian nations has been tremendously improved since the middle of the 1960s owing to various reasons, such as their economic progress, the Sino-Soviet conflict, the cultural revolution in (Communist) China, U.S. military action in Vietnam. and so on. In this sense, the Nixon Doctrine is based on a realistic evaluation of the situation in Asia. In its application, however, we think you (the U.S.) need careful handling. For example, it is a good thing to urge Asian nations to defend themselves; but it will psychologically and politically have an adverse effect if it gives Asians the impression that the United States is thinning out its security commitment. In Asia as a whole, psychological measures are sometimes more important than actual military measures. Some Asian countries may need actually less military protection in terms of modern defense ability than those in Western Europe; but they may need more psychological military presence or moral commitment by the United States for their political stability.

At Georgetown University, Washington,
July 9/The Washington Post, 7-18:(B)6.

. . . I want to make it very clear that Japan will not go nuclear, and that Japan's armed forces will not be sent to any part of Asia. All informed observers of Japanese affairs will agree with this conclusion after a careful analysis of the political trends and the tendency of the public opinion in Japan. At least they would agree that the change in this fundamental policy of Japan will not take place unless there is a very radical change in the political atmosphere in Japan, which would be desirable neither for the Japanese people nor the American people. Above all, it

315

(NOBUHIKO USHIBA)

is vitally important that the Japanese people will not feel themselves isolated in this world. I have no apprehension about such eventualities, since I firmly believe that the U.S.-Japan friendship and cooperation will continue to be the pillar of Japanese foreign policy for a very long time to come.

> *At National Press Club,*
> *Washington, Aug. 11/*
> *The Washington Post, 8-13:(A)22.*

Once we (Japan) were a garden. But in our haste to catch up with the modernized West, we have cluttered our cities, scarred our countryside and left too many of our people—especially our rural and small-town population—outside the mainstream of our new prosperity. This is, I realize, the kind of problem with which the United States is also trying to deal. And like the United States, Japan is also beginning to reallocate massive resources in order to clean up the environment, raise minimum living standards and greatly expand essential public services. We have dreams of becoming a garden once again.

> *Before Japan Society, New York,*
> *Sept. 16/Vital Speeches, 10-15:13.*

George C. Wallace
Governor of Alabama

As far as Red China is concerned, I hope that the President (Nixon) is successful in his forthcoming trip (to Peking) and that whatever he does results in world peace. However, I doubt that this will be the result of his trip. I think the China trip is going to prove to be a colossal mistake. The only thing that the President will accomplish is to be required to give some unilateral concessions to enable us to get out of Southeast Asia and then turn South Vietnam over to the Communists.

> *Interview/Nation's Business, November:75.*

Harold Wilson
Leader, British Labor Party; Former Prime Minister of the United Kingdom

With Britain, the test for recognition of

sovereign governments always has been, not if we didn't like the governments, but if they were, in effect, in control of the country. We decided in 1950 that applied in the case of (Communist) China, so we recognized its government. It makes international relations much easier if that is the test.

> *At University of Texas at Austin,*
> *April 30/The Austin (Tex.)*
> *American-Statesman, 5-1:6.*

Agha Mohammad Yahya (Khan)
President of Pakistan

I inherited a bad economy, and I am going to pass it on.

> *News conference/*
> *The New York Times, 1-31:(1)5.*

(Regarding the secessionist movement in East Pakistan): No matter what happens, as long as I am in command of Pakistan's armed forces and head of state, I will ensure the complete and absolute integrity of Pakistan. I will not allow a handful of people to destroy the homeland of millions of innocent Pakistanis.

> *Broadcast address, Rawalpindi, March 5/*
> *The New York Times, 3-7:(1)3.*

(Accusing India of artillery attacks along the border with East Pakistan): I am watching the situation. If the Indians have the idea of taking a chunk out of East Pakistan, it would mean war. We are very near to war with India. Let me warn them—India and the world—it means total war. I am not looking for war and am trying to avoid it. But there is a limit to my patience.

> *Interview, Karachi/*
> *The Dallas Times Herald, 8-11:(A)10.*

(Announcing defeat of his forces by India in East Pakistan): To all our friends we say, stand by us and rest assured the people of Pakistan and their armed forces will not cease their struggle until the aggression is ended and justice prevails . . . This is not the end. We shall fight for our country relentlessly . . . The torch of resistance to India's naked aggression shall never be allowed to be extinguished.

Broadcast address, Dec. 16/
Los Angeles Times, 12-17:(1)7.

C. K. Yen
Vice President and Prime Minister
of Nationalist China

When discussing the seating of the (Chinese) Communists in the United Nations, I'm asked, "How can you ignore the hundreds of millions of people on the mainland?" I tell them we are the true representatives of all the Chinese on these islands and the mainland, and *you* will be the one ignoring the people if you do business with the Mao Communists. When you deal with the Communists, you do not do business with the people; you are dealing with a regime that exploits people; it does not represent them. There is no personal liberty in Communism.

Interview/
Los Angeles Herald-Examiner, 7-4:(A)10.

THE WAR IN INDOCHINA

Bella S. Abzug
United States Representative, D–N.Y.

We do have a chance to set the date this year to bring the troops home. We have a new year, a new Congress and the same old war. From our President's military leaders and leading statesmen we have gotten lies and deception. They manipulate words as though they were playing parlor games instead of dealing in human suffering.
Washington, Jan. 21/Daily World, 1-22:1.

Spiro T. Agnew
Vice President of the United States

(Critics of the war are making American troops feel that) they are fighting in a "worthless" and "immoral" cause, and that we ought to abandon the South Vietnamese to their enemy. (This advice) has come to them not from Hanoi Hannah but from some of the leading members of the U.S. Senate, prestigious columnists and news commentators, academic figures, some church organizations, as well as assorted radicals, draft-card burners and street demonstrators.
Before Veterans Administration Volunteer Service, Washington, April 1/ The Washington Post, 4-2:(A)16.

It probably would be hard to find in American history a more glaring example of negative treatment of an issue than the Vietnam war. The news coverage of that war has been preponderantly negative in tone—critical of the United States and the South Vietnamese and, in that sense, helpful to the North Vietnamese and the Viet Cong. There are, of course, exceptions. But in the main, our news media have seemed obsessed with playing up our weaknesses—real or imagined—and ignoring those of the enemy.
Before Los Angeles Area Chamber of Commerce, April 7/ Los Angeles Times, 4-8:(1)26.

(Regarding the previous weekend's anti-war rally): I respect their right to dissent and demonstrate, peacefully and orderly. (But) there is something grotesque and macabre in seeing the banners of an enemy nation (North Vietnam) being carried down the streets of Washington. There's something wrong with that, in my judgment.
Los Angeles Herald-Examiner, 4-28:(A)12.

(Regarding the treatment in the U.S. of many returning Vietnam veterans): For fighting in an unpopular war, they have had to bear the brunt of its unpopularity. In no other war have we had so many Medal of Honor winners and so few recognized heroes. In no other war has the uniform been so disparaged or has the returning veteran received less citizen assistance in obtaining employment and finding his rightful place in society.
At Veterans Day ceremonies, Washington, Oct. 25/Los Angeles Times, 10-26:(1)10.

George D. Aiken
United States Senator, R–Vt.

The day has passed when the major problems of Asia can be settled in some European city, where the Soviet Union and the Western powers enjoy a protocol status far in excess of their real influence. The time has come for nations to recognize that formal peace among the parties in Indochina will only come as a result of agreement among themselves. It cannot be imposed by others.

Before the Senate, Washington, Feb. 10/
Los Angeles Times, 2-11:(1)10.

I . . . think it is folly to argue that setting a date for a (U.S.) withdrawal from Vietnam would be lending aid and comfort to the enemy. I don't swallow that.

Interview, Washington/
U.S. News & World Report, 6-28:27.

George W. Ball
Former Under Secretary of State
of the United States

I would say on the whole that I think the government is pulling out of Vietnam. I would hope they'll do it with an accelerated tempo . . . because it seems to me that there's been a full signal to the Administration now that they haven't got a great deal more time to get American troops out of this situation without a real blowup in the United States.

TV-radio interview/"Face the Nation,"
Columbia Broadcasting System, 6-27.

Birch Bayh
United States Senator, D—Ind.

Let history show that this generation of Americans ended the war in Vietnam once and for all. I have supported setting a definite timetable for our withdrawal—not just from Vietnam, but from all Southeast Asia as well.

At California State Democratic Party
convention, Sacramento, Jan. 24/
Los Angeles Herald-Examiner, 1-25:(A)9.

Lloyd M. Bentsen
United States Senator, D—Tex.

I think we have fulfilled our commitment in South Vietnam. They now have an army of 1.1 million men, the seventh largest air force in the world, the fourth largest helicopter force, the fourth largest navy in the number of ships. South Vietnam has the capacity to defend themselves without us. Whether or not they have the will is another question. We cannot be responsible for their will to defend

themselves. This is something they have to do on their own.

Austin, Tex./
The Dallas Times Herald, 7-18:(A)19.

Mme. Nguyen Thi Binh
Chief Viet Cong delegate
to Paris peace talks

Fifty battalions of American and South Vietnamese puppet troops have invaded Laos. Among them are 10 battalions of American infantry, artillery and armor—I stress infantry. The United States cannot escape through impudent sophism its heavy responsibility in intensifying and extending the war to Laos and all of Indochina.

At Paris peace talks, Feb. 11/
Los Angeles Herald-Examiner, 2-11:(A)8.

(U.S. President) Nixon has already expanded the war to all of Indochina and has suffered grave defeats. If he expands the war again, he will reap even graver defeats.

News conference, Rome, Feb. 24/
The New York Times, 2-25:4.

We Vietnamese, more than any people anywhere else, want the American troops to withdraw immediately. Last year, we demanded the immediate withdrawal of American troops. And next year we will demand that American troops be withdrawn immediately. This slogan reflects the aspirations of the people who want to settle the question immediately. It is a good slogan. But we must be more realistic, because (U.S. President) Nixon, as you know, has a lot of tricks. He wants people to believe that he has a timetable for American withdrawal in his pocket. But everybody knows it is not true. We must put up the slogan that there must be a clear date for American withdrawal. Only in this way can we force Mr. Nixon to say yes or no. If he is not able to set up any timetable, any date, that proves he does not have any timetable in his pocket.

Interview, Budapest, Hungary/
Daily World, 6-26:(M)11.

Derek C. Bok
President-elect, Harvard University

I don't know about other places, but Vietnam is still the dominant public issue here (at Harvard). I do not think the concern has gone away to any extent. There is just bewilderment about what to do, and frustration. The students feel no response from the government in terms of human life. They hear about military considerations and withdrawal rates, not about the number of people being killed in Indochina. They get back from Washington an insensitivity to the human cost of what we are doing.

Interview, Cambridge, Mass./
The New York Times, 3-27:29.

Kingman Brewster, Jr.
President, Yale University

To my mind, the basic flaw in our Southeast Asian war policy is moral. Policy seems to be shaped and is most often discussed as though America had no concern for the sanctity of human life as such, as though we cared only for American lives. The reduction of American casualties, even the withdrawal of all American combat troops, does not mitigate our moral responsibility—for the spread of the war, for the indiscriminate bombing of neutrals, for the scorching of forests and villages, for the massacre of innocents.

On Alumni Day, Yale University, Feb. 20/
The Washington Post, 3-12:(A)23.

Leonid I. Brezhnev
*General Secretary, Communist
Party of the Soviet Union*

Anyone capable of taking a realistic view of things must realize that neither direct armed intervention nor torpedoing of negotiations nor even the ever-wider use of mercenaries will break down the Vietnamese people's determination to become masters of its country. The so-called "Vietnamization" of the war—that is, the plan to have Vietnamese kill Vietnamese in Washington's interests—and the extension of the aggression to Cambodia and Laos—none of this will get the U.S.A. out of the bog of its dirty war in Indochina or wash away the shame heaped on that country by those who started and are continuing the aggression.

At Soviet Communist Party Congress,
Moscow, March 30/
The New York Times, 3-31:14.

Edward W. Brooke
United States Senator, R—Mass.

To my mind, the fact that Congress has failed to take a central part in shaping past policies toward the war is a crucial reason for authoritative action in molding our policy for disengagement. Indeed, to assert clear legislative authority over the manner in which the United States extricates itself from an undeclared and unduly-prolonged war would be a vital step toward reviving Congressional powers over the initiation of conflict.

Before the Senate, Washington/
The Dallas Times Herald, 3-5:(A)17.

David K. E. Bruce
*United States Ambassador
to Paris peace talks*

(Addressing North Vietnamese and Viet Cong delegations): Throughout your statements runs the failure to mention the long-standing and continuing massive presence of North Vietnamese forces in Laos, Cambodia and South Vietnam, sent there clandestinely, illegally, in great numbers and in defiance of the wishes of the governments concerned and of international agreements to which North Vietnam is a party . . . We will persist in our efforts to persuade you to engage in genuine negotiations. But until you agree to do so, we will carry out alternative solutions to the conflict. You have made it abundantly clear that you do not like these solutions. Yet you make no contribution to genuine negotiations. The choice remains in your hands.

At Paris peace talks, Feb. 4/
Los Angeles Times, 2-5:(1)9.

(Addressing North Vietnamese and Viet Cong delegations): . . . you ask whether we are prepared to set immediately a date in 1971 for the total withdrawal of our forces from South Vietnam. The answer is that we have long been ready to negotiate a timetable for complete withdrawals as part of an over-all settlement. But the fixing of a withdrawal date must be the result of a genuine negotiating process, not a price we must first pay just for negotiations to begin or a unilateral action we must take because you so dictate.

At Paris peace talks, July 15/
The New York Times, 7-16:2.

James L. Buckley
United States Senator, C–N.Y.

We are on the verge of achieving the success of our years of effort in blood and treasure (in Indochina). To heed the demands for a precipitous withdrawal at this time would betray the valiant efforts made to date. By simply continuing our training, logistics and air support efforts for but a brief period of time, the South Vietnamese will be capable of bearing the full weight of their own defense.

Before the Senate, Washington, April 22/
The New York Times, 4-23:7.

Ellsworth Bunker
United States Ambassador to
South Vietnam

I know what the cost of this war has been to the United States. I am aware of the moral ambiguity our presence in Vietnam poses for many, and that this is more deeply felt than in any previous war in this century. I am deeply conscious of our needs at home in every direction. But as the world's most powerful nation, we cannot escape the responsibilities of power. What we do or fail to do in Vietnam will affect our own position in Asia and the balance of power in this part of the world, and eventually will mean the difference between war or peace in Asia. I believe that our actions in Vietnam will determine the credibility of our commitment to the principles of the United Nations Charter and the credibility of our obligations under

NATO, SEATO and in other bilateral treaties. The issue that our people and our Congress must face is whether we have the patience and the will to accept the responsibilities of power. It seems to me that we have a commitment to history and to ourselves as to the kind of world we envisage—whether the rule of law shall govern or the rule of force. I deeply believe that as our resolve now weakens, the danger of an eventual wider conflict will be increased.

Interview, Saigon/
U.S. News & World Report, 7-5:25.

Robert F. Byrnes
Professor of History, Indiana University

One of the most curious aspects of the war in Southeast Asia is the entire absence of any popular interest in relief and rehabilitation. Indeed, not since President (Lyndon) Johnson launched his exciting Mekong River program has there been any serious discussion in this country of our postwar policies . . . Why do the American people—*not* the government— not begin a program such as Herbert Hoover did during and after the First World War? Where are today's Hoovers and La Guardias? Why do not our educational leaders and our scientists create a truly international Samaritan program, in which Americans could participate, to heal the wounds of war here and abroad? If peace should come quickly to that part of the world—as we all hope—we would be even less prepared to assist the peoples of those countries than we were to understand them when the fighting began.

Before Senate Subcommittee on National
Security and International Operations,
Washington/
The Washington Post, 4-25:(B)6.

William L. Calley, Jr.
Lieutenant, United States Army;
Convicted of participation in the
My Lai (South Vietnam) massacre

. . . I'm not going to stand here and plead for my life or my freedom. But I would . . . ask you to consider a thousand more lives that are going to be lost in Southeast Asia, a thou-

(WILLIAM L. CALLEY, JR.)

sand more to be imprisoned—imprisoned not only here in the United States, but in North Vietnam and in hospitals all over the world as amputees. I've never known a soldier—nor did I ever myself—ever wantonly kill a human being in my entire life. If I have committed a crime, the only crime that I have committed is in judgment of my values. Apparently, I valued my troops' lives more than I did that of the enemy—when my troops were getting massacred and mauled by an enemy I couldn't see, I couldn't feel and I couldn't touch—that nobody in the military system ever described as anything other than as Communism. They didn't give it a race. They didn't give it a sex. They didn't give it an age. They never let me believe it was just a philosophy in a man's mind. That was my enemy out there. And when it came between me and that enemy, I had to value the lives of my troops. And I feel that is the only crime I have committed. Yesterday (by finding him guilty), you stripped me of all my honor. Please, by your actions that you take here today, don't strip future soldiers of their honor, I beg of you.

> *Before court-martial jury considering his sentence, Fort Benning, Ga., March 30/ The Washington Post, 3-31:(A)12.*

Chou En-lai
Premier of Communist China

(To North Vietnam): Do not thank us for our aid. Aid is mutual. It is you who aid us by fighting in the front lines of the anti-imperialist struggle. For that, the Chinese people must thank *you*.

> *Hanoi, North Vietnam, March 5/ The New York Times, 3-9:5.*

The three Indochina countries are China's close neighbors. By willfully enlarging their aggressive war in the Indochina area, the U.S. imperialists are posing a serious threat to China. The Chinese government and the Chinese people have already seen through all the frenzied and adventurous nature of the U.S. imperialists and have made adequate preparations. The

Nixon government must be responsible for all the serious consequences arising from its unceasing expansion of the aggressive war in the Indochina region.

> *Hanoi, North Vietnam, March 5/ The Washington Post, 3-9:(A)8.*

(China and North Vietnam) are closely united to each other—like the lips and the teeth.

> *Hanoi, North Vietnam, March 5/ The Washington Post, 3-9:(A)1.*

The revolutionary situation in Indochina is unprecedentedly fine.

> *At North Vietnamese Embassy banquet, Peking/The Washington Post, 3-18:(A)9.*

(Regarding United States President Nixon's announced plans to visit Communist China): We believe that the first question that must be settled is that of Indochina; and in settling it, we will be acting not only in the interests of the Indochinese people but also of the American people. The thing which, in our view, is most called for, whether in the United States or abroad, is the withdrawal by the United States of their troops from Vietnam and the evacuation of troops of other countries that followed the United States in Indochina. It can be said that this demand for evacuation is even stronger than the call for the restoration of relations between the Chinese and American people.

> *Interview, Peking, July 20/ Los Angeles Herald-Examiner, 7-21:(A)1.*

Frank Church
United States Senator, D—Idaho

The only remedy is to bring America home again to the forgotten truth that the first mission of Federal government was never to decide which faction should govern some little country on the fringes of China, but to attend to the genuine need of the American people. The Vietnam war's fallout has debased on a far broader front the confidence of young people in their government. The credibility of the government, including the Presidency itself, has been grievously impaired.

At College and University Conference and Exposition, Atlantic City, N.J., March 26/San Francisco Examiner, 3-27:2.

J. Harlan Cleveland
President, University of Hawaii; Former United States Ambassador to the North Atlantic Treaty Organization

(The Vietnam war) has to be the most unilateral, the most unsuccessful, the most unpopular war in American history.

At international conference on the United Nations, Stanford, Calif., Jan. 12/ Los Angeles Herald-Examiner, 1-13:(D)12.

Maurice Couve de Murville
Former Foreign Minister of France

Your (America's) preoccupation is with having a non-Communist regime in Saigon. That is really what you are seeking, for reasons of prestige much more than for reasons of national interest. Why do you care? There is going to be a South Vietnamese regime; no person can say what it will be like. The only thing that you and anybody have to worry about is that it is an independent regime, not a satellite of anybody, be it of the United States or (Communist) China or the Soviet Union. As long as it stays a national regime it will be all right. The regime in the North is a national regime. It is a fact that foreign intervention, which is American intervention in Vietnam, has a way of identifying what is Communist and what is national. What I mean is that, wherever you intervene in Southeast Asia, those who are against you are the Communists. It is the same in Thailand now. With occupation, you have succeeded in creating opposition which is both national and Communist. It is the same in Laos and Cambodia. This is the real domino theory. You are developing Communists by intervening; because the only reaction against foreign intervention is the Communist resistence.

Interview, Paris/ Los Angeles Times, 9-17:(2)7.

Ronald V. Dellums
United States Representative, D–Calif.

If we're going to save face in the world, then we ought to get out of Southeast Asia as quickly as we can; and then we ought to look back on the activities of the last few years and lay the blame where it desperately needs to be laid . . . We were very aggressive in World War II in prosecuting war crimes. We ought to be just as interested in prosecuting our own.

Washington, Jan. 28/ The Washington Post, 1-29:(A)4.

Pham Van Dong
Premier of North Vietnam

Many more hardships and difficulties lie ahead of our struggle against U.S. aggression and for national salvation. Yet, we are advancing fast toward victory, and we will surely reach our goal, which will be a victory of tremendous international significance.

Before National Assembly, Hanoi, June 11/The New York Times, 6-14:6.

Hedley Donovan
Editor-in-chief, Time, Inc.

There begins to be a good deal of evidence that the South Vietnamese do more on their own behalf when the U.S. does less. For better or worse, however, they should now have to plan on the Americans being gone, instead of assuming—because U.S. leaders never quite say otherwise—that our presence can always be prolonged. It would be good to get this out in the open *before* the South Vietnamese elections. To postpone the news is to export a bit of our own credibility gap.

At dinner for executives of 500 largest U.S. corporations sponsored by "Fortune" magazine, Chicago, May/Time, 6-14:28.

Thomas F. Eagleton
United States Senator, D–Mo.

It is we, the United States, who are hung up about elections in Vietnam. We decided that this war-ravaged, backward country with no historical or current experience in the democratic process must be shaped in our image.

323

(THOMAS L. EAGLETON)

Since we elect a President, so too must Vietnam . . . It salves our conscience.

The National Observer, 5-3:4.

Daniel Ellsberg
Former government consultant,
Rand Corporation

(Concerning the effect on high government officials—in office during increased U.S. involvement in Vietnam—of secret Pentagon papers he released to the press): The punishment I want for them is that which I have had to suffer. I want them to be compelled to read every page of the 7,000 pages of the Pentagon documents, to see their own decisions laid end to end in the context of all the other decisions made during that period. Beyond that, I would like them exposed, as I was, to the human physical impact of their decisions on the people of Indochina. I would like them to know what happened as a result of the (American) bombing. I want them to see the footage that never got on television of the wounded children, of the defoliation, of the refugee camps, of the impact of the war on Indochina. And then I want them to decide for themselves what they ought to do. The aim of any inquiry on the origins of the war—and there should be an investigation—should be to help public understanding and to bring about a change in the policies these men pursued, not to add them to the victims of these policies. There are too many political prisoners already. What's really needed is not new prisoners but amnesty—amnesty for the people who are in jail right now simply for opposing the criminal policies of these officials; amnesty for the people of Indochina who might still be sentenced to death by these policies in the future; and amnesty for all our own sons who may now be sentenced to risks of killing or dying. Some papers, some facts, have now been freed from safes. I'd like to see a lot of prison cells opened too.

Interview/Look, 10-5:42.

John J. Flynt, Jr.
United States Representative, D—Ga.

I will not now or ever again vote to start or continue an undeclared war. It is wrong . . . to fight in a war we have not the fortitude to win or end. My people used to say, "Win the war." Then they said, "Win it or get out." Now, with one voice, they say, "Get out."

Before the House, Washington, April 1/
The Washington Post, 4-2:(A)1.

Gerald R. Ford
United States Representative, R—Mich.

I simply cannot comprehend how any American—especially anyone with a claim to public leadership—can stand up in this trying hour of our history to carp and criticize, snipe and sabotage, quarrel and quibble with a President (Nixon) who day-by-day and week-by-week and month-by-month (is) successfully extricating us from the war in Vietnam.

At Republican Governors Conference,
Williamsburg, Va., April 19/
Los Angeles Times, 4-20:(1)16.

J. William Fulbright
United States Senator, D—Ark.

It's what's happening to the United States at home that is of uppermost importance to me, to my own state and to this country. It's secondary to me what happens out there (in Indochina). I'm not immune to having feelings about the war; but the first thing is what it's doing to the United States. And this seems to me to be my first responsibility. I have the feeling that many people take the other view. They look at this as dissociated from our domestic problems—whether it be the turmoil of the young and the disillusionment of the young or economic difficulties, balance of payments, etc.; you name all the difficulties we are confronting . . . I don't want to see the United States go down the drain all because of Vietnam. We all would like our preferences. We would like to see a nice, friendly democratic government there. But that objective to me is not worth sacrificing the democratic system in the United States, which is very far eroded now. And if the war continues, I think it will continue to erode our democratic system, and we will turn into an authoritarian system, and I don't like that. It's too big a price to pay, in a word.

Interview, Washington/
The Christian Science Monitor, 3-17:3.

The great tragedy of the (Lyndon) Johnson Administration was its subversion of the Constitutional warmaking responsibility of the Congress by false information and deception. The President and his aides misrepresented the facts about an alleged unprovoked attack upon our naval forces in the Gulf of Tonkin on August 4, 1964. The fault of the Congress, including this speaker, was in believing the President of the United States, in having too much confidence in a man and in neglecting to insist upon the full exercise of the Constitutional powers of the Congress.

Before American Society of Newspaper
Editors, Washington, April 16/
The Washington Post, 4-17:(A)2.

James M. Gavin
Lieutenant General,
United States Army (Ret.)

Get out of there (Vietnam) as quickly as we can. I have been saying this for years; in fact, I was one of those who said in the first place: "Don't go in." We should phase our forces out as promptly as we can and then begin to set our priorities right here at home. We should do the things that must be done to make this country as strong as it can be and give it back the moral strength and confidence in its own goals that it needs.

Interview/
U.S. News & World Report, 4-26:25.

Barry M. Goldwater
United States Senator, R–Ariz.

(Regarding proposed Congressional bills to limit the President's war-making powers): Unless I am badly mistaken, there is at the bottom of much of the interest in the war-power bills a feeling, an emotional belief that they will restore Congress to its "proper" position in the

political heavens and rescue the world from the abyss of nuclear destruction. At the very core of this belief is the oft-expressed charge that the Executive has led this nation blind-folded and solely on his own authority into an ever-widening expansion of the Vietnam conflict. I want to declare right here and now that this belief is wrong. It is totally and firmly contradicted by the facts of history. It is erroneously founded on a bedrock of pass-the-buckism, convenient forgetfulness and downright falsehood. The fact is, Congress is and has been involved up to its ears with wars in Southeast Asia. It has known what has been going on from the start and has given its approval in advance to almost everything that has occurred there. Far from being the innocent dupes of a conspiring Executive, Congress has been wholly involved in the policy decisions concerning Vietnam during the entire span of American commitment there.

Before the Senate, Washington/
The New York Times, 8-25:35.

Charles E. Goodell
Former United States Senator, R–N.Y.

According to Administration spokesmen, (the U.S.-South Vietnamese operation in) Cambodia was a success, Laos was a success. How many more successes will it take for the Nixon Administration to recognize failure?

At Macalester College,
St. Paul, Minn., March 26/
The New York Times, 3-28:(1)34.

Mike Gravel
United States Senator, D–Alaska

The greatest representative democracy the world has ever known, the nation of Washington, Jefferson and Lincoln, has had its nose rubbed in the swamp by petty war lords, jealous Vietnamese generals, black marketeers and grand-scale dope pushers . . . The war is still in progress. People, human beings, are being killed as I speak to you—killed as a direct result of policy decisions we, as a body, have made. Arms are being severed, metal is crashing through human bodies, because of a public

325

policy this government and all its branches continue to support.

Washington, June 29/
Los Angeles Times, 6-30:(1)7.

(Regarding his breaking down while reading a statement on the Vietnam war at a Senate Committee session): I wept over the fact that we are killing human beings, we Americans, this wonderful great country. I wept because it hurts, it hurts to see our nation dragged in the mud. It hurts to be part of the leadership of a nation and a citizen of a nation that is killing innocent human beings. That hurts so much we should all cry over it.

TV-radio interview/"Face the Nation,"
Columbia Broadcasting System, 7-4.

Andrei A. Gromyko
Foreign Minister of the Soviet Union

Statements were recently made in Washington about an intention to withdraw American troops from Indochina. Almost every week it is reported that the strength of the American army has been reduced by so many thousands of men. Yet the war in Vietnam, Laos and Cambodia is going on—and the scale of military operations is even increasing from time to time. The United States and its mercenaries are continuing the war. The point is not how big the percentage of American soldiers is there and how big the percentage of local troops if the latter are trained, armed and sent into combat on orders from Washington. The point is that the United States should stop its interference, both military and political, in the affairs of Indochina and abandon its attempts to implant by force of arms an order which is to its liking.

At United Nations, New York, Oct. 4/
Vital Speeches, 11-1:41.

Ernest Gruening
Former United States Senator, D—Alaska

These boys who are being tried now (for the killings at My Lai, South Vietnam) are not responsible. The people who sent them down there are responsible and should be tried. We

are just as responsible as the Germans were in World War II. We're doing all the horrible things the Nazis, the Fascists and the Communists did. The only difference is we do it in the name of liberating people, democratizing them, freeing them. It's ghastly hypocrisy.

Interview, Washington/
The Washington Post, 2-8:(A)18.

Charles S. Gubser
United States Representative, R—Calif.

This war (in Vietnam) is ending and will be over soon. So I respectfully suggest that maybe the real issue involved here today is not ending the war or saving lives but who gets credit for ending it. I suggest respectfully to the people who urged the end of the war years ago, there is plenty of credit for them. There is also credit for Johnny-come-lately doves; there is plenty of credit for the Congress, and plenty of credit for the President (Nixon).

Before the House, Washington/
The National Observer, 10-30:2.

Gus Hall
General secretary,
Communist Party of the United States

Based on these documents (secret Pentagon papers published by several newspapers), now you know why for over two and one-half years (President) Nixon has not put an end to the aggression in Vietnam. And now you know why he refuses to set a date for its end. Nixon's game is to repeat the 1964 election of L.B.J. (Lyndon Johnson)—that is, to withdraw enough troops to be re-elected and then, on the basis of some new provocation, to re-escalate the war after the elections. On the basis of these papers, now you know that 50,000 U.S. youths have given their lives and 350,000 have been crippled in an illegal, immoral war. Now you know! You are paying high taxes and inflationary prices because of the overall policy of U.S.-sponsored, U.S. corporate military aggression.

Mesaba Park, Minn., June 27/
Daily World, 7-1:3.

Clifford P. Hansen
United States Senator, R–Wyo.

When history records the winning of the peace in Indochina, it must also record the great obstacles which were overcome to achieve peace. Those obstacles were not only in Vietnam; they were also in the news offices of Manhattan, generated, sadly, to millions of citizens along transmission wires.

Washington/Variety, 3-17:57.

W. Averell Harriman
Former United States Ambassador-at-Large

If we negotiate an entire withdrawal of our troops (from Vietnam) and take out the Navy and the air power, they (North Vietnam) will release our prisoners, and there will be no problem there.

Before House Foreign Affairs Subcommittee, Washington, June 11/ The Boston Globe, 6-12:9.

Vance Hartke
United States Senator, D–Ind.

. . . the (American) people know, even if their President does not, that we have stayed too long in Vietnam and have bled too much and have perpetrated too many horrors. We have sacrificed not only our men and wealth but our good standing among the civilized nations of the world. We have driven our own children into spiritual exile and thereby mortgaged the future of this society. The war must end, and it must end now.

Before Senate Foreign Relations Committee, Washington, April 20/ Daily World, 6-19:(M)3.

Mr. President (Nixon), let us remind you that America's first and highest commitment is to mankind—and in Indochina we have been violating that commitment for 15 years; and every day we stay we violate it more terribly.

The New York Times, 4-25:(4)1.

Paul Harvey
News commentator,
American Broadcasting Company

These unwinnable wars are absolutely in-

excusable. I subscribe to the old Douglas Mac-Arthur theory that there's only one conceivable excuse to ever get into a war—and that's to win it. When the outgoing Commandant of the Marine Corps confesses that he didn't know what we were doing over there (in Vietnam), then maybe we're getting closer to that day of sufficient sophistication when a President of the United States can say, "We goofed."

Interview, Chicago/TV Guide, 2-20:22.

Mark O. Hatfield
United States Senator, R–Ore.

Everybody is tired of the war. We all know that. Senators are tired of thinking about it, and speaking about it. The press is tired of writing about it. People are tired of reading about it—tired of seeing it on TV. We all just wish it would go away. But being tired about the war, and wanting to forget about it, will not stop it; in fact, it will make it easy for it to quietly go on. It becomes an innocuous, tolerable "page 12" war that kills only 30 Americans every week, that wounds only about 300 other Americans each week, that costs only $10-12 billion a year, that requires only 100,000 or 50,000 or 40,000 American troops . . . and never stops. We have all become de-sensitized by this war; our conscience has become numb. We blink at the TV pictures of Asian villagers who are maimed and burned by our bombs, and are relieved to see a mouthwash commercial flash on the screen after a few seconds. We would all rather worry about whether our breath is fresh than whether innocent people are dying in Asia as a result of our policies . . . Why is there this insensitivity? It is not because Americans do not care, or because Americans like the war. It is because they have heard and seen enough, and they want it to end. Yet, they feel helpless; the war just drags on; despite the announcements about troop withdrawals and the reduced casualties, they still see the war continuing. They are unable to stop it, so they want to forget about it. But we cannot. Every week, new young Americans are sent out to Indochina. About a quarter of a million Americans are there this very day, risking their life and limb. We must not forget them, and those who will follow.

(MARK O. HATFIELD)

Members of the Senate may wish that we did not have to talk about Vietnam again. The press may wish that they could write about something else, something more unique. But we all know better. We know the truth. We know we cannot afford to forget about this war.

Before the Senate, Washington, June 10/
The Washington Post, 6-16:(A)22.

F. Edward Hebert
United States Representative, D—La.

We should have moved in and destroyed everything—everything that was in the hands of the enemy. I decry bombing innocent civilians, but there was no impediment to our destroying the docks and harbor at Haiphong (North Vietnam). If the Pentagon had listened to us two or three years ago, we would have had a victory now with the flag waving high. Now, it's a sorry mess. You don't go out to fight Jack Dempsey with one arm tied behind your back. You don't send kids to get killed and not win. Well, that's what they did. If you get out a gun, you had better be ready to pull the trigger.

Washington/Time, 1-11:11.

Harold E. Hughes
United States Senator, D—Iowa

The President (Nixon) has indicated that he insists on disengagement from Indochina with honor—and (I) agree. There is no honor in prolonging this dreadful war another week. There is no honor in sacrificing more American lives, even at a reduced rate. There is no honor in slaughtering tens of thousands more Asians, including untold numbers of innocent civilians —men, women and children. There is no honor in reducing their homelands to a charred and cratered wasteland. The wise, honorable and humane course is to announce a date for (U.S.) withdrawal, to end the killing, to instruct our negotiators at Paris to offer plans for the exchange of prisoners, and to join with the nations which met at Geneva in 1954 and 1962 in neutralizing all of Indochina. The American people are capable of subduing any enemy in a cause in which they believe. But the people have now rejected the intervention in Southeast Asia, as a human body rejects an unsuited alien heart.

TV-radio broadcast/
American Broadcasting Company, 4-22.

Hubert H. Humphrey
United States Senator, D—Minn.

I think it is important to all of us that South Vietnam be able to maintain its national identity and its national independence; but those decisions are ultimately in the hands of the people of South Vietnam. We have been there a long time, since 1954. We have poured in a treasury of money, of men; we have poured in our manpower, our resources, our technical assistance. South Vietnam today has an army of 1,200,000 regulars, equipped by the American government and the American taxpayer. It has 500,000 regional and local forces. It has had years—ten years, since 1961—to develop a viable regime. I think we have more than fulfilled any obligation we have ever had under any treaty or any commitment that we may have ever made.

Interview/"Meet the Press," National
Broadcasting Company, Washington, 2-28.

. . . a decision to withdraw our military forces from Vietnam this year does not mean, as the President (Nixon) has suggested, that the United States is entering a new era of isolationism. To the contrary, we have extensive international responsibilities, and we will honor them. Indeed, the end of our Vietnam obsession will free the United States to assume a far more balanced and productive role in the world community.

TV-radio broadcast/
American Broadcasting Company, 4-22.

(Regarding secret Pentagon papers on U.S. involvement in Vietnam which were published by several newspapers): These papers portray (former) President Johnson as wanting to wage an all-out military offensive (in Vietnam), and that's just not true. I am a sensitive observer of the man. I (as Vice President) saw him anguish over the war. I saw him try to limit the bombing, turn down the Joint Chiefs' man-power requests and turn down bombing Hai-phong Harbor . . . He wanted to end the war and get a negotiated peace.

Interview, Washington, June 16/
The Washington Post, 6-17:(A)17.

Henry M. Jackson
United States Senator, D–Wash.

Our Party has room for hawks and doves, but not for mockingbirds who chirp gleefully at those who are shooting at American boys.

At New York State AFL-CIO convention,
New York, Aug. 10/
Los Angeles Herald-Examiner, 8-11:(A)11.

(Regarding the prospect of only President Thieu running in the upcoming South Viet-namese Presidential election): I consider the failure to have a Presidential election in Viet-nam a serious and fundamental matter. Should such an election fail to take place, I must reserve my position regarding future U.S. mili-tary and economic aid to the South Vietnam-ese government . . . It is ironic that the sabotage of this Presidential election is not by the Viet Cong–who no longer seem to be able to do it–but by the Thieu regime itself.

Before the Senate, Washington, Sept. 10/
San Francisco Examiner, 9-10:6.

Jacob K. Javits
United States Senator, R–N.Y.

It seems to me that the Nixon Administra-tion faces the same dilemma now which faced the (Lyndon) Johnson Administration in 1967. I am speaking here of the "winning" and "losing" syndrome (in Indochina) which spurred President Johnson on to those meas-ures of military escalation and insensitivity to public opinion which brought his political career to an end.

At Mid-America World Trade
Conference, Chicago, Feb. 25/
The Dallas Times Herald, 2-26:(A)3.

(Regarding the public support for Lt. Wil-liam Calley, convicted of murdering civilians at My Lai, South Vietnam): If the nation really is encouraged to believe that he did nothing wrong–indeed he is a hero–then we have changed as a people during the course of this tragic war even more disastrously than I had imagined. Medals, marches and honors for Lt. Calley, rather than sadness over what a young American was brought to do in a brutal and misguided Vietnam war, is not patriotism but anti-patriotism.

Before the Senate, Washington, April 5/
San Francisco Examiner, 4-6:11.

Herman Kahn
Director, Hudson Institute

If we (the United States) pulled out reck-lessly, South Vietnam would collapse. It's hard for me to see us doing that, by the way; but if we did, I think you'd get a political explosion in the United States. You see, the U.S. military believe they've basically won the war in Vietnam. And lots of people recognize how many Americans have lost their lives there. When you pull defeat out of victory –let me tell you–it doesn't taste good. I don't care how you feel about the Vietnam-ese–it doesn't taste good.

Interview, Washington/
U.S. News & World Report, 2-8:61.

Nicholas deB. Katzenbach
Former Under Secretary of State
of the United States

What I cannot understand is why (Presi-dent) Nixon takes upon his own shoulders the huge burden of disengagement in Vietnam, which may not end–probably will not end–up under happy circumstances, when Congress has indicated a willingness to share that bur-den with him. I simply can't understand it as a matter of politics, in addition (to) as a matter of government.

Before American Society of Newspaper
Editors, Washington, April 16/
Los Angeles Times, 4-17:(1)19.

Edward M. Kennedy
United States Senator, D–Mass.

We have now seen clearly what "Vietnam-

(EDWARD M. KENNEDY)

ization" means. The (U.S. and South Vietnamese) invasion of Cambodia, the invasion of Laos, are the children of that policy. Vietnamization means war and more war; it has nothing to do with an end to violence; it is a policy of violence . . . It is possible that we will, under Vietnamization, eventually reduce our involvement in Vietnam, only to step back and watch the ultimate agony of that place while washing our hands of it.

Before Businessmen's Executive Movement for Peace in Vietnam, Washington, Feb. 17/ The Washington Post, 2-18:(A)18.

For millions of American people, the vision of the Laos operation is scores of American helicopters shot down, the highest American casualty rates in many weeks and American troops refusing a command to engage the enemy. Above all, the vision is of South Vietnamese soldiers in headlong flight, desperately clawing for room on the skids of the American helicopters that could carry them to safety, while American airmen just as desperately push them back to the ground to wait for the next uncertain and overloaded plane. America is coming out of Laos on the skids.

Before Democratic Party state chairmen, Washington, March 25/ The New York Times, 3-26:19.

(Regarding secret Pentagon papers on U.S. involvement in Vietnam which were published by several newspapers): Too many Americans have died there; too many Asians have shed their blood in futility. The clearest lesson (from the Pentagon papers) is that many American government officials were deceiving the American people and ultimately deceiving themselves as they escalated the violence. The American people were misled, and they are entitled to this information.

The Boston Globe, 6-18:4.

Henry A. Kissinger
Assistant to the President of the United States for National Security Affairs

(The idea of South Vietnam invading North Vietnam is) a novel problem; because so far it's North Vietnam that's invaded all the neighboring countries. And the idea that any of the Indochinese countries might be invading North Vietnam would have been unthinkable, even a year ago, so that this indicates a certain evolution in the relative balance of strength.

Television interview/"Morning News," Columbia Broadcasting System, 2-26.

Herbert G. Klein
Director of Communications for the President of the United States

It's true that the number of people who want to withdraw (from Indochina) has increased. On the other hand, the tension which gripped the nation during the (Lyndon) Johnson days and at some points a year or more ago within the Nixon Administration seems to have decreased. Now this doesn't rule out that there won't be some demonstrations, perhaps with massiveness on a couple of occasions. But I think the key thing here is that, while people may answer a poll that they want to withdraw and there may be an argument in Congress over the withdrawal date, the fact is that the American people now more fully realize that the President is proceeding toward a policy of disengagement. And it is a policy that they don't doubt any more. They might have doubted it at the earlier stages. And there may have been momentary doubts when the question was raised, for example, if American troops were going into Laos on a ground-combat basis. But the fact that he has a documented record of carrying out each commitment will help us, I think, in building support for the action he has taken.

Interview, Washington/ The National Observer, 4-12:5.

Alexei N. Kosygin
Premier of the Soviet Union

We would readily help the Americans in leaving Vietnam; but, after all, what holds them there? Nothing, I think, except the desire of some United States quarters to retain in South Vietnam the anti-popular puppet regime which fulfills the will of the United States and to perpetuate South Vietnam as an American beachhead. The road out of Vietnam is open for the American Army. The Soviet Union is ready to assist further the attainment of a political settlement in Indochina.

Interview/
The Dallas Times Herald, 1-3:(A)10.

Victor H. Krulak
Lieutenant General (Ret.)
and former Pacific Commander,
United States Marine Corps

(Regarding secret Pentagon papers on U.S. involvement in Vietnam published by several newspapers): You may be sure that the men in the Kremlin rejoiced as they were able to read, word for word, the reasoning steps and successive judgments of our planners as they appraised the options as they saw them and reached sensitive conclusions affecting national policy. The decisions themselves are long since well-known, but the reasoning process should never have been made available to our enemies . . . (Several of the papers) show exactly how our planners think, exactly how they reason, exactly what our nation's basic aspirations were at any given moment in time. Such papers would—and should—command a king's ransom; but *The New York Times* gave them to the Kremlin for nothing . . . (Publication of the papers) did our national interest more harm than good (and) did not shorten the war by an instant; it did not spare one casualty. To the contrary, it probably added to them because it gave our enemies heart.

At Pacific Coast Gas Association
convention, San Francisco, Sept. 9/
The Dallas Times Herald, 9-12:(A)2.

Nguyen Cao Ky
Vice President of South Vietnam

We began three years ago to learn to live in a democracy. Your (America's) experience began 200 years ago; and even now your system is not perfect.

Plainview (Tex.) Daily Herald, 2-9:10.

The Vietnamization plan is not completed yet; so we still have many things to do, not only in the military field, but in other fields, socially, politically and economically. So, if Vietnamization means South Vietnam strong, capable to defend itself, it will take 15 or 20 more years. But if Vietnamization means only to allow the withdrawal of American troops, then you can see the Vietnamization plan will be completed next year.

News conference, Saigon, April 18/
The New York Times, 4-19:7.

(Regarding United States Senator George S. McGovern): The day he comes here, I will kick him out. He doesn't need to say, "Get out of Vietnam." I will kick him out personally.

News conference, Saigon, April 18/
The New York Times, 4-19:7.

The people have lost all faith in the government. South Vietnam is like a sinking boat with a deceptively good coat of paint; and the man who steers the boat (President Nguyen Van Thieu) is an unfaithful, disloyal, dishonest fellow. A whirl of wind and the boat will sink to the bottom.

At School of Social Welfare, Saigon,
April 19/The New York Times, 4-20:9.

There are two extremes: those who want peace through military victory (against the Communists) and those who want peace at any price, including a coalition government. I think the realistic solution is somewhere in the middle.

News conference, Saigon, May 30/
Los Angeles Times, 5-31:(1)2.

I am a nationalist. I want South Vietnam to be free—free from Communist domination and influence and free from American domination and influence.

Quote, 5-30:507.

If (President) Thieu remains at the Presidency with the present crisis of leadership, with the miserable conditions of living for the people and soldiers, there will be no possi-

(NGUYEN CAO KY)

bility of winning the war. If he indulges in dishonest elections, there will be no possibility of winning the peace.

Saigon, Aug. 4/
Los Angeles Times, 8-5:(1)20.

I'm going to destroy (President) Thieu and all his clique. If I were to give my life by destroying Thieu, then I will do it. When I decide to do it, neither (U.S.) Ambassador Bunker nor the whole American government will be able to stop me . . . In a political fight I'm not so smart, but in a military confrontation I'm a specialist . . . I told (Bunker) before I do anything I will let him know five minutes in advance. You will see, I'll keep my word.

News conference, Saigon, Sept. 3/
San Francisco Examiner & Chronicle
(This World), 9-12:14.

I would prefer to have a fixed date of the American withdrawal (from South Vietnam). If the Vietnamese are lazy and indifferent, it is because for years now—even though they are angry and afraid of the Communists—they have relied on American money and American sacrifices to protect them. A withdrawal date would provide a new motivation for our nationalists to unite and take action on their own. I said last year that I would like to see American withdrawal by the end of 1971. I still think that is the best time, but a few months' further delay would be acceptable to me.

Interview, Saigon/Time, 9-20:34.

Melvin R. Laird
Secretary of Defense of the United States

Whatever the day-to-day reports (about South Vietnamese defeats in Laos), the unassailable fact is that U.S. involvement in the war in Southeast Asia is going down, down, down, and we continue to follow that policy.

News conference, Washington, Feb. 24/
Los Angeles Times, 2-25:(1)7.

We will maintain a U.S. presence in South Vietnam just as long as the North Vietnamese hold a single American prisoner.

Television interview/
National Broadcasting Company, March 16/
San Francisco Examiner & Chronicle
(This World), 3-21:14.

The rules of warfare and the Geneva Convention are abided by in every way (by U.S. forces in Indochina).

News conference, Washington, April 13/
The Washington Post, 4-14:(A)4.

The idea that the (U.S.) Air Force and Navy will withdraw after the war is ridiculous. Our defense objectives are to train these countries to be more reliant on their own manpower, but we'll have military assistance during this time. The idea of total withdrawal is unrealistic.

Interview/Daily World, 4-29:4.

Pham Dang Lam
South Vietnamese Ambassador
to Paris peace talks

It is the Hanoi regime which has blatantly and permanently violated the independence, sovereignty, neutrality and territorial integrity of Laos. (South Vietnam's action in Laos) only involves measures of legitimate self-defense against the attacks coming from the territory of Laos . . . The government of the Republic of Vietnam (South Vietnam) has always respected the independence, sovereignty, neutrality and territorial integrity of Laos, and it will continue to do so.

At Paris peace talks, Feb. 11/
Los Angeles Herald-Examiner, 2-11:(A)8.

Lee Kuan Yew
Prime Minister of Singapore

Sending them into Laos was asking more than the South Vietnamese Army was ready to give or able to give . . . But these are the risks you must take to meet your deadline for the withdrawal of U.S. troops (by) November, 1972. The fact remains the situation is better today in 1971 than it was in 1969 for non-

Communist Asia, including a viable South Vietnam.

Interview, Singapore/
The Dallas Times Herald, 3-20:(A)1.

John V. Lindsay
Mayor of New York

The most obvious challenge for lawyers in our time is the one on which we have heard little from the organized bar—and that is the issue of the legal basis of our war in Indochina. Have we, in fact, waged a war in violation not only of international treaties, conventions and customs, but also our own laws and Constitution? Have we sanctioned acts committed by our own forces which, if committed by an enemy, we would condemn as war crimes? Have we developed techniques of mass destruction so sophisticated that they remove all responsibility and therefore all moral strictures from our soldiers who employ them?

Before American Bar Association, New York,
July 7/The New York Times, 7-8:27.

Walter Lippmann
Former political columnist

I believe he (U.S. President Nixon) will now fix a date (for U.S. withdrawal from Vietnam), which is all he ever had to do to get out of Vietnam, and get out quite honorably and decently. Not honorably and decently considering what the war has been, but honorably and decently in the sense that the (North) Vietnamese Army isn't going to march up Broadway and the (North) Vietnamese flag is not going to fly over the Capitol. Nothing like that is going to happen. It's a perfectly decent loss, but not defeat. We'll have not been defeated, but we'll have failed at an enterprise in which it was never possible to succeed.

Interview, Seal Harbor, Me./
The Washington Post, 10-10:(C)5.

Lon Nol
Premier of Cambodia

The North Vietnamese and the Viet Cong came into my country. They invade; they kill; they destroy. They pay no damned attention to international law . . . Without U.S. aid we could not have come as far as we have, and without it we could not continue.

Interview, Phnom Penh, Oct. 10/
Los Angeles Herald-Examiner, 10-10:(A)7.

(Announcing the suspension of the republic and substitution of rule-by-decree instead of constitutional law): We now reach the turning point in the history of our fatherland as we have to choose between the following two paths: whether we keep on playing the game of fruitless democracy-freedom which will inevitably lead us toward a certain fall, or whether we curtail the anarchist democracy for the sake of victory. This government has decided to follow the path which leads to victory . . .

Broadcast address, Phnom Penh, Oct. 20/
The Washington Post, 10-22:(A)12.

Allard K. Lowenstein
Former United States Representative, D–N.Y.

I think it makes a great deal of difference that we get out of Vietnam before we go down the drain. We are not God. We can't keep a government in power (in South Vietnam) that has no support from its people; and after 10 years and $150 billion and 55,000 dead Americans and all the rest of what that tragedy has represented, if they cannot stand on their own feet, then that's their problem.

TV-radio interview/"Meet the Press,"
National Broadcasting Company,
Washington, 5-2.

Richard W. Lyman
President, Stanford University

If the war could be ended by the issuance of anguished statements by university presidents, it would have ended long ago. But the war can only be ended by hard and sustained political work. Too few people in universities have been willing to do that kind of work. Instead, we have allowed a situation to develop in which the antiwar movement gets written off by large sections of the public as the aberration of a few "campus crazies."

Plainview (Tex.) Daily Herald, 3-24:8.

Mike Mansfield
United States Senator, D–Mont.

Reports of an intensified United States military role in Cambodia were not unexpected; nor were they needed to remind us that there is still a deadly war in Indochina. We are reminded by the casualties—a hundred this week, a hundred the week before, a hundred next week—the continuum stretches back years and reaches forward into the indefinite future. As members of the Senate, we know those casualties are not statistical counts. We know them as the sons, husbands and friends of our constituents . . . It is clear that we are still deeply in the war, and we are still committed to remain until the end, whenever that may be. It is the form of the U.S. involvement which has been changed, not the involvement itself. We may be in a war of different tactics, but it is still a war in which we are involved. It is still a mistaken war. Americans are still dying in that mistaken war which does not involve the vital interests of the United States.

At Senate Democratic caucus,
Washington, Jan. 21/
The New York Times, 1-22:12.

The longer this war continues—and there is no end in sight—the more we are preparing that area for the (Communist) Chinese to come in. It looks to me that the thesis that we are in there to prevent Communism from taking over may result in time in Communism taking over the area.

News conference, Washington, Feb. 20/
The Dallas Times Herald, 2-21:(A)13.

We have to face up to the realities. I think we are in an area where we have no business. We have paid too high a price. They (South Vietnam) have had their elections. They will have more elections next October. It is time for them to take over. It's their country, their future; and they have got to make the decision in South Vietnam.

TV-radio interview/"Meet the Press,"
National Broadcasting Company,
Washington, 3-28.

The Cambodian incursion (by U.S. and South Vietnamese forces) was justified largely in terms of saving American lives. That is a consideration that has always weighed heavily with me and every other member of the Senate. It was apparent then, however, and it is apparent now that the termination of our involvement in the war in Vietnam and a prompt withdrawal would save far more American lives and return our POWs more quickly than an enlargement of the area of conflict. As it was, in the brief invasion of Cambodia a year ago, 362 Americans died and 2,205 were wounded—in the process of "saving American lives." And in the process of "saving American lives," our forces in Indochina have incurred casualties of 4,000 dead and 18,000 wounded in the year since the Cambodian incursion. In the light of those grim figures, it may well be asked: Are we saving lives or saving face?

At Olivet College, Olivet, Mich.,
March 29/Los Angeles Times, 4-4:(G)3.

Vietnam was a mistake, a tragic mistake. To persist in it now is to add outrage to the sacrifices of those who have suffered and who have died in this conflict. To persist in it now is to do violence to the welfare of the nation. The need is to terminate the mistake, not to prolong it. No national commitments of this nation remain to be discharged to the governments in Indochina. We have armed, trained, financed and fought for those governments. We have done our share—far more than our share—to inject them with the elements of survival. What last-ditch effort, as we are withdrawing, is likely to do anything more? Can the dragging out of the withdrawal do other than add to the tragedy?

At Boston College commencement,
June 14/The New York Times, 6-15:3.

(Vietnam is) an area which did not, has not and never will be vital to the security of this country.

Before the Senate, Washington,
Aug. 5/
The Washington Post, 8-6:(A)7.

In retrospect, what was really achieved by the Cambodian gambit (U.S.-South Vietnamese attacks on enemy sanctuaries)? Enemy Vietnamese forces—even the "high command" —were supposed to have been killed or captured in their "sanctuary" along the Vietnamese-Cambodian border by this essay. Well, to the extent that enemy forces were there in the first place, they withdrew from the border and, since then, about all of Cambodia has become the enemy "sanctuary." Cambodia has also emerged as another battlefield of the Indochina war over which Americans are fighting and dying . . . Before the government of (Cambodian Chief of State Norodom) Sihanouk was overthrown, nothing—zero—in the way of U.S. aid was going to Cambodia. Their country was an oasis of order in war-torn Indochina. In one and a half years of coup government in Phnom Penh, the picture has been completely reversed. Cambodia is being reduced to chaos and devastation even as it is now well on its way to receiving its first billion dollars in direct or indirect support from the United States.

> *Before the Senate, Washington, Oct. 13/*
> *I. F. Stone's Bi-Weekly, 11-1:2.*

Charles McC. Mathias, Jr.
United States Senator, R–Md.

The noble motives with which we came to the aid of South Vietnam have long since been transformed by black markets and brothels, defoliants and My Lais.

> *Before the Senate, Washington/*
> *The Dallas Times Herald, 2-24:(A)2.*

Paul N. McCloskey, Jr.
United States Representative, R–Calif.

If we pull out of this country (South Vietnam) in one year or two years or three years, I suspect that that will to fight that may remain latent in the South Vietnamese and the North Vietnamese is ultimately going to result in a single Vietnam, probably ruled by the inheritors of the great national patriot recognized by both sides: (the late North Vietnamese President) Ho Chi Minh.

> *Interview, United Press International/*
> *Daily World, 3-16:4.*

The American people do not know that it is official policy to wipe out every village in northern Laos controlled by the Pathet Lao. We are using cluster bombs which spew out projectiles at varying altitudes and directions. A single bomb devastates 25 acres. Cluster bombs are designed to kill and maim as many people as possible. We are using napalm with an effective diameter of 150 feet. It burns at a temperature of 2,000 degrees for ten or fifteen minutes. We are using these sophisticated weapons against defenseless villages. If I confirm on my trip (to South Vietnam) everything that I have read, then I say we are engaged in war crimes. Such bombing violates the Hague Convention, never mind anything decided at Nuremberg.

> *Washington, April 5/*
> *The New York Times, 4-6:39.*

(The war) is best solved by the President (Nixon) adopting a single position: If we can get our POWs back, we will be out of Vietnam tomorrow, and we will end the bombing of these countries, and we will get the CIA and the Thai mercenaries and other mercenaries we're paying in Southeast Asia to end the war there. That is still the crucial issue. The President, in my judgment, is banking on the fact that the ordinary voter will not perceive that when our American casualties drop, that the war is still going on; that the American people are somehow willing to accept a war if we are killing people from 30,000 feet and not losing American soldiers' lives. In my judgment, the issue is a far deeper one. It's the moral issue as to whether weaponry, sophisticated weaponry, is used against people in rural Asian villages somewhere to save our pride and prestige and to preserve a government we seem to think our prestige is banked upon.

> *Concord, N.H., Aug. 9/*
> *Los Angeles Times, 8-10:(1)10.*

William J. McGill
President, Columbia University

As I see it, we became involved in Vietnam on rather abstract considerations of the dis-

(WILLIAM J. McGILL)

tribution of global power. We then found ourselves in an utterly brutal and ruthless guerrilla war that forced us either to get out or to
become as brutal as circumstances required.
The whole ugly business has stripped us of
our essential virtuousness. We are in danger of
losing everything we have always stood for
before the rest of the world . . . If we had
welcomed the brutalization of our lives during
the last decade, my conclusion might be different. But the revulsion that America's young
people exhibit about this war and what it has
made of us shows that there is something
fundamentally healthy about our nation. We
have been taught a bitter lesson about the
realities of modern war and modern diplomacy; but we are hardly destroyed by the
learning process.

> *At Iona College commencement,*
> *New Rochelle, N.Y./*
> *The Christian Science Monitor,*
> *6-26:(B)8.*

George S. McGovern
United States Senator, D–S.D.

It alarms me that any U.S. Senator should
talk about expanding our military operations
in Cambodia . . . Very frankly, any Senator
who talks about sending American forces into
Cambodia ought to lead the charge himself.
I'm fed up with old men dreaming up wars
for young men to die in—particularly stupid
wars of this kind that add nothing to our
security.

> *Washington, Jan. 27/*
> *San Francisco Examiner, 1-28:4.*

I think it is fair to say that (President)
Nixon came into office with a one-front war
confined largely to South Vietnam. Now he
has us very heavily involved in three areas,
Laos and Cambodia as well. Laos just happens
to share a common frontier with (Communist)
China. I see some of the same signs of danger
that faced us 20 years ago when another
American Commander sent American forces
toward the Chinese border; and the conse-

quence was the intervention of a million
Chinese and the loss of 30,000 American lives.
I think the way out of South Vietnam does
not lead through Cambodia and Laos. It leads
by a flat statement that we are getting out;
and once we make that statement, we won't
need to be fighting in Laos and Cambodia in
order to accomplish our withdrawal.

> *TV-radio interview/"Meet the Press,"*
> *National Broadcasting Company,*
> *Washington, 2-21.*

. . . I regard this war as the most barbaric
and inhuman act that our country has ever
committed. I think it is terrible that this
country has its bombers ranging all across the
face of Indochina, killing innocent men,
women and children by the tens of thousands,
paying the people of Vietnam and Laos and
Cambodia to kill each other, and doing all of
this in the name of self-determination for
them. I can't participate in that kind of thing
any more than I could go out here in the
street and start shooting down innocent people outside this door.

> *TV-radio interview/"Meet the Press,"*
> *National Broadcasting Company, 2-21.*

I suggest . . . that, in any kind of an honest plebiscite in Indochina, the people would
vote at least 10 to 1 for us to get our forces
out of there and leave them alone. And I
think the reluctance to leave has more to do
with the unwillingness of our policy-makers to
admit that they were wrong than it does with
any real concern for the welfare of the people
of Southeast Asia.

> *Interview, Washington,*
> *The Christian Science Monitor, 3-25:4.*

The very soul of this nation now demands
that we end our intervention in this destruction in Southeast Asia. The best course now
available to the United States is to terminate
all further funding for U.S. military operations
in Indochina. That is the formula of the
McGovern-Hatfield amendment. That is the
formula which 73 per cent of the American
people have endorsed in a Gallup Poll. That is
the formula which the other side has said can

lead to the release of our prisoners and assurances as to the safety of our forces while they are being withdrawn. On the other hand, President Nixon's Vietnamization formula does not lead to the release of American prisoners. It does not end the danger to our forces in South Vietnam. It does not break the negotiating stalemate in Paris. And it does not end the destruction of the countryside and the people of Indochina.

TV-radio broadcast/
American Broadcasting Company, 4-22.

(Regarding the massacre by Communist troops at Hue, South Vietnam): The slaughter at Hue was a wartime situation and probably won't be repeated in peacetime. There may be some reprisals, assassinations of village chiefs in areas if the Communists take over, but no systematic slaughter.

The National Observer, 5-3:4.

I wonder if we can really argue that the people of Asia are better dead than red. And who appointed us God to make that decision in the first place?

At University of California
at Berkeley, May 6/
San Francisco Examiner, 5-7:12.

(Regarding South Vietnam's President Thieu running unopposed in the upcoming Presidential election): The chance for the South Vietnamese to decide their own future now turns out to be a tightly-controlled one-man charade. Both the Congress of the United States and the President of the United States should seize on the October 3 election fraud as the final justification for ending our military operations here.

News conference, Saigon, Sept. 15/
Los Angeles Times, 9-16:(1)28.

I submit that the slaughter of innocent people in Cambodia, Laos, North and South Vietnam by American bombs is the worst moral catastrophe ever committed by the U.S. Indeed, except for Adolph Hitler's extermination of the Jewish people, the American bombardment of defenseless peasants in Indo-china is the most barbaric act of modern times.

Beverly Hills, Calif., Dec. 14/
Los Angeles Times, 12-15:(1)3.

William McMahon
Prime Minister of Australia

We and the free-world forces are operating in South Vietnam to give the people of that country an opportunity to determine their own future and to prevent Communists taking over through bloodshed and force.

Before Parliament, Canberra, March 16/
The Washington Post, 3-17:(A)10.

Duong Van Minh
General, South Vietnamese Army (Ret.);
Candidate for
President of South Vietnam

. . . if we cannot defeat the Communists, neither can the Communists defeat us. No one can deny the growth and maturity of our armed forces. If they are led by a good government, these armed forces will become a very sharp weapon inferior to no other army in the world.

Saigon, June 17/
Los Angeles Times, 6-18:(1)17.

Up until now, (United States) President Nixon and Ambassador Bunker have said that the United States will be neutral, that it will not mix in the (South Vietnamese) election. But the United States has a role to play in this election. The Americans should adopt a form of positive neutrality and guarantee that the elections are honest. In fact, the Americans have more than a role to play. They have a duty . . . You Americans are the champions of justice, liberty and democracy. It's the moment to prove it. Our lives are at stake in this election. But the honor and interests of the United States are also at stake. If the Americans are set on leaving hands off so that (current President Nguyen Van) Thieu can cheat, then there's no reason to have an election.

Interview, Saigon/
The Christian Science Monitor, 6-25:1.

(DUONG VAN MINH)

I have never advocated coalition government . . . I advocate coexistence with North Vietnam. But that is not the same thing as a coalition government.

Interview, Saigon/
The Christian Science Monitor, 6-25:3.

This government (of President Nguyen Van Thieu) only makes people go to the other side. The people do not have another choice; when you can no longer live in this atmosphere, you have to find another; when you are in a suffocating room, you try to get out. If I were a Communist, I would do all I could to help President Thieu be re-elected. Then their victory would be assured.

Interview/
San Francisco Examiner, 7-6:17.

If we want to continue to fight, we will have to have economic, social and political progress as well . . . When the war is over, we will need the aid of the U.S. and other friendly countries. Our resources will be exhausted. Then we will face our greatest problem, and I hope the Americans will help. But whatever aid comes in should not be directed by the Americans. If it is, we would appear as a lackey in the world's eyes.

Interview, Saigon/Time, 7-26:25.

I have decided to withdraw (from the Presidential race), because I cannot participate in this farce.

Saigon, Aug. 20/
Los Angeles Times, 8-20:(1)1.

Walter F. Mondale
United States Senator, D—Minn.

It is now clear that the President (Nixon) is widening this war, rather than ending it. If it is to be ended, if limits are to be firmly set, Congress must do so.

Washington, Feb. 25/
The New York Times, 2-26:10.

Thomas H. Moorer
Admiral, United States Navy;
Chairman, Joint Chiefs of Staff

We must remember this: The North Vietnamese are the ones who started the trouble in Laos, Cambodia and South Vietnam. If this war is to stop, let the North Vietnamese go home. Too many people want to blame this war on the South Vietnamese; and many say they're suddenly aggressive. It's the North Vietnamese who are the aggressors; they were from the start. And it's much better to fight them in Cambodia and Laos, where they had their sanctuaries, than it is to fight them inside South Vietnam.

Interview, Washington/
U.S. News & World Report, 4-5:44.

It should be noteworthy that the media have publicized very few heroes in this war; and yet, every day young Americans in uniform perform extremely heroic acts. Daily, they do feats of courage that during World War II certainly would have been in the headlines and lauded by a grateful citizenry. Public opinion has been shaped by this kind of coverage. And it's not so much that the public shouldn't receive the bad side—war is always going to have bad sides, because it's a nasty, cruel, sad business—but the press hasn't always reported the good side in terms of performance of our young people. If the press had done that, the public might have a different attitude about what has actually been accomplished.

Interview, Washington/
U.S. News & World Report, 4-5:48.

Wayne L. Morse
Former United States Senator, D—Ore.

You still don't have a decision of the (U.S.) Supreme Court that says the government has a right to kill American boys over there (in Indochina) . . . I think young men are completely justified to evade the draft. The issue is not patriotism—99 and nine-tenths of them would have rallied to the flag if American security were really at stake. But we've been the aggressor; we've been the outlaw.

Interview, Poolesville, Md./
The Washington Post, 9-9:(G)4.

Edmund S. Muskie
United States Senator, D—Maine

(Criticizing American military action in Cambodia): We're just putting our big toe over the threshold. Before we know it, the whole foot and leg are over the threshold . . .

Sacramento, Calif./
The Dallas Times Herald, 1-25:(A)1.

Some say that (Vietnamization) will work. Some say it will not work. I say it is the wrong plan in either case. If the plan does work, we can look forward to continued warfare among the Vietnamese and an indefinite American presence. If it doesn't work, this (Nixon) Administration does not exclude the possibility of attacks on North Vietnam itself. The dangers are incalculable. A plan which leaves only these alternatives, which gives only these bleak expectations, is the wrong plan.

At University of Pennsylvania/
The Christian Science Monitor, 2-26:2.

(If the majority of Americans believe that) what Lt. (William L.) Calley is convicted of having done (killed civilians at My Lai, South Vietnam) is not a crime . . . then the rule of law in America will be in grave peril. It will be in grave peril because a free and independent people can no longer distinguish between right and wrong.

Before Lehigh Valley Milk Cooperative
Association, Philadelphia, April 15/
The Washington Post, 4-16:(A)2.

(Regarding the Indochina war and the Democratic Party): Our purpose must not be to create an issue next year (during the 1972 U.S. Presidential elections) but to end the killing now . . . It is more important than politics. It is about human life and the American future. It is worth fighting for in 1971, and it is even worth losing for in 1972.

At Democratic fund-raising dinner,
Milwaukee, May 15/
The Dallas Times Herald, 5-16:(A)6.

The responsible officials may make good on a recent threat to pull the rug out from under their war critics. I think any party and every politician should be proud to stand on that rug. I think we should be proud to encourage them to pull it away. And I think we should be proud to fall flat on our political faces—if that is what it takes to bring peace.

At Washington and Jefferson
College commencement, May 29/
The Washington Post, 5-30:(A)2.

(The war in Indochina must be ended) not by lifting the specter of death from black and white shoulders and placing it on yellow shoulders—as if that could somehow bring more good, or more morality, to this war. To some officials, it does not seem to matter that the war will go on after we have left—that other human beings will still die. But it matters to the people who live there. It matters to the men and women who struggle to find the words to make a peace in Paris. It matters to the American people. And I guarantee that it will matter to the government we elect (in the United States) in November of 1972.

At Democratic dinner, Phoenix, Nov. 5/
Los Angeles Times, 11-6:(1)26.

Gaylord Nelson
United States Senator, D—Wis.

We have a situation in which we have said to the youth of America: "This is a war which does not involve the vital interests of this country, and we know now that it never did. It has not been worth the sacrifice of 50,000 deaths; the sacrifice of 300,000 wounded; the sacrifice of $150 billion in treasure; the disillusionment of the youth of America; the loss of confidence of the people of this country in the decision-making by the authorities." Every young man in America knows it. He knows that what we are doing—and it is the truth of the matter—is filibustering, seeking a pretext to get out of Vietnam and save face; get out. That is all there is to it. So we are saying to a young man, "While we are trying to devise a pretext to get out and to save the face of the political leaders of

(GAYLORD NELSON)

this country, you go over there and risk your life." I would not ask my son to do that, and I would not ask anybody else's son to do it, either.

Before the Senate, Washington, May 25/
I. F. Stone's Bi-Weekly, 6-14:1.

(Regarding secret Pentagon papers on U.S. involvement in Vietnam which were published by several newspapers): These documents do not contain any information that would endanger the national security, and it would be a disservice for any court to enjoin their further publication. Quite obviously, these documents contain information embarrassing to the political and military leadership of the country; but that is no reason to deny the public information it is clearly entitled to have.

The New York Times, 6-16:18.

Pham Kim Ngoc
Minister of Economy
of South Vietnam

The war has led to a general decline in the standards of conduct of Vietnamese toward each other as well as to foreigners. The general discipline of behavior has weakened. People's courtesy in all activity has roughened. I think this probably happens in all wars, especially when they are prolonged and bitter. Also, the inevitable element of political uncertainty created by the war probably makes people more venal, more determined to hang onto their slice of the pie than would be the case in peace time . . . I suppose the war, and the presence of large numbers of foreign troops, may have led to some degree of xenophobia, a general distrust of foreigners. I would not be prepared to admit, as some say, that this is native to the Vietnamese temperament. When one considers the size and pervasiveness of the foreign presence here, it is perhaps surprising this problem isn't worse.

The Washington Post, 6-22:(A)18.

Richard M. Nixon
President of the United States

We have not yet ended the war in Vietnam;

I had hoped we would have by this time. But we now see the end of Americans' combat role in Vietnam in sight . . . we are on the way out; and we're on the way out in a way that will bring a just peace—the kind of a peace that will discourage that kind of aggression in the future and will build, I hope, the foundation for a generation of peace.

Television interview, Washington, Jan. 4/
The New York Times, 1-6:42.

(Regarding the South Vietnamese drive against North Vietnamese forces in Laos): There were 16 good reasons against doing it, and there were only two good reasons for doing it. But if you analyzed them, the two reasons *for* completely outweighed the 16 against—which were mostly domestic political reasons, anyway.

Los Angeles Times, 2-11:(2)6.

I do not want to suggest that there are any more concessions coming from our side to North Vietnam. We are not going to make any more concessions. The time is for them to act on the principles that we have laid down.

News conference, Washington, Feb. 17/
Los Angeles Times, 2-18:(1)23.

As far as the (South Vietnamese) actions in southern Laos are concerned, they present no threat to Communist China, and should not be interpreted by (the) Communist Chinese as being a threat against them . . . The Communist Chinese have been operating in northern Laos for some time; but this action is not directed against Communist China. It is directed against the North Vietnamese who are pointed toward South Vietnam and toward Cambodia. Consequently, I do not believe that the Communist Chinese have any reason to interpret this as a threat against them or any reason, therefore, to react to it.

News conference, Washington, Feb. 17/
The New York Times, 2-18:14.

I am not going to place any limitation upon the use of air power (in the Indochina war) except, of course, to rule out a rather ridiculous suggestion that is made from time to time . . . that our air power might include the use of tactical nuclear weapons . . . this has been speculated on for a period of five years; and I have said, for a period of five years, that it is not an area where the use of nuclear weapons, in any form, is either needed or would be wise.

News conference, Washington, Feb. 17/
The New York Times, 2-18:14.

. . . as long as the North Vietnamese have any Americans as prisoners-of-war, there will be Americans in South Vietnam—and enough Americans to give them an incentive to release the prisoners.

News conference, Washington, Feb. 17/
The New York Times, 2-18:14.

If North Vietnam wishes to negotiate with the United States, they will have to recognize that time is running out. With the exception of the prisoner-of-war issue, if North Vietnam continues to refuse to discuss our peace proposals, they will soon find they have no choice but to negotiate only with the South Vietnamese.

State of the World radio address,
Feb. 25/
The Christian Science Monitor, 3-6:1.

To end a war is simple. But to end a war in a way that will not bring on another war is far from simple. In Southeast Asia today, aggression is failing—thanks to the determination of the South Vietnamese people and to the courage and sacrifice of America's fighting men . . . We are at a critical moment in history. What America does—or fails to do—will determine whether peace and freedom can be won in the coming generation. That is why the way in which we end this conflict is so crucial to our effort to build a lasting peace in the coming decades. The right way out of Vietnam is crucial to our changing role in the world and to peace in the world.

State of the World radio address,
Washington, Feb. 25/
Los Angeles Times, 2-26:(1)12.

I recall at the time we went into Cambodia . . . I said the purpose of our going into Cambodia was to cut American casualties and insure the success of our withdrawal program. Many of the members of the press disagreed with me. They thought that was not an accurate description of what would happen. They were entitled to that view. Night after night, after I announced the decision to go into Cambodia, on television it was indicated that that decision would have the opposite effect—it would increase American casualties; it would mean it would prolong the war. Now we can look at it in retrospect. Casualties are one-half of what they were before Cambodia. And our withdrawal program has continued; and actually we were able to step it up somewhat during the last of 1970. Now in Laos, the purpose of the Laotian operation was the same as that of the Cambodian operation; this time, no American ground forces, only American air power. I said then, and I repeat now, the purpose is not to expand the war in Laos. The purpose is to save American lives, to guarantee the continued withdrawal of our own forces and to increase the ability of the South Vietnamese to defend themselves without our help.

News conference, Washington, March 4/
Los Angeles Times, 3-5:(1)20.

. . . it was a political temptation when I started office to state simply that we would get out (of Vietnam) right away without any responsibility for what came next. But I knew too much about history, about Asia, about the basic feeling in the United States. If we failed to achieve our limited goal—to let a small country exercise the right to choose its own way of life, without having a Communist government imposed on it by force—if we failed to achieve this, we would not help the cause of peace. For a time, perhaps, we would be seen as a kind of hero. But soon it would be seen that we had left behind a legacy of even greater dangers for Southeast Asia and for the Pacific region.

Interview, Washington, March 8/
The New York Times, 3-10:14.

(RICHARD M. NIXON)

Those who think Vietnam is going to be a good political issue next year are making a grave miscalculation. Now I am not applying our policy there for political reasons, but for reasons of national security. Nevertheless, those who are counting on Vietnam as a political issue in this country next year are going to have the rug jerked from under them.

Interview, Washington, March 8/
The New York Times, 3-10:14.

. . . when we judge whether this operation (in Laos) is going to be labeled a success or a failure, we cannot judge it before it is concluded, and we cannot judge it even after it is concluded. We can only see it in perspective, because its goals were long-range—long-range being, first, to insure the continuation of the American withdrawal; second, to reduce the risk to the remaining Americans as we withdraw; and third, to insure the ability of the South Vietnamese to defend themselves after we have left. Those were the three goals of this operation.

Television interview/
American Broadcasting Company,
Washington, 3-22.

If our goal is a total withdrawal of all our forces, why not announce a date now for ending our involvement? The difficulty in making such an announcement to the American people is that I would also be making that announcement to the enemy. And it would serve the enemy's purpose and not our own . . . Or shall we leave in a way that gives the South Vietnamese a reasonable chance to survive as a free people? My plan will end American involvement in a way that would provide that chance . . . I know there are those who honestly believe that I should move to end this war without regard to what happens to South Vietnam. This way would abandon our friends. But even more important, we would abandon ourselves. We would plunge from the anguish of war into a nightmare of recrimination. We would lose respect for this nation, respect for one another, respect for ourselves.

TV-radio address, April 7/
The National Observer, 4-12:2.

As one who has visited Vietnam many times and as Commander-in-Chief of our armed forces, I feel it is my duty to speak up for the two-and-a-half million fine young Americans who have served in Vietnam. The atrocity charges in individual cases should not and cannot be allowed to reflect on their courage and their self-sacrifice. War is a terrible and cruel experience for a nation, and particularly for those who bear the burden of fighting. Never before in history have men fought for less selfish motives—not for conquest, not for glory, but only for the right of people far away to choose the kind of government they want. While we hear and read much of isolated acts of cruelty, we do not hear enough of the tens of thousands of individual American soldiers who have built schools, roads, hospitals, clinics and who, through countless acts of generosity and kindness, have tried to help the people of South Vietnam. We can and should be proud of these men. They deserve not our scorn but our admiration and our deepest appreciation.

TV-radio address, Washington,
April 7/The New York Times, 4-8:6.

When I say that I will not be intimidated and that Congress will not be intimidated (by antiwar demonstrations), I'm simply stating the American principle . . . that policy in this country is not made in the streets.

News conference, San Clemente, Calif.,
May 1/
Los Angeles Herald-Examiner, 5-1:(A)1.

We are very actively pursuing negotiations on Vietnam in established channels. The record, when it finally comes out, will answer all the critics as far as the activity of this government in pursuing negotiations in established channels. It would not be useful to negotiate in the newspapers if we want to have those negotiations succeed. I am not predicting that the negotiations will succeed. I am saying, however, that as far as the United States is concerned, we have gone and are going the extra mile on negotiations in established channels. You can interpret that any way you want; but do not interpret it in a way that indicates that the United States is missing this opportunity or that opportunity, or another one, to negotiate.

News conference, Washington, Aug. 4/
The Washington Post, 8-5:(A)10.

With regard to the (upcoming South Vietnamese) elections, let me emphasize our position. Our position is one of complete neutrality in these elections. Under (U.S.) Ambassador (Ellsworth) Bunker's skillful direction, we have made it clear to all parties concerned that we are not supporting any candidate, that we will accept the verdict of the people of South Vietnam. I have noted, for example, that President Thieu has invited observers to come from other nations to witness the election. I hope observers do go. I think they will find, I hope they will find, as they did when they observed previous elections in Vietnam, that by most standards they were fair.

News conference, Washington, Aug. 4/
The Washington Post, 8-5:(A)10.

(The American objective of achieving a democratic process in South Vietnam) will not be met for several generations. But at least we will be on the road . . . I think sometimes we forget . . . how difficult the process of democracy is.

News conference, Washington, Sept. 16/
Los Angeles Times, 9-17:(1)7.

. . . we would prefer, as far as South Vietnam is concerned, that its democratic process would grow faster. We believe that considerable headway has been made. We believe that the situation from that standpoint is infinitely better in South Vietnam—where they at least have some elections—than in North Vietnam, where they have none; and we are going to continue to work toward that goal.

News conference, Washington, Sept. 16/
The New York Times, 9-17:27.

Air power, of course, as far as our use of it is concerned, will continue to be used longer than our ground forces due to the fact that training Vietnamese to handle the aircraft takes the longest lead time, as we know; and we will continue to use it in support of the South Vietnamese until there is a negotiated settlement, or looking further down the road, until the South Vietnamese have developed the capability to handle the situation themselves. As far as our air power is concerned, let me also say this: As we reduce the number of our forces, it is particularly important for us to continue our air strikes on the infiltration routes. If we see any substantial step-up in infiltration in the passes, for example, which lead from North Vietnam into Laos and, of course, the Laotian trail that comes down through Cambodia into South Vietnam—if we see that, we will have to not only continue our air strikes, we will have to step them up.

News conference, Washington, Nov. 12/
Los Angeles Times, 1-2('72):(2)7

Let's look at Cambodia. We have made a conscious decision not to send American troops in. There are no American combat troops in Cambodia. There are no American combat advisers in Cambodia. There will be no American troops or advisers in Cambodia. We will aid Cambodia. Cambodia is the Nixon Doctrine in its purest form. Vietnam was in violation of the Nixon Doctrine. Because in Cambodia what we are doing is helping the Cambodians to help themselves, and we are doing that rather than to go in and do the fighting ourselves, as we did in Korea and as we did in Vietnam. We hope not to make that mistake again if we can avoid it.

News conference, Washington, Nov. 12/
The New York Times, 11-13:10.

I do not think it would be helpful to indicate at this time what we will discuss with regard to Indochina when our visits to Peking and Moscow take place. We are hopeful and continue to be hopeful that we can make progress on handling this problem ourselves, and that it may not have to be a problem that

(RICHARD M. NIXON)

will have to be discussed in those areas. Incidentally, I think it would not be well to speculate as to what, if anything, either Peking or Moscow can or will do on this matter. All that I can say is that we are charting our own course, and we will find our own way to bring it (the war) to a halt. We will, of course, welcome any assistance; but we are not counting on it from either source.

News conference, Washington, Nov. 12/
The New York Times, 11-13:10.

Frederick E. Nolting, Jr.
Former United States Ambassador
to South Vietnam

I have not seen all of the Pentagon papers (on U.S. involvement in Vietnam). The records selected for publication (by newspapers), together with *The New York Times'* interpretation, leave the impression that the Kennedy Administration was faced with a Hobson's choice in '63—either to sink with the Diem government (in South Vietnam) or support a coup d'etat. The Diem government was depicted as corrupt, oppressive, unworthy in every respect . . . I'm strongly convinced this picture of the Diem government was a false one. The Kennedy Administration was not faced with a choice of evils in '63. It deliberately abandoned a reasonably successful policy and a self-reliant ally to encourage a shameful and disastrous revolt.

Interview/
U.S. News & World Report, 7-26:67.

Nikolai V. Podgorny
President of the Soviet Union

The Soviet people have rendered and will continue to render all-sided assistance to the Vietnamese people in their struggle on all planes—military, political, diplomatic—and in the consolidation of the Democratic Republic of (North) Vietnam, an outpost of socialism in Southeast Asia.

Hanoi, North Vietnam, Oct. 3/
San Francisco Examiner, 10-4:15.

Georges Pompidou
President of France

(Regarding South Vietnamese operations against Communist troops in Laos): I deplore the events in Laos, and I condemn them; and with me, so does France . . . There can be no military solution. The solution can only be political, thus negotiated.

Los Angeles Times, 2-14:(F)7.

William Porter
United States Ambassador
to Paris peace talks

(Addressing the North Vietnamese and Viet Cong delegations): I search in vain for any organized category of South Vietnamese which supports overtly or covertly the Viet Cong or its program. I also fail to recall any prominent South Vietnamese political figure who has ever joined your group . . . You rely on terror and propaganda instead of a persuasive program to influence your people. Though these tactics have continually met abject failure, you do not get the message. You go right on doing exactly what must be done to lose friends and alienate people . . . Your tactics have failed to improve your standing and have, in fact, deprived you of political support among the people . . . I suggest that the time has come for you to follow the example of other divided countries by opening a peaceful dialogue with your fellow Vietnamese for the benefit of your people.

At Paris peace talks, Oct. 7/
The New York Times, 10-17:(4)11.

(Addressing the North Vietnamese and Viet Cong delegations): When you declare that the United States "must" do this or "must" do that you apparently overlook the fact that your military situation is unimpressive . . . Of the 300 or so district and province capitals of South Vietnam, you do not hold a single one after these many years of war and your best military efforts. You are, in fact, further from military victory than ever. In such circumstances, your use of peremptory language seems rather pretentious.

At Paris peace talks/
The New York Times, 10-17:(4)11.

Roman C. Pucinski
United States Representative, D—Ill.

I am no dove. I have been one of the strongest supporters of Vietnam and our role in Vietnam . . . But I believe with the same fervor that the time has now come to get out of Vietnam . . . We are not surrendering; we have won the battle.

Before the House, Washington, Feb. 2/
The Christian Science Monitor, 2-13:8.

Ronald Reagan
Governor of California

After 10 years of futzing around in Vietnam under Democratic Presidents, Mr. Nixon came into office and found there was no plan to create a South Vietnamese army capable of defending itself and to end American involvement. (Since President Nixon assumed office) half of our troops have been brought home, the South Vietnamese are in much better shape to take care of themselves and the President is even stepping up the withdrawal rate.

Interview, Williamsburg, Va., April 20/
Los Angeles Times, 4-21:(1)21.

If we're going to get so concerned about one-man elections (such as in South Vietnam), then we could start down the list and be concerned about several of the African countries, about Albania, the Soviet Union, Hungary, Czechoslovakia. No one seems to be saying anything about easily a score of nations that consistently have one-man elections.

Singapore, Oct. 12/
Los Angeles Herald-Examiner, 10-12:(A)3.

(Regarding South Vietnam's recent Presidential election in which only President Thieu was on the ballot): Naturally we (Americans) would favor a selection of candidates . . . (but) after hundreds of years of no democracy and colonial status and 15 years of building democracy (the South Vietnamese are making) fantastic progress, and I think more progress than in the first 15 years of our (America's) democracy.

News conference, Saigon, Oct. 15/
The Washington Post, 10-16:(A)10.

I think from all that I have heard, the principles for which Americans died in this country (South Vietnam) are still valid and that there is still reason for it. No one looks forward to it. No one wants it to happen. But there is a battle going on in this world between two philosophies. I think our side is in the fight for individual freedom and the dignity of man.

News conference, Saigon, Oct. 15/
Los Angeles Times, 10-16:(1)16.

William P. Rogers
Secretary of State of the United States

There's no reason, when the South Vietnamese are as strong as they are, why they should be under any restrictions militarily . . . It makes no sense under the rules of war, international law or equity to let an enemy occupy territory and use it against our forces and use it with impunity. If you conduct a war in which the only action you can take is defensive, then you are at the mercy of the enemy.

Before Veterans of Foreign Wars/
The New York Times, 3-9:2.

(Regarding criticism of elections in South Vietnam): The Vietnamese elections are not pristine and pure, and neither are ours for that matter.

News conference, Washington, Sept. 3/
Los Angeles Herald-Examiner, 9-3:(A)1.

Walt W. Rostow
Former Special Assistant to
the President of the United States

(Regarding secret Pentagon papers on U.S. involvement in Vietnam published by several newspapers): The Pentagon report itself is an uneven report based on partial evidence lacking the most critical evidence—that is, the President's mind, his consultations with his leading advisers and his consultation with the Congressional leadership. But the worst of it, in my judgment, is what *The New York Times* did in its first three articles. It proceeded from this limited evidence to draw conclusions

(WALT W. ROSTOW)

which are in no way warranted by the evidence itself.

Interview/Los Angeles Times, 7-7:(1)18.

If we (the United States) had walked away from Asia, or if we walk away from Asia now, the consequence will not be peace. The consequence will be a larger war and quite possibly a nuclear war . . . If you believe that, then the pain (of the Vietnam war) is worth taking.

TV-radio interview/"Issues and Answers,"
American Broadcasting Company, 7-11.

Dean Rusk
Former Secretary of State
of the United States

I think (Hanoi) relied rather heavily on the division in this country. I don't draw from that the conclusion that we shouldn't have a lively and active and even boisterous debate in this country. It's (the war) a great public issue; and in our kind of society we ought to talk these things out—in a free society. But one of the prices we pay is that these fellows in Hanoi can listen in on us. Now, Hanoi can hear about 50,000 people marching around the Pentagon calling for peace; and it would take a good deal of sophistication on their part to realize that maybe that's not the way decisions are made by the President of the United States. So I think they can be misled by our public discussion to a degree. I mean, for example, if we had heard that 50,000 people were marching around the headquarters in Hanoi calling for peace, we would think the war was over. And it probably would be.

At University of Georgia, February/
The New York Times, 3-22:31.

. . . I personally underestimated the persistence of the North Vietnamese. But there were some other considerations that were very much in our minds, and it has almost become unfashionable to talk about them any more. How much is it worth to prevent World War III? How much is it worth to try to guarantee

the reputation of the United States for fidelity to our security commitments? How much is it worth to try to avoid a basic miscalculation in places like Moscow or Peking about what the United States might do in situations that we consider vital to our own national security and national interest, or to world peace? One of the severe prices we may be paying for Vietnam is that it may have stimulated or assisted a trend toward isolationism in this country. Are the policy planners in Moscow saying to their leaders now, "Get ready, gentlemen, for a period of American isolationism"? This worries me. I don't know the answer to that question.

Television interview/
National Broadcasting Company, 7-2.

(Regarding reported peace offerings by North Vietnam during his term in office): We were never out of contact with Hanoi. But when you checked these things out with Hanoi, usually they told us to go to hell. We were not children in this business. The world was filled with candidates for the Nobel Peace Prize. All sorts of people talked with North Vietnam in all parts of the world, and many people visited Hanoi. They would come back seven months pregnant: Peace was about to be delivered. When you checked it out with Hanoi, there was nothing in it.

Interview, Atlanta, July 3/
San Francisco Examiner & Chronicle,
7-4:(A)1.

William B. Saxbe
United States Senator, R—Ohio

I am sick and tired of the war and Vietnam; and for more than two years, I have been a persistent critic of our involvement in Indochina. One thing that distresses me even more, however, is those who continually play politics with this unfortunate war. I am also sick and tired of that.

Before the Senate, Washington, April 1/
Los Angeles Times, 4-2:(1)12.

If it is fair to say that the Vietnam war has become "Nixon's war," then it is also fair to say our steady withdrawal of American troops has become "Nixon's withdrawal."

Before the Senate, Washington, April 22/
The New York Times, 4-23:7.

Hugh Scott
United States Senator, R–Pa.

I am sick and tired of seeing this war used as a political football by many of the same Democrats who, during the Democratic Administrations, were lauding our involvement in Vietnam.

Before the Senate, Washington, April 1/
The Dallas Times Herald, 4-1:(A)22.

In simple justice, will not the American people and those who interpret the news to them recognize the clear, unassailable truth— that the President (Nixon) is ending our involvement in this war at the quickest level of withdrawal consistent with the commitments made by other Administrations and with the security which, in common decency, we owe to ourselves and to those who called for our help?

Before the Senate, Washington, April 22/
Los Angeles Times, 4-23:(1)7.

Ulysses S. Grant Sharp
Admiral (Ret.) and former Commander-in-Chief/Pacific, United States Navy

(Regarding former President Lyndon B. Johnson's decision to stop the bombing of North Vietnam): With that move, we lost the major leverage we had for bringing the war to a conclusion by successful negotiations. The air war was one of the most misunderstood parts of our whole engagement. It was especially misunderstood by the civilians in the Pentagon who were making the broad decisions.

Before San Diego Council of Navy
League, San Diego, July 21/
The Dallas Times Herald, 7-22:(A)26.

Sargent Shriver
Former Director, United States Peace Corps

So many young Americans are disillusioned with the policies of their government, they refuse to volunteer for the Peace Corps . . . First of all, one would have to mention the war in Vietnam. It is very difficult for young Americans to join an organization called the Peace Corps when their country is conducting an all-out war. Secondly, it is very difficult to represent our country abroad and say that you, as an American citizen, believe in peace and (are) working for peace, working for racial and cultural equality, that you are working for the unification of mankind, when, at the same time, the government is conducting an all-out war in a remote place against people of a different racial and cultural background . . . Many American young people no longer have faith in, or understanding of, the purposes of America. The young people either fail to understand them or don't believe them. At home, the Vietnamese war and numerous examples of official duplicity in handling the news about the war and the handling of other matters connected to the war, have disillusioned millions of young Americans.

Radio interview, Tel Aviv, Dec. 28/
Los Angeles Herald-Examiner, 12-28:(A)2.

Norodom Sihanouk
Exiled Former Chief of State
of Cambodia

(In Cambodia) I wanted justice and a union of Marxism, Maoism and capitalism. I have failed to unite the country, to bring rich and poor together in fruitful cooperation. (Present Chief of State) Lon Nol is the proof of my failure . . . (U.S. President) Nixon has come to be the Grand Master of the capitalists, as Mao is the Grand Master of socialism. I tried to achieve a compromise. But with these two great pieces on the board . . . what can a pawn do, even if he happens to wear a crown?

Interview, Peking/
The New York Times, 2-4:35.

You Americans know from your own bitter experience what civil war is like. But why can't you put yourselves in other peoples' shoes? How would the Northerners have felt (in the American Civil War) if the British, say,

347

(NORODOM SIHANOUK)

had come in and kept the Confederacy going with a huge expeditionary force just as it was about to collapse? Can't you see that's what you've been doing in Vietnam all these years —spending your money to kill and to die for a lost cause?

Interview, Peking/
Los Angeles Times, 6-19:(1)13.

Had you (the United States) not supported the Saigon regime's refusal (in 1954) to abide by the Geneva accords, free elections would have been held as planned, and the two Vietnams would have been peacefully reunited. Such a nation would have been Communistic, but also nationalist—and no threat to you. But your government then was so fearful of a Ho Chi Minh victory in elections that it committed U.S. power and prestige to a hopeless cause. And look where it led you—and us!

Interview, Peking/
Los Angeles Times, 6-24:(1)223.

Without U.S. military support, (Cambodian Premier) Lon Nol would not survive a minute. My forces have liberated two-thirds of our land. We are in the outskirts of Phnom Penh; and what prevents us from entering the capital is U.S. air support . . . I am not a Communist and will not become one. Cambodia cannot become a Maoist state. We don't want to live under Hanoi's influence, either. But we are, in fact, now allied to the Pathet Lao and the Viet Cong, while before the coup Cambodia was neutral.

Interview, Peking/Newsweek, 12-20:50.

Sisowath Sirik (Matak)
Vice Premier of Cambodia

We were very happy (U.S.) President Nixon announced his decision to destroy the (Vietnamese Communist) sanctuaries (in Cambodia). That, in itself, constituted an enormous aid to us. Whether it pushed the North Vietnamese deeper into Cambodia was of no consequence. Actually, they were already all over the country, anyway, at the time Presi-

dent Nixon made his decision. They were in the plantations; they were near Phnom Penh.

Interview, Phnom Penh/
The Christian Science Monitor, 1-18:10.

Howard K. Smith
News commentator,
American Broadcasting Company

A couple of questions of the day: (1) Is *The (New York) Times* right to publish the secret Pentagon report on how we got into Vietnam? My bias is—yes. I see nothing harmful to present U.S. security in it. It may make other nations more hesitant about talking with us if they think their secret thoughts may appear in headlines, but that is the drawback of freedom and an aggresive press—both of which give us compensating strengths. Question (2) Does the *Times* report give us an accurate view of the Vietnam war? My answer is—no. It is like writing *Hamlet* and leaving out the key figure, Prince Hamlet himself.

Television broadcast/
The New York Times, 6-18:15.

Souvanna Phouma
Premier of Laos

(Regarding South Vietnamese operations in Laos): The Royal Lao government regrets that, once more, foreign troops from countries which promised to guarantee and defend the neutrality, sovereignty and inviolability of Laos have deliberately chosen Lao territory as a battlefield. To be sure, the primary responsibility rests with the North Vietnamese, who have disregarded international law—including the 1962 Geneva Accords—and who continue to violate the neutrality and territorial integrity of Laos; but that cannot constitute a justification for entry of other troops into Laos. In any case, the royal government requests all foreign troops to withdraw immediately.

Vientiane, Laos, Feb. 8/
The Washington Post, 2-9:(A)12.

John C. Stennis
United States Senator, D—Miss.

The longer we continue to deal with the origins of the Vietnam war in an atmosphere of anger, recrimination and domestic politics, the deeper will be the wounds on our society. The sooner we can have an objective and disinterested account by professional researchers on the origins, the conduct and the wide-ranging effects of the Vietnam war, the sooner we will be able to begin the healing that can only come from understanding.

Before the Senate, Washington, Aug. 6/
The Washington Post, 8-7:(A)9.

Vietnam has shown us that by trying to fight a war without the clear-cut prior support of the American people, we not only risk military effectiveness but we also strain the very structure of the Republic.

Before Senate Foreign Relations Committee,
Washington, Oct. 6/
The New York Times, 10-7:3.

Adlai E. Stevenson III
United States Senator, D—Ill.

We should make it very clear that our military involvement in South Vietnam is not endless, that we are getting out, and by that I mean withdrawing not only our ground forces but also our support forces. We should take the crutch away from the patient. I am inclined to think that this is the best way to accomplish our purpose, to help the South Vietnamese. Take the crutch away and the patient may just walk on his own two feet. He may compose his political differences. If a war must be fought, he may be able to fight it much more effectively on the ground, than he can now by relying on American firepower and artillery support. Hopefully, the South Vietnamese would be given an incentive to make peace.

TV-radio interview/"Meet the Press,"
National Broadcasting Company,
Washington, 9-5.

Samuel S. Stratton
United States Representative, D—N.Y.

The only thing our potential Presidential candidates seem to be doing so far is vying with one another in the intensity of their fervor in putting full blame for the Vietnam war onto the Nixon Administration. But this is an exercise both in futility and in rewriting history. As Senator (Hubert) Humphrey has acknowledged, both the Democrats and the Republicans share responsibility for our involvement in Vietnam. And as (Treasury) Secretary Connally—still a wise and respected Democrat, even if he is also a member of the Nixon Cabinet—reminded us recently, by the time the 1972 election rolls around, the Vietnam war won't be an issue anyway.

At Democratic meeting, Albany, N.Y./
The Austin (Tex.) Statesman, 5-3:(A)4.

Robert Taft, Jr.
United States Senator, R—Ohio

Now, when we are disengaging from Vietnam and President Nixon is committed to that course, the junior Senator (from Maine, Edmund Muskie) and some of his previously-silent colleagues—including the former Vice President (Hubert Humphrey)—have taken up the anti-war chant . . . Their silence during the '60s rings clear today. We are leaving Vietnam, thanks to a Republican President.

Before the Senate, Washington, April 1/
The Dallas Times Herald, 4-1:(A)22.

Herman E. Talmadge
United States Senator, D—Ga.

The American people are weary to the bone and fed up with this ill-conceived conflict. It has placed a dangerous drain on a precious reservoir which we once thought bottomless—the unity of spirit and purpose which has made this nation great . . . Americans have reached the end of their patience. There is a rising tide of sentiment in our land against this war. We have honored our commitment to the South Vietnamese many times over, at a cost which is staggering. Families are shattered and torn apart by the war and the ideo-

(HERMAN E. TALMADGE)

logical divisions it has created . . . It is time to put an end to this cruel and unusual war which we have never tried to win, and which is tearing at the basic fabric that holds this country together.

Before the Senate, Washington, June 15/
Los Angeles Herald-Examiner, 6-15:(A)3.

Harold Taylor
Former president,
Sarah Lawrence College

He (President Nixon) does not want the United States to lose the war, to become a "pitiful helpless giant," suffering its first defeat in its proud 190-year history. By implication, he wants it always to win at whatever game it plays—to be a pitiful successful giant.

At Southern Methodist University,
March 5/
The Dallas Times Herald, 3-6:(A)7.

Nguyen Van Thieu
President of South Vietnam

(Regarding South Vietnam's drive into Laos): When we fight pirates outside our house, only our mango and guava trees are damaged. But when we fight them inside the house, how can we keep the furniture from being destroyed?

Vungtau, South Vietnam, Feb. 22/
The Washington Post, 2-25:(A)22.

I have a duty to build democracy for the nation and a duty to help all political groups within the security and order of society in a spirit of freedom and democracy. I always encourage political groups for themselves, but not for me. For example, if I become a candidate for a second term, I will present my candidacy as an individual, an individual who loves his country . . . and do the best and not be tied up by interests of any political group.

Before national teachers' convention,
Saigon, June 13/
The Washington Post, 6-14:(A)14.

The Communists do not want to negotiate an end to the war, because if they negotiate they will be caught in the trap of acknowledging peace. And if they accept peace, they will have to retreat from South Vietnam, from Cambodia and from Laos.

At National Defense College
commencement, Saigon/
The Dallas Times Herald, 7-8:(A)14.

Maybe big powers can afford to give concessions to the Communists because they are so rich and powerful. We cannot afford to give any concessions to the Communists, because we are weak.

Saigon, July 31/
The New York Times, 8-1:5.

(Regarding his running unopposed in the forthcoming Presidential election): The Constitution says there will be an election on October 3, and there *will* be a Presidential election on October 3. The important thing remains the indisputable trust the people of South Vietnam should have in me, in my government and my policies. This trust must be shown very clearly in a free and democratic way through the size of the vote in the October 3 elections. If the result of the October 3 elections confirms clearly the trust the people have in me, I will consider that the people have given me their confidence and, consequently, I will continue for another four-year term. If the results show clearly that the people do not trust me, I will willingly decline to continue for another four-year term.

TV-radio address to nation, Saigon, Sept. 2/
Los Angeles Times, 9-3:(1)6.

(Regarding suggestions that he resign rather than run unopposed in the coming Presidential election): I am responsible to the whole country. To resign would be the act of an irresponsible man, a deserter trying to avoid his responsibilities. Such an act could severely damage the country, leaving the legal and Constitutional regime vulnerable to the Communists. To run or to withdraw is the freedom of each ticket. But the October 3 election is determined by the Constitution and cannot be changed, even if there is only one ticket. There is no legal basis for not organizing the elections. I want competition, but there is nothing I can do about it. I must carry out the Constitution and legal procedures.

TV-radio address to nation,
Saigon, Sept. 2/
San Francisco Examiner, 9-2:1.

Everyone in the countryside asked by me or others, "What is different about President Thieu (as compared with before Thieu)?", answers, "Security, prosperity; these two things." They don't care about politics, the Senate, Congress. (They care about) security, freedom of movement, miracle rice, law, land reform, tractors, fertilizers.

Interview, Saigon/Time, 9-20:33.

Despite all the controversy, I believe that everyone realizes in his own heart that this is the most democratic period Vietnam has ever known. From the dictatorial rule of only a few years ago, we have achieved democracy for this country.

Television address to nation,
Saigon, Sept. 27/
The New York Times, 9-28:6.

Le Duc Tho
Member,
North Vietnamese Politburo

The Vietnamese people want peace and independence. They do not want to make war. It is the desire of the Vietnamese people to see the soldiers home and able to live in happiness with their families. It is also the desire of the Vietnamese people to see all the captured soldiers return home as soon as possible. We understand the suffering of the mothers and wives of America whose loved ones have been captured in Vietnam. We want to see the development of friendship between the American and Vietnamese peoples. The Vietnamese people want national concord and the national reconciliation of all the Vietnamese in peace and independence. No Vietnamese wants to see a Vietnamese kill another Vietnamese.

Paris, June 24/
The New York Times, 6-25:2.

Robert Thompson
British authority on
Asian guerrilla warfare

The situation in South Vietnam now is becoming more of a police problem and less of a military problem. The Vietnamization program now is unassailable by the enemy. I don't see what the North Vietnamese can do about it. It seems likely to develop into a no-war, no-peace situation, where all the free states of Indochina can hold off the North Vietnamese. We are approaching the point of containment (of the Communist threat to Indochina). It is quite remarkable, I think, how the U.S. Administration has been able to get its approach right, in spite of the confusion in America itself.

Interview, London/
The Christian Science Monitor, 2-8:8.

Xuan Thuy
North Vietnamese Ambassador
to Paris peace talks

I propose that at this conference, this very day, or tomorrow, or another day of your choice, we discuss the question of fixing the date for the withdrawal from South Vietnam of United States forces and of those of other foreign countries in the American camp, so as to be able then to take up the question of the guarantee of the security of the United States soldiers during their withdrawal and the question of the release of the captured troops. We think that if the discussions on these questions arrive at positive results, all the troops participating in the war can then rapidly regain their homes.

At Paris peace talks, April 29/
The New York Times, 4-30:1.

If (United States President) Nixon does not set a deadline for the total withdrawal in 1971 of U.S. forces, the American people and the families of American servicemen will come to the conclusion that the U.S. government has deceived them . . . Every American new casualty or new prisoner on the Vietnam battlefield will only serve immoral objectives, in contradiction with the interests of the United

(XUAN THUY)

States and of the American people . . . It is now up to the Nixon Administration to choose the path of peace or to continue the war, to let American servicemen promptly and safely return home or to prolong the list of American casualties and prisoners.

At Paris peace talks, July 15/
The Dallas Times Herald, 7-15:(A)1.

(Regarding the upcoming South Vietnamese Presidential election): The White House (Washington) is putting on a comedy in Saigon. It is staged and directed by the U.S. Embassy. All that is needed to see it is an airline ticket to Saigon; the rest is free.

Paris, Aug. 26/
Los Angeles Herald-Examiner, 8-26:(A)4.

John V. Tunney
United States Senator, D–Calif.

The only certainty concerning Vietnam, apart from death and destruction, has been the inability of our government to face reality; and that reality is that we cannot win in Southeast Asia at a price that we are willing to pay.

Before government information officers,
Washington, Feb. 24/
Los Angeles Times, 2-25:(1)9.

The wild antics of the May Day (peace) demonstrators (in Washington) are deplorable. The demonstrators tried to trample the rights of Americans peacefully to go to their jobs, and they failed. They did succeed, however, in hardening the attitudes of those in the Administration who want to keep our bombers in the air over North Vietnam and our troops on the ground in South Vietnam.

Washington, May 3/
Los Angeles Times, 3-4:(1)4.

Lewis W. Walt
General (Ret.) and former Assistant
Commandant, United States Marine Corps

There were two turning points to this war. The first was the Tet offensive, after which South Vietnamese forces went up while the enemy went down. The second was the Cambodian operation. And now, we have a third. If the operation in Laos is as effective as I think it will be, we are going to destroy the enemy's capability to attack South Vietnam.

News conference, Los Angeles, Feb. 8/
Los Angeles Herald-Examiner, 2-8:(A)2.

Roy Wilkins
Executive director, National Association
for the Advancement of Colored People

Some black extremists have gone so far as to label this a racist war—"racist" being their favorite term applied to anything they don't like.

Before board of governors, National
Conference of Christians and Jews,
New York, April 30/
The New York Times, 5-1:30.

Ronald L. Ziegler
Press Secretary to the
President of the United States

I have said on probably 25 occasions that there are no U.S. ground combat forces or advisers being committed to the ARVN operation in Laos . . . obviously, we would have absolutely no motivation to state that policy as categorically as we have stated it and pursue another policy.

News conference, Key Biscayne, Fla.,
Feb. 12/The Washington Post, 2-13:(A)10.

(Regarding a rumored major allied thrust into Laos): The President is aware of what is going on. That's not to say there is something going on.

The Wall Street Journal, 2-18:12.

Elmo R. Zumwalt, Jr.
Admiral, United States Navy;
Chief of Naval Operations

(North Vietnam's leaders) know that we place great emphasis on the lives of our people, and that we want those prisoners (of war) removed as soon as possible from the barbaric conditions known to exist in their prison camps. They (North Vietnam), on the other hand, care nothing for their own people in prison camps of the South, where the Republic of Vietnam (South Vietnam) now holds 37,000 North Vietnamese and Viet Cong prisoners. For example, the President (Nixon) and the government in Saigon offered last December to return every one of these in exchange for all the prisoners held by the enemy in North Vietnam, South Vietnam and in Laos. We would have returned more than ten of theirs for each one of our own people. The answer to this was "No."

At San Francisco Chamber of Commerce
Military Affairs luncheon, May 13/
San Francisco Examiner, 5-14:5.

Europe

Pyotr Abrasimov
Soviet Ambassador to East Germany

(Regarding the Berlin treaty signed by Britain, France, the United States and the Soviet Union): We have come to an understanding on one of the most complicated international problems over which frictions and tensions often have arisen during a quarter of a century. All's well that ends well.

The National Observer, 9-6:4.

Ferrari Aggradi
Minister of Finance of Italy

. . . our friendship with America is the most important tie for us. The American presence in Europe is the most important point for our future. *That* you have to repeat and to repeat and to repeat.

The Washington Post, 11-26:(D)11.

Spiro T. Agnew
Vice President of the United States

(Regarding when the Greek government will return to a democracy): . . . it's not up to us to impose on another government our attitudes as to whatever schedule they should adopt. We would resent it greatly if they did that to us. The fact that other governments of both the right and the left may not be as representative as ours should not in any case prevent our cooperating fully if that's where our mutual security interests are.

News conference in flight en route to Athens, Oct. 16/
The Washington Post, 10-17:(A)2.

Salvador Allende (Gossens)
President of Chile

I had a chance to be a guest of the wonderful Soviet people. I admire their enthusiasm displayed in the tireless construction of their society, in which there are neither exploiters nor exploited—a society which is a reliable bulwark of peace all over the world.

Interview/Daily World, 1-7:10.

Raymond Aron
Professor of Faculty Letters,
Paris University

As long as the Russian Army is in East Germany, what can we do but depend on America for our security? When the United States did not want to leave Europe, perhaps it was all right for General de Gaulle to tell them to go. But now that the Americans may want to leave Europe, we should do something to keep them here.

Interview/
U.S. News & World Report, 5-3:69.

George W. Ball
Former Under Secretary of State
of the United States

If the (West) German treaties with Moscow and Warsaw should generate complacency and result in a decline of West Germany's contribution to the common defense, it would prove politically impossible for America to maintain her forces in Europe at anything like their present deployment level. On the other hand, I have too much confidence in Chancellor Brandt's integrity and realism to expect this to happen in the foreseeable future.

Interview, Washington/
Los Angeles Times, 1-4:(1)25.

While we Americans, due in large part to the mess in Vietnam, have seen our influence and authority sadly diminish, Russia, during the past few years, has taken long strides toward making its weight felt around the world. It is now more powerful than ever before in history. At long last, Russia has realized a dream it has cherished ever since the days of Peter the Great—to escape the claustrophobic encirclement of the Black Sea and establish itself as a Mediterranean power.

At Northern California World Affairs
Conference, Asilomar/San Francisco
Examiner & Chronicle, 5-9:(A)25.

The Soviet purpose, as we have seen it demonstrated again and again, is revolutionary; it is to stir up trouble, subvert governments and undermine Western ideas and Western influence.

At Northern California World Affairs
Conference, Asilomar/San Francisco
Examiner & Chronicle, 5-9:(A)25.

Winton M. Blount
Postmaster General of the United States

Where do people get the idea that France is such a hot ally of the United States? They've been kicking us in the teeth for 15 years. I wouldn't even go there when (Charles) de Gaulle was in power.

Washington, Oct. 16/
The Dallas Times Herald, 10-17:(A)35.

Willy Brandt
Chancellor of West Germany

Neither the ideological differences nor the differences between our (East and West German) social structures can be blurred, nor can differences of opinion be belittled. But these two states should also be able to achieve a peaceful modus vivendi, in which neither would patronize the other; but in which both, between themselves and in their relations with the outside world, would set an example that there could be peaceful cooperation also between such contrasting political and social systems.

State of the Nation address,
Bonn, Jan. 28.

It's very hard to tell U.S. leaders 26 years after the war that Europeans still want this degree of American engagement and presence.

But this has to do not only with protecting West Germany but the future of Europe and the United States. We are all looking for balanced force reductions between East and West, and this may become a vital theme in future years. But it wouldn't make sense to reduce the American engagement here before one enters into negotiations. If one did so, the West as a whole would be weakened, and the United States wouldn't be able to take care of its own interests.

Interview, Bonn/
The New York Times, 1-29:45.

East Germany has made remarkable progress. One has to admit that, whether one likes their methods or not. The figures show it, especially in the various branches of their industry—and the standard of living is not so bad, especially if you compare it with other countries in the Eastern bloc. The comparison with us is not so favorable; because every time they think they are getting closer to us, we move ahead, too. But apart from the material difference, there still is and will be for a long time to come a general feeling of closeness to West Germany, of belonging together because of family links, history, cultural links, etc. But those who rule that other part of Germany believe they still need a period of isolating themselves and their people as much as possible. They need it in order to get stability and to develop a kind of identity of the people with the state. Only after they have gone through this period will it be possible for them to accept the kind of communication which goes on today between the Federal Republic (West Germany) and other Communist states. This, of course, is somewhat absurd. Our people can go to Bulgaria and to Romania—hundreds of thousands do—and they meet their East German relatives on the shores of the Black Sea. This belongs to the ridiculous realities of the world. But I think the main argument for the East German government is that more communication, even if it were limited, would go against their dominating interest of stabilizing their regime.

Interview, Bonn/
U.S. News & World Report, 6-14:47.

355

(WILLY BRANDT)

(Regarding his country's attempts at easing tensions between West and East Europe): We have a special responsibility. It is not only a question of moral responsibility because of recent German history, but also the fact that peace in Europe is not possible without specific German contributions . . . Despite all the vacillations, the basis for this policy is that relatively soon after the war (World War II), the average German saw the guarantee of peace in cooperation and friendship with the West, and at the same time he saw that peace would be more secure when there was understanding with the East.

Interview/The New York Times, 10-21:16.

Trygve Bratteli
Premier of Norway

I don't think you will meet people here (in Norway) who say, "Our friends are in the East and our enemies are in the West." But you will find many who say, "We have no enemies on either side." Today the feeling of a divided Europe is less strong than it was. Nevertheless, having said this, no widespread neutralist feeling has been produced here, and NATO remains generally accepted.

Interview, Oslo/
The New York Times, 12-8:37.

Leonid I. Brezhnev
General Secretary,
Communist Party of the Soviet Union

The Soviet Union is prepared to deepen relations of mutually-advantageous cooperation in every sphere with states which for their part seek to do so. Our country is prepared to participate together with the other states concerned in settling problems like the conservation of the environment, development of power and other natural resources, development of transport and communications, prevention and eradication of the most dangerous and widespread diseases, and the exploration and development of outer space and the world ocean. And we declare that, while consistently pursuing its policy of peace and friendship

among nations, the Soviet Union will continue to conduct a resolute struggle against imperialism and firmly to rebuff the evil designs and subversions of aggressors. As in the past, we shall give undeviating support to the peoples' struggle for democracy, national liberation and socialism.

At Soviet Communist Party Congress,
Moscow, March 30/
The New York Times, 3-31:14.

(Regarding the situation in Czechoslovakia in 1968): It was quite clear to us that this was not only an attempt on the part of imperialism and its accomplices to overthrow the socialist system in Czechoslovakia; it was an attempt to strike in this way at the positions of socialism in Europe as a whole and to create favorable conditions for a subsequent onslaught against the socialist world by the most aggressive forces of imperialism. In view of the appeals by Party and state leaders, Communists and working people of Czechoslovakia, and considering the danger posed to the socialist gains in that country, we and the fraternal socialist countries then jointly took the decision to render internationalist assistance to Czechoslovakia in defense of socialism. In the extraordinary conditions created by the forces of imperialism and counterrevolution, we were bound to do so by our class duty, loyalty to socialist internationalism and the concern for the interests of our states and the future of socialism and peace in Europe.

At Soviet Communist Party Congress,
Moscow, March 30/
The New York Times, 3-31:14.

Our press, radio and television are doing much to insure quick reporting of the pressing problems of the life of the country and international affairs that really interest the Soviet people. They help to disseminate the advanced experience of Communist construction and give a rebuff to the ideological sallies of the class enemies . . . Imperialist propaganda (is sparing nothing) to delude people, to make them believe that under capitalism they are living in a near-paradise and to slander socialism. The airwaves are virtually clogged with all sorts of fabrications about life in our country and in the fraternal socialist countries. It is the duty of our propagandists to give a timely rebuff to these ideological attacks and tell hundreds of millions of people the truth about the socialist society, the Soviet way of life and the building of Communism in our country. This has to be done with purpose, convincingly, intelligibly and vividly. The voice giving the truth about the Soviet Union must be heard in all the continents.

At Soviet Communist Party Congress,
Moscow, March 30/
The New York Times, 4-5:16.

Some of the NATO countries show an evident interest, and even some nervousness, concerning the reduction of armed forces and armaments in Central Europe. Their representatives ask: Whose armed forces, foreign or national? What armaments, nuclear or conventional, are to be reduced? Could it be, they ask, that the Soviet proposals encompass all this taken together? . . . In this connection, we too have a question: Don't those curious people seem like a person that tries to judge the flavor of wine by its appearance, without tasting it? If something is not clear to somebody, we are quite ready to make it clear. All you have to do is muster resolve to try the proposals that interest you by their taste. Translated into diplomatic language, this means: Start negotiations.

Tiflis, U.S.S.R., May 14/
The New York Times, 5-15:7.

It is clear to all that the Communist Party went victoriously through this cruel test (the events in Czechoslovakia in 1968 leading up to Soviet military intervention). Czechoslovakia now stands in the eyes of the world as a firm element in the socialist commonwealth. And no one will ever be able to pull the Czechoslovak socialist republic from the socialist camp.

Before Czechoslovak Communist Party
Congress, Prague, May 26/
The Washington Post, 5-27:(A)28.

The joint coordinated efforts of the Soviet Union and the German Democratic Republic (East Germany) are aimed at ensuring that West Berlin ceases to be the trigger of tensions and crisis situations and that normal conditions for the life of the city and its people be secured—of course, under adequate consideration for the legitimate interests and sovereign rights of the German Democratic Republic. We are of the opinion that the current negotiations on West Berlin will make it possible to at first clarify the positions of the interested parties . . . I do not know what the attitude of our partners in negotiation is on this. But we, for our part, are ready to strive for a successful conclusion of this objective and to work toward the achievement and implementation of an effective agreement.

At East German Communist Party Congress,
East Berlin, June 16/
The Washington Post, 6-17:(A)26.

(Addressing Yugoslav President Tito): We both know well that in the world different forces exist which want to hinder . . . (improved) development of our relations and which strive to deepen all the differences and endeavor in this or that way to divide us. They let circulate a so-called new doctrine of limited sovereignty, spread rumors of Soviet armies which are allegedly prepared to move into the Balkans, and many other fairy tales. They assert that Yugoslavia is allegedly a gray zone, and that she allegedly goes to the West and so on. I think we should not take time to deny all these slanderous publications. Still, they lead us to conclude that Yugoslav-Soviet friendship should be protected and defended . . . The task before us is not simple. We would not be realists if we would not see that the inheritance of those years when Soviet-Yugoslav relations were seriously darkened is in some way still present with us. (But) we would not be Communists if we would not understand that our interests are, in essence, the same and that we have a joint responsibility in the struggle for peace.

Belgrade, Sept. 22/
The Washington Post, 9-23:(A)1.

(LEONID I. BREZHNEV)

The people of our two countries (Yugoslavia and the Soviet Union) stand on the same side of the barricade.

Belgrade/Time, 10-4:44.

On this continent we have seen the elements of detente, security and a better future for the European people grow and take force. This progress has evolved through the recognition of the inviolability of borders, the respect of principles of non-violence, the equality of rights and the principle of non-interference in the interior affairs of other countries.

Versailles, France, Oct. 26/
San Francisco Examiner, 10-26:1.

Alastair Burnett
Editor, "The Economist," London

If we (Britain) don't get into Europe (the Common Market), we are going to be something of an orphan child on America's doorstep. We would start behaving like a wife with very fading charms—a sort of Catherine of Aragon—beseeching the United States to show us some pity. The worst result, of course, would be for us to reach the sort of dependence on America that Austria and Hungary came to have on Germany.

Interview/
U.S. News & World Report, 5-3:71.

Nicolae Ceausescu
President of Romania

Romanian Communists and our people highly appreciate the outstanding achievements of the Soviet Union in building socialism and Communism. They consider them a major contribution to the consolidation of the might of the world socialist system and the anti-imperialist front. The conclusion last year of a treaty of friendship between our two countries opens new prospects for the all-round development of Romanian-Soviet cooperation.

At Soviet Communist Party Congress,
Moscow, April 1/Daily World, 4-3:4.

No matter how much interdependence in production between various sectors of activity of the East European countries will develop, this must not lead in any way to the transgression of national sovereignty . . . must not influence in any way the right of the Communist party of each country to decide itself its development program according to its own wish.

Constanta, Romania, July 24/
The Dallas Times Herald, 7-25:(A)3.

The working-class state has a right to interfere in literature, music and art, and to admit only that which corresponds to the interests of the socialist homeland.

The Christian Science Monitor, 11-10:9.

Jacques Chaban-Delmas
Premier of France

France is on the way to winning. We have everything in our favor. Before 10 years have passed, we shall at last have reached the threshold of economic power which will ensure our political independence and allow us to speed up social progress.

Before National Assembly, Paris,
April 20/
The Christian Science Monitor, 4-24:13.

James Chichester-Clark
Prime Minister of Northern Ireland

There is no war between our Protestant and Roman Catholic citizens. Their interests are the same and their enemies are the same. Let it be plain that the security forces and the police and Northern Ireland government will not give in to intimidation. They will never surrender to the tiny groups of Irish republicans who man machine guns and manufacture nail bombs and acid bombs. If these ugly elements really want a trial of strength, the forces of law and order will be resolute in confronting them and defeating them.

Belfast, Feb. 6/The New York Times, 2-7:(1)3.

Emilio Colombo
Premier of Italy

For a complex of historical reasons, (the

Italian Communist) Party finds itself representing various strata of the people and ruling local administrations, especially in some regions where socialist tradition was strong at the beginning of the century. (Nevertheless) the model of development and international alignment that the Communist Party proposes for Italy—an especially advanced country, deeply imbedded in the Western area and with its own system of alliances—is the antithesis of what we propose and regard as vital. I exclude (the possibility) that a government alliance between the democratic parties and the Communist Party may be created whereby the Communist Party attains power.

Interview, Rome, Feb. 14/
The New York Times, 2-15:1.

John B. Connally, Jr.
Secretary of the Treasury
of the United States

(Advocating European nations to contribute more to their defense): It isn't a question of cutting the number of troops in Europe. It's a question of who the hell is going to pay for them.

At International Banking Conference,
Munich, May 28/
The Salt Lake Tribune, 5-29:2.

Earl of Cromer
British Ambassador
to the United States

(Regarding British entry into the European Common Market): The rapid rate of growth of the Common Market countries has enabled the United States to increase exports to them nearly threefold since the Market was formed. An economically united and politically stable Europe will prove a still better trading partner for the United States than in the past.

Interview, Washington/
The Dallas Times Herald, 7-21:(A)16.

Richard Crossman
Editor, "New Statesman," London

We want a German nation that has lost the art of starting wars. Anything that keeps Germany divided is to be welcomed.

Interview/U.S. News & World Report, 5-3:71.

Suleyman Demirel
Premier of Turkey

Why should I resign? I have done nothing wrong. There are dissatisfied, disorderly people in every country. I am an elected man. I did not just take this chair; I was pushed into it by the people. I defend free enterprise. I defend the wealthy . . . but I defend social welfare, too . . . We spent 100 years fighting for freedom and democracy; and in the last 25 years we have achieved this and made the citizens—the peasants—partners in the government. We will not give this up.

Interview/Newsweek, 1-18:36.

Bernadette Devlin
Member of British Parliament
from Northern Ireland

The Catholics and Protestants (in Northern Ireland) live together very easily. They don't fight over Papal infallibility . . . They fight over exploitation. The Catholic and Protestant poor are exploited by the Catholic and Protestant rich.

At University of South Florida,
Feb. 16/Daily World, 2-24:7.

We are happy to receive capitalist money in our attempts to destroy the capitalist system. If they are stupid enough to give it to us, we are glad to use it—it is our money anyway.

Interview/
Los Angeles Herald-Examiner, 2-17:(A)10.

I don't think there's malice in Northern Ireland on the part of the people. But people are frightened, and those who are frightened are armed. And it's not a matter of sort of setting the date, dropping the flag and declaring civil war. It's a matter of when fear and frustration become intolerable that people will resort to armed defense of their own homes, their own villages, and a frightened people very quickly moves from defense to attack . . . Attacking those who they may think would do them some harm.

TV interview,
London/
San Francisco Examiner, 9-20:7.

Brian Faulkner
Prime Minister
of Northern Ireland

I regard it as my most important single aim (as new Prime Minister) to restore confidence to the entire community of Northern Ireland; because I am utterly convinced that, without that restoration of confidence, all else is futile.

> *Inaugural address, Belfast, March 23/*
> *Los Angeles Times, 3-24:(1)5.*

Talk of fighting for civil rights is . . . absolute rubbish. What the terrorists are in fact aiming to do is to bypass the democratic wishes of the people of Northern Ireland and to create a situation of such chaos and despair that a "solution" to the problem will be sought in terms of establishing an all-Ireland republic.

> *The New York Times, 6-22:10.*

(Regarding criticism of the Northern Irish government by Jack Lynch, Prime Minister of the Republic of Ireland): What is apparent now is that no further attempt by us to deal constructively with the present Dublin government is possible. Now Mr. Lynch clearly commits himself and his government to support, by political means, what the IRA seeks to achieve by violent means—the overthrow of the Northern Ireland government. (The IRA), based in the Irish Republic, was trained and organized in Eire. It sends across the border from the Irish Republic the explosives, the arms and the ammunition designed to kill and maim Ulster people.

> *Aug. 13/The Washington Post, 8-14:(A)12.*

Neither the United Kingdom nor the Northern Ireland government will be shaken in their resolve to maintain Northern Ireland as an integral part of the U.K. by any campaign—be it outright terrorism or political blackmail. The sooner everyone fully realizes that, the better for all of us—and I mean all of us.

> *Belfast, Aug. 24/*
> *The New York Times, 8-25:1.*

(Regarding internment of suspected troublemakers in Northern Ireland): Can any of us progress, can any of us prosper, while various factions of the IRA and their associates are allowed to infect the whole atmosphere in which we live? Internment is not aimed at repressing the Catholic minority. The government took the decision to introduce internment with great reluctance; we truly deplore the necessity for it. But the allegation that the internment operation was deliberately and maliciously one-sided is wholly without foundation. The instructions to the security men were—and still are—that all dangerous men about whom they had reliable information should be arrested. This is a matter which has nothing to do with politics or religion. It is a straightforward matter of public order and safety.

> *Belfast, Aug. 24/*
> *The New York Times, 8-25:13.*

(Regarding the religious and political violence in Northern Ireland): People in the Republic (of Ireland), in Britain and other places around the world have seen for themselves the injured men, the bleeding and terrified girls. Witnessing such acts, they may feel our community is willing to accept any course—even surrender—which would restore peace. They must not make such a tragic error. These deeds may appall and outrage the Ulster people, but they only increase their will to resist and reinforce their utter determination that men like these and methods like these shall not rule their lives. Those who imagine that terrorism will bring about an Ireland united against the will of the Ulster majority must now pause. Not just the government, but an entire determined community stands in the way of any such course.

> *Sept. 3/The New York Times, 9-4:2.*

(Regarding United States Senator Edward Kennedy's urging the withdrawal of British troops from Northern Ireland and the reunification of it and the Republic of Ireland): (Senator Kennedy has shown himself) willing to swallow hook, line and sinker the hoary propaganda that IRA atrocities are carried out as part of a freedom fight on behalf of the Northern Ireland people. This completely ignores the fact that free elections over the past 50 years have demonstrated the democratic wish of the overwhelming majority of the Ulster people to remain part of the United Kingdom.

Before Northern Irish Parliament,
Belfast, Oct. 21/
The New York Times, 10-22:3.

Edgar Faure
French statesman

I see that the French are replying to an Algerian threat to cut off gasoline supplies with a counter-threat to refuse to buy Algerian wine. This seems to me to be a highly appropriate exchange of reprisals as between one undrinkable liquid and another.

San Francisco Examiner, 4-20:34.

Edward Gierek
First Secretary, Communist Party of Poland

We attach particular importance to the fact that state policy must be clear and understandable to everyone; that practice should not be contrary to words; that decisions and deeds must be born in an honest, direct conversation with the working class, with the whole nation.

Address to the nation, Warsaw/
San Francisco Examiner & Chronicle
(This World), 1-10:14.

Our entire Party and our people are profoundly grateful to the Communist Party of the Soviet Union and to its leadership for their understanding of our problems and for friendly aid in settling them. This genuinely internationalist attitude to our Party, to our people, is of really priceless importance for us Polish Communists.

At Soviet Communist Party Congress, Moscow,
March 31/The Washington Post, 4-1:(A)15.

Arthur J. Goldberg
Former United States Ambassador
to the United Nations

. . . repression of any group is an ex-

pression of disregard for the opinion of mankind, and there is nothing so quick to erode mutual trust on which international understanding depends. Many Soviet Jews undoubtedly wish to remain and to live in dignity and freedom as loyal and productive citizens of their birthplace. This they are being denied. And for this denial, the Soviet Union is bound to pay the great price of alienating three million of its people, of goading them into acts of protest and of impoverishing the intellectual, artistic, scientific and economic life of the nation.

Brussels, Feb. 23/
The New York Times, 2-25:3.

Andrew J. Goodpaster
General, United States Army;
Supreme Allied Commander/Europe

Twice in this twentieth century, American Presidents and American Congresses have had to recognize that the security of Europe is vital to the security of the United States. Twice the U.S. has sent expeditionary forces to Europe to restore the military and political balance; and the price has been a big one. The premium that the American taxpayer pays today to maintain the peace and security, so expensively restored when violated in the past, is low-cost insurance for something we treasure so highly. We Americans and our NATO allies cannot afford to further reduce our already limited forces unless and until reciprocal and mutual force reductions are made by our potential adversaries . . . or until free Europe, united in the European Economic Community (Common Market), can muster greater strength to take up additional parts of the collective security burden. But until that time, let every American understand that the three hundred thousand U.S. soldiers, sailors, airmen and Marines stationed in Europe play a role which is of critical importance in maintaining and strengthening peace and is therefore strongly in our enlightened national self-interest.

At American Legion convention,
Houston, Sept. 2/
Vital Speeches, 10-1:746.

Andrei A. Grechko
Minister of Defense of the Soviet Union

We are strengthening our army—not for attack, but for defense. However, our armed forces are always ready to chastise the aggressor, and right on that territory from which he dares violate our borders. Our army is equipped with weapons of great destructive force and capable of reaching any point on the globe, on land, sea and air.

At Soviet Communist Party Congress, Moscow, April 2/Los Angeles Times, 4-3:(1)12.

Andrei A. Gromyko
Foreign Minister of the Soviet Union

The German Democratic Republic (East Germany) has firmly established itself as a real and active component of the European system of states. To be more precise, modern Europe is already inconceivable without it.

At United Nations, New York, Sept. 28/ The New York Times, 9-29:2.

Alfred Grosser
Professor of Political Science, Paris University

Western Europe is a million times more important to American interests than Vietnam. If you (America) can't afford to lose Western Europe to the Communists, then you must defend it in your own interest. And we don't even have to be grateful.

Interview/U.S. News & World Report, 5-3:70.

Edward J. Gurney
United States Senator, R—Fla.

An emphatic denial by the Soviets of an important military or foreign policy matter is more likely to mean that they are doing the exact opposite.

Quote, 1-10:25.

Rita E. Hauser
United States Representative, Commission on Human Rights of the United Nations

The persistent pattern of political discrimination and cultural deprivation over the past 30 or more years has resulted in the desire of many Soviet Jews to emigrate, particularly those with families living abroad. It is disturbing to note that any interest a Jew may evidence in Israel makes him suspect to the Soviet authorities . . . It is the considered view of my delegation that discrimination against Jews persists on a wide scale in the Soviet Union.

Geneva, Feb. 26/ The Washington Post, 2-27:(A)10.

Denis Healey
Former Minister of Defense of the United Kingdom

It only takes a five per cent credibility of American retaliation to deter the Russians. The Allies will never be satisfied with the 95 per cent possibility there will be no retaliation. And the job of diplomacy and strategy is to narrow the gap between the degree of capability needed to deter and the degree needed to reassure the Allies.

Interview, London/ San Francisco Examiner, 2-22:1.

. . . I think it is always a mistake to imagine that the Russians have only one motive for anything they do. There is undoubtedly a number of motives, some less benign than others. But my personal opinion is that the last congress of the Soviet Communist Party in March did mark a turning point on two issues. First of all, the balance of Soviet expenditure swung in favor of consumer goods against defense and heavy industry. Secondly, for whatever reason, the Russian leaders are giving a lower priority to military adventures. I believe their proposals both in the SALT talks and on mutual and balanced force reductions in Europe, as well as some limitation on the deployment of fleets overseas, all relate in part to this Soviet desire—having achieved a stand-off with the United States both at sea and in the strategic nuclear field—to stabilize the situation rather than continue the arms race.

Interview, London/ Los Angeles Herald-Examiner, 10-2:(A)10.

Edward Heath
Prime Minister
of the United Kingdom

The frontiers of Soviet ambition are not bound by the Mediterranean.

At British Commonwealth conference,
Singapore, Jan. 15/
Los Angeles Times, 1-16:(A)8.

The Soviet Union does not negotiate with the weak.

London/
The Christian Science Monitor, 3-6:8.

If the road we have taken is hard, it is only because we know by now in our hearts that there are no short cuts. It demands a steady nerve and resolution. This is what Britain needs today. That is what your government will provide.

The New York Times Magazine, 3-14:37.

Successive American Administrations have supported enlargement of the (European Common Market) because they believe wider European unity would be in their own interests, and Europe would be able to do more in its own defense. I would say that if the negotiations (to admit Britain to the Common Market) fail, the Americans, in their disillusionment, would be more inclined to say that Europe should be left to look after itself.

News conference, Bonn, West Germany,
April 6/The Washington Post, 4-7:(A)9.

Look what we (his government) have done already. We have only been in office nine months. We at once gave pensions to those who had been forgotten all these years, the over-80s. We have since increased pensions all around and brought in pensions for others who also had been left out. We have introduced Family Income Supplements. We have reduced taxes; we have begun the first great reform of taxation for half a century; we have taken 200,000 families out of the income-tax net altogether . . . society must look after those who cannot help themselves. The more fortunate must help those who through no

fault of their own are poor; the disabled, too, the old, the sick . . . We have produced a sound legal basis for the improvement of industrial relations. We have also reduced the size of government. We have greatly improved the process of decision-making. Our policy is the product of five years' hard thinking in opposition. Nobody need ask us, "What is your policy?" There it is. It is all there in black and white.

Interview, London/
The Christian Science Monitor, 4-19:7.

(Regarding British entry into the Common Market): I have a vision of a Europe once united—1,200 years ago—coming together once again.

News conference, London, July 12/
The New York Times, 7-13:3.

We have an opportunity (by joining the European Common Market) to make history happen. It is in our hands now and no one else's. For 25 years we have been looking for something to get us going again. Now here it is. We have the chance for new greatness. We must take it.

Television address to British people/
Time, 7-19:27.

We are now seeing a dramatic and welcome renewal of contacts between the United States and (Communist) China. At the same time, the U.S. and the Soviet Union are deep in conversations on nuclear matters which intimately affect the future of every citizen of this country and Europe. (All this) provides opportunities for statesmanship which, if taken, could break down barriers we have come to take for granted in our modern world . . . So the decision we are called upon to take on this great matter (British entry into the European Common Market) is not simply a decision about our own prosperity. It is also a decision whether we should join with the others in working out a European policy which would give Europe an effective voice in these overwhelming developments which vitally affect her own future.

Before House of Commons, London,
July 21/The New York Times, 7-22:3.

(EDWARD HEATH)

The Soviets may calculate that (due to the build-up of the Soviet military) eventually the sheer disparity of military strength would leave Western Europe with no convincing strategy. Political pressure, shrewdly applied and backed by the threat of greatly superior military force, could compel one of the more exposed members of the (Western European) alliance to lapse into neutrality. Then a process of disintegration could begin which would lead to the ultimate price: an extension of the Soviet sphere of influence gradually into countries at present members of (NATO), and if possible, to the Atlantic.

Before House of Commons, London/
Time, 10-18:39.

The attempt to destroy the fabric of society in Northern Ireland by violence cannot be tolerated. The sniper's shot, the bomb in the night, the use of children for cover, the intimidation and humiliation of neighbors, the killing of innocent men and women—these wanton acts of terrorism solve nothing. No doubt the roots of the troubles of Northern Ireland can be traced deep into the past. But when we come to construct a political solution—and that is what all men of goodwill must work for—we have to deal with the realities of today. The reality is that Northern Ireland exists, that it is part of the United Kingdom and that the majority of its people want it to remain so. Many Catholics in Northern Ireland would like to see Northern Ireland unified with the south (the Republic of Ireland). That is understandable. It is legitimate to seek to further that aim by democratic and constitutional means. If at some future date the majority of the people in Northern Ireland want unification and express that desire in the appropriate constitutional way, I do not believe any British government would stand in the way. But that is not what the majority want today.

At Lord Mayor's banquet, London/
The Christian Science Monitor, 11-18:2.

If, by agreement, the North and South (of Ireland) should decide to come together, not only would the present government (of Britain) raise no objection, but I cannot conceive of any future government which would want to stand in their way. All we say is that a united Ireland cannot be brought about by force and that we cannot usurp the right of choice of the people of Northern Ireland . . . In Northern Ireland there is a majority which, at present, wishes to remain within the United Kingdom. To them we say: "As the majority, you have your democratic rights. We will respect them, and we expect you to respect the democratic rights of others." There is a minority which looks toward the unification of Ireland. To them we say: "You have the right to pursue your aims by peaceful means. We will try with your help to find the right way for you to have a permanent guaranteed place in the making of decisions within Northern Ireland." There are groups of gunmen which seek to unite Ireland, not by consent but by murder and terror. To them we say: "Your methods are an affront to civilization and democracy and a disgrace to the Irish people. We are determined to defeat you, and you will fail."

Interview, London/
The Dallas Times Herald, 12-17:(A)14.

Erich Honecker
First Secretary,
Communist Party of East Germany

East Germany fully distances itself from West Germany; and their relations can only be those of two states with different systems.

Before Central Committee of East German
Communist Party, East Berlin, May 3/
Los Angeles Times, 5-5:(1)13.

Gustav Husak
First Secretary, Communist Party
of Czechoslovakia

We wish from the tribune of this congress to express our sincere gratitude to the Communist Party of the Soviet Union, the Soviet government and the Soviet people for reacting with understanding to the alarm of Czechoslovak Communists for the cause of socialism and responding to their appeal for help (during the crisis in Czechoslovakia in 1968). This international help saved our country from civil war, counterrevolution, and helped defend the achievements of socialism.

At Soviet Communist Party Congress,
Moscow/
The Christian Science Monitor, 4-9:1.

Various reformers entertain the hope that there will be a more liberal period after the (Czechoslovak Communist) Party Congress. If they mean freedom for bourgeois tendencies, for laying the foundations for a new disruption, they should not entertain any illusions.

At Slovak Communist Party Congress,
Bratislava/Time, 6-7:18.

Henry M. Jackson
United States Senator, D—Wash.

We are in Europe today because we have learned that the security of the United States is inextricably tied to the security of Europe. The American military presence in Europe is the hard nub of the Western deterrent. The chief purpose of these American forces is political—to deter a Soviet aggressive move against the NATO area by making it clear to the Russians that their forces would meet enough U.S. forces to make any crisis a Soviet-American crisis, not just a European one. This means that a token American force is not adequate. It has to be an effective American combat force—not just something to be tripped over, but a force capable of putting up a serious defense.

Interview, Washington/
The Dallas Times Herald, 7-22:(A)22.

I am opposed to unilaterally pulling back American troops from Europe so long as our allies are willing to share the burden more equitably. The primary reason we have American forces in Europe is to make it clear to the Russians that, if they move against the NATO area, they will provoke a Russian-American crisis, not just a Russian-European crisis. The potential for a Russian-American crisis deters the Russian-European crisis.

Interview/Nations's Business, November:67.

Jacob K. Javits
United States Senator, R—N.Y.

If we adopt a resolution cutting our forces (in Europe) in half by unilateral action, without consulting with the Europeans, we are giving them word which, in my judgment, will induce them to believe that the United States is no longer going to be the force in Europe which it has been for 25 years . . . that, on the contrary, the United States is pulling out as the back-up for the security of the Atlantic Alliance and that they (the Europeans) will have to look elsewhere . . . If they looked elsewhere—and in my judgment it would be necessary for them to look elsewhere—they would have to look to the East. I see this written large on the wall.

The National Observer, 5-17:6.

Roy Jenkins
Deputy leader, British Labor Party

(Prime Minister Edward Heath) has no sense of persuasion and no sense of fairness. He is an expert at demolition and at division; but at promoting cohesion and construction, he is barren. This, I believe, is because he is, to an extent greater than any Prime Minister since Neville Chamberlain, incapable of understanding the minds of those who do not agree with him or have a different background of experience.

Before House of Commons, London/
The New York Times, 2-28:(4)3.

We want a Britain which, while no longer a dominating power, nonetheless captures the imagination of others by its pattern of humane civilization and its sense of responsibility for the world outside our relatively cozy island. We want to make a reality of our traditional idealism.

At Labor Party conference,
Brighton, England/
The Washington Post, 10-9:(A)12.

Donald M. Kendall
President, PepsiCo, Inc.

By the end of the Seventies, there is a strong possibility that Europe will become a fully-integrated economic unit, with national frontiers taking on the characteristics of state lines in the United States. It is observed that Europe is already an economic giant that can stand on its own competitive feet. The question before us is whether we (the United States) can afford to have it stand on *our* feet. With the EEC, EFTA and all their relations, we are talking about the weight of 50 nations!

Before Mid-America World Trade
Conference, Chicago/
The Wall Street Journal, 3-16:16.

Edward M. Kennedy
United States Senator, D–Mass.

Ulster (Northern Ireland) is becoming Britain's Vietnam. America cannot keep silent when men and women of Ireland are dying. Britain has lost its way, and the innocent people of Northern Ireland are the ones who now must suffer . . . The tragedy of Ulster is yet another chapter in the unfolding larger tragedy of the Empire. It is India, Palestine, Cyprus and Africa once again.

Before the Senate, Washington,
Oct. 20/Time, 11-1:48.

Isaac N. Kidd
Vice Admiral, United States Navy;
Commander, Sixth Fleet
in the Mediterranean

If the Soviets introduced their own aircraft carriers into the ballgame (in the Mediterranean), I would be one very worried man . . . But I don't see any other way they can go if they're going to use the massive investment they've put into developing their Navy in the past few years. They're spending a national fortune . . . The rate of improvement of the Soviet Navy is fantastic. They are in one hell of a hurry; and I wish I knew why.

News conference aboard U.S.S. Springfield,
off Gaeta, Italy/Los Angeles Times, 5-5:(1-A)6.

Kurt Georg Kiesinger,
Former Chancellor of West Germany,

(Regarding the government of Chancellor Willy Brandt and its policy of seeking better relations with Eastern Europe): It has failed. It has won no concessions in return. It has gained no evident relaxation of tension . . . It has plunged into the hectic adventure of its Eastern policy, which the whole world and the Soviet Union itself judge to be a great political success for Moscow. It is a policy of adventurism without any compelling necessity.

At Christian Democratic Union
convention, Dusseldorf, Jan. 25/
The New York Times, 1-25:8.

Alexei N. Kosygin
Premier of the Soviet Union

Wherever encroachments are made on the freedom and independence of peoples, the position of the Soviet Union is perfectly clear: The aggressor must withdraw from foreign land. It is necessary to have strict respect for the rights of the peoples for independent development, for managing their internal affairs in accordance with the peoples' will and aspirations. Our country invariably takes sides with the states and peoples attacked by the imperialist aggressors and uphold their righteous cause.

Moscow, May 18/Daily World, 5-19:2.

The Soviet-West German treaty, just like the treaty between Poland and West Germany, is based on the necessity of proceeding on the basis of the actual situation established after World War II. That is precisely why these treaties are encountering the fierce opposition of those who are against a detente. We share the opinion recently expressed by West German Chancellor Willy Brandt that these treaties are an "example of how to achieve equal partnership in the cause of creating peace."

Moscow, June 8/Daily World, 6-11:2.

(Regarding United States President Nixon's planned trip to the Soviet Union for meetings with government officials): No one in the world should ever say that this is just two big powers ganging up to dictate their will to all the others, because this is ridiculous and would be entirely wrong. We are against that completely. We want all people of the world to know that (Soviet-American) friendship pursues the goal of insuring progress and prosperity for all nations, big or small.

Moscow, Oct. 15/
The New York Times, 10-16:13.

The total industrial and agricultural output of the U.S.S.R. in 1975 will exceed that of the United States at present. This is an important landmark in the economic competition between the U.S.S.R. and the capitalist countries.

Before Supreme Soviet, Moscow, Nov. 24/
Los Angeles Times, 11-26:(1)25.

I believe no country in the West can boast conditions equal to those offered to the Jews in the Soviet Union. There is absolutely no discrimination against them, just as there is none against any other national group.

News conference, Aalborg, Denmark,
Dec. 5/Los Angeles Times, 12-6:(1)24.

Bruno Kreisky
Chancellor of Austria

After what happened in Czechslovakia three years ago (the Soviet invasion), I am totally convinced that there is but little room for political development inside the East European Communist world. There is always some chance for more national identification inside these countries, as in the cases of Hungary and Poland. But there will only be as much freedom in the real sense as there is freedom inside the Soviet Union itself. Nationalism, yes, to a degree; but political freedom is tied to Soviet developments.

Interview, Vienna/
The New York Times, 11-14:(4)13.

Melvin R. Laird
Secretary of Defense of the United States

If the Russians have a superior military force, they can gain their political objectives

throughout the world without the use of weapons. There is no military advantage to overkill, but the political gains are tremendous.

Time, 10-18:39.

Fred Luchsinger
Chief editor,
"Neue Zuercher Zeitung," Switzerland

Europe wants to be more powerful economically and more independent politically, but still wants to remain dependent on the United States for its security. The whole situation is not rational.

Interview/
U.S. News & World Report, 5-3:70.

Joseph Luns
Secretary General, North Atlantic
Treaty Organization

It is regrettable that only the nuclear deterrent and the presence of U.S. troops in Europe has kept the peace; and it would be very rash to pretend that without these no war would have come about.

Interview, Brussels/
Los Angeles Herald-Examiner, 10-17:(A)14.

Jack Lynch
Prime Minister
of the Republic of Ireland

The Ireland Act of 1949 pledges British support (to Northern Ireland), financial and military, as well as British prestige, in a manner . . . which makes intransigence a virtue and silences reason, (and which tends) to encourage infamous conduct, represented again and again on the streets of Belfast and Derry.

At ceremony marking 50th anniversary
of Anglo-Irish truce, July 11/
The Christian Science Monitor, 7-16:2.

The sympathies of the government and of the vast majority of the Irish people, North and South, go to the nationalist minority in (Northern Ireland) who are again victimized by an attempt to maintain a regime which has

367

WHAT THEY SAID IN 1971

(JACK LYNCH)

long since shown itself incapable of just government.

The Christian Science Monitor, 8-12:2.

(The Northern Irish government) is now, and has been since it was created, directed at the suppression of (the) human and civil rights of more than a third of the population. We know that the British public, if fully aware of the facts, would turn away in horror from what they have been asked to support, financially and otherwise, all these years in Northern Ireland.

Dublin, Aug. 12/
The New York Times, 8-13:2.

Ireland is one country, one nation, one people; and I think we are both small enough and big enough to live together. We have been one for centuries and only divided (into Ireland and Northern Ireland) in the last 50 years.

News conference, London, Sept. 7/
The New York Times, 9-8:10.

They (the Irish Republican Army) have no mandate from anyone, no matter what kind of moral support they claim they have from the people . . . Every bomb exploded and every bullet fired—not only by an IRA gun, but by a British gun—and every innocent person killed in the north (Northern Ireland), no matter on what side the loss of life, put the day of reconciliation between the north and south further away . . . This government is going to pursue its aim to unite this country in a peaceful way. There is going to be no pulling back in relation to pursuing the IRA and other subversive actions.

Before Dail Eireann (Parliament),
Dublin, Dec. 17/
The New York Times, 12-18:14.

Mike Mansfield
United States Senator, D–Mont.

We've got too much over there (in Europe) —too much logistics; too many generals; too many colonels; too much headquarters. Too much. The 525,000 servicemen and their dependents could be cut by half, and they would probably be twice as effective.

Interview, Washington, May 9/
The Washington Post, 5-10:(A)1.

In my judgment, a reduction in U.S. forces in Western Europe by 50 per cent is in the interest of this nation, with or without negotiations . . . Lest we lose sight of reality in an enthusiasm for negotiated mutual reductions with the Soviet Union, I would . . . remind the Senate that the run has not been on the ruble; it has been on the dollar.

Before the Senate, Washington, May 14/
Los Angeles Times, 5-16:(A)1,6.

The U.S. is maintaining too many troops there (in Europe) and is shouldering a lopsided burden it cannot afford. The Europeans have restored their economies. The Deutschmark is strong. The guilder is strong. The pound sterling seems to be strengthening. But the dollar is less strong. We simply cannot afford the commitment any longer . . . I don't think I am against NATO. I am for it and always have been. But NATO's changed since 1949, just like everything has changed in nearly a quarter of a century. NATO used to be a shield. Today it's a symbol. And a symbol does not need so many troops and dependents.

Interview, Washington/
The Washington Post, 7-8:(A)34.

I don't regard the present level of United States forces in Europe in any sense as a "bargaining chip" in negotiating a mutual reduction (of forces) with the Soviet Union. There is no bargaining power in the irrelevant. An excessive and antiquated United States deployment in Europe and the enormous costs it entails cannot strengthen the United States position in negotiations. It can only weaken the international economic position of this nation.

At Johns Hopkins University,
Nov. 18/
The New York Times, 11-19:8.

Reginald Maudling
Home Secretary
of the United Kingdom

(Regarding violence in Northern Ireland): Those whose aim cannot be reconciled with democratic government, freedom and a lawful society have turned more and more to the use of the gun and the bomb, because they could see no other means of achieving their ends.

London, March 6/
The Christian Science Monitor, 3-13:3.

Northern Ireland is a part of the United Kingdom and will remain so as long as that is the will of her people. And so long as Northern Ireland is in the United Kingdom, our Army will do its duty there in the defense of law, order and justice.

At British Conservative Party
conference, Brighton, England, Oct. 14/
The New York Times, 10-15:3.

Eugene J. McCarthy
United States Senator, D—Minn.

I don't go along with the people who want to pull out of Europe. Our military force there made it unnecessary for Germany to have a big army. And that reassures the Russians; they're happier with an American presence on their border than a German one.

Interview, Washington/
Los Angeles Times, 1-11:(2)7.

Jean Monnet
Founder, European Common Market

We are heading toward the creation of a Europe with one policy and one currency. When that happens, the Europeans will no longer suffer from any inferiority complex, and the Americans will no longer have reason to feel any superiority complex.

Interview, Paris/
The New York Times, 1-20:33.

Thomas H. Moorer
Admiral, United States Navy;
Chairman, Joint Chiefs of Staff

The U.S. contribution to the strength in

Europe provides not only military capability, but I think it provides a clear-cut indication that the United States considers that the security of Western Europe is vital to its own interests, and that the United States is fully involved in the treaty (NATO) and intends to carry out its commitments. Now, you can make a case to show that the gross national product, for instance, of the European nations versus the Warsaw Pact, or the total population of the European nations versus the Warsaw Pact is in favor of the Western European nations . . . But I think that, in order to maintain the complete unity and viability of the Alliance, the U.S. presence is necessary.

Interview, Washington/
U.S. News & World Report, 4-5:47.

Edmund S. Muskie
United States Senator, D—Maine

I find him (Soviet Premier Alexei Kosygin) a man who is willing to talk freely and frankly. He did so in a gentlemanly, constructive way. There's no personal hostility or animosity in his attitude. He's a comfortable man to sit down to talk to. He has very firm opinions and some harsh opinions about the United States. But when he does, he expresses them in a way that makes it difficult to take offense. However, one does disagree with him, and he does not object if one does take issue with him. I responded to him very favorably.

News conference, Moscow/
The Christian Science Monitor, 1-19:4.

Gunnar Myrdal
Swedish economist

(Regarding the strike of Swedish teachers, railwaymen, civil servants and white-collar municipal workers): The organized welfare state has gone mad. (The situation is) against the whole concept of our society, because it involves a strike of well-paid government employees who shouldn't have the right to strike in the first place. It's become a class struggle, with academics and civil servants seeing the lower classes creeping up on them and not lik-

ing it at all. They see the state as being un-
sympathetic. It's an impossible situation.

Interview, Stockholm/
The New York Times, 2-26:3.

Osman Olcay
Foreign Minister of Turkey

Friendly relations with the U.S.A. coincide
with a generally pro-Western attitude of the
Turkish people. They are convinced that theirs
is a Western destiny.

The New York Times, 8-29:(4)13.

George Papadopoulos
Premier of Greece

(To United States Vice President Agnew):
Convey to the people of the United States our
faith in the principles of the political system
(democracy) which was born in this country,
and which we are working day and night to
build within the framework of the Constitution. Tell them to shut their ears to the
sirens of anarchy and to the enemies of the
world we belong to. Tell them we are building
democracy.

Athens, Oct. 23/
The Dallas Times Herald, 10-24:(A)35.

Prince Philip
Duke of Edinburgh

We used to shout "British is best," or
"Britain is best," or "Our products are the
most reliable," "Our deliveries are the most
punctual," and so on. There was a time when
this was perfectly true. It took a bit of time
before we discovered that it wasn't. Well, we
have gone to the other extreme . . . The stuff
we produce is not quite so reliable; it is not
made with such great care; it does not arrive
at the right time.

Interview/The New York Times, 7-20:38.

Nikolai V. Podgorny
President of the Soviet Union

In the military field as in other fields, we

have no secret goals that represent a danger to
peace.

Cairo/The Dallas Times Herald, 1-15:(A)2.

Georges Pompidou
President of France

(Chiding Britain for some conditions it is
asking for entry into the European Common
Market): The English are recognized for having three qualities, among others: humor,
tenacity and realism. It occurs, at times, to
me that we are still somewhat at the stage of
humor. We have no doubt that tenacity will
follow. I hope that realism will also come and
triumph. We shall do everything for that.

News conference, Paris, Jan. 21/
The New York Times, 1-22:11.

For several years now we have had this
issue of the Common Market, and we have
lived—Britain and France—in an atmosphere of
cordial feelings. Sometimes we accomplished a
few things together; but also we sometimes
sulked. And the question now is whether we
can stop sulking and whether we have the
common will to go ahead together . . . Today
it is up to Great Britain to choose Europe.
For my part, I wish profoundly that this
choice be made, that it be made sincerely and
profoundly, taking account of the changes
that it will bring to the life of the British people, in their very conception of life and of
their relations with the outside world . . .
The truth is that a conception of Europe exists, and we must know if Britain's conception
is truly European.

Television interview/ British
Broadcasting Corporation, London, 3-17.

English is not any more the language of
England alone. It is, above all, for the whole
world the language of America. In fact,
Europe will only be Europe if it is distinguished—I do not say separated—from America. The French language might be one of the
means for Western Europe to affirm its personality to America.

Interview/Los Angeles Times, 5-20:(1)19.

(Regarding Britain's entry into the Common Market): It is essential that we be in agreement on fundamentals. We must not make believe we are getting married, to divorce afterward. The countries of Western Europe—be they the Six, be they the candidates for admission—are not movie stars who change fiances every six months. If we get married, it is forever. So we must be serious about it.

Interview/The New York Times, 5-20:3.

Many people believed that Britain was not and did not want to become European and that she wished to enter the (Common Market) only to destroy it or to divert it from its goals. Many also thought that France was ready to use all pretexts to put up a new veto on the entry of Britain. Well, ladies and gentlemen, you see before you this evening two men convinced of the contrary.

After meeting with British Prime Minister Edward Heath, Paris, May 21/ The New York Times, 5-22:2.

Enoch Powell
Member of British Parliament

(Arguing against British entry into the European Common Market): Political unity (in Europe), right or wrong, is incompatible with national independence; and the will to bring Britain into the Community is the will to give that national independence up. On this each one of us must take his own resolve. I can say only what is mine. I do not believe that this nation, which has maintained and defended its independence for a thousand years, will now submit to see it merged or lost; nor did I become a member of our sovereign Parliament in order to consent to that sovereignty being abated or transferred. Come what may, I cannot and I will not.

At British Conservative Party conference, Brighton, England, Oct. 13/ The New York Times, 10-14:8.

Ranier III
Prince of Monaco

In my opinion, the value of a small state should not be expressed by means of terri-

torial size. Rather, should it be considered by the image it has been able to create in the world of today. By image, I do not mean the picture created in our minds by real estate, population figures, military power, type of government, political and economic strength. I refer, rather, to the respect it commands by its way of life, its basic moral values, its consideration for the rights of all. And also, there is the manner in which it can illuminate one corner of a darkening world through its dedication to creative human achievements in arts, sciences and social advancement of human kind . . . Where, in my opinion, our role in this world is of utmost importance is that—just by looking over our borders, or paying us a visit—the people of other countries can see what it is like to live in peace without fear of being coveted.

Before Young Presidents' Organization, Monte Carlo/Los Angeles Times, 5-16:(G)3.

William P. Rogers
Secretary of State of the United States

President Nixon has had a very careful study made of the requirements of our force levels in Europe; and at the last NATO meeting, we decided, together with our allies, that the present force levels were just right, that if we reduced our force levels . . . it would be very destabilizing. We have about enough strength there to be a deterrent to the Soviet Union to prevent any conventional attack, we believe. If we reduced our force levels in Europe at this time, we think it would be a very dangerous situation. We would want to do it in the context of a mutual and balanced force reduction. Why should we in the United States reduce unilaterally and thereby kiss goodbye to any chance that we might have to negotiate successfully to reduce the Soviet presence? The tensions in Europe could be reduced if we could have a mutual and balanced force reduction, and that is our objective.

TV-radio interview/"Meet the Press," National Broadcasting Company, Washington, 5-16.

We regret the failure of the Greek regime to move more rapidly toward a return to repre-

WHAT THEY SAID IN 1971

(WILLIAM P. ROGERS)

sentative government, and we have made our disappointment clear to the Greek government on a number of occasions. Nevertheless, we believe strongly that United States and North Atlantic Treaty Organization security interests warrant an assistance program for Greece . . .

*Before Senate Foreign Operations
Subcommittee, Washington, Sept. 8/
The New York Times, 9-9:10.*

Kenneth Rush
*United States Ambassador
to West Germany*

Nothing has struck me more forcibly during my time as Ambassador to the Federal Republic (West Germany) than the simple fact that U.S. troop presence is viewed by every German—and indeed every European—as the proof of our political commitment to the security of Western Europe.

*Before World Affairs Council,
Los Angeles, June 17/
Los Angeles Herald-Examiner, 6-18:(A)4.*

(Regarding the Berlin agreement between Britain, France, the United States and the Soviet Union): The quadripartite agreement we have signed today is the first major East-West agreement on this subject since the end of World War II. President Nixon considers the agreement an encouraging step toward relieving tensions in Europe and toward his goal of a generation of peace. The President and the American people as well welcome this agreement as a sign of the Soviet Union's desire to move from confrontation to negotiation in its own relations with the West.

*West Berlin, Sept. 3/
Los Angeles Herald-Examiner, 9-5:(A)4.*

Anwar el Sadat
President of the United Arab Republic

The Soviet Union has, through practical experience, proved its solid stand on the anti-imperialist world revolution front. It has never hesitated to extend every moral, material or financial assistance to any people struggling

for liberation. It has also proved its true desire for peace and to work hard to remove all obstacles impeding its path. It does not hesitate to put its potentialities at the disposal of developing countries which are working to develop their economies and protect their independence, without restrictions or conditions. This is a reality that we live, and not words that we hear.

*Before Peoples Assembly of Egypt,
June 10/Vital Speeches, 7-15:582.*

Leonard Schapiro
Authority on Soviet affairs

Soviet policy is unremittingly dynamic. It is not directed toward achieving equilibrium or balance of forces or peace or collective security . . . Its ultimate aim is "victory"—which means Communist rule on a world scale. However unrealistic this aim may seem, it is the case that it has been thoroughly inculcated into the minds of all Soviet leaders from Lenin onwards for over 50 years . . . There is no time factor attached to this ultimate ideological aim—in contrast in this respect, say, to Hitler or Genghis Khan. And so . . . the Soviet Union seeks to advance wherever this is possible—to gain one advantage here and another there, and to move forward or halt as advantage dictates . . .

*Before Senate Subcommittee on National
Security and International Operations,
Washington/Nation's Business, April.*

Walter Scheel
Foreign Minister of West Germany

The international monetary crisis has many causes, and I consider it a mistake to join in the chorus of complaints about the dollar. The stability of the international monetary systems is not independent of price stability, money interest policies and other factors in the United States; but we should not forget that, only recently, Europe suffered from a shortage of dollars, that only the dollar was then convertible and was desired by all.

*At International Banking Conference,
Munich, May 25/
Los Angeles Herald Examiner, 5-25:(C)6.*

For purely egotistic reasons of our own, we are interested in the further economic development of the United States. We European politicians know that we can have a happy future only when we have a strong American partner.

Interview, Bonn, Dec. 25/
Los Angeles Times, 12-26:(A)20.

Helmut Schmidt
Minister of Defense of West Germany

. . . the political and military commitment of the United States in Europe is an essential prerequisite for the balance of power in Europe during the present decade. A substantially undiminished presence of American troops in Europe is to the benefit of all those countries which are interested in maintaining a stable and peaceful Europe. Western Europe cannot replace American troops, be it militarily, politically or psychologically.

At Princeton University, April 21/
Vital Speeches, 5-15:459.

Maurice Schumann
Foreign Minister of France

What counts above all is the working together for the constitution of a harmonious and strong Europe where all historic rivalries will be out of date; and that is why the French, just as the Germans, are happy to see Britain asking to join the Six (the Common Market) and accepting the rules of the European Community.

Interview, Paris/
The Christian Science Monitor, 10-16:8.

Klaus Schutz
Mayor of West Berlin

(Regarding the Berlin Wall between East and West Berlin): We must attempt to dismantle one of the most depressing by-products of developments in Berlin in the last decade. The Western Berliners must finally be able to see their friends and their relatives in the other part of the city and in the other part of our country. Such contacts are necessary in order not to destroy the real unity of our

city, which is the unity of the people.

Broadcast on 10th anniversary of construction
of the Wall, West Berlin, Aug. 13/
San Francisco Examiner, 8-13:4.

Hugh Scott
United States Senator, R—Pa.

(Regarding a proposal to cut United States forces in Europe by 50 per cent by the end of 1971): Harry Truman doesn't like this resolution; Lyndon Johnson doesn't like this resolution; and President Nixon doesn't like it—and all for good reason. Because they, in the stillness of the night, in the loneliness of the Presidency, have seen what it means to turn back from responsibilities.

The Dallas Times Herald, 5-20:(A)1.

Margaret Chase Smith
United States Senator, R—Maine

If the relatively non-cooperative attitude of the Western European nations is the acid test —yes, we are too deeply involved in Europe . . . Certainly, Western Europe is far more important to us than Asia—but not to the extent of perpetually carrying the load of defense for those countries while they have so much economic prosperity and contribute so little to their own military security.

Interview, Washington/
U.S. News & World Report, 6-28:28.

Paul-Henri Spaak
Former Premier of Belgium

(Regarding Britain's decision to enter the European Common Market): I have waited for this moment for 30 years. Today, Europe needs Britain more than ever. How could Europe do without Britain?

The Christian Science Monitor, 11-1:1.

Axel Springer
West German newspaper publisher

Will we see in the last third of our century a *pax americana* or a *pax sovietica?* One excludes the other. *Pax americana* would mean continued hope for all mankind; *pax sovietica,* new dark ages in our times. You, our Ameri-

(AXEL SPRINGER)

can friends, after your victory in 1945, had the wisdom to help rebuild the destroyed countries of Europe, including my own, your former enemy. This is never forgotten. When shortly after the war the Soviet Union resumed its aggressive policies, you brought together world-wide alliances. Especially in Europe, they stopped the aims of the Communists and allowed the countries protected by the NATO shield to live through years of unheard-of prosperity and growth. The question is: Do we want to *work* for this *pax americana*, or are we willing to let the other side win? These are the only alternatives—a compromise is not possible. Even the Soviet term for international compromise—peaceful coexistence—does not mean cooperation, but continuation of the confrontation at other levels . . . Aggression and peaceful coexistence, disarmament talks and rapid buildup of the armed forces, subversion and cooperation, trade negotiations and trade war—all these and many other seeming opposites are for the Soviets only two different sides of one coin. As long as we refuse to realize this, we are in great danger.

Before National Press Club,
Washington/Human Events, 12-4:9.

Rod Steiger
Actor

. . . what irony it is that the entire political feeling in Russia today is pure Fascism . . . the people live by the order, by the rule, or they don't live at all. Freedom for the people? Ha! I was never so glad to get back to the Western World.

Interview, Los Angeles/
Los Angeles Times, 3-28:(F)2.

Norman St. John Stevas
Member of British Parliament

(Advocating British entry into the European Common Market): The Queen of England is more than a match for any Continental president. If we go into the Common Market, the only thing likely to happen to the Queen is that she may become the Empress of Europe.

At British Conservative Party
conference, Brighton, England, Oct. 13/
The New York Times, 10-14:8.

Nikitas A. Storis
Minister of Education of Greece

The Greek government was, from the beginning, liberal in its views; but during this period of repair of our state bureaucracy, you are obliged to limit—not democracy—but parliamentary procedures. You can never repair a car while driving with full speed.

San Francisco Examiner & Chronicle
(This World), 3-14:2.

Franz Josef Strauss
Former Minister of Finance
of West Germany

(Regarding Chancellor Willy Brandt's moves for better relations with Eastern Europe): Bismarck used to say you don't make things move faster just by setting your watch ahead. That is what Brandt is doing. The ability to wait is an indispensable prerequisite for a pragmatic policy. What was the reason right now to start a sudden new Ostpolitik? Some (Social Democrats) contend that America is getting weaker, that it is obsessed with internal problems, that it will lose its position as a world power in ten or twenty years; that the Soviet star is rising and, therefore, we Germans must settle our problems with Moscow now on the best possible terms. I don't accept this premise.

The New York Times, 1-31:(4)13.

Cevdet Sunay
President of Turkey

There is no doubt that the Turkish nation is very much in favor of the government's pro-American policy. One would have to be blind and ungrateful not to appreciate the benefits we have received from the United States. As for NATO, it is the greatest guarantee of peace that exists today. My fondest wish is that Turkey's association with NATO will continue, and I can assure you the vast majority of the Turkish nation shares this view.

Interview/The New York Times, 8-27:31.

Stuart Symington
United States Senator, D—Mo.

We have heard arguments that a reduction of our forces (in Europe) would "tempt the Russians." These arguments have always seemed specious to me.

*Before Senate Foreign Relations
Committee, Washington, May 14/
Daily World, 5-15:4.*

Josip Broz Tito
President of Yugoslavia

(Regarding possible Soviet interference in Yugoslav affairs): This is not a problem for us. There is no question of interference in our internal affairs . . . our integrity and independence are beyond question.

*News conference, Ottawa, Canada, Nov. 5/
Los Angeles Times, 11-6:(1)17.*

Walter Ulbricht
*Chairman, Council of State
of East Germany*

(The Berlin issue) should be settled in the interest of peace in Europe. Although these are complicated questions, we believe that negotiated settlements should be possible if the other side also proves, through corresponding goodwill, its serious desire for understanding.

*At diplomatic reception, East Berlin,
Jan. 9/The New York Times, 1-10:(1)69.*

C. H. von Platen
*Swedish envoy to Organization for
European Cooperation and Development*

The mental attitude of the United States' entrepreneurs is perhaps most vitally illustrated by the example of American business in Europe. On this old and fragmented continent of ours, the American industrialist approaches problems and possibilities without undue regard for tradition, without that economic claustrophobia prevalent among all too many European entrepreneurs. He deals with Europe as a whole; and the degree of American industrial penetration of Europe is proof enough that this kind of approach is possible and profitable. In comparison, we Europeans are often burdened with tradition and prejudice; we are less adaptable, less dynamic, less inclined to accept change and competition, more static, only too eager to turn to government for aid, direct or indirect, in the form of protection against foreign competition.

The New York Times, 3-19:37.

Harold Wilson
*Leader, British Labor Party;
Former Prime Minister
of the United Kingdom*

I believe it will be to the good of Britain and to the good of Europe, and to the strengthening of Europe's voice in the world, if terms can be agreed which enable us to enter the Community (Common Market). (Prime Minister) Heath, in speech after speech, enjoins a Britain to which he denies leadership to solve its own problems by standing on its own two feet. What none of us are prepared to accept is a Britain which, because of his policy to seek humiliating terms for entry into Europe, has to stand on its own two knees.

*At British Labor Party reception,
London, Feb. 13/
The New York Times, 2-14:(1)14.*

(Regarding the violence in Northern Ireland): One element in a gravely deteriorating situation is the growing appearance of a British government departing from its position of neutrality and accepting a state of alliance with a single Ulster faction. There is no future in a policy based on the repression of violence alone, unless that is accompanied by an active or intensified search for a political solution. The present government's policies in Northern Ireland are set on a dead end.

*London, Sept. 4/
The New York Times, 9-5:(1)14.*

(HAROLD WILSON)

I believe the situation (in Northern Ireland) has now gone so far that it is impossible to conceive of an effective long-term solution in which the agenda does not at least include consideration in some way directed to achieving progress toward a United Ireland. There must be a substantial term of years before any concept of unification (between Northern Ireland and the Republic of Ireland) can become reality, but the dream must be there. If men of moderation have nothing to hope for, men of violence will have something to shoot for.

Before House of Commons,
London, Nov. 25/
Los Angeles Times, 11-26:(1)5.

Todor Zhivkov
First Secretary,
Communist Party of Bulgaria

The Bulgarian Communist Party and the Bulgarian people need Bulgarian-Soviet friendship the way all living things need sun and air.

The Austin (Tex.) Statesman, 5-5:16.

Yigal Allon
Deputy Premier of Israel

I implore the Egyptian government not to repeat their earlier folly and not to advance the escalation to the point of no return . . . The cease-fire has been observed until now for one reason only: It is desired by both sides. If it was not desired by one side, it would have been broken long ago. Neither side is doing the other (a) favor.

Tel Aviv, Feb. 12/
Los Angeles Herald-Examiner, 2-12:(A)2.

All the modern developments in military technology cannot negate the importance of geographically-defensible positions. We must be sure that we have borders that will prevent a surprise attack. There is no alternative to a peace treaty and secure borders which we can defend with our own forces.

Before Israeli Labor Party youth organization,
March 19/The New York Times, 3-20:4.

We, the generation which grew up during the holocaust and its shadows, are determined that our people never again shall be the victim of anarchy, that its blood shall be shed at will. The Jewish people in its homeland knows how to defend its existence and its freedom . . . A nation which has proven capable of defending itself is also bound to know how to blaze a path to peace.

Radio broadcast, April 22/
Los Angeles Times, 4-23:(1)23.

The only Western power the Arabs think highly of today is the United States of America, despite their cries against American imperialism and so on. First, for economic reasons; because they need American help. Secondly, only America, thanks to her special position with Israel, can be helpful to bring both sides to some agreement. This is a very important key in America's hands, and it must not be wasted on imaginary solutions or unrealistic solutions.

Tel Aviv, June 5/
The Dallas Times Herald, 6-6:(A)8.

Hafez al Assad
President of Syria

There is no such thing as a peaceful settlement (of the Arab-Israeli conflict) . . . because the Zionists want to establish a state extending from the Nile to the Euphrates.

Interview, Damascus/
The Christian Science Monitor, 3-19:2.

Chaim Bar-Lev
General and Chief of Staff,
Israeli Armed Forces

What the Egyptian Army—like all Arab armies—lacks is staying power in actual battle. We have met the Egyptians on the battlefield for 24 years and in this respect I do not think they are going to change. I do not believe that the Egyptians are capable of conquering a fortified area while things are falling on the right, and on the left the commander has disappeared.

News conference, December/
The Christian Science Monitor, 1-5('72):3.

David Ben-Gurion
Former Prime Minister of Israel

Unquestionably, (the late Egyptian) President Nasser was the greatest Arab statesman. During the last years before his death, believe me, he changed completely. He saw it had been a terrible mistake to try to destroy Israel. He wanted to make up for lost time, have peace, develop his country and improve the lot of the Egyptian peasants—who are growing poorer.

Interview, Tel Aviv/
The Christian Science Monitor, 2-22:2.

377

(DAVID BEN-GURION)

Peace, real peace, is now the great necessity for us. It is worth almost any sacrifice. To get it, we must return to the borders before 1967. If I were still Prime Minister, I would announce that we are prepared to give back all the territory occupied in the six-day war except East Jerusalem and the Golan Heights—Jerusalem for history's sake and the Golan for security. Sinai? Sharm el Sheikh? Gaza? The west bank? Let them go. Peace is more important than real estate. We don't need the territory. With proper irrigation, we now have enough land right here in the Negev to care for all the Jews in the world—if they come. And they certainly will not all come. No, we don't require more land. As for security, militarily-defensible borders, while desirable, cannot by themselves guarantee our future. Real peace with our Arab neighbors —mutual trust and friendship—that is the only true security.

Interview/San Francisco Examiner, 3-25:7.

We have always been a people that resides alone, and we can only rely on ourselves and world Jewry. Our closest neighbors are our bitterest enemies, refusing to accept our existence. (But Israel) was never intended to be a Hebrew Sparta. Our strength will not be determined solely by our military power and economic wealth, but by the special content of our lives and our capacity to cling to our unique heritage.

Interview, Sde Boker, Israel/
Time, 10-18:46.

Houari Boumedienne
President of Algeria

The (Arab-Israeli) war of 1967 arose from the problem of a whole people. The Palestinians were driven away from their homes, their lands, their country, and replaced by a foreign people who settled there as colonizers. Grafted onto this situation was the influence of the great powers—and there we are. Personally, I think we must get back to the root of the evil to achieve a permanent solution. If we try to impose a solution which is not a solution, we shall have no peace, but another war. The racist

and religious state should disappear; it has no place in the latter part of the 20th century.

Interview, Algiers/
San Francisco Examiner & Chronicle
(This World), 2-21:22.

Egypt is a sovereign state and has the right to choose any policy it considers best within its borders. But neither Egypt nor Algeria can decide on behalf of the Palestinian Arabs. If Egypt recognizes Israel's existence, and this signifies liquidation of Palestinian Arab rights in their own country, we cannot accept that decision—today, tomorrow or in forty years.

Interview, Algiers/
The New York Times, 2-28:(4)13.

Habib Bourguiba
President of Tunisia

It is Israel that does not want peace (with the Arabs). They feel they are the stronger. They consider that the frontiers they acquired in (the war in) 1967 are those with which they can hold fast. I think these frontiers can only perpetuate the state of war. Yet compromise by both sides could bring Israel a true peace, a peace with all these countries, which could then unite in a federation. Such a federation could be very fruitful, since the Israelis are extremely advanced in their economy, their scientific development, their research, etc. One must envisage a federation, something bringing together all the Middle East countries. This is not yet possible because some states reject it; but I believe it is the only positive solution to put an end to the war. Perhaps they will come to accept it in 20 or 30 years.

Interview, Tunis/
The Christian Science Monitor, 11-30:4.

Leonid I. Brezhnev
General Secretary,
Communist Party of the Soviet Union

The crisis which has arisen as a result of Israel's attack on the U.A.R., Syria and Jordan (in 1967) has been one of the most intense in the development of international relations over the past (five-year) period. Together with the fraternal socialist countries, we did everything necessary to stop and condemn the aggressor. Our country has helped to restore the defense potential of the Arab states which were subjected to invasion, the U.A.R. and Syria in the first place, with whom our cooperation has been growing stronger from year to year. The Soviet Union will continue its firm support of its Arab friends. Our country is prepared to join other powers, who are permanent members of the (United Nations) Security Council, in providing international guarantees for a political settlement in the Middle East.

At Soviet Communist Party Congress,
Moscow, March 30/
The New York Times, 3-31:14.

Chiao Kuan-hua
Deputy Foreign Minister of the
People's Republic of (Communist) China

The essence of the Middle East question is aggression against the Palestinian and other Arab peoples by Israeli Zionism with the support and connivance of the superpowers. The Chinese government and people resolutely support the Palestinian and other Arab peoples in their just struggle against aggression and believe that, persevering in struggle and upholding unity, the heroic Palestinian and other Arab peoples will surely be able to recover the lost territories of the Arab countries and restore to the Palestinian people their national rights.

At United Nations, New York, Nov. 15/
The New York Times, 11-16:16.

The two superpowers (the United States and the Soviet Union) are contending and in collusion with each other there (in the Middle East). They are taking advantage of the temporary difficulties facing the Palestinian and other Arab peoples to make dirty political deals in their contention for important strategic points and oil resources at the expense of the national rights and territorial integrity and sovereignty of the Palestinian and other Arab peoples. Herein lies the crux of the matter; and that is why the Middle East question has remained unsolved for such a long period.

At United Nations, New York, Dec. 8/
The New York Times, 12-9:2.

Alan Cranston
United States Senator, D–Calif.

Disillusionment over the way things have turned out in Southeast Asia must not blind us to the fact that Israel's survival and world peace depend on our standing by our commitments (in the Middle East).

Before World Affairs Council,
Los Angeles, April 13/
Los Angeles Times, 4-14:(1)27.

Moshe Dayan
Minister of Defense of Israel

I prefer Sharm el Sheikh without peace to peace without Sharm el Sheikh.

The National Observer, 3-22:4.

I know there is a (United Nations) Security Council resolution Number 242 and there is a Rogers plan and there is a Dayan plan and there is an Allon plan and there are and will be other plans. But there is one thing bigger and greater than all of them; and that is the people of Israel returned to their homeland.

Before Israeli Labor Party, Tel Aviv,
April 5/The New York Times, 4-6:2.

The readiness for a general peace with Israel cannot be judged by the speeches or the approach of this or that Arab leader. The real touchstone is the basic attitude in the Arab nations regarding the existence of Israel; and I feel I have not detected any change.

Before Israeli Labor Party, Tel Aviv,
April 5/The New York Times, 4-6:2.

Abba Eban
Foreign Minister of Israel

Reality proves that positive statements by Arab leaders are usually followed by reservations and contradictions that cancel out positive ideas.

Before the Knesset (Parliament),
Jerusalem, Feb. 17/
The Washington Post, 2-18:(A)8.

(ABBA EBAN)

The paragraphs of a peace agreement (with the Arabs) cannot be presented to Israel ready-made, so that Israel should be called upon only to contribute its signature. Commitments must be the result of negotiations and not their prior condition.

The New York Times, 3-14:(4)1.

I am completely sure that the U.S. Administration knows that Israel will resist any pressure and will insist that security borders be reached by direct negotiations. They will not be the borders of June 4, 1967. This must be our policy and the policy of the United States. It is a very basic principle of our policy, and it has not changed since I announced it to the UN General Assembly in the summer of 1967.

News conference, Tel Aviv, March 15/
The Dallas Times Herald, 3-15:(A)1.

We don't want to be alone; but there are certain principles and positions which are crucial to us . . . We would like others to understand our positions and support them; but we will, if necessary, uphold and defend them alone. A nation must sometimes accept tenacious solitude.

News conference, Washington, March 19/
The Washington Post, 3-20:(A)6.

Those who say to us today, "You'll never get the Arabs to adjust their territorial thinking," were the people who were saying to us a year ago, "But you'll never get them to say that they would have a peace agreement with Israel or recognition of Israel" . . . If you see fruit, you should rejoice; but you don't eat it until it's ripe; and you don't try to bring this to a head until thinking has further evolved.

Interview/"Face the Nation,"
Columbia Broadcasting System, 3-21.

(Regarding Sharm el Sheikh, the promontory at the entrance to the Strait of Tiran): There is no (other) place on the map of the world in which so many crucial interests of a country (Israel) converge on a little piece of sand remote from its boundaries.

Interview/"Face the Nation,"
Columbia Broadcasting System, 3-21.

The (Suez Canal) is the only place at which the Soviet-American equation is superimposed on the Israeli-Egyptian equation; and, therefore, it is a problem not only for the Middle East but for all mankind. Therefore, if there is to be a defusing, that's the place at which it ought to start.

Interview/
Los Angeles Herald-Examiner, 4-15:(A)4.

(Regarding charges of Israeli prejudice against Christian holy places in Jerusalem): What is the point at issue? What is the terrible accusation? Churches and synagogues are being restored; institutions for fostering spiritual and religious values are being built. A Jewish as well as a Christian and Moslem fabric of life is being added in Jerusalem—and this is the cause of all the shouting.

Interview/The New York Times, 7-25:3.

If the Arab states decide that the earth is flat and not round, they will immediately have some 50 votes in the United Nations to support such a decision.

The Christian Science Monitor, 9-10:5.

(Regarding Jerusalem under Israeli control): It is one of the few cities in the world where there is peace . . . Instead of division, there is unity; instead of sacrilege, there is scrupulous maintenance of the sanctity of holy places; (instead of evidences of war) it is one of the most peaceful and tranquil places.

News conference, Los Angeles, Sept. 26/
Los Angeles Times, 9-27:(1)3.

Faisal (Ibn Abdel al-Saud)
King of Saudi Arabia

I urge my colleagues, the leaders in every Arab country, not to accept any settlement (with Israel) that does not guarantee the restitution of usurped rights, the restoration of assaulted dignity and the safeguarding of the rights of their displaced brothers.

Mecca/The New York Times, 2-18:6.

J. William Fulbright
United States Senator, D—Ark.

. . . the commitment there (to Israel) grows out of the tremendous influence that the Israelis have in our country. I mean, it isn't a formal commitment; it's sentimental, political and I don't know how personal. There's no treaty commitment; there's no legal commitment to do anything. It simply grows out of the fact that Israel as a country and a people has tremendous influence in this country and certainly in this Congress.

Interview, Washington/
The Christian Science Monitor, 3-19:3.

The principal reason that there has been no progress on a negotiated (Arab-Israeli) settlement is the belief on the part of Israel that the United States and the Senate will back it, no matter what position it takes. Its attitude is most unfortunate, because I do not see any possibility of a negotiated settlement so long as Israel believes we are completely at its disposal.

Before the Senate, Washington,
March 23/The New York Times, 3-24:10.

We, too, (along with the Russians) keep a fleet in the Mediterranean, which is a good deal farther from our shores than it is from the Soviet Union. And our main objection to Soviet "influence" in the Arab countries is that it detracts from our own. Were it not for the fact that they are Communists—and, therefore, "bad" people—while we are Americans—and, therefore, "good" people—our policies would be nearly indistinguishable.

Before Yale Political Union,
New Haven, Conn., April 4/
The New York Times, 4-5:3.

Recent visitors to the Middle East assure me that the Israelis are quite sincere in their fear of being "thrown into the sea" (by the Arabs) and in their conception of the Soviet Union as an insatiable imperialist power bent, presumably, upon the conquest and communization of the Middle East. Nonetheless, I perceive in this some of the same old Communist-baiting humbuggery that certain other small countries have used to manipulate the United States for their own purposes.

Before Yale Political Union,
New Haven, Conn., April 4/
The Washington Post, 4-9:(A)22.

Andrei A. Gromyko
Foreign Minister of the Soviet Union

. . . nobody can any longer believe that Israel is allegedly defending its "existence." The false arguments with which the Israeli ruling circles have been seeking to cover up the real meaning of their policy have fallen through, one after another . . . Israel does not want peace; and even if it does, it is an annexationist peace . . .

At United Nations, New York,
Sept. 28/San Francisco Examiner, 9-28:4.

George Habash
Leader, Popular Front for the
Liberation of Palestine

We are not a terrorist party. We are revolutionaries. We will not practice terror but revolutionary violence, taking as targets things that the common man will understand.

Interview, Beirut/Time, 9-27:45.

W. Averell Harriman
Former United States
Ambassador-at-Large

In the Middle East, both sides (the United States and the Soviet Union) want to see an end to the fighting and peace established. Each side is indulging—I think unwisely—in blaming the other side for the difficulties which are occurring, which is an issue between Israel and the Arabs, and should not be a confrontation between the Soviet Union and the United States.

News conference, Moscow,
Jan. 13/The New York Times, 1-14:10.

(W. AVERELL HARRIMAN)

(The Soviets have) used their influence to induce Egypt to move toward a peaceful solution (to the Arab-Israeli situation). No longer does Egypt talk of pushing Israel into the sea; and she appears ready to accept freedom of navigation in the Suez Canal and the Gulf of Aqaba.

Before Jewish Theological Seminary,
Palm Beach, Fla., Jan. 31/
Los Angeles Herald-Examiner, 2-1:(A)8.

Mark O. Hatfield
United States Senator, R—Ore.

Our one-sided support of Israel, to the neglect of her neighbors, has had an effect similar to our overarming ourselves to such an extent that other sectors of our economy and our relations with other countries have deteriorated.

Before Senate Foreign Relations Committee,
Washington, June 12/The New York
Times, 6-13:(1)83.

Denis Healey
Former Minister of Defense
of the United Kingdom

It has often been said that the Middle East problem consists of two countries that can't make peace being controlled by two countries which don't want war.

Interview, London/
Los Angeles Herald-Examiner, 10-9:(A)11.

Mohammed Hassanein Heikal
Editor, "Al Ahram," Cairo

The Israelis don't want peace; they want territorial expansion. They are seeking not only to secure a homeland for the Jews in Palestine, but to establish a mini-imperialist apparatus to control the Arab world. If they persist in this, they will make the present struggle an intractable one of *them* or *us*. For in spite of themselves, they are pushing Egypt to change. They are creating a power that will defeat them. The future is on our side. There are now 35 million Egyptians, and the population of the Arab world exceeds 100 million. Perhaps, in our present weakness and divisions, this strength of numbers doesn't mean very much. But I tell you that education, science and technology are not an Israeli monopoly. Whatever our shortcomings, the Egyptians—and the Arabs generally—are intelligent people, and we can and are acquiring education, science and technology. Perhaps I should worry about tomorrow; but I am not worried about the day after tomorrow; or about the final result of our struggle with Israel.

Interview/
The New York Times Magazine, 8-22:61.

Haim Herzog
Former chief of Israeli Army
intelligence

A partial withdrawal (by Israel) from the (Suez) Canal today—which would satisfy one of Russia's major strategic requirements in the area—would, militarily speaking, endanger Israel's security considerably. For this time, Israel would not be facing an Egyptian army on a desert front, but something far more serious—an Egyptian army backed by Russian forces, however limited they might be.

Radio broadcast/
The Christian Science Monitor, 2-10:11.

Hubert H. Humphrey
United States Senator, D—Minn.

Once the Arab world realizes the U.S. policy will never permit the destruction of Israel, they also will realize they do not need the Soviets telling them how to run their countries, how to fight their wars, how to identify their national goals and plan for their achievement.

Quote, 2-14:145.

The (Nixon) Administration today is relying on the Soviet Union to help us establish peace in the Middle East. That reliance might make sense were it not for overwhelming evidence that the Soviet Union does not appear to want a settlement in the Middle East. Soviet leaders do not want an all-out war. But it is clear they do not want an all-out peace. And they stand to gain from continued restlessness and tension.

The New York Times, 10-6:45.

Hussein I
King of Jordan

From time to time, we hear mention of the internationalization of Jerusalem. We believe this is connected with the 1947 Palestine partition plan of the United Nations, which means the internationalization of *both* sides of Jerusalem. If this is not the approach, then Arab Jerusalem is Arab Jerusalem. There must be total recognition of our rights of sovereignty over that side of the city. Jerusalem must be included in the Israeli withdrawal (from occupied Arab territories). At the same time, we are always ready to make Jerusalem a city of peace, and especially to ensure rights of access to the holy places for all believers. What is totally unacceptable is the loss of Arab Jerusalem; for it belongs not only to Jordan but to the Arab and Moslem world as a whole. We have to fulfill here a responsibility which has lasted 1,200 years.

Interview, Amman/
The Washington Post, 2-28:(A)17.

I . . . warn against wishful thinking by the Arabs that the conflict with Israel can be eliminated through a sort of pat solution, whereby one simply gets rid of the Americans and admits the Soviets in their place. Our goal is to maintain good relations with all nations of the world. But it is also our duty to defend our Arab identity and our national character against foreign influence.

Interview, Amman/
Los Angeles Times, 4-28:(1)14.

The disarray and weakness of the Arab world have never been worse. The Arab countries are not yet strong enough to take on Israel.

Interview, Aug. 24/
Los Angeles Times, 8-25:(1)13.

The Arab side, as such, is not prepared for war (with Israel). It is not my right to drag anyone else into war and no one is going to drag us in. We are not prepared to make one single move unless we are convinced of the reason and logic of the action.

Interview, Amman/
The New York Times, 12-12:(1)17.

Henry M. Jackson
United States Senator, D—Wash.

I was appalled at the suggestion by our State Department that we ought to consider Soviet participation in a force designed to guarantee the integrity of an inherently insecure border (between Israel and the Arab states). In my view, the Administration is courting disaster by considering a plan that would have the effect of legitimizing the Russian military presence in Egypt. We should be trying to get the Russians out of the Middle East, not designing plans to dig them in.

Before the Senate, Washington, March 23/
The Washington Post, 3-24:(A)9.

Far from driving the Russians and Egyptians apart, our State Department's irresolution has enabled the Soviets to cement their hold on Egypt with an international treaty and unwittingly helped to establish there a Trojan horse that threatens our vital interests in the strategic Middle East. It is time for the State Department to face reality and recognize that the central issue in the Middle East is not the Arab-Israeli dispute but the continuing penetration of the Soviet Union in an area toward which Russia has had historic ambitions back to Catherine the Great . . . In the resulting atmosphere of American vacillation, it is not surprising that the Soviets should have been willing to attempt a historic consolidation of their position in the Middle East.

Before Jewish National Fund,
Boston, June 13/
Los Angeles Times, 6-14:(1)5.

The situation in recent days and weeks has grown extremely grave. While the (Nixon) Administration has been withholding from Israel the arms she requires to defend

(HENRY M. JACKSON)

herself, the Soviet Union has poured vast quantities of weapons into Egypt. The over-eager—sometimes frantic—maneuvering of the Secretary of State (Rogers) has helped to make the Soviet Union a major Middle Eastern power. We have played into the hands of the totalitarians at the expense of our democratic friends . . . We have been practicing in the Middle East a carrot-and-stick diplomacy, in which the Soviet Union and the Arab states are offered the carrot while Israel gets the stick. The time to end this foolishness is long past.

Washington, July 14/
The Washington Post, 7-15:(A)12.

Jacob K. Javits
United States Senator, R—N.Y.

I am confident that the deep commitment of the United States to Israel's security and national integrity—affirmed under President (Harry S.) Truman and reaffirmed by his four successors and now reaffirmed and implemented by President Nixon—continues strong, not only in our government's policy, but also in the minds and hearts of the American people.

San Francisco, Feb. 28/
San Francisco Examiner, 3-1:7.

Moshe Kol
Minister of Tourism of Israel

The indifference of the peoples of the world when Hitler was killing European Jewry in gas ovens . . . our isolation during three wars—all constitute profound historical lessons for us when deciding our policy in the struggle with the Arabs. Our friends in the world should not be surprised at our extreme care in taking any steps or making any decisions. Alone, we achieved independence; alone, we defended our existence; and therefore, we shall not leave our fate in the hands of others.

April 21/
Los Angeles Times, 4-23:(1)23.

Teddy Kollek
Mayor of Jerusalem

This (Jerusalem) is a mixed city, a kind of mosaic. Each group will continue to have its own culture, its own way of life. Jews will live in their neighborhoods, Arabs in theirs. This is by choice. Arabs want to live around their own schools, their own restaurants; they don't want to move into some place where their neighbors have different ways. That's the way we are here—not some kind of indiscriminate melting pot, but a place where each group goes on living its own life.

Interview, Jerusalem/Parade, 10-10:5.

Alexei N. Kosygin
Premier of the Soviet Union

Israel's ruling circles are promoting a course directed at the implementation of the imperialist plans against the peoples of the Middle East, at retaining there an ominous hotbed of military danger.

Interview/The Washington Post, 1-3:(A)1.

Melvin R. Laird
Secretary of Defense of the United States

The Soviet Union has gone forward with sophisticated weapons shipments (to the Arabs). I can assure you that this Administration will see that a proper balance is maintained in the area.

News conference, Washington, April 13/
The Washington Post, 4-14:(A)4.

Mike Mansfield
United States Senator, D—Mont.

As far as American troops being used (in the Middle East), as has been suggested, I have grave doubts about that. I would be in favor of a consolidated United Nations force rather than a scattered UN force as was the case in 1967—so scattered it could not be effective . . . However, I worry and fear the possibility of American troops being concentrated in that part of the world, because I do not want to see another Vietnam. I do not want to see another participation of this kind. I think one Vietnam is one too many.

Interview, Washington/
The Christian Science Monitor, 3-23:3.

George S. McGovern
United States Senator, D–S.D.

I believe that it is the obligation of those who have led the peace movement in this country to educate our constituents to the vital distinction between preventing war in the Mideast by placing the American guaranty behind Israel's right to survive, and perpetuating the war in Indochina . . . Basically, I favor the maintenance of a balance of power in the quantity and sophistication of conventional arms, which I believe must include the maintenance of Israel's control of the air, the assurance of secure, defensible boundaries, international insistence on a directly-negotiated settlement of the dispute between Israel and its neighbors, and the deterrence of Soviet intervention in the area through (a) firm American guaranty that a Soviet threat to Israel is intolerable.

At dinner sponsored by American-Israel
Public Affairs Society and Jewish Community
Council of Greater Washington, April 29/
The New York Times, 4-30:2.

Golda Meir
Prime Minister of Israel

I'm not a pessimist by nature . . . But how can you be optimistic when you see how the Arabs behave? Three times they try to throw us out. Three times we shatter them. And yet, they go on talking about destroying us. How can you be optimistic about that? No, pessimism and optimism don't come into my state of mind. It is a matter of going on steadily and facing the facts. You know that saying—the optimist says his glass is half full; the pessimist says it is half empty. But the fact is that the drink is at the same level. The fact is that we Israelis keep going. We are carrying on as usual, planting the crops, building the roads, teaching the children, building Zion. We have come back to our home. We intend to stay,

and we shall fight to the death to stay. We shall win, because we have a secret weapon: We have no alternative.

Interview/Los Angeles Times, 1-24:(F)2.

The dangerous involvement of the Soviet Union in the Egyptian war machine has continued and deepened . . . This process has clear militant anti-Israel implications, which are not lost on either the Egyptians or the Soviets. But the process has global implications as well; and it is vital that these should not be lost on the nations of the world—and, in the first instance, on Israel's friends, who are in a position to take deterrent political measures and to aid us in procuring the tools and means that are necessary for our self-defense.

Before the Knesset (Parliament),
Jerusalem, Feb. 9/
The Washington Post, 2-10:(A)9.

The Americans know very well how much we can concede (to the Arabs), and know we cannot concede the Golan Heights, East Jerusalem or Sharm el Sheikh . . . The Americans know well that pressure, including financial, will not work; and they know that financial pressure will not force us to give up what we consider vital to our security.

Tel Aviv, Feb. 25/
The Washington Post, 2-27:(A)11.

The most important thing we think people should understand is that we want peace. The only reason the Arabs refuse to make peace is that they believe if not this war then the next—finally they will be able to destroy us. The Arabs must accept the idea that Israel will remain. They don't have to love us; they do have to live with us.

Interview, Jerusalem/
San Francisco Examiner & Chronicle,
3-7:(A)4.

The way (the Jarring) negotiations are being conducted is a comedy, where Egyptian representatives use every way possible to

(GOLDA MEIR)

avoid meeting Israeli representatives face-to-face.

Haifa, March 10/
Los Angeles Herald-Examiner, 3-10:(A)4.

1) Jerusalem shall remain united and part of Israel; 2) Israel will not come down from the Golan Heights, which dominate the Hulah Valley; 3) The Jordan River must not be open for Arab troops to cross; 4) . . . (I am) opposed to an independent Palestinian state on the West Bank; 5) Secure and recognized frontiers, to be determined by negotiation, are necessary to prevent another war. International guarantees cannot replace such borders; 6) Israel is prepared to negotiate with the Arabs on all issues, but will not be dictated to.

Before the Knesset (Parliament),
Jerusalem, March 16/
The Washington Post, 3-17:(A)10.

Recent utterances coming from Vatican circles (criticizing Jewish expansion into Arab neighborhoods of Jerusalem) are surprising. For 19 years, the world was silent when the Old City was under Moslem-Jordanian rule, when its Jewish inhabitants were killed and the survivors expelled, and the Jews were denied access to their holiest places. Why this concern now, when under Israeli rule the Arab inhabitants of East Jerusalem have remained in their homes and access is free to all religions, to all the holy places? Is it because Jerusalem is now under Jewish control?

Before United Israel Labor Party,
Tel Aviv, April 3/
The New York Times, 4-5:6.

(Regarding the possibility of Soviets flying Egyptian fighter planes): . . . if the shooting is restarted and we go out to defend ourselves, we shall not be able—when we encounter a fighter plane—to check carefully first who is sitting in the cockpit in order to

decide whether or not to take action against it.

Radio interview, Jerusalem, April 24/
San Francisco Examiner, 4-24:2.

. . . I must say I envy Egypt a little bit for the ease with which they get arms. Nobody stands in line when we want to buy. We have to work hard and negotiate.

Stockholm, May 29/
San Francisco Examiner, 5-29:6.

(Regarding Suez Canal proposals by Israel to Egypt): As part of this special agreement, Israel would be prepared to consider some pullback of her forces from the water line (Suez Canal) in accordance with the following principles: The fighting would not be resumed. Egypt would clear and operate the Suez Canal. No Egyptian and/or other armed forces would cross to the eastern side of the Canal. There would be free passage for shipping in the Canal, including Israeli ships and cargoes. Effective and agreed supervision procedures would be established. Means of deterrence against the danger of violation of the agreement would be assured. Removal of Israeli defense forces from the water lines would not be a stage leading to a further withdrawal without peace. Maintenance of the arrangement would not be dependent upon the (UN mediator) Jarring talks, but it would also not be incompatible with the holding, furtherance and aim of these talks. The new line to be held by the Israeli defense forces will not be considered the permanent boundary. The permanent boundary between Israel and Egypt would be determined in the peace treaty to be concluded between us and Egypt; and Israel would withdraw to it.

Before the Knesset, Jerusalem, June 9/
The New York Times, 6-10:9.

We demand for ourselves boundaries that we believe are safe for us and that we believe can deter a next war. What we want are two things: If and when we are attacked, the borders should be such that we will have fewer casualties; even more important, the borders should be such that every Arab leader who takes it into his mind to attack us will look at them and say, "Ah, that is difficult. Maybe we won't do that." That is all.

Interview, Jerusalem/Time, 8-30:29.

I think the crux of the difficulties of peace in the Middle East is the introduction of an imperialistic power in this area. That is the Soviet Union. I honestly believe the '67 (Arab-Israeli) war would not have taken place had it not been for the Russians.

Interview, Jerusalem/Time, 8-30:29.

Has anybody ever asked (Egyptian President) Sadat, or Nasser before him, what is it that you want to achieve? War after war? Thousands dead? Tens of thousands dead? No, he's prepared to have a million dead. But what for? What is it that we have that is so vital to the life of the Egyptian people that he's prepared to have a million dead? He thinks that we also will have to lose a million lives. Fine. Two million lives lost. For what? What is it that we have that Egypt cannot possibly get along without?

Interview, Tel Aviv/
Los Angeles Herald-Examiner, 9-28:(A)4.

(Regarding the United States' holding back delivery to Israel of more Phantom jet fighter planes): There is no basis whatsoever for the assumption that political concessions may be obtained from us by withholding the supply of the means vitally required for our security. Israel will not be prepared to agree to political conditions which undermine her security and future, even in return for a promise of the equipment needed for her security.

Before the Knesset (Parliament),
Jerusalem, Oct. 26/
The New York Times, 10-27:1.

Edmund S. Muskie
United States Senator, D–Maine

Each side (Israelis and Arabs) has what it considers a rock bottom position, and neither side concedes flexibility to the other. Yet, when I see a situation in which the greater part of the distance between two parties could relatively easily be traveled if the element of confidence in some way could be supplied, then I'm always optimistic the rest of the distance can be traveled.

News conference, Cairo, Jan. 13/
Los Angeles Times, 1-14:(1)19.

Prospects for a political settlement in the Mideast are surely not advanced by a military balance that shifts dangerously in favor of the Arabs. Neither are these prospects increased by a zig-zag diplomacy on the part of the United States which, on the theory of gaining political leverage over Israel by delaying needed military assistance, serves only to raise doubts among all parties to the conflict that the United States is truly committed to preserving Israel's security.

Washington, Aug. 1/
San Francisco Examiner, 8-2:4.

Richard M. Nixon
President of the United States

If the Soviet Union does not play a conciliatory peace-making role, there's no chance for peace in the Mideast. Because if the Soviet Union continues to fuel the war arsenals of Israel's neighbors, Israel will have no choice but to come to the United States for us to maintain the balance . . . And we will maintain that balance.

Television interview, Washington,
Jan. 4/The New York Times, 1-5:21.

I think that we are at a critical time in the Mideast—a critical time over the next few months, when we may get these talks (between Arabs and Israelis) off dead center; make some progress toward a live-and-let-live attitude; not progress that's going to bring a situation where the Israelis and their neighbors are going to like each other—this isn't ever going to happen, perhaps—but where they will live with each other, where they won't be fighting each other.

Television interview, Washington,
Jan. 4/The New York Times, 1-6:42.

(RICHARD M. NIXON)

There is still the risk of war (in the Middle East). But now—for the first time in years—the parties are actively calculating the risks of peace.

State of the World address, Feb. 25/
The New York Times, 2-26:14.

We know what our vital interests are in the Middle East. Those interests include friendly and constructive relations with all nations in the area. Other nations know that we are ready to protect those vital interests. And one good reason why other nations take us at our word in the Middle East is because the U.S. has kept its word in Southeast Asia.

State of the World address,
Washington, Feb. 25/
U.S. News & World Report, 3-8:52.

Nikolai V. Podgorny
President of the Soviet Union

You (Egyptians) can rely . . . on the support of the Soviet Union. Our military relationship does not have secret objectives which constitute a threat to peace . . .

Cairo, Jan. 13/
Los Angeles Herald-Examiner, 1-14:(A)4.

There have been many sugar-coated statements by American officials about Washington's alleged desire to restore peace in the Mideast. Sure enough, they will not object to a so-called peaceful settlement—so long as it is the kind of settlement which would enable America, through Israel, to impose her will and maintain the kind of regimes she favors in the area.

Cairo, May 26/
Los Angeles Times, 5-27:(1)7.

Georges Pompidou
President of France

We have always regarded the rights of the state of Israel to exist within the boundaries of firm and recognized borders as being tied to its duty to leave all the territories it occupied as a result of the six-day war (in 1967).

News conference, Paris, Jan. 21/
Daily World, 1-23:4.

Muammar al Qaddafi
Chief of State of Libya

We can do without Jordan in the struggle against Israel. If the Palestinians want (to) coexist, it is a matter for them. As far as the Libyan Arab Republic is concerned, there will be no reconciliation with Jordan. (Jordan's King) Hussein will remain a stooge until doomsday. He will never change.

News conference, Tripoli, Aug. 1/
The Washington Post, 8-2:(A)17.

Yitzhak Rabin
Israeli Ambassador to the United States

If there is one thing we should not do at this critical state, it is to give in (and withdraw from territory occupied in the 1967 war). I believe we simply have no other choice. Because the moment we make the slightest concession or show weakness on this score, we shall be pushed back to the 1967 lines on all fronts.

Television interview, Washington, March 12/
San Francisco Examiner, 3-13:2.

Moses traveled 40 years in the desert and picked the only country in the Middle East (Israel) with no oil.

At Yale University/
The New York Times, 3-28:(4)4.

The United States has no formal commitment to come to Israel's aid with force either in the case of a local conflagration or in the case of an Israeli-Soviet clash. But if we do our utmost to enhance a Middle East settlement, I cannot see how the American Administration and nation could stand by and permit Soviet forces to harm Israel.

Radio interview, July 3/
The Dallas Times Herald, 7-4:(A)2.

Mahmoud Riad
Foreign Minister
of the United Arab Republic

Israel must choose between peace and expansion. I think through our diplomatic relations and contacts, through our activities in the United Nations and through our positive answers to Mr. Jarring (UN mediator) . . . the image of Israel in the world has changed from a small country looking for peace to a country looking for expansion—an aggressor.

> *Interview, Cairo/*
> *The Christian Science Monitor, 3-29:13.*

If this (Israeli occupation of Arab territories) should continue and the (UN) Security Council accepts it, it will mean the end of the UN and the Security Council; and the international organization will then turn into a sidewalk cafe or a bar.

> *News conference, Paris, April 1/*
> *The Washington Post, 4-2:(A)23.*

If tomorrow Washington will come to me and say here is a plan for peace which will result in the withdrawal of Israel from our territory, we will welcome such a move. Our main effort is to reach a peaceful solution which will lead to the liberation of our territory. We will fight when we see that all doors are closed.

> *Interview, Cairo, Nov. 25/*
> *The Washington Post, 11-26:(A)1.*

Have all the American Phantoms (fighter planes) and thousands of millions of dollars which Israel received during the past four years brought Israel one inch closer to undertaking its commitments to withdrawal from the occupied territory (taken from the Arabs in the 1967 war)? Has all the U.S. support to Israel brought any cooperation from Israel to respond even to American initiative? The answers are obvious. Indeed, nothing has enabled Israel to continue to evade its obligations more than its reliance on the American support.

> *At United Nations, New York, Dec. 3/*
> *Los Angeles Times, 12-4:(1)4.*

I recall what Dean Rusk (the then U.S. Secretary of State) said to me in 1968 when I asked him about the U.S. position on withdrawal of Israel (from lands won in the 1967 Arab-Israeli war). He said, "There is no doubt that we don't want any country to annex territory of another country. This is our policy, so the Israelis should no doubt withdraw from your land." I replied, "Why, then, don't you make a public statement? That's all we want." Mr. Rusk said, "We are a superpower. We are not Upper Volta or Gabon. And if we say that Israel should withdraw, then they must withdraw." (The present U.S. Secretary of State, William P.) Rogers has said Israel should withdraw. He has said that the U.S. would use all its influence to see UN Resolution 242 implemented and the U.S.'s own plan implemented. When you hear these words from a big power—that it will use its influence—well, it's something that has big meaning. That is why we agreed to the U.S.'s playing a role. But if it turns out that the role is no more than that of a small power like Nicaragua or Costa Rica or Malawi, what's the point of receiving any American representative?

> *Interview, Cairo/Time, 12-6:37.*

William P. Rogers
Secretary of State of the United States

There is a thought that geography is the sole consideration when you are thinking about security. Now, we don't think that geography is solely responsible for security, or even to a large extent responsible for security. Certainly, in modern-day world situations, geography is ordinarily not important. What is important is the political arrangement that is made—the agreement itself, whether the parties are belligerent and hostile, or whether they have made an agreement that is understood by the international community, and whether the powers of the world are willing to take part in guaranteeing that the agreement will be kept. And therefore, we think that, although geographical considerations are important, and certainly Israel is fully justified in considering them, we think an equally

WHAT THEY SAID IN 1971

(WILLIAM P. ROGERS)

important consideration is the political consideration—what is the political climate.
> *News conference, Washington, March 16/*
> *The New York Times, 3-17:18.*

There are risks in agreeing to peace. There
are greater risks in failing to do so.
> *Tel Aviv, May 6/*
> *Los Angeles Times, 5-7:(1)1.*

Anwar el Sadat
President of the United Arab Republic

Don't ask me to make diplomatic relations
with them (Israel) . . . Never! Never! Never!
. . . Leave it to the coming generations to
do that. Not me!
> *Interview, Cairo/*
> *The New York Times, 1-3:(4)4.*

We have no objection to talking about
peace. But the way the other side (Israel)
looks at it, the Arab nation was defeated (in
the 1967 war) and part of it was occupied
and it must pay the price of this defeat. We
will not behave like a conquered nation, because we are not yet finished . . . (The
United States) did not give up after Pearl
Harbor and did not act as if they were
defeated. But again, what is good for them is
apparently taboo for us.
> *Tanta, U.A.R., Jan. 4/*
> *The Washington Post, 1-5:(A)1.*

No one agrees in this country, or all over
the world will agree, to the surrender of one
inch of the Arab land; because this is part of
our land, our dignity, our honor. (Regardless
of any peace settlement with Israel), we shall
have war after five years, because Israel wants
from the Nile to the Euphrates.
> *TV-radio interview/"Face the Nation,"*
> *Columbia Broadcasting System, 1-10.*

(In exchange for an Israeli pullback across
the Sinai Peninsula) I would guarantee to
reopen the (Suez) Canal within six months. I
would prolong the cease-fire to a fixed date. I

would guarantee free passage in the Strait of
Tiran, with an international force at Sharm el
Sheikh. (If agreement on the Canal were
achieved) we would finally be grappling with
fundamentals and a final settlement (with
Israel) would at last be in sight.
> *The New York Times, 2-15:4.*

The starting point for every Israeli attitude
is that we were defeated (in the 1967 war)
and they can, therefore, dictate whatever they
want. Our starting point is that we lost a
battle—but not the war. If their starting point
is erroneous, everything else is wrong.
> *Interview, Cairo/Newsweek, 2-22:40.*

(Israeli Prime Minister) Golda Meir once
said that peace will only come when she can
drive her car from Tel Aviv to Cairo to do
some shopping. That is a pipe-dream based on
the victory complex. America, for example,
recognizes (Communist) China's territorial
integrity, but does not have normal diplomatic
relations with Peking. The exchange of ambas-
sadors is a technicality. It's a question of
sovereignty. Each nation decides for itself. But
Israeli propaganda has used what I said to
claim that I wouldn't recognize Israel's territorial integrity. That is absolute nonsense,
designed to confuse American opinion.
> *Interview, Cairo/Newsweek, 2-22:41.*

You may think I am speaking prematurely;
but in the very near future, we will be one of
the principal petroleum producers in this part
of the world. We are not poor!
> *Interview/The New York Times, 3-25:10.*

I insisted on signing this treaty of friendship and cooperation with the Soviet Union.
Science and technology, in both military and
civil affairs, are available in full only in the
Soviet Union and the United States. One of
them is an honorable friend that stands on
our side in the darkest days, and the other
declares, even today, that it will guarantee the
balance of power in favor of Israel.
> *Before People's Assembly,*
> *Cairo, June 2/*
> *The New York Times, 6-3:7.*

The Soviet Union has not asked us for anything. We are the masters of our own will. There is no authority in our country except our own.

Before People's Assembly, Cairo,
June 2/The New York Times, 6-3:7.

The U.S. gives Israel all the essentials of life and survival. The U.S., by insisting on taking this policy line, has therefore defined its position: It is Israel's partner in aggression and hatred against the Arab nation. The continued U.S. military and financial support of Israel, while it (Israel) occupies our land, amounts to actual U.S. partnership in the occupation of our territory and aggression against the sovereignty of our country.

June 10/Daily World, 6-11:2.

The no war, no peace situation (with Israel) will not last, no matter what the sacrifices are; this decision will be made in 1971. I will not let 1971 pass without this battle being decided.

Before National Congress of Arab
Socialist Union, Cairo, July 23/
The Washington Post, 7-24:(A)1.

Everything that we do is for the sake of the battle (with Israel). The battle today and tomorrow means our life, our aspirations, our dignity and our honor. We shall pay the price. It will be high, but the United States should understand that Israel also will pay a high price. An eye for an eye, a tooth for a tooth, napalm for napalm.

TV-radio address, Cairo, Sept. 16/
The New York Times, 9-17:13.

We are passing through a decisive stage. Every hope we used to have for a peace settlement (with Israel) is finished; and we have no alternative but to fight to regain our land, our honor and our dignity. Our decision is to fight, because the battle is the only way to regain our land and honor.

Addressing Egyptian troops
near Suez Canal, Nov. 21/
Los Angeles Herald-Examiner, 11-22:(A)1.

Mohammed Ahmed Sadek
Minister of War
of the United Arab Republic

We shall wage the battle (against Israel) not because we are warmongers but due to failure of peace efforts in the face of Israel's arrogance and America's connivance.

Before graduating Egyptian pilots,
Nov. 24/
San Francisco Examiner, 11-25:6.

Saeb Salam
Premier of Lebanon

When we say we have fear of Israel, it is a genuine fear. This was for about 20 years missed by public opinion in America, Europe and elsewhere. The old picture of little Israel, with peaceful people trying to live in it peacefully, and some 100 million savages around it dying to devour it and crush it under the heel of the conqueror or throw the two million Jews into the sea, was false, absolutely false. It was Israeli Zionist propaganda that was proved fully in 1967.

Interview, Beirut/
Los Angeles Herald-Examiner, 5-9:(A)5.

Every new Jew who arrives in Israel is more dangerous than a tank, cannon or fighter plane. When population increases, expansion follows. Increase of human resources can be more conducive to aggression than weapons.

Beirut, Dec. 16/
The New York Times, 12-18:10.

Michael Stewart
Former Foreign Minister
of the United Kingdom

I wish the Arab countries would go as far as to put it absolutely beyond doubt that, once a settlement is made, they will treat Israel as a neighbor. To ask them to treat her as a friend would be asking too much; but as a neighbor, they should behave toward her as one member of the United Nations ought to behave toward another member.

Interview, London/
Los Angeles Herald-Examiner, 2-28:(A)14.

Yosef Tekoah
Israeli Ambassador to the United Nations

It never is and never will be too late for peace (between the Arabs and Israel). Efforts toward peace, however, cannot proceed successfully if they are darkened by talks of last chances, deadlines and threats.

April 19/
The Washington Post, 4-20:(A)17.

Josip Broz Tito
President of Yugoslavia

It should be made clear to Israel that its entity would not be safe if it persists in its current policy, which denies the sovereignty and entity of others.

Cairo, Feb. 14/
The New York Times, 2-19:8.

(Soviet Communist Party leader Leonid) Brezhnev has told me it is not correct to believe that the Soviet Union would remain permanently in the Middle East. It will withdraw from Egypt and other Arab countries as soon as there is a solution (to the crisis in that area).

Before National Press Club,
Washington, Oct. 29/
Los Angeles Times, 10-30:(1)2.

Shmuel Toledano
Adviser on Arab Affairs
to the Prime Minister of Israel

Our minority problem is almost unique in the world. It is a minority legitimately belonging to the Arab world yet living in the Israeli state—but Israel and the Arab world are at war . . . With all the progress that has been made economically and politically to accept the minority into society—not assimilate, but accept—the social differences remain as the most vexing of all. On the simplest level, a girl dates a boy that her parents don't approve of—that happens everywhere in the world and reflects common problems in society. When it happens here—a Jewish girl dates an Arab boy—an ordinary social problem becomes a conflict of nations.

Interview/The New York Times, 1-29:8.

Barbara Tuchman
Author, Historian

The American ignorance about Israel is abysmal . . . As a Jew, I think the race is important. It is the oldest coherent race in the world. The re-creation of the State of Israel—after the longest-known period of exile—is unique in history. For the sake of the world, survival of the country is important.

Interview, San Francisco/
San Francisco Examiner, 3-17:27.

Mohammed Abdul Salam Zayyat
First Secretary, Arab Socialist
Union Central Committee

This month will be the beginning of the end for our aggressor enemy (Israel). The people are convinced that their destiny lies in battle and that in battle there is no substitute for victory.

Before Arab Socialist Union,
Cairo, Nov. 17/
The New York Times, 11-19:10.

Spiro T. Agnew
Vice President of the United States

I've never felt, honestly, that the UN has served the interests of the United States diplomatically in any important sense . . . (But) it's good to be in the other guy's huddle.
Interview/
The Washington Post, 10-28:(A)1.

I understand the United Nations gave Red China a big hand when it denounced the United States the other day. That may be. But that wasn't half as big as the hand the United Nations has had in the pocket of the United States taxpayers for the last 26 years.
Before Illinois Agriculture Association,
Chicago, Nov. 17/
The New York Times, 11-19:16.

Kiichi Aichi
Former Foreign Minister of Japan

. . . there are two governments confronting each other across the Taiwan Straits. One of these is the government of the Republic of (Nationalist) China, in effective control of a population of some 14 million people who enjoy a high standard of living in Taiwan. The other is the government of the People's Republic of (Communist) China, in effective control of the mainland China with a population over 700 million people . . . it is beyond doubt that the expulsion or exclusion of the Republic of (Nationalist) China from the United Nations against her will (as a result of admitting Communist China) will be a matter of great injustice, contrary to the very spirit of universality, harmony and friendship of nations and inconsistent with the purposes and principles of the Charter of the United Nations.
At United Nations, New York, Oct. 19/
The New York Times, 10-20:12.

Zulfikar Ali Bhutto
Foreign Minister of Pakistan

(Addressing Yakov Malik, Soviet Ambassador to the UN): I know you are a leader of a great country. You are the permanent representative of the Soviet Union. But behave like one. The way you throw out your chest, the way you thump the table, you do not talk like Comrade Malik. You talk like Czar Malik.
At United Nations, New York, Dec. 15/
The Washington Post, 12-16:(A)16.

James L. Buckley
United States Senator, C–N.Y.

(Regarding the vote by the UN to expel Nationalist China while admitting Communist China): The action taken by the General Assembly tonight may well be recorded as the beginning of the end of the United Nations, as marking that clear moment when a majority of the member nations decided to abandon principle in order to curry favor with a government which still remains branded by the United Nations as an aggressor; a government which by precept and action repudiates provisions of the United Nations Charter.
Washington, Oct. 25/
The New York Times, 10-26:1.

William F. Buckley, Jr.
Political columnist;
Editor, "National Review"

(Concerning the UN vote to expel Nationalist China while admitting Communist China): I call on the President of the United States to instruct his Ambassador to the United Nations to cease, beginning immediately, to vote in the General Assembly. To argue there, yes; to listen, yes; to plead, to explain, to cajole, threaten, conciliate, yes; to *vote*, never. Because to participate in the vote,

393

(WILLIAM F. BUCKLEY, JR.)

given the American ethos, is psychologically to involve ourselves in the outcome of a vote which we cannot—as the only major world power concerned with ethical considerations—agree to do. Just as our official position at this juncture toward Taiwan cannot be defined by the action of the General Assembly, so on future occasions—predictably—we shall have to make our own policies, removed from recommendations of the General Assembly which come to us with parliamentary effrontery. We should, accordingly, try to free ourselves of the psychological shackles that imperceptibly inhibit us—for so long as we participate in that vote. Loose those shackles, and we can continue to participate in the affairs of the United Nations, having calmly described the nature of our relationship to it. If the United Nations wishes to expel from membership all nations that resist domination by those other nations the United Nations at any particular moment desires not to offend, why let it do so; but let it not understand itself as engaged in writing the moral law, or in making pronouncements which have presumptive weight in the chancelleries of the world—or, most particularly, in this chancellery (the U.S.). By a word, the President of the United States could effect the great reconciliation between the theoretical and the actual. If he does not give that word, he will have lost an opportunity for penetrating leadership.

At China Conference, New York, Oct. 29/
National Review, 11-19:1317.

George Bush
United States Ambassador
to the United Nations

(Regarding the U.S. resolution providing for UN admission for Communist China and retention in the UN for Nationalist China): The resolution neither says nor implies that there are two Chinas or one China and one Taiwan. It does not attempt to prejudice the status of China or of future developments between the Republic of (Nationalist) China and the Peo-

ple's Republic of (Communist) China or of relations between them. It carefully closes no doors concerning future developments. It simply provides that, given the existing state of affairs, the People's Republic of China, which is not in the United Nations, should come in and should take over the Security Council seat; and that the Republic of China, which is in, should remain in.

At United Nations, New York, Oct. 18/
Los Angeles Times, 10-19:(1)9.

In the 26-year history of the UN, no member has been expelled or deprived of its seat. Not one. In fact, the whole trend has been just the other way—so that the original 51-nation membership has grown now to 131, including an immense variety of sizes and political systems. Yet here it is proposed that a member in good standing (Nationalist China), a government representing over 14 million people, served here by decent men, with no Charter violations against its name and, on the contrary, with a most constructive record, should be expelled utterly from the United Nations and all its agencies—solely because certain other governments question its legitimacy . . . If the (General) Assembly is going to travel down that road, where do we stop? Who can predict what United Nations member could be next? Surely there is many another member in this organization which, though fully in possession of territory and governmental powers, could one day become the target of some political combination in these halls commanding a simple majority . . . aiming to throw it out of the United Nations solely because its right to govern is disputed by others. If we are going to start playing with the right of members to sit in this organization, as if that right were a chip in some international poker game, we will have started the United Nations itself down a very perilous slope.

At United Nations, New York, Oct. 18/
U.S. News & World Report, 11-1:74.

Chiang Kai-shek
President of Nationalist China

Our voluntary withdrawal from the United

Nations . . . does not mean isolation from the world. It was, rather, a step taken in pursuit of our determination to defend the principles of the United Nations Charter which we feel were violated by the admission of the Mao Tse-tung (Communist Chinese) regime. Our withdrawal also reaffirmed resoluteness in our compatriots on the mainland. We shall never compromise with evil.

New Year's Day message, Taipei,
Dec. 31/ Los Angeles Herald-Examiner,
1-1:('72):(A)4.

Chou En-lai
Premier of the People's Republic
of (Communist) China

(Referring to the UN vote to expel Nationalist China and admit Communist China): Frankly, we did not expect that the resolution would be approved by more than a two-thirds majority, much less an overwhelming majority, vote. This apparently was unexpected also for the United States government, and was also unexpected for the Chinese government. As long as the resolution has been approved, we cannot go against the wishes of the peoples represented by many countries and of the peoples of the whole world; and we are deeply thankful for this support. This was a victory, not just for China, but for the great majority of the peoples of the world, including the . . . Americans.

Interview, Peking, Oct. 28/
The New York Times, 11-9:16.

In connection with our attitude toward the United Nations, there is an old Chinese saying which goes, "Be careful when facing a problem." We do not have too much knowledge about the United Nations and are not too conversant with the new situation which has arisen in the United Nations (his country's admission to the UN). We must be very cautious. This does not mean, however, that we do not have self-confidence; it means that caution is required and that we must not be indiscreet and haphazard.

Interview, Peking, Oct. 28/
The New York Times, 11-9:16.

Chow Shu-kai
Foreign Minister of Nationalist China

It must be admitted that the United Nations in recent years has lost much of its prestige and influence. In Vietnam, it has contented itself with playing the role of helpless bystander. In the Middle East, its attempts to bring about a settlement have achieved no outstanding success. The advance toward disarmament is being decided not so much by the Geneva Disarmament Conference as by the direct result of negotiations between the Soviet Union and the United States. The recent agreement on the status of Berlin was concluded outside its walls. The inescapable conclusion is that, on the main currents of world events, the United Nations has exerted only a marginal influence.

At United Nations, New York, Oct. 8/
Los Angeles Times, 10-9:(1)19.

Inis L. Claude, Jr.
Professor of Government and Foreign
Affairs, University of Virginia

If the peacekeeping possibilities of the United Nations can be fully exploited, we shall see the confirmation of the basic proposition that the organization's usefulness does not live in its strength, but that its strength lies in its usefulness.

At international conference on the United
Nations, Stanford University, Jan. 12/
San Francisco Examiner, 1-12:4.

Colin Crowe
British Ambassador to the United Nations

My government recognized the government of the (Communist) Chinese People's Republic as long ago as January, 1950. And we have consistently voted for the so-called Albanian resolution which calls for "the restoration of the lawful rights of the People's Republic of China in the United Nations," and recognizes that the representatives of that government are "the only lawful representatives of China in the United Nations." We shall vote for that resolution again this year . . . The United Kingdom's attitude is governed by our view

(COLIN CROWE)

that the government of the People's Republic of China is the sole legal government of China and therefore entitled to occupy the place which the Charter accords to that state. There is no question here of the expulsion of a member state (Nationalist China). It is rather a question of who should represent an existing state. In the light of this, my delegation will vote against any substantive resolution or amendment which provides for dual represent-ation . . .

> *At debate on admission of Communist China, United Nations, New York, Oct. 21/ The New York Times, 10-22:12.*

Humberto Diaz (Casanueva)
Chilean Ambassador to the United Nations

The (Communist) Chinese have come to the United Nations as if they were disembarking from the moon or from Mars—as remote as mythological beings; and people want to know how they dress, what they eat, what they think and what their dreams are.

> *Welcoming the Chinese delegation, United Nations, New York, Nov. 15/ The Dallas Times Herald, 11-21:(A)20.*

Peter H. Dominick
United States Senator, R—Colo.

(Regarding the UN vote to admit Communist China and oust Nationalist China): We (the United States) pay 35% of the United Nations' support. We're being played for a sucker again, and I for one am not willing to play along with it.

> *Washington, Oct. 25/ Los Angeles Times, 10-26:(1)20.*

Alec Douglas-Home
Foreign Secretary of the United Kingdom

(Advocating Communist China's admission to the United Nations): In the Far East, we have seen that China has for too long isolated herself from the world community. When she plays her full part here in New York, a mighty voice will be added to our counsels

and a major step will have been taken toward the true representation here of the balance of world powers and world opinion, from which consensus can be hammered out, however painful at times the process may be.

> *At United Nations, New York, Sept. 29/ Los Angeles Herald-Examiner, 9-29:(A)2.*

Abba Eban
Foreign Minister of Israel

I think, for the sake of world peace and realism, it is wise to bring Communist China into the international family . . . But the organizational effects in the short term are likely to be paralyzing. In other words, the United Nations is going to be even less able to reach determinations of any weight than before.

> *Radio interview, Jerusalem/ San Francisco Examiner & Chronicle, 10-31:(A)20.*

Barry M. Goldwater
United States Senator, R—Ariz.

My only regret, when I heard the news last night (of the UN's admission of Communist China and expulsion of Nationalist China), was that my country had not joined the representatives of Taiwan in walking out on a session so farcical that it defies description . . . The time has come for us to cut off all financial help (to the UN), withdraw as a member and ask the United Nations to find a headquarters location outside of the United States that is more in keeping with the philosophy of the majority of voting members— some place like Moscow or Peking . . . In moving the admission of Red China—regardless of whether that motion was coupled with an attempt to retain Assembly membership for Taiwan—we sacrificed principle for expediency. We went on record as favoring the admission of a bandit nation which has had a long history of violating every precept of peace as outlined by the UN Charter.

> *Before the Senate, Washington, Oct. 26/ U.S. News & World Report, 11-8:108.*

Andrei A. Gromyko
Foreign Minister of the Soviet Union

More than a quarter of a century has elapsed since the establishment of the United Nations. This is a long period. In this time, the United Nations has experienced both achievements and failures. The United Nations has not always been resolute enough in matters where firmness and energy were required. But on the whole, it has proved that it can serve as a useful instrument for peace and for the development of international cooperation, provided it follows the right direction; that is, provided it strictly observes the principles of its Charter. Nevertheless, even today the question is sometimes asked what priorities should be established in the activities of the United Nations. The answer was given already at the time when the Charter of the United Nations was signed. The key task of the United Nations and the core of its activities are to preserve and consolidate peace and to prevent a new war. It was to this end that the Organization was established, and this is where the first priority of its activities lies. Nations evaluate the results of each session of the General Assembly, as well as of each session of the Security Council, by whether effective steps were taken in the attainment of that key objective.

> *At United Nations, New York,*
> *Oct. 4/Vital Speeches, 11-1:44.*

Edvard I. Hambro
Norwegian Ambassador
to the United Nations

The Security Council does not deal with conflicts before it is far too late.

> *At conference on United Nations,*
> *Stanford, Calif./*
> *The New York Times, 1-17:(1)15.*

Edward M. Kennedy
United States Senator, D—Mass.

(Communist) China should be admitted to the United Nations and to the Security Council. With a nation with one-quarter of the world's population, with nuclear weapons which we would like to see controlled, and with potential markets which might aid employment and arrest the economic doldrums in our country, we should make every effort to formalize relations. If China doesn't want to join the UN, that's its decision. But we should encourage such membership . . . I'm opposed to the present resolution which would admit Red China and throw out Nationalist China. We must maintain Nationalist China as an entity. We have traditional and historic ties with Nationalist China. Both should be represented in the United Nations.

> *Interview, Boston/*
> *Los Angeles Herald-Examiner, 5-2:(A)7.*

In light of distressing developments involving humanitarian aid to victims of the conflicts in Vietnam, Nigeria and today in East Pakistan and India, new initiatives must be taken within the United Nations to establish a United Nations Emergency Service, supported, perhaps, by a declaration on humanitarian assistance to civilian population in armed conflicts and other disasters. Such a service would exist purely for humanitarian purposes. It would function as a separate office within the United Nations—responding to a call from the Secretary General to mobilize and coordinate the vast resources of the United Nations and its specialized agencies . . . To establish a United Nations Emergency Service is a logical extension of United Nations activities in humanitarian questions—and hopefully, it would also be a means to blunt and overcome some norms of international conduct, bureaucratic inertia and diplomatic complexities reflected in the erratic and timid international response to massive human suffering in so many troubled areas.

> *At International Conference of Voluntary*
> *Agencies, New York, June 30/*
> *The Washington Post, 7-13:(A)18.*

Jacques Kosciusko-Morizet
French Ambassador to the United Nations

There is only one draft resolution that

(JACQUES KOSCIUSKO-MORIZET)

takes into account the rights and the reality of the People's Republic of (Communist) China. It asks us (in the UN) to recognize, by a simple majority, that China is the People's Republic of China, and alone qualified in this capacity to occupy the seat which for 25 years has been reserved for this state. It is to this draft resolution that our vote will go. To vote otherwise would be to disavow the vast effort of rapprochement which has grown since last year; this would be to assail, through artifices little-suited to serving the reputation of our organization, the unity and the rights of China; this would be—a more awesome consequence—to mortgage the future, to compromise the cooperation which must be established between the Chinese representation and all the delegations of the United Nations; this would be, finally, to refuse to see the world as it is, with China; to refuse to make a peaceful world, with China.

At debate on admission of Communist China, United Nations, New York, Oct. 20/ The New York Times, 10-21:18.

Henry Cabot Lodge
Former United States Ambassador to the United Nations

It (the UN) has already in the past been what diplomats call a "power fact"—a tool which has prevented the world from getting more dangerous and disorderly than it is already. If we did not have it, we would all be working to create it . . . In the past decade, the utility of the United Nations as a place for quiet diplomatic exchanges has grown. During the life of the United Nations, there has been no world war.

San Francisco, Jan. 12/ Los Angeles Herald-Examiner, 1-13:(D)12.

. . . the United Nations will only measure up to the high hopes of its founders if the great powers—notably the two super-states (the United States and the Soviet Union)

—cease having adversarial relationships. This overrides and underlies all problems.

San Francisco, Jan. 12/ San Francisco Examiner, 1-13:4.

Adam Malik
President, United Nations General Assembly

Let this Assembly resolve to become and to be remembered as an Assembly forging a true universality of membership to encompass all nations of the world, including the divided nations, without prejudice as to political ideology, social system or legal recognition.

At his inauguration, United Nations, New York, Sept. 21/ Los Angeles Times, 9-22:(1)1.

Yakov A. Malik
Soviet Ambassador to the United Nations

Attempts are . . . made to tell us that the expulsion (from the UN) of Chiang Kai-shek (and Nationalist China) is an important matter, a decision which must be taken by a two-thirds vote, whereas anybody who has any common sense will easily understand that it is a very procedural question; a decision on it must be made by a mere majority. Everybody understands that this isn't a matter of expelling a member state; what is at stake here is to expel a group of private persons who seized a seat and to restore this seat to its lawful occupants (Communist China). This procedure has absolutely nothing to do with expulsion of a member state of the United Nations.

At debate on admission of Communist China, United Nations, New York, Oct. 20/The New York Times, 10-21:18.

It is to be regretted that the principle of universality has so far in the United Nations not reached a final solution. A number of governments are awaiting the day when it will be possible for us to welcome them here as members of the Organization. I refer in this connection to the German Democratic Republic (East Germany) and certain other states. We are firmly convinced that those who have blocked the restoration in the United Nations of the principle of universality and who have blocked the admission of new states to the United Nations will find themselves in a situation similar to that in which they found themselves when they tried to block the entry of the (Communist) Chinese People's Republic.

> *On arrival at the UN of Communist China's delegation, United Nations, New York, Nov. 15/ The New York Times, 11-16:16.*

Paul N. McCloskey, Jr.
United States Representative, R—Calif.

It seems to me that, whatever type of government a nation has, we benefit by admitting every nation to the community of nations and taking our chances that that government may some day change.

> *TV-radio interview/"Meet the Press," National Broadcasting Company, Washington, 7-18.*

Nesti Nase
Foreign Minister of Albania

The People's Republic of (Communist) China publicly declared . . . on August 20, 1971, that its legitimate rights in the United Nations should be fully re-established and restored and that the Chiang Kai-shek (Nationalist China) clique should be expelled from this organization. It has rejected resolutely the American imperialists' plot of two Chinas, or of one China and one Taiwan; and it has expressed itself categorically that it will have nothing to do with the United Nations if the latter were to adopt this particular solution. We are appealing to all member states to vote in favor of this draft resolution (to admit Communist China and expel Nationalist China), because it is the only way to repair the horrible injustice committed to the Chinese people.

> *At debate on admission of Communist China, United Nations, New York, Oct. 18/The New York Times, 10-19:12.*

Richard M. Nixon
President of the United States

. . . Taiwan (Nationalist China), which has a larger population than two-thirds of all the United Nations, could not and would not be expelled from the United Nations as long as we had anything to say about it . . . Under no circumstances will we proceed with normalizing relations with Communist China if the cost of the policy is to expel Taiwan from the family of nations.

> *News conference, March/ Human Events, 11-6:2.*

John O. Pastore
United States Senator, D—R.I.

(Complaining that the U.S. pays more than its share of UN costs): Every time I go into the washroom at the UN and pull the paper towel—one, two and three—we're paying for the third one.

> *Washington, Oct. 28/ Los Angeles Times, 10-29:(1)1.*

William P. Rogers
Secretary of State of the United States

. . . the United States and 16 other countries have introduced a resolution which would seat the People's Republic of (Communist) China as a permanent member of the (UN) Security Council, while providing representation both for it and for the Republic of (Nationalist) China in the General Assembly. That resolution is based on political reality and on basic equity. It is only realistic to recognize a factual situation which has persisted for more than 20 years: Two governments now exercise authority over territory and over people who were given representation in the United Nations when China ratified the Charter in 1945 as an original member. It is only realistic that all the Chinese people who were once represented there should again be represented—and represented by those who actually govern them. It is only realistic that the Security Council seat should be filled by the People's Republic of China, which exercises control

(WILLIAM P. ROGERS)

over the largest number of people of all the world's governments. It would be unrealistic to expel from this body the Republic of China, which governs a population on Taiwan greater than the populations of two-thirds of the 130 United Nations members. Further, it would be unjust to expel a member which has participated for over 25 years in the work of this organization with unfailing devotion to the principles set forth in the Charter.

> *At United Nations, New York,*
> *Oct. 4/The New York Times, 10-5:14.*

Last night's decision to admit the People's Republic of (Communist) China as a member of the United Nations of course is consistent with the policy of the United States. President Nixon hopes that this action, which will bring into the United Nations representatives of more than 700 million people, will result in a reduction of tensions in the Pacific area. At the same time, the United States deeply regrets the action taken by the United Nations to deprive the Republic of (Nationalist) China of representation in that organization. We think that this precedent, which has the effect of expelling 14 million people on Taiwan from representation in the United Nations, is a most unfortunate one which will have many adverse effects in the future . . . Although we believe a mistake of major proportion has been made in expelling the Republic of China from the United Nations, the United States recognizes that the will of a majority of the members has been expressed. We, of course, accept that decision. We hope that the United Nations will not have been weakened by what it has done. We continue to believe in its principles and purposes, and hope that ways can be found to make it more effective in the pursuit of peace in the future.

> *News conference, Oct. 26/*
> *The Washington Post, 10-27:(A)20.*

If the United Nations is to have an effective role in peace-keeping, this (the India-Pakistan conflict) is a classic test . . . (If) the UN does not take follow-up action (after its vote for a cease-fire), if the nations involved do not pay some attention, then it suggests the UN is quite ineffective.

> *News conference, Washington, Dec. 12/*
> *San Francisco Examiner, 12-13:4.*

Carlos P. Romulo
Foreign Minister of the Philippines

(Regarding the division of China into Communist and Nationalist): It is unreal to insist that there exists "only one country" when we are faced with the obvious fact that there are two governments and two societies which have had nearly a quarter-century of independent and sharply diverging history. Questions of usurpation of seats (in the United Nations) are out of date and irrelevant. Questions of who represents China are also irrelevant and out of date. History has taken its course.

> *At United Nations, New York,*
> *Oct. 21/The New York Times, 10-22:12.*

John J. Rooney
United States Representative, D–N.Y.

Uncle Sam paid 38.3 per cent of the cost in calendar year 1970 of operating the United Nations. I think it is high time that all the member nations be made aware of the fact that Uncle Sam no longer intends to be Uncle Sap. In short, if the Republic of (Nationalist) China, a charter member of the United Nations, is expelled, there will be no money forthcoming from the U.S. Congress to pick up the biggest tab at the U.N. . . . The issue of the Republic of China's representation in the United Nations is a simple moral issue: Are we to abandon our friends, abandon our principles, to seat a dedicated Communist enemy of the United States (Communist China) and of the free world? If the United Nations cannot see the morality of this issue, then we are better off walking away from an organization which is ineffective anyway.

> *Before the House, Washington/*
> *Human Events, 10-30:3.*

Dean Rusk
Former Secretary of State
of the United States

The United Nations is an utterly indispensable organization. One of the problems is that much of its work gets very little attention. General agreement, serenity, a successful negotiation are not news. It takes a little blood and controversy to get public attention . . . The truth of the matter is that the overwhelming majority of international frontiers are peaceful. The overwhelming majority of treaties are complied with. The overwhelming majority of disputes are settled by peaceful means. Now, despite the fact that this does not appear in newspapers and TV news programs, there's an enormous amount of unseen work in international cooperation going on all the time. The United Nations and its specialized agencies play a major role in that day-to-day work of the world. Someday, we may find a way to bring that to public attention more effectively.

At University of Georgia School of
Journalism, February/
The New York Times, 3-23:35.

Salim A. Salim
Tanzanian delegate
to the United Nations

(Concerning his delegation's reaction to the admission of Communist China to the UN): We were extremely happy at the admission of Red China, but our rejoicing was at the righting of an injustice. At no point in our cheering and applauding did we consider that we were doing so to humiliate the United States.

San Francisco Examiner, 11-23:28.

Agha Shahi
Pakistani Ambassador
to the United Nations

The inescapable fact is that the People's Republic of (Communist) China is bound to be restored its rights in the United Nations soon. That is the writing on the wall which no one can refuse to read. The important question which this Assembly has to face, therefore, is whether the member states of the United Nations are going to display foresight and grace in now welcoming the representatives of the People's Republic of China or whether, by following a course which would postpone that event, we betray the impotence of all but the great powers in accelerating progress toward ends that themselves are no longer controversial. The seating of the People's Republic of China at this session will evoke a new interest in and respect for the United Nations among peoples and governments all over the world . . . (The unseating of Nationalist China would be) not the expulsion of a member state; but the departure of one delegation and the entry of another is all that is involved here.

At United Nations, New York,
Oct. 19/The New York Times, 10-20:12.

James C. H. Shen
Nationalist Chinese Ambassador
to the United States

(The UN Charter states that membership is open) to all peace-loving states which accept the obligations contained in the present Charter and, in the judgment of the organization, are able and willing to carry out these obligations. This disqualifies the Maoist (Communist Chinese) regime right from the start. The Peking regime, it should be remembered, was branded by the United Nations as an aggressor for its intervention in the Korean War in 1950 and was also found guilty of committing genocide in Tibet in 1963. Both stand on the United Nations records themselves and have never been rescinded. Is the United Nations going to set aside its previous resolutions in this respect? (The reason for Communist China's possible admission) lies in the fact that appeasement is in the air. Expediency seems to have taken over. If the Peking regime should be admitted, the question will not merely be one of whether (Nationalist China) is going to stay, but one of whether the United Nations deserves to survive once it has compromised on some of the basic principles and

401

(JAMES C. H. SHEN)

purposes on which and for which it was founded 26 years ago.

At American Legion convention,
Houston, Sept. 1/
Los Angeles Herald-Examiner, 9-2:(A)15.

U Thant
Secretary General
of the United Nations

. . . the time has come when the United Nations must be made universal. The absence of the People's Republic of (Communist) China and of the divided countries gives year after year to debates on international cooperation and disarmament in the United Nations a greater sense of artificiality. There can be no secure peace and world order until all qualified nations are part of a worldwide system of security and solidarity. On a small planet so closely knit today by communications, transportation, scientific and technological strides and faced with new global dangers and challenges, for nations to participate in global instruments and affairs is not only a right, it has become a responsibility, a very serious responsibility indeed. An international organization can only solve multilateral problems when all parties to those problems take part in the deliberations intended to work out corrective measures. Only then will all parties concerned feel bound to implement such measures. The necessity of world commitment and the aims of worldwide peace, justice and progress require a universal society of nations.

Before Organization of American
States, San Jose, Costa Rica, April 14/
The New York Times, 5-23:(4)17.

There is no easy way to discharge the duties of the Secretary Generalship, but that does not distract from the immense privilege of being allowed to attempt the job. In my view, it is the most varied, most interesting and most challenging political job on earth. In one way, the Secretary General is fortunate, for he is allowed to consider the prob-

lems of peace and war, the problems of the present and the future of mankind, from a position which is—and must be by its very nature—independent of national considerations. Impartiality, principle and objective truth are his strongest weapons.

Before United Nations
Correspondents Association, Sept. 16/
The New York Times, 9-21:37.

Those of us who believe profoundly in the principles of the Charter as the civilized and humane way of settling differences among nations are witnessing with infinite sorrow the gradual erosion of the authority and prestige of this great organization.

On the 26th anniversary of the
promulgation of the UN Charter,
United Nations, New York, Oct. 24/
Los Angeles Times, 10-25:(1)7.

George M. Thomson
Member, British Parliament;
Former Minister of State of the
United Kingdom

If the UN General Assembly were to vote for Chinese Communist membership, and Peking were to accept, it would in the short run add to the difficulties of the UN rather than reducing them. Nevertheless, the UN cannot come realistically to grips with the long-term challenge of creating a secure world order without the Peking government amongst its members.

Before Commonwealth Club,
San Francisco, April 16/
San Francisco Examiner, 4-17:4.

Tsai Wei-ping
Vice Minister of Foreign
Affairs of Nationalist China

(Regarding the recent UN vote to expel Nationalist China and admit Communist China): We are not going to draw back into a shell. Our approach will be positive and outgoing. We are prepared to have relations wherever we can, and these will be extensive. We are still recognized by 59 members and nonmembers of the United Nations and expect many will stay with us. We will continue to play a constructive role in promoting international cooperation and understanding. It is in our Constitution that we abide by the principles upon which the United Nations was founded, and we feel we did not desert the United Nations but that it deserted us.

Interview, Taipei, Oct. 27/
The New York Times, 10-28:14.

Kurt Waldheim
Secretary General-designate
of the United Nations

In order to ensure the successful functioning of the United Nations, the financial solvency of the organization is a basic requisite without which resolutions and decisions remain mere declarations of intent.

At United Nations, New York, Dec. 22/
Los Angeles Times, 12-23:(1)4.

Earl Warren
Chief Justice of the United States

The United Nations and its system of agencies still have very little ability to shape a disorderly world. The halting approach to world order begins with the fact that the most populous of all nations—the People's Republic of (Communist) China—and three significant divided states—Germany, Korea and Vietnam—are not represented. The early admission of mainland China, of the two Germanys, the two Koreas and the two Vietnams—regardless of what may later evolve in their internal relationships—are essential steps that must be taken to bring the real world and the international system together. There is also a tendency (by the UN) to avoid difficult solutions in the absence of crisis and, when violence occurs, to go no further than to freeze the dangerous status quo. This is a prescription for the continuation of the tension.

At International World Peace
Through Law Conference,
Belgrade, Yugoslavia/
The New York Times, 7-23:31.

C. K. Yen
Vice President and Prime Minister
of Nationalist China

As a founding member of the UN, the Republic of (Nationalist) China always has been faithful to both the letter and spirit of the Charter. It has carried out its obligations in the General Assembly and as a permanent member of the Security Council. The Nationalist Chinese oppose UN membership for Peking, because the Chinese Communists constitute an insurrection, not a state, and also because the Maoist regime stands condemned by the UN as an aggressor. The seating of Peking at the UN would be an act in contravention of the Charter.

Interview/
Los Angeles Herald-Examiner, 7-4:(A)10.

War and Peace

Spiro T. Agnew
Vice President of the United States

Aggression historically has been halted only by the sword, or a convincing willingness to use it.

At United States Air Force Academy commencement, Colorado Springs, June 9/
Los Angeles Herald-Examiner, 6-10:(A)6.

Unless a nation has been prepared to fight to defend its rights and resources, it has usually been forced to surrender them. War is dreadful; but the loss of freedom is the ultimate catastrophe.

At United States Air Force Academy commencement, Colorado Springs, June 9/
The Washington Post, 6-10:(A)2.

The road of history is lined with the ruins of nations which did not remain zealous in the protection of their interests.

Athens, Oct. 16/
The Washington Post, 10-18:(A)9.

George D. Aiken
United States Senator, R–Vt.

Peace, after all, is not a final solution. It is a state of affairs that permits more effort to be spent on activities of a constructive, even if competitive, nature, and less on military affairs. The normal state of relations among nations is not one of perfect harmony and cooperation. It is a state of competing and conflicting interests that are reconciled through continuous negotiation and diplomacy.

Before the Senate, Washington,
Feb. 10/
The Washington Post, 2-16:(A)12.

Omar N. Bradley
General, United States Army (Ret.)

For every man in whom war has inspired

sacrifice, courage and love, there are many more whom it has degraded with brutality, callousness and greed . . . I certainly did not welcome war. That goes without saying. I would have much preferred to have served out my years in a peacetime army and retire quietly as a colonel. Once war (World War II) came, I did welcome the opportunity to do what I was trained to do and paid to do.

Interview, Beverly Hills, Calif./
Los Angeles Times, 3-21:(B)6.

Willy Brandt
Chancellor of West Germany

(Upon receiving the 1971 Nobel Peace Prize): The young man who in his time (during the Hitler regime in Germany) was persecuted, driven into exile in Norway and deprived of his rights as a citizen, speaks here today not only in general for the cause of peace in Europe but also, most particularly, for those from whom the past has exacted a harsh toll. How much it means to me that it is my work on behalf of the German people which has been acknowledged, that it was granted me, after the unforgettable horrors of the past, to see the name of my country brought together with the will for peace.

Oslo, Norway, Dec. 10/
The Dallas Times Herald, 12-10:(AA)3.

Leonid I. Brezhnev
General Secretary,
Communist Party of the Soviet Union

Even some members of the ruling circles of the Western states are ceasing to regard the arms race as an unquestionable blessing. In this situation, growing significance is undoubtedly acquired by the Soviet-American strategic arms limitation (SALT) talks, whose positive outcome would answer, in our opinion, the interests of the people of both countries and the task of strengthening universal peace. The decisive factor of the success of these talks is strict observance of the principle of equal security for both sides (and) renunciation of attempts to secure any unilateral advantages at the expense of the other side. It is to be hoped, therefore, that the U.S. Administration will also take a constructive stand.

At Palace of Congresses, Moscow,
June 11/Los Angeles Times, 6-12:(1)2.

James L. Buckley
United States Senator, C–N.Y.

Military forces are not a luxury; they are a necessity. So long as we live in a world in which some nations feel a compulsion to dominate others, we have no choice but to maintain those levels of defense which are essential to our own survival. Great nations are not allowed the luxury of retiring from the world. For such nations, there can be no peace unless they have the power and the will to defend it.

At National Press Club, Washington,
July 14/Human Events, 7-24:5.

McGeorge Bundy
President, Ford Foundation

These (herbicides and tear gas) weapons have two kinds of importance: For today, they mean what they mean in Southeast Asia; for tomorrow, their meaning is inescapably defined by what they imply for the whole future of chemical warfare. Between these two kinds of importance, it is the future that counts most. The trial balance on what has happened in Vietnam is not clear-cut. But when we weigh the claims of the future, the scales fly up. In that future, there will be other herbicides, other riot-control agents, other gasses, in other hands. Far more important than any local tactical advantage of tear gas or herbicides is the need for the strongest possible international barrier against the gas war of the future.

Before Senate Foreign Relations
Committee, Washington, March 19/
The Washington Post, 3-20:(A)22.

William L. Calley, Jr.
Lieutenant, United States Army;
Defendant in Mylai (South Vietnam)
massacre trial

Combat is not John Wayne. You don't look up at a guy and shoot at him and he shoots at you. A combat situation is slow and inactive and boring at times. Nobody looks eyeball to eyeball. Nobody knows where the enemy is. He doesn't know where you are, either.

Interview, Washington/
The Washington Post, 1-9:(A)3.

Chiao Kuan-hua
Deputy Foreign Minister
of the People's Republic
of (Communist) China

If the Soviet government truly has the desire for disarmament, particularly nuclear disarmament, the Soviet representative (at the UN) should come forward to this rostrum and solemnly declare that, at no time and no circumstances, will the Soviet Union be the first to use nuclear weapons and it will dismantle all nuclear bases and withdraw all nuclear weapons and means of delivery from abroad. Distinguished Soviet representative, do you dare to do so? If you are man enough, you will do it.

At United Nations, New York, Nov. 26/
Los Angeles Times, 11-27:(1)9.

Chou En-lai
Premier of the People's Republic
of (Communist) China

It is quite clear, we can see, that the two big powers, the United States and the Soviet Union, having embarked on the mass production of nuclear weapons, cannot get down from the horse, so to speak. But can they thereby monopolize nuclear weapons? No, they cannot. We produced nuclear weapons by ourselves. We manufacture nuclear weapons because we are forced to do so in order to break the nuclear monopoly. And our aim is the complete prohibition and thorough destruction of nuclear weapons. And so every time we make a test, we de-

(CHOU EN-LAI)

clare that we will never be the first to use nuclear weapons. You will see what we Chinese say counts.

Interview, Peking, Aug. 5/
The New York Times, 8-10:15.

J. Harlan Cleveland
President, University of Hawaii;
Former United States Ambassador to
the North Atlantic Treaty Organization

Peacekeeping . . . is better tackled through international organizations than unilaterally; better legitimized by international consensus than by domestic decision-making; better symbolized by an international flag than the Stars and Stripes.

At international conference on the
United Nations, Stanford, Calif., Jan. 12/
Los Angeles Herald-Examiner, 1-13:(D)12.

Michael S. Davison
General and Commander-in-Chief/Europe,
United States Army

As long as we have to cope with the imperfectability of man, there are going to be conflicts of one kind or another. This is everything that recorded history tells us.

Interview/
The Washington Post, 9-12:(A)16.

Hiram L. Fong
United States Senator, R—Hawaii

. . . peace will come when all have a share in shaping the peace. Peace will endure when all have a stake in keeping the peace.

At Lincoln University commencement,
San Francisco, June 13/
San Francisco Examiner, 6-14:8.

Andrei A. Gromyko
Foreign Minister of the Soviet Union

The strategic arms limitation (SALT) talks between the U.S.S.R. and the United States of America are continuing . . . The positive outcome of the talks would meet the interests of the peoples in both the U.S.S.R. and the United States, as well as the task of strengthening universal peace. Considering the increasing importance of the talks, the Soviet side is making efforts to achieve understanding, which should of course be based on the principle of equal security. But the success of the talks depends to the same extent on the other side, too. What has been achieved in the field of limiting the arms race is only a threshold to disarmament. Important as it may be, to stop there would mean evading the solution of the fundamental problem. And we are convinced that, from the viewpoint of possibilities, this problem does lend itself to solution. The question, therefore, lies entirely in whether there is a will to solve it.

At United Nations, New York,
Oct. 4/Vital Speeches, 11-1:42.

Huang Hua
Communist Chinese Ambassador
to the United Nations

Since World War II, very profound changes have taken place in the world situation. Countries want independence, nations want liberation and the people want revolution—this has become the main trend of the present international situation, propelling the advance of history and colonial progress. The colonialists and neo-colonialists, and particularly the one or two superpowers, have not ceased their activities in practicing power politics and in carrying out aggression, interference, subversion and control against other countries and peoples . . . Since the end of World War II, although a new world war has not broken out, local wars have not ceased and tensions have occurred one after the other. There is no peace on earth. The danger of a new world war still exists.

At United Nations, New York, Nov. 23/
Los Angeles Herald-Examiner, 11-24:(A)4.

Hubert H. Humphrey
United States Senator, D—Minn.

Controlling the arms race is a political problem, requiring political solutions. It cannot be accomplished by experts, by the military, or by technicians. There are political decisions which have to be made. Stopping the arms race can only be done by leaders responsible for the overall wellbeing of their people, and who have a sufficient grasp of history and of men to end the tyranny of nuclear technology and our cowardice before it.

Before the Senate, Washington,
March 25/
The Washington Post, 4-2:(A)26.

We have enough nuclear power now to destroy all that God and man ever created. It is madness. We have enough nuclear power to burn the earth, to scorch everything. (But Russia and the United States are trying to acquire even more) like a couple of kids who are off their rocker.

Washington, Sept. 24/
Los Angeles Herald-Examiner, 9-25:(A)2.

Samuel P. Huntington
Professor of Government,
Harvard University

The risk of over-reacting to Vietnam is to end up with the conclusion that nothing is worth it. On the other hand, the so-called lesson of Munich is that you must fight every war—which, after all, is the basis of collective security. Vietnam has persuaded America that no war is worth it. The question before us . . . is to devise principles for judging first-order interests and second-order interests.

Interview, Cambridge, Mass./
The Christian Science Monitor, 3-17:17.

Gerhardt W. Hyatt
Major General and Chief of
Chaplains, United States Army

I think any believer—whether he is Catholic or Protestant or Jew, or if he doesn't have a religion—is against war. I hope so. I hope we're all against war as a satisfactory solution for problems. But mankind hasn't yet become so perfected in its morality that we're living in that environment. Mankind still looks on war as a satisfactory solution to international problems. Unless that changes, we must be prepared to deal with it.

Interview, Washington/
Los Angeles Herald-Examiner, 8-28:(A)7.

Andrew Jacobs, Jr.
United States Representative, D–Ind.

One hears it said that a continuation of intervention will mean a generation of peace—it will teach the Communists a lesson. Yet, in the very midst of our mammoth effort in Southeast Asia, did the Russians even so much as hesitate to invade Czechoslovakia (in 1968)? Who would ever believe that the underdeveloped tip of the Asian tail could wag the world? A generation of peace? A war to end all wars? I was 13 when World War II ended all wars. And I knew that sort of thing was only for my father's generation. I would be spared. And so at 18, I was sent into hell (Korea) with an M-1 rifle to help bring back a generation of peace. My little sister's boyfriends would be spared—long enough to serve in another crusade, this time with M-14 rifles and another promise of peace. And next month, my little sister's boy will be 16. A generation of peace? A war to end all wars? How about a *peace* to end all wars? . . . if our country ever goes to war again, it should be because we have to, not just because we have a chance to. And we don't have to borrow the trouble of a war to protect freedom where there is no freedom to protect. The only way to avoid future Vietnams is to recognize our error in becoming involved in this one. And that recognition—that realization—will not result from official government declarations that Vietnam has been "our finest hour."

Before Senate Foreign Relations
Committee, Washington, May 27/
The Washington Post, 5-28:(A)24.

Herman Kahn
Director, Hudson Institute

I would say that, today, most of the traditional causes of war among the major nations have pretty well disappeared. In Europe, the territorial boundaries are firmly set, and, with some exceptions, they have been accepted by public opinion. Nations no longer go to war because they have been insulted, and most of the "prestige" arguments had to fall by the wayside. The basic remaining causes of formal

(HERMAN KAHN)

war would stem from considerations of defense: one nation feeling threatened by some crisis which it could only resolve by force or because it feels threatened by the pre-emptive strike-potential of its rival. But it is highly unlikely that any military request for nuclear weapons to be used to achieve positive gains would be condoned either by the United States or the U.S.S.R. For all these reasons, it is very difficult to write credible scenarios for formal nuclear war in the 1970s or 1980s.

Interview, Davos, Switzerland/
The New York Times Magazine, 6-20:13.

Nicholas deB. Katzenbach
Former Under Secretary of State
of the United States

The more we modernize military forces, the more we encourage inevitable military solutions to political problems.

Before Joint Congressional Economic
Subcommittee, Washington, Jan. 5/
Los Angeles Times, 1-6:(1)14.

Alexei N. Kosygin
Premier of the Soviet Union

We would welcome a reasonable agreement in the field of the limitation of strategic arms which would not be of a one-sided nature, benefitting only one side. We proceed from the premise that effective measures in the field of restraining the strategic arms race and limiting strategic arms would meet the vital interests not only of the Soviet and American peoples, but also of the peoples of the whole world. The Soviet Union comes out for the implementation, also, of other measures directed at limiting the arms race—especially nuclear arms—and directed at disarmament.

Interview/The Washington Post, 1-3:(A)22.

(Regarding United States President Nixon's planned visit to the Soviet Union): To solve any problems in such a way (as) to strengthen world peace, we need mutual desire. The Soviet Union and the United States must do everything toward that end. The Moscow visit is not a one-sided meeting; it is a reciprocal meeting.

News conference, Ottawa, Canada,
Oct. 20/
The Washington Post, 10-21:(A)1.

John Cardinal Krol
Roman Catholic Archbishop
of Philadelphia

. . . when you get to the point of buildup in arms where your greatest opponent, where you both have the capacity of destroying each other five or six times, when you're building up arms to the point where the greater half of money spent is for military arms rather than for civilian needs, then I think a citizen has the right to question the values between providing for a common defense and insuring domestic tranquility. I think it was Reinhold Neibuhr who said it is the business of military strategists to prepare for all eventualities, and it is the fatal error of such strategists to create the event for which they must prepare.

News conference, Vatican City, Oct. 22/
Los Angeles Times, 10-23:(1)3.

Melvin R. Laird
Secretary of Defense of the United States

I am confident that history will recognize President Nixon as the man who led the world toward peace. His contemporaries must recognize him as one who tried—as no other President ever tried—to achieve peace.

Before Navy League, Panorama Council,
Beverly Hills, Calif., Nov. 18/
Los Angeles Times, 11-19:(1)26.

Yakov A. Malik
Soviet Ambassador to the United Nations

. . . the (General) Assembly has had an opportunity to witness a curious (Communist) Chinese-American duet of negativism in regard to the Soviet proposal for the convening of a world disarmament conference. One might have passed over this duet—let them sing together against the Soviet proposal—but we cannot pass over the attempt in the statement by the Chinese representative to distort the position of the Soviet Union in regard to disarmament and in regard to nuclear disarmament . . . As long ago as 1946 we were the first to propose that atomic weapons should be outlawed forever and that their stockpiles should be destroyed. The basis for the Soviet program for disarmament is the banning and complete destruction of all nuclear weapons and their means of delivery to the target.

At United Nations, New York, Nov. 24/
The New York Times, 11-25:22.

Forbes Mann
President, Ling-Temco-Vought
Aerospace Corporation

Surely, no sane individual desires war—least of all the military, who, we somehow seem to forget, are the ones called upon to do the fighting and dying. But if one is dissatisfied with the threat of war, the solution cannot lie in the destruction of the military any more than the solution to crime is to dismantle the police department, or that the solution to disease is to eliminate doctors.

Before American Ordnance Association/
The Dallas Times Herald, 12-5:(A)35.

Margaret Mead
Anthropologist

I think the most optimistic thing is that we are still here! We have attained the capacity to destroy the planet and haven't done it. The longer we don't do it, the better chance we have.

Interview, Los Angeles/
Los Angeles Herald-Examiner, 3-16:(A)15.

Richard B. Morris
Professor of History,
Columbia University

The last quarter century has witnessed undeclared wars assuming a shape and dimension of fearsome proportions, and with fearsome results.

Before Senate Foreign Relations
Committee, Washington, March 9/
The Washington Post, 3-10:(A)2.

Daniel P. Moynihan
United States delegate to the
United Nations; Former Counsellor
to the President of the United States

The peoples of the world have been organizing themselves into nation states whose legitimacy and purpose derive primarily from a common ethnic or religious identity. There are only a very few places on earth, however, where it has been possible to establish national borders which correspond to these identities. The map of the world may be neatly divided, but the peoples of the world are hopelessly mixed. As a result, the relatively peaceable period of nation-founding which we have been through must now be succeeded by a period likely to be far less peaceable, in which peoples seek to sort themselves out in accordance with boundaries. The best hope of the world is that there should be an end, and a quick end, to the colonial or conquered condition in which many peoples continue to live, and that simultaneously those nations, ancient or new, which find themselves torn by racial or ethnic conflict, learn the uses of diversity and acquire the art of living as multi-national states. This is a rare achievement, but it brings rare rewards. It has, however, never come easily to any nation in the past, and it will not in the future.

At United Nations, New York/
The Washington Post, 11-25:(A)22.

Naomi Nishimura
Director, Self-Defense Forces of Japan

In my view, the use of military means to protect overseas interests is not only anachronistic but useless. Protection must and can be provided, in the era of negotiation, first by diplomatic persuasion and second, if that fails and interests are violated, by economic measures such as compensation to the victims.

Before Foreign Correspondents Club
of Japan, Tokyo, Oct. 11/
The Washington Post, 10-12:(A)12.

Richard M. Nixon
President of the United States

Speaking for the United States of America,

(RICHARD M. NIXON)

I pledge that, as we sign this treaty, we consider it only one step toward a greater goal: the control of nuclear weapons on earth and the reduction of the danger that hangs over all nations as long as those weapons are not controlled.

At signing of treaty banning nuclear arms on the ocean floor, Washington, Feb. 11/ The New York Times, 2-14:(4)5.

A full generation of peace depends not only on the policy of one party, or of one nation, or one alliance, or one bloc of nations. Peace for the next generation depends on our ability to make certain that each nation has a share in its shaping, and that every nation has a stake in its lasting. This is the hard way, requiring patience, strength, understanding and, when necessary, bold, decisive action. But history has taught us that the old diplomacy of imposing a peace by the fiat of great powers simply does not work. I believe the new diplomacy of partnership, of mutual respect, of dealing with strength and determination will work. I believe that the right degree of American involvement—not too much and not too little—will evoke the right response from our other partners on this globe in building for our children the kind of world they deserve—a world of opportunity in a world without war.

State of the World address, Washington, Feb. 25/ U.S. News & World Report, 3-8:52.

I rate myself as a deeply-committed pacifist, perhaps because of my Quaker heritage from my mother. But I must deal with how peace can be achieved and how it must be preserved. I know that some national leaders and some countries want to expand by conquest and are committed to expansion, and this obviously creates the danger of war. Moreover, some peoples have hated each other for years and years . . . You can't suddenly eliminate these differences, these hatreds, just because some political leaders get together. All you can hope for is to bring about a live-and-

let-live situation. With this in mind, I am deeply devoted to a desire that the United States should make the greatest possible contribution it can make to developing such a peaceful world. It is not enough just to *be* for peace. The point is, what can we *do* about it? Through an accident of history, we find ourselves today in a situation where no one who is really for peace in this country can reject an American role in the rest of the world.

Interview, Washington, March 8/ The New York Times, 3-10:14.

. . . I seriously doubt if we will ever have another war. This (the Vietnam war) is probably the very last one.

Interview, Washington, March 8/ Los Angeles Herald-Examiner, 3-10:(A)1.

Today, despite the terrible evidence of this century, there are those who have refused to learn the hard lessons of the history of tyranny. They would tell us—as their predecessors in other times have told us—that the appetite for aggression can be satisfied if only we are patient, and that the ambitions of the aggressor are justified if only we understand them properly. I am never surprised to see these positions held. But I am always astonished to see them held in the name of morality. We know too well what follows when nations try to buy peace at the expense of other nations.

At Naval Officer Candidate School, Newport, R.I., March 12/ The New York Times, 3-13:45.

Often I am asked what single thing, above all others, I would rather accomplish as President. I always give the same answer . . . I want peace for America. Not just in Vietnam; but in the Middle East, in Europe, in the world. And not just peace for our time; but peace for a generation—a full generation of peace, something Americans have not known in this century.

TV-radio address, Washington, April 7/The New York Times, 4-8:6.

More and more, we have good grounds to believe that . . . hope for a new era of world peace will come true . . . America and the Soviet Union . . . are committed more seriously than ever before to working out an agreement that will limit strategic arms. America and mainland (Communist) China, after more than 20 years of hostility and isolation, are beginning to move to a new and more normal relationship. The nations of Europe are taking important steps toward greater unity. The truce in the Middle East will soon be a year old. (However) none of this is cause for euphoria. The harvest time for peace is not yet. What we can say, though, is that the seeds of peace are planted, and that they are germinating in a way that holds great promise. Certainly, the chances for a full generation of peace in America and the world are stronger today than at any other period in your lifetime.

Before cadets, United States Military Academy, West Point, N.Y., May 29/ The Dallas Times Herald, 5-30:(A)26.

To those who attack the morality of strength with claims that our defense establishment is "militarist" and evil, we must reply it is war that is evil, and that the vigilance which prevents war is honorable and good.

At Veterans of Foreign Wars convention, Dallas, Aug. 19/ The Dallas Times Herald, 8-20:(A)1.

(Regarding his planned trips to Communist China and the Soviet Union): We go with no false hopes, and we intend to leave behind us in America no unrealistic expectations. There are great differences between the government of the United States and the governments of the Soviet Union and the People's Republic of China. But we have much in common with the Russian people and the Chinese people. We share this earth. We share a love for our children. And we share an understanding of the ultimate futility of war. And so, while the road to a lasting peace may still be long and difficult, yet all that reasonable men may do to accomplish that lasting peace will be done.

Veterans Day radio address, Camp David, Md., Oct. 24/ Los Angeles Times, 10-25:(1)13.

I know that it has been suggested that I am taking those trips halfway around the world (to Communist China and the Soviet Union) as political junkets in an election year. Let me be very blunt on that point. These trips are not about the next election. They are about the next generation, and we all have an obligation to that next generation. No one . . . knows better than I do the great differences between the Communist societies and ours. No one . . . would go to such a conference with his eyes more open than mine will be open. They know me. I know them. Those differences are not going to be solved by these trips. Then why do we go? I will tell you why. It is a practical consideration. There are 250 million people in the Soviet Union. Their nuclear power, as far as land-based missiles is concerned, is presently about equal to ours, and possibly even a bit ahead. There are 750 million people in China. Within 15 years, if they want to do it, their nuclear power will be a very, very significant threat to the peace of the world. So we then come to this question: what do we do about it? Do we wait 10, 15, 20 years from now and continue to stand in confrontation with those that we do disagree with? Or, in other words, putting it more directly, do we talk about our differences? . . . With the advent of nuclear warfare, a President of the United States, with an obligation to future generations, has no choice but to talk about those differences—talk about them with this goal in mind: not of giving in on our system; not of making concessions at the expense of our friends; but talking about them with the great goal of seeing that the peoples of this world can have different systems but will not be engaged in nuclear destruction. That is why I am going. We are going to try.

At AFL-CIO convention, Bal Harbour, Fla., Nov. 19/ The Washington Post, 11-20:(A)12.

. . . the only time in the history of the world that we have had any extended periods of peace is when there has been balance of power. It is when one nation becomes infinitely more powerful in relation to its potential

(RICHARD M. NIXON)

competitor that the danger of war arises. So I believe in a world in which the United States is powerful. I think it will be a safer world and a better world if we have a strong, healthy United States, Europe, Soviet Union, China, Japan—each balancing the other, not playing one against the other, an even balance.

Interview, Washington, December/
Time, 1-3('72):15.

Paul VI
Pope

You, the people, have the right to be ruled and guided in such a way that your fate . . . your very lives are not disturbed by war. You have the legitimate right to expect that your leaders conduct affairs in such a way that you do not suffer. And with the terrible weapons which are at the disposal of those who promote war, you could be struck without even knowing why . . . Peace must spring from the people. *You* must be the promoters of peace.

Rome, Jan. 1/
The Dallas Times Herald, 1-3:(A)7.

Peace is not weakness; it is not cowardice; it is not tolerance of injustice; nor is it passive acquiescence to the so many sad conditions in which the world finds itself. (Peace means the) virile and magnanimous affirmation of the energy of the holy spirit; it means the victory of good over bad; it means the end of the old system of vendetta—the system of a tooth for a tooth, an eye for an eye, that still perpetuates a chain of hate and bloodshed.

Vatican City, Jan. 1/
Los Angeles Times, 1-2:(1)8.

Everybody wants peace, but not all seek it.

Vatican City, Jan. 10/
The Dallas Times Herald, 1-11:(A)2.

William P. Rogers
Secretary of State
of the United States

In all of our efforts, both in the United Nations and elsewhere, we should recall that nothing we do matters so much as the legacy we leave to those who follow—the bridge we build between past and future. There is a tendency, especially when tensions are high and tempers short, to regard the present as the focal point of all of man's history. But ours is only the latest generation, not the last generation; and nothing we can leave to future generations will matter as much as a structure of enduring peace. Peace must be achieved and maintained not by the decree of a few but by accommodation among many. Each government, in upholding its people's particular interests, must also advance the world's interest in a peace which will endure.

At United Nations, New York,
Oct. 4/Vital Speeches, 11-1:38.

When you look around, the world is a more peaceful place than it was. There is a good deal less fighting and less turmoil than there was. We're taking steps to reduce the tensions that cause trouble. And we have . . . more negotiations going on now with the Soviet Union than ever in our history. We have discussions scheduled with the People's Republic of (Communist) China. We are taking the lead in trying to bring about an interim agreement in the Middle East. The world definitely is a safer place to live in than it was 2½ years ago.

Interview, Washington/
U.S. News & World Report, 11-22:33.

Dean Rusk
Former Secretary of State
of the United States

. . . I myself believe that one of the principal pillars of peace in the world is the feeling on the part of certain capitals that "we had better be just a little careful, because those crazy Americans just might do something about it." And if that question is ever transformed into a certainty that we will not do something about it, then I think we are headed for periods of very great danger.

TV interview/
National Broadcasting Company, 7-2.

The overriding moral question is how do you avoid World War III. I can't emphasize the importance of this question, although not many people seem to be worrying about it these days. We had a chance to pick ourselves up out of the destruction of World War II and start over. We're not going to have that chance after World War III. Now, how do you do it? We came out of World War II with the notion that collective security was the key to the preservation of peace. We wrote it into Article I of the United Nations Charter, and we reinforced it by these so-called security treaties. Now that idea is eroding. My generation has become old and tired, and it doesn't grip us the way it used to when I was young. Half of our people are so young they've had no chance to live through or to remember these experiences, so it's understandable that it doesn't grip them in the same way. Now, if we are to cast aside the notion of collective security, what are we going to put in its place? I don't know; and I can't tell these young people what it will be because each generation must find its own answers to that question. But we've got somehow to find an answer, because unless we can organize world peace, there literally is no human survival.

Television interview,
National Broadcasting Company/
The New York Times, 7-14:33.

Anwar el Sadat
President of the
United Arab Republic

. . . war is a science now. It is not, as before, just bravery and so forth.

Interview/The Washington Post,
12-14:(A)17.

Maurice Schumann
Foreign Minister of France

Today, new and lofty horizons are being offered to our weary, burdened nations and to the impatient youth of the world who are astonished at our quarrels and are already tempted to break rank. Away with hegemonies, the wills of power and of superpower. The world has grown. It offers our ambitions immense, still-little-explored and under-exploited fields, such as space, the sea and the sea-bed, which science and technology are continually opening up. May these prospects help us to liquidate the sequels of past conflicts and to overcome the crises which some day will appear quite absurd. May this "shock of the future" urge us to move toward tomorrow together—all together.

At United Nations, New York,
Oct. 4/Vital Speeches, 11-1:49.

Haile Selassie
Emperor of Ethiopia

Certain people advocate peace, but only in words. In our view, it is the implementation rather than the words that is important.

Interview, Addis Ababa, Jan. 18/
The New York Times, 1-19:14.

Mitchell Sharp
Secretary of State for
External Affairs of Canada

Time is running out if the (nuclear) non-proliferation treaty is to become fully effective. It is not enough to deny acquisition of nuclear weapons to those countries capable of producing them. Unless the nuclear powers themselves put an end to the proliferation of their own nuclear weapons, in qualitative as well as quantitative terms, the full non-proliferation regime stands in danger.

At disarmament conference,
Geneva, Sept. 7/
Los Angeles Herald-Examiner, 9-7:(A)15.

Marshall D. Shulman
Director, Russian Institute,
Columbia University

Those who think nuclear war is inconceivable place too much reliance on an assumed rationality in the decision-making process. Decisions are more often the results of interplay of pressures, and the outcome does not always—perhaps not even often—correspond to what anyone would decide as a rational choice.

Interview, New York/
Los Angeles Times, 12-28:(2)7.

Lewis L. Strauss
Rear Admiral, United States Navy
(Ret.): Former Chairman, Atomic
Energy Commission of the United States

I suspect that the great wars are over. The fact that we and the Russians and the British and the French have had it (nuclear weaponry) now for this long a period without using it attests to the persuasive deterrence of nuclear armament.

Interview, Brandy Station, Va./
San Francisco Examiner, 9-3:12.

U Thant
Secretary General
of the United Nations

. . . I have my personal doubts about the wisdom of the active participation of the two superpowers (the United States and the Soviet Union) in a UN peace-keeping force, particularly in an area like the Middle East. Of course, in the future—perhaps in 1980 or 1990—the participation of U.S. Soviet contingents, and even of a Chinese contingent, may be desirable and even essential in some areas for the purpose of peace-keeping.

News conference, United Nations,
New York, Jan. 18/
Los Angeles Times, 1-19:(1)9.

Barbara Ward
Economist

Enough is being spent to blow up the planet five times over. Modest people think two times is enough.

Plainview (Tex.) Daily Herald, 4-5:4.

PART THREE

General

Amyas Ames
Chairman, Partnership for the Arts;
Chairman, Lincoln Center for the
Performing Arts, New York

Do you realize that West Germany spends $2.42 per person on the arts each year, that Sweden and Austria spend $2; that Canada spends $1.40, that Israel spends $1.34 and that Great Britain spends $1.23? Guess what the United States spends per person on the arts—seven and a half cents. That's it. Our aims really are very modest. For fiscal '71, we're only asking that the richest country in the world, as we like to think of ourselves, spend only 15 cents per person on the arts—to enrich our lives.

The Washington Post, 2-28:(F)3.

W. H. Auden
Poet

The relationship between art and life is either so obvious that nothing need be said, or so complicated that nothing can be said.

Interview, London/
The New York Times, 10-19:52.

Kenneth Clark
Art historian

The discovery of a new date or a new document has given me more satisfaction than any other achievement, because these are certainties that cannot be questioned; whereas the historical interpretation of works of art must remain subjective and speculative, and leave one with a sense—a humble sense— of being very far from the truth.

Accepting Cosmos Club Award,
Washington/
The Washington Post, 4-15:(H)3.

Salvador Dali
Artist

Painters today paint nothing. Art is collaps-ing because of the laziness and depression of artists. I am going to raise that morale because my next painting will be unique and exciting. Instead of the color being painted on the canvas, the color will be mixed in the eye. It will be something new in color that has never existed before.

Interview, Cleveland/
The National Observer, 3-15:11.

Giorgio de Chirico
Artist

I cannot bear to look at modern art. I am the only one with the courage to say so. The rest pretend to like it, to understand it. Impossible! It makes no sense.

Quote, 4-25:385.

David McAdam Eccles
Former Member of British Parliament

We shall not reduce the popularity of dirty books, pictures, films and plays by showing that they are bad art, but because, regardless of time and place, they advertise behavior which mocks at love and tenderness and at respect for other people.

Before House of Lords, London/
The Christian Science Monitor, 4-24:7.

Federico Fellini
Motion picture director

(The artist) is simply a medium between his fantasies and the rest of the world.

Interview/The Washington Post, 1-29:(C)9.

Katharine Graham
President,
The Washington Post Company

The arts that need our help most desperately are those that many of us find it difficult to understand.

Before Business Committee
for the Arts, Chicago, Feb.17/
The Washington Post, 2-18:(C)11.

H. R. Gross
United States Representative, R—Iowa

(Arguing against appropriations for the National Foundation on the Arts and Humanities and the Smithsonian Institution): At a time when this country is desperately in need of drastic savings on the part of the Federal government, when it is facing a desperate fiscal situation at home and abroad . . . I do not know how anyone can possibly justify an increase of $28,150,000 . . . in one year for the arts and humanities, when the taxpayers who have to cough up this increase will not have enough left after they pay their taxes to buy a ticket to the ballet or the opera they are forced to subsidize . . . not one major orchestra, opera or ballet company in this country is operating in the black. Obviously, if the public is so hungry for these things, that segment of the public ought to be willing to pay for them. Not long ago, Congress defeated the subsidy program for the supersonic transport. The government was subsidizing that airplane for the "jet set" by taxing the mass of the people. The mass of the people revolted and forced an end to that government subsidy. Now here you are subsidizing the arts, which the great mass of the people neither want nor patronize. You had better look out for a taxpayer revolt in this area, too.

Before the House, Washington, June 29/
U.S. News & World Report, 7-19:30.

Nancy Hanks
Chairman, National Endowment for the Arts of the United States

It is my view that unless we dedicate ourselves to competition *for* the arts—instead of what is an inordinate amount of competition *between* the arts and a vast waste of energy given to competition *in* the arts—then we're not going to have a common wealth to enjoy.

Boston/The Christian Science Monitor,
11-20:14

Thomas B. Hess
Editor, "Art News"

There is a tendency to assume that artists are working for an audience and they're mocking the audience or they're mocking other artists. (Pablo) Picasso is 90 and he started to paint around 14. That's 76 years. Nobody is going to play a practical joke for 76 years. It may sound like a trivial canard, but you see it over and over again—the artist is making fun of other artists, the critics, the public, the curators. Baloney! Maybe you could make a joke for a week, maybe you could make a joke for a month—but 76 years?

At "New York Times" panel discussion/
The New York Times, 10-25:42.

John Hightower
Director,
Museum of Modern Art, New York

My friends told me (when he took the job six months ago) it was going to be bad. "You can't get along there without a suit of armor," they told me. I knew all that cerebrally. But then I came here. And on the first day at 9:30 in the morning, there was a blowup in the curatorial department. In the afternoon, the Art Workers' Coalition came in and demanded that we open a Martin Luther King wing the next day—or face the consequences. The AWC arrived the following morning in white tie and tails and blocked the entrance with guerrilla theatre, claiming we were against blacks and Puerto Ricans. It's been a god-awful year for the museum.

Interview/Newsweek, 1-25:82.

In the late 1960s, museums in New York City were asked to be lots of things they weren't—foundations, giving grants and commissioning work from artists; government agencies, defending the rights of artists; community galleries, which some accomplished successfully, others not so. In a year, I've learned that MOMA isn't any one of those things and shouldn't be. What it is, is a harder question. For one, an institution that expands—or is sensitive to the expansion of—definitions of art; for another, an institution that preserves, hopefully for time immemorial, great works of modern culture. I'd hate like hell for there not to be a place in New York

City like the second and third floors of the Modern, where you can have your mind blown by great works of art.

Interview, New York/
The New York Times, 7-30:22.

Louis I. Kahn
Architect

Form is "what"; design is "how." In my opinion, the greatness of an architect depends more on his power to realize that which is "house" than on his ability to design a "house"—something prescribed by the circumstances.

The Dallas Times Herald, 2-14:(B)9.

Lincoln Kirstein
General director,
New York City Ballet

Culture is not about success or failure. It is about possibility. You cannot possibly talk about ballet as a money-making concern. Money—but who is making money? Is New York City making money? Compared to armaments and toothpaste?

Interview, New York/
The New York Times, 6-17:48.

Steve Lawrence
Singer

I don't think enough is done in any of the entertainment medias to uplift and educate the audiences. This applies to television, to every one of the arts. Many claim music and art have always reflected the times, and maybe that's why there's such a great expression of neurotic music and art around today. But I feel the people that are in a responsible position in the record business, in the TV industry, have an obligation and a duty to bring forth the better creators, to subscribe to and support the better writers. I really believe that this is a great lack in the entire industry; a great lack of administrative people that are around that have the courage of those kind of convictions today. I get very frightened when I see any kind of mature, adult executive, over 40, maybe even 55 or 60, who suddenly lets his hair grow and wears fringe and beads.

I'm very nervous. I have to believe that this executive's life up until then has been a fraud, or if it's not, then he's a fraud now. One of the two worries me greatly. And it's those guys I'm really addressing myself to—the guys who have the responsibility to go in and support good creative writers, good creative artists, good creative composers. It's not being done at all, in this country in particular.

Interview/
Los Angeles Herald-Examiner, 7-18:(F)5.

Peggy Lee
Singer

In each talent, there is a kind of discipline that is terribly necessary—whether it be learning to play one's instrument or studying the craft of singing, writing, painting or any form of art. If you are born with a gift and are appreciative of being alive, then it becomes necessary to follow that impulse that sends you onward and upward.

Interview, Beverly Hills, Calif./
Los Angeles Times (Calendar), 3-7:12.

John V. Lindsay
Mayor of New York

The fate of art in this country depends upon the condition of our cities. Art happens in cities. Art is preserved in cities.

At dedication of expansion of
New Orleans Museum of Art, Nov. 17/
The New York Times, 11-18:21.

Rouben Mamoulian
Former motion picture director

There's no such thing as improvisation—unless you're performing for your friends at a Christmas party. Improvisation doesn't belong in art because art requires design . . .

San Francisco Examiner & Chronicle
(Datebook), 10-24:6.

William J. McGill
President, Columbia University

Corresponding to the growing alienation of our students is a growing creative effort in

(WILLIAM J. McGILL)

painting, music and theatre. There is also a great surge of interest in medicine and law, because these professions offer opportunities for participation in social change . . . I hope society is ready for this artistic and professional ferment.

Before Economic Club, Detroit/
The Christian Science Monitor, 2-24:14.

Robert Merrill
Opera singer

If our arts organizations don't get the money they need, I don't know what will happen. In Europe, it's different—the Viennese would give up a meal to see an opera . . . The question is, can we Americans live too easily without it. I didn't see any particular sign of protest when the Met (Metropolitan Opera) almost went under last year because of the work stoppage. What if a football season is threatened? People would yell. But I'm not sure about the arts.

Interview, New York/
The Christian Science Monitor, 2-24:13.

Richard M. Nixon
President of the United States

We can spend billions on new scientific miracles, on education, on housing, on health care, highways and airports and all the other goods and services that government is expected to provide; and in doing so, we can meet very genuine needs and discharge very real responsibilities. But this alone would be like designing a violin without strings. As we look ahead, 10, 20, 30 years, we can chart the prospect of many great achievements. We have seen technological advance speed up by almost a geometrical progression. Already, we take moon landings almost for granted. Computers, industrial advances, agricultural breakthroughs —all are multiplying the goods and services our economy can produce. These material advances are important. They extend man's reach; they widen our range of choices; they make it possible to look ahead toward an end to hunger and misery and disease not only in

America but elsewhere in the world as well. But by themselves, these advances can never be enough. The engineers and the scientists can take us to the moon; but we need the poet or the painter to take us to the heights of understanding and perception. Doctors are enabling us to live longer and healthier lives; but we need the musician and the dancer and the filmmaker to bring beauty and meaning to our lives.

Before Associated Councils
of the Arts, Washington, May 26/
The New York Times, 5-27:32.

Betty Parsons
Artist

How do you decide what is art? That's a feeling you get in the solar plexus. I have it. I was born with it. If you haven't got it, you can't acquire it . . . Art can spring from many different sources of the psyche. In primitive man, it came from awe and fear, a sense of the mystery of life. I think art springs from feeling and love. Intellect is very important as a policeman for your feelings; but it should never come first.

Interview/The Washington Post, 3-17:(E)7.

Georges Pompidou
President of France

Pablo Picasso is a volcano that never ceases to erupt. Whatever he touches he recreates or at least changes. Whatever his subject—a table, a woman's face, a saucepan—he makes us discover it afresh.

San Francisco Examiner, 11-9:30.

Jule Styne
Composer

It is women, single-sexedly, who decide what people are going to be stars and what songs are going to be standards. It is also girls who made rock-and-roll and folk rock. And if the day comes when they decide against it, all the boys will go straight again, musically. The reason women have all this cultural power is that women care. They are more mature and understanding. They're reached emotionally by music and art, and they force men to accept it, even when the men would intrinsically prefer to be doing something else—like gambling or going to a ballgame. If it weren't for women, there would be no New York. There might be a Pittsburgh or a Detroit, I wouldn't know about that. But there would be no New York. Thank God. Thank God that men care for women and that women care for culture. That's what keeps art and music in America alive.

San Francisco Examiner, 6-28:31.

Fashion

Pierre Balmain
Fashion designer

In the old days, young girls tried to look like their mothers. That has changed. Now they want to dress like their fathers.

Quote, 7-25:73.

Cecil Beaton
Fashion designer

With few exceptions, I like all periods of fashion. Each one is remarkable in that it's so innately of itself. What makes a style good is what makes it suitable and fresh for each instance. There is no permanent criterion or norm. What could be *kitsch* in 1930 might be considered valid in 1970.

Interview, London/
The New York Times, 12-19:(1)62.

Bill Blass
Fashion designer

The costume party's over. As I travel around the country, I sense a growing conservatism from a newly-discerning customer. It is no longer the moment to shock. It's time for downright ladylike clothes again—for the out-and-out pretty shoe, the beautiful strand of pearls.

Beverly Hills, Calif., Jan. 18/
Los Angeles Times, 1-20:(4)1.

To sell my clothes, I travel all over this country. I don't think people realize how square this nation is. The majority of women do not wear ethnic clothes. They have never arrived at a party looking like a gypsy or a maharani. In the past couple of years, they haven't been quite sure how to look.

New York/The New York Times, 4-22:47.

Dictatorship in fashion is dead. We've learned that we can propose, but not impose.

New York/The Washington Post, 5-23:(F)3.

There is a relationship between what men and women wear. When women wear outlandish gypsy clothes, men feel that they have to be more flamboyant. But personally, I feel men should be accessories in the evening—let the women shine. I hate all those brocade and ruffled shirts.

The Washington Post (Potomac), 9-12:35.

Main Rousseau Bocher (Mainbocher)
Fashion designer

I don't believe that dressmaking is an art; but I do think dresses are an important part of the art of living, just as important as food, surroundings, work and play . . . I've always thought things had to be wearable, unless of course they were for a great occasion. I've never done eccentric things. I don't like to see people "dressed up." I've always made dresses for ladies. "Ladies" and "elegance" may have become naughty words today, but I still believe in them.

Interview, New York/
The New York Times, 6-25:41.

Marc Bohan
Fashion designer

It is cretinous to say that haute couture is dying. It is true that times have changed. Women want more liberty and fantasy. But haute couture still gives the great moments.

Newsweek, 3-29:78.

Couture will never die . . . Just because a few designers, like Saint Laurent and Cardin, say they are not going to show collections doesn't mean that the whole thing is finished. I believe that, when January comes around,

even Cardin and Saint Laurent will have something to show. We all need publicity.
New York, Oct. 21/
The Washington Post, 10-26:(B)2.

Donald Brooks
Fashion designer

(Hot pants are) just this year's hula-hoop or skateboard.
Newsweek, 3-29:75.

Andre Courreges
Fashion designer

Fashion writers should not pick here and there in a collection to find what amuses them but what is not necessarily wearable, without also being concerned with what goes on in the cells of creation, which is the future.
Radio discussion, Paris, Feb. 24/
The Washington Post, 2-26:(B)2.

Marlene Dietrich
Actress

There is no "fashion." Everybody does what they want to do. But they do not have eyes any more. They don't see themselves from behind.
London, Sept. 12/
Los Angeles Herald-Examiner, 9-13:(A)11.

Mike Geist
Fashion designer

In doing their own thing, many American women seem to have lost their ability to tell the difference between what's "in" and what's "out." They lost the reference point. How high is up when you don't know what down is? When a girl can wear hot-pants to a nightclub without attracting much attention, who's to say if she's "in" or "out" unless you have a reference point? The consumer is, of course, the one who sets this reference point. A designer is like a consumer-researcher who must understand what the consumer wants and then give it to her before she knows she wants it.
Interview, New York/
Los Angeles Times, 3-16:(4)1.

Rudi Gernreich
Fashion designer

The fashion industry as we know it is dead. The isolated couturier is dead. Women are striving toward liberation. And clothes are no longer status; they're very much antistatus. Today, fad *equals* fashion.
Newsweek, 3-29:75.

There are so many correct and incorrect things to do, the importance of how you look is diminishing.
Santa Monica, Calif., April 24/
Los Angeles Times, 4-27:(4)3.

Buyers are still searching the world for "original creativity." They cannot seem to understand that we're beyond this phase of fashion, that the designer's challenge for today is not to come up with a new sleeve, a new look, a new hem, a new status symbol, a new statement, but to edit and assemble very real, very wearable clothes at a price. This is the only legitimate fashion for today. The focus is on the body, on comfort. The minute you invent, it becomes a conspicuous invention. When kids decide, on their own, to roll up their blue jeans, that's invention. When a designer rolls up your blue jeans for you, that's nonsense.
Los Angeles Times, 5-27:(4)1.

Aldo Gucci
Fashion designer

Fashion comes and goes, but good taste remains good taste. You know, good taste really doesn't change very much.
Interview, Rome/
Los Angeles Times, 12-3:(1-B)1.

George Halley
Fashion designer

The street clothes of the '60s were one big masquerade. My wife, Claudia, and I used to give annual Halloween parties. We had to stop because all our guests were wearing costumes every day. The only fantasy left would have been to arrive in basic black with pearls and

(GEORGE HALLEY)

little white gloves. We're at that point right now in fashion. We've had so much costumerie that the only fantasy left is to be serious.
Interview, Los Angeles/
Los Angeles Times, 8-10:(4)1.

There are still enough women who will pay big prices to get individuality and luxurious fabrics. Last week in Beverly Hills, one customer bought 14 of my designs. And several women have picked out my most elaborate gowns for the opera. But the number of women who buy like that is becoming smaller every season. Maybe in times like these people don't want others to think they are extravagant or obsessed with fashion. I believe that is why Yves Saint Laurent announced that in the future he will make only a small couture collection, and he'll show it only to private customers, without publicity.
San Francisco/
San Francisco Examiner, 8-16:21.

Katharine Hepburn
Actress

(Women) have to pretend they care how they look. Now men are imitating us with all these fancy clothes. One can only assume from this that the female is infinitely superior —which I have known for some time.
News conference, Baltimore/
Los Angeles Herald-Examiner, 4-26:(B)5.

Betsey Johnson
Fashion designer

Clothes are finally just clothes. People will begin to wear only what they want—no more mini-midi controversy. Whenever I get confused about designing, I look at what's happening in the world. How can you expect sanity to come out of insanity?
Newsweek, 3-29:77.

Ted Lapidus
Fashion designer

I take the sophistication of the rich and

give it to the masses. The secret is never to modify what is expensive, but to take it, study the prototype and discover how to reproduce it. It is a matter of engineering, of mathematics, of dividing a garment into parts and teaching machines the language of beauty. It is not modern for men to spend hours doing what machines can do in minutes, and better. Why should the couture linger in the drama of the 19th century when technology has put man on the moon?
New York/
The Christian Science Monitor, 1-8:6.

Sophia Loren
Actress

The midiskirt? Yes, I am fond of it. Of course, it depends on how you are built and how you walk. You must feel like a queen at that moment.
Interview/TV Guide, 1-9:26.

Shirley MacLaine
Actress

Whatever you put on your skin is a sign of what you are. All of us who say we don't care what we wear are not being honest. When I was in London, just before the election, I went into the shops on Kings Road and saw all the depressing colors and the very covered-up clothes which left no skin showing. I began to get the feeling that the people would vote conservative. That's the way they were dressing.
Interview, New York/
The New York Times, 1-15:17.

Vincent Monte-Sano
President, New York Couture
Business Council; Former couturier

Fashion (in 1970) became a charade, a masquerade, a giant put-on. No wonder women of good taste are confused. I am critical of Seventh Avenue for dredging up the past. The look of the '30s has no place in a space and technological age; it would be as if we resurrected . . . the DC-3 to replace the 747. Never in making a major purchase has the consumer been faced with such an emotional confrontation: Is it too young, too old, too short, too ethnic, too hippie? We have succeeded in destroying the continuity of fashion in the mind of the consumer.

> *At opening of New York Couture Group's fashion week, New York, Jan. 4/ The Washington Post, 1-5:(C)3.*

Pat Nixon
Wife of the President of the United States

(Regarding hot pants): I can't even comment on them.

> *Washington, Feb. 11/ The Dallas Times Herald, 2-12:(A)2.*

Norman Norell
Fashion designer

I'm 70 years old, and I've been working in this business since I was 25. I've spent my whole life devoted to quality. I realize it's not as important as it once was, but I'm too old to change. Quality means everything to me. I would rather have a good suit and wear it for 10 years than have several cheap ones. The same thing applies to furniture: Either get the best or any wicker. The garbage lies in between.

> *Interview, New York/ The New York Times, 1-12:38.*

Emilio Pucci
Fashion designer

I look at the sky and think happy. Some designers look down and think muddy.

> *The Boston Globe, 6-30:34.*

Rosalind Russell
Actress

I think exhibitionism in women is wrong over 40—no, over 35. I just don't find it amusing. You have to keep abreast of the times, but the adjusting should be on an individual basis. You look it all over, and you find what is becoming to you in fashion. That's what being "chic" means.

> *Interview, New York/ The New York Times, 3-26:42.*

Yves Saint Laurent
Fashion designer

I did not think in a profession as free as fashion that one could meet so many people so narrow-minded and reactionary, petty people paralyzed by taboos . . . Fashion is a reflection of our time; and if it does not express the atmosphere of its time, it means nothing . . . Haute couture is bogged down in a boring tradition of sc-called good taste and refinement; and it has become a museum, a refuge for people who do not dare to look life in the face and who are reassured by tradition.

> *Interview, Paris/ San Francisco Examiner, 2-19:20.*

Other couturiers who have a ready-to-wear line have it because they're obliged to. They don't enjoy themselves. But I adore it. It's alive; it's quick; it's daring. The challenge is to make a raincoat which looks just as good on a girl of 15 as on a woman of 60.

> *Life, 10-8:93.*

Charles H. Salesky
President, HCA Industries
(Hat Corporation of America)

Hats are not on the way out. It's the styles that are way out.

> *The Washington Post, 2-21:(L)3.*

Elsa Schiaparelli
Fashion designer

I like pants; I wear them: I think they will stay. But shorts? Hot-pants? At Maxim's last night, I saw two women over 50 in lame silver shorts. It wasn't funny at all.

> *Interview, Paris/ San Francisco Examiner, 4-6:28.*

Women are afraid of fashion. You hardly ever see one who looks smart these days. There are no leaders. Sometimes I go to a party and see somebody who looks quite well. But it's always a mystery woman. When I ask who she is, nobody has ever heard of her.

> *San Francisco Examiner, 8-23:28.*

Geraldine Stutz
President, Henri Bendel, Inc.

You're sick if you need expensive clothes to establish your worth. To be "in" these days is to be "out."

Newsweek, 3-29:75.

Valentino
Fashion designer

Women are tired of gimmicks and kinky things. They are coming back to couture—not for the prestige, but because it's the only way to look elegant at the moment.

New York/The Washington Post, 3-24:(B)2.

Journalism

Spiro T. Agnew
Vice President of the United States

. . . such is the power of the national media today that of all our political, social and economic institutions, they seem to be able to cloak themselves in a special immunity to criticism. By their lights, it appears, freedom of expression is fine so long as it stops before any question is raised or criticism lodged against national media policies and practices. Nor is the national media's refusal to abide criticism reserved for utterances of a Vice President . . . or a Congressman or a member of a Presidential Cabinet. Any citizen who has suffered the frustration of being rebuffed when calling or writing to complain about inaccurate or biased news reporting knows exactly what I mean. Yet, an extremist who dignifies our adversaries and demeans our traditions is sought out and spotlighted for national attention. He is interviewed as though he were representative of a large following and is treated with the utmost deference as he unloads into millions of American living rooms his imprecations against society and disrespect for civilized law. Such attacks against American institutions are editorially lauded as healthy demonstrations of freedom of expression in a free society. Again, when the president of a prestigious university assaults our nation's judiciary by declaring that certain defendants cannot receive a fair trial in an American court, he is not charged with attempting to "intimidate" the courts. On the contrary, he is praised by important segments of the national news media for contributing to what they term "the dialogue."

Before Middlesex Club, Boston,
March 18/Human Events, 4-3:13.

A prominent member of the television medium made the comment just yesterday that he was going to take the gloves off; he was tired of being criticized by public officials. He said these words: "I want to warn you again," referring to me . . . I don't like that kind of threat—"I'm going to warn you again." That's intimidation. Let me just tell that gentleman he doesn't have to warn me. I will not be intimidated by the news media any more than they intend to be intimidated by me. In some cases, they're just as vulnerable to proper criticism as any local official, state or Federal official. They're not immune from criticism.

Before North Carolina state and
local officials, Raleigh, May 6/
Los Angeles Times, 5-7:(3)13.

We in government are wholly dependent on you who run the news media in this country to get our message to the people. There is no *Pravda* or *Izvestia* or Radio Moscow, Radio Peking, Radio Hanoi or Radio Havana in the United States of America. There's not even a BBC. But as tempting as it would be for me to have such an outlet to vent my ire some mornings, I'm glad we're dependent on a free and independent and honestly skeptical press to relay our message and to report to the people on our stewardship.

At Mutual Broadcasting System
convention, Nassau, Bahamas, June 1/
Los Angeles Herald-Examiner, 6-2:(A)8.

(Regarding *The New York Times'* printing of secret Pentagon papers on Vietnam): Legality aside, I think it important for us to worry to some extent about the reliability of people who—knowing that this information was classified, with full knowledge of that, and with full knowledge of the fact that there are ways of declassifying information so it can be published—nonetheless, in a secretive, clandestine fashion made that information available . . . This is aside from any determination of the

(SPIRO T. AGNEW)

legality of the disclosure itself. It might be completely all right to do it. Maybe the court will decide it that way. But I think the judgment factor is one the American people would do well to consider very carefully.

News conference, Los Angeles, June 16/
Los Angeles Times, 6-17:(1)21.

. . . I do find that one has to be very specific in one's comments because, if not, the press immediately shreds away all the qualifications that you put in. For instance, I said originally that those who *encouraged* the student riots were "effete snobs." Within two or three days, it had become, in the press, not the people who had *encouraged* the students, but the students themselves. Then presently it became *all* students. Then presently it became *all youth*. And that is the way it goes. People asked me why I attacked Kingman Brewster of Yale, and I said, "Well, if I don't make it specific, within a week I will be accused of having attacked *all* college presidents instead of just one college president." This is a very dangerous thing that the press does, and they do it all the time.

Interview, Washington/Look, 10-19:40.

Harold W. Anderson
President, "Omaha World-Herald"

Let me say I reject the conspiracy theory—you know, the allegation that the Nixon Administration is trying to intimidate the news media by a calculated campaign of criticism and thinly-veiled threats. Hogwash! . . . Let me say I feel that some of Vice President Agnew's criticisms of the media have been justified. I fail to understand the almost hysterical reaction to those criticisms in some quarters. So far as I know, Mr. Agnew hasn't dismantled a single TV network or cost a single TV commentator his job. And at last report, *The New York Times* was still publishing daily.

Before Senate Judiciary Subcommittee
on Constitutional Rights, Washington,
Oct. 13/The Washington Post, 10-14:(A)4.

William B. Arthur
Editor, "Look" magazine

(Vice President Agnew) is doing far more than causing the press some discomfort. He is willfully encouraging the American people in a tendency that could eventually save them not only from reality, but from any meaningful concept of what freedom of the press—freedom itself—actually is.

Before northeastern region members of
Sigma Delta Chi, Windsor, Conn.,
April 24/San Francisco Examiner
& Chronicle, 4-25:(A)24.

Lucy Wilson Benson
President, League of Women
Voters of the United States

For more than 50 years, the League of Women Voters has operated according to a belief in the value of informed participation in our system of self-government. However, of late, it's becoming more and more difficult to really be informed. We seem to be drowning in a form of informational overkill—constantly bombarded by an ever-changing kaleidescope of events, happenings and personages. Just when we feel we're beginning to grasp the meat behind a particular piece of news, it disappears from view to be replaced by another swirling set of scenes and circumstances.

At Monadnock Summer Lyceum,
Peterborough, N.H./
The Wall Street Journal, 8-24:12.

Barry Bingham, Sr.
Editor and publisher, Louisville
"Courier-Journal" and "Times"

. . . I feel no sublime assurance of the survival of newspapers, certainly not in their present form. Many people who have been reading papers all their lives suspect that those familiar journals are helping to destroy their comfortable world. At the same time, a younger generation is coming along which is accustomed to getting its information mainly from television and radio. That generation also contains at least one member out of four who does not enjoy reading or finds it an easy exercise. Will these younger Americans demand newspapers in the future as a necessary part of their lives? I think not—unless newspapers find a way to make themselves indispensable to young Americans as they seemed to their parents and grandparents.

> *At University of Wisconsin, Madison/*
> *The National Observer, 1-18:18.*

David Brinkley
News commentator,
National Broadcasting Company

Anyone who cannot stand criticism should not go into journalism—as I think anyone who cannot stand criticism should not go into politics.

> *Before Senate Judiciary Subcommittee,*
> *Washington, Oct. 19/*
> *The Washington Post, 10-20:(A)3.*

Edward W. Brooke
United States Senator, R—Mass.

What commandment, what canon, what etiquette-imperative keeps you in the news media silent about each other's foibles? . . . My objection is to blandness, sameness, homogenization of the news—the unwillingness, for example, of the networks to take on each other as well as the other titans in American life.

> *Before Massachusetts Broadcasters*
> *Association, Hyannis, Oct. 8/*
> *The Washington Post, 10-9:(C)4.*

Clarence J. Brown
United States Representative, R—Ohio

The plain fact is that the First Amendment is not limited to the truth. That amendment guarantees the right to print and speak—but the right of expression thus assured may be the truth to one and lies to another . . . the government should not and must not be permitted to control the content of programs. Fraudulent and deceptive advertising or that which is blatantly pornographic must stand on its own feet as areas for regulation; but varying viewpoints on public affairs, a multiplicity of "free" voices, must be preserved to insure the public's right to know. The free citizen must have the largest possible number of free voices from which to choose the truth.

> *Washington/Variety, 7-21:31.*

William F. Buckley, Jr.
Political columnist;
Editor, "National Review"

It has been obvious to me for a great many years that the networks are biased . . . Liberal; a left-liberal position . . . I would encourage a conscious search for intelligent and well-informed people who don't go along with the *Zeitgeist*, who would be on the air on a fairly regular basis. For instance, Howard K. Smith—who dissented from the general opposition to Vietnam—made an enormous difference in just the fact that he was there occasionally to say a few things on ABC. I wish there were somebody like that to put other issues into focus on all the networks.

> *Interview/Nation's Business, June:36.*

(Announcing that supposedly secret government papers on Vietnam printed in *National Review* were a hoax in response to *The New York Times'* printing of secret Pentagon papers on Vietnam): (It was a hoax designed) to demonstrate . . . that forged documents would be widely accepted as genuine provided their content was inherently plausible . . . Those who will want to question the methods we used in order to make our demonstration may proceed to do so. We admit that we proceeded in somewhat of an ethical vacuum. *The New York Times* has instructed us that it is permissible to traffic in stolen documents. But they have not yet instructed us on whether it is permissible to traffic in forged documents.

> *News conference, New York, July 21/*
> *The Washington Post, 7-22:(A)1,(A)6.*

Dean Burch
Chairman, Federal Communications
Commission of the United States

I am more frightened of government interference with news than I am of the news being a bit, well, let's say slanted—in terms of

(DEAN BURCH)

philosophical point of view. Insofar as a broadcaster is exercising a news function, I think he is entitled to First Amendment privilege.

San Francisco Examiner, 9-1:47.

No government agency can, or should try to, authenticate the news. Therefore . . . we (the FCC) have consistently and repeatedly stated that we will shun the censor's role and will not try to establish news distortion . . . (But) staging or slanting the news is flagrantly contrary to the public interest. Indeed, it is difficult to imagine a more effective way to destroy the very essence of democracy. Every act of deliberate distortion—in some senseless race for ratings—not only diminishes the profession of journalism or broadcasting, but also impoverishes the nation.

*Before Senate Subcommittee on
Constitutional Rights, Washington,
Oct. 20/San Francisco Examiner,
10-20:2.*

Erwin D. Canham
*Editor-in-chief,
"The Christian Science Monitor"*

For the printed word, for the journal, to survive and save society with it, editors must think harder and deeper of the implications of these great days. Let us, for a change, take time to think. It will be the most valuable time we have ever spent . . . All the human race has ever hoped for is in danger of being blown up—not necessarily by design, but ingloriously by accident. This would be an inexcusable end for man. Men who use the sharp and hard tool of the printed word should be using it to awaken humanity to its danger.

*Before Arizona Newspaper Association,
Tucson/The Christian Science Monitor,
1-20:2.*

Turner Catledge
*Former executive editor,
"The New York Times"*

I suspect that believability of the press is in serious jeopardy right now. A lot of it is beyond the control of the newspapers. They (the public in general) so resent it (wars, problems of race and the environment, etc.) and are so depressed by it . . . Our newspapers developed to their present form in calmer days. From, say, 1890 to 1954, newspapers could be relied upon to bring enough information, sufficiently impartial. But since then . . . there's been social ferment . . . It's true that there have always been great problems; but now there are a lot more of them.

*Interview, Washington, Feb. 9/
The Washington Post, 2-10:(B)1.*

Otis Chandler
Publisher, "Los Angeles Times"

Is the press objective today? Was it five, 10, 25 years ago? If you took a street poll today, I think a majority of people would say the press has lost its objectivity. But I must disagree. The press has changed. Today it is more honest than it used to be . . . There is no such thing as complete objectivity. News selection, by its very nature, is subjective. The writing and handling of the news requires subjective judgments.

*At Occidental College, Los Angeles,
March 31/Los Angeles Times, 4-1:(2)2.*

Gardner Cowles
Chairman, Cowles Communications, Inc.

(Announcing the end of publication of *Look* magazine): When it came time to make this decision, I thought back over *Look's* 35 years of constructive, responsible and award-winning journalism, and my heart said "Keep it going." But my head said "Suspend it," and there was really no other way . . . Now, at the end, we have the most interested and best-educated audience we have ever had. We tried to be serious without being solemn, entertaining without being frivolous, angry without being bitter, and hopeful without being complacent. And generally, I believe, we succeeded.

*News conference, Sept. 16,
New York/Time, 9-27:55.*

Alan Cranston
United States Senator, D–Calif.

(Regarding Vice President Agnew's criticism of the press): It is not the job of the press in a free society to say sweet things about people who wield power in the government . . . If I could be permitted to lapse into just one Agnewism, I would observe that . . . the Veep belongs to a caterwauling corps of crybabies who are only happy when being permissively patted by friendly flacks.

At San Francisco Press Club,
Aug. 11/San Francisco Examiner, 8-12:2.

Walter Cronkite
News commentator,
Columbia Broadcasting System

No one doubts the right of anyone to seek to correct distortion, to right untruths . . . but the present campaign (against the press), spearheaded by Vice President Spiro T. Agnew and Republican National Chairman Senator Robert Dole, goes beyond that. Aside from their attempts at intimidation through their reminders that broadcasting is a licensed industry, they are attacking the qualifications of the press as the single most powerful monitor of the performance of the people's government. Short of uncovering documents which probably do not exist, it is impossible to know precisely the motives of this conspiracy. But is it too much to suggest that the grand design is to lower the press' credibility in an attempt to raise their own and thus even—or perhaps tilt in their favor—the odds in future electoral battles? . . . Nor is there any way that President Nixon can escape responsibility for this campaign. He is the ultimate leader. He sets the tone and the attitude of his Administration. By internal edict and public posture, he could reverse the anti-press policy of his Administration if that were his desire . . . But the evidence today buttresses the suspicion that this Administration has gone much further—that it has conceived, planned, orchestrated and is now conducting a program

to reduce the effectiveness of a free press—and its prime target is television.

Before International Radio and Television
Society, New York, May 18/
The Washington Post, 5-19:(E)9.

Broadcast news (in the United States) today is not free. Because it is operated by an industry that is beholden to the government for its right to exist, its freedom has been curtailed by fiat, by assumption and by intimidation and harassment . . . The power to make us conform is too great to forever lie dormant. The axe lies there temptingly for the use of any enraged Administration—Republican, Democrat, Wallacite or McCarthyite. We are at the mercy or whim of politicians and bureaucrats, and whether they choose to chop us down or not, the mere existence of their power is an intimidating and constraining threat in being.

Before Senate Constitutional Rights
Subcommittee, Washington, Sept. 30/
The Washington Post, 10-1:(A)12.

Deane C. Davis
Governor of Vermont

I think television people especially have really done a job on the President (Nixon). Every single thing they say—the tone of their voice, the things they say and don't say and emphasis they place on things they view as adverse—I just don't think they are objective.

Montpelier, Vt./Variety, 1-27:28.

Nancy Dickerson
News correspondent,
National Broadcasting Company

If I had to give a girl advice about how to get into this kind of work, I'd say go out and get yourself in blackface; because they usually want one woman and one black, and if they can have them both in the same person, then good.

The Washington Post (Potomac), 2-28:11.

John D. Dingell
United States Representative, D—Mich.

(Supporting efforts by the House Commerce Committee to cite CBS-TV for contempt in not producing subpoenaed material from the documentary, *The Selling of The Pentagon*): If the Committee is denied the opportunity to secure the information it seeks, the Congress will have completely lost control over how and by whom the airways are used. The broadcasters will become trustees and fiduciaries to no one. Deceit and fraud may well run riot with no one to bid them nay.

Before the House, Washington,
July 13/The New York Times, 7-14:59.

Bob Dole
United States Senator, R—Kan.

The essential bond between the media, the people and the government should be one of trust. It rests on the implicit assumption that the news media will report events fairly and objectively, and we have every right to expect that this be done.

Washington/Variety, 3-17:57.

Corydon Dunham
Vice president and general counsel,
National Broadcasting Company

Only the corrupt and unconscionable would benefit if a government agency were to weaken the ability of television journalism. Increased FCC regulation of broadcasters has not resulted from any violation of the public's trust by broadcast newsmen, but from the regulatory nature of the Commission's doctrine. Regulation begets regulation.

At Practicing Law Institute
seminar/Daily Variety, 3-2:10.

Sam J. Ervin, Jr.
United States Senator, D—N.C.

Recent developments, including the subpoenaing of journalists by grand juries and Congressional committees, efforts to secure injunctions against certain newspapers, the use of assumed press credentials for investigative covers and new fears about the use of broadcast licensing for intimidation and censorship, have brought into sharp relief existing concern about the relationship between government and the press.

The Dallas Times Herald, 9-8:(A)26.

It sometimes appears that some government officials assume that the role of the press is to present news about government policies and actions only in the best possible light. And it sometimes appears that some members of the press unjustifiably interpret any official response to their criticism, other than acquiescence, as a threat to their freedom to criticize. It is my belief that robust criticism of government by the press and the consequent skepticism of the press on the part of government are the necessary ingredients of the relationship between the press and the government in a truly free society.

The Wall Street Journal, 10-6:12.

Most Americans have come to understand that the irritating excesses of the press are a small price to pay for a press independent of government control.

San Francisco Examiner, 10-21:40.

Reuven Frank
President,
National Broadcasting Company News

(Regarding criticism of television newsmen): We have been pushed and prodded, palpated and probed like fishmarket mackerel on a Friday morning, and we have had enough.

The New York Times, 5-9:(4)4.

It is time somebody said the Fairness Doctrine (requiring broadcasters to give equal time to all sides of controversial issues) is unfair; not to us, because that doesn't matter, but to the public. Extended to its fullest, the Fairness Doctrine is monumentally boring—this legislated need for the full spectrum of opinions on any one topic. Boring the public is cruel and should be considered unusual . . . To create a bludgeon against independent judgment in the name of some higher freedom than the First Amendment is not folly but malice, and should be so labelled.

At Sigma Delta Chi convention,
Washington, Nov. 11/
Daily Variety, 11-10:6.

I do not know how it happens that so many people miss the simple logic and historical need of including broadcast news—and especially television news—within the meaning of the First Amendment . . . If the First Amendment does not apply to television news, of what use is it today? It was written not to protect the press but to protect Americans. What does it protect them against if the evils which may not be practiced on written news are allowable if the news is broadcast? I repeat, if television news may be censored without violating the First Amendment, there is no First Amendment. It would be the first Constitutional provision repealed by technological advance—by a machine.

At Sigma Delta Chi convention,
Washington, Nov. 11/
Vital Speeches, 12-1:127.

Fred W. Friendly
Former president,
Columbia Broadcasting System News

The distrust that the Executive branch of government is spreading applies not just to the news media but to a crucial American freedom. The fallout from that distrust can be as damaging as if the Chief Executive tried to circumvent due process of civil law or military justice.

At Tufts University's Fletcher
School of Law and Diplomacy, April 16/
The Washington Post, 4-17:(A)8.

That television news suffers from overexposure and underdevelopment is certainly not due to any professional inadequacy. It is due to an awkward and often archaic system of news gathering that favors bulk footage and costly duplication, frequently at the expense of interpretive and investigative reporting. Overkill in journalism, as in war, is counterproductive. The spectacle of a half-dozen camera crews and a dozen microphones, several from the same organization, standing tripod to tripod at Andrews Air Force Base to witness the Secretary of Defense's routine departure for a NATO meeting, or to cover S. I. Hayakawa's, Abbie Hoffman's or George Wallace's latest news conference, often says more about the news gatherers than it does about the news makers. Such events have news value more because they illustrate the fact that the profession must repeatedly commit its best troops to the urgent rather than to the important in order to avoid being scooped. The price for such overkill is often paid by missing truly significant stories.

At University of Michigan, Ann Arbor/
The National Observer, 4-19:10.

Gerhard A. Gesell
Judge, United States District
Court for the District of Columbia

(Regarding the publication of secret Pentagon papers on U.S. involvement in Vietnam): Our democracy depends for its future on the informed will of the majority, and it is the purpose and effect of the First Amendment to expose to the public the maximum amount of information on which sound judgment can be made by the electorate. The equities favor disclosure, not suppression . . . In interpreting the First Amendment, there is no basis upon which the court may adjust it to accommodate the desires of foreign governments dealing with our diplomats, nor does the First Amendment guarantee our diplomats that they can be protected against either responsible or irresponsible reporting . . . There is not here a showing of an immediate grave threat to the national security which in close and narrowly-defined circumstances would justify prior restraint on publications.

Ruling denying injunction against publication
of the secret papers by "The Washington Post,"
Washington, June 21/
The New York Times, 6-22:18.

Julian Goodman
President, National Broadcasting Company

Freedom of information in a democracy

(JULIAN GOODMAN)

means just that—total, unqualified freedom. You cannot say it applies here but not there; at this time but not another. You cannot remove a part of it without threatening—and ultimately compromising—all of it. When that happens, no matter how you cover it up, you no longer have freedom of information. The regulators of broadcasting in the U.S. have set out to expand freedom by restrictions and guidelines. The result is a tangle of contradictions George Orwell would appreciate—restriction is freedom; stepping back is going forward; supervision promotes independence; a concept called the Fairness Doctrine justifies official second-guessing of news judgment.

Before Canadian Association of Broadcasters, Montreal, April 21/ The Hollywood Reporter, 4-21:1.

Erwin N. Griswold
Solicitor General of the United States

Many of the younger people in the press are not content to be observers. The press is a great part of our social structure. It has played an important and critical role in many ways. But the press will not serve its purpose unless it reports the facts. If it seeks these (First Amendment) privileges for the purpose of carrying on propaganda, it will not serve its purpose.

At State Bar of Georgia press seminar, Atlanta, Dec. 3/ San Francisco Examiner, 12-4:4.

Murray I. Gurfein
Judge, United States District Court for the Southern District of New York

(Regarding *The New York Times*' publishing secret Pentagon papers on U.S. involvement in Vietnam): The First Amendment concept of a "free press" must be read in the light of the struggle of free men against prior restraint of publication. From the time of Blackstone, it was a tenet of the founding fathers that precensorship was the primary evil to be dealt with in the First Amendment. Fortunately, upon the facts adduced in this case, there is no sharp clash such as might have appeared between the vital security interest of the nation and the compelling Constitutional doctrine against prior restraint. If there be some embarrassment to the government in security aspects as remote as the general embarrassment that flows from any security breach, we must learn to live with it. The security of the nation is not at the ramparts alone. Security also lies in the value of our free institutions. A cantankerous press, an obstinate press, a ubiquitous press must be suffered by those in authority in order to preserve the even greater values of freedom of expression and the right of the people to know.

New York, June 19/ The Wall Street Journal, 6-22:18.

H. R. Haldeman
Assistant to the President of the United States

There's a great deal of (news) reporting and editing and presentation that tends to slant one way or another, and I don't think there's any way to avoid that as long as human beings are writing stories and editing them and writing the headlines and so on. The hope would be that you would have an equal balance of bias, so that there would be as much bias for as against . . . I don't think there's any substantial amount of willful distortion or intentional distortion of a story. I do think there is an inevitable selectivity process, and there's an inevitable tendency for any individual, including a reporter, to believe what he wants to believe or what he thinks he already believes.

Interview, Washington/ The Christian Science Monitor, 10-15:2.

Paul Harvey
News commentator, American Broadcasting Company

News isn't news any more. It's hour-by-hour warnings.

Before Association of County Commissioners of Georgia, Macon/Variety, 4-28:50.

A. Andrew Hauk
United States District Judge for
the Central District of California

The duty, and incidentally the glory, of the free press is to report events accurately; that is, to let the people know what actually occurs, not to record or film a contrived spectacular. It is to report the news, and not to stage "happenings" or to publicize "non-events." And that is the essence of a free press.

Los Angeles, April 26/
Los Angeles Times, 4-28:(2)6.

F. Edward Hebert
United States Representative, D–La.

(Regarding the CBS-TV documentary, *The Selling of the Pentagon*): In no way do I assume that the news media is out of bounds by criticizing the Pentagon. As a former newspaper editor, I know that no segment of the government is, or should be, free from severe criticism by the news media. And it would be hard to find anybody in Washington who has issued more public criticism of the Pentagon than I have over the last 30 years. But presentations which are biased throughout, which are slanted to only use language and items which support that bias, and which clearly make false innuendos about individuals in order to prove the bias—such presentations detract from the media's function of being a true critic of society and make it more difficult for worthwhile criticism to be presented and accepted.

Human Events, 6-12:8.

William P. Hobby
President and editor,
"The Houston Post"

Telling the truth is frequently unpopular, and because the newspaperman guards this always-troubled frontier of truth, he is often at odds with constituted authority.

Houston/
The Dallas Times Herald, 10-8:(A)23.

J. Edgar Hoover
Director,
Federal Bureau of Investigation

Incredible as it may seem there have been instances in which the news media, particularly television, have accepted without question wildly improbable allegations made by hate groups against the police and, even when the facts have been readily accessible, certain segments of the media have, for whatever reason, chosen to ignore and disregard them. Unfortunately, the truth never seems to catch up with the "big lie," and even if it does, it is too late to undo the harm that has been done in denigrating the forces of law enforcement. The publication of drivel—while admittedly a right—is not the best way of discharging the precious responsibilities of a free press. Criticism, of course, is essential in our democratic society . . . but criticism, to be valid, must be based on knowledge and a desire to correct deficiencies. The foundation of any news media should be truth, objectivity and justice.

Before Washington chapter,
Society of Former Special Agents
of the FBI, Oct. 22/
The Washington Post, 11-16:(A)18.

Hubert H. Humphrey
United States Senator, D–Minn.

The public airwaves are repeatedly usurped by the President (Nixon) for partisan advantage, while lesser lights in the Administration are dispatched to attack and intimidate the network news organizations.

At Democratic conference on the
issues of 1972, Washington, March 24/
The Dallas Times Herald, 3-24:(A)6.

Chet Huntley
Former news commentator,
National Broadcasting Company

Right now, press conferences are beautifully made for the President to use to his own advantage. I'd like to see a President say, for instance, at the end of a question on Viet-

(CHET HUNTLEY)

nam: "Are there any more questions on Vietnam before we go on?"

News conference, San Francisco,
Jan. 11/
The Dallas Times Herald, 1-13:(AA)5.

Richard W. Jencks
President, Columbia Broadcasting
System Broadcast Group

. . . spurred by enthusiasm for access theories and by the increasingly shrill demands of partisans for a line-by-line and word-by-word accounting of fairness and balance obligations, I am afraid that the nation is moving toward the concept of a broadcast press which would increasingly be a common carrier of other people's views, with no creative or vigorous voice of its own. We may continue in this direction; but if we do, we will increasingly have, in my judgment, a broadcast press without purpose, without passion, which shuns tough issues and does not lead but merely presides.

Before Federal Communications Bar
Association, Washington, June 16/
The New York Times, 6-17:75.

Oliver Jensen
Editor, "American Heritage" magazine

Extremism is a symptom of the times, because people are impatient and angry about many things. And TV has made it possible to be an instant success as an extremist. If you're a TV newsman, and you know (NAACP executive director) Roy Wilkins will be calm and reasonable, you go cover the Stokely Carmichael show.

Los Angeles Herald-Examiner,
4-24:(A)11.

Herbert G. Klein
Director of Communications for
the President of the United States

We've heard that we're trying to intimidate the reporters of the news industry. But I can tell you as one who's had a great number of press conferences, I've yet to meet the first intimidated reporter, and I hope I never will.

Before North Carolina Association
of Broadcasters, Asheville, Oct. 19/
The Dallas Times Herald, 10-20:(A)13.

The most rapid information in the world today, I think, goes by the young people's grapevine. And you can find a false story in one sentence in a New York City radical newspaper and you'll read it in San Francisco three days later being printed in bigger form. And they believe it once they've read it in their papers. Another thing that bothers me: I think there's too little checking of facts by the news media today. Something erroneous will be printed and it gets into the newspaper libraries and I find it popping up over and over—each time more positive, and all the time it's wrong.

Interview, Washington/
U.S. News & World Report, 11-15:74.

John S. Knight
Chairman, Knight Newspapers

. . . the name of the game in Washington and in every state and local community is to raise serious doubts about the credibility of the press. In large part, the aspersions cast upon us by the Vice President (Agnew) and other disgruntled public officials are calculated to make us unbelievable to the general public. We should, I think, accept such criticism philosophically, while endeavoring to set the record straight at all times. An editor, who must or should take editorial positions on the great issues of the day, is not meant to be loved. If he seeks affection and popularity, he should be in public relations. Newspapermen who formulate policy must base their conclusions upon the facts at hand. The unvarnished truth is frequently unpleasant reading since it so often differs from the reader's preconceived notions of what the truth should be.

Before City Club,
Charlotte, N.C.,
September/Parade, 11-7:8.

Elmer W. Lower
President,
American Broadcasting Company News

If the journalist is forced to betray information obtained in confidence, whatever the immediate short-term gain for law enforcement, the long-term effect is to dry up valuable sources of information and to severely restrict the flow of information to the public.

Before Senate Subcommittee on
Constitutional Rights, Washington,
Oct. 14/The New York Times, 10-15:9.

Torbert MacDonald
United States Representative, D—Mass.

The favorite indoor sport in Washington today is a game called "kick the media." As you all know, this is a game played regularly by high Administration officials and members of Congress. The goal is "instant headlines." No special equipment or knowledge is necessary to play the game. A favorite stratagem in this game is to kick the media by blaming it for the current ills of society.

Before Southern CATV Association,
Memphis, April 5/Daily Variety, 4-6:13.

Mike Mansfield
United States Senator, D—Mont.

All the (broadcast) networks have been doing a good job, as has the press, and I hope . . . constant criticism will not have the effect of intimidating the networks . . . I think the press, radio, television and the Fourth Estate in general should have the protection of the First Amendment, which includes the right of free press and free speech and the right to report the news as they see it and contemplate it. After all, they are on the spot. If the news is biased, intemperate and untrue, they will pay a penalty by engendering a lack of confidence on the part of the public. I think the people can determine whether they should have confidence in the news media. They don't have to watch television; they don't have to read newspapers.

News conference, Washington, 3-20/
San Francisco Examiner & Chronicle,
3-21:(A)1.

Frank McGee
News commentator,
National Broadcasting Company

It is absolutely vital that the people understand that you cannot censor the press. You can only censor the people. And when (Vice President Spiro) Agnew, or anybody like him, directly or indirectly attempts to intimidate and thereby alter the way news is presented, he doesn't give a damn about me and what I say. He's not trying to censor me. He's trying to censor the people. And they're the only ones who count. The freedom that the First Amendment guarantees is not my personal property. It was put in there for the benefit of the people. And it's crucial that they understand this and realize who has the most to gain by lying to the people—a reporter or a politician? The precise moment that Mr. Agnew has any effect whatsoever on how *I* do any news story, including a story about him, he will, in part, have achieved his purpose.

Interview/Look, 10-5:13.

C. A. McKnight
Editor, "Charlotte (N.C.) Observer"

(Regarding the publishing of secret Pentagon papers on U.S. involvement in Vietnam): I would not presume to second-guess the editors of *The New York Times* on their decision to print the Pentagon documents; but I have very definite ideas on another issue that has arisen. I am appalled at this exercise of prior-restraint censorship by the government. At the same time, I agree with the decision of *The New York Times* to obey the temporary Federal court restraining order. I have great faith in our Federal courts, and I am confident that this unprecedented effort at government censorship will ultimately clarify still further the responsibility of a free press in a free society.

The New York Times, 6-17:19.

William E. Marshall
United States Representative, R—Ohio

Many of us have witnessed television and radio crews actually encouraging and even re-

(WILLIAM E. MINSHALL)

hearsing demonstrations by protestors, or recording only one point of view at Congressional hearings. We have seen the actual meaning of an interview distorted, even turned about-face, by sequences cleverly taken out of context. I shall always vigorously protect the freedom of the news media. By the same token, I shall with equal vigor protect the right of the American public to know the truth. The two are not—and should not be permitted to become—incompatible.

Washington, March 30/
The New York Times, 3-31:78.

John N. Mitchell
Attorney General of the United States

(Regarding the news media): We find emotion and intuition in the saddle, while truth is trampled in the dust.

At Southern Methodist University,
April 30/The New York Times, 5-1:21.

Edward P. Morgan
News commentator,
American Broadcasting Company

We in the news media are so crisis-oriented —and, particularly in the United States, so profit-oriented—that unless an event is bizarre, sensational or controversial, it doesn't have much chance. If Martha Mitchell (wife of the U.S. Attorney General) posed as Jeanne d'Arc for the centerfold of *Playboy* magazine, there might be some interest in it.

Panel discussion at Washington
and the Arts conference, Washington,
May 25/The Washington Post, 5-26:(C)1.

Frank Moss
United States Senator, D—Utah

(Explaining that he favors the First Amendment rights of broadcasting):—The right to develop, shape and disseminate news and public-affairs programming, free of the yoke of bureaucratic harassment, free of the chilling threat of Congressional process and free of the surge toward thought control by an Adminis-

tration paranoid with fear, suspicion and loathing of a free and undomesticated press.

Washington, May 24/
Daily Variety, 5-25:11.

J. Edward Murray
President-elect, American
Society of Newspaper Editors

(Regarding the publishing by several newspapers of secret Pentagon papers on U.S. involvement in Vietnam): (While not) privy to the inner councils where, I am sure, many considerations, including national security, were weighed before a decision to print was made, I am confident . . . that the men who made those decisions . . . are just as loyal, just as patriotic as any man in this room or in the White House . . . I think our (newspapers') truth record in the Vietnam war is better than that of the Executive branch. And I hope one by-product of publication of the (Pentagon) papers will be to restore public confidence in the traditional axiom that you can believe what you read in your newspaper.

Before House Government Information
Subcommittee, Washington, June 25/
San Francisco Examiner, 6-25:4.

Wade Nichols
Editor,
"Good Housekeeping" magazine

The death of every established magazine I've known anything about in over 30 years has had precisely the same cause—the incapacity, lack of commitment or just plain stupidity and greed of top management.

Los Angeles Times, 9-19:(H)1.

Richard M. Nixon
President of the United States

. . . nowadays they (young reporters) don't care about fairness; it's the "in" thing to forget objectivity and let your prejudices show. You can see it in my press conferences all the time. You read the (John) Kennedy press conferences and see how soft and gentle they were with him, and then you read mine. I never get any easy questions—and I don't want any. I am quite aware that ideologically the Washington press corps doesn't agree with me. I expect it. I think the people can judge for themselves when they watch one of my press conferences. It's all there. I can tell you this: As long as I am in this office, the press will never irritate me, never affect me, never push me to any move I don't think is wise . . .

Interview, San Clemente, Calif.,
March 30/Look, 10-19:52.

I'm not like Lyndon (Johnson, former President) as regards the press—we're two different people. The press was like a magnet to him. He'd read every single thing that was critical. He'd watch the news on TV all the time. And then he'd get mad. I never get mad. I expect I have one of the most hostile and unfair presses that any President has ever had; but I've developed a philosophical attitude about it. I developed it early. I have won all my political battles with 80 to 90 per cent of the press against me. How have I done it? I ignored the press and went to the people. I have never called a publisher, never called an editor, never called a reporter, on the carpet. I don't care. And you know?—that's what makes them mad. That's what infuriates them. I just don't care. I just don't raise the roof with them. And that gets them.

Interview, San Clemente, Calif.,
March 30/Look, 10-19:52.

(Addressing news correspondents): Don't give me a friendly question. Only a hard, tough question gets the kind of an answer—you may not like it—but it is the only one that tests the man. And it is the responsibility of the members of the press to test the man, whoever he is. You have done that. You have met that responsibility. And I, of course, will try in my own way to meet mine . . . I benefit from your probing, from your criticism. And if I succeed, that means that—if the country succeeds in these great goals also—it will be due not simply because of what I did or my advisers helped me to do, but will then be due in great part to the fact that the members of the press examined searchingly everything that I suggested, every recommendation

that I made . . . so thanks for giving me that heat. And remember, I like the kitchen. Keep it up.

Before White House Correspondents
Association, Washington, May 8/
The Boston Globe, 7-1:4.

Robert (Shad) Northshield
Executive producer, National
Broadcasting Company News

Every day, news on television demonstrates that our technology is way ahead of our consciousness. It proves that things happen before we are conditioned to accept them. It shows us things which are bad. But good or bad or dull, the reporting of news is essential. Newsmen, when they are good, tell what's going on, what's happened. We don't, when we're good, tell anyone what to do about it. We deal with what is significant, and that often is not happy. We deal with change, because that's what news is.

Before Knox College graduating class/
Variety, 6-9:1.

Newbold Noyes
Editor, "The Washington Star";
President, American Society of
Newspaper Editors

. . . we of the press are allowing ourselves to be manipulated by various interests—some for change and some against it; some powerfully in support of the system, some destructively seeking to tear it down; all clever in the business of playing on our weaknesses, our laziness, our superficiality, our gullibility. In this process of letting the kooks on both sides determine for us what constitutes tomorrow's news—and the kookier their activity, the bigger the news—in this process . . . we are giving our readers a view of society and its problems that even we know to be false. Can we blame our readers for sensing that something is wrong with our performance?

Before American Society of Newspaper
Editors, Washington, April 14/
Los Angeles Times, 4-15:(1)12.

Charles A. Perlik, Jr.
President, American Newspaper Guild

Once the public's right-to-know is abridged by governmental censorship of the press and denial of information to its elected representatives, two consequences are inevitable, both of them equally disastrous to a free society. We become, to the extent of that abridgement, less of a representative democracy than we profess to be. And the credibility of the press and, more important, the government itself, is destroyed.

Before House Government Information Subcommittee, Washington, June 25/ San Francisco Examiner, 6-25:4.

Paul A. Porter
Former Chairman, Federal Communications Commission of the United States

I have at long last become weary of the constant refrain that "the airwaves belong to the people." Of course, they do. But this should not become a cliche to support any small group, either on the right or left, claiming to act in the people's name to throttle free expression of opinion or responsible reporting on the people's air. Broadcasting has, I think, reached a state of maturity where it can be trusted.

At Peabody Awards luncheon, New York, April 21/ The New York Times, 4-22:83.

Dan Rather
News correspondent, Columbia Broadcasting System

(Regarding Presidential use of the broadcasting medium): Kennedy, who was the ground-breaker, had the knowhow but not the determination. Johnson had the determination but not the knowhow. Nixon, however, has both.

Variety, 3-3:35.

Harry Reasoner
News commentator, American Broadcasting Company

I like to read the news. I have a great deal of pride in doing it professionally. But I'd say that if you were an old-time talent scout and intended to select the men who would get (audience) acceptance, you'd never have selected David Brinkley, Walter Cronkite or me. In the old days, you would have looked for Gregory Peck or Henry Fonda. What's happened is that the real reporters have surfaced. It is a very natural development.

Interview, New York/ San Francisco Examiner & Chronicle (Datebook), 5-2:13.

There is only one proper place for journalism in relation to government, or for that matter, to any special group. That is arm's length, or maybe a few inches longer. And there is only one professional position for one journalistic organization in relation to others, and that is unremitting competition in finding out the news and unassailable unity in defending the right to get it.

The Dallas Times Herald (TV Times), 6-13:50.

Good, objective reportage often writes its own editorial.

At Southwest Journalism Forum, Southern Methodist University, Oct. 22/ The Dallas Times Herald, 10-24:(A)13.

George E. Reedy
Former Press Secretary to the President of the United States

Actually, Presidents really don't have "press problems." What they have are political problems. But there's a very natural human tendency to confuse bad news with the man who brings the bad news. And when political leaders start thinking in those terms, it is the press that they blame rather than the intractable world that isn't going to go along with their finest schemes and their plans and their dreams.

New York/The Dallas Times Herald, 4-11:(A)6.

Elton H. Rule
President, American Broadcasting Company

Today, more than ever, the controversy

(over TV news) rages. The reason is simple. There is much bad news. TV shows reality in a vivid, uncompromising way . . . TV is too often the scapegoat when the images it shows are less than the image of Snow White. Many would rather their mirror on the world was a mirror that said: "You are the fairest of them all"—no matter what it reflected . . . One result of the current climate is the feeling that somewhere, under pressure, an egg is about to hatch. Out will come an electronic ostrich. This electronic ostrich will keep its head in the sand and its tail in the blue sky. What it showed its viewers would be carefully pre-screened and pre-controlled by some pre-selected censor. It would drug the brain and lull the senses. Of course, it would not change reality; it would not alter truth.

Before ABC affiliates, Los Angeles,
May 3/Daily Variety, 5-4:9.

Government attempts to suppress publication of the (secret Pentagon) Vietnam papers by *The New York Times* and *The Washington Post* are further examples of the highest official pressure against the guarantees of the First Amendment. This is a time for every member of the journalistic fraternity—whether his tools be typewriter, microphone or television camera—to respond to the alarm quickly, firmly and effectively by insisting on the Constitutional right of a free press to function and a free public to be fully informed.

June 22/The Hollywood Reporter, 6-23:9.

Richard S. Salant
President,
Columbia Broadcasting System News

(Regarding the House Commerce Investigations Subcommittee inquiry into the CBS documentary, *The Selling of the Pentagon*): There have been lots of words on what the Congressional investigation and the subpoena are all about. But when you cut through all the words, it comes down to one stark fact: The government, through a legislative committee, proposes to sit in judgment on our editing and our accuracy; it proposes to decide whether we have met its notions of proper

journalism. The First Amendment does not discriminate between good intruders and bad intruders.

At Boston University School
of Public Communication, April 28/
The Washington Post, 4-29:(F)11.

Pierre Salinger
Former Press Secretary to the
President of the United States

If there is one certain fact about the relationship between the press and the Presidency, that fact is that the relationship will be hostile.

Los Angeles Times, 4-11:(A)2.

Dwight E. Sargent
Curator of Nieman Fellowships,
Harvard University

The jet-age newspaper preaches to more people than American preachers, argues with more people than American lawyers, reaches more people than American politicians, educates more people than American educators, spends more time on information—as against entertainment—than television and radio combined, and talks with more people than all of America's bartenders and, I might add, does so in an atmosphere of sobriety.

At Wayne State University, Detroit/
Quote, 8-22:182.

John Scali
News correspondent,
American Broadcasting Company

I'm a firm believer in telling the truth when the news is bad. In that way, you have more people ready to believe you when you tell them the news is good.

Newsweek, 4-19:95.

Walter A. Schwartz
President,
American Broadcasting Company Radio

By today's standards of judgment, had a radio and television crew been around to cover the firing on Fort Sumter, the networks

(WALTER A. SCHWARTZ)

would have been blamed for starting the Civil War.

Before South Carolina Broadcasters Association, Columbia, Feb. 17/ Los Angeles Times, 2-19:(4)18.

John Searle
Professor of Philosophy, University of California at Berkeley; Member, President's Advisory Commission on Campus Unrest

I watch television news not to find out what's happening, but what *other people think is happening.* Any time you're personally involved in a news event—as I have been at Berkeley—and then you later see it on television, you're often struck by the fact that, somehow, they just didn't get the story quite straight. There's a structural reason for that. TV news departments are in the business of providing dramatic entertainment based on current events, not pictures of an independent reality. If they did, the news programs would be dull.

Interview/TV Guide, 1-30:8.

Rod Serling
Writer

. . . we have our President (Richard Nixon) somewhat soulfully acknowledging that he is the least popular President when it comes to his treatment at the hands of the press. He accuses the news media of deliberately and predatorially distorting facts in some kind of vast network of subversion. To President Nixon I would simply say that he is far from being the least popular President, nor has he received any unduly harsh treatment from the press. For historical proof of this, he need only look back to Lincoln, Wilson or Harry Truman, just to name a few. These gentlemen were pilloried, pounced upon and nailed to the wall . . . I submit to you that it is the job of the press to question, to embarrass, to drag out the truth by its ears.

At Emerson College, Boston/ Variety, 6-16:28.

William Shawn
Editor, "The New Yorker" magazine

Is *The New Yorker* "with it"? No. Being "with it" means running after somebody else's fashionable "it." We've never been interested in that. The aim of *The New Yorker* is to report on, comment on and cast light on what's happening in the world, and to do it with grace and with style. Is *The New Yorker* set in its ways? No. It's constantly changing. The changes have come about gradually, not through any specific intention but through the changing interests of the magazine's artists, writers and editors, including me. What remains the same is our standards and our principles. We publish more material today that deals with the issues and problems of our times than we did 20, 15 or even 10 years ago. It would be sheer affectation to take a 1920s attitude, or even a 1960s attitude, toward the 1970s.

Interview, New York/ The Washington Post, 3-7:(D)3.

Neil Sheehan
News correspondent, "The New York Times"

Ours is not the highest of callings. We (journalists) do not serve humanity with the selflessness of the priest or the life-saving gift of the physician. We frequently do evil. We publish falsehood, our own and that of others. We bring pain and embarrassment to those who are named in our often erroneous accounts of events. In his decision in June of 1971 upholding our right to publish the "Pentagon Papers" (on U.S. involvement in Vietnam), Judge Murray Gurfein of New York spoke of "a cantankerous press, an obstinate press, a ubiquitous press." Those are not pleasant words, and I suspect that Judge Gurfein did not mean them to be entirely complimentary. Yet I choose to regard them as one of the finest compliments that can be paid free journalists. For those words imply that, whatever our faults, we seek, when we can, to do our duty as we see that duty to the best of our ability.

Those words imply that, whatever evil we do, we do a greater good.

Accepting Drew Pearson Prize,
Washington, Dec. 13/
The Washington Post, 12-14:(B)4.

William Sheehan
Vice President and director of news,
American Broadcasting Company
Television

I have never experienced what I consider improper pressure from the White House. Never has there been a threat. It is perfectly proper for the White House Press Secretary to take exception to a story; but it's never been anything beyond that.

Los Angeles, May 5/
Daily Variety, 5-6:13.

J. Kelly Sisk
Publisher,
"Greenville (S.C.) News"

There is a new movement whose members call themselves "The New Journalists." Their basic argument is that the reporter has the right to render judgments from the facts he gathers. To do less, these newsmen say, reduces the reporter to the status of a moral eunuch. It is impossible, they say, to put simple unvarnished facts into perspective. It is necessary, they contend, to put their independent intelligence to work to wrest meaning from the torrent of events. Total objectivity is impossible, they say, because all men have opinions which get in the way of objectivity. What they apparently do not recognize is that there is considerable difference between having an opinion and imposing that opinion on someone else. These New Journalists are not content to be observers. They are determined to exert an influence, to be opinion-makers. They are not content to express their opinions on editorial pages or during editorial air time. They insist they have a moral commitment to decide what is truth and present it as fact. Beware of the man who speaks of moral commitment. Inevitably, he is the man who has bought a point of view. He is then no longer a reporter. He is a propagandist. I don't think

this is right. I don't think this is a newsman's job. I also don't think the bulk of the newsmen in this nation agree with the New Journalists' position. Most of them still prefer to think of objectivity as (their) goal. To be sure, it is harder to be objective than to be opinionated; but that difficulty goes with the job. Unfortunately, the voices heard from the nation's news media most often are the voices of the New Journalists. And as they are the only ones heard, it is no wonder that some public officials have found most responsive audiences for their attacks on the media.

At Clemson University, Feb. 11/
Vital Speeches, 4-15:406.

Harley O. Staggers
United States Representative, D–W.Va.

(Regarding his investigation of the CBS-TV documentary, *The Selling of the Pentagon*): The sole question under inquiry here is one which is clear, definite and objectively ascertainable. That is, are the producers of television news documentary programs engaging in factually false and misleading filming and editing practices, consisting of rearranging, staging or misrepresenting events, giving viewers an erroneous impression that what they are seeing has really happened, or that it happened in the way and under circumstances in which it was shown?

News conference, Washington, April 20/
The Washington Post, 4-21:(A)3.

(Regarding the refusal of CBS to provide film clips relating to their TV documentary, *The Selling of the Pentagon*): No segment of the broadcasting industry has the right to insist that its affairs be held sacrosanct and immune from public scrutiny and criticism. It seems somewhat ironical to me that the First Amendment—that great guarantor of the people's right to know—should now be raised as a bar to a public inquiry.

At House Commerce Investigations
Subcommittee hearing, Washington/
The Christian Science Monitor, 6-29:8.

Frank Stanton
President,
Columbia Broadcasting System

(Regarding a House subcommittee subpoena of material connected with the CBS-TV documentary, *The Selling of the Pentagon*): We at CBS have rejected, in principle and in fact, this government invasion of this country's oldest and most fundamental freedoms—and we have rejected it totally . . . We will take every step necessary and open to us to resist this unwarranted action of a Congressional committee and to keep broadcast journalism free of government surveillance. Too much is at stake for us to do less.
Los Angeles/Variety, 4-28:40.

Stuart Symington
United States Senator, D–Mo.

The Vietnam war is the first war ever to be covered by television. It is a new kind of actuality reporting, presenting to the entire public the immediate realities of battle, the reactions of troops in the field, the unofficial as well as the official versions of strategies, tactics and their effects; the version of events given by military and governmental officials compared with actual results. The novelty of this type of presentation—that is, placing the unfiltered view of events on a level with the official picture—may be unsettling to policymakers who have never confronted this problem before. But it meets a basic principle in our system; namely, that the right of the public to independent information about government action is superior to the desire of government officials to protect their policies. This issue will not be resolved by criticizing the media. In due course, the facts invariably turn up to speak for themselves; and such criticism will not make the public more willing to believe the government. The government will be believed only when it demonstrates that it is willing to be exposed to the light of honest independent journalism—to accept the criticism as well as seek the praise.
Before the Senate, Washington/
The Wall Street Journal, 5-12:14.

Vincent T. Wasilewski
President,
National Association of Broadcasters

There have been suggestions that broadcasting news is such an important element in the total news function that it should be subject to government surveillance in order to assure its "objectivity." Apparently, the reasoning goes that the more important the service, the greater the need for surveillance; the more important the service, the less that service is entitled to First Amendment protection. In our judgment, that is precisely backwards—a mirror image of the situation. In our judgment, the more important the news service, the more important it be free from government control . . .
Before Broadcast Advertising Club
of Chicago/Variety, 5-26:26.

Av Westin
Executive producer, American
Broadcasting Company Television News

I think television news is an illustrated headline service which can function best when it is regarded by its viewers as an important yet fast adjunct to the newspapers. I know what we have to leave out; and if people do not read newspapers, news magazines and books, they are desperately uninformed.
The New York Times, 11-12:82.

Charles W. Whalen, Jr.
United States Representative, R–Ohio

There have been attempts during the last year to bring into the courts the notes, unedited film and tapes of newspaper and television reporters. Such actions clearly are a threat to freedom of the press and the time-honored right of newsmen to protect confidential sources . . . In my view, too few people—including the press itself—are reacting sufficiently to the threat to the free and uninhibited functioning of the American press and to the First Amendment guarantees upon which its independence is based. It will be too late to cry "fire" when the barn is already burned to the ground.
Before the House, Washington, Feb. 10/
The Washington Post, 3-21:(B)6.

Tom Wicker
Associate Editor,
"The New York Times"

We are . . . being told at exalted levels that the American press has something of a Marxist function—that it's our duty to serve the interests of the state. More specifically and absurdly, that it's our duty to serve the interests of a briefly-authorized national Administration and of a particular policy. Let's make it clear—and I believe we never have fully done so—that the press of America is not an adjunct of politics or an appendage of the government, but an estate of its own, with its own responsibilities and its own commitments.

At Robert F. Kennedy Journalism
Awards, Washington, April 28/
The Washington Post, 4-29:(F)1.

J. Russell Wiggins
Editor and publisher,
Ellsworth (Maine) "American"

Facts were never at a higher premium in the market-place of ideas than they are today. Facts were never more elusive, complicated and evasive. Facts were never more needed, never harder to come by. The foremost political, economic and social controversies (of) our day cry out aloud for facts. When a reader finds a single, solitary, undisputed, indubitable, inescapable and undebatable fact gleaming like a lost needle in a haystack of windy rhetoric, he is likely to be overcome.

Before New England Press Association,
Boston/The Wall Street Journal, 6-21:8.

Thomas Winship
Editor, "The Boston Globe"

I'd like to give my definition of "objectivity." Objectivity is what we gave Joe McCarthy before a great group of reporters took their gloves off, and before Ed Murrow's TV show. Objectivity is what we gave cancer-producing cigarettes before the Surgeon General's report. Objectivity let the most unexplained war in history go on without challenge until one-and-a-half million people were killed. Objectivity let industrial wastage almost clobber to death the face of America; Ralph Nader and Rachel Carson blew the whistle, not our great newspapers. That's our definition of "objectivity." I say it's spinach and I say to hell with it . . . We all know why objectivity as a debate is on the American Association of Newspaper Editors' dance card this year. It's because ever since (Vice President) Agnew yipped at us, many editors have been more "objective" than ever. I call it a nice, quiet backslide. Objectivity is such a nice trip for an editor. Every morning he swallows his little objectivity pill. It turns him off from all that paranoia among the long-haired kids in the city room who whisper dirty talk over the water cooler—words like "Nader," "Hanoi" and "Panther." Objectivity is a code word for playing it safe, covering up and superficiality.

Before American Society of Newspaper
Editors, Washington/
The National Observer, 7-12:15.

Ronald L. Ziegler
Press Secretary to the
President of the United States

In the last two years, people have been suggesting the (Nixon) Administration has an intent to intimidate the press. This is not our intent. We respect the free press. But just as government should be criticized and should be self-critical, criticism of the press in itself does not suggest intimidation. In my personal view, there has been too much sensitivity by the press.

News conference, Washington, Sept. 28/
The New York Times, 9-29:58.

Literature

Conrad Aiken
Poet

This is a very bad period for poetry writing now. Young poets today are given to too much fragmentation which doesn't really relate to anything but themselves.

Interview, Brewster, Mass./
The Boston Globe, 7-10:5.

W. H. Auden
Poet

What now seems to happen is this appalling thing of artists asking themselves, "Is this relevant for 1971?" Well, it may be important what I wrote at the age of 64, but it's absolutely unimportant what I write in 1971. This slavery to the moment is far more tyrannous than any other constructions I can think of. The artist ceases to ask the personal question of "What is right for me to do?" and asks instead, "What is right for 1971?"

Interview, London/
The New York Times, 10-19:52.

Saul Bellow
Author

There is today an extraordinary interest with the data of modern experience per se. Our absorption in our contemporary historical state is very high right now. It's not altogether unlike a similar situation in 17th-century Holland, where wealthy merchants wanted their portraits done with all their blemishes included. It is the height of egotism, in a sense, to think even one's blemishes are of significance. So today, Americans seem to want their writers to reveal all their weaknesses, their meannesses, to celebrate their very confusions. And they want it in the most direct possible way—they want it served up neat, as it were, without the filtering and generalizing power of fiction. The truth is, we've not really developed a fiction that can accommodate the full

tumult, the zaniness and crazed quality, of modern experience. Some of us continue to work at it. Others have turned away, at least for now. But of course, even the non-fiction successes of writers like Truman Capote and Norman Mailer would have been unthinkable without their novelistic antecedents—and here I am talking about these writers' training as novelists and their audiences' experience as readers of novels.

Interview, Chicago/The New York
Times Book Review, 5-9:14.

Anthony Burgess
Author

I am a bad reader. I think most writers are bad readers. We just cannot immerse ourselves in a book. Our own thoughts get in the way; we start thinking what we would do if we had the book to write ourselves.

Interview/The Washington Post
(Book World), 3-21:2.

Melville Cane
Poet

You can't set hours and then write by the clock. You catch it on the fly, and at most inconvenient times. I might be sitting here and looking out of the window and suddenly see something moving or static that gives me a feeling of wanting to express it. I might make notes here of my immediate impressions, and then go home or off in the country and develop it.

Interview, New York, March 29/
The New York Times, 3-30:24.

Agatha Christie
Author

I get some of my best ideas for stories while doing some monotonous chore around the house. As a matter of fact, some of my best plots have come to me at the sink.

San Francisco Examiner & Chronicle (This World), 12-12:38.

Robertson Davies
Author; Master of Massey College, University of Toronto

One thing I am very proud of is the fact that I have never received any kind of handout or grant. Any awards I got came along after I was well and truly started. When I look at the government of my country, I would rather die than accept money from it. I do not think people ought to take this kind of governmental assistance unless they need it terribly. This kind of help may be fine for the performing arts, because they are so expensive. But you cannot give somebody some money and say, "Write a good book." It just doesn't work that way.

Interview/Publishers' Weekly, 4-5:23.

Paul Engle
Writer; Director, University of Iowa Writers' Workshop

The most difficult attribute for beginning writers to acquire is self-criticism. They must learn to commit a critical act on their own work, develop that sense of the difference between "interesting material" and creative art. Too often, writers feel that the subject is enough. But it's what happens to the material when an imaginative intelligence works with it that's important—the focused eye of the talent. Writers must learn that art is something made, not revealed.

Interview, Asilomar, Calif./ San Francisco Examiner & Chronicle (This World), 7-18:34.

Theodor Geisel (Dr. Suess)
Author

. . . I do not want to write for adults, even though writing for children is harder. Adult humor today in this country is based on superiority, contempt, even meanness.

Interview, La Jolla, Calif./ Los Angeles Times, 8-30:(4)8.

Graham Greene
Author

(Regarding his writing): I generally have the beginning, the middle and the end in my head, and hope that there are some surprises in between to amuse myself. The end sometimes alters; one's got to leave enough liberty to one's characters; one can't be absolutely sure what point they'll have reached at the end of the book. At the opening of a book, one is thinking of the mood in which the whole book will move—the signature tune. In something written as an entertainment, one wants a quick mood, to excite the reader, keep him on the edge of his chair. For a book that is going to be slightly brooding, I think one wants to prepare by a slow movement at the beginning. For depressed moods, it becomes very unpleasant writing.

Interview, Antibes, France/The New York Times Book Review, 9-12:2.

Joseph Heller
Author

I write very slowly. I can't go on with a page if there's anything in the page I've just written I feel can be improved. It's not that I'm aiming at immortality, or even aiming at good reviews. When I'm writing it, I forget everything except me and the work. That may be why I have a work span of about two hours a day with fiction. After two hours I'm exhausted, and my mind runs completely dry. It may be because it engrosses me so thoroughly. When it comes to rewriting, I can go eight hours a day. It's my work and I love it.

Interview/ The Washington Post, 8-25:(C)2.

James D. Hodgson
Secretary of Labor of the United States

I am an unabashed Anglophile when it comes to arts and letters. I suppose there is a maturity, a humor and a grace about British fiction and poetry that I admire tremendously. I can recall, immediately after World War II, when my wife and I began married life together, that one of my great joys was read-

447

(JAMES D. HODGSON)

ing in succession the principal works of British authors such as Huxley, Evelyn Waugh and Firbank . . . Firbank, I remember, had the reputation of attending a state dinner and eating a single pea as his entire meal. He was an oddball. Waugh was brittle, humorous and biting; Firbank was one step beyond that, very closely approaching the absurd.

Interview/
The Washington Post (Book World), 1-3:2.

William Jovanovich
Chairman, Harcourt Brace, Jovanovich,
publishers

In a recession, people will stop buying a second car or a new television set—but they will continue to buy books.

The New York Times, 2-7:(4)8.

Robert Lowell
Poet

Almost no movies are first-rate, the novel is in decline, it's a sad age for criticism, you snap your fingers at journalism but it's in passable shape, so what's poetry in decline to? Any of these categories I've named would feel the same about poetry, yet I don't think any of them are much better off. I happened to get into poetry, and I feel a thanksgiving I didn't get into one of these other things. They all seem much sicker than poetry, poor sick poetry. What's *not* in decline?

Interview, University of Essex, England/
The New York Times Book Review, 4-4:31.

I suppose a poet is content to be a minority. The public is a lost cause.

Interview, University of Essex, England/
The New York Times Book Review, 4-4:31.

Norman Mailer
Author

. . . a good skier never worries about a route; he just goes, confident that he'll react to changes in the trail as they happen. It's the same thing in writing; you have to have confidence in your technique. But you also have

to assume that you're going to grow in the writing of a piece of work; so you've always got to take on more than you are able to do at the moment. If you take on something you know you can do, all your contempt for yourself will get into it very quickly.

Beverly Hills, Calif./
Los Angeles Times (Calendar), 2-14:56.

The great difference between a novelist and a journalist is that the novelist doesn't know his own ending. He doesn't have all that NASA material laid out for him; and it takes two or three times as long to write a novel for just that reason. Writing is like playing chess. In a good chess game, you might have five interesting continuations at one point, three at another and, at a certain point, you might be lucky enough to reach 18 continuations.

Interview, Beverly Hills, Calif./
Los Angeles Times (Calendar), 2-21:12.

Bernard Malamud
Author

With me, it's story, story, story. Writers who can't invent stories often pursue other strategies, even substituting style for narrative. I feel that story is the basic element of fiction—though that idea is not popular with disciples of the "new novel." They remind me of the painter who couldn't paint people, so he painted chairs.

Interview, Vermont/
The New York Times Book Review, 10-3:22.

Rod McKuen
Poet

(Critics attack his poetry) because it's understandable. I always think everything should have a beginning, a middle and an end. A while ago it was announced that I would come out with a paperback of new poetry. I got bad reviews from *Publishers' Weekly* and *Book World* and a rave from *Coronet,* and I still have not written one word of the book.

Interview, San Francisco/
San Francisco Chronicle, 7-14:48.

V. S. Naipaul
Author

Writing isn't just a matter of acquiring a skill and then looking round for material or a subject. To willingly wish on oneself the sort of panic of which it partakes is not something I could do now. When I was younger, of course, it was nice to write a book. But now the thought of having to go into that other mood . . . People who are not artists have this vision of the creative life as being a rather attractive extension of themselves. I was quite unhinged when I finished my last book. One doesn't want to overdramatize it, but if writing at my time of life (39 years of age) means that, how horrible to have to go through that when one is 50.

London/The New York Times, 11-26:38.

Beverley Nichols
Author

I never had any doubts about how my life would go; simply because I had never had a failure. Everything I wrote was promptly published. I'm not saying I had any profound feelings about being a great writer. I merely knew that I was capable of making a perfectly good living out of it.

Interview, Richmond, Surrey, England/
The Christian Science Monitor, 9-2:13.

Erich Segal
Author

You can't even find on the record—or off the record—or anywhere testimony to the effect that I thought that *Love Story* was a worthy piece of literature. This is not so. It was to me something I had to do. You know, sometimes things happen to me in a day and I've just got to go out and run 10 miles to just get it over with. *Love Story* was this same kind of thing. I heard this true story, and instead of running it out, I wrote it out. And it was for me I wrote it; and I was not depressed when nobody wanted to publish or film *Love Story*. I wasn't. I had written it, and that was the important thing, and it was over. And when people printed it, I thought that was really nice. And when people liked it, I thought that was nicer still. And when people started to put it down, well afterward I said that they, too, had their rights because it doesn't matter. You know, it did what it

did for me, and it can do what it does to them.

Interview/
The New York Times Magazine, 6-13:36.

Georges Simenon
Author

The ideal condition for the reader is to have time to read a whole book in one evening. You never think of going to see a play— one act today, the second act a fortnight later, and the third in a month. You see the whole play in one evening. It's the same for today's novel.

Interview, Epalinges, Switzerland/
The New York Times Book Review, 10-24:4.

I'm a bit like a sponge. When I'm not writing, I absorb life like water. When I write, I squeeze the sponge a little—and out it comes, not water but ink.

Interview, Epalinges, Switzerland/
The New York Times Book Review, 10-24:20.

William Stafford
Poet-in-residence, Library of
Congress of the United States

Often students bring something to you, saying, "I don't know whether this is really good, or whether I should throw it in the wastebasket." The assumption is that one or the other choice is the right move. No. Almost everything we say . . . or write . . . comes in that spacious human area bounded by something above the forgivable. We must accustom ourselves to . . . writing without achieving *Paradise Lost*. We must forgive ourselves and each other much . . . When you write, simply tell me something.

Before Women's National Democratic
Club, Washington, Feb. 8/
The Washington Post, 2-9:(B)3.

Irving Stone
Author

The basic function of a writer is understanding mankind and the world, to plunge in-

(IRVING STONE)

to the future and to sketch a better world. A writer must extract the essence of the world.

On receiving honorary Doctor of Literature Degree from the California State Colleges, Los Angeles/Los Angeles Herald-Examiner, 3-25:(B)2.

Jacqueline Susann
Author

There's a great thing you get creatively when you've written a chapter and it's right, and you know it's right. There's no feeling like it in the world.

Interview, New York/ San Francisco Examiner & Chronicle (Datebook), 2-21:6.

You never make a name for yourself by writing good reviews, but by being caustic and turning a phrase at the author's expense. Why should some guy who's never written anything more in his life than a book on bird watching in Africa, and sold 27 copies, be assigned to review a novel by Leon Uris? There's built-in jealousy, envy, spite in that kind of system.

The Wall Street Journal, 6-9:10.

Barbara Tuchman
Author, Historian

(Regarding contemporary literature): There should be a beginning, a middle and an end, plus an element of suspense to keep a reader turning the pages. As a historian, I'm not a Ph.D. type, someone who feels he must include everything . . . Historians who put in everything, plus countless footnotes, aren't thinking of their readers. Subsequently, they're not readable. They're simply safeguarding their trail so no other historian will criticize them.

Interview, New York/ The Christian Science Monitor, 3-24:(B)7.

Being a wife and mother—that, in people's minds, is enough to establish you as an amateur. It's difficult to get time to write, or respect for the closed door. In a woman, writing is regarded—at least until you make a success—as a sort of gardening. You're a dilettante, whom anybody can interrupt.

Interview/ The Washington Post, 9-12:(E)11.

John Updike
Author

Once I had lots of theories about how to write. I've forgotten most of them. Yet I do feel the novel is where my work's at now. The novel is like an empty box: You can do anything you want if you can do it.

Interview, Martha's Vineyard, Mass./ San Francisco Examiner & Chronicle (This World), 8-8:37.

Leon Uris
Author

I've learned to live with the critics. I personally don't care any more what the hell the critics say about my "tin ear" or anything else. But they do bother the hell out of my new wife, who's only 23 and doesn't have any experience putting up with them.

Washington/The National Observer, 1-11:22.

Ernest van den Haag
Lecturer in sociology and psychology, New School for Social Research, New York

. . . the expert says that a certain work isn't pornography; it's great literature. I have come to the conclusion that many experts are so strongly against any kinds of controls that they are willing to call something "great" when they know perfectly well it isn't. Every literary critic I've ever known realizes that *Lady Chatterley's Lover*, written by a great writer, is not a great work of literature, it's a silly novel. But when they go to court, they say: "Oh, no—it's great."

Interview/ U.S. News & World Report, 1-25:73.

Kurt Vonnegut, Jr.
Author

I am in the dangerous position now where I can sell anything I write. I am like an animal in a wicker cage, if you want to know what my life is like now. I'm scrambling. For so long money motivated me, and now there is nothing to move me off center. I don't know what to do.

The New York Times Magazine, 1-24:17.

That American writers are unhappy is well known. What is interesting about American writers is how many of them are drunks. I did not know Jack Keroac when he was a writer; I only met him when he was a drunk. Ernest Hemingway was drowning something and finally shot it. Faulkner was drowning something, too. And Fitzgerald was doing it mawkishly. All of them seemed to feel that they could not be socially useful people . . . So let's have a drink.

At Publishers' Publicity Association seminar/Publishers' Weekly, 3-22:27.

Irving Wallace
Author

(Writers reach success) in the historic way: by applying the seat of the pants to the chair; by sitting in a little lonely room or a big lonely room for ceaseless lonely hours; and sweating and cursing and writing word after word, sentence after sentence, alone.

Interview, Los Angeles/ Los Angeles Times, 4-1:(2)1.

Tennessee Williams
Author

Luxury is the wolf at the door, and its fangs are the vanities and conceits germinated by success. When an artist learns this, he knows where the dangers lie. Without deprivation and struggle, there is no salvation and I am just a sword cutting daisies.

Interview, New Orleans/ Esquire, September:220.

Herman Wouk
Author

I write a "traditional" novel—which is rather unfashionable—and I've taken a lot of kicking for it. The critics may be right and yet in my judgment the classic novel was not killed by Joyce and Proust. That's the way literary people think today, with the result that I'm writing an extinct form and doing it only for money—that's the way the anti-Wouk line goes. I think they're wrong. I believe the classic novel is alive, and that we're experiencing the end of the experimental period, and that the classic novel will come back very strongly. Whether my books will live is another question entirely. But the strength of my work comes from this intense grounding in the 18th- and 19th-century novelists.

Interview/The Washington Post (Book World), 12-26:14.

Medicine and Health

Spiro T. Agnew
Vice President of the United States

Without a lot of fanfare, without a panoply of promises no one knows how to keep, we have been looking at the whole range of issues and challenges that combine to produce the current (health care) crisis . . . (The Nixon health-care program) will build on not just the best judgments of the experts but also the sincere hopes and ambitions of a nation that places health among the first of its high ideals.

At dedication of Martin Anthony Sinatra Medical Education Center, Palm Springs, Calif., Jan. 15/Los Angeles Times, 1-16:(2)1.

The language of extremism attracts attention; but if the Senator (Edward Kennedy) hopes to ride to the Presidency on a charge that Americans are getting poor medical care and the whole system should be replaced with nationalized medicine, he is riding a mighty frail horse . . . I do not believe that even his colleagues among the doom-sayers, who have other favorite catastrophes to panic about, will agree to diverting up to one-fourth of the national budget to health financing.

Before Political Action Committee, American Medical Association, New Orleans, Nov. 28/ The Washington Post, 11-29:(A)2.

Christiaan Barnard
Surgeon

You ask me why I have not performed a heart transplant for two years? I could do a transplant today—if I had a patient. Doctors are just not referring patients to me. They'd rather send them home to die.

Interview/Newsweek, 5-3:53.

Birch Bayh
United States Senator, D—Ind.

Public health implications related to the abuse and misuse of barbiturates is shocking. While the current focus of concern today is on heroin addiction, it would be folly to overlook the present and prospective role of barbiturates.

Before Senate Judiciary Subcommittee on Juvenile Delinquency, Washington, Dec. 15/The Washington Post, 12-16:(B)3.

Winton M. Blount
Postmaster General of the United States

(Calling for an American boycott of French products to force a crackdown in France on heroin production and exportation): The State Department, by its very function, must act through diplomatic channels to accomplish its goals. I believe that diplomacy will not do the job quickly enough, and this is why I believe American citizens, must involve themselves and deal with the matter not diplomatically through government representatives, but directly . . . Is it more important to avoid embarrassing the French, or is it more important to act firmly and forcefully against a problem that the President has called Public Enemy Number 1? For myself, I am willing to see French pride and the narcotics trade in France sacrificed to the welfare and health of American children.

Before National Association of Postmasters, Anaheim, Calif., Oct. 7/ Los Angeles Herald-Examiner, 10-8:(A)6.

Walter C. Bornemeier
President, American Medical Association

The AMA has, for some time, taken the

position that health programs without economic barriers must be developed for the poor and near poor. We endorse the principle that it is the basic right of every citizen to have available to him adequate health care.

Chicago, Feb. 18/
The New York Times, 2-19:19.

Edmund C. Casey
President-elect, National Medical
Association of the United States

All the health plans before Congress have addressed themselves to how we are going to pay the doctor. This is not our concern . . . Our concern is how are we going to deliver health care. Our approach is not insurance companies; our approach is not Social Security; our approach is not private insurance; our approach is really not health maintenance organizations. Our approach is deliverance of health care to all the people, particularly in areas where there are no physicians.

At National Medical Association
convention, Philadelphia/
The New York Times, 8-15:(1)22.

Morris Chafetz
Director, Division of Alcohol Abuse,
National Institute of Mental Health
of the United States

We tend to look down our noses at a biological fact—a need of man to alter his reality. Even a baby in his crib will spin himself around until he is dizzy. But we also have a problem in America of equating drinking and intoxication as one and the same thing. There is a difference between altering reality and getting drunk.

San Francisco Examiner & Chronicle
(This World), 4-4:2.

Sidney Cohen
Director, Center for the Study
of Mind-Altering Drugs,
University of California at Los Angeles

If 1966 was the year of "acid," 1968 the year of "speed" and 1970 the year of "smack" (heroin), then 1972 may well become the year of the "downer" (barbiturates) . . . For the youngster, barbiturates are a more reliable "high" and less detectable than "pot." They are less strenuous than LSD, less "freaky" than amphetamines and less expensive than heroin.

Before Senate Juvenile Delinquency
Subcommittee, Washington/
Los Angeles Herald-Examiner, 12-19:(A)6.

John A. Cooper
President, Association of
American Medical Colleges

Harnessing the atom and the space program were largely technological challenges built upon a firm base of fundamental scientific knowledge. In cancer, we do not yet possess the equivalent of Einstein's formulation of the fundamental relationship between matter and energy.

Before Senate Health Subcommittee,
Washington, March 9/
The Washington Post, 3-10:(A)3.

Edward E. David, Jr.
Science Adviser to the President
of the United States

To isolate the cancer effort would prejudice the very outcome we seek. The problem of cancer straddles virtually all of the life sciences: molecular biology, biochemistry, virology, pharmacology, toxicology, genetics. Any of these, or all of them, will contribute to the final solution. No one is wise enough to pick and choose just those components of the total bio-medical spectrum that will be vital. Who knows what new discovery will become vital even next year?

Before Association of American
Medical Colleges, Chicago, Feb. 13/
The New York Times, 2-14:(1)1.

Charles C. Edwards
Commissioner, Food and Drug
Administration of the United States

Our goal is to have all drugs that are marketed in the United States do what it is

(CHARLES C. EDWARDS)

claimed that they will do. And to bring this about is going to take three to five years. This is a big, big undertaking. Although it isn't as dramatic as some of the things that are happening in the field of medicine today—such as the heart transplant and things like that—it probably will have more impact in terms of good medical care than anything that's happened in medicine in the last 50 or 60 years.

Interview, Washington/
U.S. News & World Report, 4-19:53.

We are a drug-culture society . . . psychiatrists, sociologists, psychologists—all share with us a deep concern that this trend, this attitude, may be one of the causative factors in our drug-abuse problem. Now, how did all of this come about? I think there are perhaps several reasons: the increasing complexities and stresses of modern society; the postwar discovery of chemicals that allegedly help the average person cope with these stresses and frustrations; the tremendous wave of advertising over the media, especially TV, creating an environment in which the consumer feels that reaching for a pill, tablet or capsule is a panacea for all of his ills. The advertising industry took advantage of the first two factors . . . to promote and advertise these drugs in such a way as to actually create a climate of need.

The Christian Science Monitor, 8-26:16.

Roger O. Egeberg
Assistant Secretary for Health
and Scientific Affairs, Department
of Health, Education and Welfare
of the United States

The American system of health care is literally on trial, and the verdict at this point is in doubt. (The trouble is in medicine's) inability to deliver decent health care to all who need and deserve it . . . (The problems can be solved) without taking the kind of extreme and ill-conceived action being proposed by the advocates of a national system of compulsory health insurance . . . (plans) that would ap-

pear to promise instant solutions, that give the American people the erroneous impression that passing a law and setting up a new Federal health program will take care of everything in a flash.

At Salerni Collegium dinner, Los Angeles,
Feb. 17/Los Angeles Times, 2-18:(2)8.

John Finlator
Deputy Director, Bureau of Narcotics
and Dangerous Drugs, Department
of Justice of the United States

I wish I could say drug abuse has reached its peak and is dropping off, but I can't. We had hoped it would slow down in the late '60s, but in the last two years heroin use has greatly increased . . . In the '60s, the hippies said they would use marijuana and LSD but never turn to heroin. But just two years later, it's common knowledge that heroin is our major drug problem . . . The sad thing is that many young people today think heroin is the ultimate drug experience. Really, it's the last drug experience.

Interview, Kansas City/
The Dallas Times Herald, 9-1:(A)26.

William H. Foege
Director, smallpox eradication program,
United States Center for Disease Control

(Regarding smallpox): This will be the first time in history that a disease has been eradicated in the world, and I doubt if we'll see another instance of complete eradication in our lifetime.

The Dallas Times Herald, 10-7:(A)33.

Jack A. L. Hahn
President, American Hospital Association

Health care in America is a study in contrasts. We have great medical centers, utilizing the most advanced medical technology in the world, where persons can have vital organs repaired or transplanted. At the same time, we also have persons dying from diseases long conquered, because of geographical or environmental isolation. We live in a society where malnutrition rubs elbows with obesity.

Before Commonwealth Club health problems committee, San Francisco, Dec. 7/San Francisco Examiner, 12-7:12.

George Himler
President-elect, Medical Society of the State of New York

(Large group practice is) the most costly method of rendering medical care that has yet been devised . . . Personally, I am convinced that solo and small group practices still have a useful, and perhaps even an essential, role to play in our health-care system.

Before house of delegates, Medical Society of the State of New York, New York, Feb. 14/ The New York Times, 2-15:15.

Charles A. (Carl) Hoffman
President-elect, American Medical Association

The great problem today is the public not understanding the problem facing the physician. I go to work at 8 o'clock every morning. I come home at 8 o'clock every night. Every physician has a great dedication to his patients. The physicians I know are putting in long hours and seeing many patients, almost to the point of fatigue.

News conference, Atlantic City, N.J., June 24/The Washington Post, 6-25:(A)2.

Harold E. Hughes
United States Senator, D–Iowa

The time has come for the government to move into the drug scene with controlled distribution of methadone, or some comparable synthetic drug, to counter the growing heroin addiction and the crime it inevitably causes . . . The blunt fact is that heroin addiction and the vast crime that it creates are simply unacceptable to our society. We must move with the best alternative possible. Heroin

Boulevard is a one-way street to national disaster.

At Chicago Conference on Brotherhood, Feb. 28/Los Angeles Times, 3-1:(1)4.

John E. Ingersoll
Director, Bureau of Narcotics and Dangerous Drugs, Department of Justice of the United States

Many studies show that, while cannabis (marijuana) isn't physically addicting, it can be psychologically habituating, often resulting in an antimotivational syndrome in which the user is more apt to sit and contemplate a flower pot rather than try to solve his problem.

Before National Commission on Marijuana and Drug Abuse, Washington, May 17/The New York Times, 5-18:10.

John Kaplan
Professor of Law, Stanford University

If the marijuana laws worked, I would be strongly in favor of them; but they, like Prohibition, do not work. They divide the young from the old and are propelling us to a national crisis of confidence of major dimensions. Therefore, they must go.

Before National Commission on Marijuana and Drug Use, Washington, May 18/ U.S. News & World Report, 5-31:68.

Edward M. Kennedy
United States Senator, D–Mass.

The pittance we spend on cancer is dramatic evidence of the urgent need to reorder our national priorities. At present, we spend $410 per person per year on national defense, $125 on Vietnam and $19 on the space program; but we spend only 89 cents on cancer research.

Washington, Jan. 25/ The Dallas Times Herald, 1-25:(A)8.

(EDWARD M. KENNEDY)

There appears to be a health crisis to me. The President has stated it. The Secretary (of Health, Education and Welfare) has stated it. People who have to wait hours in hospital emergency rooms, mothers who see their children die feel there is a crisis. There are examples after examples by individuals of what they consider to be a crisis.

> *Before Senate Health Subcommittee,*
> *Washington, March 15/*
> *The Washington Post, 3-16:(A)1.*

After 40 years, the providers and financers of health care in America have established a dismal record of performance—a record characterized by inequity, inefficiency, ineffectiveness, inflation and, worst of all, by inhumanity. Too often, the system is an obstacle course for the consumer, not a path for better health.

> *Before Senate Health Subcommittee,*
> *Washington, March 15/*
> *The Washington Post, 3-16:(A)10.*

(Health care in the 1970s) is the fastest-growing failing business in the nation—a $70 billion industry that fails to meet the urgent needs of all our people . . . The way (health) insurance premiums are rising, fewer and fewer Americans will be able to afford (it). We have an industry in which the hospitals have been protected. We have an industry in which the doctors have been protected. We have an industry in which insurance companies have been protected . . . It is time to change all this. We can't leave it to the insurance industry, as (President) Nixon proposes. Nor can we leave it to the doctors, to the hospitals or to any of the currently-reigning health powers. Only the consumer can pull it together.

> *Before New England Hospital Assembly,*
> *Boston, March 29/*
> *The Dallas Times Herald, 3-29:(A)11.*

The American Medical Association puts the lives and well-being of American citizens below its own special interest in ordering its priorities. It deserves to be ignored, rejected and forgotten.

> *At Senate Subcommittee on Administrative*
> *Practices hearing, Washington, July 14/*
> *Los Angeles Herald-Examiner, 7-15:(A)10.*

John H. Knowles
General director,
Massachusetts General Hospital

When you tie a physician's income to what he does or doesn't do to a patient, you're asking for trouble. It's been shown time and again that if you prepay persons on a capitation basis—so much per person per year—the rate of surgery and unnecessary hospitalization drops. I'm not polemicizing or inflating the rhetoric. Those are facts. Therefore, the system has got to change its method to more prepayment, more capitation, less reliance on high-cost acute treatment, less hospitalization.

> *The National Observer, 1-25:17.*

. . . I cannot support the present (Kennedy health plan) bill in front of the Senate because I do not agree with the committee that is backing this bill, which deals in sweeping absolutes: All hospitals are mismanaged; all private insurance companies are full of greedy, avaricious merchants; all doctors are just trying to make a buck. All of this, all of that. Such is not the case. There are many fine insurance companies that are now exercising a fine social conscience. The same is true of doctors. And the same is true of hospital directors; there are a few good ones around; and hospital trustees that work assiduously in the public interest. I do not want to see regional self-determination and voluntarism go down the drain.

> *Radio broadcast, Boston/*
> *Human Events, 11-27:4.*

Earl F. Landgrebe
United States Representative, R—Ind.

It has been said that there is no longer a question of whether we need national health insurance. The debate now centers upon what kind of health program we will have. There have been numerous proposals—from the

Administration, from various Congressmen and Senators, even from the American Medical Association. But while everybody is devising ways to pay for the ever-rising cost of medical care, perhaps we should pay more attention to the causes and bring the costs into line.

Human Events, 5-15:13.

Philip R. Lee
Chancellor, University of
California Medical Center

For any chance of success, the anti-cancer campaign must be able to draw not only on the cancer specialists in the National Cancer Institute, but on other specialists in other parts of the National Institutes of Health. Among these are the experts in virus diseases, genetics, aging, endocrinology, molecular biology, pharmacology and immunology. We do not need more separation. We need more intimate interchange of ideas and interaction among investigators. We do not know where the breakthroughs will come.

Before Senate Health Subcommittee,
Washington, March 9/
San Francisco Examiner, 3-9:6.

William P. Longmire, Jr.
President,
American College of Surgeons

If we can find the secrets of rejection, proper cross-matching, good preservation and handling of organs, surgery already has the techniques to expand the transplant field enormously . . . However, before we advance to this phase, a lot of good, sound scientific investigation and reporting will be necessary. But there is no doubt expansion of transplants is coming.

Interview, Dallas/
The Dallas Times Herald, 11-21:(A)44.

Donald B. Louria
Chairman, Department of Public Health
and Preventive Medicine, College of
Medicine and Dentistry of New Jersey

We are on a continuum that starts with legitimate prescription use . . . then extends to over-prescribing by physicians for a variety of discomfort-relieving agents. The next step is over-the-counter self-medication, sometimes used sensibly, often indiscriminately. At the end of the continuum is illicit use of pleasure-giving agents. Let no one delude himself into thinking there is no nexus between excessive self-medication and use of illegal drugs. Good epidemilogic studies show that parents who use inordinate amounts of medicaments breed children who have a far greater likelihood of using illicit drugs.

The Christian Science Monitor, 8-26:16.

Reginald Maudling
Home Secretary of the United Kingdom

It is a strange anomaly that it is perfectly legal for me to drink myself to death but wholly illegal to drug myself to death. I believe this to be right, but I find it terribly difficult to justify the logic of it.

San Francisco Examiner, 5-27:36.

Thomas J. McIntyre
United States Senator, D–N.H.

(Regarding high-pressure advertising of over-the-counter and prescription drugs): I was under the impression that drug pushing is an illegal activity, punishable in every one of the 50 states . . . I have discovered that the more sophisticated forms of drug pushing are not only legal but flourishing in this country.

Plainview (Tex.) Daily Herald, 10-27:4.

John N. Mitchell
Attorney General of the United States

. . . for what my opinion is worth, I would suggest that we have almost become a country with a drug culture. I don't mean necessarily narcotics and dangerous drugs; but I'm referring to all these pills that are sold. If you've got a cold, you take some pills; if you can't get to sleep in 10 minutes, you take some pills; the next day, you take a pep pill to keep you awake. We've become a nation of pill poppers. And I have a feeling that this

(JOHN N. MITCHELL)

may have some relation to the boom in drug use.

Interview, Washington/
U.S. News & World Report, 3-22:41.

Jean Munzer
Psychiatrist, Columbia University

. . . a lot of people kid themselves that going to "encounter" groups is emotional therapy. It's not. It's like going to the gym for a workout.

Interview, Los Angeles/
Los Angeles Times, 2-5:(2)1.

Edmund S. Muskie
United States Senator, D—Maine

The first medical right of all Americans is care within their means. (The second right is) care within their reach. Even if we guaranteed the payment of health costs, millions of our citizens could not find sufficient medical services.

At Albert Einstein College
of Medicine Commencement, May 27/
The New York Times, 5-28:37.

Richard M. Nixon
President of the United States

I will . . . ask appropriation of an extra $100 million to launch an intensive campaign to find a cure for cancer, and I will ask later for whatever additional funds can effectively be used. The time has come when the same kind of concentrated effort that split the atom and took man to the moon should be turned toward conquering this dread disease. Let us make a total national commitment to achieve this goal.

State of the Union address,
Washington, Jan. 22/
The Washington Post, 1-23:(A)12.

America has long been the wealthiest nation in the world. Now it is time we became the healthiest nation in the world.

State of the Union address, Washington,
Jan. 22/The Washington Post, 1-23:(A)12.

I realize this is controversial, but I can see no social or moral justification whatever for legalizing marijuana. I think it would be exactly the wrong step. It would simply encourage more and more of our young people to start down that long, dismal road that leads to hard drugs and, eventually, self-destruction.

News conference, Washington, June 1/
The New York Times, 6-2:24.

I believe that the most expensive plan that has been offered in the current discussion on health care in America—a plan for nationalized compulsory health insurance—is the plan that would actually do the most to hurt American health care.

Before American Medical Association,
Atlantic City, N.J., June 22/
The New York Times, 6-23:1.

If there is any single institution that symbolizes the tragic isolation and shameful neglect of older Americans, it is the substandard nursing home—unsanitary and ill-equipped, overcrowded and understaffed. Many of our nursing homes are outstanding institutions; but altogether too many are not. And that is why so many are described as little more than warehouses for the unwanted, dumping grounds for the dying. I have even heard of doctors who refuse to visit some nursing homes because they get too depressed. Too often it seems that nursing homes serve mainly to keep older people out of sight and out of mind, so that no one will notice their degradation and despair.

Before National Retired Teachers
Association-American Association of
Retired Persons joint convention,
Chicago, June 25/
The New York Times, 6-26:11.

The real problem fundamentally gets down to why: Why do people take them (drugs)? There we find the fundamental challenge of our time, a challenge that opinion leaders have to meet. If individuals have something to live for, if individuals have something to believe in, then the tendency to throw up their hands, to retreat, to give up on life, is substantially reduced. But as a society comes to the point where there is negativism, defeatism, a sense of alienation, it is inevitable that younger people will give up. They will turn to drugs, to any other kind of activity that is, of course, disruptive of a society.

Before newspaper, TV and radio executives, Kansas City/ The National Observer, 7-12:2.

Patrick Cardinal O'Boyle
Roman Catholic Archbishop of Washington, D.C.

Today, a man who has himself sterilized is praised. A woman who avoids pregnancy for no better reason than that she wishes to retain her girlish figure is admired. A physician who performs thousands of abortions is made into a sympathetic folk hero . . . (American culture is) polluted by a sick hatred of human bodily life.

At National Wanderer Forum, St. Paul, Minn., June 18/ The Washington Post, 6-20:(D)6.

Max Parrott
Chairman, board of trustees, American Medical Association

Many of our health problems (in the United States) . . . are more factors of our society and economy than the absence of medical treatment . . . one of the most damaging blows to our health statistics comes from the very affluence of our society . . . The truth is our fat standard of living does create health problems. We ride in cars when we should be on a bicycle or on foot. We overeat. We overdrink. We smoke cigarettes. This affluent life style relates directly to some of our most depressing medical statistics. Up to the time when a person is 45 or so, the most common cause of death is an accident—in a car, on the job or at home. After a person survives his mid-40s, heart disease takes over as the number one killer, and heart disease . . . links up very closely with the affluent standard of living most of us "enjoy."

Human Events, 5-15:15.

Abraham A. Ribicoff
United States Senator, D–Conn.

If private health insurance is to survive, it must change its basic philosophy and act as an advocate on behalf of those in need of medical care, and not as a neutral independent conduit which simply distributes money throughout the system.

Washington, Feb. 19/ The New York Times, 2-20:28.

Elliot L. Richardson
Secretary of Health, Education and Welfare of the United States

Our most recent estimates disclose that some 10 million Americans are dependent on alcohol—a shocking figure that yet does not begin to reveal the damage to the nation in terms of achohol-related diseases, broken families, economic ruin and death.

Washington, Jan. 11/ The New York Times, 1-12:15.

(Regarding a proposed totally Federally-financed health insurance program): The proponents of such a system seem to assume that radical intervéntion by the Federal government in health care, in an inflexible, predetermined and monolithic manner, is the only way to solve health organization and delivery problems. I suggest that we are more likely to attain our common health objectives by stimulating competition and by promoting consumer education and freedom of individual choice, rather than by resorting to fiscal coercion and unrealistically global schemes.

Before House Ways and Means Committee, Washington, Oct. 19/ The Washington Post, 10-20:(A)10.

Nelson A. Rockefeller
Governor of New York

Group (medical) practice allows the doctor to work in the most modern medical setting. It enables him to have the latest diagnostic tools, technicians and consultation of his colleagues at his fingertips. It allows him to concentrate, not only on healing, but on pre-

(NELSON A. ROCKEFELLER)

venting sickness—which is the most practical way to cut down our spiraling medical costs. And because he is salaried, the physician can devote himself wholly to the practice of medicine, rather than the economics of medicine.

Before his Social Services Steering Committee, New York, April 15/ The New York Times, 4-16:1.

Peter H. Rossi
Professor of Social Relations, Johns Hopkins University

The one great problem of marijuana is that it might lead to cigarette smoking.

Plainview (Tex.) Daily Herald, 3-7:(A)12.

Russell B. Roth
Speaker of the house of delegates, American Medical Association

More people are getting more and better (medical) care from more and better physicians in more and better facilities. That's hardly a crisis.

Before Senate Health Subcommittee, Washington, March 15/ The Washington Post, 3-16:(A)1.

Robert Seidenberg
Clinical Professor of Psychiatry, State University of New York at Syracuse

Being unable or unwilling to sleep, apparently irrespective of cause, has been converted into an important "disease" . . . The imperative to sleep, and within the prescribed time, has in America become a puritanical obsession which drug companies are happily encouraging and profiting from. They continue to frighten people, knowing full well that sleeplessness, except in rare and extraordinary instances, is not harmful to mind or body. Many people would enjoy lying awake if the threat of thereby harming themselves were removed.

Before Senate Monopoly Subcommittee, Washington, July 23/ The Washington Post, 7-24:(E)1.

Howard K. Smith
News commentator, American Broadcasting Company

We know it costs $40 to $60 a day for a (hard drug) addict to get his fix. At the lower figure, it costs him $14,000 a year. We know many or most resort to crime to get the money. More than 50 per cent of all hard crimes, like violent robberies in our cities, were done by heroin addicts. So, while we are waiting to find the ultimate remedy, Edward Bennett Williams, the famous criminal lawyer here in Washington, proposes this one. It is not new; it is the British way: Let government register addicts, without punishment. And let government maintain the addict with a daily dose of, say, methadone, at cost—not at street prices inflated by illegality. It is admittedly far from perfect. But almost anything is better than what is happening now. Official maintenance would cost at most $2,000 a year per addict; that is $12,000 less than at present. When you add to that the saving in crime and policing, and the drying up of a main source of Mafia income . . . it is a good interim plan, indeed. Whenever we find that ultimate answer, we can always switch over.

TV commentary/"Nightly News," American Broadcasting Company, Washington, 7-9.

Jesse L. Steinfeld
Surgeon General of the United States

Nonsmokers have as much right to clean and wholesome air as smokers have to their so-called right to smoke, which I would redefine as a right to pollute . . . Evidence is accumulating that the nonsmoker may have untoward effects from the pollution his smoking neighbor forces upon him. It is high time to ban smoking from all confined public places, such as restaurants, theatres, airplanes, trains and buses. It is time that we interpret the Bill of Rights for the nonsmoker as well as the smoker.

Washington, Jan. 11/ The Washington Post, 1-12:(A)1.

S. Leonard Syme
Professor of Epidemiology,
University of California

The whole focus of medical care in this country is on disease, the physician and his stethoscope, early detection, training more medical personnel, methods of financing and the whole business of providing medical care for all. But this is like closing the barn door after the horses are out. The focus is on the repair of people who are already broken . . . We must not only treat people who are sick, but we must treat what causes them to be sick.

Los Angeles Herald-Examiner
(California Living), 3-14:38.

John V. Tunney
United States Senator, D–Calif.

(Drugs) is a terribly serious sociological problem in this nation. It wouldn't be such a problem, I think, if we didn't give young people the reasons to want to cop out. I think the reason they do it is the distortion in the society around them. Mass advertising has developed a state of mind that drugs are the cure-all for everything. Adults in this country also have contributed to the drug culture—they need pills to go to sleep, pills to keep them awake and pills to calm their nerves. There is a substantial portion of people who just can't cope with the stresses of life in a super-industrial state—where one's identity is confused, his role is undetermined and decisions have to be made hourly.

Washington/Los Angeles Times, 7-18:(E)6.

John G. Veneman
Under Secretary of Health, Education
and Welfare of the United States

Too many hospitals today are in wasteful competition with one another. You don't need two open-heart surgery teams in town if one can handle the traffic, and you don't need five maternity wings in five hospitals when each one is operating at only 50% of capacity.

Before Lutheran Hospital Society of
Southern California, Los Angeles,
Dec. 15/Los Angeles Times, 12-17:(1-C)6.

Leonard Woodcock
President, United Automobile
Workers of America

We do not intend to let President Nixon decry the crisis in health care in 1969 and stand silent in 1971, while he prescribes poor, penny-pinching solutions based on ill-conceived, catastrophic insurance concepts which benefit the few rather than meet the basic, unmet health needs of the many. We do not intend to let the American Medical Association get by with its "Medicredit" malarkey that would do little for the public and further compound the health-care crisis. We do not intend to let the insurance industry skim its billions of profits from premium payments and continue to provide payment for only about a third of the nation's medical bills . . . We can no longer tolerate skyrocketing costs, shortages of health-care personnel, lack of adequate care and the inadequacies of private health insurance solely because we don't have a national system for providing health care.

Jan. 1/Daily World, 1-2:5.

The (Nixon) Administration's own (health insurance) bill, now that we finally have a look at it, reminds me of the old Buffalo policy. There are deductibles, co-insurance clauses, exclusions, loopholes and gaps—so much fine print that it resembles the policy that covers you only when you are run over by a herd of Buffalos in downtown Detroit at high noon.

Before Senate Finance Committee,
Washington/The New York Times, 4-28:31.

Mitchell R. Zavon
Clinical Professor of Industrial Medicine,
University of Cincinnati College of Medicine

Don't be stampeded into believing that all disease is of environmental origin, any more than you would believe that environment plays no role in disease.

At symposium sponsored by Oregon Academy
of General Practice, Portland, Jan. 30/
The New York Times, 1-31:(1)44.

The Performing Arts

MOTION PICTURES

Woody Allen
Actor, Director, Writer

So much of the comedy films being made today are like Muzak; they just fill space. If people have nothing to do, they drop in.

Interview, Los Angeles/
Los Angeles Herald-Examiner, 5-16:(F)1.

Robert Altman
Director

Nobody has ever made a good movie. Some day someone will make half a good one.

The New York Times Magazine, 6-20:47.

James T. Aubrey, Jr.
President,
Metro-Goldwyn-Mayer, Inc.

Everybody was caught in the new-found freedom (in films). The industry wallowed in it. But while permissive films might have been successful six months ago, they aren't now. The whole country has undergone a big reversal of taste—one of the most remarkable in recent times.

Interview/The Washington Post, 3-31:(B)4.

Lex Barker
Actor

If you're an actor, it's always hard to be married. If your wife is young, she's almost bound to be jealous and insecure. If she's an actress, it's worse, because you're inevitably in competition. And let's face it—actors are impossible; we're all terribly self-centered.

Interview, Los Angeles/
The Washington Post, 3-22:(B)10.

Ingmar Bergman
Director

Movies . . . are fantastic media with which to touch other human beings, to reach them,

to either annoy them or to make them happy, to make them sad or to get them to think; to get them started emotionally. That's probably the truest, deepest reason why I continue to make movies. There is also something about the work itself that you get very dependent upon. You are part of a group. If you are a relatively inhibited, shy and timid person like me, who has difficulty establishing deeper relations, it is wonderful to live in the collective world of filmmaking; or a group in the theatre that is working on a play. The reason is that nothing else is of importance to the group; you devote yourself completely—no less is acceptable—and you have to stake yourself for better or for worse, and you have to accept taking the chance of making a fool of yourself. You have to take the chance that people will laugh at you, which actually makes no difference. But through making films and staging plays, you constantly come into contact with other people—one intrudes into the problems of others. Performers, the members of the crew, everyone is forced into a form of emotionalness that is very worthwhile and very amusing. And constantly fascinating, because the great stimulation one has all the time is that one is with people. Living people.

Interview/
Los Angeles Times (Calendar), 8-15:22.

Joan Blondell
Actress

Who's a movie star these days? Today there are no contract players. You do a picture at an independent studio; they take whatever juice they want out of you; and then they don't care what happens to you. In the old days, it was like a family, and that I do miss. The guard at the studio gate would say, "Hi, Joanie, have a good day." And if one person had a sorrow, *everybody* had it. When all that ended, it was like standing on a raft in the middle of a rough sea.

Interview/Life, 2-19:62.

Claire Bloom
Actress

. . . acting is probably the only profession where there is no sex discrimination. I've been earning a living in it since I was 14, and I've never been discriminated against. Actresses are totally equal, and many times they're a lot better off than men.

Interview, New York/
The New York Times, 2-7:(2)1.

Peter Bogdanovich
Director

When I direct, I become an actor. I discover things that way. Otherwise I don't know what to tell my actors to do.

Life, 11-26:44.

Charles Bronson
Actor

(Hollywood) used to be called the movie capital of the world. The rest of the world used to be fascinated by life in this country. Now most of those places have the things we have. On top of that, American pictures have become narrowly nationalistic, in that they mostly show only our worst problems. Ninety per cent of the pictures being made are either subtly or indirectly anti-American. It can be just the selection of the actors in a film. They can be overly effeminate or overly something else—and it's unattractive . . . I don't think people around the world want pictures like that from us. They want to see the kind of pictures we don't seem to make much any-more—strong, meaningful stories where a prob-lem or a conflict is presented, then worked through, resolved. They want to see interest-ing, fully-developed characters—people who don't just take off all their clothes and jump into bed together at the bat of an eye.

Interview, Beverly Hills, Calif./
Los Angeles Times, 9-4:(2)8.

Genevieve Bujold
Actress

If acting is what you want, need, what you are, there's a tendency for it to be all-embrac-ing, so you find it hard to have a life of great harmony. And sometimes it creates dissatisfac-tion in others, so that reflects on you. But sometimes, maybe if you're in the super-market shopping, and having a bad day, and somebody knows you and says something nice to you, it gives you a chance to be outgoing; it stops you for a second and makes you think, so maybe that's good.

Interview, New York/
Los Angeles Herald-Examiner, 12-31:(A)14.

Frank Capra
Former director

I visit the front offices (of film companies) and I don't feel anything. But let me go on a soundstage again and, oh, that's something else. There's a smell on those stages—musty, dusty, mixed with stale perfume and old makeup and ozone—ozone, you know, from the arcing when they unplug the big lights—and it all gets to me. But I'd be scared to death to go back at it again. Because you don't just direct, or I didn't. You put a lot of yourself into a film, and you leave a lot of yourself there. It's a young man's game. You need that energy and that strength to tell everybody else to go to hell.

Interview, Los Angeles/
Los Angeles Times, 5-7:(4)1.

You know what I tell people today about the scarcity of laughter—of real comedy—on the screen? When people say to me, especially the young moviemakers, "What is there to laugh at?" I say, "Look at yourself in the mirror."

Interview, New York/
The New York Times, 6-24:32.

I have never been in favor of government subsidies, but the government and big business should do something about saving this great industry which is the greatest salesman this country has ever had. Movies made here have

(FRANK CAPRA)

Americanized the world. That's why foreign governments give subsidies to their moviemakers. They want to combat this Americanization. I'm really surprised U.S. industry hasn't come to the aid of the movie industry. It opened the door for their products everywhere.

Interview, Los Angeles/
Los Angeles Herald-Examiner, 8-1:(E)4.

All I can say is that the great motion pictures are yet to be made. I talk to a lot of the kids, and I tell 'em, "This is your bag, and it's a big one. The stakes are very high." If anything at all, I have shown that it can be done. I have shown that you can be successful, that you can deal with controversial subjects, that you can survive. If I can do it, these young people can; because it's a young man's game. It takes a lot of *chutzpah*.

Interview, New York/
Publishers' Weekly, 8-2:33.

To young filmmakers, I say: Don't compromise. Only the morally courageous are worthy of speaking to their fellow men for two hours in the dark.

At San Francisco Film Festival, Oct. 9/
San Francisco Examiner, 10-11:28.

Claudia Cardinale
Actress

It's time there were deeper stories about women in the movies. Mostly, women are put there because the public likes to see a woman in a picture. Love scenes and nude scenes— that's what we're supposed to be for. You don't find many good scripts written about us. Why? Because the writers are mostly men; and, naturally, they know men better than women. Also, to know women deeply, you have to like them or love them. Our movie profession is filled with men who *don't* like women.

Family Weekly, 11-14:7.

John Cassavetes
Director

. . . I always thought it was the writing

that was the most important thing to a film. I never believed ₄a director could make that much difference . . . It is what is being said that is important.

Interview, Los Angeles/
The Dallas Times Herald, 2-14:(E)1.

Charles Chaplin
Former actor-director

In the cinema, as in the other arts today, there is a great deal of amateurism. It is not permanent; the cinema is in transition. I find all the sex stuff very dull. Well, you expect that at my age; I'm 82, you know. Let's say sex in films doesn't interest me. People should make more entertaining films. I enjoy all my own pictures. Frankly, I don't think I have made a bad one. Well, at least not a dull one.

Interview, Cannes, France/
San Francisco Examiner, 5-25:27.

James C. Corman
United States Representative, D–Calif.

We must make it our national policy to save this vital American industry without further delay. The motion picture industry is, after all, the industry which has "sold America" to the world by a graphic display of the American system and of the productivity of free competitive enterprise. It is the motion picture industry which has opened up new vistas of international communication, and it is most directly responsible for much of the development of art and culture in this country.

Before the House, Washington/
Daily Variety, 3-16:12.

Sherrill C. Corwin
Chairman, Metropolitan Theatres Corporation, Los Angeles; Former president, National Association of Theatre Owners

People are sick to death of the explicit language, unnecessarily used, and of the sexual situations dragged in by the heels (in motion pictures). I think that everyone is regaining his senses, and we're going back to some of the values that mean so much to us, without losing the freedom of the screen. I personally call it the "No, No, Nanette" syndrome.

The New York Times, 4-20:48.

Costa-Gavras
Director

Editing is the most important point in a picture; it is the director really writing the picture with his editing. All films are divided into three periods: Number 1, the writing of the script; Number 2, the shooting–when something happens, your feeling becomes materialized with the actors' personalities and, how you say, *le decor*, the sets. Yet a different thing with all the material is when you're editing, the third step. *Alors, le film, le vrai film commence*, which is absolutely different from what it was in the beginning, not at all what it had been in the shooting.

Interview, New York/
The Christian Science Monitor, 1-26:10.

Once people went to the cinema only to be amused. Today, they also go to learn. Of course, people still find entertainment films more attractive; they alleviate their guilt. But pictures are becoming more meaningful. However, political films, like amusement films, must be made for all spectators, despite the difference in spirit and aim.

Interview, Paris/
The New York Times Magazine, 3-21:46.

Joseph Cotten
Actor

We (actors) make a living out of acting and pray we don't get associated with too much junk. But we've got to go on working, otherwise the public easily forgets us. We may want to be selective, but in the end all we hope to reach is a high standard of compromise!

Interview, London/San Francisco Examiner
& Chronicle (Datebook), 8-15:7.

George Cukor
Director

It's easy–in fact too easy–to dismiss the old-time studio czars as tasteless buttonhole-makers. Most of the writing about them is done by people who weren't here at the time. Whatever else they may have been–in personal idiosyncrasies, four-letter words, dictatorial

rule–they came to make movies and they made them. They'd gamble millions on an idea they really couldn't understand, if they sensed something big in it. They had an instinct for what would sell; but that doesn't mean they couldn't tell good from bad, and they wanted it good as well as colossal. They didn't always get what they paid for, but they tried. A lot of us owe them respect and thanks for their willingness to bet on us. It was fun making films. Dreariness and defeat set in when we got too serious about ourselves. The young filmmakers (today) are mostly so taken up with their message, and so self-righteous about it, that they leave out the entertainment.

Los Angeles/
The Christian Science Monitor, 8-27:4.

Tony Curtis
Actor

(Regarding the virtues of home film cassettes): There are very few nice cinemas. They're pushing candy on you all the time, when it's bad for your teeth; people are smoking cigarettes all the time, which is bad for your lungs; then on top of that, they push a commercial, a short that's junk and coming attractions that are rubbish–when all you wanted to go and see was some guy making it with some girl. I don't wanna do that. Do you wanna do that? I don't wanna go through all that getting into the car and driving to the theatre; being pushed around in line. And then to have someone breathing on top of me and someone else belching; and there are all the noises and smells of people.

Interview, London/Los Angeles Herald-
Examiner (California Living), 2-28:30.

Nigel Davenport
Actor

. . . I really don't think I've ever done anything particularly dangerous (as an actor). But even in our jobs, actors take risks, especially if we're married, with kids. The bullet is never far away. Being out of work and not wanted can happen at any time, whether you're the biggest star or the smallest extra. If we live

(NIGEL DAVENPORT)

our lives this way, rather than going into something safe, like banking or law, I reckon we take enough risks juggling with our own destiny without having to prove ourselves in other ways.

Interview, Naivasha, Kenya/
San Francisco Examiner & Chronicle
(Datebook), 3-14:12.

Bette Davis
Actress

There is too much realism (in films) today. One doesn't even have to go to the theatre. You can stand on the street corner watching the people and save the price of a theatre ticket.

Interview. Houston/Variety, 3-24:7.

Kirk Douglas
Actor

Movie-making is an important resource of our country. Movies were once synonymous with America. A lot of that has gone away, because there's a suicidal critical attitude: If it's made here, it can't be good, say the critics.

Interview, Beverly Hills, Calif./
Los Angeles Times (Calendar), 2-14:11.

After you've been a star for 20 years, you realize that making movies isn't like working in an assembly line. What keeps you alive is variety. That's why they can't really type me to anything. After *Lust for Life*, John Wayne came up and said, "What the hell, Kirk. What's a guy like you playing a weak guy like (Vincent Van Gogh) for? There's only a few of us left." I explained to him I was trying to become an actor.

Interview, Oban, Scotland/
San Francisco Examiner & Chronicle
(Datebook), 4-18:15.

I think that we have a tendency to forget that the greatest contribution picture making can do is to entertain. Nothing in filmmaking

is more important than the therapeutical value of an audience being taken out of its own problems in a movie . . . However we do it, the end result must be that the audience loses themselves in the picture that they're seeing.

Interview, Los Angeles/
The Hollywood Reporter, 8-6:12.

Melvyn Douglas
Actor

Playing an interesting role is like having a love affair. When you have a love affair in your teens, you think it is the most important that will ever happen to you. In your 20s, you know better, because a richer, more rewarding experience has come along; and so on into later years. It is like that with actors. Each role is your love of the moment.

Interview, Los Angeles/
Los Angeles Herald-Examiner, 1-17:(F)1.

One hears that your price goes up if you win a prize (such as the "Oscar" award), but that has never been my experience. One also hears about the conniving, the exploitation of soliciting votes, so that also puts you off in a way. But if I win (for his role in *I Never Sang For My Father*), it would be inhuman to say I wouldn't be gratified. But on the other hand, I really don't think there is any such thing as "the best" of anything. Actors can't be compared; roles can't be compared. It would make more sense if awards were set up like the honors list in school. Everyone could then be recognized for the contributions they've made.

Interview, New York/San Francisco
Examiner & Chronicle (Datebook), 1-24:5.

Clint Eastwood
Actor

(His goal in films): Maybe it's a swear word today—but just to entertain. I don't feel I have any major social message to impart. But if there is an underlying message in the film, fine. It's the difference between the saber and the foil.

Interview, New York/
The Washington Post, 3-31:(B)1.

466

Blake Edwards
Director

It used to be that there were 10 directors you were sure of. Now, a guy has one great success and three failures and you look back and say, "What did I ever see in him?"
The New York Times Magazine, 6-20:11.

Alice Faye
Former actress

I don't go to movies much any more. I don't understand the Jane Fondas; I don't understand the *I Am Curious—Yellows*. I went to see that thing with a girl friend in San Francisco, and we had to have three double martinis afterwards. I don't live in the past, but the old movies are still the ones people remember. I watch them on TV and cry like a slob.
Interview, New York/
The Washington Post, 5-2:(K)2.

Jane Fonda
Actress

I want to see actors and actresses enlisted in a boycott of sexist movies. And I also want to see the practice of producers chasing girls around the desk abolished in our industry.
Interview, Los Angeles/
Los Angeles Herald-Examiner, 2-25:(B)5.

Bryan Forbes
Director

I'm a very unshowy director. I don't believe that you should flash your technique to the detriment of the actors. In the last analysis, performance is everything. I don't think it matters a damn what camera lens you're using or how well you can spin the camera on the end of an elastic band. I mean, that's jolly nice for a lot of mad movie buffs. The point is, all you remember is performances, whether it's Spencer Tracy and Katharine Hepburn, or Garbo.
Interview, New York/
The New York Times, 10-24:(2)11.

John Frankenheimer
Director

For many years, movies could be made that went out and broke even or earned a few hundred thousand dollars, the comfortable little pictures that kept things going between big hits. Not anymore . . . There doesn't seem to be room for the qualified success. The public will still go to see good movies. But I don't have the answers, and I don't know anyone who does. Nor do I know where the audience is. It comes out for *Airport* and *Love Story* and then disappears again. There seems to be a mysterious underground that lets people know in advance if a picture will be a hit. Thereafter, the successful movie seems to take on a life of its own.
Interview, Los Angeles/
The Dallas Times Herald, 7-16:(A)27.

William Friedkin
Director

I don't think people want to see personal expressions by directors. I don't think they want to see stars. They want to see stories that move them emotionally. My attitude may seem cynical but it isn't. It's as practical as I can make it.
Interview, Boston/
The Christian Science Monitor, 11-15:13.

James Garner
Actor

. . . I'd like to see some of the glamor stay in movies. They've taken all the magic out of motion pictures. The mystery's gone. I remember when no one would think of going up to a movie star and slapping him on the back. They'd do it to a TV actor—he's only a foot high on their screens and he's in their home all the time. In a movie, the guy's head is 21 feet tall up there on the screen. No one's going to play games with that!
Interview/San Francisco Examiner
& Chronicle (Datebook), 8-8:13.

467

John Gielgud
Actor

I do enjoy making films. One arrives, after a long journey, in some totally strange location and is whisked into a costume and instantly has to perform. Not like the theatre at all, with all the preparations, fittings and rehearsals. I remember arriving in Spain for Orson Welles' *Falstaff*. Everything was in chaos. Welles just flung these old robes on me . . . but it all worked somehow. As I was due to leave, Orson suddenly realized he hadn't got a reaction shot he needed. "Look here and here and there and here," he said. I did, and of course there was nothing to look at. But it was marvelous when it was edited into the film. Of course, it helps if you are something of a genius like Welles.

Interview, Los Angeles/
Los Angeles Herald-Examiner, 12-19:(F)1.

Paulette Goddard
Actress

Hollywood is now a place to retire to. Even the producers are itinerant today—they have no home base. The reason for the "stars" is that they always had the studio. Look how Clark Gable was groomed by MGM. If he had just run from one movie to the next, I'm sure his ears would have looked bigger than they were. Stars need somebody responsible for their career, who protects them from everything bad. Now, everybody's on a one-shot deal.

Interview/Life, 2-19:63.

Dagmar Godowsky
Former actress

I don't know why it is (that silent screen stars were more beautiful than those of the present day cinema). Maybe it's because we were chosen for beauty, and the standards were more classic. I know it sounds conceited, but when I was in Amsterdam as a girl they had to get police to protect me. This was before I was in films. Barbara La Marr, Corinne Griffith, Margaret Livingstone, Dolores del Rio—you don't see beauty like that on the screen today.

Interview, London/
Los Angeles Herald-Examiner, 1-2:(B)9.

Lee Grant
Actress

There are people (in films) who have been successful "doing nothing"—like Carole Lombard and Jean Arthur. But to "do nothing" is not easy. Today, the "do nothing" girls are in trouble, because the public will have a love affair with these girls for a year or two, and then they fade. To be respected by the whole American public at first, and then not be loved for the very same dimples they loved you for before, is very heart-breaking.

Interview, Los Angeles/
The Hollywood Reporter, 4-29:6.

Peter Graves
Actor

Movie stars, as we knew them, no longer exist; but I think they can again. For the past 10 years, everything has been anti-hero, but I sense a change. The heroes of the '60s were the John Kennedys or the John Glenns. People now want a hero they can identify with or admire. Once the motion pictures straighten themselves out, the first girl to make three good pictures in a row will be a star.

Interview, Los Angeles/
Los Angeles Times (Calendar), 2-28:15.

Conrad Hall
Cinematographer

. . . very shortly there is going to be a machine out where you go down to the store and buy a movie like you buy a record. You take a cartridge and stick it into your TV set . . . It's so much more fun to go over to a friend's and sit down and watch a movie and have a cup of coffee and sit with your feet up and discuss it. It's a much better way of watching movies than going into a theatre that smells, and where the bathroom is a long ways away, and is probably dirty, and the sound is not the way you want it. At home, you have the controls right there. I think that theatres are out, as soon as this new equipment comes in. Then you'll have a collection of movies, and you'll exchange with someone else who has a collection of movies. Let me see *2001* tonight, and I'll show you *Birth of a Nation.*

Interview/
The Wall Street Journal, 6-14:12.

Laurence Harvey
Actor

One is always striving to do more, to do diverse things, to create excitement and shock the audience. But at the same time, you are always risking the loss of reputation you had prior to that. You have to experiment, and that sometimes requires—or necessitates—failure . . . Whereas a scientist can go on experimenting, and if he fails he fails in the privacy of his laboratory, an actor fails in public . . .

Interview, London/
The Albuquerque Tribune, 5-10:(C)6.

Charlton Heston
Actor; President,
Screen Actors Guild

The generally-accepted image of a movie actor is wildly distorted, I'm afraid. In the public mind, he is pictured as enormously affluent—the possessor of large sums of money and a glittering public image, both of which he squanders around fur-lined swimming pools largely populated by naked starlets. The truth, I'm afraid, is a long way from that. The film actor is a hard-working professional, though he has not had the opportunity to work so hard in recent years as he would like. In fact, he's not had enough work to feed his family. Last year, 76% of the membership of the Screen Actors Guild made less than $3,000 under the Guild's jurisdiction for the year. That is, as you may know, below the official poverty level set by Federal standards.

At Federal Communications Commission
panel discussion, Washington, March 18/
Daily Variety, 3-19:29.

Nudity is never erotic, except in the bedroom. On film, it is merely decorative, and then only when photographed well.

Interview, San Francisco/
San Francisco Examiner, 8-20:24.

The time has come for the American people and the American government to recognize that the American film industry is one of our nation's most vital assets and that this industry is in desperate need of Federal assistance. A disastrous decline in domestic film production, coupled with a decrease in the weekly audience from 80 million to 17 million, begins to look like the collapse of the American film industry . . . Historically, this country has always refrained from government sponsorship of the arts. For the past decade, however, we have joined the rest of the world in recognizing that this is an important area of governmental responsibility. Each year, increasing sums of Federal money are disbursed to support music, dancing, architecture and so forth. To date, however, none of this money has been given to film producers.

Before House General Subcommittee
on Labor, Los Angeles, Oct. 30/
The Hollywood Reporter, 11-1:1.

Alfred Hitchcock
Director

Actresses are all children under the skin, some nice, some nasty—but most of them stupid. I remember an actress imploring me on the set one day to "Photograph my good side," to which I replied, "Madame, you're sitting on it."

Interview, London/
Los Angeles Times, 3-22:(4)17.

Some of the films now are full of tricks for the sake of tricks. Some are full of cliches, too—flowers in the foreground that are just a blur, things like that. Where cinema is concerned, I am a puritan. I believe in telling a story visually. I believe in using the medium for what it is—the medium of montage, of cutting. A lot of films are only photographs

(ALFRED HITCHCOCK)

of people talking, merely extensions of the theatre. To me, the visual is first and the oral is supplementary.

Interview, London/
The New York Times, 6-18:24.

Dustin Hoffman
Actor

I always used to think I wanted to be an actor, when all along what I really wanted, deep down, was to be a movie star. It's something you just don't admit even to yourself.

Cornwall, England/
The Hollywood Reporter, 2-22:2.

Dennis Hopper
Director

Most great movies are bombs, because the audience has not been educated to receive them. Art lives beyond its own time.

Interview, Los Angeles/
San Francisco Examiner, 10-29:3 ..

Ross Hunter
Producer

How sad, how terrible that showmanship seems to have lost its true meaning. All too many people have taken the word "show" out of showbusiness. In Hollywood, our industry is dominated in many areas by people who manufacture stoves and breakfast foods and refrigerators and petroleum products. To most of them, making movies is only a question of profit and loss. They rely on banks of computers that go blip and brr and zip and zap in order to find out what kind of movies the people want. When the computer is proven wrong, they turn to research experts and market surveyors for more answers. Then they analyze the clinical reports with slide rules and mathematical equations and gradation scales and frequency curves. Where did all the creative people go? Who was supposed to pick up the banners of Louis B. Mayer and Sam Goldwyn and DeMille and Lasky and the others? Do you know who took their places? I'll tell you who did: ogdoads. That's a $10 word I found in the dictionary, and it means

something that has eight heads—an executive committee, for instance.

Accepting Producer-of-the-Year award
at National Theatre Owners Association,
Texas branch, convention, Dallas/
Daily Variety, 2-11:14.

I once thought I could never be ashamed of an industry I love so deeply; but I've been ashamed of the movie business for several years. I am deeply and painfully embarrassed by the screen filth being passed around as movie entertainment. There is no rhyme or reason for filthy movies being projected in neighborhood theatres. Hard-core pornography in films has but one place—the back alleys of show business—and it should be kept there. I think the sun is beginning to shine again. The novelty of screen pornography is decreasing. The shock value is wearing off. The public is finally realizing that behind the nudeness and the lewdness, those movies are really pretty lousy. But while we all can applaud the fact that X-rated films are on the decline, we must remember that the customer who was offended by some of that screen pornography is probably still mad. He's a much more elusive patron than he used to be. Because of dirty movies, it's going to take a lot more hard work to get him back into that theatre seat.

Accepting Producer-of-the-Year award
at National Theatre Owners Association,
Texas branch, convention, Dallas/
Daily Variety, 2-11:14.

Glenda Jackson
Actress

(How it feels to be an "Oscar" Award nominee): It's like being pregnant with a child someone else may have for all your labor pains.

The Hollywood Reporter, 3-22:2.

Herbert Jaffe
Vice president in charge
of worldwide production,
United Artists Corporation

The tragedy of the recent past for all the (film) industry has been that the $6 million picture has come in at $8 million. You might have come out even at the lower figure, but you're dead at $8 million. We laughingly call ourselves an art-form, but our problems are the problems of any manufacturer.

Los Angeles Times, 12-31:(2)2.

Leo Jaffe
President, Columbia Pictures Industries

From our viewpoint, the prime objective is to make the customer feel that motion pictures is still one of the least expensive forms of entertainment, and that he hasn't been cheated by the presentation of inferior or distasteful product . . . There is no such thing as a built-in audience today, such as we had the last three to five years; it's selective, flexible and subject to change, as indicated in the present trend away from flesh pictures to the family type.

Before Variety Clubs International,
Las Vegas, Nev., April 28/
The Hollywood Reporter, 4-29:3.

Stanley Jaffe
President,
Paramount Pictures Corporation

A picture pulling in $20 million is making a mess of money. If it turns out to be only enough to break even, then you've done it all wrong. Even with $10 million worth of business you should make money.

Interview, Beverly Hills, Calif./
Los Angeles Times (Calendar), 1-24:20.

Deborah Kerr
Actress

(In the Hollywood of the late 1940s) we all worked and had a kind of security. Things were done. They knew what the audiences wanted. At least they thought they knew. Things were done with a kind of nice secure plan. You knew what to expect if you made a certain kind of picture—what kind of response and what kind of money. Now, nobody knows or has any kind of an idea what will go and what won't go. That's very healthy!

Interview/
The Washington Post, 8-22:(K)10.

Jack Klugman
Actor

I don't like Hollywood. In New York, you produce a play, and the aim is to have the best writing, the best acting, the best directing. Here, they want a guy who looks good on a horse. It doesn't matter if he can't act.

Interview, Los Angeles, 2-6:29.

You can't learn how to act in movies. You can learn your best side or how to light yourself. But all acting is remembering what you did on the stage. The good actors, like Olivier and Tracy, were on the stage. They try to say, "Back away from the camera." I say the hell with the camera. Move the camera away from me. Don't interfere with the actor.

Interview, Los Angeles/
Los Angeles Times (Calendar), 8-0:13.

Veronica Lake
Former actress

I felt it (the "new Hollywood") would give the youngsters a chance—the competition with television, the lack of (a) "star system." And it has. But it seems to be a dangerous thing. Young talent comes to the top in three years; then they have the rug pulled out from under them. Now it can *truly* be said that you're only as good as your last picture.

Interview, San Francisco/
San Francisco Examiner & Chronicle
(Datebook), 4-18:17.

Claude Lelouch
Director

All good things are brief. On a movie, as with a couple, things start coming apart after about five, six weeks. People begin finding fault, quarreling. You've got to reduce time to the minimum to keep that first fine flush of enthusiasm and excitement. Every movie for me is like a love affair between the director,

471

(CLAUDE LELOUCH)

crew and actors. It's got to be short to be good.

Interview, Paris/
Los Angeles Times (Calendar), 9-26:16.

Jack Lemmon
Actor

Actors are really like children, you know. We're always looking for a new way to be something different from ourselves.

Interview, Los Angeles/
Los Angeles Herald-Examiner, 10-3:(F)4.

Jerry Lewis
Actor, Director

Sex, greed and incompetence have hurt films more than any other factor.

London/Variety, 4-28:31.

I can't blast American audiences; they've been very good to me for years. But as for the critics, well, we don't have many *real* critics in this country anyway—only about half a dozen—and I've gotten blasts from all of them. The question is, I suppose, how do I feel when I get blasted? Naturally, I don't like it. But as long as critics really examine my work, I have to respect what they have to say as their sincere opinions.

News conference, Washington/
The National Observer, 6-28:18.

Joseph Losey
Director

(Regarding directors who submit to restrictions imposed by producers): There are three categories of such directors: young directors with no money; commercial directors; and salaried directors who are kept men, puppets paid by their masters. Unfortunately, the situation in cinema, as far as the financial side goes, is always the same. Few directors have been able to acquire a certain amount of freedom: Bergman, Fellini and perhaps Resnais. Bunuel did what he wanted to do, and finally he was accepted. If I live another 15 years, I hope to become part of this select group.

Interview, Rome/Variety, 1-27:24.

Shirley MacLaine
Actress

Hollywood and television, with very few exceptions, are totally out of touch with the culture. (The public) is freer; it's more liberal. It's willing to take a lot more than Hollywood is willing to give them. If some of the producers in Hollywood would make more of the films they believe in, you'd find more of a fusion with the culture.

At Yale University/
The Hollywood Reporter, 12-31;8.

E. G. Marshall
Actor

I have known performers who actually resent being asked to grant an interview or to give an autograph. They believe it is an invasion of their privacy. No one forced them to get into this business. And every time a performer refuses these requests, it serves to alienate someone. Interviews and autographs are part of show business. So, to those actors who live in ivory towers, I can only say that you are in trouble when the press and the public *don't* ask.

The Dallas Times Herald (TV Times), 4-25:4.

Walter Matthau
Actor

Today, the moviegoing public accepts the idea that you don't have to be extremely beautiful, and you don't have to stand very tall, and you don't have to look like you're a cigar store constipated Indian, or be a great beauty, to have a love affair. They realize that it's possible now for an ordinary fellow to be accepted in a role where he has something to do with a female. He can kiss the girl, or he can say, "Hello, darling," without looking stupid or constipated, and the audience will believe it if the guy is a good enough actor.

Interview, Los Angeles/Parade, 5-16:9.

When you become a "movie star," the very things the critics liked about you when you were unknown and obscure, they now despise. The "dry humor" that critics liked about me is now termed "sour presence." And those little "nuances" they loved, they now accuse me of using like a "phony."

Daily Variety, 6-7:2.

Andrew McLaglen
Director

The Western includes love, bad, good, right and wrong, heroes and villains. Any story can be transformed to a Western simply by providing the background. We (in the United States) haven't the heroes of antiquity that belong to Europe or the Orient. So men of the Old West are our prime legends.

Interview, Los Angeles/
The Dallas Times Herald, 1-1:(C)2.

Burgess Meredith
Actor

(The new wave of frankness in films) has been supressed for so long; and anything natural which is blocked up will eventually explode. That's what has happened, and it causes a lot of distress and pain. There is an awful lot of cheapness coming out, and that's too bad; but that's the price you pay. We get all kinds of bad by-products as a result of our own greedy natures, as well as from suppression. As a matter of fact, with the people who are in the ascendency now, we'll probably see stronger attempts at suppression of the arts.

Interview/Los Angeles Herald-
Examiner (California Living), 4-11:25.

Douglas Netter
Executive vice president,
Metro-Goldwyn-Mayer, Inc.

It's very obvious from the reaction of the public and theatre owners that they are sick and tired of excessive violence, excessive sex, nudity and profanity. There seems to be little or no interest in films dealing with the contemporary social issues—race problems, college, revolution. The trend, certainly, as we see it, is a return to entertainment.

Daily Variety, 12-3:1.

Richard M. Nixon
President of the United States

(Samuel Goldwyn) proved you could have a movie that was good boxoffice, that was entertainment, that was exciting, that was not dull, and still was not dirty.

Presenting the Medal of Freedom to
Samuel Goldwyn, Beverly Hills, Calif.,
March 27/Daily Variety, 3-29:1.

Gregory Peck
Actor

I am finding I get restless just acting. It's not as stimulating as organizing, planning and arranging for production. Creating a film is far more engrossing than just projecting the stellar role in it.

Los Angeles Herald-Examiner, 7-22:(D)3.

Eugene Picker
President, National Association
of Theatre Owners

Films are not made to be shown in a vacuum. Their first responsibility is to entertain. Any message expounded must be of secondary significance. There are vast numbers of people waiting to return to our theatres, if we can only find the chemistry to convince them that we have the kind of entertainment which provides them with the rewarding and satisfying experiences they used to know of old.

At Show-A-Rama-14 convention,
Kansas City, March 9/Variety, 3-10:18.

(Regarding the Motion Picture Association of America's film rating system): It demonstrated to public officials that we were mindful of our responsibilities to the community. It showed we acknowledged a commitment to the welfare of the youngsters. It proved we were legitimate businessmen and not pornography specialists—and as such were entitled to run our theatres free of legal restraint and official embarassment.

Variety, 7-28:46.

It's already apparent to most producers that

(EUGENE PICKER)

garnishing the story line with moral garbage is no longer the automatic path to the fast buck. More compelling considerations than ethical zeal have persuaded the filmmakers of this verity. The public has been speaking at the boxoffice; and what it has been saying is that gratuitous sex and violence are not satisfactory substitutes for a superior story.

At National Association of Theatre Owners convention, New York, Oct. 25/ Variety, 10-27:3.

Roman Polanski
Director

People ask why I do . . . this or that film. Why? Why do I eat fish and not steak for lunch? I don't know why. There are layers of experience, and not only artistic experience. Making a film is separate from life, but it is made by a human being, and whatever happens to me has got to have an influence in what I do. A film sums up the experiences of my life. You absorb the experience, you assimilate it and you make a decision. A film sums up everything—whom I see, what I drink, the amount of ice cream I eat. It is everything. Do you understand? Everything.

Interview, London/ The New York Times Magazine, 12-12:36.

Anthony Quayle
Actor

If you're an actor, you walk a tightrope between two extremes, between justifiable pride and humility. You have to cultivate a complete carelessness of yourself, in a way, or else become an egotistical, introspective monster.

Interview, New York/ The New York Times, 3-14:(2)15.

Tony Randall
Actor

A good actor must truly sublimate his own ego. Actors cannot afford the flaming self-adoration of an Ev Dirksen or a Billy Graham. They must lose themselves in their roles—

unless they're just playing themselves in make-up.

Interview, New York/ San Francisco Examiner & Chronicle (Datebook), 4-25:13

Ronald Reagan
Governor of California; Former actor

The United States is virtually the only country in the world where the pictures of all the world are free to play with no restrictions, no quota and no special taxes assessed against them which aren't assessed against our own pictures. In every other country in the world, they restrict the amount of pictures we can show; they restrict the playing time given to those pictures; they have extra added taxes against American pictures.

News conference, Sacramento, Jan. 19/ The Dallas Times Herald, 1-20:(A)32.

Rachel Roberts
Actress

Everybody in England knocks Hollywood, so I went there with a great deal of trepidation. But I'll tell you this—I got better and more professional treatment there than at any other time in my 20-year career. Better make-up, better coaching, better lighting. I had to play golf in one scene, and they even sent me to the Bel-Air Country Club for golfing lessons. I like the feeling of being pampered. English film studios are very poorly equipped, you know. You don't even get air conditioning. When I did *This Sporting Life*, I had to wash my own hair over a dirty sink.

Interview, New York/ San Francisco Examiner & Chronicle (Datebook), 2-14:12.

Ken Russell
Director

Filmmaking is an odyssey. You never know what is going to happen. You set out on a journey, meet all sorts of monsters on the way, and, in the end, you either win or get wounded.

The New York Times, 4-19:54.

(His philosophy of filmmaking): This is not the age of manners. This is the age of kicking people in the crotch and telling them something and getting a reaction. I want to shock people into awareness. I don't believe there's any virtue in understatement.

Time, 9-13:53.

George C. Scott
Actor

There are only two kinds of actors, in my opinion: risk actors and safe actors. Safe actors hold back, experiment not, dare not, change nothing and have no artistic courage. I call them walkers.

The Washington Post (TV Channels), 3-7:32.

I think you have to be a schizoid three different ways to be an actor. You've got to be three different people. You have to be a human being. Then you have to be the character you're playing. And on top of that, you've got to be the guy sitting out there in Row 10, watching yourself and judging yourself. That's why most of us are crazy to start with, or go nuts once we get into it. I mean, don't you think it's a pretty spooky way to earn a living?

Time, 3-22:63.

Actors are the world's oldest underprivileged minority. For centuries, we've been looked upon as nothing but buffoons, one step above thieves and charlatans. Those awards ceremonies simply compound the image for me. A lot of people sitting around making an exhibition of themselves. What I hate is that whole superstructure and the phony suspense and the crying actor clutching the statue to his bosom and all of that crap. It's all such a bloody bore.

Time, 3-22:66.

(Regarding the Academy Awards): I have nothing against anyone in any profession being honored by their peers. The other awards do it and get it over. They decide, and then it comes out that Joe Bosotz won. Great. What I dislike is making a two-hour television spectacular out of it. Putting actors in competition with each other—that should never be . . . Those close-ups of the wife crying and all that nonsense—I won't be a party to it. I am a commercial actor. I enjoy being paid, and I earn my money. But I don't like being used as a freak. And I don't like it for my colleagues.

Interview, Nerja, Spain/
Los Angeles Times (Calendar), 3-28:43.

God knows, you go to weird, marvelous places (making films). And from time to time, you get a chance to do something important. But there's so much time wasted waiting for things to happen. Overall, you begin to wonder if it's a very important profession.

Interview/Look, 4-20:83.

(Regarding screen nudity): I'd never do it; no, not for any role. I'm not a skin-flick actor. Even years ago, when I looked a little better with my clothes off, I wouldn't have done it. The whole thing is just one of those dumb phases our business goes through for exploitative reasons. I don't approve of exhibitionism on or off the screen.

Interview, Los Angeles/
Los Angeles Times (West), 11-7:5.

The essence of art should be life and change—and that can't be where movies are concerned. The film freezes your art forever. No matter how much better you become, there is no way to improve a performance you've done for the camera. It's locked. And there's a certain, sad death in that.

Interview, Los Angeles/
Los Angeles Times (West), 11-7:5.

Walter Seltzer
Producer

I think gratuitous nudity and vulgarity (in films) are on their way out. But the language and sex emphasis will be with us for a long time. Pictures reflect our society. Television

(WALTER SELTZER)

doesn't. That's the difference.

Los Angeles Herald-Examiner, 12-27:(B)4.

Leon Shamroy
Cinematographer

The obtrusive camera is like a chattering woman. It's okay for the camera to join the conversation, but it must never dominate. It must never distract from the story. The real art of cinematography lies in the camera's ability to match the varied moods of players and story or the pace of the scene.

Interview, Los Angeles/Los Angeles Herald-Examiner (California Living), 4-11:19.

Melville Shavelson
Writer, Director, Producer

Eighty-five per cent of the Screen Actors Guild in Hollywood are now unemployed, with the average member making less than $3,000 annually; meaning that the income of the average member is below the National Poverty Level. But the problem is that for so many years Hollywood spent its energies glamorizing its image, that who now is going to help "poor little Hollywood?"

Interview/San Francisco Examiner & Chronicle (Datebook), 4-25:3.

Stirling Silliphant
Screenwriter

Humphrey Bogart told me one afternoon in New York toward the end of his life that the only thing that matters in the film business is a continuity of success. To achieve this, he said, was to survive, and the people who are really successful are the survivors. Just hang in there, kid, and if you're still around 20 years from now, somebody will have to notice you, hand you a gold cup, and write a column about you. I've put in 14 years as a writer, so I'm in my second decade. If I can survive 30 years and do some good things and some bad, that's better than having written one brilliant thing 20 years ago.

Interview, Los Angeles/ Los Angeles Times (Calendar), 12-5:27.

Carrie Snodgress
Actress

I'm not interested in just staying up there on the silver screen. I want to make films because they say something, because they're honest. Movies are one of the largest communicative devices this country has; and we must use them to talk about the problems of the times, to talk about the difficulties of communication, to talk about the hostility that lies in people. If it's just another Western or a movie that doesn't tell the truth, I can't do it.

Interview, Los Angeles/ Los Angeles Herald-Examiner, 2-14:(G)5.

Sam Spiegel
Producer

It's too bad that when actors become stars, too many cease being actors.

Los Angeles/Daily Variety, 12-21:2.

When I finish a picture, I always sit down and consider how large is the gap between my original concept of the film and what's on the screen. If the gap is big, you'd better not release it. If the gap is tolerably small, you have a success.

Interview, Los Angeles/ Los Angeles Times, 12-23:(4)8.

Donald Ogden Stewart
Former screenwriter

. . . in 1929 a thing happened which was called the Depression, the crash and so forth. As far as Hollywood was concerned, it never happened. Or, rather, it was a very good thing; because people needed a dream world to get away from the awfulness of the reality around them—breadlines and all that. And boy, did we know how to give them dreams!

Interview, London/ The Washington Post, 4-8:(D)1.

James Stewart
Actor

The picture business is in trouble . . . Big studios find it impossible to continue. Television, football and baseball and other entertainments have come up to fill the additional spare time that people have. We are no longer at the top of the heap. Movies used to be *the* recreation. Now we are in a niche. Now we must get back in a different operating status. One thing hindering this is not enough variety. We are getting tagged too much as a sort of permissive, stag-movie type medium. The way people tell us this is true is to stay away. I don't think Hollywood is an industry just to make movies for the family. We are not a national baby-sitting organization. I think it would be just as bad to have all Disney pictures as it would be to have all stag pictures. I think the medium can stand all sorts of pictures.

Interview, Los Angeles/
San Francisco Examiner, 6-30:29.

Gordon Stulberg
President, Cinema Center Films

The number of paid admissions in the U.S. this year will be the lowest in the history of the movie business since the advent of sound.

Daily Variety, 2-4:2.

Mel Torme
Singer

The era of film musicals is over. They'll still make pictures like *Fiddler on the Roof* and *Man of La Mancha,* but those are stage plays put on screen. The day of films such as *Singing in the Rain* and *The Bandwagon* are over, too trivial and naive for today's audience that wants more relevant themes. I don't agree, though; I loved those films, and it is sad that we can't enjoy that land of escapism.

Interview, Dallas/
The Dallas Times Herald, 3-21:(E)8.

There's been a great change in the entertainment field since I entered it. Naturally, the economy dictates change. But, aside from that, this is a time when what is sought is rapid prosperity rather than posterity. If you look at the movies, we used to develop stars who became household words. They had some kind of longevity. Now, with TV and records,

and entertainment so easy to obtain, stars and fads get instant recognition, and, as instantly, depart. They come and go. It's sad.

Interview, Los Angeles/
Los Angeles Herald-Examiner, 4-20:(D)4.

Francois Truffaut
Director

I laugh from morning till night—while I'm filming, I mean. It is the only way to keep morale high. If things go wrong, I don't show it. With 40 people standing around watching you, the director must always be buoyant, always look happy.

Interview, London/
San Francisco Examiner & Chronicle
(Datebook), 1-3:6.

Lana Turner
Actress

. . . this whole business was built upon illusion—to give the public a chance to escape from the realities of life for a little while. It is escapism. But now the people cannot; hell, they live in the same situations that are on the screen. Now nobody can tell me that's escapism. That's what the whole business was built on, for beauty. Give the people back their dreams. It's tough enough as it is.

Interview, Beverly Hills, Calif./
The Washington Post, 6-6:(K)3.

Peter Ustinov
Actor, Writer, Director

Film is a hybrid form at the moment. The critics treat it as an art form, but it really isn't an art form. It's a cocktail of artistic sympathies. It is, to my mind, at its best a poignant and appealing form of journalism set on an artistic base.

Interview, New York/
Publishers' Weekly, 10-25:17.

Roger Vadim
Director

I am now determined that I will not work for a major studio again. After all, the reason I decided to become a director in the first

(ROGER VADIM)

place was because I wanted to be my own boss on a creative level. You cannot be that with a big studio. They always think they know better than you do.

Interview, Malibu, Calif./
San Francisco Examiner, 3-10:28.

Jack Valenti
President, Motion Picture
Association of America

You read a national (film) critic for the pyrotechnics of his prose—what Bacon calls "the sweet falling of words." But if you're looking for advice on a movie to see, you get much better advice from your peers.

Interview, Washington/Newsweek, 2-1:74.

We will need the help of the government. I have never felt before this way, but I am convinced of it now. The problems are too heavy to carry without some kind of government recognition that the film industry is a national resource and therefore: 1. There should be a Congressional bill which should encourage more pictures to be made in this country; 2. Government assistance in treating the motion picture industry, on the matter of taxes, like other industries in this nation. Both are very much needed.

Before Society of Motion Picture and
Television Engineers, Los Angeles,
April 26/The Hollywood Reporter, 4-27:1.

In the five years I have been in the motion picture business, I have determined that the most pressing need in this business is for leadership, for men with vision, for men with ideas, for men with the courage of their convictions; because an idea is worthless unless it is given sinew and strength and is brought to life and is able to do whatever it is that an idea strives to do.

At National Association of Theatre
Owners midwest convention, Milwaukee,
Aug. 18/Daily Variety, 8-20:1.

. . . a number of pictures have been made which have a more insular content than possibly would have been the case 20 years ago. This is not necessarily a pejorative statement. I am not necessarily speaking about art, quality or enduring merit. I am talking about the audience value of a film, which means how many people go to see it. One of the things that oftentimes an audience senses, that even a creative man overlooks, is the dramatic impact of a film. I mean the sense of conflict, suspense, building up of plot, holding our interest, which is the ancient way of telling a story, which has captivated people since the dawn of time. Many times the creative man today is more intent on developing the subtle nuances of character and stream-of-consciousness, which results in a piece of valuable art, great merit and even enormous skill, but which fails to affect the viewer with this ancient tonic you call "interest." Many times this results in a spate of lyrical reviews—and justly so—about pictures that great numbers of people simply have no interest in seeing . . . Let's realign ourselves with the dramatics of story-telling as it has captured people's interest for a thousand years. Be like the ones around the campfire telling stories, like the book you can't put down because you can't wait to find what happens on the next page. Let's have a balance of innovative and specialized pictures and movies for all audiences, telling a good story with dramatic intensity and interest. This does not mean a creative man can't have a message; there are messages by the ton to choose. But it should all be interwoven in a seamless web of dramatic continuity.

Interview/Los Angeles Times, 8-23:(2)7.

. . . the biggest thing that needs to be done is to make pictures that people want to see. That's really the crux of it. You can change your distribution system; you can clean it out and do all sorts of things to it. But unless you have movies that people want to see, it's of no avail. The bottom line, the key, the gut and and core and heart of this business is making movies that enough people want to see to cause that movie to be a success, a financial success, so that you can produce more movies.

*Interview, Los Angeles/
The Hollywood Reporter, 10-4:11.*

The (MPAA film) ratings have been well received by the great majority of the American public. It's only within the industry and the critical field that so much adverse criticism is heard. The ratings make a tempting target, an easy bell to clang. During three years, we have rated 1,400 films. No more than 20 or 30 of them have become controversial, in that their ratings were questioned. I think that is a good record.

The Dallas Times Herald, 12-30:(A)23.

King Vidor
Producer, Director

Because of a newly-found freedom, there are many people making films who don't have the background that is necessary, either in their individual lives or in their lives as filmmakers. They jump in half-ready, and the results are disorganized, incomplete and badly-constructed films. However, I'm very pleased with anything that shatters accepted conventional conditioned hypocrisy. You can't sit on progress; and I feel encouraged by the new freedom, because it breaks away from old patterns. It's bound to lead to free use of cinema, which will show better when the new movement is perfected or there is more awareness of what's going on.

*Interview, San Sebastian, Spain/
Daily Variety, 7-29:3.*

Hal B. Wallis
Producer

I suppose that if anything at all unifies the body of my work, it is the constancy of my approach to filmmaking. It is very simple, really—though I realize it is fashionable these days for filmmakers to speak of deep social problems that influence their work. In my case, this approach begins with a deep reverence for the cinematic form. I've always had it. Although I am almost a lifetime removed from the small, suggestible boy in a darkened Chicago movie theatre, caught up in the magic of the flickering screen images, I never enter a movie theatre, or even a studio projection room, without experiencing a sense of wonder. I am always aware, as the blank screen is filled in, of the medium's power to move and affect and shape and change.

*Interview/San Francisco Examiner &
Chronicle (Datebook), 5-23:9.*

John Wayne
Actor

The men who control the big studios today are stock manipulators and bankers. They know nothing about our business. They're in it for the buck. The only thing they can say is, "Jeez, that picture with what's-her-name running around the park naked made money, so let's make another one. If that's what they want, let's give it to them." Some of those guys remind me of high-class whores . . . In their efforts to grab the box office that these sex pictures are attracting, they're producing garbage. They're taking advantage of the fact that nobody wants to be called a bluenose. But they're going to reach the point where the American people will say, "The hell with this!" And once they do, we'll have censorship in every state, in every city; and there'll be no way you can make even a worthwhile picture for adults and have it acceptable for national release.

*Interview, Newport Beach, Calif./
Playboy, May:76.*

Life, death, courage, good and evil. No nuances. Give 'em a little scenery, a little action. And then, if you've got a good personal story and good characterization, you've got a (film with) universal appeal.

The Dallas Times Herald, 6-20:(F)4.

Richard Widmark
Actor

Television is taking over an area of entertainment that I think is needed at this time; because the movie business is making pictures for a minority segment of the audience. There are more people than just kids. But to get the

(RICHARD WIDMARK)

others out of their homes and into the theatres is pretty tough. *I* don't like to go out to movies very much any more.

Interview, Los Angeles/
The New York Times, 3-7:(2)17.

Elmo Williams
Vice president in charge of worldwide production, 20th Century-Fox Film Corporation

Motion pictures should entertain. Unless they do, they are failures . . . Essentially, audiences want escape from reality in a movie. They don't want politics, social problems and moral lectures.

Interview, Los Angeles/
Los Angeles Herald-Examiner, 5-23:(F)5.

Robert Wise
Director

Critics don't give me enough credit for some of the qualities my films have, beyond the fact that they're commercially successful. I'm not an "auteur" director, and I'm not a Bergman or a Fellini. I've grown up in a different milieu. I've grown up in the studios, and we do have commercial considerations; we do take into account the people going to see the film. But I've never consciously gotten into something because I thought that it was a trend or going to be successful. I do consider the audience once I'm interested in an idea. I do try and project as best I can whether there is an audience for it—but only after I'm convinced it's worthy.

Interview, Los Angeles/
Los Angeles Times (Calendar), 4-11:16.

Keenan Wynn
Actor

The word "actor" is used too loosely. In our profession, there are a lot of people but few actors. A number of them fool around but can't act. Some of them stay around a long time. They sell. Clark Gable, a very fine

actor, became a star and wasn't allowed to act.

Interview, Los Angeles/
Los Angeles Herald-Examiner, 8-19:(A)15.

Frank Yablans
President,
Paramount Pictures Corporation

I think (film) critics are incredibly good when they write a good review; when they don't, I wonder why newspapers have them.

Milwaukee/Variety, 6-9:24.

We're losing our audience. I think some of it is because of the so-called visceral films. Overt sex and profanity aren't helping any, but they're passing things. People aren't paying to be offended. I don't advocate that every film be a *Mary Poppins*, but there is a vast and quite untraveled territory between *Poppins* and *Sexual Freedom in Denmark* . . . How do we get the people back? Once you've lost them, lost their faith, it's very hard to get them back. One thing we've got to do is roll back prices at the box office. Put on midweek specials. Look, the filmgoing audiences are all Jewish eaters—they only go where the food is good. Right now, the food isn't good.

Interview, Los Angeles/
Los Angeles Times (Calendar), 8-22:24.

Darryl F. Zanuck
Former chairman, 20th Century-
Fox Film Corporation

I've known this business from the silent days, when I started as a boy of 19 writing scripts. I've lived with this industry. I'll never live without continuing to make a contribution. The fact that I stepped down in one capacity (chairman of 20th Century-Fox) may lead to my stepping up in another. My heart, my body and my brain belong to the production of motion pictures.

At 20th Century-Fox stockholders
meeting, Wilmington, Del., May 18/
The Washington Post, 5-19:(E)1.

Adolph Zukor
Founder and chairman emeritus,
Paramount Pictures Corporation

There's nothing wrong with the picture business that can't be handled. But those in charge of it must study the temperament and tempo of the people. Most movies I see these days are shown in a projection room. But when a big one comes along—such as *Sound of Music, Midnight Cowboy* or *Patton*—I go to the theatres. That's the only way to judge the reaction of the public; and it's a thing I've been doing much of my life. Too many studios spend too much time evaluating techniques, the script, the brainpower behind production. They forget the audience—which makes you or breaks you.

Interview, Beverly Hills, Calif./
Los Angeles Herald-Examiner
(California Living), 4-11:10.

The whole world is getting educated through motion pictures. And the more the world sees motion pictures, the more they will know what is going on, will be much wiser, more informed than in the past. I don't know of any instrument that keeps the world so informed as films.

Interview, New York/
The Hollywood Reporter, 11-26:1.

MUSIC

Daniel Barenboim
Pianist, Conductor

If the public in America really valued music the right way, the government would give more money. America is the only place in the world where they talk about great orchestras all facing the threat of nonexistence. That's why in America music is an anachronism and in Europe it isn't. The Berlin Philharmonic isn't an anachronism; it gets a lot of money from the city of Berlin. Bad as conditions are in London—and they are terrible, the whole set-up is completely amateurish—none of the London orchestras faces the threat of nonexistence.

Interview, London/
The New York Times, 1-24:(2)15.

Tony Bennett
Singer

I'm only interested in great songs. Most of the songs by today's writers are not great at all. Very few of today's writers are capable of writing songs that will last . . . and I don't care how high they get on the charts. Aside from a few fellows like Burt Bacharach and Jimmy Webb, there are very few young writers who can write songs which can survive as long as those written by men like George Gershwin, Irving Berlin, Dick Rodgers, Cole Porter and many others who were doing their thing in the 1930s, '40s and '50s.

Interview/
Los Angeles Herald-Examiner, 7-3:(B)9.

Pierre Boulez
Musical director-designate,
New York Philharmonic Orchestra

The death of (Igor) Stravinsky means the final disappearance of a musical generation which gave music its basic shock at the beginning of the century, and which brought about the real departure from romanticism . . . The glory of Stravinsky was to have belonged to this extremely gifted generation and to be one of the most creative of them all.

Los Angeles Times, 4-9:(4)10.

The great works of music can accept the very direct kind of understanding; they can also stand the very investigative understanding. The great works are those which remain for each generation to understand anew.

Washington, July 13/
The Washington Post, 7-14:(B)8.

One of the difficulties in modern music is its lack of symmetry. Structural symmetry began to disappear with Wagner. Until Wagner, we had certain guideposts: a powerful first theme, a melodic second theme, a period of disorder when the two conflict. The conflict was finally resolved by repeating the beginning. Contemporary music is not based on repetition, so you must do the repeats yourself by listening more than once. As the initial shock is absorbed, you recognize this figure or that theme, finding your way in the music like a child going from home to school.

Before Fortnightly Musical Club,
Cleveland/Life, 11-12:46.

(Without reforms) concert halls will become more and more like museums—and bad museums. Firstly, because the performances are often not all that good. And then because, if you look at the pieces that are performed in the standard repertory, they are getting fewer and fewer. A good museum doesn't only consist of great masterpieces, such as Rembrandt's "Night Watch." It contains a lot of other paintings of the same period that form the background to his work and help you to understand more precisely why that particular work is a real masterpiece. It's the same in the concert hall. You've got to play Telemann as well as Bach's cantatas and the Brandenburg concertos.

Interview, London/
The New York Times, 11-14:(2)15.

Alfred Brendel
Pianist

A hundred years ago, one played almost always the music of one's own time. Today, with historicism creating a situation in which the bulk of the available repertory is the music of the past, it takes a special concentration of energy to perform the music of the present as well.

Interview, Los Angeles/
Los Angeles Times, 2-18:(4)12.

Maria Callas
Opera singer

From the beginning, singers must learn music; and music means technical things, like being on pitch and how to phrase. A singer's job is more difficult than an instrumentalist's. A violinist has a trill, period. But we don't have a trill, period. We have an emotion to express: fear, fury, anxiety . . . I have been criticized for singing sharp, shrill, hard phrases. But the drama or the comedy of an opera can ask for those sounds. You can't always just make a luscious sound—the drama comes first.

At the Juilliard School, New York/
The National Observer, 2-15:24.

I feel that opera is really in trouble. You have only to see performances all over the world. The training just isn't good enough. Singers are put on stage too early; they accept engagements before they are ready. In my time, it was far more difficult to make a career, simply because you had to be an accomplished musician. You had to have a voice to begin with. Then you had to have a personality, and hopefully, the looks. In my opinion, opera is the most difficult of all the

arts. To succeed, you must not only be a first-rate musician but a first-rate actor. It goes without saying that you must also be able to cope with your colleagues—with the conductor, with the other singers, with the stage director. Opera is a vast unit where everyone plays a vital role.

Interview, New York/
The New York Times, 10-31:(2)15.

Fiorenza Cossotto
Opera singer

It used to be that, in Europe, a singer's vocal technique was the great test—you know, one wrong note and the tomatoes would start flying. Now, the audiences at, say, La Scala, respond more to the dramatic interpretation, to the emotions of a singer. I think it was Callas who made the Europeans realize that there was more to opera than just bel canto. She taught them that high-voltage dramatics could be just as exciting as singing perfectly-pitched phrases.

Interview, New York/
The New York Times, 2-14:(2)20.

Bob Crosby
Bandleader

My job has involved so many things the audience doesn't know about . . . Being a bandleader is trying to get a baby sitter for a trumpet player (so) his wife can come to the gig; otherwise, she'll give him hell and he won't be in the mood to play. It's helping the trombonist find his lost suitcase, and advising the pianist whether to get a divorce.

Interview/
Los Angeles Times (Calendar), 8-29:47.

Hal David
Music lyricist

The lyricist might very well have been the romantic poet of another century. The way he makes his living today is writing the romantic lyric—like Shelley and Keats. Lyric writing at its romantic best is in that genre; but I also think it must serve the music. But the music must serve the lyrics, too.

Interview, New York/
The Christian Science Monitor, 1-4:13.

WHAT THEY SAID IN 1971

Edward Eliscu
*President, American Guild
of Authors and Composers*

The music industry without the writer is just a gigantic factory with nothing to make.

*Before American Guild of Authors
and Composers, Los Angeles, Feb. 17/
Variety, 2-24:47.*

"Duke" Ellington
Musician

Our (musicians) most unique point is that we're the only people in the world who do something 52 weeks a year without a holiday, a weekend or a vacation. We never leave it. We don't lock an office door and walk away from it and go breathe fresh air. We breathe our fresh air through music. It is what I enjoy; that is all.

*Interview, New York/
The Dallas Times Herald, 9-12:(E)4.*

Arthur Fiedler
Conductor, Boston Pops Orchestra

There's a great deal of snobbism in music, such that you have to go along with the musical elite. They belittle light music—as if you can only love Shakespeare and Proust, but not O. Henry, and even *Playboy!* Well, I have trained myself to understand all *kinds* of music. *I'm* not like a horse with blinders on!

Interview/TV Guide, 7-24:16.

Dietrich Fischer-Dieskau
Singer

I think that giving concerts, especially recitals, means much more to a musician (than opera). In opera, you are part of a large machine, and many nonmusical aspects are involved. When you stand alone on a concert platform, you are your own director and your own instrumentalist; there is nothing between you and your voice.

*Interview, Hamburg/
The New York Times, 1-17:(2):31.*

Goeran Gentele
*General manager-designate,
Metropolitan Opera, New York*

Opera is not a place where you should force people to do things. It's a question of creating a climate of enthusiasm, of having fun together and of making people feel the excitement that comes when you create art. There are so many tensions involved in any creative activity—for technical people as well as artists—that it is terribly important to make people feel as comfortable as possible, since most of them are terribly uncomfortable inside. So when there is a catastrophe, you never indicate that you think the end of the world has come. You examine it and say, "Well, this is a fine new catastrophe. Now, what else is important today?"

*Interview, New York/The New York
Times Magazine, 9-12:131.*

Jakob Gimpel
Pianist

When I was a boy, people would bring whistles to the concerts; and if they didn't like the performance, they would blow into them and disrupt it. There would be chaos. Now it is very different. The audience just sits and listens, and afterwards says "very interesting," even if they don't like it or understand it. People are the same way about modern art —afraid to express their own feelings.

Los Angeles/Los Angeles Times, 4-13:(4)6.

Jerry Goldsmith
Composer

There's a special technique of writing music for films. You have to have the sense of the drama. Not all composers can write for the movies; they can't submerge their own particular creative urges to serve the whole. And they don't recognize the fact that most people aren't going to listen to the music anyway. You sometimes want to stand up and say, "Why don't you listen; it's great music." But that's not what a film composer is there for. So to make up for all of this, we all try to put on an air of legitimacy by predicting all the great things we're going to do, apart from the cinema, sometime in the future.

Interview, Los Angeles/
Los Angeles Herald-Examiner, 3-21:(D)5.

Lionel Hampton
Musician

I'm playing a lot of swing these days, because people let me know they want to hear it. Swing is jazz, and jazz builds something as a musician improvises from his mind. You have to have a good musical background and be a good technician to do this. It's like an artist creating a painting. Why, even the young people like it, because it's something new to them; and they act like they just discovered jazz, swing and me.

Interview, Los Angeles/
Los Angeles Herald-Examiner, 1-30:(B)9.

Jascha Heifetz
Violinist

If I don't practice one day, I know it; two days, the critics know it; three days, the public knows it.

San Francisco Examiner & Chronicle
(Datebook), 4-18:21.

Rafael Kubelik
Music director,
Metropolitan Opera, New York

I think the whole stage business is overrated today. A director cannot go and stage an opera as if it were a drama. It's not a play. Opera has a special law, a special musical form. It's never as realistic as a stage play. It's not like a movie, either. Of course, one cannot have performers who are physically unsuitable for certain parts. One cannot have old-fashioned movements and all that nonsense, either. The director must try to keep things in good shape esthetically and dramatically. But the main effort should be concentrated on the score. This means that the conductor is a constructive element in an opera house and that he must share the responsibility for the over-all result.

Interview, New York/
The New York Times, 10-17:(2)17.

Peggy Lee
Singer

Everything now (in entertainment) is instant. (The performer has) no preparatory period to go on the road, learn about theatre and training and presence; and suddenly you're standing out there in front of 20,000 people. That must be frightening. Those who survive it are the ones who, seeing the value of their talent, try to protect it by honing it, polishing it, learning to become craftsmen.

Interview, Beverly Hills, Calif./
San Francisco Examiner & Chronicle
(Datebook), 3-21:7.

Eric Leinsdorf
Orchestra conductor

Orchestras today are corporate bodies. There are women's auxiliaries and board meetings and fancy offices. Instead of artistic meetings, there are endless business meetings that have little to do with music.

New York/The Washington Post, 12-29:(B)6.

John Lennon
Musician

The bigger we (the "Beatles") got, the more unreality we had to face. The most humiliating experiences were like sitting with the Mayor of the Bahamas, when we were making *Help!* and being insulted by these f—ing, junked-up middle-class bitches and bastards who would be commenting on our work and our manners. One has to completely humiliate oneself to be what the "Beatles" were, and that's what I resent.

Interview/Time, 1-18:34.

Alan Jay Lerner
Music lyricist

If I don't like a melody, Fritz (his collaborator, Frederick Loewe) never plays it again. If he doesn't like a lyric, I never use it again.

Palm Springs, Calif./Newsweek, 12-20:55.

Guy Lombardo
Orchestra leader

Ballroom dancing will come back. It's too

(GUY LOMBARDO)

good to go away. It is romantic, think so or not, to hold a girl in your arms. I bet more girls got engaged on dance floors than in the back seats of cars . . . People get a chance to dress up. And let me tell you one thing I notice: People are dressing up more now than they did a couple of years ago. People want to get out and dance again. They have had TV! They want to get out again, dress up, mingle. I would say the mood of the country is one of togetherness again.

Interview/Los Angeles Times, 12-31:(2)19.

Christa Ludwig
Opera singer

You ask how I find the interpretations for my roles. I cannot really answer that; because no matter how much I study a role, no matter how much research I do, my real and only guide is that first intuitive experience with singing the role. The interpretation and the vocal results just come . . . and I never know *where* they come from. I, myself, am astonished at the way things fall into place. Actually, it is the unconscious part of you that must respond in some way so that everything jells and becomes whole. This is something you cannot measure—it's pure magic. I believe very strongly in the magic and psychic part of art— the part we don't understand, and really *shouldn't* understand.

Interview, New York/
The New York Times, 1-31:(2)22.

William Masselos
Pianist

When I prepare a- new score, say, by Copland or Ben Weber or by William Mayer, I begin by sight-reading it. It's like taking your first walk in a forest path, and you're very aware and alert, because it's a first, and it's a fresh experience. Then, little by little, things fall into place; and suddenly, you know where you are; things become familiar. I like it when that happens—when I get that feeling of knowing exactly where I am and what is to

be—in one total picture. It's also like meeting someone you don't know but whom you instinctively like—some person who may be saying something you yourself have wanted to say.

Interview, New York/
The New York Times, 3-14:(2)26.

Johnny Mathis
Singer

. . . there are a great many good songs around today. The problem is, there's too many bad performers around doing this good material.

News conference, Dallas/
The Dallas Times Herald, 1-24:(D)4.

Gian-Carlo Menotti
Composer

Music (today) is in the hands of people who are either snobbish or ignorant. If I were still young, I would get on a horse and play the role of a St. George and the Dragon. As it is, I am past middle-age and I look ridiculous in a suit of armor.

New York/
San Francisco Examiner, 8-31:24.

Robert Merrill
Opera singer

There's such a thing as being too professional. Maybe one of the best things that happened to me as a young man was being turned down for a scholarship to study at Juilliard. Technically, I believe I was qualified; but the judges got the impression that I knew too much already. It seems to me now that if I'd won that scholarship I wouldn't have flourished. I needed to be developed as an individual.

Interview, New York/
The Christian Science Monitor, 2-24:13.

Darius Milhaud
Composer, Conductor

Once I heard a Boulez first performance, *Visages Nuptiales*, a very difficult work. He brought a tape to the public and spoke for more than one hour describing all the tricks and beauties in the piece. After his words, we heard a piece 15 minutes long! That bored me. For the public, analyses are nothing. That's why I never accept to write program notes—only the history of the piece, how and why it was written. But all those little details on the music, I think it's stupid!

Interview, San Francisco/
San Francisco Examiner & Chronicle
(This World), 4-25:33.

Richard M. Nixon
President of the United States

Country music speaks to what is tried and true for many Americans. It speaks of the common things shared by all: the happiness of a family, the pains of a broken heart, the mercy of God and the goodness of man.

Washington, Oct. 14/
Los Angeles Times, 10-15:(1)26.

Ewald Nyquist
New York State Commissioner of Education

Today we live in a world which is dominated by an outpouring of a vast variety of images and sounds. And the sound which speaks the most universal language, and communicates with and captivates the great masses of the youth we teach, is the sound of music. It is a menu for all seasons. One would have to be virtually deaf to ignore music today. Never in history has there been such an outpouring—such a mass availability—of musical sounds and noises. They bombard us from all sides, every day of our lives, thanks to progress in electronics and the communications media. Music pursues us into the supermarkets, the buses, the barbershops, the air terminals—even into the public washrooms. There is a danger of our becoming calloused by the ceaseless exposure and of seeking silence in some quiet place. But some intruder would be sure to follow with a transitor radio!

Before New York State Council
of Administrators of Music Education,
Kiamesha Lake, N.Y., Nov. 30/
Vital Speeches, 1-15('72):202.

Patti Page
Singer

Hard rock, acid rock, dirty rock—they are all just quick, passing fancies. I could never sing music like that, because there is no excuse for poor taste. And when you get down to the so-called "nitty-gritty," good music will always drive out bad.

Quote, 1-24:73.

Gregor Piatigorsky
Cellist

In the old days, people had time to sit around, discussing things, drinking, joking. Right around here we had Schoenberg, Stravinsky, Huxley, Heifetz. Now, people dash in for a concert and away again. There's been a loss of unity, of purpose in the profession of music . . . Nobody in this business communicates. Composers distrust performers, both distrust managers, and everybody dislikes critics.

Interview, Los Angeles/
Los Angeles Times, 1-26:(4)10.

Andre Previn
Composer, Conductor

(Regarding writing music for motion pictures): I have a feeling (that) in these hysterical days of the demise of the film, they're (filmmakers) all too anxious to have not a film score but simply a theme that can be recorded by whatever current pop group is around the charts.

Interview/
The Washington Post, 8-15:(G)8.

Richard Rodgers
Composer

A lyric is a problem, and I enjoy trying to solve it.

Interview, New York/
The Christian Science Monitor, 1-6:19.

Beverly Sills
Opera singer

I think American singers are the best-educated and best-trained in the world. When I sang *La Traviata* in Naples, I had a very interesting review from a critic there, who said it took an American to "come here and teach us how to sing that role." This is because there are no singing teachers left in Europe.

Interview, Washington, Jan. 31/
The Washington Post, 2-1:(C)3.

Georg Solti
Music director,
Chicago Symphony Orchestra

. . . the problem at the Met (New York's Metropolitan Opera) is a question of his (general manager Rudolf Bing) basically not understanding opera. Because opera is music, not a drama. At least music! Bing's belief, which is utterly wrong, and is the reason why I never went back to the Met, is that if you collect five or six big names, you automatically get a good performance. You don't! You don't!

Interview, Chicago/
The New York Times, 4-25:(2)13.

Isaac Stern
Violinist

(Igor Stravinsky's) passing is proof of what we lack today in music—a really great talent.

Los Angeles Times, 4-9:(4)10.

Joan Sutherland
Opera singer

To survive as a diva, you have to be absolutely like a horse.

The Washington Post, 5-16:(K)1.

Michael Tilson Thomas
Musical director,
Buffalo Philharmonic Orchestra

The quality I especially admire in (Leonard) Bernstein is the way he demands that every note, every second of music be super-intense and alive. With Bernstein, even very slow pieces have staggering presence at every instant. I want to approach music in the same way. I'd like to have the feeling that the orchestral players and the conductor, together,

are really speaking through the music.

Interview, Washington, March 16/
The Washington Post, 3-17:(E)1.

I like to rehearse, and in a very detailed way. The way to be popular with an orchestra is to go through the piece and say, "A little louder here and a little softer there," and that's it. But I can't do it. I was rehearsing the Schumann Third Symphony with the Berkshire Music Center Orchestra recently and I drove them crazy trying to get the phrases exactly the way I wanted them. But the performance turned out so well that in the end they were happy. One has to be that way. If you really know a piece, it means knowing how every single note goes, and that takes a *lot* of rehearsing.

Interview/
The New York Times Magazine, 10-24:47.

Virgil Thomson
Composer

You can't go into a royal palace or a peasant hut today without finding a radio on somewhere. In the old days, the rich had restaurants with a little trio, and the poor had their beer gardens. Now there's cocktail music, dinner music and after-dinner music. The first is a little goosey, the third is a little dancey, and the dinner music is pure boned mackerel.

Interview, New York/
The Washington Post, 11-25:(C)3.

I find (opera) the most interesting thing around in music today, because it is least bound by schoolmasters and school-book minds. It's show business, and therefore has to work.

Interview/Time, 12-6:84.

Alexis Weissenberg
Pianist

A piano is definitely not a she. I think a piano has the potential of a bull, and to dominate it is one of the most exciting things for a pianist.

Interview, New York/
The New York Times, 8-15:(2)11.

THE STAGE

Edward Albee
Playwright

I go back to my theory that all critics should be judged by their betters, that is, the playwrights. And if they don't measure up, they should be shot.

Time, 4-12:41.

Musicals and escapist plays are always going to do better at the box office than serious plays . . . Most people go to the theatre to get out of their lives; and the purpose of serious theatre is to put them more into it—which is a proposition most don't like.

Interview, New York/
The Washington Post, 4-25:(E)9.

Wouldn't it be awful if I woke up one day and decided to go to my typewriter and realized I didn't have an idea in my head? Of course, some people say that already.

Interview, New York/
The Washington Post, 4-25:(E)9.

Most critics are honorable and sober men . . . limited by two factors. One, the fact that most of them have got to make value judgments about a piece of theatre in an hour, which can't be done. And all critics, of course, are limited by their intelligence. Unfortunately, a lot of critics are of no more use to you than your uncle.

Television broadcast, New York, Sept. 5/
Los Angeles Herald-Examiner, 9-6:(B)4.

Judith Anderson
Actress

Sure, I'm old; but I am sick and tired of . . . writers who keep dwelling on that. I want people to see me and not be thinking of how old I am. What I do on the stage is what counts. There are a lot of young people who never have seen me perform. My age isn't important to them.

Telephone interview, Evanston, Ind./
The New York Times, 1-3:(2)3.

Burt Bacharach
Composer, Musician

You put in all that blood and sweat. That's one thing that bothers me about the theatre. You feel it's so impermanent. It takes you two months to train an orchestra—then there are 11 subs (substitutes) one night, even the conductor. A good performance and next a lousy performance. You've lost it. That's the impermanence of it. On film, it remains; you do it, and it will stay there. When you do it for TV, it's always there, too; you wait for the rerun but, anyway, it's there. The theatre bugs me.

Interview/Los Angeles Herald-
Examiner (TV Weekly), 3-14:6.

Brian Bedford
Actor

To be perfectly honest, I don't think about the theatre very much. I think about the things that *I* do myself. I get involved in my *own* roles, in my *own* projects. Frankly, I've stopped going to the theatre, because it bores me.

Interview, New York/
The New York Times, 3-28:(2)14.

Maurice Bejart
Director, Ballet of the 20th
Century, Brussels

It is ridiculous to say, as some do, that there is not a large public for ballet. There is. But for the large public, ballet must change as much as music and painting have in the 20th

489

century. The traditional balletomanes are like the ruined families of Europe who like to imagine they are powerful, although they have no more money. But young people—young people can be touched by ballet as by no other art form. Dance is so immediate and speaks to them so powerfully.

Interview, Brussels/
The New York Times, 1-24:(2):3.

Larry Blyden
Actor

Broadway is finished for our lifetime. Don't expect anything but musicals and comedies, for three reasons: greed, stupidity and the times. Greed, because the producers are strictly after the buck, not wanting to gamble. Stupidity, because of the formula thinking. Most people in theatre today came in on the big wave of the realistic thrust that began with Ibsen. They never realized that there was a limit as to how far theatre realism could be pushed. So when realistic drama stopped working, these people got nervous and went into producing safe little comedies.

Interview, Dallas/
The Dallas Times Herald, 6-15:(A)26.

Peter Brook
Director

Theatre can have only one purpose, which is to give you something you can find nowhere else. Critics, audiences and theatre people lost their balance for a number of years, because they saw that society was moving in a technological direction and theatre was not a part of that mainstream. Films and television were. But now there is an instinctive understanding among writers and directors—an intuitive world conspiracy, if you will—that the strength of the theatre is not in going with the mainstream of technology. On the contrary, its strength lies in making certain little concentrated events in which one can participate—the unique quality of living events that

technology makes more and more inaccessible.

Interview, London/
The New York Times, 1-15:20.

(Speaking of Shakespeare): No other playwright offers the actor or the director such dynamic elements with which to create a miniature real world in all its complexities and richness. And like the real world, his plays have a looseness and openness that go beyond the strict vanity of form. They lend themselves to endless permutations, without in the least destroying the basic fabric of the work. In fact, nothing of Shakespeare exists until it is performed in the place and period and space in which the actors are working. His plays are as contemporary or as old-fashioned as making love or eating an apple. The sperm or the juice emerges where or when the act takes place.

Interview, New York/
The New York Times, 1-17:(2)15.

There is only one interesting difference between the cinema and the theatre. The cinema flashes on the screen images from the past. As this is what the mind does to itself all through life, the cinema seems intimately real. Of course, it is nothing of the sort—it is a satisfying and enjoyable extension of the unreality of every-day perception. The theatre, on the other hand, always asserts itself in the present. This is what can make it more real than the normal stream of consciousness. This also is what can make it so disturbing.

New York/
The Washington Post, 1-31:(E)3.

Mel Brooks
Playwright, Comedian

One of my cardinal rules for writing is I really want to bang my head on the table on the way down to the floor, laughing. I don't want to ever say, "I think they'll like this." I want to first laugh so much I can't write it down, then hope to remember it so I can. I want to be able to say, "If they don't like this, they're crazy."

San Francisco Examiner, 7-13:33.

490

Abe Burrows
Playwright, Director

I don't think people should come to the theatre relaxed or for relaxation. They should come to pay attention.

> *At "Playbill" magazine-sponsored luncheon, New York/Variety, 2-24:1.*

Carol Channing
Actress

There is a great difference in preparing for a musical compared to a straight play. You have to get in shape and work at it. You have to get muscles moving that you haven't moved in some time. That's the reason I hate to miss any performances; even one day off and I find that I have to get my muscles limber again. The theatre can be, oh, so exciting and thrilling and full of great rewards—but it is never easy.

> *Interview, Dallas/ The Dallas Times Herald, 7-4:(D)7.*

Paddy Chayefsky
Playwright

The only point the recent Off-Broadway strike made was to prove to audiences that they do not have to come to the theatre . . . One of the horrors of being a playwright is that the audience is too tiny to kill off. Theatre, if it continues, will be cultist.

> *Interview, San Francisco/ San Francisco Examiner & Chronicle (Datebook), 1-10:3.*

John Cranko
Director-choreographer, Stuttgart Ballet

Some people think it's a sin to tell a story in ballet. I disagree. You can look at Shakespeare and see only incest, murder and rape—if you're a fool. But you can also find a world of psychology and poetry.

> *Interview/ The Washington Post, 8-1:(H)1.*

Marlene Dietrich
Actress

I don't think it (nudity) has any place in the theatre. If you can't do it without being nude, you ought not to do it at all.

> *Quote, 11-7:434.*

Melvyn Douglas
Actor

. . . at my age, it is easier to make a film than to appear in a play, even though I have never the same kind of personal satisfaction from movies. There's something about exposing yourself eight times a week to an audience that has a built-in tension all its own.

> *Interview, New York/ San Francisco Examiner & Chronicle (Datebook), 1-24:5.*

Helen Hayes
Actress

I'm alarmed at what is happening to the world I've known the best and loved the most—the theatre. I would like to see some kind of concentrated effort begin to rid the theatre of such undisciplined nonsense as plays without words, story, meaning or clothes.

> *Dallas/ The Dallas Times Herald, 3-17:(C)1.*

I find a thin, dulling veil of snobbism creeping into the theatre, and I resent it terribly. Give me a play with a beginning, a middle and an end, and characters that are recognizable and that send you out of the theatre knowing a little more, perhaps, about yourself and the people who live in the world with you. I'm tired of seeing audiences punished instead of being entertained.

> *Interview, Los Angeles/ Los Angeles Times, 3-19:(4)14.*

. . . some of the best theatre in New York is Off-Broadway, and has been for some time. Actors work for peanuts; but they are fulfilled and happy. Seems the critics are kinder to their efforts—and that is something in this day of the cynical and destructive review.

> *Interview, Los Angeles/ Los Angeles Herald-Examiner, 4-11:(E)3.*

491

Katharine Hepburn
Actress

Film separates; but the life-spark in the theatre is the relationship between you and the part and the audience.

Interview, Baltimore/
Los Angeles Herald-Examiner, 4-26:(B)5.

John Houseman
Director

... the new theatres being built around the country, and the several that will be along in New York fairly shortly, can be an answer to what's ailing us. Why on earth should people go to those crowded, uncomfortable theatres that have outlived their time? They're damned unpleasant places to go. These new theatres are pleasant places to be. I'm bullish about this; I believe that our new regional theatres are producing new playwrights and new audience attitudes that soon will be reflected in New York.

Interview, Washington/
The Washington Post, 11-14:(H)

William Inge
Playwright

Playwriting is a selfish art. Writers who write to fulfill themselves, but with an audience in mind, achieve respect and success. Those who write just for an audience, turn out television and bad novels and are doomed to be forgotten.

Los Angeles Herald-Examiner
(California Living), 9-26:6.

Danny Kaye
Entertainer

There are hundreds of local symphonies, and business leaders are proud to be on the board and help subsidize them. That is not so with theatre groups, however. The cultural attitude toward the stage is different. Theatre actresses are considered "loose" women.

At "Playbill"-sponsored luncheon,
New York, May 20/Variety, 5-26:48.

David Merrick
Producer

Of course, it's no substitute for a good play (the new 7:30 p.m. Broadway curtain time). I've found that if you have a hit play, you can put it on at 4 a.m. and get an audience.

The New York Times, 1-10:(4)10.

Financially, some (plays) just don't (make it). *Take Me Along* ran 448 performances over at the Shubert and still didn't get out of the red. What is a hit and what isn't, anyway? *Variety* listed *Take Me Along* as a failure . . . You can't tell me that if people go to a play for over, well, 200 performances, that it wasn't worth producing.

Interview, New York/
The Washington Post, 11-30:(B)2.

Ray Milland
Actor

I don't understand actors. In the theatre, they must do the same thing precisely with their eyeball or pinkie each performance or they forget their lines. So you fall into a dreadful rut. Some actors . . . love the theatre and the interplay with the audience. Not me; I hate live audiences. I'll never work in the theatre again as long as I live.

Interview, Los Angeles/
The Dallas Times Herald, 9-21:(A)19.

Agnes Moorehead
Actress

My repertory experience was the most valuable of my life. One week, I'd play a leading role; and the next, I'd do a walk-on as a maid. The trick is to be the best maid or cook or spear-carrier that you can. Talent without self-discipline is pathetic. Today, the film and TV world is run over with talented young people completely undisciplined. In this day and age, there's no time for self-indulgence. An actor must be totally prepared to do anything, anywhere, at any hour. The only way to the top is work, work, work.

San Francisco, March 30/
San Francisco Examiner, 2-1:31.

John Osborne
Playwright

. . . I look on the theatre, in a way, as an act of aggression . . . The very fact that you create a conflict with the audience . . . it is all an act of war.

*Interview/Los Angeles Times
(Calendar), 1-24:57.*

Joseph Papp
Producer, New York Public Theatre

Our first responsibility is to the playwright, then the actors, the directors and the audience. I can't build this theatre on the Broadway idea of having hits. We don't mind hits, but I don't believe in long runs. I'm against them artistically; they don't give a new play a chance of getting on the boards. I do shows I think are worthy of being done. I hope the audience agrees with our choice. But we cannot just take the audience as an abstraction and try to satisfy them.

The National Observer, 3-29:20.

I want theatre that is doubting, questioning. We're not a newspaper. Don't waste your time in the theatre if you leave without having something about you changed. Go roller-skating. Make love. But don't go to the theatre.

Time, 11-15:71.

Harold Pinter
Playwright

It may sound childish, but I tend to regard the audience as my enemies. In other words, they're guilty until they're proved innocent. What is required is simply an act of concentration, and they so rarely seem disposed to give it. Half the time, I wonder what the hell, why do they bother to go to the theatre. I'm not at all convinced that the main bulk of a given audience is really interested in the theatre. But when I'm in the audience, I have great sympathy with the audience for having to submit to the terrible things on stage.

Sometimes I feel dreadfully with them in our mutual suffering.

*Interview, New York/
The New York Times Magazine, 12-5:135.*

Harold Prince
Producer, Director

I have to make money to stay in the theatre. But I'm not in the theatre to make money.

Newsweek, 7-26:68.

Anthony Quayle
Actor

(Regarding repertory): You do get to evolve a style and an understanding of your fellow actors and directors. But if it gets too permanent, you turn into civil servants and tend to sit on your, ah, bottoms and think you're fine. I think, perhaps, a semipermanent company is the best idea—people always coming in, others going, rather like a bath being emptied and filled at the same time.

*Interview, New York/
The New York Times, 3-14:(2)15.*

Tony Randall
Actor

. . . I think back 29 years, to when I got the part of a coal miner in Ethel Barrymore's company of *The Corn is Green.* When I reported to the theatre, the stage manager took me aside and instructed me on how to behave around the First Lady of the Theatre. One disappeared into the shadows when her car pulled up to the theatre; one never spoke to her unless she addressed one—and if she did, one stood at attention; one tiptoed and whispered when passing her dressing room; and one had to watch oneself even when she was not backstage—she had spies in the company and knew everything. She never let you forget that she was Royalty. She was also a bad actress—that plangent voice, posey, stagey, fake. But she did what she had been trained to do, and she did it with nobility. It was a hell of an experience for a kid like me,

493

(TONY RANDALL)

that tour with the First Lady. I have only one regret—I never met Miss Barrymore.

Interview/TV Guide, 1-2:19.

George C. Scott
Actor

One of the most important attributes for an actor to cultivate is a sense of analysis of himself and his audience. The audience is a dark thing, a peculiar animal, an enemy that must be assaulted and won. That's the big competition right there—not between you and the other actors, but you and the audience. The only measurement of fine acting is so simple, yet so many actors get fouled up about it. It's this: Does the audience feel it? It doesn't matter a damn what the actor does or does not feel—it's what the lady with the blue hat down there is feeling. You as an actor can suffer the agonies of the damned; but unless that's communicated to the people who paid $9.90 to see it, you've failed.

Time, 3-22:66.

Neil Simon
Playwright

Critics. Some of them are very helpful. As a group, I don't find them very consistent. Some of the notices for *Gingerbread Lady* were very strange. "Why doesn't Neil Simon go back to writing those wonderful comedies?"—from people who couldn't stand those "wonderful comedies" when they first came out. I can accept the most severe review when the man behind it seems to be saying, "I want what you're doing to be good, but it isn't good and here is why." But I can't accept the kind of notice that starts off with, "What you're doing couldn't possibly be any good because it's Broadway"—and then goes on to tell you why, sure enough, it isn't any good.

Interview, New York/
Los Angeles Times (Calendar), 2-28:32.

Maggie Smith
Actress

The theatre, in the end, is *it* for me . . .

(In films) I never get over the empty, unfulfilled feeling of having once said the lines, moved through the paces, extracted the momentary emotion from a particular scene . . . then knowing I'll never see it again. I mean, it might be cut, or edited, or moved to a different sequence. As a creation it is gone. You can never go back and improve it. You get another chance in the theatre—every night. There is that new chance to do it better, work on the laugh, hear it succeed, feel it fail.

Interview, Spain/
Los Angeles Times (Calendar), 11-28.24.

Robert Stephens
British actor

One hopes that theatre in the provinces of America finally will help to feed Broadway the way theatre in the provinces of England feed London. After all, Shakespeare started at Stratford-on-Avon, not the West End. New York is too parochial. This is an enormous country, and it would be nice if New York could feed off the size of it.

Interview, Los Angeles/
The New York Times, 4-15:36.

David Susskind
Motion picture-stage-television producer

I don't think the American theatre is a temple. I think it is a whorehouse.

London/San Francisco Examiner, 9-4:34.

Gloria Swanson
Actress

(Regarding Broadway in the 1920s): There was an excitement about everything . . . You had beautiful restaurants and lovely ladies dressed for the occasion—not looking like they were going to a gym.

The New York Times, 8-22:(4)3.

. . . I don't read any reviews (of her performances). I don't believe I've read, in my whole life, 10 all the way through—even if they're flattering . . . The only way I'll listen to one is if somebody holds me down and reads it to me.

Interview, New York/
The New York Times, 10-10:(2)13.

Edward Villella
Ballet dancer

The closest thing to ballet, I guess, is the (boxing) ring and basketball. But being a dancer is a lot different. My parents could never see where the winning and losing is in ballet; but it is there, only it is just not visible and it is much more elusive. The athlete can accomplish his feats in any way best suited to him. The dancer has to win within the framework of a technique, of a musical phrase, of a dramatic idea. He has to make what he does alive and beautiful through the power of the movement and the delicacy of the control.

Interview, New York/
Sports Illustrated, 9-27:100.

Dale Wasserman
Playwright

I am very fond of the musical, but not in the conventional way. I'd like to make it encompass a range of subjects that it just hasn't dealt with in the theatre. The musical can wield and hold any subject that anyone wants to use it for. Music for me is one more dimension of theatrical expression. I think we are going to see more and more progress to the serious musical form.

Interview, New York/
The Dallas Times Herald, 7-15:(D)3.

TELEVISION AND RADIO

Steve Allen
Television entertainer; Humorist

(Concerning humor on television): Some of the best humor of the new school of comedians involves social criticism. It is calculated to offend one social group or another. And since television is an advertising medium which almost by definition is dedicated to the proposition that not a single viewer should be offended, we are presented with a problem which is essentially incapable of solution.

Before Pacific Pioneer Broadcasters,
Los Angeles, Nov. 19/
The Hollywood Reporter, 11-22:5.

Amyas Ames
Chairman, Lincoln Center for
the Performing Arts, New York

The truth is that commercial television and radio have developed a system that functions extremely well to its purpose—which is sales. But this highly-evolved system rejects the quality programs of arts and humanities exactly as the human body resists a transplanted organ . . . Since the multi-million audience can only be attracted by certain types of entertainment, the arts, education and many subjects of broad national interest are blanked out by what is, in effect, a monopolistic dominance of television by mass-appeal programs. Because many of the wonderful things in life fail to meet the commercial test of "instant broad appeal," we all become underprivileged.

The New York Times, 10-9:29.

Pearl Bailey
Entertainer

There are two things about television. Its sameness, the repetition of ideas. You can blame that on the attitude that it can't be done if it hasn't been done. Then, they have

this strange way of handling talent. They're attracted to you because you are what you are. When they get you, they want to change you. You have to fight to stay yourself.

Interview, Los Angeles/Los Angeles Herald-
Examiner (TV Weekly), 2-7:4.

Lucille Ball
Actress

When I started on TV, you couldn't show a pregnant woman. Now, you can show her and also show how she got that way.

Receiving award from International
Radio and Television Society/
San Francisco Examiner, 3-17:41.

Gene Barry
Actor

The only excitement in TV is making the pilot, seeing it get on the air and then waiting to find out whether it will succeed. If it does, then you're stuck in a hit show.

Interview/Family Weekly, 4-4:15.

Richard Boone
Actor

Television is a strange monster. The people who are necessarily in executive positions are business executives and salesmen. So when you walk in to talk about a creative idea, you're talking to the wall. It's not that they don't want to understand, or that they want to make bad television—they just don't know. But they're forced to make creative decisions every day. In non-commercial television, you've got academicians and politicians instead of businessmen and salesmen—and I don't know if that's any improvement.

Interview, Los Angeles/
TV Guide, 9-25:16.

Dean Burch
Chairman, Federal Communications
Commission of the United States

The nation's bets always have been placed on a commercially-based (broadcast) industry to assay a higher incidence and a higher quality of public service than any theoretical public alternative. And that is where my bets remain.

Before National Association
of Broadcasters, Chicago, March 31.

Robert C. Byrd
United States Senator, D–W.Va.

. . . over 10 years have passed since Newton N. Minow, in his role as Chairman of the Federal Communications Commission, told the National Association of Broadcasters that television was "a vast wasteland." America has just endured the first week of television's new offerings, and it appears obvious that Mr. Minow's words ring as true today as they did a decade ago. A full 20 of the 56 prime time hours of our three major networks are occupied by detective shows—blind detectives, fat detectives, private detectives and detectives upholding the honor of local, state and Federal governments. If our streets were as amply patrolled as our prime time TV hours, we could all sleep a lot better at night.

Before the Senate, Washington,
Sept. 20/
The Wall Street Journal, 9-29:12.

Kitty Carlisle
Actress

I have found a home in television. It has done more for me than any other medium. I am relaxed on the show *(To Tell the Truth)*, and it gives me personal contact with people because they respond as if I'm a friend. How else could New York have been turned into a village for me? Guys pop out of manholes to shout, "Hello, Kitty, how are you?" And when I get into the elevator at Saks, it turns into a cocktail party.

Interview, Los Angeles/
Los Angeles Times (Calendar), 1-10:41.

Dick Cavett
TV talk-show host

I once thought I'd always be nice to people if I ever became a star, because I saw so many stars who weren't. I still try to be polite; but I understand it all better now. People want you to become part of their lives.

Interview, New York/Family Weekly, 4-25:18.

Paddy Chayefsky
Playwright

. . . the trouble is that TV is dedicated to the largest audience possible. Its executives explain they want meaningful but commercial programs. That's why it's hopeless. Television has no self-respect. It should think of America as something more than *Hee-Haw*.

Interview, San Francisco/
San Francisco Examiner & Chronicle
(Datebook), 1-10:3.

Most of the drama on television is garbage. You can't call those series "drama"—week after week, the same dialogue coming out of the same stock characters. There's nothing for me there.

Interview, New York/
San Francisco Examiner & Chronicle
(Datebook), 5-30:14.

Tony Curtis
Actor

Movies and television are the same. All this talk about the big screen and the small screen is nonsense . . . When I watch television, my eye absorbs the images just as it would at the movies. You forget what medium it is you're watching. You lose the size of the screen. Your eye adjusts to the size. I found no special approach was needed in my acting . . . I can't understand how an actor could look down on television. If he does, he has his head in the ground. He's playing an old L. B. Mayer record.

Interview, Los Angeles/Los Angeles
Herald-Examiner, 9-6:(B)2.

Michael H. Dann
Vice president, Children's Television workshop; Former vice president in charge of programming, Columbia Broadcasting System Television

I take no joy in predicting a gloomy future for the networks, because the system has been good to me and is providing significant contributions to our national life. But the times they are a'changing, and the networks are not; and the name of the game in TV is change.

Before New England Broadcasting Association, Boston, Feb. 25/
Daily Variety, 2-26:23.

You know, I just don't believe people when they say they never watch television, that there's nothing worth watching. Don't kid yourself; there's almost always something to watch.

Interview, New York/
The National Observer, 3-1:20.

. . . television is no longer a new toy; it has to compete equally with every facet of the communications industry. It really is now facing the same crunches that all other American businesses are facing; and in television that poses a real challenge. Like any other management in the entertainment industry, television management can't rest with the bookkeepers or the business administrators. Sound business principles are okay and good and great as long as you don't have to be creative. But when things start to get tough, then that kind of management no longer serves the best interest of the broadcast industry and the people as a whole.

Before New England Broadcasters Association, Boston/Variety, 3-3:32.

Bob Dole
United States Senator, R–Kan.

Most TV programs are 30 minutes or an hour long. They all have one thing in common: At the beginning of the program they build a problem. Maybe it's minor, but often it is the problem of peace or war, or famine, or law and order. But, regardless of its magni-tude, 30 or 60 minutes later the problem is solved. Every day and every night for most of their lives, your children and mine have watched the major problems of the universe solved in 30 or 60 minutes. Is it possible . . . part of the unrest in this country, part of the dissatisfaction with government and with our leaders is that, as far as our children are concerned, they do not solve problems fast enough? The smog that is here today is here tomorrow. And so is the civil rights problem. And so is the war. And you name it. In real life, problems are solved and go away very slowly. Are our children having trouble separating the immediacy of television from the reality of life? Are they demanding more than we can ever deliver, or more than they will ever be able to deliver? Is TV creating a frustration with reality that can only be relieved by threats and demands for change, and that failing, by violence? I don't know the answer, but I suggest that we think about it.

Tucson, Ariz./
The Wall Street Journal, 12-9:16.

Mike Douglas
TV talk-show host

(Regarding motion picture actors appearing on TV talk shows): Take a script away from some screen actor, rob him of the protective cloak of a characterization, put him in front of a TV camera just being himself, and he may freeze so cold even his own mother wouldn't recognize her Charm Boy.

Interview, Beverly Hills, Calif./
Los Angeles Herald-Examiner, 8-22:(E)3.

Alex Dreier
Former news commentator

Radio is the most imminent communications media there is. You have nothing to rely on in capturing your audience other than your voice. Your audience can't simply sit back in a chair and watch you present that which you have to say. You've got to capture him, make him lean forward so he won't miss a word, while still entertaining him.

Interview/San Francisco Examiner
& Chronicle (Datebook), 4-25:15.

Don Durgin
*President, National Broadcasting
Company Television*

(Regarding the selling of 30-second commercials): Television was once sold by the carload, then by the case, then by the can, then by the potful, now by the cup—and some people want to sell it by the sip.

*Before Broadcast Advertising
Club, Chicago, Jan. 12/
The New York Times, 1-13:49.*

The biggest single problem (in TV programming) is trying to maintain enough flexibility. Our audience has color TV; it has black and white TV. It is wealthy; it is poor. It is male; it is female. It is employed; it is unemployed. It is old; it is young. How do you program for a profile like that? You need tremendous variety. Your challenge is to really "broadcast" rather than "narrowcast."

*Interview, Los Angeles/San Francisco
Examiner & Chronicle, 8-22:(B)4.*

Dave Garroway
Television personality

. . . the American people for some reason have done a very funny thing. You wouldn't think of taking a book off the shelf and reading it without looking at the title, or going into a movie without looking at the marquee to see what's playing. And yet, that's what we mostly do with TV—we turn it on and watch whatever comes out.

*Interview, Los Angeles/
The New York Times, 7-18:(2)20.*

Nicholas Johnson
*Commissioner, Federal Communications
Commission of the United States*

When our homes fill up with junk appliances and toys, our stomachs with empty calories and chemical additives, and our heads with conspicuous-consumption commercials, it is big broadcasting that is the pusher . . . We are all by now quite familiar with what the big business-big broadcasting-big government axis has done to this country.

*At Windham College commencement,
Putney, Vt./Variety, 5-26:27.*

One of the most vicious of television's predatory habits is its stalking of the poor. The affluent have nothing to lose but their money and control over their own lives and personalities. The poor are not so lucky. They must sit there, without even the depressing knowledge that money can't buy happiness, and be constantly told that their lack of material possessions is a badge of social ostracism in a nation that puts higher stress on monetary values than moral values. Occasionally this frustration breaks out in violence on the streets. Then, for an evening or two, we get a distorted picture of what the problem is, as television brings us the "news"—followed by another evening of series shows and commercial messages urging conspicuous consumption as the mark of success in life.

*Weinstock Lecture,
University of California at Berkeley/
The New York Times, 6-13:(2)19.*

Getting 100 million people to watch Westerns, soap operas and other prime-time junk is a political achievement that ranks with the Roman circus. The networks want to keep you stupid so you'll watch more of their programs. They are trying to get you to turn yourself off and turn them on.

*At International Design Conference,
Aspen, Colo., June 23/
The Washington Post, 6-25:(B)9.*

Chuck Jones
*Director of children's programming,
American Broadcasting Company Television*

The ultimate in children's television is to get children to do other things than watch television. If I do a show on Mark Twain . . . it's to inspire children to go out and build a raft.

*Interview/San Francisco Examiner
& Chronicle (Datebook), 1-10:15.*

Jack Klugman
Actor

Television isn't the place for an actor to learn how to act. It's not possible to start in TV and expect to get a good foundation that way. There are occasional shows . . . where you're fortunate to have lots of rehearsal; rehearsal is what works you into a part. In most cases of tape and film television, rehearsal is held to a minimum . . . TV doesn't let you eat and sleep a role. You can learn how to hit your mark, that you look better from this angle or that angle. But these are the mechanical and not the organic aspects of acting.

Interview, Los Angeles/Los Angeles Herald-Examiner, 2-17:(A)17.

Robert E. Lee
Commissioner, Federal Communications Commission of the United States

I think the stations do a good job in public service programming. It is easy to say they should do more, but the first obligation of a station is to make money, because if it does not, it won't be on the air . . . I would accept a station telling us it is going to do very little public service programming in a place where it could show there is plenty already. That would be broadcasting in the public interest.

Look, 9-7:49.

Robert F. Lewine
President, National Academy of Television Arts and Sciences

(Television) has had to be an art form, a fountainhead of entertainment, a symphony hall, a Broadway stage, a classroom, a newspaper, a sociological source of information and the best reserved seat for hundreds of sporting events each year. Unlike other industries, it must turn out its product around the clock, come hell or high water. The luxury of shutting down to catch one's breath will never be enjoyed in the broadcasting industry.

Before Century City Chamber of Commerce, Los Angeles/Variety, 3-3:34.

Art Linkletter
Television personality

Parents too often use the television as a baby sitter. They too often use this as a substitute to reading and active participation. Worst of all, I will indict television for this 100 per cent—because it is a very seductive play toy. And television in the average American home has practically killed conversation. Parents and families go through years of being in the same room every night, and they never say anything to each other except, "Turn the channel."

Before National Congress of Parents and Teachers, Oklahoma City/ Los Angeles Times, 6-4:(4)18.

Guy Lombardo
Orchestra leader

People have often said to me that they enjoyed the big dance bands on the radio because they found it left something to the imagination. They visualized the big ballroom. Radio had an air of mystery to it. You would hear a singer and wonder what he looked like. When you came to town, you wanted to see him . . . You can wear yourself out on TV so fast. Unfortunately, TV has proven itself a vicious medium. (It) just eats up talent.

Interview/Los Angeles Times, 12-31:(2)19.

Shirley MacLaine
Actress

I don't agree that TV necessarily hurts the cinema box office. If you make it on TV, you really grab the hearts of the people watching. And if they like you in the living room, they are even more likely to go out and see you in films. I believe the task of the stars is to raise the medium to help films. I don't believe they should stay away from television.

Los Angeles Herald-Examiner, 5-5:(A)14.

John W. Macy, Jr.
President, Corporation for Public Broadcasting

. . . we have conducted a fundamental, down-to-the-bones analysis of public broadcasting to determine what our proper role is and how we may best serve. And we have concluded—not surprisingly—that our chief value to the nation lies in education. Not only in education that complements classroom activity; not only in education for the young; not only in education tied to books—but education in all its forms; for the young, the old and the in-between; education both formal and informal, tied to the classroom in some cases and in others tied only to the question of what life is all about.

Before National Association of Broadcasters, Chicago/Variety, 3-31:32.

D. Thomas Miller
President, Television Stations Division, Columbia Broadcasting System

Slowly but inexorably, the mass media have been dying off. Motion pictures now reach relatively small audiences. Magazines, once courting national audiences, now are far more limited, appealing to specialized audiences in most cases. Even major metropolitan newspapers no longer reach far into the suburbs; for instance, there are some 30 papers in the greater Los Angeles area. Early this year, *The New York Times* quoted NBC officials as saying that "radio, except for newscasts and occasional special events, is economically no longer a mass medium." In fact, radio's recent resurgence can be attributed to its appeal to specialized audiences—news, talk and various music formats. Only television remains today as a truly mass medium.

The National Observer, 9-18:13.

Roger Mudd
News correspondent, Columbia Broadcasting System

Our broadcasts have not improved. If anything, their quality has declined. The tube has become a trip, a national opiate, a baby sitter who charges nothing, something to iron by, and to shave to, and to doze over.

At Washington and Lee University, Lexington, Va./Quote, 8-22:185.

Ralph Nader
Lawyer; Consumer rights advocate

The top 10 problems of our country—such as pollution, Vietnam, inflation, campus demonstrations, drugs—should all be on television, instead of the candyland of dedicated doctors and lawyers who supposedly help the poor. How many of you know a truly dedicated doctor?

Los Angeles/ The Hollywood Reporter, 5-5:1.

Leslie Nielsen
Actor

Television is making craftsmen of actors. It's a birth by fire. You have to know your craft as an actor better for TV than movies because of the pressure . . . the pressure forces everyone to trust his first impression and intuition. In pictures, you have second thoughts, which aren't usually as good as the first insight.

Interview, Los Angeles/ The Washington Post, 9-29:(D)5.

Virginia F. Pate
National president, American Women in Radio and Television

The invention of radio, followed by television, must stand in the first rank—comparable in importance to the advent of the automobile, the airplane and moveable type—when measured in terms of its influence on all of us.

The Washington Post, 4-29:(F)4.

Anthony Quinn
Actor

(Why he is doing a TV series): I have always believed that an actor must have an audience no matter what the medium—be it the legitimate stage, motion pictures, records, radio, television or cassettes; an actor belongs where the audience is. Unlike the artist who can paint in his studio and exhibit to a few friends, or the pianist who can derive satisfaction from performing alone, the actor *must* have an audience. Without it he is nothing. And the

(ANTHONY QUINN)

biggest, most influential, powerful audience today is undeniably in TV.

Interview, Los Angeles/
The Hollywood Reporter, 8-30:6.

Elton H. Rule
President,
American Broadcasting Company

News is the foundation of television's credibility. And that credibility extends to areas of entertainment, to the commercials we show, to every nuance in the relationship between ourselves and our audience. If we lose that trust, if a credibility wedge is driven between us and the people we are pledged to serve, then we have not only lost face, we've lost the ball game.

Before ABC affiliates, Los Angeles,
May 3/Los Angeles Times, 5-5:(4)22.

Walter A. Schwartz
President,
American Broadcasting Company Radio

As broadcasters, we are the most vulnerable, for we have been subject to a regulatory body (the FCC) all along—one that, in keeping up with the trend to tear at the structure of the entire business establishment, sees itself in a new and more powerful role. So responsive had it become to the zealots within its own ranks and to the fanatical reformers who hammer petition after petition on its doors, that it has taken on the character of the great inquisition.

Before South Carolina Broadcasters
Association, Columbia, Feb. 17/
Los Angeles Times, 2-19:(4)18.

Rod Serling
Writer

(Regarding TV's Emmy Awards): They do it without dignity, in a back-slapping fashion. It is repugnant and ridiculous.

At Merced (Calif.) College/
Los Angeles Times,
4-27:(4)15.

Sid Sheinberg
President, Universal Television

The only times when I've ever fallen on my face are when I tried to play it safe. There's too much caution in this business. You get too cautious and you lose your bright young talent—writers, directors, producers. What attracts them is the opportunity to be bold, not cautious . . .

Interview, Los Angeles/
Los Angeles Times, 4-1:(4)27.

Barry Sullivan
Actor

There's never been a tougher school (than television). Here's the repertory company of today. It fulfills the basic credo I respect—that the reward for good deeds is more punishment.

Interview, Los Angeles/
Los Angeles Times (TV Times), 1-10:2.

Ed Sullivan
TV variety-show host

(Regarding cancellation of the 23-year-old *Ed Sullivan Show*): What it narrows down to is one thing—the people just finally got tired of the variety format. Vaudeville on television just finally died out. I remember not too long ago, when we kind of felt that the reaction to the show wasn't the same, that the old public enthusiasm and acceptance was declining, I was reluctant about admitting what was wrong. But Sylvia, my wife, sensed the trend instantly. She said to me, "Ed, people don't want it any more. You'll have to get yourself a new idea" . . . Here is how it is after 23 years—I leave on a note of pride; and I want to be back.

Interview, New York/
San Francisco Examiner, 3-20:32.

David Susskind
Motion picture-stage-television producer

. . . cable television is going to be just the same thing as regular television, only worse. *Real* television—dreary and hackneyed and boring and gutless as it is—is at least run by professionals. All the guys in the cable-television companies are the guys who aren't good enough to make it in real television. I've got cable television at the apartment. You know what's on it? Old British movies I've seen a thousand times before. My wife had it put in; heaven knows why. I don't think she watches it either. You know what's going to happen to cable TV? Well, first, the cable guys have to get a lot of people to watch it. Then the advertising guys are going to start buying in. Then the high-price help from the networks are going to start professional programming. Then they'll start censoring movies to protect the public's mental health or something. And then everybody will stop watching cable television, too.

Interview, New York/TV Guide, 4-3:9.

Peter Ustinov
Actor, Director, Writer

It seems strange that movies have become so permissive while TV goes Victorian . . . Television has taken the place of the half-aspirin which Edwardian nursemaids used to give children. Come to think of it, I'm not sure TV isn't worse.

Interview, London/TV Guide, 3-13:24.

Huw Wheldon
Managing director, British
Broadcasting Corporation Television

It is quite common to hear commercial television in the United States dismissed out of hand, especially by Americans, as a wilderness of monkeys. This is not my own experience. I have thoroughly enjoyed watching baseball matches and American public affairs programs. I have enjoyed many a movie or comedy on American television. I also like those extraordinary late-night shows they have. What becomes gradually and—to me, at all events—even hatefully evident is the almost total absence of the voice of the writer. I believe it is true to say that, during the last calendar year, the three great commercial networks in America, each of them transmitting 18 hours a day, 365 days a year, did not between them put on any commissioned or contemporary

plays at all. Careful research might prove me technically wrong, on a .01% basis, but broadly this is certainly the position. Locked in all-out commercial competition, what seems to be altogether missing are the voices of Bernard Malamud and Saul Bellow, of Norman Mailer and Norman Podhoretz, of John Updike and Nabokov. The voice of the novelist and the scholar and the playwright is not there. They appear as celebrities, of course; but they do not write or make programs.

London/Los Angeles Times, 5-7:(4)19.

Richard Widmark
Actor

(TV talk shows) are a menace. I look at them all the time; they fascinate me. But I'll never go on one of them. I think a performer should do his work and then shut up. If a talk show wants to buy a performance, then it should pay the going rate, not $290. What has happened with all overcommunication is that the most valuable thing a performer can have—his personal privacy—gets destroyed. When I see people destroying their own sense of privacy—what they think, what they feel—by beaming it out to millions of viewers, I resent it. I think it cheapens them as individuals; it cheapens the whole reason for their work. As Bogart said, the only thing you owe your public is to do a good job. Just because you're an actor doesn't mean you have to give your whole life to a bunch of unseen faces.

Interview, Los Angeles/
The New York Times, 3-7:(2)17.

Robert D. Wood
President, Columbia
Broadcasting System Television

The importance and the dimensions of television are so fantastic, I'm excited with every minute of it. I can't dream of anything more challenging and more fulfilling, with more personal satisfaction, when you guess right (with programming). It's worth any gamble to be part of it.

Interview/San Francisco Examiner
& Chronicle (Datebook), 10-17:14.

Personal Profiles

Spiro T. Agnew
Vice President of the United States

I think in time the people will come to know what a warm, sweet, lovable person I really am.

On "Dinah's Place," National
Broadcasting Company Television, May 5.

Woody Allen
Actor, Writer, Director

No matter what I'm working on, I like to do what I'm not doing. No single project is ever satisfying.

Interview, New Orleans/
The Dallas Times Herald, 4-25:(F)1.

Lucille Ball
Actress

I don't abuse anybody, scream at people, break laws or cheat. Maybe that's part of staying young and feeling vital. I just try to be good.

Family Weekly, 12-5:4.

Samuel Barber
Composer

. . . years ago, someone wrote a book about me, and when it was done, the proofs were sent to my sister. She sent me a telegram saying, "Have this book stopped. You're dull, but not *that* dull."

Interview, Mt. Kisco, N.Y./
The New York Times, 10-3:(2)30.

Birch Bayh
United States Senator, D–Ind.

I'm very easy going and matter of fact. I like Dairy Queens, and I have an old guitar I like to play. I keep it in the trunk of my car when I go to parties. I sang in a quartet at Purdue. I like work; I'm strong, young, ener-

getic, and I can take any burden that comes my way. I don't think I have given enough time in my 43 years to making any money, but we have enough. I severed my law-firm connections, but I get a few bucks from my farm income. I'm not a materialist. I wear baggy pants—that's another fault.

Interview, Washington/
The Washington Post, 6-20:(G)9.

Warren Beatty
Actor

(Regarding seeing himself in films): . . . I don't mind at all. I just think I look great. I've never been bothered by any fear of the public image. I can cope with these things, even at the expense of being called arrogant.

Interview, Vancouver/San Francisco
Examiner & Chronicle, 7-18:(B)4.

Hugo L. Black
Associate Justice,
Supreme Court of the United States

Perhaps I'm a rocky, stodgy old fella as some people say. But I don't feel that way about myself.

News conference, Washington/
The Washington Post, 2-27:(A)2.

Claire Bloom
Actress

Let people think of me what they like. I just want them to come and see my work, and then leave me alone. I'm not a big personality or star.

Interview, New York/
The New York Times, 2-7:(2)9.

Leonid I. Brezhnev
General Secretary,
Communist Party of the Soviet Union

I love driving. When I am driving, I relax.

When I am behind the wheel, I have the feeling that nothing will happen.

Interview, Paris/
Los Angeles Times, 10-27:(1)18.

Richard Burton
Actor

We (he and his wife, Elizabeth Taylor) have genuine adoration and love for each other. Love may be a curious word to use in this permissive age. But I am still, at 46, despite my wildness and rampant youth, enormously disgusted by permissiveness. As for Elizabeth, she is really a very prudish girl, which is one of the reasons she has been married five times. She would not go to bed with a gentleman unless he was married to her.

Interview/Newsweek, 12-6:51.

Robert C. Byrd
United States Senator, D–W.Va.

I am a perfectionist who falls far short of perfection.

The New York Times Magazine, 2-28:53.

Maria Callas
Opera singer

I am a very normal human being. I am healthy-minded, and I have good judgment. When I'm off-stage, I'm just like any other normal woman who goes shopping, goes to the movies, and shames her friends because she comments on a lot of things or screams with laughter or cries like an idiot. It's true, I have very few friends; but the few I have are very good friends. Of course, I have many acquaintances, and some of them *think* they are my friends—and so I let them think that. But unfortunately, I see right through them. To them, I'm only the famous woman. To them I'm only "La Divina." They usually only see the gold that glitters. They never see the hardship that goes with it. They do not see the pain, the work, the dedication. To tell you the truth, I do not like being called "La Divina." I resent it. I am Maria Callas. And I am only a woman.

Interview, New York/
The New York Times, 10-31:(2)28.

Vikki Carr
Singer

I haven't reached the point where I sing just for money, like a machine. My eyes give me away; and I couldn't stand it if I didn't sing with my heart and look people in the eyes.

Interview, Framingham, Mass./
The Christian Science Monitor, 4-6:(B)15.

Dick Cavett
TV talk-show host

I'm thought of as a writer who turned performer, rather than a performer who used writing to get into performing, and knew that all the time I was a performer.

Interview/San Francisco Examiner
& Chronicle (Datebook), 4-18:22.

(Regarding his identity): If I have one, it's a kind of dimpled winsomeness masquerading as sophistication; a combination of wit and earthiness, as if Voltaire and Jane Russell had had a child.

The Hollywood Reporter, 5-26:10.

Emanuel Celler
United States Representative, D–N.Y.

Chronologically I may be old. But I am mentally young, and that is what counts. One doesn't count his years unless he has nothing else to count. I have been asked, "How do you grow old so easily?" I reply: "Very easily. I give all my time to it."

On his 83rd birthday, Washington,
May 6/The New York Times, 5-9:(1)89.

Charles Chaplin
Former motion picture actor-director

I've lost interest in what society does and what the world does. There used to be a song, "Let the Rest of the World Go By"—this is how I feel at the moment.

Interview, Vevey, Switzerland/
San Francisco Examiner & Chronicle
(Sunday Punch), 11-7:5.

The nice thing about being rich is that I

(CHARLES CHAPLIN)

can do exactly what I want. Being, ah, distinguished gives me a few more liberties; and being old lets me get away with absolute hell.

Interview, Vevey, Switzerland/
Life, 12-3:94.

John B. Connally, Jr.
Secretary of the Treasury-designate
of the United States

(Why he accepted the position of Secretary of the Treasury): (President Nixon) convinced me, after many hours of conversation, that I could contribute something significant to his Administration, and thus to the welfare of this country. I was vain enough to believe him, and silly enough to try it. That's why I'm here.

At his confirmation hearing before Senate
Finance Committee, Washington, Jan. 28/
The Washington Post, 1-29:(A)14.

Alain Delon
Actor

Next to being an actor, I would have enjoyed being a gangster.

Los Angeles Herald-Examiner, 1-17:(F)2.

Bernadette Devlin
Member of British Parliament
from Northern Ireland

Contrary to popular opinion, I'm quite capable of standing in one place for an hour and behaving like a civilized human being.

San Francisco Examiner & Chronicle
(This World), 2-28:2.

Kirk Douglas
Actor

I'd hate to think I could never duck out of the spotlight. But if I walked down the street and nobody recognized me, it would give me a hell of a jolt. I've been a star too long to want to give up that easy . . .

Interview, Oban, Scotland/
San Francisco Examiner & Chronicle
(Datebook), 4-18:15.

William O. Douglas
Associate Justice,
Supreme Court of the United States

Perhaps my real claim to distinction is that I have never traveled at government expense.

San Francisco Examiner, 1-4:34.

Hugh Downs
Television talk-show host

I hate to waste opportunity. I don't have a miser complex, really, but there's something inside me which yearns uncontrollably to achieve the difficult. I hoard those chances . . .

New York/The Boston Globe, 7-6:16.

Clint Eastwood
Actor

(Things he likes): Casual clothing; Mexican and Japanese food; beer; green colors; women with little or no makeup; dawn, when it isn't too painful; the sound and smell of pine trees and oceans; the feel of polished wood, swimming and all other sports. (What he dislikes): Pressures; pickles and cucumbers; scotch whiskey; blizzards and big winters; women with grating voices; the confined feeling of staying too long in big cities; people who constantly bother you to do something you have to say no to—they bug the hell out of me.

Interview, New York/
The Washington Post, 3-31:(B)1.

Arthur Fiedler
Conductor, Boston Pops Orchestra

I think I am a romantic under the skin. I'm a person who likes excitement. I like exciting music. I like exciting sports. Going to a fire is like going to an Indianapolis auto race. It's the speed that counts. I want to see how *fast* man can fight the forces of nature. I *hate* placidity. I hate *evenness*.

Interview/TV Guide, 7-24:16.

Henry Fonda
Actor

Acting is putting on a mask. The worst

torture that can happen to me is not having a mask to get in back of.

TV Guide, 5-8:33.

Indira Gandhi
Prime Minister of India

My public life started at the age of three. I have no recollection of games, children's parties or playing with other children. My favorite occupation as a very small child was to deliver thunderous speeches to the servants, standing on a high table. All my games were political games; I was, like Joan of Arc, perpetually being burned at the stake.

The New York Times, 11-5:10.

Ruth Gordon
Actress

I think I'm *terribly* interestin'. I'm a classic. The wonderful thing about a classic is that a classic never gets old; a classic is eternally modern. Would ya believe it, I never think of myself as old. And *I* think I should be playin' all the *young* parts. Just 'cause I look old and everythin', that doesn't really matter . . .

Interview, San Francisco/
The New York Times, 4-4:(2)13.

Billy Graham
Evangelist

A minister never retires—although admittedly I can't keep up this crusade work all my life. But I hope to be preaching and writing on the day I die.

Interview, San Francisco, July 20/
San Francisco Examiner, 7-21:15.

Lee Grant
Actress

There are two types of people acting. Yes, they're different; but one isn't better than the other. Some have a strong sense of identity. In others, that sense is weak. Those with a strong identity become personality actors, and they're good at it. Those who don't have this sense of their own identity pass the day being

300 kinds of people. I'm that. I don't have a strong self-image at all.

Interview, Los Angeles/
Los Angeles Herald-Examiner, 2-11:(B)4.

Graham Greene
Author

My chief sickness is getting easily bored—a symptom of manic depression. What I cherish most is probably escape from boredom, especially from oneself. That can come from loving somebody, or from a good wine, or from travel.

Interview, Antibes, France/
The New York Times Book Review, 9-12:2.

Katharine Hepburn
Actress

I'm like an old building, and people say, "You're not going to tear that down." Or like an old top that's still spinning, and people say, "Oh, see it spin; see it go down the street; follow it."

News conference, Baltimore, March 1/
The Washington Post, 3-2:(B)1.

Hildegarde
Entertainer

If antiques get more valuable when they're older, why shouldn't I be more valuable when I get older? And isn't old brandy better than young brandy and an old Hildegarde better than a young Hildegarde?

Family Weekly, 12-5:5.

James D. Hodgson
Secretary of Labor
of the United States

To me, life is so damned fascinating as it is that I don't find much desire to get away from it. Just sticking around and watching what happens next is the element of my fascination.

Interview/
The Washington Post (Book World), 1-3:2.

507

Trevor Howard
Actor

. . . I'm frightfully restless. I always will be. I feel if I'm away running around the world, then I'm not wasting my time. But if I'm sitting at home for any length of time, I get bored. And I can't stand boredom, just as I can't stand bores.

Interview, London/San Francisco Examiner & Chronicle (Datebook), 1-10:2.

Glenda Jackson
Actress

. . . I don't want to wake up one morning and find myself stuck in the hermetically-sealed, centrally-heated, show-biz world, which can destroy you. You need very strong root-lines to so-called everyday living. I wouldn't like to think that I couldn't go to the launder-ette when I felt like it.

Interview, London/ The Christian Science Monitor, 2-11:13.

Lyndon B. Johnson
Former President of the United States

I could have been a school drop-out. It was only the applied psychology of my mother that led me to go on, or I would have been an elevator operator.

At Southwest Texas State University commencement, Aug. 15/ The Dallas Times Herald, 8-15:(A)7.

I want to keep fit, young, interested and happy. I've been shoved around all my life, and now I want to do things without anybody crowding me and the phone ringing.

The New York Times, 10-10:(1)51.

Nicholas Johnson
Commissioner, Federal Communications Commission of the United States

I never have decided what to do when I grow up.

Interview, Washington/ Los Angeles Times, 1-17:(A)2.

Barnaby C. Keeney
Chairman, National Endowment for the Humanities of the United States

I'm an arrogant, effete, Eastern intellectual—and a WASP to boot. I'm also a snob. I think it's a fine thing.

The Washington Post, 1-14:(G)1.

Veronica Lake
Former Actress

I was a pretty young freak in the Hollywood days. Now, I'm a tough old actress, and I'm not ashamed of it. There have been people—even doctors—who told me I ought to have a face job; but I just laughed at them. This is my face. It's been lived in—*well* lived in, mostly, I think. I've earned it, and I'm going to wear it.

Interview, New York/ The Washington Post, 3-17:(E)7.

. . . I can live in a matchbox as long as it's clean.

Interview, San Francisco/San Francisco Examiner & Chronicle (Datebook), 4-18:17.

Gina Lollobrigida
Actress

I don't think (there) exists one man that is good for me. I think I'm too complicated for a man. I think the men like simple, nice, quiet, unsophisticated girls, not independent girls like me. If you're independent, you don't need a man. It's a problem.

Interview, Beverly Hills, Calif./ Los Angeles Times (Calendar), 8-29:64.

Mairin Lynch
Wife of the Prime Minister of the Republic of Ireland

When we retire from this job there will be no tears. It'll give us time to see all the things we never saw, hear the music we never heard, read all the books we have never read. This is a lonely, lonely job, and I am automatically in a lonely position.

San Francisco Examiner, 12-17:38.

Groucho Marx
Actor, Comedian

My obituary will probably say, "Had been a moderately funny comedian." I don't want to be remembered. I don't want flowers or bouquets. I just want to die when I die.

Interview, Beverly Hills, Calif./
San Francisco Examiner & Chronicle
(Datebook), 11-14:2.

William Masselos
Pianist

There are so many sides to our natures. I used to think I was a quiet guy—contemplative, easy-going. Actually, there is a violence in me—a terrible violence that I let loose in, say, Charles Ives. The music of Ives releases so much in me! I'm always terribly surprised to find how much anger there is in me. It's then I realize that, inside, I'm really not such a quiet fellow after all.

Interview, New York/
The New York Times, 3-14:(2)26.

Marcello Mastroianni
Actor

For me, life without love is meaningless. But always in my life romance was amusing for me; perhaps because I did not give very much of myself. Then I fell in love and gave everything, and got hurt. It was better, I think, when romance was merely amusing. You see, I am not really such a good Latin lover.

Interview, New York/
San Francisco Examiner, 1-9:9.

I don't like myself. I never did, even physically. I don't like my body when I look at myself naked. These childish legs and arms. I don't like my face, with this short nose and these fleshy lips. I'm cute. And a man must not be cute.

Time, 8-30:30.

Walter Matthau
Actor

Most people don't recognize me. I don't look like an actor. I could be anyone from a men's room attendant to a guy from Erie, Pa. I try to live the life of a guy who earns maybe $150 a week. I go to the grocery. I go to the drug store. I walk around town. I get on a bus. Sometimes I get strange looks. Someone will come over and say, "Aren't you Walter Matthau, the movie star?" And I'll say, "Yes, I am." And they'll say, "What are you doing here?" And I say, "Why shouldn't I be here?" They'll say, "You must be rich." I say, "I'm not rich. I have enough money to hire a limousine if that's what you mean, but I would rather ride in a bus. I like it better." And some people say, "Gee, that guy is cheap. He uses the bus."

Interview, Los Angeles/Parade, 5-16:7.

My public image is that of an extroverted, happy-go-lucky, spaghetti-throwing lout. On the other hand, my image to my wife is that of a very romantic, kind, sweet, gentle, considerate, reasonable, selfless—and oh yes, sexy—husband and father.

Interview, New York/
Los Angeles Herald-Examiner, 5-22:(B)8.

Roddy McDowall
Actor

I don't really know what I'd like to be remembered for. I think of a man like Claude Rains—everything he did, he did well. Whatever it was, he did everything with a measure of style, dignity, insight, distinction and humor. He was always good. I like it simple, you see. People I admire never cop out. The real people don't sulk if they miss out. The way I see it, I'd like to be, well . . . good.

Interview, London/San Francisco
Examiner & Chronicle (Datebook), 8-22:12.

Frank McGee
News commentator,
National Broadcasting Company

. . . I came into broadcasting when news was supposed to be a deadly serious affair. I've always had what I think of as a funereal aspect. Well, maybe it's time I trotted out the real me.

I'm not all that gloomy a fellow. I've even been known to tell a joke.

Interview, New York/
Los Angeles Times, 7-12:(4)12.

Golda Meir
Prime Minister of Israel

I have inner strength? . . . I? When I go down to the (Suez) Canal area and I see our boys there, I know they are the ones who have inner strength. And more than that, when I see their mothers and the young widows I know it is true of them. One the other day told me, "I have two little children. I will not let my home be a sad home." That is inner strength . . . The day before Independence Day, I went as Prime Minister to the Mount Hertzl military cemetery. The women standing near the graves of their sons called out to me, "You should be strong. You should live to be 120." Then I felt small . . .

Interview, Jerusalem/San Francisco
Examiner & Chronicle, 3-7:(A)4.

Karl A. Menninger
Psychiatrist; Founder, Menninger Clinic

I don't think about age, don't believe in getting old. Stretching out on a chaise longue or lying on the beach is fine for crocodiles and turtles; it's torture for me. I need to be going, contacting people, moving.

Plainview (Tex.) Daily Herald, 5-4:10.

Melina Mercouri
Actress

I live where I work, and I always keep three suitcases packed so I can move on quickly.

Interview, New York/
The Washington Post, 10-13:(B)6.

Robert Mitchum
Actor

. . . I could go forever not working. I don't enjoy work. I wouldn't work at all if I didn't have an elegant ballroom and wife to support.

Interview, Los Angeles/San Francisco
Examiner & Chronicle, (B)4.

Paul Newman
Actor

My own personality is so vapid and bland, I have to go steal the personalities of other people to be effective on the screen.

Interview, Los Angeles/
The Dallas Times Herald, 4-11:(F)3.

Pat Nixon
Wife of the President
of the United States

Someone said that being married to a Milhous-Nixon was enough of a job without having to be the President's wife, too. Well, someone was wrong. Dick is the easiest man in the world to live with. Outside, with the problems he has to face, he may seem very serious, even forbidding to some. But when he comes home to me and the girls, he comes whistling and joking.

Interview/Los Angeles Times, 1-19:(1)12.

Richard M. Nixon
President of the United States

I don't stomp around. I don't believe in public displays of anger. I don't raise hell. I'm never rough on the staff about things just for the sake of being rough, or making an effect. But they know how I feel. The things we've faced in this Administration have taken a lot of hard decisions, and I've had to be firm about things; but I've *been* firm—I haven't shouted about it. There are some people, you know, they think the way to be a big man is to shout and stomp and raise hell—and then nothing ever really happens. I'm not like that, with the staff or with the press. I never shoot blanks.

Interview, San Clemente, Calif.,
March 30/Look, 10-19:52.

Rudolf Nureyev
Ballet dancer

I've never married because I'm married to dancing.

Interview, Argentina/
Los Angeles Times, 3-23:(1)2.

John Osborne
Playwright

. . . I have no real idea how other people see me at all. Obviously, they don't see me as I am. But one is always terribly maligned by the uninformed. I know if I meet new people they still expect me to snarl at them. Even fairly smart people are surprised that I'm civilized and polite and friendly and charming.
Interview/
Los Angeles Times (Calendar), 1-24:57.

Farah Pahlavi
Queen of Iran

. . . most people in America don't understand royalty. The picture which comes out and the one they have of a queen is that she is living in a big palace and wearing a crown and nothing more. But it's a real job. It's hard work. I work seven hours a day every day. I'm the president of 24 different organizations, and I have to deal with so many things which are really not my business, too. I see a lot of our ministers because of my position in social organizations which deal with their areas. In fact, I'm getting grey hairs already.
Interview, Teheran/
The Washington Post, 10-9:(C)3.

Prince Philip
Duke of Edinburgh

(On being a prince): I look at it as a job. And I imagine I do it at much the same pressure I would any other job.
Plainview (Tex.) Daily Herald, 7-14:4.

Pablo Picasso
Artist

(Regarding his upcoming 90th birthday): They will annoy me terribly next month when I will be one year older. They insist on offering me tributes usually paid to very old persons and to the dead ones.
September/
The Washington Post, 10-26:(B)7.

Georges Pompidou
President of France

I like to please people. I don't like to hurt anyone. In the position I am in, I spend my time giving every now and then and refusing most of the time. I suffer, I suffer . . . I remember some advice that General (Charles) de Gaulle gave me at least 10 times: "Be tough, Pompidou." I try, but it's hard for me.
Television interview/
The New York Times, 6-25:40.

Otto Preminger
Motion picture producer-director

My reputation for firing people is all the product of publicity. I am a sweet, lovable, gentle man.
Interview, Los Angeles/
Los Angeles Herald-Examiner, 12-19:(F)3.

Tony Randall
Actor

When I think of Tulsa, I remember the girls I dated. The girls always smelled of vinegar. I liked that. They all washed their hair and rinsed it in vinegar. I love to think of all those girls with vinegar in their hair.
Interview, New York/San Francisco
Examiner & Chronicle (Datebook), 4-25:13.

Elliot L. Richardson
Secretary of Health, Education
and Welfare of the United States

Before I began to watch my weight, I used to eat twice as much as most people. There was a time when I could go to three political campaign dinners a night and eat everything set before me. I guess it was really my New England conscience; I never could bear to see anything go to waste.
Interview, McLean, Va./
The Washington Post, 1-3:(F)1.

Rachel Roberts
Actress

I used to be a very good actress. Then I married Rex Harrison and got lost. I just

(RACHEL ROBERTS)

ceased to exist. We led a very aristocratic life in Paris and on yachts and in our villa in Portofino—walking the dog for two hours, then taking a nap, then having friends by for drinks, with the most unbelievably beautiful scenery in the world just outside the window. There's nothing like it, if you like that kind of life . . . But I couldn't live on one more yacht for one more day. I'm Welsh, and I come from 500 years of poverty, where we had to work all our lives. And without work, without creating anything with my own life, I just turned into a vegetable. So I gave it up; but in its place, I found myself.

Interview, New York/San Francisco Examiner & Chronicle (Datebook), 2-14:12.

Artur Rubinstein
Pianist

If you are in Poland, call me Artur. If you are in New York, call me Arthur. If you happen to meet me on the street in Rome, please say, "Hello, Arturo!"

Newsweek, 11-29:47.

Julius Rudel
Director, New York City Opera

I've been married to the same girl for more than 25 years. I have a family—two married daughters and a teenage son. I don't go having affairs. I don't dance around from jet to jet. I have a very small circle of intimates . . . I'm not going to stand on my head to attract attention. Of course, I want glamour; I'd be a liar if I said I didn't. But I don't know what price I'm prepared to pay for it.

*Interview, New York/
The New York Times, 2-7:(2)36.*

William Saroyan
Author

I took to writing at an early age to escape from meaninglessness, uselessness, unimportance, insignificance, poverty, enslavement, ill health, despair, madness and all manner of other unattractive, natural and inevitable things.

*San Francisco Examiner & Chronicle
(Datebook), 1-31:6.*

George C. Scott
Actor

Acting is easy, is difficult, is frustrating, is rewarding, is hellish, is enjoyable, is tedious, is exciting. In other words, it is—has been—my life.

*San Francisco Examiner & Chronicle
(Datebook), 6-20:15.*

Erich Segal
Author

I'm a good guy, a serious man . . . I've never done an immoral thing in my life.

*Washington, Feb. 10/
The Washington Post, 2-11:(C)1.*

Norodom Sihanouk
*Exiled former Chief of State
of Cambodia*

I've been a king—at 18—an editor, composer, film director, saxophonist, chief of state—even a pretty good amateur cook. I've been proclaimed a national hero and denounced as a national traitor. What's left for me? Perhaps it's time I retired.

*Interview, Peking/
Los Angeles Times, 6-24:(1)23.*

Beverly Sills
Opera singer

I'm not a nervous woman. I'm a very energetic woman. I prefer to be out meeting people on days when I'm to sing. I thrive on that. I just get so bored sitting in my hotel room, staring at things.

*Interview, New York/
The New York Times, 10-24:(1)84.*

Georges Simenon
Author

I can't imagine myself in a position of great responsibility, political, military or anything.

Indeed, my ambitions are small—easily satisfied, and I would put them on the same scale as my pleasures. The first pleasure is when the maid opens the shutters in the morning. She opens the shutters and I see the sky, see if the sun is shining or if it's raining. If it's shining, I revel in the sunshine; if it's raining, I revel in the rain.

Interview, Epalinges, Switzerland/
The New York Times Book Review, 10-24:22.

Frank Sinatra
Singer, Actor

(Regarding his announced retirement): I've been a saloon singer all my life, and it's appropriate that I started quietly and I end quietly.

Los Angeles, June 13/
The New York Times, 6-20:(4)7.

Albert Speer
Former Armaments Minister
of Nazi Germany

Intellectually, I have accepted that it is wrong to be proud of such things (his role in building the Nazi war machine). But emotionally, I still feel a surge of pride when I think of the obstacles I overcame and the goals we achieved. I would be dishonest if I said otherwise.

Interview/
The New York Times, 5-16:(4)3.

David Susskind
Motion picture-stage-television producer

What will remain (when he dies) is a marker with year of birth and death, and maybe it will also say: "He did television." Someone passing in 100 years will say: "He did what?" If I had my life again I think I would rather have been a surgeon—to have reached into pain and removed it. A surgeon knows if the patient has died or been cured. When I am finished, I don't quite know.

London/San Francisco Examiner, 9-4:34.

Virgil Thomson
Composer

One of the nice things (about being 75 years old) is that you don't have to go out so much. You can be very close to composers like Beethoven and Mozart and Bach, Haydn and Schumann, but that doesn't mean you have to run uptown all the time to hear them played. They're in your mind, like your grandmother.

Interview/Time, 12-6:84.

Josip Broz Tito
President of Yugoslavia

(Regarding himself): Some people may think that the old rifle can no longer be fired. But let me assure you that this old rifle has plenty of ammunition and can still shoot straight.

Los Angeles Times, 5-11:(1)2.

Lawrence Turman
Motion picture producer-director

I'm always in a state of inner conflict. Some guys live in a straight line. I live zigzag. I speak too quickly. My voice pitch is too high. I don't sound at ease to myself. I would give anything to drive more slowly and not flagellate myself over some error. I write myself notes about things I know I'm going to remember. And it took me five years to tell my father I didn't like the fabrics business. Any other guy would have told his father in six months.

Interview, Los Angeles/
The New York Times, 1-24:(2)13.

Robert Young
Actor

As far as I can remember, I was afraid—of some imagined disaster that never did eventuate. When I was a child, I used to hide in the crooks of trees, just to be alone. When I became an actor, I constantly felt I

(ROBERT YOUNG)

wasn't worthy, that I had no right to be a star. All those years at Metro, and even later on *Father Knows Best,* I hid a black terror behind a cheerful face.

Interview, Beverly Hills, Calif./
The New York Times, 1-17:(2)23.

Ronald L. Ziegler
Press Secretary to the President
of the United States

I've never written down a plan or a course in life I wanted to take. Life is more complex than that . . . If I have my eight years as a Press Secretary, I don't see that as exactly the end of my life.

The Washington Post (Potomac), 7-4:15.

Spiro T. Agnew
Vice President of the United States

Young Americans too often are represented as crying out as a class for recognition and as asking for special attentions. In response, many members of the older generation—my generation—have come to regard this cry as a class and have chosen to shower on "youth" generally the special attention that they thought youth wanted. Our reply to the demands of young people should not be programs, special committees, special offices . . . our reply should be to accept young men and women . . . as full members of the community . . . ready to take on a great deal more in the way of responsibilities and burdens than they generally have been given today.

Before delegates of Senate Youth Program, Washington, Feb. 3/ San Francisco Examiner, 2-4:2.

George Allen
Former football coach, Los Angeles "Rams"

The achiever is the only individual who is truly alive. There can be no inner satisfaction in simply driving a fine car or eating in a fine restaurant or watching a good movie or television program. Those who think they're enjoying themselves doing any of that are half-dead and don't know it. I see no difference between a chair and the man who sits in the chair unless he is accomplishing something.

The Washington Post, 1-10:(C)4.

Neil A. Armstrong
Former American astronaut

Technology does not improve the quality of life; it improves the quality of things. Things can improve the convenience of living: power stations, automobiles; the experience of living: television, spaceships; and even the duration of living: vitamins, X-ray machines. Things can also degrade the environment of our living: power stations and automobiles—again!; and reverse the fact of our living: guns and bombs. Improving the things that surround living can be achieved by the application of knowledge. Improving the quality of life, however, requires the application of wisdom.

Interview/ U.S. News & World Report, 1-11:32.

W. H. Auden
Poet

Political history is far too criminal a subject to be a fit thing to teach children. Art history, literary history, yes—but not political history.

Plainview (Tex.) Daily Herald, 1-5:8.

Pearl Bailey
Entertainer

Fame, my dear children, is not an easy mantle to wear.

At Neval Thomas School, Anacostia, Va., April 27/ The Washington Post, 4-28:(B)2.

Roger Baldwin
Founder, American Civil Liberties Union

That whole cold war business, what a lot of nonsense it all turned out to be. Communism wasn't going to be able to take over the world. There isn't even an international Communism movement left. Nationalism has always been a lot stronger than any ideology—Communism, Fascism or whatever. When it comes down to it, people stick together.

Interview, Chilmark, Mass./ Los Angeles Times, 9-10:(2)7.

Jack Benny
Entertainer

I don't indulge in nostalgia. To hell with the past. It's gone. Thinking about it makes you older quicker than anything. I'm only concerned with how good my last show was and how good my next two will be.

Interview, London/
Los Angeles Times, 5-3:(1)9.

Bernard L. Berzon
President,
Rabbinical Council of America

Nudity, indiscriminate promiscuity, obscenity and pornography are taking over our society. Today we have an orgy of sex but a dearth of love. We accuse the television and movie industry of sex exploitation for monetary profits while contributing to a total breakdown of morality in our society. The supposed new morality is destroying the family unit and has contributed to marital unhappiness, divorce and to the emotional disturbances of young people. Emotional health is derived from wholesome family life. The unhappiness of modern youth, their fits of depression and boredom, their craving for drugs, their clinging together for bits of warmth in communes, are all results of the breakdown of the family structure.

Interview, New York, Oct. 15/
The New York Times, 10-16:51.

Pierre Boulez
Musical director,
New York Philharmonic Orchestra

Look around you. Happiness is a function of blindness. The more you see, the less happy you can be. Happiness is a soap bubble.

Interview/Newsweek, 10-11:91.

Omar N. Bradley
General, United States Army (Ret.)

. . . my boyhood experience gave me a sense of responsibility. If I didn't cut the firewood, we didn't have firewood. If I didn't clean the lamps, we didn't have clean lamps. One trouble with modern living is that chil-

dren don't have that opportunity. The furnace goes on automatically, and you flip a switch to get light. If a child doesn't learn responsibility by having responsibility, first of all to his own family, how will he ever develop a sense of responsibility to his community and his country?

Interview, Beverly Hills, Calif./
The Dallas Times Herald, 3-21:(A)9.

James L. Buckley
United States Senator-elect, C–N.Y.

My proposition is that a well-ordered society is the only free society.

Interview/
The Washington Post, 1-10:(B)2.

Maria Callas
Opera singer

Love is so much patience between two people. But it takes work, and you have to give a lot and have to receive, also, like a flower. It is also somewhat of a disease.

Quote, 1-3:1.

Byrum E. Carter
Chancellor, Indiana University
at Bloomington

It has become customary in many quarters to disparage (college) commencement exercises as no longer relevant, and to raise doubts of the rationality of formal ceremonies expressing the symbolism of the past. But men are not bound together solely by rationality. Symbolism and ritual have always played their role in the development and maintenance of civilization, and through that very role have made their own unique contribution to the possibility of rationality.

At Indiana University commencement/
The National Observer, 9-6:7.

Pablo Casals
Cellist

We must tell the children, when they are 8 or 9, when they can understand the sense of the words: We *are* a miracle, every one of us. Look what our hands can do! Tell the children: Beethoven, Michelangelo, Bach, all great people, were once children like you. You can be a Michelangelo. You are a unity. This is what parents and teachers must tell children. There never has been and never will be another child like you. But then we tell them, "Kill or be killed. That is the law." The law makes me kill; the law says I can kill. I don't respect the law in that sense. They say we have discovered so many things. True. Science has made it possible for us to do such things —to go to the moon. It is fantastic. But the world is at the disposal of the Russians and the Americans, who have all those wonderful things to destroy and to kill.

Interview, Washington, May 16/
The Dallas Times Herald, 5-17:(A)30.

Fidel Castro (Ruz)
Premier of Cuba

The history of everything has to come out; but the men who participate in one way or another . . . all the protagonists of history, don't dwell on their place in history. History is not an objective. In each case, it is a result. That is, the history of individuals is not an objective. It is a by-product of the life of man, of the life of peoples and of the drama of man. No one sets out to write history, to make history. One sets out to do things.

News conference, San Miguel, Chile/
Los Angeles Times, 12-2:(1)24.

Dick Cavett
TV talk-show host

I . . . find amusing certain aspects of women's liberation. Any humorless movement invites humor. Awfully good jokes came out of the American Revolution, and Churchill got laughs during World War II.

Interview/San Francisco Examiner
& Chronicle (Datebook), 4-18:22.

Charles Chaplin
Former motion picture actor-director

There's so much humiliation in being poor; but it's not really possible to appreciate luxury without it.

Interview, Vevey, Switzerland/
The New York Times, 12-12:(2)3.

Shirley Chisholm
United States Representative, D–N.Y.

Relentless lobbying by women is going to be necessary, because men aren't going to extend rights to them of their own free will. Why? Because they are basically antifeminist. When you say that many women really have more strength and spirit than men, it's true; but what man wants to hear that? They would rather keep them in a certain kind of box, and, like blacks, most women have accepted that. They are wrapped in a pink blanket at birth; and later on they are encouraged by guidance counselors to become homemakers, secretaries, nurses. This inferiority is built in and has to be thrown off.

Los Angeles Times, 3-21:(E)16.

Kenneth Clark
Historian

We have had a complete revolt against all institutions, all old rules. It is an understandable revolt because the old had really shown up pretty badly. You couldn't do much worse than the old institutions and rules did in the last 49 years. A very, very great revolution is going on. I see great value in young people questioning any number of exhausted beliefs. Attack on all institutions is a very serious need. I am not a great believer in civilizations. I like to see them questioned. Public men with their evasions and lies should be constantly shown up; and I have had my fill of public hypocrisy. But if you knock it all away, you have nothing to hang onto; and the result from that will be reaction and an authoritarian regime.

Interview/
Los Angeles Times, 9-24:(2)7.

I hold a number of beliefs that have been repudiated by the liveliest intellects of our time. I believe that order is better than chaos; creation better than destruction. I prefer gentleness to violence; forgiveness to vendetta. On the whole, I think that knowledge is better than ignorance; and I am sure that human sympathy is better than ideology. I believe that, in spite of the recent triumphs of

(KENNETH CLARK)

science, men haven't changed much in the last two thousand years; and, in consequence, we must still try to learn from history.

From film series, "Civilization"/
Quote, 12-12:557.

A. W. Clausen
President, Bank of America

Almost all genuine human progress has been the result of rational thought working in an environment of compassion. Pure rationalism sounds cold and unappealing, and, without compassion, it is. But rational thought, tempered by the human spirit, still offers our best hope to improve the quality of life for all people.

Before Association of California
School Administrators and California
School Boards Association, San Francisco,
Dec. 6/Los Angeles Times, 12-7:(2)4.

Norman Cousins
Editor, "Saturday Review"

Whether in the U.S. or Paraguay, Great Britain or Russia, youth seems to be speaking with a single voice. They are saying, "We live in an irrational world; human life is fragile and precarious; and the means of sustaining life are increasingly irrational, too; and the human consciousness is being submerged under this life."

San Francisco Examiner & Chronicle
(This World), 3-14:2.

Archibald Cox
Professor of Law, Harvard University;
Former Solicitor General of the
United States

Freedom of speech is indivisible. You cannot deny it to one man and save it for others . . . The price of liberty to speak the truth as each of us sees it is permitting others the same freedom.

At Harvard University, March 26/
The New York Times, 3-29:31.

Jules Dassin
Motion picture director

What I respect in the young people is the revolutions they are groping for. I don't think any of them know where they are going. But their striving is basically moral. They really mean it when they say, "Look, life should be beautiful." And I believe them when they say it . . . I'd kind of like to be around to see what they find eventually.

Interview, Paris/
The Washington Post, 4-4:(H)5.

Doris Day
Actress

I don't think about the past, and I don't think about the future. That makes a great sandwich, but not much else. I live for today. Life is just one long day. It gets light and it gets dark, and time is relative.

Interview, Los Angeles/
San Francisco Examiner & Chronicle
(Datebook), 11-28:15.

Kirk Douglas
Actor

I used to say, "Virtue isn't photogenic. What is it to be a nice guy? (It's) to be nothing, a write-off, a big fat zero with a smile for everybody . . ." I still hold to that. You've got to have some sort of impact. Love me or hate me, just don't be indifferent to me. That would be the biggest insult.

Interview, Oban, Scotland/
San Francisco Examiner & Chronicle
(Datebook), 4-18:15.

Rene Dubos
Professor of Microbiology,
Rockefeller University

One has to be free, but one has also to accept the constraints of the social order. As a scientist, I believe in determinism—but, as a human being, I believe that at each moment of life one has freedom. In social affairs, we need as wide a range of freedom as possible; but, on the other hand, without some constraints the social structure would collapse and we would collapse along with it.

Interview/
Modern Maturity, Aug.-Sept.:60.

Faye Dunaway
Actress

It's the American dream that, when you reach success, you'll be happy. It's just not true. Your relationships with friends don't change. Your feelings about yourself don't change—although, admittedly, they're soothed a bit. The danger is in believing in the adulation that is suddenly paid you. But self-esteem can't be built on that. Suddenly, the adulation is gone, and you say, "My God, now I'm nothing again."

Interview, Los Angeles/
Los Angeles Herald-Examiner, 1-10:(F)4.

Abba Eban
Foreign Minister of Israel

A nation must be capable of tenacious solitude.

News conference, Washington,
March 19/The New York Times, 3-20:1.

John Kenneth Galbraith
Professor of Economics,
Harvard University

So often in the (United) States I've seen a first-class woman scholar fall in love with a man who has half her brains . . . (and) he takes her off to Gallup, N.M. or Peoria, Ill. In effect, he drags her down to his level of intellectual incompetence.

London/The Dallas Times-
Herald, 5-17:(A)27.

It's very hard to admit errors if you're basically wrong. But it's not hard to admit errors that are cosmetically wrong. You can get a great deal of psychological pleasure out of saying, "God, what a broad-minded man you are, Galbraith."

Interview, Newfane, Vt./
The New York Times, 8-25:33.

James Garner
Actor

I can't go (along with) this business of actors on the march, making speeches and carrying banners. I think it is particularly wrong for "stars" for this reason: Unlike college students, professors, others of the intelligentsia, or even millionaires if they are so minded to get involved in protests, a screen star projects *two* images—the personality he has made famous on the screen or TV, and the person he really is. The great majority of the public knows us as that fella they see in the movies. Most of these roles are very flattering. So when the "star" gets on his soapbox about whatever cause he or she happens to be hysterical about at the time, he's throwing an unduly strong and virtuous image behind it. It's like what he is saying as a "person" must be right because he's always Mr. Right in front of a camera.

Interview, Los Angeles/
Los Angeles Herald-Examiner, 4-25:(F)3.

Billy Graham
Evangelist

The most prominent place in hell is reserved for those who are neutral on the great issues of life.

Quote, 4-4:313.

Loneliness is probably the foremost American illness among young people. Many psychiatrists agree to this. It is no respecter of persons as it devastates the young and the old, the rich and the poor, the educated and the illiterate, the famous and the unknown, the ghetto dweller and the suburbanite and the farmer. It is getting worse every year.

San Francisco Examiner & Chronicle
(This World), 8-8:2.

Arthur Hailey
Author

Age and wisdom are not synonymous. There are more old fools than young ones. As

(ARTHUR HAILEY)

much as we hate to admit it, greater wisdom can reside in those much younger than we.

Before Commonwealth Club,
San Francisco, June 11/
San Francisco Examiner, 6-12:5.

W. Averell Harriman
Former United States Ambassador-at-Large

I'm afraid our country, as a whole, hasn't made very much headway in preparing people for retirement. We have to educate people about what to do when they retire . . . The most important computer is the human brain. Good judgment comes from years and years of that brain's storing up millions and millions of important impressions. A wise decision comes when a man who has lived a long time is able to dig deep into that brain. To throw away people who have developed such magnificent mental computers is a great waste.

Interview, Washington/
Modern Maturity, December:12.

Katharine Hepburn
Actress

That's one of the troubles today—people are afraid to face up to responsibilities. Work is the only thing that ever made anybody happy. The notion that work is a burden is a terrible mistake.

News conference, Baltimore/
Los Angeles Herald-Examiner, 4-26:(B)5.

Alfred Hitchcock
Motion picture director

Good wine should be drunk on one's own. The enemy of good wines—and good food—is conversation. It's quite pointless to serve either at a dinner party.

San Francisco Examiner, 11-17:44.

Eric Hoffer
Philosopher

We have the rudiments of reverence for the human body, but we consider as nothing the rape of the human mind.

Quote, 5-2:409.

Dustin Hoffman
Actor

. . . I certainly am aware of fame and money; but they have nothing to do with any vacuums you have inside. When success comes, it is no magic land. You are still the same person with the same crazies running around inside you.

Interview, New York/
The Boston Globe, 6-27:53.

Paul G. Hoffman
Administrator, United Nations
Development Program

A person who has problems in his family doesn't, or shouldn't, for that reason neglect the problems of his community. In the same way, richer countries can ignore only at their peril the increasing disparities between their high and steadily improving standards of living and the abysmal conditions of life of the vast majority of the world's people. This is a moral as well as a material issue. It means that we have to do what is right as well as what is essential in practical terms of our own economic and political survival. Perhaps this sounds "preachy"; but can anyone nowadays make a real distinction between what conscience and reason tell us? Just try it.

Interview/Vista-The Magazine
of the United Nations Association,
May-June:15.

It is appalling to contemplate the fact that in large parts of our planet poverty and poverty of opportunity still kill and permanently cripple quite as many people as would be killed or permanently crippled in a conventional war . . . It simply mocks reason that the wealthier nations are devoting some $200 billion every year to building their defense capabilities and less than $15 billion to helping their poorer next-door neighbors combat the poverty and poverty of opportunity which are major sources of international tension.

Before UN General Assembly
economic committee, New York/
Los Angeles Times, 10-25:(2)6.

Bob Hope
Entertainer

There's nothing terrible about being "square." The "squares" are the ones who make the clothes, bake the bread, build houses, and even make the motorcycles.

> *At St. Bonaventure University commencement, May 30/ San Francisco Examiner, 5-31:12.*

John A. Howard
President, Rockford College

I think a large proportion of the college-bound youth have somehow come to believe that man fulfills himself by being freed from all obligations and limitations. I happen to believe that this is exactly upside down; that man fulfills himself as he recognizes that limitations are necessary for humans to live together.

> *Interview, Washington/ U.S. News & World Report, 9-6:45.*

Trevor Howard
Actor

The answer to the whole thing is people, not places. The world has run out of paradise. But it's still no bloody use going to a beautiful place on your own. If you're with the right people, anywhere in the world is better than loneliness.

> *Interview, London/ San Francisco Examiner & Chronicle (Datebook), 1-10:2.*

Hussein I
King of Jordan

It would be madness to face life without thinking that things will work out.

> *Interview, Amman/Time, 7-5:27.*

Pyotr L. Kapitsa
Physicist

Young people, not having to fear for tomorrow, lack the necessity to fight for their existence, and this gives rise to a situation in which they face no problems that require their strength and will. All this, taken together, deprives the life of young people of any permanent inner substance.

> *San Francisco Examiner & Chronicle (This World), 8-8:2.*

Henry A. Kissinger
Assistant to the President of the United States for National Security Affairs

I believe in the tragic element of history. I believe there is the tragedy of a man who works very hard and never gets what he wants. And then I believe there is the even more bitter tragedy of a man who finally gets what he wants and finds out that he doesn't want it.

> *Interview/The New York Times Magazine, 11-14:112.*

Jerzy Kosinski
Author

I believe life will go on; therefore, I am a pessimist. Civilization has been nothing but the inevitability of one disaster created to solve another. Nazi Germany was a disaster solved by the disaster of World War II, which we solved with the atomic bomb. When we don't have a disaster, we create one. Now, when there isn't talk of a new war, we have pollution. But this is nothing compared to what happens in Pakistan (civil war and famine). But we sit here looking at one fish in a Long Island pond and say, "I told you so, the world is ending."

> *Interview, New Haven, Conn./ The Washington Post, 8-30:(B)1.*

Lee Kuan Yew
Prime Minister of Singapore

I think that in every democratic country freedom is limited. If you say you want complete freedom in an emergent country, I can give you two examples: one is India, another is Ceylon. Both countries are now in chaos.

> *Time, 5-31:71.*

Alan Jay Lerner
Music lyricist

There are so many bad things that people are doing to "succeed." They are lying, cheating, living an image. Although I've probably done some of them, I try to avoid that. It's so sad. And it all ends in dying.

San Francisco Examiner & Chronicle,
11-12:36.

John V. Lindsay
Mayor of New York

I do not know which is more difficult—art or politics. I do not know which is hardest to achieve—beauty or change, the cathedral at Chartres or the Bill of Rights. But I do know that today there is a hunger for both beauty and change. And I know that neither is achieved easily or often.

At dedication of expansion of
New Orleans Museum of Art, Nov. 17/
The New York Times, 11-18:21.

Walter Lippmann
Former political columnist

. . . I believe . . . that the human being, just as he somehow evolved the capacity to learn language and to speak . . . has acquired in the course of eons of time an inherited code of civility, I call it, by which man has learned that nobody can exercise absolute power, that power has to be exercised with some respect to the consent of the other powers. People must be able to express their feelings, they must be represented in decisions and so on. Men are not comfortable and not happy in a society which violates these, and, what is more, a society won't last, will be overthrown, if that code is violated.

Interview, Seal Harbor, Me./
The Washington Post, 10-17:(C)5.

Bernard T. Lomas
President,
Albion (Mich.) College

I think there are some real dangers and very real perils in an atmosphere of complete tolerance. If we want to keep this atmosphere to live in, we still have to be alert to its perils and learn to avoid its pitfalls. What we have to see is that tolerance in our day, by itself, can become extreme like any virtue. It can move over so far that it ceases to be a virtue and becomes a corrupting and enervating force. One of the pitfalls of this easygoing tolerance is neutrality. Someone said that, while our fathers had convictions, today we have opinions. That is the first danger signal in the atmosphere of complete moderation—loss of conviction, moral laziness. Trying to escape the extreme bigoted narrowness, we sometimes get enervated into an easygoing halfheartedness; trying to be open-minded enough to see both sides of the question, we are apt to attach ourselves to none; trying to be all things to all men, we may end up being nothing to any man.

Inauguration address/
The National Observer, 7-5:13.

Clare Boothe Luce
Playwright; Former diplomat

Woman knows what man has too long forgotten—that the ultimate economic and spiritual unit of any civilization is still the family.

Quote, 4-18:361.

Konosuke Matsushita
Chairman, Matsushita Electric
Industrial Company of Japan

It is very hard for anybody to achieve anything without constant and conscious effort. But the important thing is that everyone has a unique, natural gift. We must make every effort to develop the gift. Sometimes this is easier to do than at other times. Let me elaborate with a personal example. Even with a gift for electrical and electronics work, that alone would not have brought me success. Fortunately, when I got into business, the age of electricity was just dawning. I was blessed with good timing.

Interview/Nation's Business, January.

Charles P. McCarty
Mayor of St. Paul, Minn.

My philosophy is that if you wake up in the morning and the sun's there, you've got the world by the tail. I'm a crazy sonofabitch, maybe; but I believe in enjoying life.

Newsweek, 2-8:59.

Frank McGee
News commentator,
National Broadcasting Company

One of my cherished beliefs is that a man cannot be held in double jeopardy. And damn it, it seems to me that my generation, which is now middle-aged, is in double or even triple jeopardy. When I was a kid, if you turned out badly, well, it was your own fault. So said society. So I grew up and I didn't turn out too badly. Then I look around and, guess what? Now they were telling me that if my kids turned out badly, it would not be their fault. It would be my fault. That's jeopardy number two, right? And finally, now I hear some old people saying that their lives are meaningless, barren and empty, and again it's my fault. Jeopardy number three. By God, I've had enough jeopardy. I want everybody off my middle-aged back.

Interview/Look, 10-5:15.

George Meany
President, American Federation of Labor-
Congress of Industrial Organizations

Yes, I am a plumber. I don't know how humble I am, but I always try to stress the importance of the plumbing business. I say plumbers, in a good many cases, are more important than lawyers. You can put millions of people in a great city and get along without lawyers; but you couldn't put them in there without plumbers. So I must warn you never to underestimate the importance of a plumber. In fact, I know anyone who has ever got a bill from a plumber doesn't underestimate them.

Before labor convention, Miami Beach/
The Wall Street Journal, 6-11:6.

Jacques Monot
Biologist

We have no right to have no hope; because if we have no hope, there is no hope. The basic ethics for the modern man conscious of what humanity is running into is to firmly stick to the will of doing something about it, and therefore the belief that something can be done about it; although there is the famous maxim of William of Orange: "It is not necessary to hope in order to undertake, nor to succeed in order to persevere."

Interview, Paris/
The New York Times, 3-15:6.

Gunnar Myrdal
Economist

Society does not need rebels and ardent reformers any longer, and neither does it have any place for the diehard philosophers of reaction. It has, instead, use for large cadres of practical tacticians, organizers and bureaucrats.

Interview, Stockholm/
Nation's Business, April.

Ralph Nader
Lawyer; Consumer rights advocate

The concept of an individual with a conscience is one whose highest allegiance is to his fellow man.

Before National Council of Jewish
Women, Beverly Hills, Calif./
Los Angeles Times, 3-22:(4)16.

Richard M. Nixon
President of the United States

It is really easy to be for what is right.

(RICHARD M. NIXON)

What is more difficult is to accomplish what is right.

Eulogy for Whitney M. Young, Jr.,
Lexington, Ky., March 17/
The Washington Post, 3-18:(A)6.

(People must) have something to believe in, something to hold to, something to turn to when life is not what they think it ought to be. The worst thing that can happen to a young person is to believe in nothing but himself.

Washington, March 26/
Los Angeles Herald-Examiner, 3-27:(A)2.

Olof Palme
Prime Minister of Sweden

I am extremely suspicious when I hear talk of the empty materialism of our time. Those who complain are often people for whom abundance and a high living standard have been a banal matter of course.

The New York Times, 6-20:(4)6.

Alan Paton
South African author

. . . in what way can one's highest loyalty be given to one's country? Surely only in one way; and that is when one wishes with all one's heart and tries with all one's powers to make it a better country, to make it more just and more tolerant and more merciful and, if it is powerful, more wise in the use of its power.

At Harvard University
commencement, June 17/
The New York Times, 6-18:16.

Paul VI
Pope

Liberty is extremely precarious and delicate. It is true that conscience must be one's guide; but conscience itself must be guided by the science of things both divine and human. It is true that liberty must be able to operate without obstacles; but it must be directed toward good, and this direction is called sense

of responsibility, it is called duty. It is true also that liberty is a personal right; but it cannot fail to respect the rights of others. It cannot be divorced from charity.

Castel Gandolfo, Italy, Aug. 18/
Los Angeles Herald-Examiner, 8-19:(A)5.

Nathan M. Pusey
President, Harvard University

The problem for us mortals is always how to blend determination and modesty, how to hold together certainty and doubt, how to persevere in the face of defeat and racalcitrant resistance, how to hold on to hope in the face of a realistic appraisal of one's self and one's world without being enraged by failure or enfeebled by despair . . .

Harvard University baccalaureate
address, June 15/
The Boston Globe, 6-16:10.

Hyman G. Rickover
Vice Admiral, United States Navy

A half-truth is like half a brick: You can throw it farther.

Plainview (Tex.) Daily Herald, 7-15:10.

Mickey Rooney
Actor

Fame is like a good meal. You either digest it or it gives you indigestion. But you're hungry 24 hours a day.

Quote, 7-18:49.

Dan Rowan
Comedian

Ever since I reached maturity, I've known there is no escape from problems. But maybe there can be postponements.

Interview, Los Angeles/
Los Angeles Times, 3-31:(3)2.

Vermont C. Royster
Editor, "The Wall Street Journal"

This idea that it's only the young who are not sure what to do with their lives is an illusion of youth.

San Francisco Examiner & Chronicle
(This World), 1-17:2.

Artur Rubinstein
Pianist

(Regarding a suicide attempt many years ago): My love of life was born on that day. I decided that nothing would stop me from being happy; that I would even be happy on my deathbed. We must get rid of the "ifs" in life —if I had this job, if I had this girl—and be unconditionally happy just to be alive.

At luncheon marking his 84th birthday,
New York, Jan. 28/
Los Angeles Times, 1-30:(2)7.

. . . I have a feeling that we have a power in us. You know, there is always a word that nobody has been able to explain; there is no *explique*—nothing to lead you toward an answer as to what it means; yet all the languages use it so frequently that it has become an everyday word: the word "soul," *"l'ame," "anima"*—what the hell is *"anima"*? Where is it? We know pretty well the anatomy; we know pretty well what we are doing and how it functions and all that. But what the devil is the soul, you see? Well, this soul appears to be so frightfully necessary—as religion is necessary, or seems to be; we must have it; and in all the cultures, as far as we can trace, there was always something there to worship; there were all those totems and God knows what. Well, soul is a kind of power.

Interview, New York/Look, 3-9:54.

Adela Rogers St. Johns
Author

(Regarding Women's Liberation): I don't understand the women of today. They have everything in the world that they're trying to get rid of as fast as they can. That's not liberation.

Interview, Beverly Hills, Calif./
Los Angeles Herald-Examiner, 2-7:(E)3.

George C. Scott
Actor

The most necessary qualities a woman must possess to be appealing are honesty, straightforwardness and total lack of guile. Sex appeal is terribly necessary, but you can't pin it down; it differs from woman to woman. A humorless woman, though, is the saddest thing one can encounter. She's the most pathetic creature on the face of the earth. And as for Women's Lib, it's total hysteria. Any woman I've ever known who was a woman didn't feel oppressed.

Interview, Los Angeles/ Los Angeles
Times (West), 11-7:5.

Glenn T. Seaborg
Chairman, Atomic Energy Commission
of the United States

We must show youth that knowledge is not a tool of oppression—of the mind, body or spirit—but rather the key to greater physical freedom.

San Francisco Examiner, 2-18:30.

Eric Sevareid
News commentator,
Columbia Broadcasting System

Human beings are not perfectable. They *are* improvable. So are the conditions under which they live. Human problems are rarely solved, American folklore to the contrary notwithstanding. They can be and often are ameliorated. Anybody who can do that with his own life is living successfully, indeed.

At Congress of American Industry,
New York/Quote, 4-4:321.

It is perfectly clear that people, given no alternative, will choose tyranny over anarchy, because anarchy is the worst tyranny of all.

At Stanford University commencement,
June 13/Parade, 7-18:16.

John R. Silber
President, Boston University

All over the nation we hear cries of alarm about the pollution of air and the pollution of water; but we hear little or nothing about a pollution far more serious—that of time itself. We can, after all, recycle air and water through filters. But we cannot recycle time. We can live meaningfully—though painfully,

(JOHN R. SILBER)

unpleasantly and briefly—in dirty air, drinking dirty water. But when the structure of time is destroyed, the basis for significance in our own lives is likewise destroyed. All meaning is lost in the instantaneous. The pollution of time is most obvious in our loss of a sense of history, in a loss of the recognition of the past as our own, in the loss of the awareness of any past, the loss of the past in general. We see the pollution of time in the loss of the myths of childhood. As rationalistic devotees of scientism, we cannot afford to rear our children on Grimm or Andersen, on the myths of Santa Claus and Bethlehem or of Easter and Passover. We do not believe that there is a time and a place for everything—a time to be born, a time to be a child, a time to be an adult, a time to be old and a time to die. We cannot take time to observe the rites of passage. Only 30 years ago, long pants for boys was such a rite. Now long pants are issued to toddlers. So how does a boy know when he is a man? In this instant culture, little attention is paid to the rites of baptism, confirmation, engagement, marriage, or even of death. What then is left of the meaningful structure of time? Time, that great river of life, is polluted and fouled to a degree threatening all possibility of meaning in human existence.

At his inauguration/
The National Observer, 8-9:13.

Stephen G. Spottswood
Chairman, National Association for
the Advancement of Colored People

You cannot pursue togetherness by trying to get separated from everybody else. Some of the loudest calls for "getting together" come from people who want to be exclusive. They say that we'll get together without white people, or poor people, or educated people, or the men or the women, or anybody over 30, or anybody under 20. Sometimes these apostles of exclusiveness want to make it together without government, or political process, or legislatures, or courts, or policemen. Others want to get it all together

without business, or corporations, or organized labor, or banks. In fact, if you listen to this line of talk long enough, you will realize that what is being said is, "I don't actually want to get together with anyone but myself, because nobody else is old enough, or young enough, or white enough, or black enough for me—except me."

Minneapolis, July 5/
Vital Speeches, 8-15:663.

Gloria Steinem
Author

(Regarding women being treated as inferior by men): There can only be real love between equals. Unequal love causes insecure feelings. It causes the wife to be afraid her husband married her so he could have a full-time housekeeper and a part-time prostitute. It causes the man to be afraid his wife married him so she could have wall-to-wall carpeting.

At National Food Editors Conference,
Chicago/
The Dallas Times Herald, 10-10:C.

Elizabeth Taylor
Actress

Marriage is like a very good recipe. After you've made it and put in every ingredient, you can't let it sit in the icebox too long. You have to stir it occasionally, and add a touch of this or that flavor.

Interview/
The Washington Post, 3-26:(B)2.

U Thant
Secretary General
of the United Nations

. . . it is my personal conviction that we must strive . . . at forming a total man, nourished not only by material aspirations but deeply intrenched in morality, tolerance, unselfishness and understanding for his fellow men. In the world of tomorrow, which will comprise many billions of people, our best chance, and perhaps our only chance, to secure a peaceful, just and orderly society is to rely heavily on the peace, the behavior, the sense of justice, the tolerance and the kindness of individuals. Institutions and political structures are only servants of the people. No institution, however vast and powerful it may be, will ever be able to match the value of the individual human life.

Before Organization of American States, San Jose, Costa Rica, April 14/ The New York Times, 5-23:(4)17.

William R. Tolbert, Jr.
President of Liberia

I always like to give consideration to what is good in the old and have faith in what is best in the new.

Interview/ The New York Times, 11-9:14.

Barbara Tuchman
Author, Historian

History has fascinated me all my life. From the age of six, I've read it. Why? Because it's real. It's the way things happen; the way men behave. It tells us a lot about ourselves, our capabilities and limitations. It singles out the great figures, the ones who rise to the top, though not necessarily for anything good they may have done, but for something dramatic and effective that had an influence on their time. The result is that they have built-in reader interest, unlike so many of the anti-heroes novelists write about today —alcoholics, drug addicts or perverts.

Interview, New York/ The Christian Science Monitor, 3-25:(B)7.

People get mixed up. They say, "Why should the rich have all the privileges?" Well, because that's what being rich is. At some point, these were people of greater ability and energy, and that's why they're rich. Even the robber barons who robbed the poor showed they were more capable of that, more something. There's a rationale to it.

Interview/ Los Angeles Times, 11-25:(6)11.

John V. Tunney
United States Senator, D—Calif.

Monolithic Communism is a myth, no longer the dire threat that it was in the immediacy of the post-World War II era.

Before Los Angeles World Affairs Council international forum, Aug. 13/ Los Angeles Times, 8-14:(1)20.

Leon Uris
Author

Because of the (birth-control) pill, which is great in the right hands, too many girls are going to the altar with as many as 40 affairs behind them—and every bit of romance bashed out of them.

San Francisco Examiner, 12-24:22.

Peter Ustinov
Actor, Director, Writer

I have discovered that people with the reputation of being difficult are usually so considered simply because they're intolerant of stupidity.

Interview, Los Angeles/ Houston Chronicle, 3-30:(2)5.

Luchino Visconti
Motion picture director

Women's liberation? Put them all in jail! What liberation do they want? They should be *women* . . . that's enough, if they do it well. Bed, kitchen, mother. All of us have our place, our duty, our job. Their job is to get man to eat the apple, to *compromise* man.

Interview, New York/ The New York Times, 6-27:(2)17.

John Wayne
Actor

We must . . . look always to the future. Tomorrow—the time that gives a man or a country just one more chance—is just one of many things that I feel are wonderful in life. So's a good horse under you. Or the only campfire for miles around. Or a quiet night

527

(JOHN WAYNE)

and a nice soft hunk of ground to sleep on. Or church bells sending out their invitations. A mother meeting her first-born. The sound of a kid calling you Dad for the first time. There's a lot of things great about life. But I think tomorrow is the most important thing. Comes in to us at midnight very clean, you know. It's perfect when it arrives and it puts itself in our hands. It hopes we've learned something from yesterday.

Interview/Playboy, May:92.

Glenn Yarbrough
Singer

When I was a kid, I figured, like everyone else does, that the more money I had the more things I'd possess and the happier I'd be. Well, I was lucky. I obtained the material things when I was relatively young. And it didn't take long to figure out what a ridiculous goal that was.

Los Angeles Times, 2-21:(A)21.

Susannah York
Actress

I used to think that when I reached the age of 21 things would be lovely and settled, and that I would have realized all the single threads in myself. But, in fact, I have exceeded that age by eight years; and I certainly don't feel that I have no more threads to draw on. I now realize—though this may sound a very selfish thing—that one will always need to fulfill oneself. Once you stop feeling that you're discovering things, then you will know that you're at the end, so far as being a creative artist is concerned.

Interview, East Sussex, England/
The Christian Science Monitor, 3-27:12.

Franco Zeffirelli
Motion picture director

Materialism is a barren philosophy. Mechanical inventions have eased our daily life, but lulled us into a stupefying inertia. I prefer an air-conditioned office to a stuffy room, but if air conditioning were the price of my freedom, I'd rather sweat.

Interview, Rome/
The New York Times, 9-3:12.

John J. Akar
*Former Ambassador to the United States
from Sierra Leone*

The church in Africa, by assuming a see-nothing, hear-nothing and say-nothing attitude on contemporary African politics, has achieved nothing, is nothing and has alienated the African intelligentsia and reduced itself to nothing more than a Sunday fashion show. The church in Africa is incapable today of provoking social consciousness, because it has been muted by fear, ineptitude and complacency, notwithstanding the few shining stars to the contrary.

*At World Methodist Conference,
Denver, Colo., Aug. 19/
The Washington Post, 8-21:(B)9.*

J. C. Michael Allen
*Dean, Berkeley Divinity School,
New Haven, Conn.*

The church needs men and women . . . not to be priests, not to be ministers, but just to be men, just to be women. This is the job the seminaries have to do; but we have not done it very well to date. We have turned out too many technicians and not enough men of God.

*New Haven, Jan. 24/
The New York Times, 1-25:25.*

Bernard L. Berzon
*President,
Rabbinical Council of America*

(The current anti-Semite) refuses to be identified as such and declares fervently that he has no prejudice against Jews. (Instead) he has now become an anti-Zionist, placing himself in the camp of those who consistently denounce Israeli "imperialism" as some sort of nefarious world conspiracy from which he is seeking to save peace-loving world humanity.

*At Rabbinical Council of America
conference, Lakewood, N.J., Jan. 19/
The New York Times, 1-20:16.*

Frank J. Bonnike
*President, United States National
Federation of Priests Councils*

In the United States, we are losing five diocesan priests by death, retirement and resignation for every two ordained. You can keep shuffling the deck, moving around priests to meet your needs; but sooner or later the American church is going to run out of cards. We are in favor of ordaining married men, because we are afraid the American Catholic laity (will) end up not only with a shortage of priests, but with an older clergy trying to care for a population half of whom will be under 25 by 1975.

*Vatican City/
Los Angeles Times, 10-29:(1)16.*

John N. Burgess
Episcopal Bishop of Massachusetts

I think the future of the church will depend a great deal upon how successful we are at breaking down the barrier between what people like to call "spiritual" and what is called "worldly." There are those who think the church ought to stick to Gospel; yet we know very well the Gospel cannot be expressed except through structures of the world. There are those on the other side who feel we can be involved in action and humanism without a theological structure to support us. I think the churches, as we have known them, have got to help people to understand how the world and the spirit are intertwined. I think this is our biggest task,

529

(JOHN N. BURGESS)

to break down these barriers, this polarization.

Interview, Boston/Los Angeles
Herald-Examiner, 3-20:(A)11.

Leo Byrne
Roman Catholic Coadjutor Archbishop
of St. Paul-Minneapolis

No argument should be used to exclude women from any service to the church if it stems from male prejudice, blind adherence to merely human traditions that may have been rooted in the social position of women in other times, or questionable interpretation of scripture.

Vatican City, Oct. 22/
The Washington Post, 10-23:(A)12.

Jose Cardinal Clemente (Maurer)
Archbishop of Sucre, Bolivia;
Head of Bolivia's Roman Catholic Church

At all levels, one notices a true concern that the church be and appear as one of the poor in the service of the poor. A true poverty gives the church authority and credibility.

Los Angeles Times, 7-29:(1)2.

William Cardinal Conway
Roman Catholic Primate
of all Ireland

We should not deceive ourselves by saying we do not want optional celibacy but only some change in the law under certain conditions. In the modern world, where public opinion is often subject to pressures of a violent kind, such conditions would be washed away like stones in a river.

U.S. News & World Report, 11-1:33.

Terence Cardinal Cooke
Roman Catholic Archbishop
of New York

(Regarding the recent Supreme Court decision against government aid to parochial schools): . . . if this right (to free exercise of religion) is given and cannot be used, the right is given in vain. (Such a situation is comparable to saying that) a whale has the right to fly to the moon or that an elephant has a right to swim under the North Pole. We cannot tell (Catholic) parents that they can have genuine freedom of choice in education only as long as they can—in addition to paying their taxes to Federal, state and local governments for public schools—also pay for parochial schools entirely out of their own pockets. What good is that freedom if parents, to exercise it, must suffer severe economic penalties or else see it priced out of existence?

Before Knights of Columbus,
New York, Aug. 17/
The New York Times, 8-18:23.

Billy Graham
Evangelist

Our (U.S.) government heads may disagree violently on political matters; but they are together in feeling the need for the Lord and spiritual emphasis in our country. Some of these men are red-hot Christians.

The Dallas Times Herald, 2-17:(A)2.

I warn you that, as (in) the Soviet Union, secularization will lead to a rising tide of anti-Semitism and ultimately anti-Christianity. Many have been surprised that the new anti-Semitism rising in America comes from the far left. I am not surprised. Much of the far left is secularistic, humanistic and even atheistic. It is intolerant toward any kind of faith in God. This push toward secularization must be halted and reversed if democracy and freedom are to survive in this country.

Upon receiving the International
Brotherhood Award of the National
Society of Christians and Jews,
Cleveland, March 14/
The Dallas Times Herald, 3-15:(A)11.

Word is already getting around that the drug and sex themes of the 60s will be replaced in the 70s by religion . . . Millions are rejecting the materialism, the secularism, the skepticism and the agnosticism of their elders. They are on a gigantic search for reality, purpose and meaning. I seriously doubt if there has ever been a time in history when so many young people are professing conversion to Christ as at this very hour.

Before National Association of Evangelicals, Los Angeles, April 22/ The New York Times, 4-25:(1)56.

John Cardinal Heenan
Roman Catholic Primate of Britain

The state of virginity as such is not in itself virtuous. It is a physical thing . . . virtue is an attitude of the mind—the reason why a person has chosen virginity. Some people are virgins, men or women, simply because no one will have them; they may have tried time and again to get married. You cannot say, because this person is a virgin, therefore he is a better man or more virtuous than a married man. And that goes for the clergy, too. Just because I am a celibate priest, it does not mean I am more virtuous in the eyes of God and man than a person with a wife and family.

Television interview/ "A Chance to Meet . . .", British Broadcasting Corporation.

R. J. Henle
President, Georgetown University

When we accepted freshmen in our Catholic colleges 20 years ago, we assumed they were, for the most part, solid in their faith. They were Christians in practice and belief; and they recognized sin, even when they committed sin. Our problem in the colleges and universities was to put intellectual substance into their belief, to ground it and found it rationally, to give them an intellectual control over their internalized system of values. But we can no longer do this. We have to assume that it doesn't make any difference what Catholic high school they come from or what Catholic homes they come from. We have to assume that the majority of our freshmen come to us already with a crisis of faith. Our task is not to elaborate the faith into a rational system, to give it substance, to expand it or increase it. Our problem is a missionary problem: to re-establish the faith, to re-establish their belief, to help the young people find and internalize a sound system of values for themselves. The present problem of Catholicism with regard to most of our young people is to re-establish some belief in fundamental values and to work toward some kind of a basic consensus with regard to values. The conflict which our young people have seen in their parents between a secular set of values—money, the good life, the *Playboy* philosophy—and a religious set of values—Mass on Sunday, Christian words, statements—has been devastating to many of our young; and they move in both directions. So we have in this country, and in the Western world, a real crisis with regard to fundamental convictions.

At President's Dinner, Washington Alumni Club/ The Wall Street Journal, 3-1:8.

Theodore M. Hesburgh
President, University of Notre Dame

I do not discount the possible contribution of married priests, particularly in certain areas of contemporary life. But they will not be the shock troops that carry the day against the monumental powers of darkness that presently threaten the people of God.

San Francisco Examiner, 3-30:28.

Gerhardt W. Hyatt
Major General and Chief of Chaplains, United States Army

. . . over the years, I've developed a consciousness that religion is life. Life without religion is a very shattered fact. Religion without life is a mockery.

Interview, Washington/ The Washington Post, 8-14:(B)5.

Lyndon B. Johnson
Former President of the United States

Men in the pulpit have a place in the political leadership of our people, and they have a place in our public affairs.

Quote, 4-25:385.

Gerald Kennedy
Bishop, Los Angeles area,
United Methodist Church

Preaching only gets dull when fellows forget what the Gospel is. It's the most exciting news there is. It takes a real gift to make preaching boring—but we can do it.

Interview, Minneapolis/
The Washington Post, 4-17:(F)3.

Franz Cardinal Koenig
Roman Catholic Archbishop of Vienna

(Regarding the stress and frustrations of the position of Pope): When we elect a new Pope, we shall very likely have to force him to accept the job.

Plainview (Tex.) Daily Herald, 3-11:10.

Timothy Manning
Roman Catholic Archbishop
of Los Angeles

I'm very optimistic about the church. I think some grand things have happened to her. More and more, she is finding out what her real mission is. She's always known this, of course; but she is in the process of restating what she is, what she stands for, her mission of service. She is discarding superficial things that she inherited in her passage through human cultures and with which she was identified, that were not at all part of her message or her mission.

Interview, Los Angeles/
Los Angeles Times, 3-21:(C)1.

John Mbiti
Anglican theologian, Makerere
University College, Kampala, Uganda

The days are over when we will be carbon copies of European Christians. Europe and America Westernized Christianity. The Orthodox Easternized it. Now it's our turn to Africanize it.

The New York Times, 3-12:10.

Margaret Mead
Anthropologist

(Criticizing churches and synagogues as "suburban social organizations"): Parents moving out of cities (after World War II) joined the suburban churches and synagogues so their children could get into dancing class. Now those children are dancing right out of church. (The upshot is a) generation with no access to historical religion. Young people want to build a new religious movement, but they lack the liturgy, poetry, imagery of the historical church.

At University of Rhode Island/
The New York Times, 2-9:64.

Jacques Monot
Biologist

. . . the scientific attitude implies what I call the postulate of objectivity—that is to say, the fundamental postulate that there is no plan, that there is no intention in the universe. Now this is basically incompatible with virtually all the religious or metaphysical systems whatever; all of which try to show that there is some sort of harmony between man and the universe and that man is a product—predictable if not indispensable—of the evolution of the universe. Of course, naive faiths, fundamentalist beliefs in the Bible do just that. They put man in the center of the universe and believe that, for some reason, there is a necessity everywhere under God's command. In more elaborate modern versions of Christianity, you find speculations like those of Teilhard de Chardin, which gave an evolutionist interpretation of the universe in which man is a sort of achievement which had been predicted from the beginning. It is, again, an interpretation which denies the principle of objectivity.

Interview, Paris/
The New York Times, 3-15:6.

Paul VI
Pope

Little by little, even we followers of Christ classified as faithful Catholics often look for an easy and conformist Christian life, practically excluding mortification, sacrifice, the cross of our clerical clothes.

Rome, Feb. 24/
Los Angeles Times, 2-25:(1)16.

It is not easy for us men of today to retrace our steps away from the turbulent and frequently disillusioning road that has led us to modern materialism and seek, instead, the path that leads to the truth and beauty of religion.

Vatican City, Feb. 28/
The Washington Post, 3-1:(C)5.

(Regarding priests who defect from the church): One must distinguish case from case and show understanding, pity, forgiveness, patience perhaps in waiting for the return, and always love. But how can one fail . . . to weep from the deliberate abandonment by some and the moral mediocrity which thinks it natural and logical to break a long premeditated promise solemnly taken?

Rome, April 8/
Los Angeles Times, 4-9:(1)13.

From the heart of the church, even among our dearest sons, there arises unrest, intolerance and defections. It is an hour of storm.

Before conference of Italian
bishops, Rome, June 19/
Los Angeles Herald-Examiner, 6-20:(A)11.

. . . the bishops of the entire Catholic world wish to retain intact that absolute gift by which the priest is dedicated to God; and a not unimportant part of that gift—in the Latin Church—is sacred celibacy.

Before Synod of Bishops, Rome, Nov. 6/
The New York Times, 11-7:(1)1.

Today, more than ever before, the throng rises up and presses forward and declares: "We have no need for this salvation. We do not know this Savior. We do not want to recognize him." Is not this the attitude of today's radical secularism, of our proud and intolerant self-sufficiency? As at the hour of His birth for His Mother Mary, so today for mother church, who gives Him birth in the new society, the sentence is sealed: There is no room for Him; let Him be turned away.

Vatican City, Dec. 25/
Los Angeles Times, 12-26:(A)12.

Huston Smith
Professor of Philosophy,
Massachusetts Institute
of Technology

The so-called "youth culture" is emphatically religious. I have been teaching 25 years, and I have never seen so religious a generation as this one.

Interview, Los Angeles/
Los Angeles Times, 1-17:(F)6.

Colin W. Williams
Dean, Yale Divinity School

There's a crisis facing the Christian church today. Ministers don't get adequate training under the old system to prepare them for conflicts, people and situations that life is all about today, and they're lost.

New Haven, Conn., Jan. 23/
The New York Times, 1-25:25.

John Joseph Cardinal Wright
Prefect of the Sacred Congregation
of the Clergy, The Vatican

Men and women of authentic religious vision, persons capable of spiritual leadership, are conspicuously absent from the American press, the university world, political life and, we might as well admit it, the pulpit. I have some idea of the brickbats that will come in reaction to this observation—but they prove my point.

Interview, Rome/
Los Angeles Herald-Examiner, 3-20:(A)9.

533

Space · Science · Technology

Spiro T. Agnew
Vice President of the United States

There has been too much productive by-product from space exploration to quash it—our whole burgeoning computer industry, communications satellites, medical advances, miniaturization. The nay-sayers will lose this one.

Before Los Angeles Area Chamber
of Commerce, April 7/
Los Angeles Times, 4-8:(1)3.

(Regarding criticism of spending money on space projects): I have no doubt that when Spain's Queen Isabella decided to finance Columbus in his quest to prove the world is round, she was told the money could be better spent in the slums of Barcelona . . . There is no reason why we shouldn't put a man on Mars by the end of this century. To abandon such an objective would be contrary to the attitudes that made the United States a great nation.

Interview, Washington/
Los Angeles Herald-Examiner, 10-10:(B)8.

Robert Anderson
President, North American
Rockwell Corporation

Suppose we give in and abandon the national space program. Suppose we shut down the whole NASA establishment, and we leave Cape Kennedy to the swamps from which it emerged less than 20 years ago. Suppose we turn loose the engineers and scientists and technicians and wipe out hundreds of thousands of supporting jobs. Suppose we darken all the university laboratories that support our space research and development effort. The result would be a saving of three billion two

hundred and seventy million dollars a year . . . Does anyone seriously think that the United States, after that drastic action, would be a better place in which to live? That the poor would be less poor? That slums would disappear? That suddenly our rivers would be clean and our air as fresh and untainted as a spring breeze? Quite the reverse is true. More poverty, more pollution, more congested highways, a permanent cancer of high, unyielding unemployment could be the result if we were to lose this battle and wipe out the aerospace industry. In space programs, in commercial aircraft development and in military aircraft development, this nation is faced with grave decisions. Should those decisions be wrong, the errors will haunt this nation for decades—perhaps forever.

At Humane Resource Allocation
Symposium, Los Angeles, April 14/
Vital Speeches, 6-1:503.

Neil A. Armstrong
Former American astronaut

The *Apollo* (space) program demonstrated how really dedicated the American can be after he has accepted a challenge. The entire project team would absolutely not stop working. Everywhere you looked, people were working late at night and across the weekends, usually without pay, as if their life—or, more importantly, the life of their country—depended on it. They believed in their goal, and they knew every man had to give more than his share to make that goal a reality. I only hope we can agree as well on other goals and see that kind of "American spirit" more often.

Interview/
U.S. News & World Report, 1-11:32.

I believe space exploration "is" and never will become "was." It is part of our mutual lives now and will remain so for the remainder of the history of man.

Aug. 25/San Francisco Examiner, 8-26:20.

James R. Arnold
Professor of Chemistry,
University of California at San Diego

I like to think that *Apollo 14* was like the third voyage of Columbus, when he started mapping his course and didn't just "feel" his way to the New World. You might even compare *Apollo 14* to the Spaniards' first visits to the Sugar Islands or even to Cortez' landing in Mexico.

The Washington Post, 2-14:(C)1.

Georgy T. Beregovoy
Soviet cosmonaut

Let's daydream a minute. In the next ten years, I think long-term orbital (space) stations will become common. Scientists and specialists would work on them. Transport ships would cruise between the stations and earth, carrying relief crews.

San Francisco Examiner & Chronicle
(This World), 5-2:16.

Hale Boggs
United States Representative, D–La.

I am for urban mass transit. I am for the poverty program. I am for model cities. I am for aid to education. I am for building hospitals. I am for cleaning up the slums. I am for helping the small towns and farms of this country. I am for cleaning up the environment. But none of this will happen if we do not maintain the scientific ingenuity of this nation . . . When the time comes that we in America turn back on that quest for knowledge, when we say we do not have the know-how, we do not have the resources and we cannot do it, then we shall cease to move ahead. There is no such thing as a static society.

Before the House,
Washington, March 18/
Congressional Record, 3-18:H1737.

Omar N. Bradley
General, United States Army (Ret.)

There is no reason people should worry about losing their individuality. Machines haven't made us surrender anything as humans that we are unwilling to surrender. I see it the other way around; machines have expanded human opportunities. One obvious example is that now we have the opportunity, because of technology, to go to the moon if we want to. That's a gain for the individual, not a loss.

Interview, Beverly Hills, Calif./
The Dallas Times Herald, 3-21:(A)8.

Lewis M. Branscomb
Director, National Bureau
of Standards of the United States

(Regarding current criticism of technology): Science is, perhaps, some kind of cosmic apple juice from the Garden of Eden. Those who drink of it are doomed to carry the burden of original sin.

Plainview (Tex.) Daily Herald, 4 0·6.

Robin Brett
Manned Spacecraft Center, National
Aeronautics and Space Administration
of the United States

Going to and from the moon, the astronauts (on *Apollo 14*) were test pilots. Their first day on the moon, they were physicists; the next day, geologists. And when it was all over, they became tourists, took pictures and played a little golf. I think that, altogether, the use of man was very well demonstrated by this mission.

The Washington Post, 2-14:(C)1.

Michael Collins
Former American astronaut

After *Apollo 11*, we toured 22 foreign countries. Never did I hear a foreigner say the space program is irrelevant. Only Americans say that . . .

Before World Affairs Council, Los Angeles/
Los Angeles Herald-Examiner,
2-24:(A)13.

Barry Commoner
Professor of Biology,
Washington University, St. Louis

I'm not anti-science; but science is not something that was handed down in golden tablets from a mountain. It is essential that scientists re-examine how they operate and the way in which they separate the disciplines. Our technology is fragmented and aimed at increasing productivity and profits, without taking into account resources and ecology. We need a renaissance in science and technology, directing it toward human welfare.

Interview, New York/
Los Angeles Times, 12-19:(A)20.

Jacques-Yves Cousteau
Underwater explorer

Science has taken itself too seriously. Scientists thought they were special people dealing with nature in a kind of esoteric way, and the result was they became cold fish and dry bugs. Now we are beginning to humanize science a little bit, to reconnect it with daily life. What is a scientist after all? It is a curious man looking through a keyhole, the keyhole of nature, trying to know what's going on. It's a very human feeling.

Interview, New York/
The Christian Science Monitor, 7-21:17.

Walter Cunningham
American astronaut

The (U.S.) space program is receiving smaller and smaller support with appropriations from Congress. I think that's a terrible mistake. I think we find ourselves in the space program in the position of having built the dam, and it's filling up behind it, and there's precious little interest in putting the turbines in at the bottom to take out the energy, take out the resources we've built up.

Announcing his resignation,
Houston, June 17/
Los Angeles Herald-Examiner, 6-18:(A)8.

Edward E. David, Jr.
Science Adviser to the President
of the United States

A limitation on (scientific and technological) experimentation, in whatever cause, is the beginning of a wider suppression. Already we see timidity in new undertakings. If these trends progress, our society will become dull, stodgy and altogether stagnant.

At National Academy of Sciences, Washington,
Feb. 24/The Washington Post, 2-25:(A)3.

John Z. DeLorean
General Manager, Chevrolet Division,
General Motors Corporation

The concern which I have pertains to the abandonment of technology by some of the best minds in America, the men and women with the conscience, the motivation and the dedication to apply their lives to the solution of the problems which cripple the democratic process. Without technology, it is no contest. They will be using the wooden plow, while the opposition would be splitting the atom. The leaders of this movement in America would be well advised to re-evaluate their arguments against technology and to carefully and deliberately separate the consequences of the improper applications of technology from the art itself. If a beautiful Stradivarius is played badly, is it logical to smash the instrument? Or change the instrumentalist? You can still argue against water pollution and learn how to adapt the processes to bring about clean water. Technology need not be the enemy of the campus or the liberals. If housebroken and tamed, it can provide the means of a more equal distribution of goods and services. If understood and innovated, it can open the gates to the utopias of which mankind has dreamed since the beginning of recorded time.

At Emory University, Atlanta/
The Wall Street Journal, 4-27:18.

Rene Dubos
Professor of Microbiology,
Rockefeller University

The fundamental aberration of scientific

technology during the past 100 years is embodied in the motto of the 1933 Chicago World's Fair: Science Finds/Industry Applies/Man Conforms. In fact, man still lives with the genes of the Old Stone Age hunter and the New Stone Age farmer. We must make industry conform to man by adapting it to his genetic limitations. For example, we know that the temperature of the human body varies from day to night and from summer to winter. Yet the air-conditioning industry has given us a completely constant environment to live and work in. Look at London. For 200 years, it was the most polluted city in the world. (Because of strict pollution laws) they have not had a pea-soup fog for six years, and last year they had 50% more sunshine than they had ten years ago. Songbirds are returning to the parks; fish are being caught again in the Thames.

Interview/Time, 5-31:51.

Wallace B. Edgerton
Acting Chairman, National
Endowment for the Humanities

Scientific knowledge, important as it has been for achieving American goals, is increasingly recognized as incapable of responding to all of the emerging issues of American life.

Before Senate Appropriations Subcommittee,
Washington, March 18/
The New York Times, 3-19:39.

James C. Fletcher
Administrator, National Aeronautics
and Space Administration
of the United States

Our priorities are out of whack when, as a nation, we pay people more not to work and more in farm subsidies than we spend on space research, a program which impacts our national economy. I do not need to be told that our sense of priorities is dangerously lopsided when, here in Los Angeles, some of the most talented members of our technological team are driving taxis for a living while we are slipping behind Europe in aeronautical engineering and the Soviet Union is pulling ahead of us in many areas of space exploration. As a

scientist, I know that the answer to many of our social problems—worldwide as well as domestic—is to be found through technology.

At Los Angeles Area
Chamber of Commerce
Aerospace luncheon, Oct. 1/
Los Angeles Herald-Examiner, 10-1:(A)3.

Dennis Gabor
Nobel Prize-winning physicist

The triumph of technology and science has brought us face to face with irrationality. We have to fight not nature but man's nature.

At University of Bridgeport (Conn.)/
The New York Times, 11-5:29.

Paul W. Gast
Chief of Planetary and Earth Sciences
Division, Manned Spacecraft Center,
National Aeronautics and Space Administration
of the United States

I think you begin to see, from the kind of descriptions they *(Apollo 14* astronauts) gave and the kind of comments that they made, that their eyes worked, their brains worked and they were not seriously impeded by their spacesuits and by the way in which they have to work. I think this is a very encouraging and very important result of this mission—that every time we go, we see that the adaptation of man to the lunar surface seems to grow. He is functioning better and better, so that his capability as a field geologist on the surface should not be sold short . . . Let them make some of the decisions up there as to whether or not it's worthwhile to go to the edge of the crater or whether it's worthwhile going to a certain point. They clearly seem to me to be able to do this.

News conference, Houston, Feb. 8/
Los Angeles Times, 2-10:(1)3.

H. R. Gross
United States Representative, R—Iowa

Anyone would have to have rocks in his head to believe there is any austerity in the (American) space program. We now have the rocks and moon dust down here. How much more of this do we need? Let some other country that has a lot of money do this.

San Francisco Examiner, 1-18:20.

Edward J. Gurney
United States Senator, R—Fla.

There are those today here in Congress who want to stop technological progress and bury our heads in the motionless sands of status quo. This nation is not ready for that kind of defeatism. We should reject that kind of thinking out of hand.

The Dallas Times Herald, 6-29:(A)5.

George S. Hammond
*Chairman, division of chemistry
and chemical engineering,
California Institute of Technology*

I believe that science is still a baby, with great potential for further growth . . . When I look at us and the universe around us, I see much more that I do not understand than I understand. Science is far from finished. Too much of our attention is centered on what we know fairly well, and too little on things about which we know very little.

Los Angeles Herald-Examiner, 2-8:(A)15.

Philip Handler
*President, National Academy
of Sciences of the United States*

Science is more than just a record of observations and empirical fact; it is knowledge organized in such fashion as to permit insight into all natural phenomena and forces, so that, from the relatedness of facts, it creates unity out of diversity. It is this recognition of connections—where none appeared to exist before—that is the essence of scientific creativity. Although the requirements of precision and logic, the necessity of conforming to facts, the methodology of testing of concepts and ideas, may create the impression of scientific activity as an impersonal exercise, nothing could be further from the truth. Science is a truly human experience; it pro-

gresses because of the pleasure and excitement of personal involvement which underlies scientific creativity.

*Before American Iron and Steel
Institute, New York, May 26/
Vital Speeches, 9-15:716.*

It is very difficult for me to believe that mankind would be better off if no one knew that E=MC2. Clearly not. With that piece of information we made the atom and hydrogen bombs. That is a very high price we paid for that piece of information, and the knowledge cannot be exorcised. We are in it forever. We are doomed to live with that piece of information. That is a price. On the other side of the ledger, we have nuclear energy for the power plants we are going to have to have unless we want to cut back our standard of living seriously; and we have radio isotopes that have enabled medical research to make life more bearable. If there's a failure, then the failure is man, who can't manage his own interpersonal relations in a way that keeps him from using those weapons. But I find it almost impossible to believe that it is to the benefit of man, or even in the nature of man, that he should refuse to know. I would rather be knowledgeable with all the risks it brings than be ignorant with a quite different set of risks. My grandfather's ignorance of how water moves under the surface got my mother typhoid. Our knowledge of E=MC2 led to the hydrogen bomb. So both knowledge and ignorance are dangers. Given the choice, I would rather have knowledge.

*Interview, Washington/
Los Angeles Times, 12-5:(L)7.*

C. Lester Hogan
*President, Fairchild Camera
& Instrument Corporation*

. . . technological change has been a dominant feature in our society for a good number of years, particularly during the period since World War II. However, as our technologies have become increasingly more complex, they also have been more difficult for laymen to understand, and science's susceptibility to attack has increased as a result. We have now reached a point where science is in danger of being incorrectly blamed for many of the world's ills—such things as air and water pollution, and overpopulated cities and highways. I believe this is a very dangerous presumption. The true situation is that man—not his technology—is the primary cause of most difficulties in our environment. Those problems which can be linked to technology are not the direct result of science itself, but only of man's improper use of what he has discovered and developed. In fact, achievements in such fields as space, medicine and agriculture demonstrate that most of today's societal problems will more than likely have to be resolved by our resident technologies. Therefore, technology cannot and must not be shunned. Instead, it must be encouraged through conscious, intelligent leadership.

Before The Conference Board, New York,
Oct. 20/Vital Speeches, 12-15:140.

James B. Irwin
American astronaut

We're just beginning to learn about the moon. We've spent all these billions of dollars to build this transportation system to the moon, and we ought to press on and get every value from the investment. The *Apollo* flights are not just space spectaculars. They're scientific explorations to gain knowledge about the birth of the moon, our earth and our solar system. They seek basic insights into man, why he is here, where is he going. To unravel the mystery, man must know his relation to the sun. By studying the moon, we study the sun. For the sun has bombarded the moon for billions of years and etched its history in the lunar rocks.

Cape Kennedy, Fla./
San Francisco Examiner, 7-16:24.

James R. Killian, Jr.
Honorary chairman, Corporation of the
Massachusetts Institute of Technology;
Former Science Adviser to the
President of the United States

(Regarding criticism of science and technology): This tendency to deprecate reason will not long survive in our society. We have too long a record of finding answers and solutions.

Interview, Cambridge, Mass./
The New York Times, 8-8:(1)42.

Arthur Kornberg
Nobel Prize-winning biochemist

A scientist isn't a politician or a PR (public relations) man. He shouldn't be asked to judge the economic and moral value of his work. All we should ask the scientist to do is find the truth—and then not keep it from anyone.

Interview, Stanford, Calif./San Francisco
Examiner & Chronicle, 12-19:(A)22.

Christopher C. Kraft, Jr.
Deputy Director, Manned Spacecraft Center,
National Aeronautics and Space
Administration of the United States

Today, putting a scientific package into space takes a real long lead-time. A scientist has to figure out what he wants to do; he has to tell someone what he wants to do in minute detail; he even has to predict the results in order to get approval for funding. Then, when he builds his space package, he has to build it perfectly—the first time. It cannot fail. So it's a very expensive piece of equipment. Today, all those aspects make the average scientist and the average engineer shy away from space. Oh, they support our efforts in the abstract; but they know it's difficult to do, so they stay away.

Interview, Houston/
Los Angeles Herald-Examiner, 2-7:(B)2.

Hans Krebs
Nobel Prize-winning biochemist

In the past, research grants in the U.S. have been generous. Now they are inadequate. The young scientists are hit hardest. They have great difficulty in getting started in basic research—and the basic research of today is the applied science of tomorrow. The policy of cutting back funds is short-sighted. Because of reductions, the United States is falling behind much of the rest of the world.

News conference, Dallas, April 20/
The Dallas Times Herald, 4-21:(A)18.

George M. Low
Acting Administrator,
National Aeronautics and Space
Administration of the United States

. . . today there is every indication that we (the United States) will lose (space) leadership; and once we do, we may not again have the capacity to catch up . . . It is important that we move out now with the space program that we proposed for the 1970s, so that . . . we can at least point to the new capabilities that will soon exist.

Before Senate Aeronautical and Space
Sciences Committee, Washington, March 30/
Los Angeles Times, 3-31:(1)9.

W. McNeil Lowry
Vice president for humanities
and the arts, Ford Foundation

Over 150 years . . . we have learned that industrial progress, in and of itself, is not the source of beneficence. The very instruments of technical progress threaten man's own supremacy over them. The balance remains to be struck between the technical and the materialistic processes and the human beings they are intended to serve.

Washington, March 28/
The Washington Post, 3-29:(B)2.

Norman Mailer
Author

(Regarding the public image of astronauts): If they were presented to the public as the swashbuckling guys they are, they would be more interesting . . . You're asking this country to love saints, and Americans are not noted for that.

San Francisco/
The Washington Post, 1-31:(A)24.

Spyridon Marinatos
Professor of Archeology,
University of Athens

To excavate is to open a book written in the language that the centuries have spoken into the earth.

The New York Times, 1-11:12.

William F. May
Chairman, American Can Company

For the ordinary man or woman, the computer may seem a dubious blessing—if indeed it seems a blessing at all. We know that it handles our magazine subscriptions and our reservations for transportation and hotels and our credit cards and charge accounts. It handles them by the untold millions. When all goes well we don't even notice it. But when error creeps in, we are practically paralyzed from frustration. The computer then seems to take on the nastiest characteristics of mankind. Once it makes an error, it becomes mean and unforgiving and stubborn. It holds grudges. We are nervous about what it may be falsely swearing about us in areas where our good character and integrity are most important. And what drives us nearly mad is that it won't talk to us on the telephone and it won't answer our letters. Moreover, the computer is hard to understand. A man who has never quite figured out how an electric can-opener works, or a woman for whom a carburetor represents the ultimate mystery, is baffled by computers. The binary theory sounds vaguely medical, and digital computers must have something to do with fingers, and analog computers suggest word games. There is even a lot of talk about "generations of computers"—as though the things multiplied like the Schmoos in *Li'l Abner*. Computers even contribute to the generation gap. More than one father is torn between paternal pride and deep humiliation as he observes his 22-year-old daughter, fresh out of college and looking like a cheerleader, launching a career of training *grown men* in the ever-broadening applications of the computer—at a salary, one might note, that approaches the one he put her through college on! However, the role of the computer in such matters as subscriptions and charge accounts—important though those functions may be—is not the management function that concerns us here. What does concern us, as modern managers and businessmen, is the role of the computer in decision-making, in the identification of alternatives, in the very tricky business of establishing priorities. For if there is anything this poor old battered world needs, it is all the help we can get in establishing our priorities.

Before Chamber of Commerce of Metropolitan St. Louis, Dec. 15/ Vital Speeches, 1-15('72):206.

Kenneth Mellanby
Scientist; Director, Monks Wood Experimental Station, England

Most scientific research has no significance, and most scientists are profoundly unimportant.

San Francisco Examiner, 9-14:32.

Edgar D. Mitchell
American astronaut

Man is a total being; and I refuse to say science should be divorced from religion or from humanity. It's all one big kettle of fish.

Time, 2-8:10.

Dropping space programs now would be like breaking the wheel shortly after it was invented.

Plainview (Tex.) Daily Herald, 5-6:12.

Edmund S. Muskie
United States Senator, D—Maine

I have very real doubt that the manned space program needs to be continued at this time. Unmanned flights should be the level of our efforts in the immediate future.

Before Democratic Party state chairmen, Washington, March 26/ The Washington Post, 3-27:(A)2.

Pyotr S. Neporozhny
Minister of Energy of the Soviet Union; President, World Energy Conference

The age of nuclear power has not come. It would be a serious mistake to think that. I estimate that by the end of the century, nuclear fuel will constitute about 20 per cent of all energy fuels used.

Interview, Bucharest, Romania/ The New York Times, 7-18:(1)48.

Richard M. Nixon
President of the United States

This nation is first today in the space program, and we must remain first in space. That is the way that we will continue to be a great nation.

At dinner honoring Apollo 14 astronauts, Washington, March 1/ The Washington Post, 3-3:(C)2.

W. R. Persons
Chairman, Emerson Electric Company

There is . . . a need to build equipment for space warfare. Space capsules from Russia are filling the universe, and we'll have to get them out of there.

Before Dallas Investment Analysts Association, Feb. 10/ The Dallas Times Herald, 2-12:(D)6.

Rocco A. Petrone
Director, "Apollo" program, National Aeronautics and Space Administration of the United States

. . . Russia's efforts show that she clearly sees space as an arena in which she can compete and demonstrate her wares and show the capability of her system versus ours. The fact that she is willing to invest money in unmanned landers to the moon and in those many missions into earth orbit clearly shows that she recognizes space as the frontier of the future. The question of whether we (the U.S.) keep up in the arena in which we certainly have had a lead very much depends on the will of the people of this country to compete. Do they want to be first in this new

(ROCCO A. PETRONE)

frontier? I personally feel we must. And if the vote of the people is "No," I fear for the future of the country in terms of our willingness to be taking a second seat, and doing it voluntarily. Space, as a new frontier, is going to have ramifications in the field of national security. How it's used will very much depend on future developments. If we aren't up there, it isn't going to make it any safer for us. We've never accepted second-best. I sincerely hope we don't accept second-best ever in the space frontier.

Interview/
U.S. News & World Report, 8-2:22.

Derek J. de Solla Price
Professor of the History
of Science and Technology,
Yale University

One gets the impression, from quantitative studies of the literature, that the U.S. share of science (productivity) has declined over the last six or seven years, from about 35 per cent of the total to about 30 per cent. This, of course, is to be expected, as other countries develop their scientific resources. What concerns me, however, are indications of a migration to centers of excellence abroad. The numbers are small, but increasingly Americans are moving to leading (scientific) centers in the English-speaking countries, Scandinavia and Israel. They are going where the action is.
The Washington Post, 11-21:(C)2.

Ronald Reagan
Governor of California

(Regarding the U.S. space program): Little men with little timid dreams are telling us not to reach out to the stars, but to busy ourselves, instead, building subways; to quit trying to match the eagle in the sky, but to take the money and invest it in welfare.
At Republican dinner,
St. Paul, Minn., March 26/
The New York Times, 3-28:(1)34.

Nevitt Sanford
Psychologist; Director, Wright
Institute, Berkeley, Calif.

The values of the Industrial Revolution are irrelevant in the post-industrial age. Horatio Alger is dead. Virtues important to industrialism—productivity, punctuality and so forth—don't pay off the way they once did. You can do everything you're supposed to, then the company moves out and leaves you behind. Technological advances are adding new and terrible dimensions to the cost of efficiency in terms of human dignity and welfare.
U.S. News & World Report, 4-19:92.

David R. Scott
American astronaut

(Regarding his recently-completed *Apollo 15* mission to the moon): I hesitate to use the words like bare and desolate in talking about the moon; because to the three of us (astronauts), it was dynamic, it was beautiful and it had character. It was a fascinating place.
News conference, Houston, Aug. 12/
The Washington Post, 8-13:(A)4.

Glenn T. Seaborg
Chairman, Atomic Energy Commission
of the United States

. . . I would say if atomic energy hadn't been discovered, civilization as we know it would slowly grind to a halt. Atomic energy was discovered just in the nick of time to furnish the huge amounts of energy that are going to be needed in the future to sustain our civilization.
TV-radio interview/"Meet the Press,"
National Broadcasting Company,
Washington, 8-8.

(Regarding youth's cynicism toward science and technology): What is ironic is that the very things the young people want to change can best be done through their understanding and mastering of technology, of making technology their servant.
Time, 9-13:60.

John H. Shaffer
Administrator,
Federal Aviation Administration
of the United States

Not long ago, an angry research physicist told me that the "in" dirty word among some people in Congress this year is research. Whenever certain Congressmen see the word "research" in a budget request, he said, his first impulse is to cut. Sadly, even a superficial review of Congressional appropriations across the entire broad spectrum of technology will show that all too often Congress has followed that impulse. Unquestionably, technology is on trial today; and so far, it has been the prosecution who has been winning the victories. In light of these factors, consider the potentially disastrous effects the anti-technology movement could have on our nation, on our security, on our way of life. Consider what would happen to us if we purposely abdicated our position of world leadership in technology, if we turned our backs on the technology that has been the source of our strength, our success and our greatness. Yet, there are people in this country today who are thinking precisely along those lines.

At National Aerospace Conference,
Dayton, Ohio/
The National Observer, 8-16:13.

Alan B. Shepard, Jr.
American astronaut

In looking back over the last 10 years, I'm disappointed we don't still have the same momentum we had (in the space program). We know what scientific discovery means. We know that advanced technology and advanced science benefit all the taxpayers. I wish we could explain it better.

News conference, Houston, Jan. 9/
The New York Times, 1-10:(1)49.

S. Fred Singer
Deputy Assistant Secretary for Scientific
Programs, Department of the Interior
of the United States

Why has there been so much fuss raised about the SST? Why is the conflict focused on this particular new technology? I think the answer is complex. But perhaps one of the important reasons is that the SST has become a symbol. In my view, we are witnessing here a general reaction against all technological progress, and against basic science itself, on the part of a coalition of people which—paradoxically—includes scientists.

The National Observer, 3-8:2.

C. P. Snow
Writer

Technology . . . is a queer thing: It brings you great gifts with one hand, and it stabs you in the back with the other.

February/
The New York Times, 3-15:35.

Arnold Toynbee
Historian

Technological wizardry is not an end in itself. It is desirable only if it makes for human welfare; and this is the test that any tool ought to be made to pass.

San Francisco Examiner & Chronicle
(This World), 3-28:2.

Wernher Von Braun
Deputy Associate Administrator,
National Aeronautics and Space
Administration of the United States

For the past eight years, we have become spoiled and mesmerized by the fact that a President told us, "We will land on the moon." Year after year, the funds were there and kept on coming just as and when needed. During the last few years, we hardly ever had to put up a fight to get our budgets through. But now that we have landed on the moon, we must not make the cardinal mistake of imagining that all this can go on forever. No one will offer us Mars on a silver platter. That's why I say we must become viable. We need to get on a "bread and butter basis."

Interview/
The New York Times, 2-21:(1)75.

(WERNHER VON BRAUN)

It isn't the young people, the students, who are really to blame for the attitude of hostility to science and technology. They are simply misguided by certain social philosophers, cultural historians and the like, whose teachings and published works provide only a very lopsided view of science and technology pictured as causing the downfall of man. When you teach impressionable and idealistic youth that the rational, logical, puritanical work approach to life is bankrupt, and that technology serves only to erode the quality of life, you are bound to ring responsive bells in many minds of a generation that has never known the deprivation, the want and the poverty of some older generations.

Before Aviation-Space Writers Association/
The Wall Street Journal, 11-5:6.

We realize there are other pressing needs in this country. But research and development is not the kind of thing that can be turned on and off like a faucet.

Plainview (Tex.) Daily Herald, 12-3:6.

Earl Warren
Former Chief Justice
of the United States

Science has revolutionized both the physical environment and human society so substantially in such a short period of time that our attitudes, our habits and our institutions have lagged far behind. Discontent and demands for change come not only from our youth, but from those of all ages who see the methods and institutions on which society depends unresponsive to the needs of today and grossly inadequate to the needs of tomorrow. It is our political systems that have been most reluctant to yield to pragmatism and move toward toleration and accommodation. Happily, many of the technological facts that have been increasing economic interaction among nations are hard at work in the political field as well. The flow of international communications and contacts, for example, is increasing geometrically. The mounting effi-

ciency and declining costs soon to be ushered in by space communication will make attempts to control the international movement of ideas not only futile but silly and self-defeating. Even the ecological threats arising from the advance of technology provide new impetus toward political cooperation. The most rigid isolationist, the most dogmatic ideologue, now must recognize that the very air we breathe is an international resource. I am suggesting to you that the shapers of laws and the architects of institutions have been overtaken by science and technology. We have grown up in the comfortable sense that politics is the art of the possible. Few of us have faced the fact that science has transformed politics into the art of the indispensable.

At International World Peace Through
Law Conference, Belgrade, Yugoslavia/
The New York Times, 7-23:31.

Putney Westerfield
Publisher, "Fortune" magazine

Daily exposure to scenes of war and the destructive capabilities of science and technology, combined with growing awareness of environmental problems, and technological breakdowns in power, transportation, telephone service and so on, has made many increasingly anti-science. Critics of many ages and hues, who see science as a huge, ineffective juggernaut, try to ease their disenchantment with efforts to reduce funds and programs, which could cripple research and scientific progress. If this happens—and we believe this very deeply at *Fortune*—the U.S. can become a second-rate power and a third-rate place to live.

Before Northern California Chemical
Industry Council, San Francisco, April 22/
San Francisco Examiner, 4-23:7.

Jerome B. Wiesner
Provost, Massachusetts
Institute of Technology

Modern information technology provides the potential to add to our general well-being and to enhance human freedom and dignity, if properly used, by extending our muscles, brainpower and material resources; and yet, it also threatens to ensnarl us in a social system in which controls could essentially eliminate human freedom and individual privacy. Improperly exploited computer and communication technology could so markedly restrict the range of individual rights and initiatives that are a hallmark of a free society and the foundation of human dignity as to eliminate meaningful life as we appreciate it.

In other words, 1984 could come to pass unnoticed while we applauded our technical achievements . . . I suspect that it would be much easier to guard against a malicious oppressor than to avoid being slowly but increasingly dominated by an information Frankenstein of our own creation.

Before Senate Constitutional Rights
Subcommittee, Washington/
Los Angeles Times, 3-21:(G)3.

Sports

Henry Aaron
Baseball player, Atlanta "Braves"

I think baseball is running a poor third for the black player. Baseball was first a long time ago; but now it's running behind pro basketball and pro football in its treatment of blacks after our playing days are over . . . If a guy can do a good job, that's the guy I would want to work for me if I was running a ball club, no matter what his color. But for as long as baseball has been integrated—and baseball was the first pro sport to integrate—we haven't had a black manager and (there are) very few blacks in the front office.

Interview, West Palm Beach, Fla.,
March 6/The Washington Post, 3-7:(C)4.

I characterize myself as a hitter who likes to get out of the chute fast. It's simply that you want to excite yourself early. If you get off slow, you have a tendency to keep saying to yourself, "Well, I'll get better . . . well . . . well . . ." And then you look up, you've run out of days, and you've had a bad year.

Sports Illustrated, 4-26:62.

Muhammad Ali (Cassius Clay)
Former Heavyweight Boxing Champion
of the World

I say get an education. Become an electrician, a mechanic, a doctor, a lawyer—anything but a fighter. In this trade, it's the managers who make the money and last the longest. I know if I become the father of a boy, he won't be a prizefighter.

The Sporting News, 1-16:4.

If Joe Frazier ever whup me, I'll crawl on my hands and knees, look up at him and say, "You are the greatest." Then I'll crawl back and go home.

New York, March 8/
The New York Times, 3-9:29.

I was paid $2.5 million (for his fight with Joe Frazier). But the white man in Washington took $1.5 million from me the next day. New York State put a lien of $389,000 against each of us; and that left me $620,000. Then, I had to pay my trainer, sparring partners, expenses, hotels, airplanes and everything, so I came out with about $450,000. Then I had to buy my home, furnish it, landscape it and take care of my mother, father and brother . . . and when I break it all down, I'm almost busted.

At Chicago State College/
Los Angeles Times, 4-1:(3)3.

George Allen
Former football coach,
Los Angeles "Rams"

Winning is the science of being totally prepared. And preparation can be defined in three words: Leave nothing undone. No detail can be too small; no task is too small—or too big. The difference between success and failure is so tiny it can't be perceived by most of us. Nowadays, there is practically no difference between one team and another in the NFL. And usually, the winner is going to be the team that's in better physical condition and better prepared.

The Washington Post, 1-10:(C)4.

To me, a lot of things are more brutalizing than football. Your chances of being hurt are nine times greater driving an automobile than playing football. The game is not brutal. It seems that way because people don't understand the wonderful feeling it is to play a great game and win and take a shower and come out. You always feel exhilarated.

Interview, Washington/
Los Angeles Times, 11-14:(G)7.

Richie Allen
Baseball player, Los Angeles "Dodgers"

I'm no slugger. People just think I am. Maybe you can't blame them, because I'm naturally strong and I do hit a lot of balls out of the park. But every time I get a home run, I'm as surprised as the next guy.

Interview, Vero Beach, Fla./
The Christian Science Monitor,
4-2:(B)10.

Sparky Anderson
Baseball manager, Cincinnati "Reds"

Baseball is a simple game. If you have good players, and if you keep them in the right frame of mind, then the manager is a success. The players make the manager; it's never the other way.

Interview, Tampa, Fla., March 10/
Los Angeles Times, 3-11:(3)2.

Mario Andretti
Auto racing driver

The crashes (are what) people remember, but drivers remember the near misses. Sometimes they aren't even apparent to the spectators, but the driver knows. When there's a near miss, when I am able to drive my way out of trouble or "luck" my way out, the first thing I think of is "Thank God," because I always figure that when something like that happens, I wasn't the only one responsible for avoiding it. And the second thing is that I'm sort of relieved, because I figure, "Gee, that's the one for today."

Interview, Phoenix, Ariz.,
March 15/
Los Angeles Times, 3-16:(3)6.

Roone Arledge
President, American Broadcasting
Company Sports

(Sports) announcers are like politicians and actors. They're always aware that they're being heard all over the world. They don't want their images screwed up by saying things that will hurt someone's feelings. Frankly, I wish there were a lot more bite

in the business. There are damned few working now who are willing to be abrasive.

The Sporting News, 10-9:6.

Carmen Basilio
Former Welterweight and Middleweight
Boxing Champion of the World

I love boxing. I loved every minute of it, every round in the gym, every skip of the rope and every foot on the road. The fights were the dessert.

Los Angeles Herald-Examiner, 5-18:(D)4.

Manuel Benitez ("El Cordobes")
Spanish matador

It is not bravery (to fight the bull). You must prepare your body and your mind for the encounter. It is believing in yourself; and that thing nobody can teach you. I have never heard of a University of Bravery.

Interview, New York, March 7/
The New York Times, 3-8:66.

Vida Blue
Baseball pitcher, Oakland "Athletics"

I'm not trying to break any records or strike out a lot of people. I just want to win. I'm not a real pitcher, not yet. I haven't really mastered my craft. I just want to do the best I can. I want to be a good professional. I want to be good at what I'm doing. I want to be the best.

Time, 8-23:44.

All I want now is to get away on an island with a mermaid and forget the rest of the season. I'm tired of the whole season, and I'm tired of being a superstar. I just wanted to be an average pitcher on a winning team.

Los Angeles Times, 8-31:(3)2.

Mikhail Botvinnik
Former world chess champion

Chess is not a science, but a sport—an intellectual sport; to be more exact, a mathematical sport. It is a game in the widest sense of the word, in the way it is under-

(MIKHAIL BOTVINNIK)

stood by cyberneticists. And if you are fortunate enough to create an original game and it survives, then it is an art, too.

Los Angeles Times, 11-5:(1)18.

Jim Brown
Former football player,
Cleveland "Browns"

I don't feel that pro football exploited me. And the reverse is true, too. People have to realize that it is a business as well as a sport. If you have that understanding, then everything is all right. I fought for my contracts and for other things. This didn't stop me from enjoying the game.

Cleveland/
The Christian Science Monitor, 2-12:5.

Michael Burke
President, New York "Yankees"
baseball club

A baseball club is part of the chemistry of the city. A game isn't just an athletic contest. It's a picnic—a kind of town meeting.

New York, March 25/
The New York Times, 3-26:47.

Fidel Castro (Ruz)
Premier of Cuba

An attempt has been made to present Cuba as using sports as an instrument of politics. Really, it's just the other way around; politics is an instrument of sports. That is, sport is not a means, but rather an end, like every other human activity, every other activity that has to do with man's well-being, just as education, health, material living conditions, human dignity, feeling and man's spiritual values are all the objectives of politics.

The New York Times, 8-22:(5)4.

Wilt Chamberlain
Basketball player,
Los Angeles "Lakers"

Basketball is fun when you play in the school yard. As the stakes get higher, the fun goes out of it. You derive pleasure and satisfaction out of playing well and winning—but not fun.

Interview, Los Angeles/
The Washington Post, 3-7:(C)8.

Bob Charles
Golfer

I have no strategy; I just swing and hope for the best.

Interview, Greensboro, S.C./
The New York Times, 4-2:17.

Howard Cosell
Sports commentator,
American Broadcasting Company

I am Honest Howard Cosell. When I broadcast a football game, I do not resort to a lot of mumbo jumbo. Pro football is sending a fast kid out to catch a pass against a slow kid. That may be the highest kind of "strategy" to some broadcasters, but to me it's only common sense.

Interview/
The Christian Science Monitor, 12-2:20.

Bruce Crampton
Golfer

I think we have the cleanest professional sport of all. In baseball, if a guy traps a ball, he doesn't call it on himself; he tries to fool the umpire. We (golfers) police ourselves. I've seen people call two-stroke penalties on themselves when it meant a $150,000 tournament.

Interview, Los Angeles/
Los Angeles Times, 1-10:(D)1.

Joe Cronin
President,
American (Baseball) League

There'll be no changes in baseball's playing rules. We're not about to seek phony ways to hypo hits or scoring. There's nothing wrong with the game, except in the eyes of those who are neither part of it nor fans of it. We're not going to tinker with it. Sure, there have been a lot of suggestions for basic changes, such as designated pinch-hitters and runners, the extended foul lines and going to three balls and two strikes instead of what it has been for some time. We gave them all a trial, either in spring training or the minors, and none stood up to the test, in our estimation.

Minneapolis/
The Sporting News, 5-29:12.

Joe DiMaggio
Former baseball player,
New York "Yankees"

I think the greatest change (in baseball) has come with the disappearing of the minor leagues. Expansion, of course, has caused this; but too many kids today are playing major league ball and don't belong there.

The Dallas Times Herald, 3-21:(C)2.

Of course Willie (Mays) will make the Hall of Fame; but I don't know if I'll be around to see it. You know, the rules require a five-year wait after retirement to become eligible—and who knows when this man will ever retire?

At Willie Mays' 40th birthday party/
Sports Illustrated, 5-17:17.

Mark Duncan
Director of personnel,
National Football League

Officiating (at football games) breaks down into two parts. First, there's mechanics and rules. Second, there's reaction under pressure. Mechanics and rules can be learned just as one learns to drive a car; anyone can do that in time. Reaction under pressure is putting principle into practice. You've learned to drive, but now you're driving in the Indianapolis 500 every day. Now it's on the line. And that's what makes a good official: not losing his composure at the wheel.

The Christian Science Monitor, 11-20:16.

Sam J. Ervin, Jr.
United States Senator, D–N.C.

In basketball, I believe the existence of two leagues (NBA and ABA) has benefited everyone. Attendance at games is higher than it has ever been, and basketball is becoming the

best-attended of all sports . . . I believe that this healthy competition has enriched the sport.

Los Angeles Times, 10-22:(3)5.

Charles O. Finley
Owner, Oakland "Athletics"
baseball club

There's no doubt about it—the salaries (for players) are out of line. If the owners continue paying unjustified salaries, the price of tickets will go beyond what the fan can pay. The fans will stay away. That's what I'm afraid of—a strike by the fans.

The New York Times, 3-28:(5)6.

Charley Fox
Baseball manager,
San Francisco "Giants"

I don't have any figures to prove it, but there's no doubt in my mind that the average age of big-league (baseball) players (is) now the lowest in history. We've often talked about the "age of youth" and now we have it, more than ever before. Of course, we should say three cheers, because where would the game be without these kids? Youth has rejuvenated the whole big-league picture . . . nobody wins these days unless one or two youngsters come through for them.

The Christian Science Monitor, 11-20:16.

Joe Frazier
Heavyweight Boxing Champion
of the World

(Regarding his upcoming bout with Muhammad Ali): I'm no politician. The only thing I care about is that he's there to fight me. After that, I couldn't care what he does or what happens to him. All I want is to have him there so I can beat him to a pulp.

Philadelphia, Jan. 12/Los Angeles
Herald-Examiner, 1-12:(C)2.

(After defeating Muhammad Ali for the world championship): I'm champ of the whole big wide world. Ain't nobody can say Ali is better than me now; ain't no way, man . . . I

549

WHAT THEY SAID IN 1971

(JOE FRAZIER)

know about some of you writers out there. You don't think I can win. You don't think I can whip Muhammad Ali. Well, I can read a little; and I wonder what you're going to say now. Yes, I wonder what you're going to say now.

Interview, New York/The Christian Science Monitor, 3-11:13.

Roman Gabriel
Football player, Los Angeles "Rams"

I think all professional football players resent the fact that there's too many pre-season games. If you talk to a majority of the pro football players, they'd tell you that the season should start in August. Three of the six pre-season games should count as regular-season games . . . If you're going to play 'em, let 'em count. The only reason we're playing them is so the owners can make money.

Fullerton, Calif./ The Dallas Times Herald, 8-18:(B)7.

Frank Gifford
Sports commentator,
American Broadcasting Company;
Former football player

. . . the claims of some newspaper people —predicting the death of football due to television overexposure—are ridiculous. These writers are drawing some kind of kooky parallel with boxing. Yet pro football, with its TV commitments, has never been more popular. It's the perfect spectator sport for the type of world we live in. It's a violent sport; it's fun, it's exciting; it's something with which we can become emotionally involved.

Interview/ San Francisco Examiner, 9-8:41.

Pancho Gonzalez
Tennis player

I'm going to walk out on the court (at the 1972 U.S. Open tournament) in a colored shirt. If they tell me I can't play, I won't. I'll default. If it means taking a strong stand to

make the game more colorful, I'll do it.

The Sporting News, 11-27:4.

Bud Grant
Football coach, Minnesota "Vikings"

. . . football is a team game. Nothing functions in football if the team isn't functioning. In baseball, a pitcher can win with a no-hitter and a home run. In football, a passer can throw strikes all day and lose by 50-0.

Interview/ Los Angeles Times, 9-17:(3)5.

A good coach needs a patient wife, a loyal dog and a great quarterback, but not necessarily in that order.

Los Angeles Times, 10-25:(3)2.

Abe J. Greene
Commissioner,
World Boxing Association

(Regarding private boxing promoters who have entered the game): I am extremely disturbed at the new phase of ancillary boxing control. I refer to the (Joe) Frazier-(Muhammad) Ali match, which netted fabulous sums to private promoters, pre-empted the stage, shunted aside boxing men who have given their lives to the sport, and contributed nothing to the commissions or boxing administrations for improvement of the sport.

The Dallas Times Herald, 8-17:(C)3.

Calvin Griffith
President, Minnesota "Twins"
baseball club

The reserve clause is the salvation of our sport. Without it, we can't protect our own players. With the incomes of some teams that draw two million fans a year, those teams would dominate the leagues. If they needed a second-baseman, they'd go out and deal for one. But what about the teams that don't have that kind of money?

The Dallas Times Herald, 10-21:(C)9.

Dan Gurney
Former auto racing driver

(The race track is) a hostile environment. I don't mean the drivers, for they have certain ethical boundaries, and they observe them. I mean the cars. They're hot and rough. I lost 12 pounds in one race, and, in another, I saw guys come in after an hour with their hands bleeding. The idea of going that fast staggers your mind. It's difficult to maintain precise vision with the wind buffeting your helmet and goggles. What you're really doing is controlled fury.

Interview, New York, Jan. 16/
The Washington Post, 1-17:(D)5.

Bob Hollway
Football coach,
St. Louis "Cardinals"

In my mind there are three types of football players. First, there are those who want to make the team. Second, there are those interested in individual success. And third, there are those who are totally for team success. I'm looking for the third kind.

Los Angeles Times, 3-29:(3)2.

Bob Howsam
General manager, Cincinnati "Reds"
baseball club

I don't believe in multi-year contracts. I think it's fair to both the player and management to sign for one year. If a player has a good year, he's entitled to a raise. But the players of today expect to be paid high salaries regardless of their performance . . . I've seen many a ballplayer fail to equal a great performance. What I'm saying is that the greatness must be maintained over the years before a player gets to the top plateau in salary. He should work his way up to the level.

Interview, Tampa, Fla./
The Washington Post, 2-24:(D)1.

Eugene Kinasewich
President, Western Hockey League

Certainly, aggressiveness is a very important part of the game. It's built into hockey, and it constitutes one of the attractions of the game because it takes place at such high speed. But when you begin to digress and sell hockey and try to promote it as a violent sport—like wrestling and roller derby—it detracts from the game.

Interview, Seattle/
The Christian Science Monitor, 4-27:6.

Billie Jean King
Tennis player

Now that we've (women) got a tournament circuit of our own, I think women's pro tennis could become very big. I think we've finally arrived. I know everybody on the tour is excited about it. I'm not at war with the men who play tennis for a living. But when we used to share the same tournaments, they drew the crowds, got most of the publicity and practically all the money. If you were a woman tour member, it was discouraging. But now, people are coming out to see us, and they just aren't other women, either. The men like us, too. I can't tell you how many men have approached me in the past nine weeks and said: "We hope you girls make it on your own. We enjoy watching you play. What took you so long?"

Interview/
The Christian Science Monitor, 3-31:11.

The greatest time in life (as a tennis player) is when you're fourth or fifth, and young. You're getting a lot of attention from everyone. Each day there's so much hope—the unknown's out there! And there's this great desire in you. You're finding out all about yourself, and you're getting so close to your goals. Before I ever won Wimbledon, I'd have dreams of winning it and accepting the trophy afterwards. But when you've won it, you're so tired. It's really a sense of relief more than anything. Then the next day it starts all over again. That one fleeting moment was worth it—and maybe it doesn't even last a full minute.

San Francisco Examiner & Chronicle
(California Living), 6-6:22.

(BILLIE JEAN KING)

(Regarding tennis fans): Let 'em move around. Do they have to sit on their hands during a basketball game? Instead of the "establishment" pitty-patty applause, why not encourage fans to whistle and holler as they do in Italy or in the bleachers at Wrigley Field?

The Christian Science Monitor, 10-7:4.

Bill van Breda Kolff
Basketball coach, Detroit "Pistons"

(Announcing his resignation): The player today in the pro game—and even in college and high school—is worried about himself and not the team. No pro team really has a team spirit. The pro says to himself, "I've got to play or I'll lose my value." I guess that's a realistic outlook; but it's not mine.

News conference, Detroit, Nov. 1/
Los Angeles Times, 11-2:(3)5.

Sandy Koufax
Former baseball pitcher,
Los Angeles "Dodgers"

A guy who throws what he intends to throw—that's the definition of a good pitcher.

Los Angeles Times, 3-31:(3)6.

Thomas H. Kuchel
Former United States Senator, R—Calif.;
Basketball leagues' representative at
Congressional hearings on their merger plans

The business of professional basketball is in deep trouble. Many of the teams in the two leagues (ABA and NBA) are consistent money losers. It is unrealistic to expect that owners will continue to subsidize them regardless of economic considerations. It is unrealistic to believe that the laws of economics will be permanently ignored . . . Unless merger is promptly consummated, it is my belief that a substantial number of franchises may fail. After the inevitable shaking out and shrinking down, professional league

basketball would be confined to a relative handful of the largest cities. That would be to the detriment of the basketball fans of America, and of the players, many of whom would no longer have the opportunity to be a part of this great sport . . . The conditions presently confronting professional basketball result from the annual rites of self-destruction between the two leagues. Teams are quite literally forced, by the need to maintain league status, to bid against each other annually for those college players entering professional ranks with reputations as potential superstars. The yearly bidding war, with its fantastic contracts for a limited number of untested rookies—contracts which bear no relationship to basketball economics—will inexorably end in ruin. Yet, neither league can unilaterally retreat from that war, for to do so would be equally ruinous.

Before Senate Antitrust and Monopoly
Subcommittee, Washington, September/
Los Angeles Times, 10-21:(3)5.

Bowie Kuhn
United States Commissioner of Baseball

. . . if profits and losses were balanced out over the entire big-league map, the financial result would level off to about the break-even point. Only about half—and probably less than that—of the teams make money. There are many so-called hidden costs in the rising expense tide of the American and National Leagues. You hear about salary increases all along the line; but that's only part of the story. Hotel, food, transportation costs, the price of equipment, and maintenance inside your parks, the ticket-printing tab—you name it—they keep going up and up, with little hope of a checked inflation. The situation is far closer to the alarming stage than anyone outside the game realizes. Something must be done, and soon.

Interview, Boston, January/
The Christian Science Monitor, 3-6:15.

(Regarding the failure of the Baseball Writers Association to name any new members to the Baseball Hall of Fame this year): I had two reactions, one as a fan and another as commissioner. I was disappointed as a fan, because I like to see worthy candidates honored. But as commissioner, I felt that in the failure there was a vote for the integrity of the system. Nobody should get to Cooperstown with ease.

The Christian Science Monitor, 2-3:15.

We're not naive about the threat of drugs, the nature of the problem or the fact that in baseball there has been some use of pills in the amphetamine and barbiturates group. We don't intend to let that develop . . . We want to let all baseball personnel know what baseball's attitude is toward the problem in the interest of the players' health, their performance, the game itself and the integrity of the game.

New York, Feb. 18/
Los Angeles Times, 2-19(3)8.

Daryle Lamonica
Football player, Oakland "Raiders"

. . . football players talk about the confidence they have in themselves, and people call them cocky or conceited. But that's not really the way we are. You've got to believe in your own ability. We won games this season after a lot of people had walked out of the stadium and were in their cars. We just didn't believe it was over. We never quit.

Interview, Los Angeles/
The Dallas Times Herald, 1-24:(C)6.

Tom Landry
Football coach, Dallas "Cowboys"

We are in an era where the top teams are getting beat. It's hard to sustain your momentum from week to week. I'm not sure what it is. Perhaps it is the approach to things of our young people. They don't have as much of a driving force as they used to. There's a lot of complacency on the athletic field like everywhere else. There's a tendency not to work hard. In athletics you must work hard or you'll get your head knocked off.

The New York Times, 12-12:(5)2.

Frank Lane
General manager, Milwaukee "Brewers" baseball club

The players are going to price themselves out of the market. We have built up ball players as heroes—and that is good—but they can easily lose the sympathy of the fans, some of whom give up the price of needed new shoes to see a player who is objecting to a $105,000 salary.

The New York Times, 3-28:(5)6.

In the early years of the century, there were so many roughnecks in baseball . . . But now they've vested so much authority in the umpires that the game has become so pallid and emasculated that it has lost much of its attraction. A manager or player can't open his mouth before he's thrown out. They won't even let anyone holler from the bench. What they ought to do is give the game back to the players and fans. Furthermore, there are two attitudes in the calling of plays—one for the contending clubs and the other for the teams at the bottom. If you belong to the have-nots, the umpires have a so-what attitude. If in doubt, call 'em out. That's their credo.

The Sporting News, 7-24:5.

Every team sport has its forgotten men—those drones that labor in the background, acquiring and fitting the pieces together that eventually mean a championship. However, I don't think there's any other event in any other professional game that has as many forgotten men as baseball does at this time of year. The managers don't put World Series clubs together. Neither do the owners. Teams are shaped by the organization men—from the scouts and other minor-league farm operators to the general manager and his aides. But who remembers this once the World Series gets under way? Not the public. Not the press. Only baseball men know all about it. This is the one time of the year when the public and press often applaud the wrong people.

Pittsburgh/
The Christian Science Monitor, 10-12:17.

Earl Lloyd
Basketball coach, Detroit "Pistons"

Coaches don't win games; it's the players who do that. The primary job of a coach is to make sure his team doesn't lose games it should win.

News conference/
The Christian Science Monitor, 11-15:15.

Willie McCovey
Baseball player,
San Francisco "Giants"

Baseball is behind all other sports in (player) salaries. Big salaries haven't come quick enough. Look at basketball players just off the campus getting $1- and $2-million. Football players play just once a week. We play every day. Baseball is supposed to be our national pastime. Our super stars should be the highest paid in the world.

The New York Times, 3-28:(5)6.

Hugh McElhenny
Former football player

Football's a great life. It's much easier than working for a living. Just think—they pay you good money to eat well, stay in shape and have fun.

Interview, San Francisco/
Los Angeles Times, 11-22:(1)29.

John McHale
President, Montreal "Expos"
baseball club

. . . spring training has gone through several major phases during the last half-century. In the beginning, training was little more than grunting, sweating sessions to melt down extra weight accumulated during a winter of loafing. It took a while for clubs to realize the value of publicity that flowed back home, getting fans aroused and ready for the regular season. Babe Ruth and the New York *Yankees* showed baseball the cash value of long exhibition schedules; so barnstorming became a regular thing. And somewhere along the way, resort areas came to appreciate the attraction offered by the big-leaguers. Out of this grew the fat financial guarantees which most resort towns now offer invading teams.

The Christian Science Monitor, 2-23:11.

Marvin Miller
Executive director, Major League
Baseball Players Association

There is no evidence to indicate that (player) salary increases in baseball are disproportionate to what is happening in the rest of the country in other industries or in other years in baseball. If baseball is being run into the ground economically, it's because of the outrageous increases of executive salaries and other expenses not related to player salaries. To say the players are pricing themselves out of the market is absurd talk—nonsense . . . What disturbs me most is that so little is ever presented in all these stories. If a club executive says player salaries have skyrocketed, no one ever seems to ask the executive how much. From that stems the next lament—we are all losing money. And that's said when no one has ever seen any audited statements. It should be realized that it is common negotiating practice for the employer to always cry. It's standard operating procedure. What an owner pays he pays because he thinks he's going to make out well paying that kind of salary. Any time player demands are so uneconomic an owner can't pay it, he won't pay it.

New York, May 1/
Los Angeles Times, 5-2:(D)5.

Clint Murchison, Jr.
Owner, Dallas "Cowboys"
football team

A man has to be out of his mind to go into pro football to make money. You buy a team because you're kind of an addict.

Sports Illustrated, 3-22:18.

Stan Musial
Senior vice president and former player,
St. Louis "Cardinals" baseball club

On an all-star team, I vote for players of

one kind—those I enjoy watching the most when the ball is hit or pitched in their direction.

Interview, St. Petersburg, Fla.,
March 29/Los Angeles Times, 3-30:(3)1.

Jack Nicklaus
Golfer

I know it sounds selfish, wanting to do something no one else has. But that's what you're out here for—to separate yourself from everyone else. I think winning the most major championships would be a quality achievement.

Interview, Palm Beach Gardens, Fla./
The Christian Science Monitor, 3-3:11.

Richard M. Nixon
President of the United States

I believe in competitive sports, as a spectator or as a participant. I believe in the spirit that an individual develops—either as he watches or as he participates—in competition. I don't go along with the idea that all that really matters is jogging in place and having a good physical appearance. What really matters, of course, is the spirit as well as the body.

Before members of President's
Sports Advisory Conference, Washington/
Sports Illustrated, 3-1:13.

The beauty of bowling is that it takes very little time, it's very good for the stomach muscles and it doesn't cost much.

News conference,
Washington/Time, 9-27:50.

Parry O'Brien
Two-time Olympic shot-put champion

You'd be surprised what fantastic interest there is in international sports outside the United States. It's not really right, but people place a value on Americans as a race on the basis of what we do in these competitions. If the Russians win, they'll say they won because their system is better.

Interview, Los Angeles/
Los Angeles Times, 4-9:(3)2.

Peter O'Malley
President, Los Angeles "Dodgers"
baseball club

I believe (player) salaries are at their peak; not just in baseball, but in all sports. It's quite possible some owners will trade away, or even drop entirely, players who expect $200,000 salaries. There's a super-star born every year . . . But still there is no way clubs can continue to increase salaries to the level some players are talking about.

Interview, Vero Beach, Fla./
Los Angeles Herald-Examiner, 3-25:(D)3.

Walter F. O'Malley
Owner, Los Angeles "Dodgers"
baseball club

We (in baseball) have been hurt by philosophy differences in the two leagues; we have never been quite able to get together. For instance, when the *Yankees* were the hottest team in baseball, the National League asked for inter-league play. We were turned down. When the *Yankees* cooled off and good teams developed in the National League, the Americans asked for inter-league play. And the Nationals turned them down. We keep going in different directions. We have National League teams in San Francisco and Los Angeles, and the Americans move franchises into those areas. The American League has a franchise in the New York area, and the Nationals move a team there. In New York and L.A., the consequences haven't been serious. But duplication, generally, is stupid.

Interview, Vero Beach, Fla./
Los Angeles Herald Examiner, 2-25:(C)1.

Jesse Owens
Former Olympic track champion

When I won the 100 (meter) in 10.3 (in 1936), it also equalled the world record. Do you know where that time would have gotten me at Mexico City in the last Olympics? I would have been eighth.

Interview, New York/
The New York Times, 4-28:53.

Jack Pardee
Football player, Washington "Redskins"

. . . the only time age will ever hurt a team is when all the old players quit at the same time.

The Washington Post, 1-29:(D)2.

Wes Parker
Baseball player,
Los Angeles "Dodgers"

I think $200,000 for one year is the limit any star can hope to make. I also think that the player who seeks and gets that much may be pricing himself right out of the game. If I were an owner, I'd take high salaries to a point and then say the hell with it. I'd trade off or just get rid of the high-salaried players. It's getting to the point where I can't blame an owner if he says, "To heck with this. I'm going with the kids."

Interview, Vero Beach, Fla./
Los Angeles Times, 3-24:(3)1.

Floyd Patterson
Former Heavyweight Boxing Champion
of the World

Every time I fight some fighter who's lost a few, my trainer . . . tells me how easy it's going to be; and I come back to my corner after a round or two and tell him they must have stuck somebody else in there while we weren't looking. If a guy has one fight left in him, he seems to save it for me. None of them are easy.

Interview, New York/
The Washington Post, 8-15:(D)7.

Richard Petty
Auto racing driver

People don't understand that driving racing cars requires real athletic skill. You take football—they platoon, they have time outs, quarters, half-times. In basketball you get to sit down now and then. In baseball you work half an inning, then sit down. But in my sport, it can often mean four solid hours of work without letup. I have to be in top physical shape for that kind of work; and that's what it is—real hard work demanding the best of condition.

New York/
The Washington Post, 11-6:(D)2.

Gary Player
Golfer

I have won $120,000 (in 1971). Eighty thousand of that will go to taxes, and expenses will set me back $25,000. Profit: $15,000. If I had a bad year, I could be in trouble.

Interview, Johannesburg, South Africa/
The New York Times, 8-15:(5)11.

Tommy Prothro
Football coach, Los Angeles "Rams"

I never knew a coach who could get everything he wanted (from management). I've always been able to accept a "No," but not a "Let's wait and see." I don't mind authority, but I don't like procrastination.

Interview/
Los Angeles Times, 1-4:(3)6.

If what the psychologists say is true—that the mature human wants peace, relaxation and contentment—then all of us in athletics are immature, because we're seeking accomplishment and recognition.

Interview, Long Beach, Calif./
The New York Times, 1-31:(5)3.

. . . to me, one of the greatest things about football is its discipline—and whether it's "child-like" or "dehumanizing" or whatever it is. I don't believe that everything ought to be discipline; but I think whenever a group of people is striving to reach a goal, they have to have discipline. There isn't any way that a squad of 40 people can all think exactly alike. So they've got to have a constituted authority, and they've got to go in the direction of that constituted authority. Now that doesn't mean they can't change that constituted authority, but there has to be a constituted authority. And I think, really in American life today, we don't have an over-abundance of discipline; we have an underabundance of it. We need more of it.

Interview/
The Dallas Times Herald, 7-4:(C)4.

Ronald Reagan
Governor of California

There's something about football that no other game has. There's sort of a mystique about it. It's a game in which you can feel a clean hatred for your opponent.

San Francisco Examiner & Chronicle
(This World), 12-19:2.

Paul Richards
Vice president, Atlanta "Braves"
baseball club

I'm speaking of young baseball players when I tell you that college is a waste. In fact, it's worse than that. Usually, it's fatal to a career in baseball. College is for football players, girls and others who can't play baseball . . . because early training is decisive in a career like baseball, where everything depends on physical and mental skills—on sharpening those skills. The young high-school graduate is at a perfect age to learn baseball, if he devotes his life to it. If he splits his time between baseball, football, sociology, basket weaving and rock concerts, he can never be the ball-player he might have been.

Interview/
Los Angeles Times, 3-18:(3)1.

I think the ability to hit a baseball is the greatest gift in the power of the Almighty to bestow. Nothing physical is harder. The best athletes in the world are the handful who hit .300 or so year after year in times like these—with the big gloves, the big parks and night ball. The oldtimers who hit .340 and .360 couldn't approach that today. I doubt if anyone is born with enough brains to hit .360 very long.

Interview/Los Angeles Times, 3-18:(3)9.

Oscar Robertson
Basketball player, Milwaukee "Bucks"

If people only knew, only took time to realize, that 48 minutes of a game are not a man's life. Some fans say black players look so casual out there . . . The game has been good to me, but it's still Whitey's game . . . A black man has to fight for respect in basketball, season after season. And I measure that respect in the figures on my contract. What if ol' Oscar broke his leg tomorrow; who would be taking care of him? Tell me. Milwaukee would forget in a minute.

Interview/Look, 4-6:70.

Brooks Robinson
Baseball player,
Baltimore "Orioles"

. . . a guy can be the greatest fielder of all time, and he's not going to get that much publicity—or maybe even that much of a chance to play. And you can only go so far moneywise with fielding. To make money in baseball, you've got to be able to do something offensively. Being a great glove man isn't enough.

Interview, Anaheim, Calif./
Los Angeles Times, 4-26:(3)6.

Frank Robinson
Baseball player,
Baltimore "Orioles"

I don't think any place is barred to a black manager. I think this is the same situation as it was when the first black player (Jackie Robinson) broke into the majors. I think they're trying to find the right person and the right situation. I think the climate keeps changing. Each year they get a little closer to it, and the chances of it happening get better. I foresee it happening in the next few years. But I wouldn't predict myself as the first one.

Interview, Fort Lauderdale, Fla.,
March 13/
The New York Times, 3-14:(5)1.

(Regarding fraternizing between players of opposing teams): There's too much of it, particularly in the American League. There's absolutely no way you can go barreling into second base and dump a guy on a double

(FRANK ROBINSON)

play, like you should do, when you've been fraternizing with him before a game.

Sports Illustrated, 4-12:21.

Jackie Robinson
Former baseball player,
Brooklyn "Dodgers"

Black players have saved baseball, kept baseball on top. But I think football and basketball have moved beyond baseball in race relations; in many instances, they hire a man to do a job regardless of his skin color. Baseball is still wallowing around in the 19th century, saying a black can't manage, a black can't go into the front office . . . I think baseball is very vindictive. I think, very frankly, that a black man who is willing to accept their dictates and do what they want him to do can get along beautifully. But if you're a man and you stand on your own two feet, then look out. I think this is basically the problem today with baseball.

The New York Times, 12-5:(5)5.

Will Robinson
Basketball coach,
Illinois State University

I want a team that is sound; and so strong that if the referee cheats we'll win, and if we go south we'll win, and if we play UCLA at UCLA we'll win. Winning is the thing. If it wasn't, they wouldn't keep score.

The Christian Science Monitor, 1-9:8.

Art Rooney
President, Pittsburgh "Steelers"
football team

It doesn't seem too long ago when we could settle every pro football problem in a quick discussion around a table. The guys who ran the league were Bert Bell, Tim Mara, George Marshall, George Halas and myself. We ran it pretty well, too. Nowadays, though, the owners don't arrive at a league meeting by themselves as we once did. Each is accompanied by a squad of lawyers, accountants, tax experts and more advisers than I even can name. When we were struggling to survive, pro football was a fun thing. The bigger we get, though, the less fun there is in it.

The New York Times, 9-5:(5)2.

Pete Rozelle
United States Commissioner of Football

You pick up the newspaper and 90 per cent of what we read on the front page, the business page, the editorial page is depressing today. And I think that, well, football is not the answer to the world, but it is one of the things that gives us an opportunity to get our minds off the depressing things. It gives us an emotional outlet . . . It has a definite place, particularly in these times.

Interview, New York/
The National Observer, 7-26:20.

We're in an era when everybody will have to sacrifice something to make pro football prosper. Everybody would like total freedom; but pro football players, for instance, can't have it. The draft and the one-year option are essential. Otherwise, there would be nothing to stop wealthy owners like Lamar Hunt and Clint Murchison from going through a Pro Bowl program and ordering out of it like a Sears Roebuck catalog. All they'd have to say is, "I'll have two of those (receivers) and three of these (linemen) and that guy (quarterback). Club owners today must make sacrifices. These are self-imposed. The owners have agreed voluntarily not to sell their interests to a corporation or to go public. They could make more money either way, but the loss in stability would be disastrous to pro football. Corporations are in business to make a profit, whereas football today tries to be both sport and business . . . Finally, the fans have to sacrifice. They may have to go to night games in cold weather or rain occasionally, and they may have to wait for 9 p.m. kickoffs. They also have to accept (TV) blackouts. In return, they get most of the Monday night games on television. Football today is an exercise in compromise and a balance of sacrifices, and if the scales are tipped too heavily for any group—players, owners or fans—it could destroy the game.

Los Angeles Times, 12-15:(3)4.

Johnny Sain
Baseball pitching coach,
Chicago "White Sox"

You have no idea the pressure a young pitcher is under. I've walked out to the mound in the middle of an inning and the pitcher couldn't tell me his telephone number. By walking out, you calm him down . . . Yelling at a boy from the bench is confusing and ridiculous.

Interview/
The Christian Science Monitor, 4-14:12.

Howard J. Samuels
President, New York City
Offtrack Betting Corporation

It's Alice in Wonderland. When the commissioners (of various professional sports, such as baseball, football, etc.) oppose legalized betting on sports, I am convinced they are not dealing with the real world and real people . . . I'm not here to get into a controversy with the leaders of organized sports. In my judgment, however, the commissioners have ignored reality and shut their eyes to the unpleasant truth that organized crime has an exclusive franchise for wagering on sporting events . . . The real world, as Candide discovered, is not always a pleasant place. It is inhabited by real people with real vices, real lusts, real ambitions. It's time to stop the pious preaching, the sanctimony, and support new policies instead of old platitudes . . . I'm not suggesting we set up slot machines or casinos. I'm merely saying we should take the business that's already there—$20 billion or more a year . . . Billions of dollars already are being bet . . . illegally—by people who are willing to violate the law. Yes, people go to sports events for entertainment. But a little bet can increase the fun. We're just saying, "Play the game with us."

New York, May 29/
The New York Times, 5-30:(1)9.

Gene Sarazen
Golfer

I think it's ridiculous the way they keep stretching (golf) courses. They are making golf a game of sheer brute strength. Finesse and shot management mean nothing any more. To win, you have to be able to overpower a course. Few can do it.

West Palm Beach, Fla., Feb. 23/
The Dallas Times Herald, 2-24:(B)1.

George Sauer
Former football player,
New York "Jets"

The whole structure of football is ridiculous . . . Football does not do what it claims to do. It claims to teach self-discipline and responsibility, which is its most obvious contradiction. There is little real freedom. Instead, the system—the power structure of coaches and people who run the games—works to mold you into something easy to manipulate. It is a sad thing to see a 40-year-old man being checked into bed at night.

April/Los Angeles Times, 7-21:(3)6.

The game can really touch you as a human being if you are permitted to touch others as human beings. But this is difficult when you have the . . . coach hollering at you to hate the opponent, who really is just a guy like you in a different color uniform.

The Washington Post, 4-19:(D)1.

Tom Seaver
Baseball player, New York "Mets"

The baseball players' relationship with the owners is probably as bad as it's ever been in sports. A player is bound for life to a team, unless that team wants to trade him, and then he has no control over the trade. And you have big corporations coming in and taking over sports teams. Instead of having someone in charge of a team who fully understands the problem of the players and was brought up in baseball, you have some corporation president running the show. The players make a good living; that point can't be argued. But under

(TOM SEAVER)

the current system, a player who can't reach agreement with a team has nowhere to go.

Interview, Greenwich, Conn./
The Washington Post, 2-6:(C)3.

Erich Segal
Author

A friend of mine told me that almost everything I write about on athletics deals with the athlete as the protagonist. I don't do it consciously, but all of athletics are really metaphors for things which are enigmatic in real life.

Interview, New Haven, Conn./
The New York Times, 4-4:(5)6.

Pancho Segura
Tennis player

Fifteen years ago, there were more people playing high caliber tennis than there are today. But this condition is only temporary. The sport has been held down by foolish rules. Now that tennis is open and so much opportunity is offered, it is only a matter of a few years until this thing becomes bigger than ever.

Los Angeles Herald-Examiner, 1-25:(C)1.

Bill Sharman
Basketball coach,
Los Angeles "Lakers"

Basketball players have to be in better shape than any other athletes. Football players, baseball players—even hockey players—only have to go in spurts. But basketball players are constantly running, running, running, stopping, jumping, running again. That really takes a lot out of you. If you're not in condition, it catches up with you in the fourth quarter; and that's the most important part of the game, the last four or five minutes. That will decide about a third of your games. So conditioning is a big part of my philosophy.

Interview, Philadelphia/
Los Angeles Times, 12-12:(D)1.

Bill Shoemaker
Jockey

(What he likes best about being a jockey): The races. The people. The rapport I have with most of the jocks. And the anticipations—the looking forward to a good horse that I might ride into a great one. Anticipation, I guess, is the best of all—being part of the development of a fine horse.

Los Angeles Times, 4-23:(3)1.

Robert Short
Owner, Washington "Senators"
baseball club

We've established the fact that it's safe inside the (ball) park. We spent $87,000 on inside security last year, just to cut down on what I call "nickel-dick" robbery. The father sends his kid for a couple of hot dogs, and some bigger kids take his money. There've been a lot of incidents like that in baseball, but they haven't been publicized. It would be very bad for the game. The clubs have taken measures to prevent the robberies. We've spent more than $1,000 per game, about 10 cents per customer.

The New York Times, 4-22:49.

Duke Sims
Baseball player,
Los Angeles "Dodgers"

When a ballplayer makes all that money, he is only making it harder for himself in later life. He develops a high standard of living and drives a Cadillac. Will he be able to adjust later to a Pinto?

Interview, Vero Beach, Fla./
Los Angeles Herald-Examiner, 2-24:(D)1.

Dean Smith
Basketball coach,
University of North Carolina

A lot of coaches won't agree with me, but kids do go to college for financial security; and if they get a chance at a good contract (with a pro basketball team), they should take it. To me, it's just like a student majoring in business administration having a chance to leave school and become a vice president at General Motors.

Sports Illustrated, 4-12:36.

Sam Snead
Golfer

That little white ball is always staring back at you, daring you to make a mistake.

The Washington Post, 2-28:(C)1.

Eddie Stanky
Baseball coach,
University of South Alabama;
Former manager, Chicago "White Sox"

There's no place like the athletic field for a young fellow. It's one of the few places left where a boy can learn discipline. If I cut my squad, I leave 30 or 40 kids roaming around with nothing to do but get into trouble.

Sports Illustrated, 5-3:62.

Willie Stargell
Baseball player,
Pittsburgh "Pirates"

I'm always amazed when a pitcher becomes angry at a hitter for hitting a home run off him. When I strike out, I don't get angry at the pitcher; I get angry at myself. I would think that if a pitcher threw up a home run ball, he should be angry at himself.

The Sporting News, 7-17:4.

Casey Stengel
Former baseball manager

Pitchers can't pitch without catchers. When the ball gets lively, now what are you gonna do? I don't want guys in the stands catching that ball. I want my right fielder to get it, not some guy in a bow tie that had to pay his way in.

Interview, Los Angeles/
Los Angeles Times, 4-2:(3)4.

Baseball is different today. They got a lot of kids now whose uniforms are so tight, especially the pants, that they cannot bend over to pick up ground balls. And they don't want to bend over in television games because in that way there is no way their face can get on camera.

Pittsburgh/
The Christian Science Monitor, 10-14:1.

Lee Trevino
Golfer

I love this game. It's an easy game to play, but it's not easy to make a living at it. Go to a pro, if you can, to learn how to play. I never had professional help, and that's why I have so many faults in my swing. I played and played, and that's how I got so I could make a living. I used to hit one thousand practice balls a day. At night, in my motel room, I chip and putt. Sometimes I have to replace the carpet, but it's worth it. I try to keep in shape. I watch television lying on my stomach; I do pushups during the commercials.

Tucson, Ariz./
Los Angeles Herald-Examiner, 2-22:(C)4.

I've got a lot of people rooting for me, because there's more poor people than rich people. You look at my galleries. You'll see tattoos. Plain dresses. I represent the guy who goes to the driving range—the municipal player, the truck driver, the union man, the guy who grinds it out. To them, I am someone who worked hard, kept at it and made it. Sure, I go out of my way to talk to them. They're my people.

Time, 7-19:48.

People keep putting up money for golf, so I'll play golf. I'll play on a dirt road if they offer money. I'll putt with a Dr. Pepper bottle; I can do that. A lot of writers have fouled that line up. They say that I will putt with a Coke bottle. That is wrong, wrong, wrong. I putt with a Dr. Pepper bottle; I like the contour better. Nobody can putt with a Coke bottle.

San Francisco Examiner, 7-23:50.

Morris K. Udall
United States Representative, D–Ariz.

The jokes about the endless football-

WHAT THEY SAID IN 1971

(MORRIS K. UDALL)

watching weekends of the American male are not funny anymore. They have become real; and they are damaging our country and, more importantly, our children . . . Virtually every professional sport in this country is now controlled, coached and managed by television. American sports today are big businesses, and getting bigger. Football, baseball and basketball franchises are marketed around the country like so many hamburger stands. New stadiums are being built in cities that can't afford schools; and sadly, some have stood vacant when owners decided that the cash was greener in another ballpark. The irresistible attraction of the television dollar is altering every facet of the sports world that has given us so much of our social and cultural history . . . Viewers with color television sets are in for a chromatic shock this spring. The Chicago *White Sox* are no more. They will be wearing red socks, and shoes too. And the Baltimore *Orioles* will be an even more-flamboyant orange. The shoes of our *Senators* —baseball *Senators*, that is—will be red, white and blue this year. The reason? A better contrast with the overly-green artificial turf will be beaming out of those color tubes. In a television triple play, a network in the business of broadcasting baseball games ended up the owner of a major-league club last year. Nagging minor points? Or symptoms of deeper, more disturbing changes in the entire fabric of the sports world? Here's what a good sports writer, Francis Stann of the *Washington Star*, says about the change: "Only the very naive have been unmindful that TV has been calling all sports shots for a decade or more. TV dictates the time contests will start, the length of time required to play, say, football, and, in the final analysis, who makes how much money. Live gate receipts are never unimportant; but what baseball, football, basketball, golf and now tennis and track have going for them is the television dollar. Dollar? The television millions."

Before the House,
Washington, March 29/
The Washington Post, 3-30:(A)14.

(Regarding the effect broadcasting has had on sports): . . . the National Basketball Association playoffs are now under way. In case the memory has faded with the passage of time, the season got under way half a year ago, on October 13. If we . . . and the players . . . are lucky, April will see the crowning of a champion, and both players and fans can take a break. Last year, I sweltered in the stands in August and froze in January, watching professional football. The sports pages overflow now with the news of 24 major league baseball teams, not 16. The Grapefruit League moves earlier into the winter, and we have lengthened the season to play those extra teams; we have added playoffs, and now the World Series is almost an anticlimax. We watch baseball being snowed-out in October—when once the first blustering November storm meant the last kickoff and the start of the basketball season. In 1960, there were eight professional basketball teams; now there are 25. And now that season warms up in September and runs down in April. Now we have 25 professional football teams, not the 21 of 1960. Expanded leagues mean expanded schedules. Baseball, a few years ago, played a 154-game schedule. Now, the teams play 162 games spread out over half a year—before entering those drawn-out playoffs. Pro football has inbred a system of conferences and cross-schedules that look more like algebraic equations than a system of testing skill and athletic prowess. Baseball, not to be outdone in this race for longer seasons and more-complex scheduling to postpone the dullness of the late-season doldrums, is going the same direction. Next year, we'll see six divisions in the two leagues. We have been provided with a slight break in that schedule, to be sure. It's called February—the shortest month of the year. That's when—for now at least—they play neither football nor baseball. But television does bring us basketball and bowling and wrestling and skating and skiing and hockey, to say nothing of the frenetic tours of professional tennis and golf.

The National Observer, 4-5:12.

Bob Uecker
Former baseball player,
Philadelphia "Phillies"

Philly fans are so mean that one Easter Sunday, when the players staged an Easter egg hunt for their kids, the fans booed the kids who didn't find any eggs. They even boo the National Anthem.

Los Angeles Times, 4-1:(3)3.

Al Unser
Auto racing driver

I am a race driver, and pride goes with what I do just as it does with any other professional. The same goes for the other drivers here (at the Indianapolis 500). I'd venture to say that, if Tony Hulman (Speedway president) walked down pit row next Saturday morning and told us no prize money would be paid on this race, 95 per cent of the drivers would fire up their cars and race without a dime. And I'd be the first to hit the track.

Interview, Indianapolis/
Los Angeles Herald-Examiner, 5-23:(C)1.

You may drive the freeways daily at top speeds with confidence and skill. But that doesn't qualify you as a race driver. Put an ordinary driver in an Indy-type race car and he'd probably crash before he got out of the pit area.

San Francisco Examiner, 8-11:54.

I want to stay right where I am, on top. The thing is, the more you win, the more you got to keep winning. It seems like whatever you do, you got to do it again and keep on doing it. That's the pressure. It's a long way down and you don't want to fall off; you don't ever want to hit bottom. That's what scares you: not dying —losing.

Interview/
Los Angeles Times (West), 8-29:18.

Bill Veeck
Former owner, Chicago
"White Sox" baseball club

Baseball is like our society. It's becoming homogenized, computerized. People identify with the swashbuckling individuals, not polite little men who field their position well. Sir Galahad had a big following—but I'll bet Lancelot had more.

Interview, Easton, Md., Feb. 9/
The Washington Post, 2-11:(K)1.

Harry Walker
Baseball manager, Houston "Astros"

The owners and general managers aren't as tough as they used to be, because they want to make the players happy. There are guys (players) in the $50,000 class who hit .300 one year, .260 the next and wind up with raises. With that kind of situation, there's no way to make a player do extra work or drive himself if he doesn't want to. Whether we like it or not, fear is the thing that still governs all of us, and the fear of getting cut is disappearing. That leads to a situation in which the player doesn't intend to lose his drive, his incentive, but starts losing it anyway. It's not intentional; it's unconscious. But it begins to happen, because some of the incentive is gone.

Interview, Cocoa, Fla./
The New York Times, 3-14:(5)3.

Nobody pays much attention to inexperience any more. As long as a boy can get the job done, what difference does it make? I'll pull a kid down out of one of those fruit trees if he shows me he can play ball.

Interview,
Cocoa, Fla./
The New York Times, 3-20:11.

Ted Williams
Baseball manager,
Washington "Senators"

Anybody who has a chance to make it

563

WHAT THEY SAID IN 1971

(TED WILLIAMS)

in basketball, football or baseball usually goes for basketball or football. Why? Because baseball is the hardest one of them all in which to become recognized or excel in. A football player doesn't have to do as many

things well as a baseball player.
Interview, Pompano Beach, Fla./
Los Angeles Herald-Examiner, 2-28:(C)7.

Hitting is 50 per cent above the shoulders.
The Christian Science Monitor, 7-26:11.

The Indexes

Index to Speakers

A

Aaron, Henry, 546
Abel, I. W., 121, 178
Abernathy, Ralph D., 43, 243
Abrasimov, Pyotr, 354
Abzug, Bella S., 157, 208, 318
Adams, Eva, 157
Adams, Walter, 58
Aggradi, Ferrari, 354
Agnew, Spiro T., 32-33, 43, 86-87, 121,
    136, 157, 178, 208, 225, 243, 252,
    262, 288, 318, 354, 393, 404,
    427-428, 452, 504, 515, 534
Agnew, William G., 121
Ahlbrandt, Roger S., 58
Aichi, Kiichi, 288, 393
Aiken, Conrad, 446
Aiken, George D., 137, 318-319, 404
Akar, John J., 271, 529
Albee, Edward, 489
Albert, Carl, 137, 157, 178, 225, 288
Ali, Muhammad (Cassius Clay), 546
Alinsky, Saul, 44
Alioto, Joseph L., 226, 243, 262
Allen, George, 515, 546
Allen, J. C. Michael, 529
Allen, James B., 44
Allen, James E., Jr., 102
Allen, Richie, 547
Allen, Steve, 496
Allen, William R., 102
Allen, Woody, 462, 504
Allende (Gossens), Salvador, 277-278, 354
Allon, Yigal, 377
Altman, Robert, 462
Ames, Amyas, 417, 496
Amin, Idi, 271
Anderson, Harold W., 428
Anderson, Judith, 489
Anderson, Robert, 534
Anderson, Sparky, 547
Anderson, Wendell R., 121
Anderson, William R., 157, 208
Andretti, Mario, 547
Andrews, George, 226
Aranguren, Miguel, 278
Arbatov, Georgi A., 137
Arends, Leslie C., 208
Arledge, Roone, 547
Armstrong, Neil A., 515, 534
Armstrong, Willis C., 58
Arnold, James R., 535

Aron, Raymond, 354
Arthur, William B., 102, 428
Ashbrook, John M., 137, 157, 226
Ashmore, Harry, 33
Askew, Reubin, 44
Assad, Hafez al, 377
Aubrey, James T., Jr., 462
Auburn, Norman P., 102
Auden, W. H., 417, 446, 515
Awana, Charles Onana, 271

B

Bacharach, Burt, 489
Bachman, William D., 252
Bagge, Carl E., 33
Bailey, Pearl, 496, 515
Bailey, Stephen K., 102
Bain, Helen Pate, 102
Baldwin, Roger, 515
Ball, George W., 58, 319, 354-355
Ball, Lucille, 496, 504
Balmain, Pierre, 422
Banda, Hastings Kamuzu, 271
Bandaranaike, Mme. Sirimavo, 288
Banzer (Suarez), Hugo, 278
Barber, Anthony, 137
Barber, Samuel, 504
Barenboim, Daniel, 482
Barker, Lex, 462
Barker, R. F., 59
Bar-Lev, Chaim, 377
Barnard, Christiaan, 271, 452
Barnes, Ben, 121, 226
Barnes, Earle B., 121
Barnett, Robert W., 289
Barr, Joseph W., 179
Barry, Gene, 496
Basilio, Carmen, 547
Bayh, Birch, 44, 122, 158, 226, 262, 319,
    452, 504
Bazelon, David L., 199
Beaton, Cecil, 422
Beatty, Warren, 504
Bedford, Brian, 489
Beirne, Joseph A., 179
Bejart, Maurice, 489
Bell, Daniel, 158
Bellow, Saul, 446
Bendetsen, Karl R., 122
Ben-Gurion, David, 289, 377-378
Benitez, Manuel, 547

I

J

M

Index to Subjects

A

ABA—see American Basketball Association
ABC—see American Broadcasting Company
ABM (antiballistic missile)—see Defense
Abortions—see Medicine
Acheson, Dean, 152
Achievement, 515
Acting/actors, 462, 463, 465, 466, 467, 468, 469, 470, 471, 472, 473, 474, 475, 476, 480, 483, 490, 491, 492, 493, 494, 498, 500, 501, 503, 506, 507, 509. 511, 512, 513, 519, 547
Adams, John, 200
Advertising—see Commerce
Aerospace industry—see Space
Affluence (see also the Rich), 47, 65, 185, 245, 246, 256, 265, 459, 499
AFL-CIO—see American Federation of Labor-Congress of Industrial Organizations
Africa (see also specific countries), 43, 56, 149, 271-276, 296, 345, 366, 450
    Communist subversion in, 271
    French colonial territory in, 275
    religion in, 529, 532
Aggression—see War
Agnew, Spiro T., 43, 46, 56, 102, 226, 231, 234, 241, 370, 428, 431, 436, 437, 445
    on running for Vice President in 1972, 225
Agriculture—see Commerce
Agriculture, U.S. Secretary of, 61
Aid, foreign—see Foreign Affairs
Air Force, U.S.—see Defense
Airport (film), 467
Alabama, 55
Albania, 345, 395
Alcoholism—see Medicine
Alger, Horatio, 542
Algeria, 271, 378
Ali, Muhammad, 549, 550
Allende (Gossens), Salvador, 278, 285
Allon, Yigal, 379
AMA—see American Medical Association
American Association of Newspaper Editors, 445
American (Baseball) League, 552, 555
American Basketball Association (ABA), 549, 552
American Broadcasting Company (ABC), 429
American Civil Liberties Union, 229
American dream, 265, 519
American Federation of Labor-Congress of Industrial Organizations (AFL-CIO), 178, 181, 184, 189
American Jewish Congress, 49
American Medical Association (AMA), 452, 456, 457, 461

American scene, the, 32-42
Americas, the (incl. refs. to Latin America) (see also specific countries), 149, 273, 277-287
    democracy in, 282
    foreign investment in, 282
    governments, similarity of, 285
    Marxism/Communism in, 282
    military in, 283
    seizure of U.S. fishing boats, 285
    subversion in, 280
    U.S. assistance to, 286
    U.S. neglect of, 283
    U.S. relations with, 284, 285, 286
Amsterdam, Netherlands, 468
AMTRAK—see Transportation
Anarchy, 34, 168, 206, 275, 370, 377, 525
Andersen, Hans Christian, 526
Andrews Air Force Base, 433
Annapolis, Md., 219
Antiballistic missile (ABM)—see Defense
Antitrust—see Commerce
Apartheid—see Civil Rights
Apathy, 42, 106, 227, 233, 234
Apollo program—see Space
Appalachia, 65
Appeasement, 46, 300, 310
Aqaba, Gulf of, 382
Arabs—see Middle East
Architecture—see the Arts
Arizona, 249
Arms race/control—see Defense
Army, U.S.—see Defense
Arthur, Jean, 468
Art Workers' Coalition, 418
Arts, the (see also the Performing Arts), 36, 417-421, 464, 473, 496
    architecture, 419
    art/artists, 358, 361, 447, 470, 475, 477, 478, 484, 485, 486, 500, 522, 528
    culture, 263, 265, 418, 419, 420, 464, 472, 492
    discipline in, 419
    financing of, 417, 418, 420
    government sponsorship of, 469
    improvisation in, 419
    modern art, 417, 484
    museums, 418, 419, 482
    painting/painters, 417, 418, 419, 420, 482, 483, 485
Asia (incl. refs. to Pacific area) (see also specific countries and Indochina), 76, 88, 136, 137, 138, 145, 148, 149, 152, 153, 210, 273, 288-353, 379, 388, 405, 407
    collective security, 300

E

K

L

N

U